uides

C000182329

take the kids

FLORIDA

& Walt Disney World® Resort in Florida

MELANIE DAKIN

Snapshots of Florida

Nature lovers

1 Everglades, Southeast Florida
2 Horseback riding
3 Calusa Trail, Fort Myers, Southwest Florida
4 Botanical Gardens, St. Petersburg, West Central Florida
5 Everglades, Southeast Florida
6 Glass-bottomed boat, Silver Springs, Northeast Florida

Animal magic

1 Ikakia killer whales, Sea World, East Central Florida
2 Shark and ray, Florida Aquarium, West Central Florida
3 Sea Turtle

4

5

6

7

10

9

8

4 Elephant, Animal Kingdom®, Walt Disney World® Resort
5 Rhino rally, Busch Gardens, West Central Florida
6 Flamingos, Animal Kingdom®, Walt Disney World® Resort
7 Parrot Jungle Island, Miami, Southeast Florida
8 Swimming with dolphins, Hawk's Cay, Southeast Florida
9 Manatee, Sea World, East Central Florida
10 Alligator

Big thrills

1

2

3

4

1 Spiderman, Universal Studios Islands of Adventure, East Central Florida
2 Cat in the Hat, Universal Studios Islands of Adventure, East Central Florida
3 Men in Black ride, Universal Studios Islands of Adventure, East Central Florida
4 Entrance, Universal Studios Islands of Adventure, East Central Florida
5 Dr Seuss Landing , Universal Studios Islands of Adventure, East Central Florida
6 Surf's up, Universal City Walk, East Central Florida
7 Kumba ride, Busch Gardens, West Central Florida
8 Incredible Hulk Coaster, Universal Studios, East Central Florida
9 Red Baron, Busch Gardens, West Central Florida

THIS
WAY
TO
McElligot's
Pool
5

6

BUSCH GARDENS
TAMPA BAY, FLORIDA
7

8

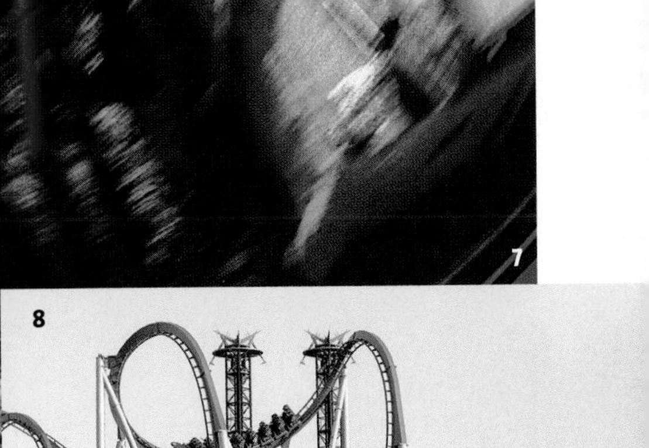

9

Big thrills

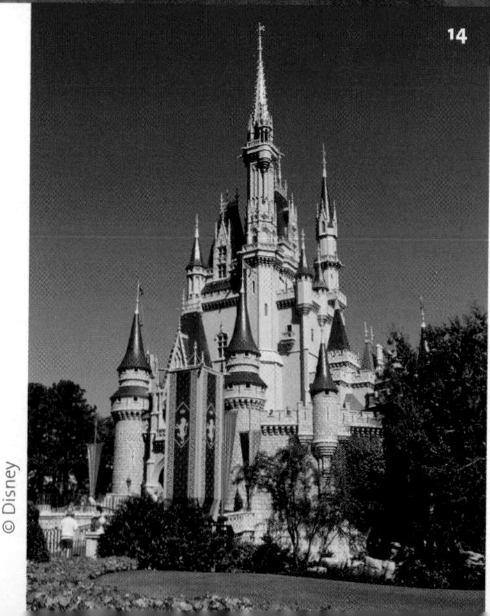

10 Astro Orbiter, *Magic Kingdom®*, Walt Disney World® Resort
11 Norway Pavillion, *Epcot®*, Walt Disney World® Resort
12 Space Mountain, *Magic Kingdom®*Walt Disney World® Resort
13 Princess Room at *World of Disney®*, Walt Disney World® Resort
14 Cinderella Castle, *Magic Kingdom®*, Walt Disney World® Resort

15

15 Indy Speedway, Walt Disney World® Resort
16 The Magic Carpets of Aladdin, *Magic Kingdom®*, Walt Disney World® Resort
17 Rock'n Roller Coaster, Disney-MGM Studios, Walt Disney World® Resort
18 Spaceship Earth and Monorail, *Epcot®*, Walt Disney World® Resort
19 Junior Chefs, *Epcot®* , Walt Disney World® Resort

16

18

19

17

Buckets and spades

4

5

7

6

1 Sandy shores, Captiva Island, Southwest Florida
2 Sand Key, St. Petersburg, West Central Florida
3 Key West, Southeast Florida
4 Daytona Beach, East Central Florida
5 Sand Key, St. Petersburg, West Central Florida
6 Ft Lauderdale, South East Florida
7 Daytona Beach, East Central Florida
8 St. Pete's Beach, West Central Florida
9 Family fun, Daytona Beach, East Central Florida

8

9

On the town

8

9

10

1 Shuttle launch, Cape Canaveral, East Central Florida
2 Daytona USA speedway, East Central Florida
3 Marine Science Center, Science Center, East Central Florida
4 Animal show, Florida Aquarium, West Central Florida
5 Museum of Arts and Sciences, Daytona Beach, East Central Florida
6 Hemingway Estate, Key West, Southeast Florida
7 Lighthouse, Key West, Southeast Florida
8 Vans Skate Park, East Central Florida
9 Baseball game, St. Petersburg, West Central Florida
10 Science Center, Orlando, East Central Florida
11 National Museum of Naval Aviation, Northwest Florida
12 Edison Estate, Fort Myers, Southwest Florida

11

12

Make a splash

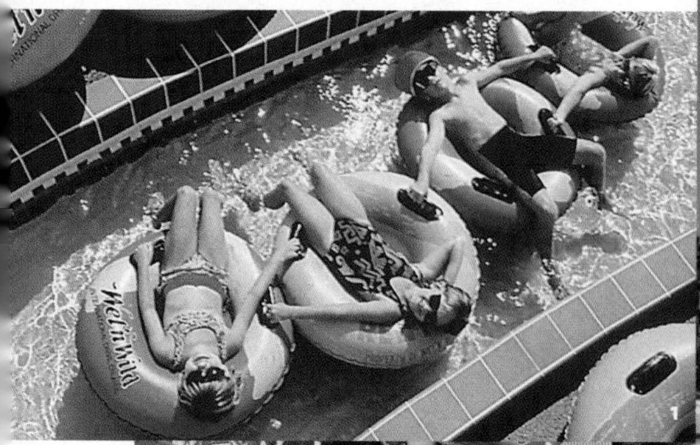

1

2

3

4

5

6

7

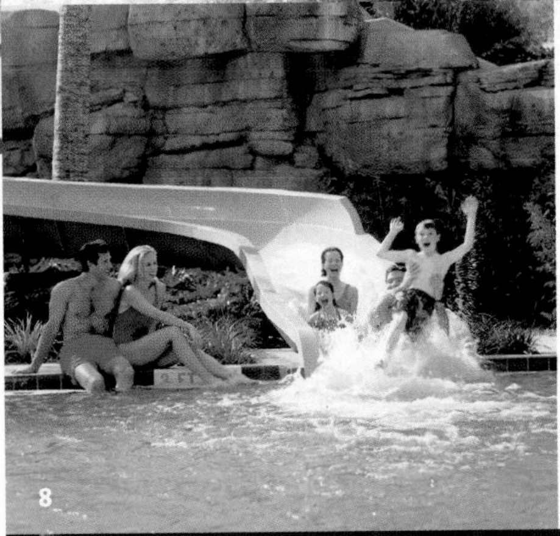

8

1 Wet 'n' Wild, East Central Florida
2 "The Blast", Wet 'n' Wild, East Central Florida
3 Raintower, East Central Florida
4 Coolzone Sun Splash Park, Daytona Beach, East Central Florida
5 Sea World, East Central Florida
6 Blizzard Beach, Walt Disney World® Resort, East Central Florida
7 Water-skiing
8 Water slide, Caribe Royal
9 Boating, East Central Florida
10 Snorkelling

9

10

Photo acknowledgements

Title page
© Lee County Visitor & Convention Bureau/www.FortMyersSanibel.com, St Petersburg/Clearwater Area Convention and Visitors Bureau, Edison Estates

Nature lovers
1,5 © Visit Florida; **2,6** © Orlando Tourist Board; **3** © Lee County Visitor & Convention Bureau/www.FortMyersSanibel.com; **4** © St Petersburg/Clearwater Area Convention and Visitors Bureau

Animal magic
1,9 © Sea World; **2** © Florida Aquarium; **3** © St Petersburg/Clearwater Area Convention and Visitors Bureau; **4,6,7** © Melanie Dakin; **5** © Daytona Beach Area Convention and Visitors Bureau; **8** © Hawk's Cay; **10** © Visit Florida

Big thrills
1–4,8 © Universal Orlando; **5-6,9,15** © Melanie Dakin; **7** © Daytona Beach Area Convention and Visitors Bureau; **10** © Alamy images; **11-14,16-19** © Disney

Buckets and spades
1 © Melanie Dakin; **3,6** © Visit Florida; **2,5,7,8** © St Petersburg/Clearwater Area Convention and Visitors Bureau; **4,9** © Daytona Beach Area Convention and Visitors Bureau

On the town
1,10,11 ©Orlando/Orange County Convention & Visitors Bureau, Inc.; **2,3,5** © Daytona Beach Area Convention and Visitors Bureau; **4,5,11** © St Petersburg/Clearwater Area Convention and Visitors Bureau; **6,7** © Visit Florida; **12** © Edison Estates

Make a splash
1,2,3,5,8,9 © Orlando/Orange County Convention & Visitors Bureau, Inc.; **2** © Daytona Beach Area Convention and Visitors Bureau; **6** © Melanie Dakin; **7, 9** © Visit Florida

This page © St Petersburg/Clearwater Area Convention and Visitors Bureau

About the series

take the kids guides are written specifically for parents, grandparents and carers. In fact, they're the perfect companion for anyone who cares for or about children. Each guide not only draws on what is of particular interest to kids, but also takes into account the realities of childcare – from tired legs to low boredom thresholds – enabling both adults and their charges to have a great day out or a fabulous holiday.

About the author

Melanie Dakin is a freelance travel writer. Over the years, she has contributed to numerous magazines and guidebooks including Time Out's *Europe by Air* and *London for Children*, *take the kids England*, Toys R Us magazine, as well as writing a regular film column and travel articles for *Angels & Urchins* magazine. Melanie is the former editor of *Kids Out* magazine and prior to that Listings editor of *City Life* magazine in Manchester. Although it was not intentional, Melanie has become something of a theme-park guru over the course of her career, which has stood her in good stead with her own children. Daughter Eve, aged 10, and John Hunter aged four, have whirled around on roller coasters, plunged down water slides and flumes, ridden the river rapids and splashed around in wave pools. Between them they have also, for the purpose of this book, kissed a dolphin, seen an alligator in the wild, been licked by a giraffe, sailed at under the starts at night, hugged Buzz Lightyear and Prince John and exprienced the beauty of islands, Everglades, magroves, manatees, sea turtles and fresh orange juice. They have enjoyed travelling on Greyhound buses and Disney shuttles, by Yellow Cab and steam train, monorail and safari jeep and most of all, they were fascinated by their journey from Key West to Miami by prop-plane. Melanie has spent a good deal of time travelling with children and being a non-driver, she is proud to say that most of it has been conducted on public transport. Florida, naturally, was something of a challenge without a car but getting around largely by using other methods of conveyance, just made the exprience more enjoyable.

Author's acknowledgements

For my dad who taught me how to travel and my mum who let me go.

For my family Stephen, Eve and John who agreed to come along on this adventure with me and who have aided, abetted and enhanced this book through their comments, critical appraisals, input, research and advice. Not to mention having put up with me, living, breathing and sleeping Florida for many months.

Thanks to my sisters Ali, Pip, nieces Lauren (a future journalist if ever there was one), Alice and Phoebe and nephew Thomas for their support, advice and help with compiling this book. Thanks too, to my friends for still being my friends after all this.

Thanks also to Esther Williamson from Visit Florida for her kind assistance and essential support. Thanks to my editor Antonia Cunningham for her patience. Thanks to Jennifer Huber, Lee Rose, Wrenda Goodwyn, Holly Johnson, Suzie Sponder, Wit Tuttel, Zaneta Hubbard, Ellen Marchman, Lindsay Dufresne, Louisa French, Sally Shifke, Stuart Kirby, James Litson, Laura Gray and Lisa Cole, plus all the other people who helped with this book.

And finally, I want to thank the parent who asked me what else there was to do in Florida apart from Disney. I hope I've answered that one.

CONTENTS

Cadogan Guides
2nd Floor, 233 High Holborn,
London, WC1V 7DN
info@cadoganguides.co.uk
www.cadoganguides.com

The Globe Pequot Press
246 Goose Lane, PO Box 480, Guilford,
Connecticut 06437–0480

Cover photographs: © Visit Florida, Daytona Beach Area Convention and Visitors Bureau, St. Petersburg/Clearwater Area Convention and Visitors Bureau, Mel Dakin, Universal Orlando, Brandon Cole Marine Photography/Alamy, Charlotte Thamo/Alamy
Colour maps: © The Globe Pequot Press, drawn by XNR Productions Inc.
Chapter 6–11 maps: © The Globe Pequot Press, drawn by Rusty Nelson
Chapter 13 maps: courtesy of Econoguide Travel Books, www.econoguide.com
Additional cartography: Angie Watts

Art direction: Sarah Rianhard-Gardner
Managing Editor: Natalie Pomier
Editor: Antonia Cunningham
Editorial Assistant: Nicola Jessop
Proofreading: Ali Qassim
Indexing: Isobel McLean
Printed in Italy by Legoprint

ISBN 1-86011-218-8

A catalogue record for this book is available from the British Library

Please help us to keep this guide up to date. We have done our best to ensure that the information in this guide is correct at the time of going to press. But places and facilities are constantly changing, and standards and prices in hotels and restaurants fluctuate. We would be delighted to receive any comments concerning existing entries or omissions. Authors of the best letters will receive a copy of the Cadogan Guide of their choice.

Introduction

01

INTRODUCTION

Every child should get the chance to go to Florida – it is practically a birthright. Abundant wildlife, glistening beaches, warm water and almost year-round sunshine – as well as thrilling theme parks and wild water rides – make it the ideal children's playground.

Florida is roughly the same size as England with a total land mass of over 54,000 sq miles, more than 4,000 sq miles of water in the form of lakes, rivers and streams, 156 state parks and 1,200 miles of sandy beaches and countless islands. Within this vast space there are many distinct locales from laid-back Key West and cosmopolitan Miami to the breathtaking beauty of the evergreen Everglades and the white-hot beaches of the sizzling Florida Panhandle. Florida has many faces and there's never a lack of things to do – you can even spend the day over on Captiva Island doing pretty much nothing at all, just soaking up the lovely atmosphere.

Both UK and US families flock to Florida for their holidays. In 2003 Florida opened its doors to more than 74 million visitors, around 1.3 million of them British holidaymakers.

Brits head off to Orlando and Tampa in droves seeking out theme-park thrills and a whole host of attractions, including water parks, dinner theatres, canoe outposts and wildlife reserves. Americans, meanwhile, tour pretty much all over the state for their vacation fix. Southern folk from Georgia, Carolina and Alabama come over the border to weekend in Northern Florida and enjoy the remoteness of the wilderness combined with the amusements that are strung out along the coast from Panama City to Pensacola Bay. North Americans swing on down the west coast to Naples, Fort Myers and east to Miami and Key West for some fun in the sun. Disney, of course, is there for everyone to enjoy, 365 days a year. 2005 marks the 50th anniversary of Disney parks worldwide, so you can expect even more people to join in the party when Florida celebrates the 18-month long Happiest Celebration on Earth at Walt Disney World® Resort.

I had always thought of saving a trip to Florida with my kids for when my son was old enough to enjoy all the rides but having whirled them around the theme parks of England and Europe I guessed they were ready for bigger and better things. At four years old my son has displayed a remarkable memory for what we did in Florida (he thinks we live there, actually) and watching the look on his face as he embraced his cartoon character heroes will stay with me a while. His ten-year-old sister took it all in her stride from eating mussels in Miami to waving at Jasmine and the other Disney princesses in Orlando. Florida may be a long way from home and a long-haul flight but we're definitely going back.

Guide to the Guide

This book is intended to be a straightforward guide for anyone going to Florida with children in tow and the information has been sourced specifically with families in mind, although these places are fun for adults too.

The book is arranged in 14 chapters, the first four dealing with background to Florida and the practicalities of travelling and organizing a holiday with kids. Chapters 6–11 are the travel guide and have been split into broad geographical areas, snaking from east to west from the northeast down to the southeast, and detailing all the sites and amusements in each area. Walt Disney World® resort, which takes up much of central Florida has two chapters to itself.

Major towns are focused upon and sights in reasonably close proximity are detailed in a subsection called 'Around and about'. If a small town close by has a variety of attractions, it is simply treated as a town to be visited; if, on the other hand, attractions are not found in one place, they are grouped under thematic headings, such as 'Buckets and spades' for beach and water amusements, 'Look at this!' for museums and sites of historical interest and 'Nature lovers' for walks and trails. You will find a list of places to eat in each area at the back of each area chapter. Throughout these chapters, there is a smattering of Did you know? and Can you spot? boxes to entertain your children.

History

02

HISTORY

Florida's first visitors arrived 12,000 years before today's tourists and encountered a land very different from today's hot and happening Sunshine State.

In 10,000 BC, the sea level was much lower and the peninsula was twice the size it is now. Nor was the famous sub-tropical climate yet in place – although it was much more temperate than the Ice Age, which drove the first settlers in from Eastern Asia.

The first Floridians were simple hunter-gatherers, settling where they found consistent supplies of food, water and wood for fire. The struggle was constant and only around 3570 BC did the natives establish what is thought to be the first permanent, year-round settlement in North America, near the mouth of the St John's River (*see* p.79).

The Floridians evolved in complete isolation from the great civilizations and religions of Europe and Asia. Small groups traded with others and as the centuries passed, villages and temples appeared. Yet Florida remained essentially wild and free, most of its land uncharted and undisturbed, until the arrival of Juan Ponce de León in 1513.

The Reign of Spain

In 1498, six short years after Columbus set sail for the New World, European eyes gazed on Florida for the first time, Englishman John Cabot viewing what may have been Biscayne Bay, as he sailed for Cuba. Fifteen years later, Juan Ponce de León, a Spanish explorer and adventurer who sailed with Columbus on his second voyage, waded ashore and set soggy foot on what is now the state's northeast coast sometime between April 2nd and 8th, 1513. He named the area *La Florida*, after Spain's Easter feast of flowers – *Pascua Florida* – and went on to sail to the Keys and the West Coast, when he returned in 1521, determined to found a colony.

Ponce de León brought 200 would-be settlers and 50 horses but had not reckoned on the ferocious Indian attacks in retaliation for his first imperious visit. He fled and died of his wounds in Cuba.

Undeterred, others soon followed in his stead. In 1539 Hernando de Soto landed near Tampa Bay (*see* p.108) with 600 men and led an exploration of central and northern Florida. A third Spaniard, named Tristan de Luna y Arellano, arrived in 1559 and managed to establish a settlement at Pensacola Bay (*see* p.69). However, he, too, left within two years, beaten not by Indians but by hurricane damage to his ships and supplies.

Spain under attack

Next came the French, led by protestant Jean Ribault in 1562 and, two years later, by Rene Goulaine de Laudonnière, who established Fort Caroline (*see* p.85) on the St John's River and set in motion three centuries of bloodshed as the Spanish and French, later to be joined by the British and Americans, battled each other, the natives and the elements for control.

Spain's Pedro Menendez de Aviles arrived in 1565 to reclaim the French advances and establish at St. Augustine (*see* p.88), which proved to be the first permanent European settlement on land that is now part of the United States. The French, led by Dominique de Gourgues, struck back in 1567 but the Spanish colonization continued across North Florida and up to the area we now know as South Carolina, their missionaries converting natives to Catholicism as they went.

Now the British got involved. In 1586 Sir Frances Drake burned down St. Augustine, but it took until 1702 and the establishment of a British colony in Carolina before Colonel James Moore was able to attack Spanish Florida, lay siege to St. Augustine and effectively bring the mission era to an end.

With the French making fresh forays, having captured Pensacola in 1719, Florida's destiny remained in the balance for the next 50 years. Spanish Florida grew weak from the almost constant onslaught on its territories throughout the period known as the French and Indian War (1754–63, also known as the Seven Years' War) when Spain joined forces with France against the British in order to gain control of North America. This ill-fated alliance allowed Britain to move on Havana, the capital of Spanish Cuba, which the British then used as a pawn to annex more territory on the mainland. A straight swap was performed and the Spanish left Florida.

Britain in control

The first thing Britain did was to rid Florida of its Spanish influences. The province was divided into two: West Florida with Pensacola as its capital and East Florida with St. Augustine. A truce was made with the Seminoles, descendants of the Creek Indians with whom Britain had formed an alliance in Canada. Yet the War for American Independence (1775–83) had weakened the British and, as an ally of France, Spain regained control of Florida in 1783. It was now the turn of the British to evacuate the land that had held such promise for them. The two Florida's (East and West) had remained loyal to Great Britain all through the War of American Independence and now, faced with an influx of Spanish colonists and settlers from the newly formed United States, they did the only thing possible – they became Americans. American patriots had proclaimed their own republic in Fernandina, Northeast Florida, in 1812. Two years later the American General Andrew Jackson took Britain's Spanish-authorized naval base at Pensacola. By 1818, Jackson was leading campaigns against the Indians in what would become known as the first Seminole War.

Three years later Spain finally relinquished control to the United States and Jackson established a new territorial government in Florida on behalf of the United States.

Once the two Floridas had become one territorial state with Tallahassee as its capital, a flood of immigration swelled its population. Many new arrivals came from the southern plantation states such as Georgia, Carolina and Virginia and, mindful of the state's potential as an agricultural centre, pressured the government to remove their main stumbling block – the Indian population who occupied much of this desirable land.

The Creek and Miccosukee Indians, original natives of Florida had opened their doors to provide sanctuary for African American refugees and runaway slaves from the northern states, were offered land in Oklahoma if they would relocate but many refused. Seven years of the bloody Second Seminole War would follow. Some 4,000 Indians and blacks were repatriated to Arkansas, although there are still Indian reservations today at Immokalee, Hollywood, at Brighton (near Okeechobee) and along the Big Cypress Swamp.

Now a vast slave population – almost half the 50,000 total population – helped build the state's infrastructure as roads and railways appeared across the state, as well as manning the plantations now creating a vast agricultural economy in Middle Florida.

United we stand

On March 3rd 1845 Florida became the 27th state of the United States with William D. Moseley as its first state governor. As the white population grew, so did that of the African American slaves. By 1850, 39,000 of the 87,445 population of Florida were slaves. This was an overriding issue in the new state. There was a growing opposition to slavery in the north and when anti-slavery supporter Abraham Lincoln became president in 1860 without a single Floridian vote, the Florida legislature began moves to withdraw from the Union. In the Civil War that followed, some 15,000 Floridians fought for the Confederate South and 1,290 for the Union North. By the end of the war and the abolition of slavery in 1865, some 5,000 of those men had died.

With centuries of localized conflict over, Florida boomed in earnest. Entrepreneurs snapped up cheap land, some of it in the south, where the swamps were being drained. The growing of citrus fruit became a signature Florida industry. And the first tourists appeared, tempted by steamboat tours along the spectacular rivers and coastline. Not even World War I could stop the growth. Florida's climate of year-round sun made it an ideal state for military training camps and many of the men who served in Florida returned at the end of the war, seduced by sun and sea. By 1924, scores of new cities had sprung up and the population, around 50,000 just 60 years earlier, was over 1.25 million. Though the Great Depression and World War II put brakes on the growth, they proved only temporary. By 1960 there were nearly 5 million Floridians, among them the astronauts of the new North American Space Agency at Cape Canaveral and the first refugees from Fidel Castro's newly Communist Cuba. In 1971 they were joined by possibly the most famous adopted-Floridian of them all, Mickey Mouse, as Walt Disney World opened its gates, creating the tourist sprawl that is modern-day Orlando.

Although often battered by tragedy – countless savage hurricanes, the space shuttle Challenger's implosion in 1986 – and controversy – the fiasco of the state's count in the 2000 Presidential election – Florida continues to boom. With almost 16 million citizens it is the fourth most populous state in the US and one of the wealthiest. And perhaps no other state offers its inhabitants and visitors alike such a variety of experiences, each one formed by the incredible partnership of man and nature.

TIMELINE

EXPLORATION AND THE BATTLE FOR FLORIDA

10,000 BC	The Ice Age brings nomadic tribes from Eastern Asia to Florida's West Coast.
1513 –	Juan Ponce de León, seeking the mythical Fountain of Youth, sights land on March 27. He names it 'La Florida' in honour of its discovery during the 'Pascua Florida' – the Feast of Flowers, or Easter.
1521	Ponce de León returns with 250 men and 50 horses but fails to establish a colony.
1559	Don de Luna y Arellano founds a colony on the shores of Pensacola Bay but abandons it after two years due to hurricane damage.
1564	Rene Oulaine de Laudonnière of France builds Fort Caroline on the St John's River.
1565	Pedro Menendez de Aviles of Spain lands at St. Augustine. He leaves some of his troops there to found what will be the first permanent European settlement in Florida, and goes on to capture Fort Caroline, which is renamed San Mateo. Aviles' men massacre shipwrecked French forces at Anastasia Island.
1566	Jesuit priests from St. Augustine begin missions to convert the local Indians to Christianity. Nine years later, the Franciscan friars begin missionary work.
1567–68	The French, led by Dominique de Urgues, retake San Mateo and hang the Spanish settlers.
1586	Sir Francis Drake takes St. Augustine and burns it to the ground. But Spanish colonization continues across Florida.
1698	Pensacola is permanently resettled.
1702–1704	The British attack Spanish settlements, laying siege to St. Augustine. As Governor James Moore of Carolina invades middle Florida, the mission era comes to an end.
1715	Ten Spanish treasure ships are driven onto reefs on the east coast.
1719	The French move into the Gulf Coast west of Pensacola.
1740	The British invade Florida from the new colony of Georgia but fail to take St. Augustine in the searing summer heat.
1763	Britain gain control of Florida in return for giving Havana to Spain. The Spanish withdraw, leaving Florida with a total population of less than 1,000. Florida remains loyal to the British throughout the American War of Independence.
1783	The Spanish regain control of Florida as part of the treaty, which ends the American Revolution. Florida's first newspaper, the *East Florida Gazette*, is published in St. Augustine.
1812	American 'patriots' proclaim their own republic in Fernandina, North–East Florida. Britain establishes a naval base at Pensacola.
1814	General Andrew Jackson takes Pensacola for the Americans.
1817	Scottish mercenary Gregor MacGregor, takes Fernandina and threatens St. Augustine. MacGregor is replaced by Luis Aury who attempts to claim Amelia Island for Mexico but surrenders to American troops.
1818	Jackson leads campaigns against the Indians in the first Seminole War.
1819	America and Spain reach an agreement which gives East and West Florida to the United States. Spain gets full claim on Texas.
1822	William P. Duval becomes the first Territorial Governor and 13 citizens form the first legislative council. Thousands of settlers arrive. Many Seminoles reject a government offer of land in Oklahoma and choose to stay and fight in Florida.
1824	Tallahassee, halfway between the major centres of St. Augustine and Pensacola, becomes the state capital.
1830	Florida's population is 34,730, of whom 18,395 are white.
1836	The St. Joseph to Lake Wimico line becomes the first railroad to go into operation in Florida.
1835	The Second Seminole War begins with the massacre of US troops under Major Francis L. Dade.
1837	Seminole leader Osceola surrenders to the Americans and is imprisoned.
1838	Florida's first constitution is drafted.
1842	The Second Seminole War ends. Nearly 4,000 Indians and blacks are sent to Arkansas.

FLORIDA, USA

1845 Florida becomes the 27th state of the USA. William D. Moseley is the first governor.

1855 The Internal Improvement Act stimulates Florida industry by offering cheap land to entrepreneurs and allowing swampland in the southern part of the state to be drained. The Third Seminole War takes place.

1860 After Abraham Lincoln is elected president, the Florida legislature begins moves to withdraw from the Union and raises $100,000 for state troops.

1861 Florida withdraws from the Union on January 10. In the Civil War that ensues, 15,000 Floridians fight for the Confederate South and 1,290 for the Union North. At least 5,000 die by the end of the war in 1865, when slavery is abolished.

TOURISM BEGINS

1870s Florida becomes a tourist destination for visitors from the Northern states. Steamboat tours are a popular attraction. The citrus industry booms, as does road and railway construction.

1881 Industrialist Hamilton Disston buys four million acres of the Everglades for 25 cents an acre, signalling the beginning of the development of peninsular Florida.

1906 Hundreds of rail workers die as a hurricane rips through the Keys and Miami.

1914 The world's first scheduled airline service, which runs from St. Petersburg to Tampa, begins.

1917 Florida becomes a giant training centre for US troops, particularly the Air Force, in World War I.

1924 Beginning of the Florida land boom. Scores of new cities are established as visitors choose to stay and become residents. The population rises to 1,263,540.

1926 A hurricane devastates Miami, nearly 200 die. 1,500 drown in 1928 as a hurricane drives water from Lake Okeechobee; 400 die in 1935 when storms hit the Keys, wiping out Henry Flagler's railroad.

1929 The Great Depression puts a brake on tourism. Thousands lose their jobs.

1946 The end of World War II signals a statewide boom. The tourist industry revives.

1950 A federal census counts 2,771,305 Floridians.

1958 NASA opens at Cape Canaveral and launches the USA's first earth satellite, Explorer 1.

1959 Fidel Castro takes Cuba and the exodus of refugees to Miami begins.

1960 Florida now has a population of 4,951,560.

1961 On 5 May America's first astronaut, Alan Shepard, is launched into space from Cape Canaveral.

1965 The Miami Seaquarium opens.

1965 Walt Disney unveils a $700 million plan to build Disney World in the Orlando area.

1966 Death of Walt Disney on 15 December.

1967 Busch Gardens opens in Tampa. American football's Miami Dolphins play first game.

1969 On July 16 Apollo 11 lifts off from the renamed Cape Kennedy, carrying the first men to the moon.

1971 Walt Disney World® opens on 1 October.

1973 A record 22.5 million tourists visit Florida. The Cuban 'freedom flights', which have brought 260,000 refugees from Castro's regime into Miami, end after seven years. Miami Dolphins become the first ever, undefeated team to win the Super Bowl. SeaWorld® Florida opens.

1980 The controversial Mariel boatlift brings another 140,000 Cubans to Miami. Florida's population is now 9,746,981.

1982 The $800 million Epcot® (Experimental Prototype Community of Tomorrow) opens.

1983 The space shuttle Challenger launches from Kennedy Space Centre.

1986 The space shuttle Challenger explodes shortly after take-off, killing all seven astronauts aboard. The TV series *Miami Vice* premieres.

1989 Disney-MGM Studios and Typhoon Lagoon open.

1990 Universal Studios® Florida opens.

1992 Hurricane Andrew kills 58 and makes over 80,000 Floridians homeless.

1995 Blizzard Beach water adventure park opens.

1998 Disney's Animal Kingdom® and DisneyQuest® open.

FLORIDA TODAY

2000 Controversy over Florida voting delays the election of President George W. Bush.

2004 Hurricanes Charley, Jeanne, Ivan and Francis wreak havoc across Florida.

2005 With a population of 15,982,378, Florida is the fourth most populous state in the USA. Disney celebrates 50 years of theme parks with the Happiest Celebration on Earth 18-month extravanganza of events, enhancements and even more magic at Walt Disney World® Resort Florida and across the Disney universe.

Travel and Preparation

03

TRAVEL AND PREPARATION

Choosing your holiday

Infants

They're portable, they sleep a lot but they can also cry, especially during a long-haul flight. If possible, breastfeed or give your baby a bottle to settle them during take-off and landing when air pressure might be a problem for them. The Florida sun is intensely hot for most of the year, so choose accommodation with air-conditioning and bring sun block and a shade for the pushchair. Try and give your baby a bath at night or a wash with wet wipes to cool them down before bed, even if they've had plenty of shade. Pop-up sun protection tents are a good idea for the beach and double up as a discreet place in which to breastfeed your baby. A pop-up travel cot with a fine mesh mosquito net is also handy for the plane and if you're likely to be on the move whilst on holiday. Baby food is a fine art in America with organic and additive-free varieties for all age groups from weaning to teething and textures to finger foods. Check out **www**.earthsbest.com, **www**.beechnut.com and **www**.gerber.com for some inspiration. Nearly everywhere you go to eat in Florida you'll pick up little pots of apple sauce – which is a great stop gap if your child has graduated to solid foods. Many brands are the same in the US as in the UK, particularly when it comes to juices and yogurt. Although you might like to bring some essential items from home, resist the urge to pack too much. Check to see if your accommodation has a kettle, steam sterilizer, baby-food warmer and what meals are provided for young visitors. Then bring along only what they've left out.

Toddlers

Toddlers are by far the most active age group to travel with but also the most easily distracted. It's not unheard of for children who have flown short distances many times to suddenly freak out on a long-haul journey. Eight or nine hours is a long time in the air and it's a good idea to have back up for dealing with scenes, tantrums and short attention spans. Here are some handy tips:

1. Ask for a children's meal when booking your flight and confirm this in the airport. Kids' meals come out first and are often more palatable to them than the main meal.
2. Ask if there are any kids' packs on board. A new cuddly toy or a puzzle can often make all the difference to a fractious child. Pack a couple of new books, a small toy or a set of new pens and paper; the novelty will be appreciated.
3. Engage your child in the journey. Buy a travel book or a game to play that will get them in the mood for the trip. Bring along some postcards of your destination and get them to study the flight path indicator on the seat back.
4. Bring lots of bottled water. If they can suck water through the top or through a straw it can help ease air pressure. Pop in some snacks like raisins and cut pieces of fruit for them to chew on – it may be a bribe but at least it's a healthy one.
5. Let them watch the in-flight movie over and over again if they want to.
6. Encourage them to sleep. Read a bedtime story and bring along a small sleep pillow. Let them open up the pack with the blanket and eyeshade in and make a big deal over putting them to bed.

School age children (5–11)

Depending on the maturity of the child, this is either going to be really easy or an absolute nightmare. As children get older they lose their irrational fears but often replace them with an inability to adapt. The plane journey may well be a breeze but when they get to their dream destination all they do is moan for days about the food and how hot it is. The best tool a parent can have at his or her disposal is reason. Be prepared to point out to them that opening a window is not conducive to the smooth running of the air-conditioning system and that chips are not all made equal. Tell them clearly why there may be delays to your journey; in fact, be ready to explain everything and anything and you'll do just fine. American immigration queues are a case in point. A school-age child will ask why they have to wait in line while other people have a fast track through to the other side – if you've done your homework, you should be able to give them a potted version of the updated laws governing international travel before it's time to hand over your passports.

Many of the toddler tips are still applicable here, which can be coupled with some efficient planning before you leave home. School-age children will enjoy having some input into your travel arrangements. They might like to look at brochures or at internet sites to see where they're going and make some of the choices along with you. Ask them what they think about two-centre breaks and touring holidays; should you buy flip flops or sandals and whether they'd rather go snorkelling or cycling. Get them on side and you'll have an ally for the whole holiday.

Teenagers

Well firstly, congratulations on getting them to agree to come along. Secondly, magnify all the aforementioned points about letting them help choose the holiday. Why not just let them go ahead and decide it all for you and just go along for the ride? It's definitely a case of the line of least resistance. Seriously, however, teenagers will have a great time if the can do as they please for part of the time away. It's important to point out the risks of being in another country (crime, guns, licensing laws etc) but also to choose a destination where they have some freedom within a secure environment. Resort hotel complexes with several pools, clubs for different age groups and interconnecting rooms are ideal for letting teenagers mix with others their age while not having to fret about them getting lost or encountering a hostile atmosphere. Make sure you maintain good lines of communication with teenagers throughout the trip. Mobile phones need to be tri-band to work in America and some chargers will not work in US plug sockets, so you'll need to buy a US adaptor.

Buy them a magazine or a good book for the plane and plan a shopping trip together or a special meal out while you're away. And let them choose the desserts.

Specialist holidays

Theme Park Holidays, **t** 0870 062 1022, **www.**themeparkholidays.com

Pure Vacations, **t** (01227) 264 264, **www.**purevacations.com

Surfing breaks for all the family.

Go Fishing Worldwide, **t** (020) 8742 1556, **www.**americaasyoulikeit.co.uk/fishing

Fishing holidays in family friendly resorts.

CruiseAmerica, **t** 0870 514 3607, **www.**cruiseamerica.org.uk

Mobile home holidays.

Holidays Afloat, **t** (01756) 693607, **www.**holidaysafloat.co.uk

Self-drive and sailing holidays.

Camping holidays

Reserve America, **t** 1 800 326 352, **www.**ReserveAmerica.com

Provides camping and cabin accommodation in State Parks for several destinations in Florida. See, www.floridastateparks.org for downloadable park guides.

Disabled access holidays

Access Travel, **t** (01942) 888844, **www.**access-travel.co.uk

Blue Skies Florida, **t** (01256) 812870, **www.**blueskiesflorida.com

National Holiday Fund for Sick and Disabled Children, **t** (01341) 280486, **www.**nhfcharity.co.uk

Eco friendly holidays

Where possible, the companies listed in the sightseeing pages of this book have been recommended because they are environment-friendly. For articles and advice on eco-friendly Florida and a directory of eco-friendly tours visit www.ecofloridamag.com

Contact the tourist information office for details of eco-friendly breaks.

Orlando Tourist Information Bureau Ecotours, 49 Winterridge Circle, Orlando, **t** (407) 415 7283, **www.**orlandotouristinformationbureau.com

Miami-Dade Park and Recreation Department Eco-Adventure Tours, 275 NW 2nd Street, Miami, **t** (305)755 7800, **www.**miamidade.gov/parks

As a general rule, try to find activities that do not increase levels of pollution such as kayaking, bike riding, canoeing or hiking. Although touring in Florida might demand the use of a car try to use it for long distances only. Bus, train and other shared forms of transport are listed in the sightseeing pages for getting around. *See also* Camping Holidays for details of accommodation in Florida's 156 State Parks. Support local firms, particularly those dedicated to maintaining and improving the local environment and take the kids to museums and nature attractions that promote care and protection of the environment. Several of these are listed within the pages of this book.

Please note that in Florida some attractions, such as swamp buggy or airboat rides designated as being eco-friendly actually are wildlife-spotting opportunities that are more intrusive to natural habitats than others – where possible go for small tour boats or, preferably, choose a walking tour of the Everglades or a canoe and kayak trip. Here are some other tips for helping to keep Florida clean.

- **Do not feed the birds or animals – it is very tempting for children when they see birds asking for food but burger buns and crisps are not part of their natural diet.**
- **Do not drop litter and clear up after your visit; items that are especially harmful to wildlife are drinking straws, fishing line, chewing gum and broken glass.**
- **Do not light fires other than in barbecue grills provided.**

Everglades tours

Footloose, t 0870 444 8735, **www.footloose.com**

Offers family adventure holidays in America (minimum age 8 though 6–7 year-olds can be considered for some trips on request), the latest addition to their portfolio is an eight-day Florida Discovery trip starting in Orlando and covering Sarasota, the Everglades, Key West, Miami and the Kennedy Space Centre with an option to stay in Orlando for a few days either before or after your trip. Optional activities include snorkelling, kayaking, swimming and roller blading. A Key West sunset cruise and Everglades tour are part of the experience.

Virgin Holidays Florida, t 0870 220 2788, **www.virgin.com/holidays, www.virginholidays.co.uk**

Families with children aged 6 and above can book an Eveglades Encounter holiday starting from Miami and visiting the Everglades National Park. In the park visitors will stop off at the visitor centre and at various points for wildlife watching. The trip includes three nights in Flamingo Lodge inside the park, plus kayaking or canoeing, a cruise through the mangrove swamps or families can opt for a fishing trip or bike tour.

Villas and house swaps

www.holidaylettings.co.uk
www.homes-seekers.co.uk
www.holswap.com
www.4homex.com

Youth hostels

www.hostelsweb.com
www.youth-hostels-in.com

Discounts and passes

See Practical A–Z p.19 for theme park ticket savings and Disney Need to Know p.227.

The good news for families visiting Orlando is that they can make savings of up to $500 with an **Orlando Magicard**. The card is valid for up to six people and is accepted at over 100 locations from attractions, hotel rooms, restaurants and dinner theatres to car rental, golf courses and shopping. Cards can be downloaded from the Orlando/Orange County Convention & Visitors Bureau website, **www**.orlandoinfo.com/magicard

Travellers to Key West can save money on attractions, eating out and shopping with a **Key West Passport**. Visitors can book online at **www**.historictours.com/keywest/

Macy's department stores is now offering a **Welcome International Savings Card**, which entitles overseas visitors (on proof of international ID) to an 11% discount on most goods in store, including sale items. To request a card before you travel, call **t** (020) 7253 0254.

Climate and when to go

Florida weather is seldom extremely cold (or at least not compared to the English climate) but it can be windy and cool at night, particularly in the north and coastal areas between November and March. Daytime winter temperatures are in the mid-70s (20°C) in southern and central Florida and 60s (15°C) in the north. At night temperatures in the north can dip as low as 41°F (5°C) but they usually remain at a comfortable 66°F (18°C) in the south. In summer, daytime temperatures in the south hover between the high 80s and reach into the 90s (30°C) inland. The summer are characteristically hot and wet and the winters slightly cooler and dry.

Winter is high season in Florida when retirees from other parts of the US (known affectionately as snowbirds) flood the state in search of milder weather. At Easter their younger relatives swarm in for Spring Break – a traditional college holiday that usually results in drinking binges and high spirits. Daytona Beach and Panama City are particularly busy at this time and, more recently, Fort Myers

Good to know

Average temperatures

	Nov–Mar	Apr–Oct	(high Jun–Sept)
Orlando	70°F	80°F	90°F
Miami	70°F+	80°F	80°F+
Key West	70°F	80°F	90°F+
Pensacola	60–70°F	70°F	80°F
Jacksonville	60–70°F	80°F	80–90°F

Beach is proving to be a favoured stomping ground. Summers are hot but the kids are on holiday and along the coast at least there is some respite from soaring temperatures, plus some attractive rental rates. Late August to early September, the queues at the major theme parks start to thin out and the temperatures ease off. The October half term is ideal, providing the stormy season has passed over the state by then. Christmas is busy but early December and New Year to early Jan can be quieter and the weather is stable if not always hot.

Hurricanes

Tropical storms and hurricanes occur in Florida between June and November with the majority putting in an appearance in September. 2004 had more than its fair share of major storms and the worst of them hit between August and September – Hurricane Charley ploughed into Charlotte County on the west coast in early August causing widespread damage and resulted in a few fatalities. Later in the month Frances toured from Hutchinson Island on the Atlantic Coast over to the West Coast around the Big Bend (between Crystal River and Apalachicola). In September, came Hurricane Ivan, which devastated the northwest Panhandle and finally Jeanne wreaked havoc in Hutchinson Island in mid-September. The development of hurricanes is closely monitored, follow TV and newspaper weather reports and look for up to date information on the National Hurricane Centre website – **www**.nhc.noaa.gov

Lightning

During May–September, Florida's low-lying bands of hot, wet air can cause some pretty powerful lightning storms. If you see dark clouds rolling in and hear rumbles, stay indoors. If you're caught out of doors it is best to stay put either in a building or inside your car until the storm passes over. Theme parks have regular storm warnings but you should check local weather reports for conditions before setting out.

Getting there

By air

Florida's main gateways are Miami, Orlando and Tampa. Airlines with direct flights include American Airlines, **t** 0845 7789 789, **www**.aa.com, British Airways, **t** 0870 850 9850, **www**.britishairways.com and Virgin Atlantic, **t** (01293) 747747, **www**.virgin-atlantic.com. Others with indirect flights include: Continental Airlines, Delta Air Lines, KLM/Northwest and Icelandic Air.

Florida welcomed more than 74.5 million visitors in 2003 and 1.378 million of these were British holidaymakers. Many of the larger airlines, including British Airways and Virgin Atlantic provide special on-board services for families, which can include children's meals (ask for these when booking your flights and again at check-in), designated flight attendants, play packs, seat-back computer games and children's TV channels, although some services will not be available to economy class passengers. Charter flights can be considerably cheaper but there may not be as much legroom and you'll have to make your own entertainment.

Transatlantic flights leave from **Heathrow Airport**, **t** (020) 8759 4321 and **Gatwick Airports**, **t** (01293) 535353. Direct charter services depart from a number of UK regional airports, check for local departures when booking.

An international air ticket for a child aged two or under should cost 10 per cent of the adult fare (one child reduction per adult, although some airlines do allow children to travel free so long as they don't take up a seat (or any baggage allowance). Between the ages of 3 and 11, child fares vary between 50% and 85% of the full adult fare, but once over 12, children are classed as adults. Carry-on baggage allowance is 40lbs (18kg) per person.

Pushchairs are usually carried free of charge on airlines and can often be taken up to the point of boarding. Carrycots, however, are not supposed to be brought on board, although some airlines will allow the collapsible kind. It makes more sense to

TOUR OPERATORS

Airtours Holidays, t 0870 238 7777, **www**.mytravel.com
America As You Like It, t (020) 8742 8299, **www**.americaasyoulikeit.co.uk
America Direct, t 0870 043 4248, **www**.americadirect.co.uk
American Travel Service, t (020) 7499 7299, **www**.northamericatravelservice.co.uk
Bon Voyage, t 0800 316 3012, **www**.bon-voyage.co.uk
British Airways Holidays, t 0870 850 9850, **www**.baholidays.com
Club Med, t 0700 2582 932, **www**.clubmed.co.uk
Delta Vacations, t 0870 900 5001, **www**.deltavacations.co.uk
Ebookers, t 0870 043 3934, **www**.ebookers.com
Eclipse Direct, t 0870 243 4300, **www**.eclipsedirect.co.uk
Erna Low, t (020) 7594 0290, **www**.bodyandsoulholidays.com
First Choice, t 0870 850 3999, **www**.firstchoice.co.uk
Florida by Phone, t 0870 99 06 880, **www**.floridabyphone.co.uk
Florida Vacations, t 01582 469661, **www**.vacationsgroup.co.uk
Funway, t 0870 444 0770, **www**.funwayholidays.co.uk
Jetlife Holidays, t 0870 787 5957, **www**.jetlife.co.uk
Jetsave, t 0870 161 3402, **www**.jetsave.co.uk
jmc Holidays, t 0870 750 5711, **www**.jmc.com
Just America, t (01730) 266588, **www**.justamerica.co.uk
Keith Prowse, t 08701 23 24 25, **www**.keithprowsetickets.co.uk
Kuoni, t (01306) 747 004, **www**.kuoni.co.uk
Peregor Travel, t 0845 345 0003, **www**.peregor-travel.co.uk
Premier Holidays, t 0870 043 5950, **www**.premierholidays.co.uk
Thomas Cook, t 0870 750 5711, **www**.thomascook.com
Thomas Cook Signature, t 0870 443 4582, **www**.tcsignature.com
Thomson Holidays, t 0870 165 0079, **www**.thomson.co.uk
Tradewinds Worldwide Holidays, t 0870 751 0003, **www**.tradewinds.co.uk
Travel City Direct, t 0870 990 4816, **www**.travelcitydirect.com
Travelpack, t 0870 121 2010, **www**.travelpack.co.uk
Unijet, t 0870 850 3999, **www**.firstchoice.co.uk/unijet
Virgin Holidays Florida, t 0870 220 2788, **www**.virgin.com/holidays **www**.virginholidays.co.uk

pre-book a sky cot, availability permitting, or to bring a large baby sling and walk up and down the aisle to rock the baby off to sleep.

By boat

For details of reliable travel agents in the UK offering Florida cruises visit www.abtanet.com, for information on cruise companies visit www.cruising.org or try the port websites below. Contact the ports direct for private charter boats for making your own sailing trip for example out of Miami and down to the Keys, a week's sailing for a family of four will cost you around £1,500 including food and, of course, seven nights accommodation at sea.

Port of Miami

1015 North America Way, Miami t (305) 371 7678, **www.miamidade.gov/portofmiami**

The cruise capital of the world, Port of Miami serves 4 million passengers annually from eight terminals. Cruise companies include: Carnival Cruise Line, Norwegian Cruise Line, Royal Caribbean International, Oceania Cruises, and Windjammer Barefoot Cruises – offering a variety of cruise destinations such as the Bahamas, Mexico, Caribbean, South America, Europe, The Far East, and around the world.

Good to know

Make sure you have all your hotel details, flight arrangements and passports handy when you fly. There are immigration and customs forms that you need to fill out on the plane, so having all your flight and hotel details to hand is much better than having to root through your suitcase to find them in the airport.

Port Everglades

1850 Eller Drive, Fort Lauderdale t (954) 523 3404, www.broward.org/port

It's not in The Everglades; it actually spans Fort Lauderdale, Hollywood and Dania Beach.

Cruises vary from round the world cruises to traditional seven-night Caribbean vacations and day-trips to the Bahamas. Cruise companies include: Carnival Cruise Line, Celebrity Cruises, Costa Cruises, Crystal Cruises, Cunard Line, Discovery Cruises, Holland America Line, Imperial Majesty Cruise Line, Mediterranean Shipping Cruises, Orient Lines, Princess Cruises, Radisson Seven Seas, Regal Cruises, Royal Caribbean International, Royal Olympic Cruises, Seabourn Cruise Line, SeaEscape, Silversea Cruises and Windstar Cruises.

Port of Tampa

1101 Channelside Drive, Tampa t (813) 905 7678, www.tampaport.com

The largest seaport in Florida with 4, 5, 7, 10, 11 and 14-day itineraries to Mexico and the Caribbean with Radisson, Carnival Cruise Line, Holland America Line, Royal Caribbean Cruise Line and Celebrity Cruises. Some itineraries call in at Key West.

Port Canaveral

P.O. Box 267, Cape Canaveral t (321) 783 7831, www.portcanaveral.org, www.portcove.com

Known as Florida's Fun Port, Port Canaveral offers partial and multi-day cruises. The two-storey terminal is attractively decorated with tropical vegetation and waterfalls. The port is also home to The Cove, a waterfront recreational area with restaurants, shops, charter boats and attractions. Terminal 8 is Disney territory where you'll find a 90-foot high glass observation tower, a children's play area, games arcade and a café. Carnival Cruise and Royal Caribbean International, Holland America, Norwegian Cruise Line, Princess Cruises and Disney Cruise Line offer cruises to the Bahamas and the Caribbean.

Passports and entry to the USA

UK citizens do not need a visa for the USA provided:

- **They hold a machine-readable passport with a barcode on the photograph page (this includes children who were previously included on their parents' passports)**
- **They have a valid return or onward ticket**
- **Their stay is for no more than 90 days**
- **Their stay is not primarily for business.**

Visa waiver forms are available at check-in desks and on planes and, together with your customs declaration, must be completed before entry into the USA.

Increased security measures mean visitors over the age of 14 must have a photograph and two fingerprints taken by an inkless scanner on arrival.

Unsurprisingly, all this leads to lengthy queues, so be ready to spend at least one hour in the arrivals area and have books or favourite toys at hand to occupy smaller travellers.

Passports do not need to be valid for more than six months for entry to Florida. Check with the US Embassy for updates, **www**.usembassy.state.gov

Getting around

By air

See sightseeing chapters for details of Florida's regional airports.

By bus

Greyhound (from the UK), **t** (214) 849 8100, (in America), **t** 800 231 2222, **www**.greyhound.com Greyhound buses operate across Florida with services to and from destinations including Big Pine Key, Bonita Springs, Bradenton, Clearwater, Clewiston, Cocoa, Crystal River, Daytona Beach, Delray Beach, Fort Lauderdale, Fort Myers, Fort Pierce, Fort Walton Beach, Gainesville, Homestead, Islamorada, Jacksonville, Jupiter, Key Largo, Key West, Kissimmee, Marathon, Melbourne, Miami, Naples, New Smyrna Beach, Ocala, Orlando, Palatka, Panama City, Pensacola, Sanford, Sarasota, St. Augustine, St. Petersburg, Tallahassee, Tampa, Titusville, Venice, Vero Beach and West Palm Beach.

If you're planning on doing a lot of touring by bus, opt for a Greyhound Discovery Pass: International 4–60-day passes available with discounts for children under 12. Fares from £70. Passes are available from UK travel agents including STA Travel, for more details visit **www**.discoverypass.com

Regional bus services vary dramatically from city to city but most major destinations in Florida do have a bus, trolley or monorail system that links the downtown areas to the main resorts. America's car culture does mean that bus travellers tend to be either American tourists from other states, international travellers or local workers and individuals who cannot afford to run a vehicle. Buses are a very cheap way of getting from A to B (fares $1.25 on most services), see sightseeing chapters for details of regional services.

See Disney Need to Know p.228 for shuttle/courtesy buses.

By car

America is most certainly a car culture and driving distances in Florida are so vast that it is by far and above most convenient mode of transport. Petrol is also cheaper than in the UK but recent oil increases are beginning to take their toll.

Rental cars have now stopped having big signs in the back advertising the fact that tourists are on board because thieves can easily identify their targets. Check your rental for any giveaway signs and ask to change a car if you're not happy with it.

The State of Florida is about the size of the UK and with all the attractions relatively far apart a rental car will allow you to make the most of everything on offer

Driving distances from Orlando to other Florida destinations

Tampa – 90 miles
Clearwater – 105 miles
St Peterburg – 115 miles
Sarasota –127 miles
Port Charlotte – 127 miles
Fort Myers – 160 miles
Naples – 187 miles
Marco Island – 202 miles
Everglades National Park – 290 miles
Daytona – 29 miles
Fort Lauderdale – 209 miles
Cocoa Beach – 50 miles
St Augustine – 90 miles
Key Largo – 268 miles
Key West – 371 miles
*All Driving distances are approx.

Florida speed limits

- **Towns and cities, residential and office districts 30**
- **Rural interstates and reduced access highways 70**
- **Other highways and roads 55**
- **School districts 20**

Drivers must be at least 21 years of age to hire a car in the US and local charges will apply to any driver is under 25. You need a full British Drivers Licence or International Driving Licence to rent a car in the state of Florida. There is no minimum time for having had a licence. You must have your original with you and if you have the new style photocard, both parts are required. A faxed copy is not acceptable.

- **On US roads make sure you drive on the right**
- **Lane discipline is not strictly adhered to. Slower traffic should keep to the right but overtaking on the inside is common practice, so watch out for cars passing on either side.**
- **Right turns, unless otherwise stated, are permitted at a red light but only if the way is clear and only after making a complete stop.**
- **Watch out for overhead suspended traffic lights.**
- **When approaching an intersection slow down and do not pass or change lanes.**
- **Street signs are suspended on overhead wires. The street sign facing you at a junction is the name of the road you are crossing over – not the road you are on.**
- **Most roads have both numbers and names and run either east/west or north/south.**

Motoring checklist

If you belong to a motoring organization, you should check to see whether you are automatically covered when driving in the US.

AA, t 0870 600 0371, **www**.theaa.com
RAC, t 08705 722 722, **www**.rac.co.uk

Familiarize yourself with the road signs – which in America, are based on words rather than pictures. You will need to purchase a good Florida road map; available at London's largest map shop, **Stanfords**, 12–14 Long Acre, Covent Garden, WC2, **t** (020) 7836 1321. Visitors can also download maps from the Visit Florida website: **www**.visitflorida.com

Wearing front and back seatbelts is compulsory in the US and children under five must be seated in a proper child restraint.

Car rental firms

Most rental companies require that the person driving be over 21 (or over 23–25 in some cases) and that they have held their license for over a year. By law, the company should provide adequate child seats on request. Check that car seats have been properly fitted and that you know how to operate them before setting off. You will need to bring a valid driving license with you when visiting Florida. You don't need to carry your papers with you all the time but, if stopped, you will usually be asked to present them at a police station within five days.

Car hire operators

Alamo, t 0870 400 4562, **www.**alamo.co.uk
Avis, t 08700 100 287, **www.**avis.co.uk
Dollar rent-a-car, t 0800 085 4578, **www.**dollar.co.uk
Hertz (Worldwide reservations), **t** 08708 44 88 44, **www.**hertz.co.uk

The NeverLost® enables Hertz customers to receive onboard driving directions to specific addresses and destinations, including local restaurants, gas stations, hotels, emergency services and tourist attractions. Renters can use their NeverLost® unit anywhere in the US. The package includes a Full Coverage map database from Navigation Technologies, the leading supplier of navigation databases in North America. The database includes all named roads in the US and detailed coverage of all major metropolitan areas. Customers also receive detailed route guidance to any programmable address in the US and a Travel Assistance directory with airline telephone numbers, radio station guides, and telephone numbers for local weather and traffic.

Taxis

Yellow Cab taxis can be found throughout city centres in Florida and at most airports.

The Mears Transporation Group also offers shuttle and taxis services within central Florida, **t** (407) 423 5566, **www.**mearstransportation.com

By rail

Amtrak, t (800) 872 7245, **www.amtrak.com**

Average fare £20–30. Look out for online discounts and mid-week savings.

America's car culture has left national rail services standing in their tracks and long-distance routes such as Tampa to Tallahasee or Pensacola can involve a bus journey for at least one leg of the journey. The hurricane that hit the Keys in 1935 took out Flagler's rail service, which was replaced by US Highway 1. The route now ends in Miami but it's a fantastic journey that runs a fair way up the Atlantic Coast before heading inland to Orlando and on up to Jacksonville in the north. Still, there's loads more leg room than you'd get in the UK, there's lots of interesting scenery to point out to the kids along the way and overnight services are available.

Journey times by rail

Jacksonville to Orlando	(+3 hours)
Orlando to Tallahassee	(+7 hours)
Orlando to Pensacola	(+11 hours)
Orlando to Miami	(+5–7 hours)
Miami to Jacksonville	(+8–10 hours)
Tampa to Fort Myers	(+3 hours)
Tampa to Miami	(+5 hours)

Walking

It's a depressing thought but the advice is, don't do it unless you're off the beaten track in the Keys or right in the middle of the city centre or wandering the wilds of a nice big State Park on a hiking trail. Cars will honk their horn at you and crossing places may be few and far between. It is an offence to walk on the Expressways in Florida.

Further reading

For kids

Hoot by Carl Hiassen

A funny and meaningful story about a group of kids trying to save a nesting site for Florida burrowing owls.

Strawberry Girl by Lois Lenski
A fascinating account of pioneer life in Florida written in dialect, great for reading aloud or for older readers.

The Yearling by Marjorie Kinnan Rawlings
Both the novel and film version of this moving tale of a boy who befriends a deer are well worth buying for your trip.

Florida by Sandra Friend, a history and nature book about Florida for children.

For adults

Anything by Carl Hiassen but most especially Native Tongue, Stormy Weather and Team Rodent.

The Everglades: River of Grass by Marjory Stomeman Douglas
A mesmerizing account of the Everglades written in 1947.

The Tropic of Cracker by Al Burt
Stories and anecdotes from people who shaped Florida's past.

Tales of Old Florida edited by Frank Oppel and Tony Meisel
True tales of daring feats and memorable visits, it includes an account of travelling on Flagler's railway down to the Keys and includes some remarkable pictures.

Films, TV and videos

It's worth pointing out that kids may be in for a shock when renting videos or watching TV in America. The English accents used in programmes such as *Bob The Builder* and *Postman Pat* have all been overdubbed by American ones. It's enough to make you choke on your microwave popcorn. Below are some films and TV series that have either been shot in Florida or cover different aspects of life in the state both past and present.

TV for adults

CSI Miami
Reruns of Miami Vice

Films for adults

Adaptation
Where The Boys Are
There's Something About Mary
Cocoon
GI Jane

Films for children

The Yearling
The ***Tarzan*** movies starring Johnny Wiesmuller
The Creature from the Black Lagoon
Parenthood
Ace Ventura Pet Detective
Edward Scissorhands
Doc Hollywood
Matinee
Contact

Practical A–Z

04

Babysitters

Although larger hotels may have their own babysitting services, several companies offer babysitting in your hotel room or vacation home.

Statewide

Sunshine Babysitting Agency, t (407) 421 6505 or (888) 609 8979, www.sunshinebabysitting.com

In Orlando

All About Kids, t (407) 812 9300
American Childcare Services, t (407) 354 0082
Anny's Nanny's, t (407) 370 4577
Super Sitters, t (407) 382 2558

Breastfeeding

United States Breastfeeding Committee, **t** (202) 367 1132, **www**.usbreastfeeding.org

Camping

Camping is a popular pastime in Florida, especially in the State Parks and on designated beach areas but it is not allowed everywhere. It's important to observe camping restrictions and rules, which will vary from site to site. Facilities also vary but usually a maximum of eight people are allowed for the one camp fee – an average daily cost for a family of four is $24 per night. Some campsites have designated family areas, boat access and both caravan (trailer) and tent pitches. Many sites also have cabins for hire. **ReserveAmerica** (Florida State Campgrounds, Reservations: **t** 800 326 3521. Customer Service: **t** 888 622 9190) allows campers to make reservations by phone or via their websites (**www**.ReserveAmerica.com and **www**.ReserveUSA.com). The websites have interactive maps for searching among sites, you can check availability, learn about the camp rules and regulations, search for driving directions and pay for accommodation in advance. Campsites are hugely popular, especially around Kissimmee and Orlando, so where possible book several months in advance.

Ecology

Sea turtles

Be sure to obey signs on beaches indicating where turtles are nesting. Sand dunes in Florida are protected environments. There are hefty fines for picking the sea grasses that maintain the dunes and even digging, sliding or playing on them is prohibited. Please make children aware that these are vulnerable habitats and that they are to be observed and not walked on.

Shells

When collecting shells make sure that the creature that inhabits the shell is not still living in it – removing live shells from Florida beaches is strictly prohibited. Certain shells cannot be collected even if they are empty. For details about Florida's endangered species visit http://endangered.fws.gov

Electricity

Electric power in the USA is 110–115 volts AC, 60Hz. Most plug sockets accept two flat pins and most UK appliances can be used with the adaptors on sale in UK chemists and departure airports. Older appliances may need a power converter to make them compatible with 60Hz current.

Embassies

UK visitors planning a Florida holiday should first look for information updates on the US Embassy website, **www**.usembassy.org.uk or Foreign and Commonwealth Office, **www**.fco.gov.uk

In Florida

British Vice-Consulate, Suite 2110, Sun Trust Centre, 200 South Orange Avenue, Orlando, t (407) 581 1540, www.britainusa.com/consular/orlando

The British Vice-Consulate in Orlando is responsible for the whole State of Florida and deals with issues such as provision of emergency passports, assistance for British nationals in distress and consular protection of all British nationals detained within the state. Offices are open Mon–Fri 9–5 for general enquiries and from 10–12 noon and 2–4 for emergency passports.

Emergency numbers

The US emergency number, as you'll know from movies and TV, is 911. Other useful emergency numbers in Florida:

Sheriff's Office, t (239) 332 3456 or (239) 477 1200

Florida Highway Patrol, t (239) 278 7100
Florida Marine Patrol, t (239) 332 6971 or t 800 342 5367
US Coast Guard, t (239) 463 5754
American Red Cross, t (239) 278 3401 or t (239) 261 8903
Help Link, t (239) 433 5000

This is an information referral service, that will provide contact numbers for services such as temporary shelter, emergency food and transport in the event of a hurricane or other major emergency.

Age Link, t (239) 433 3900

As above, providing the same information for seniors 60 years plus.

AMEUROP, t 800 452 4220

As above, providing assistance in all major European languages.

Emergency Management Office, t (239) 477 3600
Florida Poison Information Centre, t 800 222 1222

Insurance

It's vital that you take out travel insurance before your trip. As a minimum it should cover the following: hospital treatment and medical evacuation to the UK, accidents, lost/stolen belongings including luggage and passports, personal liability, legal expenses, travel delays and cancellation of your holiday because of illness. You don't have to buy insurance from the same travel company that sold you your holiday, and it's worth shopping around.

Most insurance companies offer free insurance to children under the age of two as part of their parents' policy. When travelling, always keep the insurance company's 24-hour emergency number close to hand – if you have a mobile phone, store it in the memory.

Always report stolen or lost items, however trivial, to the police so you can make a claim when you get back home.

Some useful numbers:

In the UK

Association of British Insurers, t (020) 7600 3333
The Insurance Ombudsman Bureau, t 0845 600 6666

The government-appointed regulators of the insurance industry, who are able help with complaints.

ABC Holiday Extras Travel Insurance, t (toll free) 0800 171 000
Columbus Travel Insurance, t (020) 7375 0011
Endsleigh Insurance, t (020) 7436 4451
Medicover, t 0870 735 3600
World Cover Direct, t toll free 0800 365 121

In North America

Access America, US, toll free, t 1 800 284 8300
Canada, toll free, t 1 800 654 1908
Carefree Travel Insurance, US and Canada, toll free, t 1 800 323 3149
Travel Assistance International, US and Canada, toll free, t 1 800 921 2828
MEDEX Assistance Corporation, US, t (410) 453 6300

Insects and other annoyances

Mosquitos

Come prepared for mosquitoes, in places with standing water, like the Everglades, they're a problem all year round. Some insect repellents, especially ones containing DEET, aren't suitable for use on children, so look out for brands such as Autan Family. Plug-in insect repellents are available in most UK airports and chemists. If you're travelling with a baby, pack a mosquito net for the pram or carrycot. Try to stay indoors at dawn and dusk and wear long-sleeved shirts and trousers in the evening.

Sand flies

Referred to by locals as 'no-see-ums' these irritating insects lie in wait in the sand and leave a nasty bite, which, if scratched, can leave a scar. Avoid hitting the beach after sunset unless you've liberally applied some insect repellent first.

Fire ants

In the wooded areas of Florida's State Parks and in grassy meadows, you may come across these tiny red creatures. Urge children not to kick at mounds in the grass and to walk carefully along dirt paths because these diminutive insects really do pack a punch. A chicken pox like rash and swelling is common, which then turns into an itchy blister. Keep an eye on children for severe reactions such as vomiting and nausea, which must be treated by a medical professional straight away.

Sea lice

These itchy jellyfish larvae are common in Florida waters between March and August with highest levels occurring from April–July. In the water the larvae resemble dots of black pepper. As a precaution, women are better off wearing two-piece swimming costumes. All swimming gear should be removed directly after bathing and the skin showered thoroughly with salt water should you suspect that you've picked up lice. The lice can stay in the material, so either discard an infected costume or put it through a rigorous wash and dry machine cycle.

Stingrays

During spring and summer it's important to take care when splashing in the waters along The Gulf Coast. Stingrays frequent the shallow waters of the bays and beaches, lying partly buried in the sand. If you step on one it will retaliate by stabbing you with its razor sharp tail spine. The barbs are coated with poison making the sting all the more painful. Should you be stung it's important to seek medical attention in case any barbs have remained in the skin. To avoid injury, make sure that children wear jelly shoes and adopt a slow, shuffling gait whilst in the water, which will allow the ray enough time to make a quick exit.

Internet

Internet cafés are available in most towns and cities. Most business class hotels offer free Internet access including wireless services in certain areas of the hotel. Printers, photocopy stations and airports often have Internet facilities and some hotels have on-site business centres.

Jet lag

This is generally worst on the return journey to the UK. To avoid excessive jet lag, plan to arrive and depart from the US as late in the day as possible (bearing in mind immigration queues can take up to an hour or longer, which may be taxing for young, tired children). Let the kids sleep on the plane and, if arriving early, get straight in to the local routine. If arriving mid-afternoon or early evening keep them up as late as possible on the first night to get into the swing of things as smoothly as possible. If you can allow a day for recovery when back in the UK it is useful to do so. Be patient, jet lag can manifest itself in irritability and tearfulness for up to a week after returning home.

Laundry

Most hotels have laundry services and apartment complexes, condos and resorts often have laundry rooms for guests' use. Supermarkets stock handy-size washing powders; so don't feel the need to bring your own along.

Lost children

Should the unthinkable happen and you get separated from your child, call the police immediately. At the beach report the missing child to the lifeguard station. For details of theme park lost children's services *see* pp.145 and 231 but as a general rule report the missing child to the first member of staff you can find and ask them to direct you to the guest services/lost child centre. Carry a recent photograph of your child with you at all times and remind them of the dangers of wandering off or going out without permission. Give your child a piece of paper with your name and phone number on it and your hotel address.

More information is available from the Florida Department of Law Enforcement website, **www**.fdle.state.fl.us/

Maps

There's a full-colour road map in the back of this book but visitors are encouraged to buy an atlas or road map if touring around. Most city centres have free visitor maps, which you can pick up from the information desk at the airport or the local tourist office (*see* p.27).

Medical matters

Medical treatment in the USA is very expensive and the British Embassy and Consulates will not assist with medical bills. Comprehensive travel and medical is a must. *See* INSURANCE.

(MASTA) operate a Travellers' Health Line, t 09068 224 100 (premium rates apply), www.masta.org

Federal holiday calendar

	2005	2006	2007
New Year's Day	1 January	1 January	1 January
Martin Luther King Day (3rd Monday in Jan)	17 January	16 January	15 January
Presidents Day/Presidents' Week (from 3rd Monday in Feb)	21 February	20 February	19 February
Memorial Day (last Monday in May)	30 May	29 May	28 May
Independence Day	4 July	4 July	4 July
Labor Day (1st Monday in Sept)	5 September	4 September	3 September
Columbus Day (2nd Monday in Oct)	10 October	9 October	8 October
Veterans' Day	11 November	11 November	11 November
Thanksgiving Day (4th Thursday in Nov)	24 November	23 November	22 November
Christmas Day	25 December	25 December	25 December

In the US contact the Centre for Disease Control and Prevention (CDC), **t** (877) 394 8747, **www**.cdc.gov

Minor ailments

Bring items like teething gel, junior paracetamol, antihistamine tablets or creams, zinc-based nappy creams and any other over the counter items you or your child might need. Prescription drugs and even tubes of common ointment can be very expensive to buy in America. Plasters, sewing kits and other first aid items are available in most hotels or can be purchased in supermarkets.

Money and banks

Have a supply of cash with you at all times to cover emergencies, but behave as you would in a big city at home. Pickpockets prey on tourist hot spots, so keep wallets in your front trouser pockets or money belt and hold purses and bags close to your body. Do not drape handbags on the back of your chair or buggy and avoid putting valuables into the small front pockets of large of small rucksacks – these can easily be opened by someone walking close behind you in a big city crush.

Only large banks will exchange foreign currency, so take travellers' cheques in US dollars – which will be accepted in major stores as well as banks – and credit cards. Remember to inform your credit card provider before travelling to the USA as many have fraud prevention programmes which will automatically close down your card after a certain number of purchases in a foreign country unless notified in advance.

Write down the emergency numbers for your bank and credit cards and keep them in a safe place so you can report loss or theft quickly and limit any liability.

US currency is the dollar; denominations are $1, $5, $10, $20, $50 and $100 notes and cents 1c, 5c, 10c, 25c, 50c and $1 coins. The current exchange rate is $1.86 per British pound sterling.

Natural disasters

Hurricanes and tropical storms can strike the southern and eastern coastal states of the US from Texas to Maine and the Caribbean between June and November. Air services can be disrupted during heavy storms and in worst cases may not return to normal for several days. You are strongly advised to follow advice from the local authorities on preparing for a hurricane, and on evacuation and seeking shelter when one is close. You can obtain information about the progress of hurricanes and tropical storms by visiting the National Weather Service website at, **www**.nhc.noaa.gov and reading the public advisories posted there.

National holidays

All banks, many attractions, businesses and shops are closed on US Federal Holidays, the equivalent of the British Bank Holiday.

Opening hours

Florida shops open between 9am and 10am and close at either 5 or 6pm from Monday to Saturday. However, department stores and shops in larger shopping malls will usually remain open until 9pm or later. Petrol stations are a good place to buy supplies out of hours.

Banks are open on weekdays from 9am to 3pm and some open until noon on Saturday. Museums are generally open from 9am–6pm Monday to Saturday and 10am–5pm on Sundays. Cinema screening times are roughly 11.30am–9pm, although most have midnight 'late shows' on Fridays and Saturdays.

Office hours are the standard 9am–5pm on weekdays.

Post

Stamps for letters and postcards home are widely available in shops and vending machines but the best place to buy them is in a post office, where staff will know the correct international rates. Post Offices are open from 9am-5pm on weekdays and 9am-12pm Saturdays.

The US Postal Services' dark blue mailboxes are sited outside all post offices but appear on many street corners – just don't mistake them for litter bins.

Restaurants

American dining is generally a casual affair, which is perfect for family groups. Restaurants vary from fast-food outlets and coffee shops to fine dining establishments and specialist cuisine. If you are unsure of a restaurant's policy and facilities for family dining, a quick call can put your mind at ease. Hotel owners are happy to suggest recommended local restaurants and in some cities it is even possible to order takeaways to your room for anything from pizza to Chinese banquets. Florida's proximity to Mexico and Cuba means that there are no shortage of authentic Caribbean and Mexican restaurants and Mediterranean influences are also widespread. Since many holidaymakers come to sample the beauty of Florida's beaches, you'll also find a number of seafood restaurants on offer. Local delicacies include stone crab, Florida lobster and the ubiquitous fried grouper sandwich – all are very tasty indeed. In St. Augustine you may come across Spanish dishes flavoured with spicy datil peppers and in Key West it's imperative to try out the Key Lime Pie (it's a more exotic version of lemon curd pie and authentic Key limes are yellow not green, so the paler the pie the better).

Restaurants rates

Inexpensive	below $10
Moderate	$10–$20
Expensive	$21–$30
Very expensive	$30+

See **Where to Eat** sections in all of the sight-seeing chapters for details of specific restaurants and unless otherwise stated, all restaurants are open for lunch and dinner. Advance booking is recommended to avoid disappointment.

Road safety awareness

If you are intending to drive in the US, make sure that you learn the traffic laws. Remember that speed and drink driving limits are lower than in the UK. An international driving licence is recommended. Always bring a UK driving licence for each driver on a fly-drive holiday, and always take out adequate insurance cover with the car rental company to cover not only the occupants of your own vehicle, but also any third party claims including personal injury. You should ask directions from the rental company and stay on main highways. It is worth-while buying a detailed road atlas of the areas through which you are travelling. If hit from behind while driving, indicate to the other driver to follow you to a public place and call for Police help.

Safety

The vast majority of visits to Florida are completely trouble-free. Use the same precautions as you would take in any major European city:

- **Carry only as much money as you need. Travellers' cheques or credit cards are best.**
- **Shop with care. Be discreet about displaying large amounts of cash, expensive jewellery or your flashy mobile phone in public. A camera around your neck picks you out as a tourist; stow it.**
- **Use outside ATM machines only during the hours of daylight unless absolutely necessary. If possible, use the ATM in a busy store or bank. Keep your card concealed and make sure you block the view of others as you enter your PIN number.**

- Always close windows and lock doors when you leave the car, even if you'll only be a few minutes.
- Take care when walking in unfamiliar areas away from main roads and shops, especially after midnight.
- At night, park in a well-lit, visible place or use a valet parking service when available.
- Lock valuables and packages in the boot.
- Do not sleep in your car on the side of the road or in rest areas.
- Use main roads and avoid short cuts through unfamiliar territory.

Shopping

Shops in Florida charge a 6% sales tax on top of the cost of your purchases. There are several large department stores, which stock everything from furniture and toys to luggage and designer outfits. Macy's **www.**macys.com stocks an extensive range of children's clothes up to age 6–7 including labels such as Phat Farm, Baby Phat, Guess and Polo Ralph Lauren. There's a separate Juniors range for older children featuring the JLO by Jennifer Lopez range and chic separates from American Rag, among others. JCPenney **www.**jcpenney.com provides home furnishings, including nursery items and accessories, plus children's clothes for ages up to 16. Dillard's **www.**dillards.com has a large range of toys for travelling with children, plus clothing and shoes for all the family. Shop at Sears **www.**sears.com for electrical goods, games and music, toiletries, clothes and car accessories. Beall's of Florida **www.**beallsflorida.com is a local department store chain with around 70 outlets. You'll find a large range of baby clothes and layettes, swimwear and sleepwear, plus character T-shirts and brand name clothing such as Sketchers, Quiksilver and Converse.

Supermarkets such as Wal-Mart and Publix sell food, flowers, cosmetics and pharmacy items, alcohol (be aware of restrictions that persons buying alcohol must be over 21 and carry ID), household goods and clothing.

Useful shopping contacts before you go

Young Explorers

01789 414791, www.youngexplorers.co.uk

Tiny sleeping bags and travel luggage including mini washrooms and kids' backpacks. Best buy: LifeVenture Hip pack.

Children's clothing sizes

UK	1	2	5	7	9	10	12
US	2	4	6	8	10	13	15

Women's sizes

UK	8	10	12	14	16
US	6	8	10	12	14

Children's shoes

1–3 yrs – toddler sizes 9–10
3–4 yrs – toddler sizes 10–11
4–5 yrs – toddler sizes 11–12
5–6 yrs – toddler sizes121/2–1
7–8 yrs – kids' sizes 1–3
8–9 yrs – kids' sizes 3–5
9–10 yrs – kids' sizes 5–7

Great Little Trading Company

0870 850 6000, www.gltc.co.uk

Handy for travel toys and in-car accessories, sun and wetsuits, lightweight clothing, travel games and water bottles. Best buy: Bug Bands – insect repellant snap-on remedies.

Neal's Yard Remedies

0845 262 3145, www.nealsyardremedies.com

Stocks a range of aromatherapy oils and blends, spritzers and roll-ons, herbal drinks and a homeopathic travel kit. Best buy: Treat Your Feet gift box.

Tisserand

01273 325666, www.tisserandshop.com

Stocks aromatherapy pick-me-ups and soothing treatments for all the family. Best buy: lavender wet wipes.

Lion in the Sun

01483 565 301, www.lioninthesun.com

Swim shoes, wet and dry suits, board shorts, T-shirts and jackets with UV protection. Best buy: UV surf beads that glow when it's time to cover up.

Sun-togs

01733 765030, www.sun-togs.co.uk

Rain and sun proof clothing with UV protection for children and adults including adult-size legionnaires hats and surf suits for teens, insect repellents and travel aids. Best buy: Water resistant multi-function Casio Baby G Watch.

For Discounts – *see* p.12

Smoking

Most hotels and restaurants provide some non-smoking areas and many are now smoke-free. In theme parks, you can only smoke in designated areas. Smoking on buses, trains and planes, among other forms of transport is strictly prohibited.

Special needs

Most large hotels and all Orlando's major tourist attractions have excellent facilities for those with special needs. Some useful telephone numbers:

In the UK

Council for Disabled Children, t (020) 7843 6000 Information on travel health and further resources.

Holiday Care Service, 2nd Floor, Imperial Building, Victoria Road, Horley, Surrey RH6 9HW, **t** (01293) 774 535

Provides information sheets for families with disabilities. All sites have been visited and assessed by Holiday Care representatives.

RADAR (Royal Association for Disability and Rehabilitation) Unit 12 City Forum, 250 City Road, London EC1V 8AF, **t** (020) 7250 3222

Open Mon–Fri 8–5; provides specialist advice and publishes a guide to facilities at airports called 'Getting There'.

Royal National Institute for the Blind, 224 Great Portland Street, London W15 5TB, **t** (020) 7388 1266

Advises on travel matters.

In the US

American Foundation for the Blind, 15 West 16th Street, New York, NY 10011, **t** (212) 620 2000; toll free, **t** 1 800 232 5463

Mobility International, PO Box 3551, Eugene, Oregon 97403, **t** (541) 343 1284

SATH (Society for the Advancement of Travel for the Handicapped), 347 5th Avenue, Suite 610, New York 10016, **t** (212) 447 7284

Sports

Contact **The Florida Sports Foundation**, **t** (850) 488 8347, **www**.flasports.com for a comprehensive guide to sports, sporting festivals and events in Florida,

Fishing

Although children under age sixteen can fish free in Florida, adults must purchase separate salt- and freshwater licenses.

Florida Fish & Wildlife Conservation Commission, www.floridaconservation.org

Florida Fishing and Boating, www.floridafishing-boating.com

Florida Trail Association, www.florida-trail.org

State parks

Florida has 145 state parks, which couple breath-taking scenery with opportunities to enjoy hiking, riding, water sports and picknicking. Roughly half allow camping and fees range from $8–$20 per site per night. Larger parks have cabins for rent ($40–$125 per night). Additional fees for apply for electricity, waterside sites and large parties. Many parks now require advance booking through Reserve America, toll free, at 1-800-326-3521. A Florida State Park Guide is available on the Internet at, **www**.dep.state.fl.us/parks, **www**.florida stateparks.org, or by calling, **t** (850) 488 9872.

Sunburn

Try to avoid the sun at its strongest, from 11am-3pm. Use a waterproof sunscreen with a high protection factor specifically designed for children and apply it liberally and often, particularly after swimming. Make sure children wear hats outdoors and protect babies with sunshades and hats. In hot weather everyone will need to drink plenty of water.

Teen issues

Make sure teens are careful where they use their mobile phone. Let them know it's not worth a fight if someone tries to steal it.

The legal age for alcohol consumption in Florida is 21 and being 'carded' – asked to show a passport, driving license or other government form of ID including proof of age – is commonplace. Giving teenagers a sip of your wine with a meal might be *de rigeur* in Europe but is frowned upon here.

Illegal drugs are available in many parts of Florida but penalties are tougher than they are in Europe. Even a small amount of marijuana could land you in jail and the USA's strict entry policy excludes those convicted of drug offences. In the UK, look out for the leaflet 'Drugs Abroad'. For more information in the UK call:

The National Drugs Helpline, t 0800 77 66 00

Warn teenagers who are going out in the evening alone of the dangers of drugs and alcohol. They may be unaware of the danger of swimming when drunk or that the risk of dehydrating in nightclubs is greater in the heat. *See* Water Safety, p.28.

Telephones

The USA's international dialling code is +1 and the outgoing code is 011. Dial 01144 for the UK, removing the first 0 of the domestic phone number. Mobile networks cover most of the country, including all urban areas, however unless you have a tri-band phone it is likely your cellular phone from home will not work in the United States. A better option is to hire a phone for the duration of your visit.

Tickets

Concert, sport and theatre tickets can be obtained from the following websites:
www.ticketmaster.com
www.frontrowusa.com
www.stagefront.com

Theme park tickets

Attraction Tickets Direct, **t** 0845 130 3876, **www.attraction-tickets-direct.co.uk**
http://disneyworld.disney.go.com
www.onlineflorida.co.uk
www.best4attractions.co.uk
www.orlando-ticket-deals.co.uk

Time

The US is divided into six time zones and most of Florida, is in the Eastern Standard Time zone, five hours behind Greenwich Mean Time. Parts of Northwest Florida (west of the Apalachicola River) are in the Central Time zone (six hours behind GMT). Clocks go forward and backward in summer and winter in line with British Summer Time.

Tipping

A standard tip of 15% is common in taxis, restaurants, bars and upscale hotels, although there is no need to tip in fast-food restaurants. Particularly good service should be rewarded with a 20% tip. Many restaurants automatically add between 15% and 20% to their bills; do not be shy to ask whether service is included.

Toilets

Toilets in the US are largely spotless and have individual seat liners and good washing facilities available. Watch out for self-flushing toilets, which flush after a certain amount of time has elapsed.

Tourist offices

Tourist Offices are generally called Convention & Visitors Bureaus (CVBs) and are open, from 9–5 weekdays and sometimes on Saturdays as well, staff can provide information about events, tours, museums, restaurants and hotels. In a small town the tourist office will often go under the local Chamber of Commerce. See sightseeing chapters for details of address and phone numbers for local CVBs in Florida.

Tourist office contacts in the UK

www.VISITFLORIDA.com. This is official state website for travel planning in Florida. Weather and news updates, plus information on special deals and packages are updated regularly.
Daytona Beach, **t** (01737) 643 764, **www.daytonabeach.com**
Florida Keys & Key West, **t** (01564) 794555, **www.fla-keys.com**
Greater Fort Lauderdale, **t** (01737) 643791, **www.sunny.org**
Greater Miami, **t** (01444) 443355, **www.miamianbeaches.com**
Kennedy Space Centre, **t** (020) 7328 5003, **www.kennedyspacecenter.com**
Kissimmee St Cloud Tourism Bureau, **t** (01732) 875 722, **www.floridakiss.com**
Beaches of Fort Myers and Sanibel, **t** (01737 644722, **www.fortmyers-sanibel.com/uk**
Orlando Tourism Bureau, **t** 0800 018 67 60, **www.orlandoinfo.com/uk**
Palm Beach, **t** (020) 8876 2742, **www.palmbeachfl.com**
Sarasota/Bradenton CVB, **t** (020) 7257 8891, **www.sarasotafl.org**, **www.floridasislandbeaches.com**
St Petersburg/Clearwater, **t** (020) 8651 4742, **www.floridasbeach.com**

Tampa Bay, t (020) 7729 8147, www.visittampabay.com

Water safety

Make sure children are aware of the dangers posed by the sea and by swimming pools and that they never go swimming alone.

Before you swim, always check that it is safe to do so and observe beach warning flags and signs. Lakes and rivers connected to the hydroelectric system can be lethal when the dams are opened as the water level can rise dramatically. Currents can be stronger than you realize, and seemingly shallow beaches can slope away from the shore quite steeply. Warn children about rip tides (strong underwater currents) and do not swim in water that appears cloudy or choppy.

Contact the Clean Beaches Council, **t** (202) 682 9507, **www**.cleanbeaches.org for details of beach standards in Florida and a list of the state's best beaches.

Water quality

Water quality varies considerably from county to county. To be on the safe side, visitors should only drink bottled water and boil tap water thoroughly for making hot drinks. Some hotels have water purifiers and some provide bottled water in your room (though not always for free). For more information, visit, **www**.floridaenvironment.com and **www**.epa.gov/safewater

What to take

The golden rule with long-haul holidays is to not take too much with you. Leave behind your hair tongs and make-up, your high heels and clutch of novels, your evening gowns and dinner jackets. This is not going to be a holiday where you'll need them. Bring a cover up like a cardigan or wrap or a light jacket for breezy nights along the coast. If visiting the north of Florida in winter, pack a couple of long-sleeved tops and a lightweight and breathable waterproof jacket, which will also come in handy for the summer rainy season in all part of Florida. Take a pair of comfortable shoes or trainers and pack plenty of pairs of socks for the kids. Walking shorts, jeans, skirts and summer dresses are all appropriate for the Florida weather and loose fitting clothes are preferable to figure hugging outfits. The Florida sun is very hot, so each member of the family should have a hat and a pair of sunglasses (UVA, UVB and UVC 400nm) with them. Sun lotion is widely available so don't feel the need to load your bag up with it for the trip. A small bottle for applying after you step off the plane will be sufficient.

Clothing is inexpensive to buy in America, so you can easily pick up items like beach shoes and sun tops pretty much anywhere. Leave a bit of room in your suitcase for souvenir clothing or for those must-have items for your kids that are much cheaper to buy in the US. Clothes make great souvenirs, especially hats, T-shirts and dresses that remind your child what a great time they had.

Most hotels provide towels; so don't feel the need to bring one for each member of the family. A couple of big beach towels should do.

Even the smartest restaurants have a fairly flexible dress policy, which means you can leave formal wear at home and go for a smart casual look. Providing no one is wearing swimwear at the table, you should be fine. Even at beach bars its advisable to cover up while having a meal.

Fun things for kids

- **Paper and day-glo pens**
- **Zip lock bags for treasures (though urge children not to take artefacts or live creatures/plants home with you)**
- **Pack of cards – The Green Board Game Company, (01494 538 999, www.greenboardgames.com) has an Around the World Snap game so kids can learn about other countries while on the go. They also stock a handy Travel Wheel where young kids can place reusable stickers on a picture board and move the dial round as their journey progresses.**
- **Magnetic boards – Dowling Magnets (www.dowlingmagnets.com available in the UK through Mail Order Express t 08700 12 90 90, www.mailorderexpress.com) make great travel-size boards with a variety of themed magnets for kids to play with in transit. Best of all the pieces don't fall off and get lost under the seat.**
- **Compass/stopwatch**
- **Mini torch**
- **Travel journal with souvenir pockets**

Sleep

05

Space may be the final frontier for some but it's not an issue in Florida. You will usually find big rooms and a variety of accommodation, especially in popular places such as Orlando and Miami, from luxury resort hotels to log cabins, cruise boats to condo rentals – so there's bound to be something to suit every pocket and need. Families might also want to consider a two-centre or two-hotel holiday. So, for example, you can combine a couple of nights in an upmarket hotel on Miami Beach with a week camping in the Keys or a few days at Disney's Animal Kingdom® Lodge with a week's villa rental in Kissimmee.

The easiest way to book is by email or on the internet. You can see what is available and often, if you email a hotel and they have no vacancies, they will suggest alternative accommodation to you.

It is best to book your accommodation several months in advance, especially if you want to stay at a particular hotel. All-in packages with car hire, hotel and flights are available often up to a year ahead but you won't necessarily end up saving money and may not have much control over the accommodation you receive. One option is to do the groundwork on the internet to see what a DIY holiday would cost if you sourced the flights, car hire and accommodation direct. Then go to your travel agent and see what they can do. Often travel agents will be prepared to negotiate the price in order to get the sale.

If you choose to book your accommodation direct, a call to ask about the hotel's best rate can often save you up to half the price quoted in brochures or online but make sure you receive an email to confirm. When booking on the internet, be sure to print your confirmation email and take it with you when you travel, in case what you've booked is not what you get. If you've booked a package, bring the brochure along and be prepared to take it up with the rep, if the room you've been allocated is not up to standard. Florida, especially Orlando, is bristling with hotels, so there's always somewhere else you can go if you don't like what you see.

The options below range from the grand to the comfortable but all have been selected for their suitability for families. Many independent hotels have been included because of their innovative kids' programmes and unique facilities. Chain hotels with children's services are also mentioned below. *See also* Travel p.11 for a list of UK travel agents that offer holidays packages and special interest holidays/accommodation in Florida and Disney Need to Know p.238 for Disney accommodation.

Good to know

Many Florida resorts let kids under 12 (and sometimes older) stay free when sharing a room with parents. Be sure to give the number of children and their ages when you're making reservations. If travelling with toddlers, ask about safety features in hotel rooms and if plug socket covers, door latches and nightlights are available. Make sure you stipulate whether you want a balcony or ground floor room and confirm this when you check in.

Room rates

Inexpensive	below $90
Moderate	$90 to $150
Expensive	$151 to $200
Very expensive	above $200

Hotel chains

Some of the hotel chains in America, such as Best Western and Holiday Inn, will be familiar to UK holidaymakers and should prove a safe bet. Book through their UK websites or call the UK reservation line. Most rooms are priced per room per night and offer twin double beds or a double sofa bed for kids. Family suites or rooms with built-in partitions are more common in chain hotels, which attempt to mix business with pleasure and attract families, as well as their professional clientele. For an updated list of chains visit, www.hotel-chains-online.com

Inexpensive

Comfort Inn

www.choicehotels.com

Part of the Choice Hotels Group (Clarion, Sleep Inn, Econo Lodge, Quality Inns) this value-for-money chain offers free breakfasts, newspapers and local calls.

Days Inn

www.daysinn.com

Self-catering serviced apartments with lounges and kitchens. The longer you stay the cheaper the price. Online discounts are also available.

Super 8 Motels

www.super8.com

Affordable motel accommodation.

Moderate–Expensive

Best Western

www.bestwestern.com

Kids clubs, free breakfasts and resort amenities are available at select destinations.

Hilton

www.hilton.com

In-room amenities include games and movies for kids, plus children's programmes at larger resorts, *see* Hilton Fontainbleau, Miami p.48

Holiday Inn Hotels, Resorts, Express

www.hionline.com

Larger Holiday Inn Resorts feature Kidsuites where two or up to three children sleep in their own screened off space complete with TV, video games and CD player. Kidsuites also offer coffee-making facilities, a microwave and fridge. Other facilities vary from resort to resort but most include family activity sessions or children's meal deals. *See* in particular the Nick Hotel in Orlando, p.42.

Radisson

www.radisson.com

Kids' clubs available at larger resorts.

Sheraton Hotels, Inns, Resorts and Sleep Inns

www.sheraton.com

Weekend family packages include kids' meal deals, late check out and other child-friendly facilities depending on the resort.

Very expensive

Loews Hotels

www.loewshotels.com

The Loews Loves Kids programme includes kids' menus, information on family amusements and baby-sitting services, plus a free gift bag for children under 10. The programme also offers lending game libraries, tours and supervised play programmes. Children under 18 stay for free. Room childproof kits are available for kids under 4, and cots and roll-away beds are provided at no extra charge.

Ritz-Carlton

www.ritzcarlton.com

The Ritz Kids' programme is for children aged 5–12 and includes stimulating activities ranging from arts and crafts and cookery to water sports and outdoor games). If you imagine your dream playgroup setting complete with teepee tent and cookout, play area, puppets, costumes and lots of toys and books then you're close to Ritz Kids. There's even a kids' night out experience at weekends where children can enjoy dinner and a movie without their parents.

NORTHWEST

Apalachicola

Gibson Inn

51 Avenue C, Apalachicola, **t** (850) 653 2191, **www.gibsoninn.com** (*inexpensive–expensive*)

Listed on the National Register of Historic Places, this small Victorian hotel has 30 rooms, several with four-poster beds, as well as private baths and cable TV. From horse riding by the sea to kayaking off the coast, there are several ways of relaxing here. Spoil the family with a gourmet breakfast in bed.

Old Salt Works Cabins

1085 Cape San Blas Road, Port St. Joe, **t** (850) 229 6097 (*moderate–very expensive*)

One of several cabin resorts in the area, these offer unique and surprisingly modern accommodation. Nature trails, a fort and a mini museum are fun for the kids. Kayaking, canoeing, surf fishing and swimming are just some of the activities on offer.

Destin and Fort Walton Beach

Leeside Inn and Marina

1350 Highway 98 East, Fort Walton Beach, **t** (850) 243 7359, **www.leesideinn.com** (*inexpensive–moderate*)

Standard rooms in this comfortable beachside hotel contain two queen-size beds. Rooms with kitchenette units, king-size beds and poolside

Good to know

When arriving in Florida, you need to give an address on your immigration form for at least your first night. If you're planning to tour, book the first few nights to get settled and phone ahead if travelling to remote areas. It is possible just to turn up somewhere like Key West (in the off-season) and get a room but the more remote barrier islands are less likely to have last-minute accommodation.

views are also available for family use. Golfing, sailing, fishing and tennis are all in walking distance of the hotel, as well as the Gulfarium (*see* p.68) and outlet malls.

SunDestin Beach Resort

1040 Highway 98 East, Destin, t (850) 837 7093
(*moderate–very expensive*)

This friendly hotel offers easy access to all area activities, dining and shopping. The front desk is open 24hrs and guests can make use of two pools, outdoors and in (heated seasonally). There's disabled access to the beach and a video games room. All rooms feature fully equipped kitchens, cable TV, VCR, free video rental, and either balconies or patios. Children's activities are available in season.

Panama City

The Boardwalk Beach Resort

9450 South Thomas Drive, Panama City Beach, t (850) 234 3484, www.boardwalkbeachresort.com
(*inexpensive–expensive*)

Two hotels in one, with a total of 320 rooms including connecting rooms for families, as well as family rooms fitted with bunk beds for kids. Two pools are available, one heated, and there's also a children's pool. Kids eat free in the restaurants and there are a range of kids' clubs for different age groups and a playground nearby.

Edgewater Beach Resort

11212 Front Beach Road, Panama City Beach, t 800 874 8686, www.edgewaterbeachresort.com
(*expensive–very expensive*)

This premier beach resort offers luxury one to three bed accommodations. The hotel also offers facilities such as a lagoon pool, restaurant, golf, tennis, and a complete children's recreational programme to give parents some time out. A spa and fitness center is also available on site.

Flamingo Motel

15525 Front Beach Road, Panama City Beach, t (850) 234 2232, www.flamingomotel.com
(*inexpensive–expensive*)

Family owned and operated, rooms accommodate two to eight people. Amenities include a swimming pool and a spa pool, plus the Gulf World Marine Park is just across the road, *see* p.65.

Marriott Bay Point Resort Village

4200 Marriott Drive (off Thomas Drive), Panama City Beach, t (850) 234 3307, www.marriottbaypoint.com
(*expensive–very expensive*)

This lovely bayside resort offers 78 luxury one to two bedroom villas, as well as 356 individually appointed rooms and suites, some with disabled access. Other amenities include a spa and fitness centre, on-site Discovery Center, (offering golf, spa, water sports and refreshments). The hotel also offers a choice of four restaurants, one indoor and three outdoor pools plus spa pool and a private bay beach area.

Pensacola

Best Western Perdido Key

13585 Perdido Key Drive, t (850) 492 2755
(*moderate*)

Conveniently located for the beach, the hotel offers non-smoking rooms, cable/satellite TV and a swimming pool and hot tub. Free continental breakfast is available.

Clarion Suites Resort

20 Via de Luna, Pensacola Beach, t (850) 932 4300
(*inexpensive–expensive*)

There are 86 suites, all fitted with full kitchen facilities, two phones and two TVs. The master bedroom has a queen-sized bed and there's a separate living area with sofa bed, making it a good choice for families. Extra activities such as volleyball, cycling and Playstations are available. Accommodation includes use of the outdoor pool, depending on the season. Children aged 18 and under stay free when sharing a room with their parents.

The Dunes

333 Fort Pickens Road, Pensacola Beach, t (850) 932 3536, www.theduneshotel.com
(*inexpensive–very expensive*)

All 76 rooms have private balconies and are available as non-smoking. Volleyball nets on the beach, a bike path and a heated pool are just some of the facilities offered. Golf packages are available. Three newly remodelled King Executive rooms are provided for those who require disabled access. Children aged 18 and under stay free when sharing a room with their parents. A nanny service is also available.

South Walton County

Sandestin Beach Hilton

4000 Sandestin Boulevard, Sandestin, **t** (850) 267 9500, **www.sandestinbeachhilton.com** (*moderate–very expensive*)

600 spacious suites, 400 of which contain bunk beds for children. Golf facilities, as well as 15 tennis courts, three swimming pools and a spa pool are all available, along with the world-class spa and fitness centre.

Sandestin Golf and Beach Resort

9300 Emerald Coast Parkway West, Sandestin, **t** (866) 293 4816, **www.sandestin.com** (*moderate–very expensive*)

One to four bedroom condominiums, villas, town homes, hotel rooms and suites all are all available at this resort complex. A beautiful beach, tennis courts, 73 holes of golf and bike rentals are just some of the amenities on offer. The Kid Zone programme that's available in the summer, along with the pirate ship playground and nature play park, available year round, make this an ideal destination for a family holiday.

Seaside Cottages

P.O. Box 4730, Seaside, **t** (850) 231 2222, **www.seasidefl.com** (*very expensive*)

More than 270 cottages in pristine Seaside are available for a perfect, seaside holiday with the kids. Families will have plenty of scope for an active break with access to three large swimming pools (one adult only) and two toddler pools, six tennis courts and a croquet lawn, as well as kayaking, sailing and golfing facilities. Also adults' bicycles, wagons, beach cruisers, geared bikes and tandem bikes are available for rent. Cots and highchairs are provided for younger children.

Suwanee River

Miller's Marine and Suwannee Houseboats

Route 349 South of Highway 19/98, Suwannee, **t** (352) 542 7349 (*very expensive*)

Accommodation for real nature lovers, the houseboat sleeps up to eight adults comfortably. A number of water activities are available; the river is even wide enough for kids to help drive the boat. On-site lodging is also on offer.

Tallahassee

Double Tree Hotel

101 South Adams Street, **t** (850) 224 5000 (*moderate*)

This newly renovated hotel offers 243 rooms including five two-bedroom suites. The hotel is wheelchair accessible, has an outdoor pool with sundeck and an on-site fitness centre. There are highchairs and cots for children, as well as a kids' menu and a free chocolate chip cookie on arrival.

Governors Inn

209 South Adams Street, **t** (850) 681 6855, **www.thegovinn.com** (*moderate–very expensive*)

This beautifully decorated hotel has 40 rooms and suites each named after a former Florida governor. Kids will love the twin four-poster beds and loft bedrooms. Room service and continental breakfasts are also available. All suites come with sofa beds to accommodate families.

Wakulla Springs

Wakulla Springs Lodge

Wakulla Springs State Park, 550 Wakulla Park Drive, Wakulla Springs, **t** (850) 224 5950 (*inexpensive*)

Another residence on the National Register of Historic Places, this authentic 1930s' lodge offers 27 beautifully furnished rooms in a lovely countryside setting. Biking and canoeing facilities are available and there are lots of wildlife activities in the surrounding parkland to keep the kids occupied.

NORTHEAST

Amelia Island

Amelia Island Plantation

Route A1A, Amelia Island, **t** (904) 261 6161, **www.aipfl.com** (*expensive–very expensive*)

An award-winning children's programme makes this a great place for a family holiday. Kids aged 3–10 can enjoy **Kids Camp Amelia**, which includes the Just for Kids supper parties featuring hayrides and the chance to make their own video. The **Teen Explorer** programme, offers activities such as bowling, basketball, barbeques and bonfires. Parents can relax at the spa or golf course, know ing that their children are having just as much fun as they are.

Florida House Inn

22 South 3rd Street, Fernandina Beach, Amelia Island, t (904) 261 3300 (*expensive–very expensive*)

Another gem from the National Register of Historic Places, this charming B&B offers 15 rooms with wrought iron beds and handmade rugs and quilts. A few have large Jacuzzi tubs and 10 have working fireplaces. Families might also like to stay at the rustic and beautifully furnished one- and two-bedroom carriage houses next door, both with living rooms and kitchens and available for daily or weekly rentals. Scooters are also available for rent.

The Ritz-Carlton, Amelia Island

4750 Amelia Island Parkway, Amelia Island, t (904) 277 1100, www.ritzcarlton.com (*very expensive*)

Located beside a championship 18-hole PGA golf course and overlooking the Atlantic Ocean, this combines the natural beauty of a barrier island with luxury accommodation. The best part of staying at one of the Florida Ritz-Carlton resorts is The Ritz Kids' programme (*see* under hotel chains p.31). There is also has a nanny service for under-5s. Golf and spa facilities lie in wait for the adults or the whole family can opt for a bike ride, swim or play tennis. There is a separate children's pool, a playground and children's meals are available. Rooms feature children's entertainment channels; games and VCRs and videos are available to rent.

Atlantic Beach

Sea Turtle Inn

1 Ocean Boulevard, Atlantic Beach, t (904) 249 7402, www.seaturtle.com (*moderate–very expensive*)

The Sea Turtle has more than 190 guestrooms, all with fine furnishings and lovely views. Oceanfront rooms have balconies, king-size beds and microwave ovens. Beachfront dining can be had at the award-winning Plantains Restaurant and the pool has the cabana bar and veranda. There's also a lounge with live entertainment.

Gainseville

Bambi Motel Budget Host

2119 Southwest 13th Street, t (352) 376 2622 (*inexpensive*)

This offers 34 fully air-conditioned rooms, both smoking and non-smoking and has a children's playground and pool.

Sweetwater Branch Inn

625 East University Avenue, t (352) 373 6760, www.sweetwaterinn.com (*inexpensive–expensive*)

Victorian elegance in the heart of the historic district, this B&B is arranged over two houses with 15 lovely rooms, including two interconnecting ones. Two furnished apartments nearby, available for day, weekly or monthly rentals, may be more suitable for families with younger children.

Jacksonville

Hilton Jacksonville Riverfront

1201 Riverplace Boulevard, t (904) 398 8800 (*moderate*)

Another luxury Hilton hotel, all 291 rooms and suites include the niceties of home but with better views. The hotel has an on-site pool and fitness centre, as well as a walking and jogging track. Children's activities are very popular and kids' menus, cots and highchairs are all available.

Ponte Vedra Beach

Ponte Vedra Inn & Club

200 Ponte Vedra Boulevard, Ponte Vedra Beach, t (904) 285 1111, www.pvresorts.com (*very expensive*)

This 1920s' beach club resort has 250 rooms and suites, plus two 18-hole golf courses, an on-site spa offering lots of pampering, four pools and tennis courts. Cycling, sailing and fishing are also on offer. There's an activity programme for kids featuring pizza parties, storytelling, crafts, bingo and even etiquette. The playground has swings, slides and ropes and a play boat for the little ones.

Sawgrass Marriott Resort and Beach Club

1000 PGA Tour Boulevard, Ponte Vedra Beach, t (904) 285 7777, www.sawgrassmarriott.com (*very expensive*)

This luxurious resort offers 508 guest rooms, 24 VIP suites and 80 two-bed villa suites. It is also home to five championship golf courses. The resort has three outdoor pools and two spa pools, a sauna, on-site spa and fitness facilities, as well as a beauty salon. The Sawgrass Grasshopper Gang , the children's programme for 5–12 year olds, is run by youth-education specialists, so parents can be assured that their children are under experienced supervision. Activities range from sandcastle sculpting to 'pizza & pool' parties.

Silver Springs

Holiday Inn – Silver Springs

5751 East Silver Springs Boulevard, t (352) 236 2575 (*inexpensive–moderate*)

Over 100 rooms are available some with spa baths, plus an on-site restaurant, which provides room service until 11pm. Pets are not permitted in rooms but kennels are available. There's also a pool and an exercise room.

St. Augustine

Casa Monica Hotel

95 Cordova Street, t (904) 827 1888, www.casamonica.com (*very expensive*)

Built in 1888 as a flagship Flagler hotel, and restored in 1999, this pink-turreted, castle-like hotel combines Spanish architecture and décor with modern comforts, such as a business centre, in-room internet access, cable TV and a second-floor pool, sundeck and spa pool. There are 138 unique guest rooms some of which have twin queen beds or a king-size bed and sofa bed. The hotel can arrange a tour of its classic car collection, horse-drawn carriage rides and an Adventure Package that is perfect for families. This includes room accommodation, a gourmet breakfast in 95 Cordova (*see* Where to eat p.102) and tickets to A Ghostly Experience (*see* p.93). The hotel can also arrange bike rentals, horse riding, sailing, fishing and golfing. Guests also have access to the Serenata Beach Club, a private oceanfront club on Ponte Vedra Beach, with fitness equipment, family pool, adult pool, poolside bar and food, beach equipment rentals and recreational activities.

Days Inn Historic

2800 Ponce de León Boulevard, t (904) 829 6582 (*inexpensive–moderate*)

This serviced apartment building is in the heart of the historic district with 124 rooms, and on-site pool and restaurant. It's beside the departure point for the sightseeing tram and within easy reach of all the main attractions.

Yogi Bear's Jellystone Park

1051 Southwest Old St Augustine Road, Madison, t (850) 973 8269, www.jellystoneflorida.com (*inexpensive–expensive*)

Heaven for Yogi Bear fans, this resort provides cabins that sleep 2–10 people, as well as camping grounds for tents and caravans. This is definitely a holiday destination for the kids with facilities such as volleyball, basketball and paintball, as well as a pool with a huge waterslide, a mini golf course and a games room. Themed weekends run Mar–Oct.

WEST CENTRAL

Anne Maria Island

Rod & Reel Motel

877 North Shore Drive, t (941) 778 2780, www.rodandreelmotel.com (*inexpensive–expensive*)

Small retreat offering beautiful scenery and wildlife. Close to the beach.

Seaside Inn and Beach Resort

2200 Gulf Drive North, Bradenton Beach, t (941) 778 5254, www.seasideresort.com (*moderate–very expensive*)

Private balconies and private beach, this beautiful resort is small but charming. The rooms are all tastefully decorated and include a newly renovated penthouse. Para-sailing, wind surfing, jet skiing, sailing, boating, deep sea fishing excursions and bicycling are just some of the activities on offer.

Bradenton

Behind the Fence

1400 Viola Drive, Brandon, Florida, t (813) 685 8201 (*inexpensive*)

One of Florida's best kept secrets, this lovely B&B offers tranquility with all the modern touches of home. A lagoon-like pool and homemade Amish rolls for breakfast are some of the best things on offer. The owners, Larry and Carolyn Yoss keep the 1800s' charm authentic and welcome their guests with the warmth of the era. Under 10s stay free.

Holiday Inn Riverfront

100 Riverfront Drive, t (941) 747 3727, www.holiday-inn.com (*moderate–expensive*)

153 rooms, each with a private balcony, and most offering river views. There's an outdoor pool and spa pool and kids eat forfree in the on-site restaurants.

Clearwater

Best Western Sea Stone Resort

445 Hamden Drive, Clearwater Beach, t (727) 441 1722 (*inexpensive–moderate*)

This casual bayside resort has over 40 rooms, including several deluxe rooms with lovely views and two-room suites with kitchenettes. There's an outdoor pool, restaurant and bar. Pets are allowed.

Marriott Suites Clearwater Beach on Sand Key

1201 Gulf Boulevard, Clearwater Beach, t (727) 596 1100, www.clearwaterbeachmarriottsuites.com (*expensive*)

Overlooking Clearwater Bay, this hotel has 220 suites all with a separate living area and a double sofa bed. There's a heated pool with cascading waterfalls, an aquatic playground, a salon and spa and varied dining facilities. Lisa's Klubhouse, named after the resident parrot, is specifically for kids and offers a daily programme of fun activities for ages 4–12, run by qualified staff.

Hilton Clearwater Beach Resort

400 Mandalay Avenue, Clearwater Beach, t (877) 461 3222, www.hiltonclearwaterbeachresort.com (*expensive–very expensive*)

This family-friendly beach resort has 425 rooms, many with balconies and beautiful views of the Gulf of Mexico. There are a limited number of suites. The Kids Fun Factory programme caters for children from 4–12 with activities that vary from arts and crafts sessions to boat excursions.

The Palm Pavilion Inn

18 Bay Esplanade, t (800) 433 7256, www.palmpavilioninn.com (*inexpensive–moderate*)

Blink and you're on Miami's South Beach. This Art Deco landmark has a lovely exterior but indoors the style is more executive comfort than boutique hotel. There's a pool, sundeck and beachside facilities include a shop, grill and bar with live entertainment. There are 29 new bedrooms, some with a separate kitchen and living space, microwaves, tea and coffee facilities and lovely views. An affordable option that's right on the beach.

Crystal River

Port Hotel and Marina

1610 Southeast Paradise Circle, off Highway 19, t (352) 795 3111, www.porthotelandmarina.com (*inexpensive–moderate*)

This hotel complex sits on the river. Paddle boats, manatee dives and a sizeable outdoor pool are all available (additional fee for the boat and equipment rental). Waterfront dining is also available at the Crystal River Ale House, family restaurant.

Dunedin

Holiday Inn Express

975 Broadway (Alternate Highway 19), t (727) 4501200 (*moderate*)

This easy-access hotel has 76 rooms and suites, including Kidsuites (*see* p.31). An outdoor heated pool and spa and fitness centre are on site, with nature trails, golf, windsurfing, jet skiing, fishing and sailing all within walking distance.

Homosassa

Homosassa Riverside Resort

5297 South Cherokee Way, t (352) 628 2474 (*moderate–very expensive*)

The Homosassa River provides winter shelter for the West Indian Manatee, so it is likely that you will spot one of these beautiful creatures while here. The double-decker monkey bar provides a chance to enjoy the local wildlife allowing views of monkeys, dolphins and manatees in their own habitat. Boats and other water sports equipment are also available.

Lido Key

Helmsley Sandcastle

1540 Ben Franklin Drive, Lido Key, t (941) 388 2181, www.helmsleysandcastle.com (*moderate–expensive*)

Located on lovely Lido Beach, this hotel is popular with UK families, offers 179 rooms, including two junior suites, most with beach views and balconies and is is convenient to the celebrated shops of St. Armand's Circle and Sarasota's many attractions. There are two heated outdoor pools, a restaurant, café and volleyball court. Wind-surfers, sailboats and aqua-cycles are available at the beach.

Lido Beach Resort

700 Ben Franklin Drive, Lido Key, t (941) 388 2161, www.lidobeachresort.com (*very expensive*)

This former Radisson resort offers a beautiful garden with waterfalls and a Koi pond, two heated free-form swimming pools, three poolside jacuzzis, a private white sand beach and a fitness centre. Most of the 222 rooms and suites have fitted kitchens; all with fridges, hairdryers, microwave ovens and tea and coffee making facilities.

The Ritz-Carlton Sarasota

1111 Ritz-Carlton Drive, Lido Key, t (941) 309 2000, www.ritzcarlton.com (*very expensive*)

You could be in a hotel, or maybe you've skipped off to paradise. Everything here is lovely, from the waterside views to the state-of-the-art spa, spa pool, sauna, steam room, relaxation area and the well-appointed rooms of the VIK (Very Important Kid) registration desk. Dining options are a casual terrace café, steakhouse restaurant, beachside grill and Vernona, an American fine-dining establishment, open for all meals and offering a fabulous brunch on Sundays. There's a special kids' menu that includes plenty of fresh fruit and vegetables. Treats are allowed too – don't be surprised to see children wandering along munching on oversized cookies – they don't mind if you drop crumbs, they practically encourage it. The biggest thrill here is taking a golf cart over to the Member's Beach Club (exclusively for members and hotel guests) home to the Ritz Kids programme and a breathtaking infinity pool and sundeck. There's a private beach, fitness classes, a huge sunset terrace, separate kids' pool and a choice of restaurant or bar dining.

Longboat Key

The Colony Beach & Tennis Resort

1620 Gulf of Mexico Drive, t (941) 383 6464, www.colonybeachresort.com (*expensive–very expensive*)

Anyone for tennis? The Colony is rated number one in the US for its tennis facilities, which include 21 hard and clay courts; some lit for night play. All levels are catered for, whether you want a competitive tournament or just to learn how to play. Even if tennis is not your game you can still relax and enjoy the lovely beachfront, pool, spa and fitness centre. There are one- and two-bedroom suites that feature a living room and kitchen with a dishwasher, whirlpool bath, steam shower room and accommodation over two floors. Family packages are available that include a welcome gift, $50 daily resort credit per suite per day, beach gifts for children under 12 and complimentary breakfast (two per suite) There are two resort programmes for kids, the 'Kinder Kamp' (ages 3–6) and 'Kidding Around' (ages 7–12) with activities ranging from beach games, swimming, fishing and shelling to creative art projects and tennis instruction. Families can choose casual or fine dining in the hotel.

Sarasota

Sun N Fun Resort

7125 Fruitville Road, t 9941) 371 2505, www.sunnfunfl.com (*inexpensive–expensive*)

Large canalside RV (caravan) and holiday home park set in beautiful wooded grounds with a restaurant, huge swimming pool, separate children's pool, two hot tubs, a lake with boat dock and a fishing dock, pitch and putt and mini golf, tennis courts and play area. There's also an alligator pond and a chapel. You can rent a room or suite by the day, week or month.

Siesta Key

Captiva Beach Resort

6772 Sara Sea Circle, t (941) 349 4131, www.captivabeachresort.com (*moderate–expensive*)

This small beachside resort is family-owned and run and very family-friendly. The 20 rooms all have a kitchen with microwave, a separate bath and toilet, colour TV with satellite, BBQ grill, and bottled-quality tap water. There is also a communal outdoor sitting area and laundry facilities. The hotel has shared use of a pool within this quiet cul-de-sac resort and the lovely beach is minutes' away. Fruit from the owner's garden is provided on arrival and guests are offered home-baked cakes and use of a book club and beach toys. Attention to detail here makes all the difference.

Tropical Breeze Resort & Spa

5150 Ocean Boulevard, t (941) 349 1125, www.tropicalbreezeinn.com (*moderate–very expensive*)

This resort is more like a small town with a range of properties for different family groups. Some units are on the beach while others are clustered around shady gardens. All have TVs, VCRs, microwaves and fridges and all suites offer fully equipped kitchens. Deluxe condos with private pools are also available.

St. Pete's Beach

Blue Water Cottages

8105 West Gulf Boulevard, Treasure Island, Sunset Beach, t (727) 3607993, www.bluewatercottages.com (*inexpensive–expensive*)

Cosy 1–2 bedroom cottages, all beautifully decorated. The resort offers a heated pool (with a spa cove and fibre-optic lighting at night), beach pavilion, playground and BBQ grills. This family owned resort is a peaceful destination for a quiet family holiday.

Don CeSar Beach Resort & Spa

3400 Gulf Boulevard, t (727) 360 1881, www.doncesar.com (*expensive–very expensive*)

This elegant and enormous pastel confection has been known as Florida's Legendary Pink Palace since 1928. Now part of the Loews Hotel Group, the resort has 227 recently renovated rooms, including 50 suites and two penthouses, plus a new pool and sun deck. The hotel offers 'Camp Cesar', a kids' programme for ages 5–10, with activities ranging from jewellery-making to discovering marine life. The hotel also offers the Loews Loves Kids programme (*see* hotel chains p.31). Kids can run about on the beaches and enjoy the gardens, as well as take part in activities such as beach crafts and seashell hunts to ice cream socials and Friday night themed dinner parties. For parents, there's a 24-hour spa and fitness centre and fishing facilities. Family packages offer buffet breakfast and a half-day session at the kids' camp.

Sirata Beach Resort & Conference Center

5300 Gulf Boulevard, t (727) 363 5100, www.sirata.com (*expensive–very expensive*)

The resort offers something for everyone; three heated pools, two spa pools, a water activities kiosk, playground, paddleboats, hammocks, fitness centre and several choices of dining. There are 380 suites and rooms, most with balconies for beautiful views of the area, especially at sunset. Rooms and suites for the disabled are also available.

Tradewinds Island Grand

5500 Gulf Boulevard, t (727) 367 6461, www.tradewindsresort.com (*expensive–very expensive*)

There's one thing that's guaranteed – the kids will love it here. The Island Grand is one of three adjacent Tradewinds properties thatcommand a sizeable chunk of beachfront between them. This sprawling, effortlessly family-friendly resort has spacious suites with balconies and ocean views, four pools, including a children's pool, two spas, a business centre, fitness centres, beachfront hammocks and paddle boats. Some facilities require the purchase of an Explorer Pass to gain access. There's also a choice of casual and fine-dining restaurants, a deli sandwich bar and a coffee and cocktail bar in the lobby. Children will be like the KONK Club (Kids Only No Kidding!), a supervised programme of activities for ages 4–11 with crafts, games and themed daily fun sessions. Pre-registration is required, there's a nominal fee for the service and space is limited. Older kids and adults are welcome to join the T.A.Z. Team for on-site games, including glow-in-the-dark volleyball or sand-sculpting contests. The fun continues after the sun sets, as Capt. RedBeard and his crew take the stage at Pirate Island and entertain with songs, jokes and a search for buried shark's teeth. Families can then enjoy a 'dive-in' pirate movie in the heated pool. The beach is just steps away and, in summer, boasts a huge inflatable beach slide, an adrenalin assault course and a bouncy house. Frisbees, buckets and spades, floats and beach games are always available.

St. Petersburg

Renaissance Vinoy Resort

501 5th Avenue Northeast, t (727) 894 1000, www.renaissancehotels.com (*very expensive*)

This luxury resort is situated in St. Petersburg's up-and-coming waterfront area. Another addition to the National Register of Historical Places, the 1920s' resort building has been fabulously restored with opulent public rooms and contemporary bedrooms. Some rooms come with balconies and most feature tea- and coffee-making facilities, a bath and separate shower, hairdryer, satellite TV, pullout sofa, rollaway bed and cot. The resort offers fishing, a fitness centre and two large, heated, outdoor pools, complete with a dramatic cascading waterfall and three outdoor spas. There's an 18-hole golf course, 12 tennis courts and a private marina that offers sailboat rental, lessons and charters.

Hilton St Petersburg

333 First Street South, St. Petersburg, t (272) 894 5000, www.stpetehilton.com (*expensive–very expensive*)

In keeping with its address, the hotel boasts 333 rooms and 16 beautifully furnished suites. The outdoor courtyard has a heated pool, oversized jacuzzi and a sundeck. Families can choose to dine at Café 333, Pizza Hut Express or Brandi's Lobby Bar. The hotel health club and fitness centre also allow access to jogging paths and waterside parks.

Hilton St. Petersburg Carillon Park

950 Lake Carillon Drive, t (727) 540 0050, www.hiltonhotelstpete.com (*expensive–very expensive*)

Opened in spring 2005, this purpose-built resort offers stunning views of The Lake Carillon wildlife habitat and nature preserve and Tampa Bay. The hotel has 217 rooms (including 45 suites) fitted with either two queen- or king-size beds, a heated pool and spa and spacious restaurant. The hotel is 15 minutes' away from the areas attractions and downtown area and also provides a complimentary shuttle service to Tampa and St. Petersburg–Clearwater Airports.

Tampa

Holiday Inn Tampa – Busch Gardens

2701 East Fowler Avenue, **t** (813) 971 4710 (*moderate–expensive*)

Only five minutes' away from the famous Busch Gardens theme park, this Holiday Inn features a games room and two outdoor pools. There's a children's pool with pirate-ship slide, spouting whale and rain mushroom, plus a large heated outdoor pool. There's also a games arcade and a well-equipped fitness centre. The hotel has 408 rooms, including the highly popular Kidsuites (see hotel chains, p.31).Children under 12 stay free. There's an on-site TGI Friday's for family meals.

Saddlebrook Resort

5700 Saddlebrook Way, Wesley Chapel, North of Tampa, **t** (813) 973 1111, **www.saddlebrookresort.com** (*moderate–expensive*)

This beautifully landscaped getaway offers 800 rooms (all redecorated for autumn 2005) and 1–3 bedroom suites; children under 13 sharing room with adult stay free. There are two 18-hole golf courses, an impressive array of 45 tennis courts, a fitness centre, spa and sauna, volleyball and basketball courts and three pools, including the central 'Super Pool'. The S'Kids Club for 4–12 year olds allows parents and kids to do their own thing between 9–4 with themed active sessions for kids on different days of the week, such as Underwater Thursday.

Wingate Inn USF

3751 East Fowler Avenue, **t** (813) 979 2828 (*moderate*)

This clean and comfortable hotel is popular with the business crowd but also very friendly for families. They operate a free shuttle service to Busch Gardens and other destinations within a five-mile radius. There's an outdoor pool, business centre and an innovative aqua massage unit. The hotel has 85 rooms including three one-bedroom suites and features a complimentary breakfast bar.

Tarpon Springs

Westin Innisbrook Resort

36750 Highway 19, North Palm Harbor, **t** (727) 942 2000, **www.westin-innisbrook.com** (*expensive–very expensive*)

Amenities include four 18-hole championship golf courses, 11 tennis courts and six swimming pools, including the Loch Ness Monster pool, designed for kids, which features winding water slides, sandy beaches, jets and a cascading waterfall. The resort also offers a kids' programme featuring games and pool activities, a playground and mini golf course.

Venice

Hampton Inn and Suites Venice

881 Venetia Bay Boulevard, **t** (941) 488 5900, **www.hamptoninnvenice.com** (*expensive*)

Modern business-style accommodation with 76 rooms and 34 suites, complimentary continental breakfast, an outdoor heated pool, hot tub and fitness room. Under 18s stay free with parents.

Weeki Wachee

Comfort Inn Weeki Wachee

9373 Cortez Boulevard, **t** (352) 596 9000 (*inexpensive*)

Non-smoking and disabled-access rooms are available at this affordable lodging, which offers a fitness facility, outdoor pool and free continental breakfasts.

EAST CENTRAL

Cocoa Beach

Hampton Inn

3425 North Atlantic Avenue, **t** (321) 799 4099, **www.hamptoninncocoabeach.com** (*expensive*)

This beachfront hotel offers miles of golden sands, beautiful views and comfortable rooms. There's a fitness room and an outdoor heated pool. Beach equipment rental is available.

Wakulla Resort

3550 North Atlantic Avenue, **t** (321) 783 2230, **www.wakulla-suites.com** (*inexpensive–expensive*)

These bright, clean and attractive suites offer families a quiet space in which to relax whilst taking in the attractions of the Space Coast and Cocoa Beach. There are 116 suites with kitchens, cable TV and movies, breakfast area and lounges. There's a heated outdoor pool, shaded courtyard and tiki hut, BBQ area and direct access to the beach. Carrie Lee's gourmet coffee café serves up fresh coffee, pastries, sandwiches and salads.

Daytona Beach

Audrey's Beach House

2237 South Atlantic Avenue, Daytona Beach Shores, t 800 253 4920/, t (386) 252 4920 (*very expensive*)

Restored, exclusive oceanfront home under the same ownership as the Tropical Manor (*see* below). Colourfully decorated, this house has room for up to seven people, making it ideal for family holidays. Large outdoor patios provide plenty of space for relaxation or *al fresco* dining. The property also offers a large heated pool, kids' pool, shuffleboard court and daily maid service.

Hilton Daytona Beach Resort at Ocean Walk Village

100 North Atlantic Avenue, Daytona Beach, t (386) 254 8200, www.hilton.com

Situated on Daytona's only traffic-free beach, this resort offers 742 rooms featuring a Florida tropical décor and beach setting. It also offers high-speed internet linking, in-room movies and Playstation games. Restaurants, bars with entertainment and a complete fitness centre are also available.

Perry's Ocean Edge Resort

2209 South Atlantic Avenue, Daytona Beach, (386) 255 0581, www.perrysoceaaanedge.com (*moderate*)

One of the largest and most popular Daytona hotels, this offers extensive accommodation, including the Kids' Beach Suites with king-bedded room, double pullout sofabed and separate room with bunk beds, TV and private balcony. With a full-time Activity Director on staff, together with indoor and outdoor pools for adults and children, this hotel has something for everyone.

Plaza Resort

600 North Atlantic Avenue, Daytona Beach, t (386) 255 4471, www.plazaresortandspa.com (*very expensive*)

This beachfront hotel has a spa,and runs a family recreational programme in season. The programme caters for children from 5–12, offering crafts, movie nights, ice cream socials and water aerobics.

The Shores Resort and Spa

2637 South Atlantic Avenue, Daytona Beach Shores, t (386) 767 7350, www.shoresresort.com (*moderate–very expensive*)

Luxury accommodation comprising 214 rooms with flat screen TVs and a beach cottage feel. This resort offers swimming pools, including a kiddies' pool, restaurants, spa and fitness centre, a new for 2005 beachfront restaurant offering al fresco dining and bars. The resort offers a babysitting service and children under 18 stay free when accompanied by parents or grandparents.

The Tropical Manor

2237 South Atlantic Avenue, Daytona Beach Shores, t (386) 252 4920, www.tropicalmanor.com (*inexpensive–moderate*)

Family owned and operated property offering spacious suites for family accommodation. The site also offers a large heated swimming pool with water slide on the oceanfront and a heated kiddies' pool. Children's play turtle, shuffleboard court and gazebos also feature.

Kissimmee

All Star Vacation Homes

Office: 7822 West Irlo Bronson Highway, t (407) 997 0733, www.allstarvacationhomes.com (*moderate–very expensive*)

Do you want to live like a celebrity? Even if only for a week or two, you, too, can receive star treatment at these quality vacation homes, which are just three miles away from the theme parks. Many of the homes on offer have up to seven *en-suite* bedrooms and all come with superior furnishings, massive widescreen televisions, laundry rooms, fully-fitted kitchens, through-lounges, patios with screened pools, BBQ grills, private pools and spas as standard. Top-of-the-range homes also come with their own games room. Rentals are perfect for larger families and for staying with friend. They are available by the week with car hire also available. Internet deals include seven nights for the price of six and free car hire. When weighed up against nightly hotel rates, especially for a family, you get a lot of privacy and amenities for your money.

Dream Homes

Office: 5511 West Irlo Bronson Hwy, (Hwy 192), t (407) 396 2233 (*inexpensive–very expensive*)

Less then 10 minutes' to Disney World, these beautiful 3–6 bed homes all have private pools and the 2-3 bed condos have a community pool and spa, sauna, games room, weight room, theatre, snack bar, children's playground, plus tennis, basketball and volleyball courts. All units are equipped with smoke detectors, emergency lighting and fire extinguishers.

Gaylord Palms Resort

6000 West Osceloa Parkway, t (407) 586 0315, www.gaylordpalms.com (*expensive–very expensive*)

If you like your hotels on the big side, then this whopping 1,406–room mega resort is the place to go. Apparently, it was a popular spot for locals during the 2004 hurricanes and its easy to see why – the complex is virtually an enclosed town rather than simply just somewhere to lay your head. Among the rooms there are a staggering 115 suites and nine presidential suites divided into three themed zones representing the island life of Key West, historic St. Augustine and the wilds of the Everglades – complete with live alligators. The resort also has its own shopping mall, spa and fitness centre, spa water fountain, family fun pool and La Petite Academy Kid's Station, a special resort within the resort, which caters specifically for kids. This 4,000-sq-ft facility welcomes kids from 3–14 and features an art studio, video games space, contruction bricks, karaoke stage, reading corner and soft play space. Staff are also on hand to provide a range of stimulating activities throughout the day.

Lake Buena Vista

Holiday Inn Sunspree Resort

13351 Route 535 (exit 27 off I-4), Lake Buena Vista, t (407) 239 4500, www.kidsuites.com (*inexpensive–expensive*)

A family based hotel that believes space is needed for a successful family vacation, and designed its Kidsuites so that children's bunk beds and media centers are separated as cubby holes from the rest of the room. All kids eat free either with their parents or at their own kids-only restaurant. The video arcade with its own computer island, kids swimming pool, playground and a kids-only check-in desk make sure this is a holiday for the children. There's also a tropics pool, two Jacuzzis and a fitness center so the adults feel special too.

Prestige Vacation Homes Inc

Office: 101 Thousand Oaks Boulevard, Davenport, t (863) 424 7400, www.prestigevacationhomes.com (*moderate–very expensive*)

AAA and three diamonds rated, the highest rating possible for self-catering accommodations, Prestige has 67 vacation homes. All are company owned with private pools and the estates feature several deep-water lakes. Thousand Oaks is a peaceful and secluded development, just eight-and-a-half miles from Walt Disney World® Resort. Low season prices available for nearly two thirds of the year. Local car and passenger van rental are also available.

Lake Wales

Westgate River Ranch

3200 River Ranch Road, River Ranch, t (863) 692 1321 (*inexpensive–moderate*)

Western style hotel, offering tennis, badminton, golf, fitness equipment, pools, and of course horse riding, rodeos, and BBQs. Hotel rooms, suites and cottages are all available, as well as space for caravans and mobile homes.

Orlando

For Disney hotels please *see* p.238, visit the chain hotels websites at the start of this chapter for other Orlando options.

Nick Hotel

14500 Continental Gateway, t (407) 387 5437, www.nickhotel.com (*expensive–very expensive*)

Nickelodeon has teamed up with Holiday Inn® Hotels & Resorts to bring the first Nick-themed hotel to Orlando, which opened spring 2005. Featuring kids' Nick-themed bedrooms such as SpongeBob SquarePants, Rugrats, Rugrats: All Grown Up, Fairly Odd Parents, Jimmy Neutron and Danny Phantom, the rooms include bunk-beds, kid-size pull out sofabed or two twin beds, 20" TV, DVD player, game system, CD/cassette player and activity table. Movie and game rentals, a games arcade, kids' check-in desk and a Nick specialty retail shop are also available. Nicktoons Café offers a character breakfast buffet, sharing the first meal of the day with SpongeBob SquarePants, Patrick, Dora the Explorer, Fairly Odd Parents and more. The Lagoon and the Oasis are interactive water playgrounds, with slides, flumes, dump tanks and water towers, as well as a sand pit and shaded play area for younger children. Another fantastic feature of this child friendly hotel is the Kids' Spa, providing manicures, temporary tattoos, facials, glamour photos and general pampering for fabulous young visitors.

Reunion Resort & Club of Orlando

1000 Reunion Way, t (407) 662 1000, Kids Crew reservations, t (407) 662 1605, www.reunionresort.com (*very expensive*)

This 2,300-acre resort features a Kids' Crew programme, which is located at the Resort's Seven Eagles Pool Pavilion and makes use of both the pool and surrounding facilities for a variety of interactive exercises. Sessions include: Waterworks, a variety of aquatic centered fun; kids cookery classes; plus space and movie role-playing games. The cost is $35 per for a four-hour session and $10 each additional hour and includes lunch and dinner, depending on session length, served in official Kids' Crew lunch boxes. One and three-bedroom suites are available with balconies or patios, featuring fully-fitted kitchens, living room/dining areas and corner tubs and baths or families can opt for villa or vacation home accommodation with private swimming pools. Resort amenities include 54 holes of golf, a fitness centre, tennis courts and a spa and wellness centre is scheduled for 2006. Best of all for families is the Water and Swimming Pavilion with its own lazy river, interactive children's pools, waterfalls, waterslides and poolside ice cream parlour and bar. They can even arrange to have your groceries delivered to your door or you can dine at the resort restaurants. Need you go anywhere else?

Port St Lucie

Club Med Sand Piper

3500 Morningside Boulevard, Port St Lucie, t (772) 398 5100, www.clubmed.com (*very expensive*)

Comprising of 227 two-storey bungalows, this resort offers a full programme of activities for children. Particularly valuable is the Baby Club Med providing activities for guests as young as 4-months-old. For older children, the resort offers scuba experiences, circus activities and the full range of Club Med sporting opportunities. Special family rates are also available.

Stuart

Hutchinson Island Marriott

555 Northeast Ocean Boulevard, t (772) 225 3700 (*expensive*)

Offering a range of accommodation from its 276 rooms, the Hutchinson Island Marriott is set on a 200-acre site with 18-hole golf course, marina, swimming pools, restaurants, tennis courts and bars.

Universal Theme Parks

Hard Rock® Hotel at Universal Orlando

5800 Universal Boulevard, t (407) 503 7625, www.universalorlando.com (*expensive–very expensive*)

Let's rock! Wannabe pop stars and rock chicks will love staying at this memorabilia-studded temple to all things musical. The kids will certainly be all right hanging out by the huge pool with its underwater stereo vibes, 260-ft slide, interactive fountains and private poolside cabanas (including themed Beatles' Yellow Submarine and Stevie Wonder's Musicquarium cabanas). Take time out to get it on in the Games Room and get kitted out for a night out at the Hard Rock® store. Restaurants and lounge bars vary from the cool but casual to sophisticated New York steakhouse fare at the Palm Restaurant and the all-new ultra-hip The Kitchen where celebrity rock stars may drop in to turn chef for the night and rustle up some rocking good grub. The hotel has 650 rooms, including 29 suites, some purpose-built for families. If the budget can run to it, stay in the Graceland Suite and live like The King. Elvis has definitely not left the building.

Portofino Bay Hotel at Universal Orlando

5601 Universal Boulevard, t (407) 503 1000, www.universalorlando.com (*expensive–very expensive*)

Mediterranean themed resort village with cobblestone courtyards and al fresco cafés, 750 elegant guest rooms, including Garden Rooms that can sleep up to five and two-bedroom Kid Suites, which have video and CD cassette players and TVs just for the kids. There are also three themed swimming pools – including a beach pool with Roman aqueduct slide and children's pool; a secluded villa pool featuring private cabanas and a hillside pool. The resort offers eight different places to eat – the latest addition to the dining scene being the celebrated Italian, Bice, as well as more rustic eateries serving pizza, pasta, ice cream, espressos and deli sandwiches. The resort also features the Mandara Spa, several boutique shops and an art gallery.

Royal Pacific Hotel at Universal Orlando

6300 Hollywood Way, t (407) 503 3000, www.universalorlando.com (*expensive–very expensive*)

This Loews Hotel has an enormous lagoon swimming pool with its own sandy beach and an interactive children's water playground. There are several resort restaurants – from the Polynesian-inspired Wantilan Luau with its dinner buffet and South Pacific show to the upmarket Emeril's Tchoup Chop serving nouvelle Asian cuisine, as well as casual beach bars and ice cream parlours. Standard rooms feature on demand in room movies, twin queen beds among other facilities and suites with separate living rooms and sofa beds are also available.

Vero Beach

Driftwood Resort

3150 Ocean Drive, t (772) 231 0550, www.thedriftwood.com (*inexpensive*)

Built of ocean-reclaimed timbers, this charming, unique resort offers an old-world charm allied with all modern amenities. As well as the usual pools and restaurants, this resort houses an extensive collection of beautiful and interesting artefacts. Note: due to hurricane damage, not all areas were fully operational at time of going to press; check before booking.

Good to know – Universal access

All of the Universal hotels feature a kids' activity centre. Other benefits include: bypassing the regular queues at both Universal Orlando® theme parks during your stay, free transport, including water taxis connecting the hotels and theme parks, priority restaurant seating at select restaurants, resort-wide charging privileges and package delivery services. Resort guests also receive complimentary transport to Discovery Cove, SeaWorld Adventure Park, and the Wet 'n' Wild water park (*see* pp.135, 137 and 138).

Winter Haven

Grenelefe Golf and Tennis Resort

3200 State Road, 546 Haines City, t (863)422 7511, www.grenelefe.com (*moderate–very expensive*)

This sporty resort has 850 rooms and suites sleeping 1–4 people, plus three golf courses, 20 tennis courts, four pools, three restaurants and a fitness club. They also offer a full service lake marina and supervised kids' programme.

SOUTHWEST

Boca Grande

Palm Island Resort

7092 Placida Road, Cape Haze, t (941) 697 4800, www.palmisland.com (*very expensive*)

This island retreat has 160 luxurious one to three-bedroom air-conditioned villas featuring fully fitted kitchens and washer/dryers and private homes with up to six bedrooms. With boat, bicycle and water sports equipment rentals, full service marina, 11 tennis courts and five swimming pools, the resort also offers a kids' programme so parents can get some time to themselves.

The Innlet

1251 Twelfth Street East (P.O. Box 248), Boca Grande, t (941) 964 2294, www.innletonthewaterfront.com (*moderate–expensive*)

This smart waterfront hotel offers 32 beautifully decorated rooms with access to miles of good sandy beaches that are great for shell collecting. There's a pool, restaurant and play area all onsite. Boat accessible location.

Captiva Island

Jensen's Twin Palm Cottages & Marina

Captiva Drive (PO Box 191), t (239) 472 5800, www.gocaptiva.com (*moderate–expensive*)

Historic, simple white cottages with kitchens and screened porches or decks, the Twin Palm Cottages offer a peaceful, natural alternative to a hotel, with plenty of wildlife, including dolphins, pelicans, otters and manatees. The resort also features a private fishing pier and full Marina services, including boat trips, fishing cruises and boat hire.

South Seas Resort

North Captiva Island (PO Box 194), t (239) 472 5111, www.south-seas-resort.com (*expensive–very expensive*)

Spacious and varied beach accommodation, including hotel rooms, suites, villas, cottages and homes. Activities include sailing, fishing, golf, scuba diving, nature tours and day cruises, together with an extensive, supervised kids' programme.

Englewood Beach

Weston's Resort

985 Gulf Boulevard, Englewood Beach, t (941) 474 3431 (*inexpensive–expensive*)

Accommodation is in 1–3 bedroom units and the resort offers two pools, tennis courts, BBQ grills and shuffleboard facilities. Boat slips and rentals are also available.

The Everglades

Billie Swamp Safari

Big Cypress Indian Reservation, (I-75 to exit 14, north 19 miles), Clewiston, t (954) 966 6300, www.semknoletribe.com (*inexpensive*)

The Seminole Tribe offers guests authentic thatched chickees (small sleeps two, dorm sleeps eight or 12). This Indian Reservation offers adventurous family getaways in the Everglades, featuring animal shows, campfire storytelling and airboat rides.

Fort Myers

Holiday Inn Riverwalk

2220 West First Street, Fort Myers, t (239) 334 3434 (*moderate–expensive*)

Located on the Caloosahatchee River, this riverfront hotel offers 145 rooms and suites (some with jacuzzis). Close to local attractions such as the Edison and Ford Winter Estates and Museum, the hotel features an outdoor pool and free kids' meals.

Sanibel Harbour Resort & Spa

17260 Harbour Pointe Drive, Fort Myers, t (239) 466 4000, www.sanibel-resort.com (*expensive–very expensive*)

Overlooking Sanibel and Captiva Islands, this resort offers 401 accommodations, including rooms, suites and waterfront condominiums. An on-site spa and fitness centre are also available, together with a Kids' Klub programme of supervised activities with different themes for each day, including beach games, treasure hunts, pool games, nature hikes and mystery games. The Kids' Klub is open seven days a week from 10–4 and caters for 5- to 12-year-olds. Babysitting service also available.

Fort Myers Beach

Best Western Pink Shell Beach & Bay Resort

275 Estero Boulevard, Fort Myers Beach, t (239) 463 6181, www.pinkshell.com (*very expensive*)

Comprising 192 villa accommodations, this resort is at the quieter end of the beach. The resort offers three heated pools, fishing and water sports facilities, butterfly garden, spa and a range of on-site dining facilities. A kids' programme, Kidds Kampp, is also available to give parents some time out.

DiamondHead

2000 Estero Boulevard, t (239) 765 7654, www.diamondheadfl.com (*very expensive*)

This upmarket, all-suite luxury resort features 124 one-bedroom designer suites equipped with living rooms with a queen-size sofa bed, two cable TVs with pay-per-view movies available and a kitchen/dining area. Other facilities include an under-counter refrigerator, microwave, dishes, dishwasher and coffee maker. Complimentary cots and high chairs are available on request. The resort has a heated Gulf-side pool and spas, a fine dining restaurant and beachside bar and grill. The lovely white sand beach also provides water sports equipment such as parasailing and Jet skis, beachfront cabana rentals, plenty of scope for collecting beautiful shells. Family activities, trolley service and tours are also available.

Marco Island

Marriott's Marco Island Resort Golf Club & Spa

400 South Collier Boulevard, t (239) 394 2511, www.marcomarriottresort.com (*expensive–very expensive*)

Offering oversized guestrooms with private balconies, this resort has some of the best golf facilities in the area. Convenience store and fast food outlet, restaurants, spa, fitness, tennis and golf facilities, swimming pool and beauty salon are all on site. Amenities include a miniature golf course, two playgrounds and a kids' pool and recreation programme available for the younger guests.

Radisson Suite Beach Resort

600 South Collier Boulevard, t (239) 394 4100, www.marcobeachresort.com (*moderate–very expensive*)

This sizeable beachfront hotel offers 59 comfortable guestrooms that sleep up to four people, and beautiful suites that sleep 6–8. Marco Island Watersports is located on site for parasailing, Jet skis, sailing and other liquid leisure activities. The Fun Factory kids' club provides a programme for children aged 4–11, to give parents some time out.

Naples

Lemon Tree Inn

250 Ninth Street South, Naples, t (239) 262 1414, www.lemontreeinn.com (*inexpensive–moderate*)

This hotel offers a glimpse of old Florida with 34 smart and affordable rooms, plus a pool and courtyard garden with lounge chairs. The inn is within walking distance of fine dining, good shopping and beautiful beaches. The hotel runs an annual Art for Adoption art show and garden party event to raise money for orphanages in China.

Naples Beach Hotel & Golf Club

851 Gulf Shore Boulevard North, t (239) 261 2222, www.naplesbeachhotel.com (*very expensive*)

The Naples Beach Hotel & Golf Club features 318 guest rooms and suites, onsite championship golf, an award winning Tennis Centre, large beachside swimming pool, complete fitness centre and a world-class Spa. The resort also offers four restaurants, a sunset beach bar, five shops and a complimentary children's club. The Beach Klub for Kids caters for 5–12s with themed activities such as Pirates Day with buried treasure hunts, swimming, crafts, beach walks and movies. Teenage children are also entertained with volleyball tournaments, golf and tennis clinics.

The Registry Resort & Club

475 Seagate Drive, Naples, t (239) 597 3232, www.registryresort.com (*very expensive*)

395 Guestrooms and 29 Tower Suites decorated in a Tuscan style make up the gracious accommodation of the Registry Resort & Club, together with 49 Garden Suites adjacent to the award-winning tennis courts. For an additional charge, the resort offers an extensive range of children's activities in the Camp Registry club for children aged 4–12. Trained counsellors oversee activities including art and craft, scavenger hunts, seashell and sand dollar hunts, face painting, watersports and themed nights out. All-day sessions run from 9–4, Tues–Sat. Qualified nannies are also on call for babysitting, allowing parents to relax for the evening without worrying about their little ones.

The Residence Inn by Marriott Naples

4075 Tamiami Trail North, Naples, t (239) 659 1300, www.marriott.com (*moderate*)

The Residence Inn offers spacious suites with separate sleeping and living areas. This resort also provides a complimentary hot breakfast buffet, together with Wednesday night cookouts and Mon–Thu evening hospitality hour which includes a light meal, beer, wine, iced tea and lemonade. The resort also offers a tropical pool, heated spa and sport court. At just one mile from the beach, with complimentary transport, the Residence Inn provides home-from-home comfort with all modern amenities.

The Ritz-Carlton Naples

280 Vanderbilt Beach Road, North Naples, t (239) 598 3300, www.ritz-carlton.com (*very expensive*)

The sunkissed terracotta walls of the Ritz-Carlton, Naples welcome visitors with a total of 463 guest rooms including 22 suites and 70 club rooms and suites. All suites and club level rooms also have private balconies and views of the Gulf of Mexico. The Ritz-Carlton offers an extensive range of supervised children's activities in the Ritz Kids Day Camp. The Camp can be attended on full or half days for children aged 5–12. Sessions run from 9–4 and include sports and games, swimming pool play, adventure programmes, special dinner movies (6–9 for an additional $50) and arts and crafts activities. Spa, golf and swimming pool facilities are also available.

Vanderbilt Inn

11000 Gulf Shore Drive, t (239) 597 3151, www.vanderbiltinn.com
(expensive–very expensive)

Offering 147 rooms and 16 Gulf Front rooms with spectacular views, the Vanderbilt Inn is family oriented, providing free meals for children aged 12 and under from the kids' menu, when dining with parents. Golf, tennis and boating activities are all within easy reach. Children under 18 also stay free with parents.

Punta Gorda

Fishermen's Village Villas

1200 West Retta Esplanade, t (941) 639 8721, www.fishville.com *(moderate–expensive)*

Restoration work is being carried out on the 2-bedrooms units, all of which sleep up to six, following hurricane damage. See website for details of the all-new amenities. This compact resort features a full service marina, clay tennis courts, bicycles and swimming pool all available onsite. The village also contains a shopping area and a choice of restaurants.

Sanibel Island

Gulf Breeze Cottages

1081 Shell Basket Lane, t (239) 472 1626, www.gbreeze.com *(expensive–very expensive)*

If you like the sound of it so far then this bijou collection of clapboard beach huts decorated in pastel colours and weathered by the sun will not disappoint on closer inspection.

Is it the washing up bowl for rinsing your shells on the front step that makes it so special or the short walk to the lovely, undeveloped beachfront? Accommodation ranges from one-bedroom cottages that sleep up to four to two bed cottages sleeping six and three bed duplexes for larger groups. All feature fully equipped kitchens, lounge rooms with TVs and VCRs (there's an on-site video lending library) and dining room areas. If you're seeking an island paradise, you've come to the right place.

Sundial Beach Resort

863 East Gulf Drive, t (239) 472 4151, www.sundialresort.com
(expensive–very expensive)

This resort offers the choice of 270 studio, one or two-bedroom suites or two-bedroom suites with den. The Sundial Beach Resort also features the Explorer Kids' Club Camp, which provides fun-filled days for children aged 4 to 11.The camp includes lunch, crafts, beach games, pool games and more (there is swimming in both the day and night camps if weather permits). Each child also receives a one time Explorer Kids' Club gift. With plenty of eco-friendly activities including a touch tank in the on-site environmental centre, this resort caters for the whole family.

SOUTHEAST

Boca Raton

Boca Raton Resort & Club

501 East Camino Real, t (561) 395 3000, www.bocaresort.com *(very expensive)*

Children will be spoilt for choice at this beautiful and exclusive resort, which offers three different kids' clubs: Boca Tots for ages 3–5, Boca Bunch for ages 6–11 and Boca Sport for ages 12–17. Amenities include a new golf practice range and putting green, renovated tower pool, redesigned restaurants (gourmet baby food available on request), new playground and an enhanced fitness centre. Half a mile of beautiful private beach and tennis and golf facilities await deserving adults.

Delray Beach

Crowne Plaza Oceanfront

3200 North Ocean Drive, Singer Island, 800 475 1396, www.oceanfrontcp.com
(expensive–very expensive)

This beautiful tropical-style hotel is situated on famous Singer Island and offers 193 newly renovated guestrooms with 'sophisticated style and comfortable elegance'. This boutique style hotel stretches across five acres of lush landscaping and includes 850-ft of private beach. There's also a choice of dining from the casual snack to 4-course meal, outdoor pool, golf, water sports and tennis facilities.

Delray Beach Marriott

10 North Ocean Boulevard, Delray Beach, t (561) 274 3200, www.marriott.com (*expensive–very expensive*)

The hotel offers 180 rooms and 88 suites, all well furnished and comfortable. Golf, spa and fitness facilities are all available on site, as is a heated pool, hot tub and spa pool. Activities such as kayaking, horseback riding and cycling are available nearby, as is Boomer's Family Entertainment Center (*see* p.207) for family fun.

Delray Beach Residence Inn by Marriott

1111 East Atlantic Avenue, Delray Beach, t (561) 276 7441, www.marriott.com (*very expensive*)

All 95 suites come with pool or ocean views and with a beautiful beach nearby. Complimentary hot breakfast buffet is available. Pets are allowed. Golf, spa and fitness facilities are also available, as are pool, hot tub and spa pool. See above hotel for nearby attractions.

Sundy House Inn

106 South Swinton Avenue, Delray Beach, t (561) 272 5678, www.sundyhouse.com (*expensive–very expensive*)

A choice of guestrooms, garden apartments and a freestanding luxury cottage await at the Sundy House. There's an on site restaurant and tropic pool for fishing with tropical fish! Sundy House is situated in the middle of the fragrant Taru Gardens, which offer breathtaking views and a relaxing atmosphere.

The Colony Hotel and Cabana Club

595 East Atlantic Avenue, Delray Beach, t (561) 276 4123 (*expensive*)

Delray's oldest hotel and although keeping in time with modern facilities, the lobby is still original. There are 70 guestrooms including 22 suites, all comfortable and stylish with access to a private beach.

Fort Lauderdale

The Atlantic

601 N. Fort Lauderdale Beach Boulevard, t (954) 567 8020 (*very expensive*)

With 124 guestrooms, 58 suites and five penthouses, this Starwood Hotel is part of their Luxury Collection portfolio. The Atlantic offers an oceanfront pool (with private cabanas), European style spa and fitness centre and a gourmet restaurant and bar.

The Best Western Pelican Beach Resort

2000 North Ocean Boulevard, Fort Lauderdale, t (954) 568 9431, www.pelicanbeach.com (*expensive–very expensive*)

This family friendly resort is 100% non-smoking and offers 180 guestrooms including 117 suites. The grounds feature two heated pools, one with a lazy river, private beach, fitness centre, vintage ice cream parlor, on-site dining and the Funky Fish kids' programme for a complete family-orientated holiday.

Embassy Suites Fort Lauderdale

1100 Southeast Seventeenth Street, t (954) 527 2700, www.embassysuitesftl.com (*very expensive*)

Beautiful suites offering all the comforts of home are on offer at this hotel that is within easy reach of the airport. Amenities include pool with waterfalls and tropical setting, paddle tennis table, fitness room and pool table. Cots, highchairs, children's menu and babysitting services complimentary buffet breakfasts are all available.

Harbor Beach Marriott Resort & Spa

3030 Holiday Drive, t (954) 525 4000, www.marriottharborbeach.com (*very expensive*)

Listed in the '100 Best Spas of the World' this resort offers a large free-form pool, water-sports rentals and a kids' recreational programme. It is close to the beach with wonderful views all round and has been renovated recently.

Sans Souci Hotel

618 North Birch Road, Fort Lauderdale, t (954) 564 4311, www.sanssoucihotel.com (*inexpensive*)

All rooms have beautiful views of the pool and garden, as the buildings are set in a U shape. Makes access to the pool easier, and allows guests to reach their rooms quickly for toilet trips or naps. Family excursions are all just a short drive away.

The Seminole Hard Rock® Hotel & Casino

1 Seminole Way, Hollywood, t (866) 502 7529, www.seminolehardrockhollywood.com (*moderate–very expensive*)

This large hotel features 500 guestrooms including 63 suites, all luxuriously decorated and very spacious. The main source of entertainment is of course the casino, which offers more than 2,100 gaming machines and 50 poker tables. The hotel also offers a large lagoon pool, with waterfalls, slides and hot tubs, a shallow pool for younger guests, volleyball, spa and fitness centre, as well as numerous dining choices, including the world famous Hard Rock Café. The Hard Rock Live, opening summer 2005, is the new entertainment centre for live music events, which has the capacity to seat 5,000.

Miami

Alexander All-Suite Oceanfront Resort

Kennedy Causeway, Suite 703, Miami Beach, t (305) 865 6500, www.alexanderhotel.com (*very expensive*)

With luxury all-suite accommodations, two lagoon-shaped pools, poolside cabanas and an onsite steak house, this beachfront resort is both intimate and exclusive. Children up to the age of 12 stay free and there is also an exclusive kids' registration and gift package, together with free milk and cookies for children upon arrival. There is a range of dining options are on offer and children aged five and under eat free. Fitness centre, spa and salon and a wide variety of water sports ensure that there is something for everyone at the Alexander.

Crystal Beach Suites

6985 Collins Avenue, t (305) 865 9555, www.crystalbeachmiami.com (*inexpensive–moderate*)

This North Beach hotel offers affordable and spacious suites with Caribbean style décor, sofa beds for the kids and a separate bedroom for parents. Bathrooms are basic but the kitchen comes fully stocked with plates and crockery, microwave oven and coffee machine. There's also a complimentary on-site breakfast bar for a quick bite. The sizeable outdoor pool and fitness area makes this a very good choice if you're on a budget. Renovations are being made to the lobby area, so it can only get better.

Doral Golf Resort & Spa

4400 Northwest 87th Avenue, t (305) 592 2000, www.doralresort.com (*moderate–very expensive*)

Top class golf and spa facilities, as well as 11 tennis courts, stadium and children's pool. The Blue Lagoon water park also includes Camp Doral a recreation programme for ages 5–12, featuring ball games, arts and crafts, competitions, and poolside and beachside events. Babysitting for under-5s is also available. Range of dining choices on-site, as well as room service.

Eden Roc Renaissance Resort & Spa

4525 Collins Avenue, t (305) 531 1000, www.edenrocresort.com (*very expensive*)

Situated on Miami's Middle Beach this gorgeous contemporary resort features large and spacious accommodation in all of the 349 guest rooms and suites. Most have balconies with dramatic ocean views and provide plenty of relaxation and living space. Alternatively, as the ultimate in luxury, there are three penthouse suites with spectacular wrap-around balconies and whirlpool tubs. The resort also offers an Olympic size swimming pool and an oceanfront spa and restaurant. The Aquatica restaurant also features two porthole windows looking into onsite pools for a funky underwater experience. Specifically for children, Camp Eden Roc provides an extensive range of sporting and fun activities including scavenger hunts, badminton, rock climbing, ping pong, croquet, squash, poolside games and a variety of water sports. Lemonade and fresh-baked cookies are also available daily at no extra cost.

Flamingo Lodge and Outpost Resort

1 Flamingo Lodge Highway, t (239) 695 3101, www.flamingolodge.com (*moderate–expensive*)

Offering a choice of lodge rooms or self-catering cottages, the resort features a screened pool and lots of space for the kids to burn off some energy. Continental breakfast included.

Hilton Fontainbleau

4441 Collins Avenue, t (305) 538 2000, www.fontainebleau.hilton.com (*expensive–very expensive*)

This is more like a small city than a resort hotel with accommodation available in both the 1950s Chateau (15-storey, 555 rooms) and Versailles (17-storey 365 rooms) buildings and the new Fontainbleau Tower, a 36-storey complex offering a further 462 rooms. Room and suites have a choice of king or double/double beds, wide variety of city or water views, some with terraces. One and two-bed suites come with balconies; coffee makers, 27" TV with in room movies are all standard amenities throughout the resort. Another recent addition to this landmark Middle Beach hotel is Kids' Cove, a supervised children's playroom designed with an underwater theme, offering a variety of activities for kids ages 5 to 12. Cooking, movies, arts and crafts are just some of the activities available both during the day and in the evening.

The family friendly resort offers children's menus in many of its restaurants and through room service. In addition, toys, games and a wide variety of sports equipment are available to borrow while staying at the resort. Other services include babysitting, cots, high chairs, and playpens. Visitors have a choice of dining areas including a large beachside bar and grill. Private beach equipment is also available. Naturally, a resort of this size is going to be busy, so if you want to spend the day sunning yourself on the terrace, make sure you're up with the lark and reserve your sun loungers with something other than the same hotel pool towels that everyone else is using. In addition, two levels of beach cabanas (available for rent to resort and non-resort guests) open onto the Cookie's World children's play pool overlooking the Atlantic Ocean. Perfect for spending the day at the beach or pool, the cabanas feature a ceiling fan, sofa, storage space and table and chairs. Room service is available, as well as the adjacent Cookie's Corner snack bar. The Cookie's World pool features a giant squirting octopus water play area, a lazy river tube ride and slides. The main pool also has shallow areas for family swimming.

Loews Miami Beach Hotel

1601 Collins Avenue, Miami Beach, t (305) 604 1601, www.loewshotels.com (*very expensive*)

Accommodation in this superior hotel is ranged between the lovely old Art Deco St Moritz and the purpose-built main hotel building. All rooms have luxury modern fittings with huge bathrooms featuring massive claw-foot baths, separate toilet and a power shower. Twin-bedded rooms with extremely comfortable fluffy white beds are available for families, as well as 62 suites in the Tower Building. The hotel is located just off Miami's swanky South Beach and provides beachfront access and a private gated sun terrace, beach bar and a lovely large swimming pool. Loews Miami Beach Hotel also offers visitors the opportunity to select special programmes such as Loews First, Generation G and Loews Loves Kids (*see* above under hotel chains). Special family packages are available and advance booking through the Family Concierge, is recommended. The hotel can provide a range of supervised recreational programmes together with special children's menus, welcome gifts (for under 10s), game lending library and tours. Additionally, childproof kits are available for children under four, and cots and foldaway beds are free of charge.

Sheraton Bal Harbour

9701 Collins Avenue, Bal Harbour, t (305) 865 7511, www.sheraton.com (*expensive–very expensive*)

This luxury resort on up-and-coming North Beach features 645 superior rooms and suites. This 4-diamond resort also offers a fantasy pool with Jacuzzis and a waterslide, spa and fitness centre and a children's programme. On-site and even poolside dining facilities are also available.

Silver Sands Beach Resort

301 Ocean Drive, Key Biscayne, t (305) 361 5441, www.silversandsmiami.com (*expensive–very expensive*)

Mini-suites and beach cottages, most with beautiful beach views. Pool and tennis courts are also available and bicycle and water equipment rentals are located close by.

Sonesta Beach Resort

350 Ocean Drive, Key Biscayne, t (305) 361 2021, www.sonesta.com (*expensive–very expensive*)

This large beachside resort occupies a commanding position in lovely, wooded Key Biscayne with 300 rooms offering ocean, island or bay views. Facilities include a spa and salon with sauna and steam room; Olympic style heated pool, two spa pools, nine tennis courts (three are lit at night) and volleyball and basketball courts. Several kids' programmes are on offer; 'Just For Us Kids' for ages 5–13, 'Just For Us Little Kids' for ages 3–4, and babysitting services for the youngest guests.

North Palm Beach

Palm Beach Shores Resort

181 Ocean Avenue (Route A1A), Palm Beach Shores, t (561) 863 4000, www.palmbeachshoresfl.com (*moderate–very expensive*)

Beach Buddies entertains the youngest kids with toys and games, and the older kids with night-time parties and off-campus field trips. There are 257 suites, all two-room and suitable for a family holiday. Other amenities include tennis, watersports, golf, swimming pool and tiki bar.

PGA National Resort & Spa

400 Avenue of Champions, Palm Beach Gardens, t (561) 627 2000 (*very expensive*)

This golf resort offers 339 luxurious guestrooms and suites. Dining options are numerous, with eight on-site restaurants and lounges. Golf takes the main priority in this resort (five different courses) with spa, tennis and fitness facilities taking close second.

Palm Beach

The Breakers

1 South County Road, t (561) 655 6611, www.thebreakers.com (*very expensive*)

Although founded in 1896 and on the National Register of Historic Places, this resort offers 560 newly renovated guestrooms, including 57 suites, all magnificently decorated. The Breakers Golf Academy for ages 6–15, and The Tennis Junior Programme for kids as young as three, allow younger guests to get in on the sporting action at this superior resort. Other amenities include four oceanfront swimming pools, fitness centre, Jacuzzi and on-site tennis and golf facilities.

Chesterfield Hotel

363 Cocoanut Row, Palm Beach, t 800 243 7871, www.redcarnationhotels.com (*expensive–very expensive*)

Part of the Red Carnation hotel group who own the Chesterfield Mayfair and other exclusive hotels in London, The Chesterfield offers a 'little bit of England on Palm Beach'. Families can opt for the Kids Getaway Package ($712 for four days and three nights), designed for a family of four, which features a goody bag of bath treats, milk and cookies and bedtime stories, a visit to child Dreher Park Zoo and the Science Museum, plus the chance to enjoy hands-on workshops such as a make your own teddy bear sessions. There are 53 sumptuously furnished guestrooms all with access to Jacuzzi spa and heated swimming pool. In-room children's movies are free and babysitting services are available.

The Colony Hotel

155 Hammon Avenue, Palm Beach, t (800) 521 5525 or (561) 655 5430, www.thecolonypalmbeach.com (*very expensive*)

Guests have a choice of hotel rooms, suites or villa accommodation at this gorgeous, high-class hotel. VIP guests have included presidents, royalty, movie moguls and rock stars. The Polo offers exquisite fine dining and the Bimini Bar provides poolside snacks and drinks. There's also a pool, plus beach and bicycle rental facilities.

Four Seasons Resort Palm Beach

2800 South Ocean Boulevard, Palm Beach, t (561) 582 2800, www.fourseasons.com/palmbeach (*expensive–very expensive*)

Guestrooms, suites and family or disabled rooms are all available. Children under 18 stay for free in their parents' room. The hotel also offers on-site dining, spa and fitness, golf and tennis facilities. Heated, oceanfront pool, with Jacuzzi and cabanas nearby. Provide the hotel with names and ages of younger guests and they can prepare child-size bathrobes, complimentary baby and children's toiletries, children's menus at on-site restaurants, items to childproof guest rooms, cots and/or roll-away beds (no extra charge), complimentary use of video game units, games and toys, nappies and bottles. Kids' and Teenager programmes and babysitting services are also available.

The Heart of Palm Beach Hotel

160 Royal Palm Way, Palm Beach, t (561) 644 3878 or 800 521 4278, www.heartofpalmbeach.com (*very expensive*)

This recently fully-renovated hotel offers 88 rooms and seven newly built suites. Other additions include a full-service spa and salon, newly refurbished pool, pavilion areas and high speed internet access. On-site dining at The Grille features the work of Palm Beach's resident artist Clemente Mimun. A heated pool, tennis and golf (offsite but nearby) and bicycle and snorkel rentals are some of the other amenities on offer.

Ritz-Carlton Palm Beach

100 South Ocean Boulevard, Manalapan, t (561) 533 6000, www.ritz-carlton.com (*very expensive*)

This luxury resort features 270 guest rooms including 56 suites, 26 club accommodations and two Ritz-Carlton suites. Amenities include a massage and fitness centre with an extensive spa menu, outdoor pool, oceanfront dining, seven acres of gorgeous beach, golf and tennis facilities and even yoga classes. The Ritz Kids Day Camp for 5–12 year-olds, offers either a full day or half a day of freedom for both parents and kids.

Sailfish Marina & Resort

98 Lake Drive, Palm Beach Shores, t (561) 844 1724, www.sailfishmarine.com (*inexpensive–moderate*)

Guest rooms are brilliantly decorated and most are fitted with full kitchenettes for families or extended stays. New pool, two restaurants, nearby shops, water taxis and bike, boat and water sports equipment rentals. Camp Sailfish is available for ages 8–13 (must be a strong swimmer).

West Palm Beach

KOA Kampground

2000 Lion Country Safari Road, Loxahatchee, t (561) 793 9797 (*inexpensive–very expensive*)

Campsite that combines a drive-through wildlife preserve and entertainment park with holiday attractions such as a petting zoo, paddleboats, carousel, mini-golf, pool, shuffle board, basketball, volleyball and playgrounds. Boat ride safari tours and animal theatre entertainment also available. Cabins also available.

New Grandview Gardens

1608 Lake Avenue, West Palm Beach, t (561) 833 9023, www.grandview-gardens.net (*moderate–expensive*)

All accommodations have their own private entrances and private terraces overlooking the pool amid tropical garden scenery. Children aged 12 years and under stay free when sharing room with their parents. Bicycles (guided tours on request) available for use, tennis, basketball and shuffle-board available across the street, and there's even a piano on for musically talented guests.

Tropical Gardens B&B

419 32nd Street, West Palm Beach t (561) 8482422, www.tropicalgardensbandb.com (*inexpensive*)

Enjoy the relaxed Caribbean atmosphere of this Key West-style guesthouse that is conveniently situated for exploring the museums, beaches and dining and shopping areas of West Palm Beach. Located in the Historic Old Northwood neighbourhood, the colourful 1937 Tropical Gardens complex features a main guesthouse with two guest rooms and two separate poolside units. Each of the beautifully decorated rooms has air-conditioning and cable TV. The public areas of the main guest-house are bright and breezy and surrounded by shady foliage. The Coconut Cottage, which has its own sitting room is the best for families. Otherwise you would need to rent two units. The B&B is best suited for those with older children.

West Palm Beach Marriott

1001 Okeechobee Boulevard, West Palm Beach, t (561) 833 1234, www.marriott.com (*expensive–very expensive*)

The resort has recently undergone a $10-million renovation, and now offers 352 rooms, all with a contemporary and comfortable feel. Facilities include on-site restaurants and bars, including a Starbucks Coffee House, a heated pool, plus golf and fitness centre. Activities available nearby include fly-fishing, kayaking and horseback riding.

The Keys

Big Pine Key

Big Pine Fishing Lodge

Oceanside at Mile Marker 33 (P.O. Box 430513, Big Pine Key 33043), t (305) 872 2351 (*inexpensive*)

Well maintained campground as well as motel so you can either rent a room or bring your own. Marina, boat rental, fishing charters and a pool are all available.

Islamorada

Cheeca Lodge Resort

Mile Marker 82 (P.O. Box 527), Islamorada, t (305) 664 4651, www.cheeca.com (*very expensive*)

The Cheeca is a classy residence with a reputation built on environmental awareness. Kids' activities are all outdoor-based: snorkeling, swimming and fishing and show young visitors how to have fun and be environmentally responsible into the bargain. Private beach, swimming, tennis, golf, boat charters and spa facilities are all available.

Holiday Isle Resort and Marina

Mile Marker 84, 84001 Overseas Highway, Islamorada, t (305) 664 2321, www.holidayisle.com (*moderate–very expensive*)

Made up of four hotels, this resort offers 178 rooms, efficiencies, cottages and suites along a gorgeous sandy beach. The resort features shops, playgrounds, restaurants, pools, rental boats and endless entertainment.

Key Largo

Key Largo Bay Marriott Beach Resort

Mile Marker 103.8, 103800 Overseas Highway, Key Largo, t (305) 453 0000, www.marriottkeylargo.com (*expensive–very expensive*)

153 oversized rooms, including 20 suites (two–bed). Wide variety of activities including water sports, golf, fitness, spa and tennis facilities and kids programme The Kids' Club. Onsite dining includes 'Flipper's Poolside Tiki Bar' and Gus' Grille.

Key West

Hyatt Key West Resort & Marina

601 Front Street, Key West, t (305) 296 9900 (*very expensive*)

With a newly renovated marina dock, water sports facilities of all kinds are now available at this 120-room complex. Amenities include a heated outdoor pool, spa pool, ping pong and pool table, exercise room, bicycle and scooter rentals and an on-site restaurant.

Pier House Resort and Caribbean Spa

One Duval Street, t (305) 296 4600, www.pierhouse.com (*very expensive*)

Delightful and comfortable resort accommodation that's right in the heart of the historic district with waterfront views available. Harbour-front rooms all have private balconies and offer great views of the famous Key West sunsets. There's a small private beach and hotel pool, spa, sunset terrace and shady gardens. Breakfast is available in the award-winning One Duval Restaurant, which offers nightly fine dining or in the on-site coffee shop.

Sunset Key Guest Cottages at the Hilton Key West Resort & Marina

245 Front Street, Key West, t (305) 292 4376, www.sunsetkeyisland.com (*very expensive*)

37 elegantly appointed 1–3 bed cottages, situated on a private island. All come equipped with kitchen, living and dining areas, a library and even a private chef upon request, plus in-room grocery delivery. Concierge service offers water sports activities. Complimentary breakfasts are all freshly prepared.

Wyndham's Casa Marina Resort

1500 Reynolds Street, t (305) 296 3535, www.casamarinakeywest.com (*very expensive*)

There has to be a very special reason for choosing accommodation on the other side of Key West to the historic district and this wonderful, private beach resort is it. The resort has 311 rooms all with individual climate control, TV with cable movie channels, in-room pay movies, mini-bar, coffee maker, hair dryer and many rooms have balcony/patios overlooking the ocean. There are three spectacular, oceanfront pools with a Pool Concierge service offering fresh fruit trays, reading matter and poolside drinks. The resort also provides a children's programme for ages 4–12. In addition there are tennis courts and a golf course nearby and water sports, from sailing to windsurfing to snorkelling or scuba diving off Key West's spectacular barrier reef.

Marathon

Hawk's Cay Resort and Dolphin Research Center

Mile Marker 61, North of Marathon, 61 Hawk's Key Boulevard, Duck Key, t (305) 743 7000, www.hawkscay.com (*very expensive*)

There are 161 rooms and 16 suites in the inn and a further 295 charming villas in the grounds. With a marina and full service spa, swimming pool and saltwater lagoon with beach, the resort also offers facilities such as golfing, sailing and tennis. The dolphin encounters are a once-in-a-lifetime experience that the whole family will love. Sadly, the resort is let down by a few unhelpful members of staff and the main building could do with an update.

Conch Key Cottages

Mile Marker 62.3 Oceanside, 62250 Overseas Highway, Walker's Island, t (305) 289 1377, www.conchkeycottages.com (*expensive–very expensive*)

Charming, secluded and serene, these 12 oceanside cottages have access to a small beach, pool and boat docks.

Northwest Florida

06

The Northwest

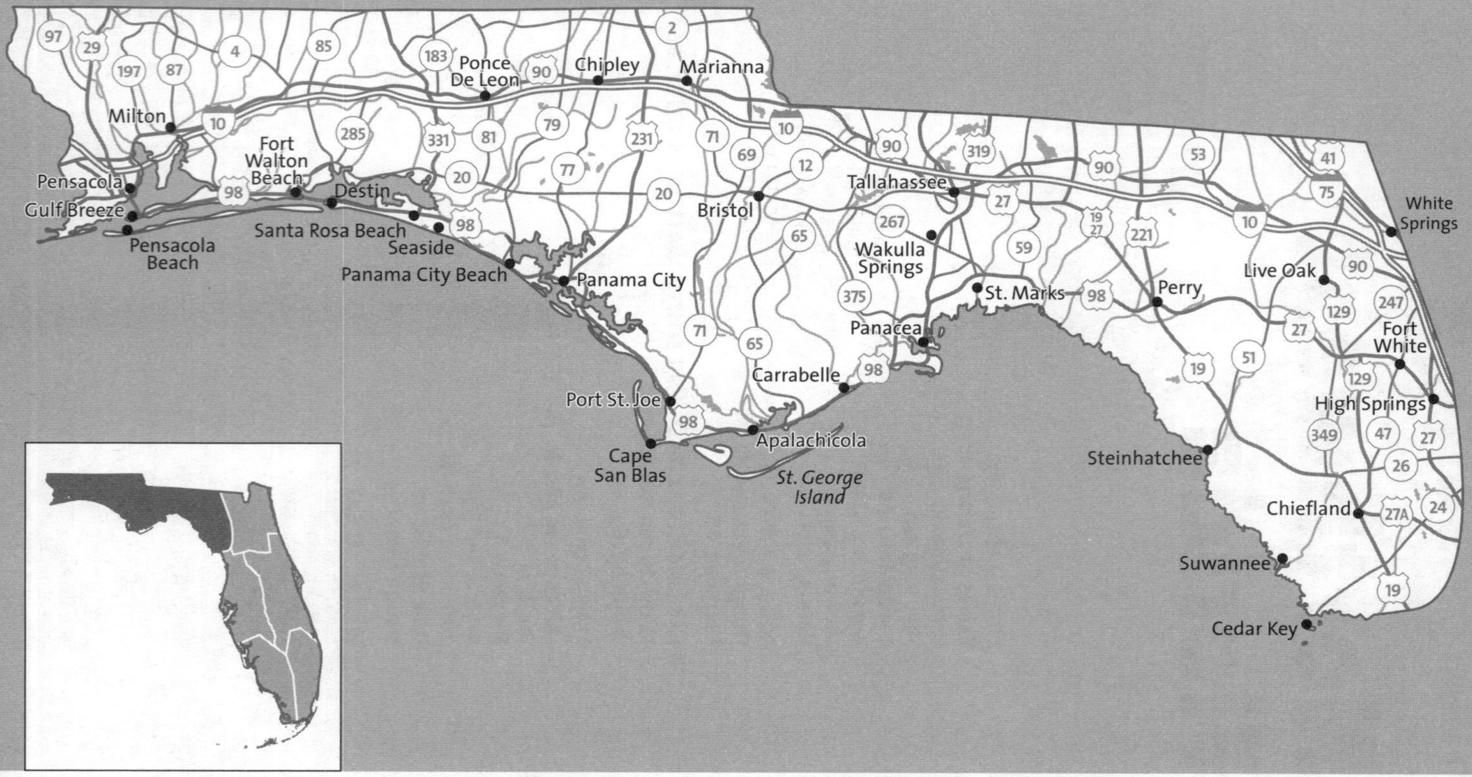

THE NORTHWEST

The coastal reaches of the northwest are known as the Emerald Coast, on account of the aquamarine waters that lap the coastline from **Pensacola** to **Apalachee Bay**. The area has also, somewhat less romantically, acquired the moniker of the 'Redneck Riviera', as a result of the historic migration of people from neighbouring Southern strongholds, such as Georgia and Alabama. What most visitors come for are the beautiful, blinding white **quartz beaches** and the vast tracts of **wilderness** that prevail here, the exception being **Panama City**, Florida's answer to Southend, which is bristling with arcade-style amusements and sprawling coastal resorts. The most beautiful beaches can be found to the south along the **Florida Panhandle**, so-called because from the air, this skinny, white stretch of sands resembles the curved handle of a frying pan. Paleo-Indians first populated the area around 9,000 BC. These nomadic peoples came by boat from across the Gulf of Mexico to occupy northern Florida, gradually moving south as the climate changed and the west coast of the peninsula moved some 100 miles inland.

The northeast remained a tribal territory until the Spanish laid claim to the area in present-day Pensacola in 1559 under the leadership of Don Tristán de Luna y Arellano (*see* History pp.4 and 6). Although Luna brought families, livestock and supplies to settle the area, a devastating hurricane meant they were unable to establish a base and Spanish eyes turned to the east coast and St. Augustine instead (*see* Northeast p.88). The region was all but abandoned until French and British interest in Florida spurred the Spanish to make a couple of reconnaissance trips. Spain decided that it would be in her interests to establish a fortress to defend the deep port at Pensacola. Despite a royal order in 1694, nothing was done to secure the province and it remained a strategic target for foreign interests. The French ruled briefly and the British finally got their hands on Florida following the Seven Years' War (*see* History p.4). Pensacola was made capital of the new territory of **West Florida**, which was divided from East Florida by the **Apalachicola River** and extended west as far as present-day Alabama and Louisiana. By the time that Spain ceded to the US in 1821 the western boundary of the state had moved back to Pensacola and, soon afterwards, Florida returned to being a single state, much as we see it today.

The Panhandle region sees more weather variations than further south. Temperatures can vary from an average of 83 degrees in summer to a chilly 50 degrees in winter, made to feel even colder by powerful coastal winds. Occasional flurries of snow have also been known. Hurricane Ivan made its mark in 2004 on the northeast's parks and nature reserves but advance warning of inclement weather is given in the danger period from June to October. It's a good idea to call beforehand if you're thinking about visiting some of the more remote places just to be sure facilities are fully operational following major storms.

Highlights

A capital day out at the Old and New Capitol Buildings, Tallahassee, pp.58–59
Living with history, Tallahassee Museum of History and Natural Science, Tallahassee St, p.59
To the Batmobile! Tallahassee Antique Car Museum, p.59
Beach treats, St. Joseph Peninsula State Park, Cape San Blas, p.61
All a flutter at the Marks National Wildlife Refuge, St. Marks, p.62
Getting away from it all, St. George Island State Park, St. George Island, p.62
Being cave dwellers at the Florida Caverns State Park, Marianna, p.63
Taking a dip in the crystal waters at Wakulla Springs State Park, Wakulla Springs, p.64
Glass Bottom Boats, Panama City Beach, p.65
Fly boys and girls at the National Museum of Naval Aviation, Pensacola, p.70
Walking through time, Pensacola Historic District, Pensacola, pp.70–72

TALLAHASSEE

Tallahassee became the state capital in 1824 for no better reason than that it was halfway between the two most prominent settlements in the north at the time – and indeed in the whole of Florida – Pensacola and St. Augustine. Under British rule these became the capitals of West and East Florida, respectively. After the British returned Florida to Spain and Spain passed it on to America, politicians got tired of traipsing back and forth from one state capital to the other and decided to journey inland. Tallahassee is where they met up and thus it

Special events

January

Civil War Re-enactment, Eden State Gardens, Point Washington, **t** (850) 231 4214, **www**.friendsofedengardens.org

Mardi Gras, Pensacola, **t** 800 874-1234, **www**.pensacolamardigras.com

February

Olustee Battle Festival and Re-enactment, Lake City, **t** (386) 752 2031 or (386) 758 0400

March

Natural Bridge Battlefield Reenactment, Tallahassee, **t** (850) 922 6007

April

Springtime Tallahassee Parade, Tallahassee, **t** (850) 224 5012, **www**.floridaconservation.org/festivals

Seaside Easter Egg Hunt and Activities, Seaside, **t** (850) 231 5424

Interstate Mullet Toss, t (850) 492 6838, **www**.florabama.com

Wakulla Wildlife Festival, Wakulla Springs State Park, **t** (850) 224 5950

May

Suwannee Bicycle Festival, Live Oak, **t** (386) 397 2347, **www**.suwanneebike.org

ArtsQuest, South Walton County, **t** (850) 237 0885, **www**.CulturalArtsAssociation.org

Tallahassee Wildlife Festival, t (850) 528 0823, **www**.TallahasseeWildlifeFestival.com

June

Fiesta of Five Flags Pensacola, t (850) 433 6512, **www**.fiestaoffiveflags.org

Sprint Billy Bowlegs Pirate Festival, Fort Walton Beach, **t** (850) 244 8191

July

Blue Angles Air Show, The National Museum of Naval Aviation, Pensacola, **t** (850) 452 3604 **www**.navy.com/blueangels

September

Pensacola Seafood Festival, Bartram Park, **t** (850) 433 6512, **www**.fiestaoffiveflags.org

October

Pensacola Interstate Fair, t (850) 944 4500, **www**.pensacolafair.com

Back to Nature, South Walton Beaches, **t** (850) 314 3749, **www**.beachesofsouthwalton.com

The Destin Seafood Festival, t (850) 837 6241, **www**.destinchamber.com

Destin Fishing Rodeo, Destin, **t** (850) 837 6734

Indian Summer Seafood Festival, Panama City Beach, **t** (850) 233 5070, **www**.panamacitybeachguide.net

Monarch Butterfly Festival, St. Marks National Wildlife Refuge, **t** (850) 925 6121, **www**.fws.gov/saintmarks

Florida Panhandle Birding and Wildflower Festival, Port St. Joe, **t** (850) 229 9464, **www**.birdfestival.org

November

Spooky Springs, Wakulla Springs State Park, **t** (850) 224 5950

Village Christmas Tree Lighting, Sandestin, **t** (850) 267 8117

December

Christmas Candlelight Open House, Eden State Gardens, Point Washington, **t** (850) 231 4214, **www**.friendsofedengardens.org

ZOOLights, Gulf Breeze Zoo, **t** (850) 932 2229, **www**.the-zoo.com

became the new state capital of Florida on the basis of a geographical compromise.

The city has profited greatly from its position and is now home to two fine **Capitol Buildings**, the **Florida State University** and a clutch of fine **museums** and elegant residential streets.

The area surrounding Tallahassee is famous for its beautiful **canopy roads**, where mighty oaks form a tunnel above your head. The Convention and Visitors Bureau stocks the *Guide to Scenic Leon County*, which outlines the best driving routes through the district. For a self-guided tour take a trip down Centerville, Miccosukee, Meridian, Old St. Augustine and Old Bainbridge Roads and imagine the forest paths where Spanish conquistadors once marched in search of gold and glory.

Getting there

By air Tallahassee Regional Airport, 3300 Capital Circle, t (850) 891 7800, www.ci.tallahassee.fl.us, is seven miles southwest of the city's central business district. Continental, Delta, Gulfstream, Northwest and US Airways service the airport with daily flights to Houston, Atlanta, Miami, Tampa and Orlando among other US destinations. The airport has a café and several fast-food outlets,

shops, a visitor information station and lounge area. For things to do while awaiting your flight, there's an art gallery, a massage centre, plus an arcade featuring video games and pool table.

By rail Amtrak, Railroad Avenue, **t** (850) 224 2779, **www**.amtrak.com, connects Tallahassee with east–west services with limited stops in LA, New Orleans, Jacksonville, Orlando, Pensacola and Miami.

By bus Greyhound Bus, 112 West Tennessee Street, **t** (850) 222 4249, **www**.greyhound.com, links the capital with Fort Walton Beach, Panama City and Pensacola, as well as destinations in east, west and southern Florida.

By road Interstate 10 links Tallahassee with Pensacola to the west (192 miles) and Jacksonville to the east (163 miles).

Getting around

By bus TalTran City Bus, 111 West Tennessee Street, **t** (850) 891 5200, is an extensive local public transit system with over 20 routes connecting the downtown district with shopping malls and Florida State University facilities

Tourist information

Tallahassee Area Convention and Visitors Bureau, 106 East Jefferson Street, **t** (850) 413 9200, **www**.seetallahassee.com

Things to see and do

Alfred B. Maclay State Gardens Park

3540 Thomasville Road, **t** (850) 487 4556, **www**.floridastateparks.org
Getting there ½ mile north of I–10 on US 319
Open Daily 8–dusk
Adm Jan–May, Adult $4, children $2, Jun–Dec $4 per car

Alfred B. Maclay designed these gardens at his winter home in the 1920s and they mainly flower in winter and spring with a dazzling display of camellias, azaleas and dogwoods. The many paths and plantings make for a harmonious visit at any time of year, and the adjacent **Lake Hall** offers scope for swimming, fishing, canoeing and kayaking.

Downtown Historic District

There are more than 25 historic and cultural sites within the 10-square area surrounding the **Capitol building** and **City Hall**. Two of the districts, **Calhoun Street** and **Park Avenue**, are listed in the National Register of Historic Places. The visitor centre has free brochures for self-guided tours around the district. There's an easy to follow map pinpointing all the sights and a separate brochure for children.

Florida Supreme Court

500 South Duval Street, **t** (850) 414 1154. For Oral Argument Experience and Historical Tours **t** (850) 488 8845, **www**.floridasupremecourt.org
Open 8–5 for drop-in self guided tours. Mock Oral Argument Experience: Thu at 9, 10.30, 1.30 and 3, Fri 9 and 10.30 and Historical Visits are both by appointment only
Adm Free

Pick up a leaflet for a self-guided tour of this beautiful 1940s courthouse. The areas open to the public include the upper and lower rotunda areas, courtroom, clerk's office, library, portrait gallery and lawyer's lounge. Guided Historical Visits are available to groups but must be booked in advance. To participate in Mock Oral Arguments, groups must call the Marshall's office but the public can observe the sessions without prior booking.

Goodwood Plantation

1600 Miccosukee Road, Tallahassee, **t** (850) 877 4202, **www**.goodwoodmuseum.org
Getting there Corner of Miccosukee Road (Route 146) and Medical Drive, 3 miles north of the Tallahassee Antique Car Museum
Open Mon–Fri 10–4, Sat 10–2. Museum: Mon–Fri 10–3.30, Sat 10–2, Gardens: Mon–Fri 9–5, Sat 10–2
Adm $5, under 3s free

One of the few remaining plantation estates in Florida, Goodwood was established in the 1830s to produce corn and cotton. Once covering over 2,400 acres, the 19-acre site comprises the main **plantation house**, 13 outbuildings, lawns and gardens. There's also a **roller rink** and a **reflecting pool**. The house, which retains original antiques and furnishings, is now a museum. The **visitor centre** is housed in the old kitchen and contains the site shop. Take a stroll in the lovely gardens, which retain their original 1920s plantings of perennials and roses.

Lake Jackson Mounds State Archaeological Site

1022 DeSoto Park Drive, Tallahassee, **t** (850) 922 6007, **www**.floridastateparks.org/lakejacksonmounds
Getting there Two miles north of Tallahasse off I–10 take US 27 to Crowder Road and Indian Mounds Road
Open Daily 8–dusk; **Adm** $3 per vehicle

This archaeological site has six Native American **temple mounds** and a **burial mound**, the largest of which is 36 feet high and measures 278 ft x 312ft at its base. Artefacts found here include jewellery, copper breastplates and more unusual finds such as cloaks preserved in the peaty soil. A **nature trail** takes in wetlands, upland pines and a ravine forest. In January, the site hosts the **Winter Encampment** living history programme, which recognizes the dig site's significance as a camp for Hernando de Soto and his crew in the 16th century on their travels through northern Florida.

Mission San Luis Archaeological and Historic Site

2020 West Mission Road, Tallahassee, t (850) 487 3711
Getting there US 90 at the intersection of Mission Road and Ocala Road, approximately 2 miles west of downtown Tallahassee
Open Mon–Fri 9–4.30, Sat 10–4.30, Sun 12 noon–4.30. Tours: Mon–Fri 12 noon, Sat 11 and 3, Sun 2
Adm Free, including tours

A Spanish Catholic Mission founded in 1656 stood on this site, which is undergoing excavations and a reconstruction programme. The **visitor centre** has an interesting display of goods from the site, including Native American and imported ceramics, metalwork and weaponry and there are on-site **reconstructions**, include a timber-framed mission church and village where guides in period dress occasionally demonstrate Spanish pioneer life as part of a living history programme. There is also a reconstruction of a circular Apalachee Indian council house, which measures 120 feet in diameter. Visitors can also enjoy free one-hour **guided tours** detailing the site's history.

MOAS, Mary Brogan Museum of Art and Science

Kleman Plaza, 350 South Duval Street, t (850) 513 0700, www.thebrogan.org
Open Mon–Sat 10–5, Sun 1–5
Adm Adult $6, children (3–17) $3.50

This facility has strong links to the Smithsonian Institute; there are two floors devoted to **interactive science experiences**, together with a world-class **Art museum**. Recent science exhibits include **Tech City** where kids can build, test and modify their own buildings, bridges and dams, and **CSI: Tallahassee**, where they can become forensic detectives, gathering and analysing evidence from a crime scene. The second floor houses permanent displays of hands-on, 'minds-on', exhibits for kids of all ages and on Saturdays there are special **Super Science** and **Smart Art experiences** involving the whole family, but arrive early as these are very popular.

Did you know?
Tallahassee is closer to Georgia than it is to Pensacola and Jacksonville? It's over 100 miles in either direction to get to the other cities in northern Florida but Thomasville and Valdosta in Georgia are only 35 miles and 63 miles away.

Museum of Florida History

500 South Bronough Street, t (850) 245 6400, www.flheritage.com/museum
Open Mon–Fri 9–4.30, Sat 10–4.30, Sun 12 noon–4.30
Adm Free

The museum acts as an umbrella organization for five sites in Tallahassee: the **Main Gallery**, the **Old Capitol**, the **Union Bank**, **Mission San Luis de Apalachee** and the **Knott House**, each of which showcase a different period of Florida's history. Visitors can take self-guided tours of the buildings and participate in scheduled hands-on activities and events. The Museum's permanent collection comprises 44,000 items that trace the development of Florida from prehistoric times to the present day. Exhibits that highlight periods of historical and cultural significance include furniture from the Old Capitol Building and portraits of Florida Governors from Andrew Jackson onwards, which once hung in the Capitol. George W's cousin, John Ellis Bush, will have a portrait here at the end of his term. There's also a huge skeleton of a 12,000-year-old mastodon, a collection of colonial gold coins from two ship-wrecked, 18th-century Spanish treasure ships, displays of Civil War weaponry and battle flags and artefacts from World War II, such as uniforms, weapons, medals, and photographs.

New Capitol

South Monroe and Apalachee Parkway, 400 South Monroe Street, t (850) 488 6167
Open Mon–Fri 8–5. Group tours available by reservation
Adm Free

The observation deck, at the top of this 1970s' skyscraper offers panoramic views of the cityscape and its environs. Visit the **Florida Artists Hall of Fame**, which celebrates writers, artists, actors and musicians who have shaped the state, including Ernest Hemingway and Ray Charles. This working state building gives visitors the chance to sit in on actual legislative sessions and houses the **Tallahassee Visitor Information Center**.

Old Capitol

400 South Monroe Street, **t** (850) 487 1902
Open Mon–Fri 9–4.30, Sat 10–4.30 and Sun 12 noon–4.30
Adm Free

Restored to its former early 20th-century glory days, the exterior sports fetching candy-striped awnings, whilst the interior and exhibits faithfully preserve the historic legislative chambers.

Tallahassee Antique Car Museum

3550A Mahan Drive (Route 90), **t** (850) 942 0137, **www**.tacm.com
Open Mon–Sat 10–5, Sun 12 noon–5
Adm Adult $7.50, children (under 11s) $4, (11–15) $5

A wonderful private collection assembled by a dedicated car enthusiast and champion of free enterprise. All the big American Classics are here; T- Bird, Corvette, Mustang, Cadillac, Buick, Pontiac and De Lorean, along with a collection of antique motorcycles and bicycles. The vast collection of antique toy vehicles display of antique pedal cars are delightful but pale in comparison with several original Batmobiles, Batcycles and, most bizarrely, the Penguin's Duck vehicle, from *Batman Returns*.

Tallahassee Museum of History and Natural Science

3945 Museum Drive, **t** (850) 576 1636, **www**.tallahasseemuseum.org
Getting there Close to Tallahassee Regional Airport off Route 371. From downtown Tallahassee, take Pensacola Street to Lake Bradford Road. Head south to Orange Avenue, turn right and onto Rankin Avenue and follow signs
Open Mon–Sat 9–5, Sun 12.30–5
Adm Adults $8, children (4–15) $5, under 3s free

A fantastic and thought-provoking experience for the whole family, this 52-acre site has a great deal to offer so plan to spend at least half a day here. Kids will love the **Big Bend farm**, a recreated 19th-century working farm, complete with corn crib, gristmill, cane and syrup shed, potato house and privy. The **museum** promotes living history and kids are encouraged to try their hand at a range of routine farm activities and domestic chores. At weekends authentically dressed guides run the farm and feed the animals. The fabulous **Natural Habitat Zoo** houses over 100 indigenous animals, including many endangered species. Here you can see Florida panther, black bears and red wolves. The zoo is a model of good practice, is actively involved in conservation and has a very successful breeding programme that is saving several species from extinction. The **Discovery Center** offers the chance to learn about ecology and natural science through fun, hands-on activities and exhibits. Will you dare to touch the creatures in the **Wet Lab Exploratorium**? Outdoors, the **nature trail** passes through swamp and under cypress trees to get to an authentic **Seminole Indian encampment**. Who can spot a gopher tortoise burrow? Stop off for lunch in the on-site **Trail Break Café**, which serves sandwiches and hot food, as well as a Bug Bites children's meal, which comes with a free toy.

Entertainment

Civic Center

505 West Pensacola Street, **t** (850) 487 1691. Box office: **t** (850) 222 0400, **www**.tlccc.org
Open Box office: Mon–Fri 10–5.30
Adm Tickets individually priced

Giant multi-purpose leisure facility, with a 13,500-seat arena that stages Broadway-style musicals, ice shows, concerts and sporting events, including the FSU basketball series.

Shopping

Bradley's Country Store

10655 Centerville Road, **t** (850) 893 1647, **www**.bradleyscountrystore.com
Open Mon–Fri 8–6, Sat 8–5

Pop over to Bradley's for a taste of real Florida, including homemade smoked sausages, hand-milled grits, jams, jellies, sugar sweets and moon pies – a favourite American snack that consists of a chocolate coating over marshmallow and a cracker base.

Governor's Square Mall

1500 Apalachee Parkway Tallahassee, **t** (850) 671 4636, **www**.governorssquare.com
Getting there From US 319 (Capital Circle) left onto US 27 (Apalachee Parkway), Governor's Square is on the right
Open Mon–Sat 10–9, Sun 12.30–5.30

Here you'll find the usual American department stores such as **Macy's**, **Dillard's**, **Sears** and **JC Penney**. There are speciality stores, including **Abercrombie** – the trendy clothes stores for ages 7–14, **Kids Foot Locker**, **Gymboree** and **PlaySmart** for toys and **EB Games** and **Games Stop** for computer and console games. **Sam Goody and the Suncoast Motion Picture Company** stock music videos and films. There's also a great choice in clothes shops for adults and teens including **Pac Sun** for casual wear, **Banana Republic**, **Gap** and **Gap Body**, **Abercrombie & Fitch** and **Aéropostale** for jeans, T-shirts and swimwear.

The food court offers a range of cafés and restaurants serving burgers, pizza, Mexican dishes and smoothies. Stop off for a gourmet drink between shopping at **Barnie's Coffee and Tea Co** or melt in the mouth ice creams from **Häagen Dazs**.

Special trips

Apalachicola

Much closer to home, about an hour's drive from Tallahassee on Highway 319/98, you come to the vast expanse of the **Apalachicola National Park.** Here visitors can hike, fish, swim and camp overnight for a minimal fee. The **barriers islands** along this stretch of coast are predominantly state parks and wildlife refuges providing scope for many wilderness adventures for families on holiday. The former private hunting ground of **St. Vincent** is now designated as a National Wildlife Refuge, **t** (850) 653 8808. It can only be accessed by boat and trips must be arranged in advance. Back on the mainland, scenic **Apalachicola** may have left behind the heady days of cotton-, lumber- and sponge-trading but it has retained its attractive waterfront warehouses and colonial homes, many of which now are boutiques, art galleries and seafood restaurants. While in the area, take a trip to **Eastpoint** and cross **Bryant Patton Bridge** to **St. George Island** for a quiet day of fishing or just playing on the beach. On the other side of the Apalachicola River is **Port St. Joe** with its paper mills and fishing boats, home of Florida's first meeting to form a state constitution. Further round the coast, **Mexico Beach**, unlike neighbouring Panama City, is an easy-going and relatively cheap place to stay while exploring the area.

John Gorrie State Museum

6th Street, Apalachicola, **t** (850) 653 9347
Getting there 1 block east off US 98
Open Thu–Mon 9–12 noon and 1–5
Adm $1, under 6s free

At the height of its prominence as a port of trade, Apalachicola attracted many young entrepreneurs, among them a doctor named John Gorrie. While tending yellow-fever patients, he experimented with methods of cooling their rooms, and developed primitive air conditioning and refrigeration units. A replica of Gorrie's mechanical ice-making machine, patented in 1851, is on display at the museum, as well as exhibits detailing the industrial development of 19th-century Apalachicola.

Suwanee River

'Way down upon the Swanee River, far, far away'... This is the first line of the Florida State Song and travelling the 100-odd miles to get here is a major detour. Geographically the river lies much closer to Gainesville than Tallahassee but technically it's in the Northwest. The river is immortalized in the song 'Old Folks at Home', but composer Stephen Collins Foster, a native of Pittsburgh, Pennsylvania, never visited the area, he merely chose the river to fit the poetic meter of his lyrics and it was conveniently located in an atlas. In the song, the **Suwanee River** was changed to Swanee. Nevertheless, the song drew many tourists to the area in the 1880s, seeking the rural idyll conjured by those words and thus the song gained its status in its own right.

Suwannee Canoe Outpost

Spirit of the Suwannee Music Park, 2461 95th Drive, Live Oak, t (386) 364 4991, www.canoeoutpost.com
Getting there **Exit 283 off I–10 and head north on US Highway 129 for 4½ miles. At I–75 take exit 451 go 4 miles and watch for signs**

Did you know?
That crossing the Apalachicola River from east to west helps you save time? The Tallahassee side of the river is in Eastern Standard Time (EST) and the Panama City side is in the Central Standard Time (CST) zone, one hour behind. Remember to adjust your watches back or forward depending on which way you're going. West = back, East = forward as you cross over the river.

Open Daily; call for times
Canoe rentals Adults from $9–$16, children (3–12) $4.50–$8, depending on the length of the trip

This wilderness centre offers adventure packages for families (*see* Sleep p.33) and provides day and overnight canoe rentals and a shuttle service for visitors staying off-site.

Suwannee River State Park

20185 County Road 132, Live Oak, t (386) 362 2746
Getting there 13 miles west of Live Oak, off US 90
Open daily 8–dusk; **Adm** $3 per car

The source of this powerful river lies over the border in **Georgia's Okefenokee Swamp** and these upper reaches can be explored by **canoe**, though check for details of water levels before setting out. The river courses through Florida for 235 miles, through several counties, and culminates in this 1,800-acre park. When water levels are low, you can see bubbles rising from the numerous springs that feed the river. **Civil War earthworks** and industrial artefacts from the days of paddle steamers line the banks and an ancient cemetery recalls the history of the area. Five **nature trails** of varying length from ¼ mile to 18 miles, loop through the adjacent forest and provide panoramic views of the rivers from a rocky overlook. There's also a playground, picnic areas, cabin rentals and campsites.

The Suwannee County Historical Museum

208 North Ohio Avenue, Live Oak, t (386) 362 1776, www.suwanneechamber.com
Open Mon–Fri 9.30–12 noon and 1–4.30
Adm Donations welcome

Situated inside the old Train Depot in Live Oak, the museum has displays of antique jewellery, home-made household items, a 1940s dentist chair and kitchen set, 1950s telephonic equipment, a copper moonshine still, the carriage used by Governor Drew, the first Governor of Florida, old school books, memorabilia and photographs pertaining to Suwannee River life.

Port St. Joe

The Constitution Convention State Museum State Park

200 Allen Memorial Way, Port St. Joe
Getting there Off Highway 98 east of Port St. Joe, **t (850) 229 8029**
Open Museum tours: Thu–Mon 9–12 noon and 1–5
Adm $1, under 7s free

Discover the fascinating history of the town of St. Joseph, a mid-1930s boomtown, that was, in effect, wiped out by storms and disease only a few years after holding the state's first constitution convention in 1938. Take a self-guided tour through displays and exhibits, including a replica convention hall where audio-animatronic mannequins play the part of delegates Robert Raymond Reid, William P. Duvall, David Y. Levy and Thomas L Baltzell, who, along with 50 others, met to draft a state constitution. It took four more conventions before Florida was finally admitted to the Union in 1845 as the 27th state. St. Joseph is where it all began.

St. Joseph Peninsula State Park

8899 Cape San Blas Road, Port St. Joe, t (850) 227 1327
Getting there On US 98 (heading east) turn onto SR30A, travel to SR30E to the park. **Open** 8–dusk
Adm $4 per car, $1 per bike or pedestrian

This lovely beach, perched on the end of the cape between the Gulf of Mexico and St. Joseph's Bay, offers scope for fishing trips and swimming and snorkelling. Rated one of top beaches in the United States, it's a great place for sunbathing backed by high dunes and scrubland. There's also a playground, toilets and a nature trail for families to follow. Sporty types can enjoy canoeing, kayaking, hiking and cycling. The park also offers good opportunities for bird watching and boating around the coastal peninsula. There are both fully serviced and primitive camping facilities within the wilderness preserve, as well as eight cabins for overnight accommodation.

St George Island

Journeys of St. George Island

240 East 3rd Street, St. George Island, t (850) 927 3259, www.sgislandjourneys.com
Open Call in advance for reservations
Adm 7–8 hour boat trips: $450 per tour (max 8 people). 4–5 hour kayak trips: Adults $60, children (under 12) $40. Kayak rentals: from $20 per day

Try this friendly excursion company for inventive and informative trips out on the water to discover the lesser-known parts of the barrier islands around Apalachicola Bay. Trips vary from an eight-hour boat trip to St. George and St. Vincent Islands for nature hikes, snorkelling and shelling to fishing trips, kayak trips and summertime 'kid only' educational excursions.

St. George Island State Park

1900 East Gulf Beach Drive, St. George Island, t (850) 927 2111
Getting there 10 miles southeast of Eastpoint, off US 98
Open 8–dusk
Adm $5 per car, $1 per bike or pedestrian

If you're looking for the natural, untamed side of Florida look no further than St. George Island's vast tracts of undeveloped coastline. You can just sit and take it all in or, if you really have to be doing something, run off excess energy among the ponds and marshes on nature trails, hunt for shells on the beach, go swimming, canoeing, boating, hiking or fish for sea trout, pompano, whiting, flounder (don't tell the kids!) and mackerel. There are picnic areas with grills, plus camping facilities and toilets.

AROUND AND ABOUT

Look at this!

Gulf Specimen Marine Laboratories Aquarium

222 Clark Drive at Palm Street, Panacea, t (850) 984 5297, www.gulfspecimen.org
Getting there 30 miles south of Tallahassee. Take US Highway 98 to Panacea, turn east on Rock Landing Road and follow signs to the left
Open Mon–Fri 9–5, Sat 10–4, Sun 12 noon–4
Adm Adults $5, children (under 12) $3

Touch tanks allow you to observe and handle sea anemones, whelks, octopi, clams shrimp, starfish and sand dollars, among others species native to Florida waters. New specimens are added often.

The tanks and aquariums hold over 200 sea creatures, including seahorses, hermit crabs, emerald eyed spiny boxfish, electric rays and red and white spotted calico, as well as sponges, anemones, lobsters and fish such as sharks, skates, moray eels and black sea bass.

Natural Bridge Battlefield Historic State Park

7502 Natural Bridge Road, t (850) 922 6007, www.floridastateparks.org
Getting there 15 miles southeast of Tallahassee off Route 363
Open 8–dusk; **Adm** Free

Relive one of Florida's largest Civil War skirmishes, where Confederate troops repelled three attempts by Union soldiers to capture Tallahassee in 1865. Thus Tallahassee remained the only Confederate capital east of the Mississippi to avoid falling into Union hands. The battle comes to life every year in March as re-enactors take up the positions of the opposing forces, which left 21 Union men and three Confederate soldiers dead. Visitors can view authentic Confederate and Union encampments during the event and can enjoy the tranquility of the site and its picnicking facilities year round.

The **St. Marks Historic Railroad State Trail** passes through the park offering 20 miles of paved and unpaved trails, between Tallahassee and St. Marks, that are perfect for hiking, cycling and horse riding.

San Marcos de Apalache Historic Site

148 Old Fort Road, St Marks, t (850) 922 6007
Getting there South end of Route 363
Open Thu–Mon 9–5; **Adm** is $1, under 6s free

At the junction of the Wakulla and St. Marks Rivers, this site was originally an important centre for the Apalachee Indians and in the 1500s was on the route of both Panfilo de Narváez and Hernando de Soto. Wooden forts were erected here in 1679 and 1718 but it wasn't until 1763 that a stone fortification guarded the confluence. This fort became a strategic line of defence in the Seminole Wars when it stood against the Creek Indians and the Civil War, when Conferdate forces held the fort against invading Union troops (*see* History pp.5–6). Today, the **visitor centre** displays exhibits detailing the area's military history, built upon the foundations of a former marine hospital that replaced the Spanish fort. Outdoors you can follow a trail through the remains of the **historic fortifications**.

St. Marks National Wildlife Refuge

1255 Lighthouse Road, St. Marks, t (850) 925 6121, www.fws.gov/saintmarks
Getting there Off Highway 98
Open Visitor Centre: Mon–Fri 8.15–4, Sat, Sun 10–5
Adm $4 per car

This 68,000-acre refuge comprsises coastal marshes, tidal creeks, estuaries and islands and includes sections of seven of north Florida's rivers. The **St. Mark's Unit** houses the **visitor centre**, which provides information on wildlife habitats and access to a seven-mile **nature drive** through freshwater and saltwater environments. The road winds down to the foot of **Apalachee Bay**. Here you'll find the historic **St. Marks Lighthouse**, still used today, and boat ramps, birding nature trails and a picnic area. This is the spot to observe the orange and black monarch butterfly, which arrives in fluttering clouds each year (Oct–Nov). Other parts of the park offer facilities for boating and walking along nature trails – the most family-orientated is the **Panacea Unit** where visitors can explore pine and oak forests interspersed with freshwater lakes via primitive walking trails. At the **Otter Lake Recreation Area**, families can stop for a picnic, launch boats and make use of the toilet facilities. The Panacea Unit is west of the **Wakulla Unit** on Highway 98.

Nature lovers

Adventures Unlimited

8974 Tomahawk Landings, Milton, t (850) 623 6197, www.adventuresunlimited.com
Getting there Exit 22 off I–10 and go left onto Highway 281 north to Highway 90. Turn right on Highway 90 for 2 miles and then left onto Highway 87 north for 12 miles and follow signs
Open Daily; hours vary according to the season
Adm From $20 per person in a 2-man canoe for 1½ hours; children (under 12) free, in the centre of the boat. Day trips and overnight camping canoe trips are also available; prices vary

The gentler waters of the Coldwater and Blackwater Rivers are more suitable for family trips than the more challenging course along Juniper Creek. This 88-acre private park also offers tubing and kayaking down freshwater streams and facilities for camping, log cabin accommodation and group retreats.

Blackwater River State Park

7720 Deaton Bridge Road, Holt, **t** (850) 983 5363
Exit 45 off I–10. 15 miles northeast of Milton off Highway 90
Open 8–dusk
Adm $2 per car, $1 per bike or pedestrian

The town of **Milton** is a self-proclaimed canoe and kayaking paradise and this scenic state park is where many vacationers flock. The sandy bottom of the riverbed and clear water also makes it a good place for **swimming**, **paddling** and **fishing**. There are shaded **campsites** nearby and visitors can picnic near the riverbank. There are lovely nature trails through undisturbed natural habitats, including towering stands of Atlantic white cedars.

Can you spot?
A Monarch butterfly fluttering by? Between late October and November look closely at the trees because what you think might be dried orangey-brown and black leaves covering a branch could be hundreds of Monarch butterflies. These delicate creatures follow the same migratory patterns each year, south from Canada to the same areas in Florida, the coast of Texas and in Mexico to feed on milkweed plants. In spring, they return north to reproduce but once they have laid their eggs they leave it to successive generations to make it back the 5,000 miles to these feeding grounds.

Falling Waters State Park

1130 State Park Road, Chipley, **t** (850) 638 6130, **www.**floridastateparks.org
Getting there 3 miles south of Chipley and I–10, off State Road 77A
Open Daily 8–dusk
Adm $4 per car, $1 per bike or pedestrian

Almost a thousand feet of boardwalks climb, descend and encircle the limestone **sinkholes**, before snaking through upland pine forests to the main event itself – a waterfall in a cylindrical sinkhole with a 73-ft drop. Visitors can observe native and migrating butterflies in the **butterfly garden**; cool off in the lake or hike among the rolling green hills. Rangers host a range of activities in the **amphitheatre**, check for details. You can **camp** overnight and there are also two acres of lake and white sand **beaches** for swimmers to enjoy and shaded areas nearby, offering toilets and picnic tables.

Florida Caverns State Park

3345 Caverns Road, Marianna, **t** (850) 482 1228, **www.**floridastateparks.org
Getting there 3 miles north of Marianna. Off of US 90 take State Road 166. From I–10 take Marianna Exit 136 or 142 north and follow signs to the park
Open Daily 8–dusk. Cave tours: Daily between 9–4 (last ticket sales at 1pm)
Adm Park $4 per car, $1per bike or pedestrian. Cave tours; Adults $6, children (under 13) $3

The park rangers give guided tours of the **cave networks**, so take this 45-minute underground excursion and add soda straws, flowstones and draperies, to your current knowledge of stalagmites and stalactites. The caves are naturally airy making a very pleasant diversion from the Florida sun; learning has never been so cool. The **visitor centre** offers an audio-visual presentation of the caves and other areas of natural beauty, which may be more suitable for visitors with young children to watch and those who would find the cave tour a bit too strenuous. The park also has facilities for **canoeing, boating, hiking, fishing and swimming**.

Torreya State Park

2576 Northwest Torreya Park Road, Bristol, t (850) 643 2674, www.floridastateparks.org
Getting there 13 miles north of Bristol. From I–10 take State Road 12 and go west on County Road 1641
Open Park: daily 8–dusk. House tours at 10am daily and also at 2 and 4pm at weekends
Adm $2 per vehicle, nominal extra fee for house tours

Built in 1935–42 by the Civilian Conservation Corps, this 12,000-acre park was part of a federal scheme to provide work during the Depression. As part of the project, the entire **Gregory Plantation House** (fully furnished; tours Mon–Fri at 10 and 2, Sat–Sun at 4) was dismantled and taken across the wide Apalachicola River, where it was reconstructed, hard work for only $30 a month. Park activities include **boating** and a challenging **hiking trail** over the bluffs. There are also extensive **camping** facilities.

Wakulla Springs State Park

550 Wakulla Park Drive, Wakulla Springs, t (850) 224–5950
Getting there 15 miles south of Tallahassee on Route 61 and west of St. Marks. From Highway 98 take Route 267 to Route 61
Open 8–dusk
Adm $4 per car, $1 per bike or pedestrian. Boat tours: (45 mins) Adults $6, children (under 12) $3

Used as a location for some of the Tarzan movies starring Johnny Weissmuller, this is 'tarzan country'. The dazzlingly clear waters of **Wakulla Springs**, one of the world's largest and deepest freshwater springs, give scope for **fishing**, **canoeing** and **kayaking**. There are designated swimming areas, which you should not swim out of, and an **observation deck** at the springhead for great views. The springs feed the Wakulla River, which passes through areas of cypress swamp, maples and palm trees. The area is abundant with birds, including apple snail-eating limpkins, anhingas and ospreys. **Glass-bottomed boat trips** allow visitors to explore the pristine habitats both in and around the river, where wading birds and warblers feed and alligators, manatee and turtles can be seen. There are plenty of picnic spots *en route* through the park, which connect to **nature trails**. Rangers provide a programme of activities at the park; call the office for a list of current events.

PANAMA CITY

Panama City has amusements, including arcades along the 27-mile-long stretch of **Panama City Beach**, family activity parks and a few nature attractions.

Front Beach Road and **Panama City Beach Parkway** are the all-singing-and-dancing, bleeping-and-flashing entertainment hubs athough **Miracle Strip Park** is due to close and its wooden Starliner roller coaster moved to either Cypress Gardens in Winter Haven (*see* p.140) or Valdosta, Georgia. It gets very busy here at weekends and Easter when college kids from next-door states hit town. Aim for a mid-week visit, avoiding April if possible, and then head to the beaches of the Panhandle for the weekend.

Getting there

98 miles west of Tallahassee on Highway 98

Tourist information

Panama City Beach Convention and Visitors Bureau, 17001 Panama City Beach Parkway, t (850) 234 6575, www.thebeachloversbeach.com

Things to see and do

Cobra Adventure Park

9323 Front Beach Road, t (850) 235 0321
Open 10–12 midnight; Adm Prices per ride

Try your luck on the snaking 4-level tracks in 9-horsepower go-karts. Smaller children can ride with an adult. The **Snow Shot Racers** offer a unique experience to drive snowmobiles along a track. Finish with a trip to the arcade or a flight simulator ride.

Coconut Creek Family Fun Park

9807 Front Beach Road, t (850) 234 2625, www.coconutcreekfun.com
Open 9–late
Adm $15 2-day ticket, under 5s free. Golf free for under 6s

The kids can get lost in humungous fenced-in labyrinth of the **Grand Maze** or play a round of mini-golf on one of the park's two challenging 18-hole courses.

Dan Russell Municipal Pier

16101 Front Beach Road, **t** (850) 233 5080
Open Daily 24 hours (passes available 9–3)
Adm Fishing: Adults, $5, children (under 12), $2, spectators $1, under 6s free

For a spot of quiet contemplation along the northwest's busiest strip, head out to this 1600-ft concrete pier to hook yourself some mackerel, red fish, cobia, flounder, pompano or other local species. Rod rentals, bait and tackle are all available on site.

Glass-Bottom Boat Tours

Treasure Island Marina, 3605 Thomas Drive, **t** (850) 234 8944
Adm Adults $15, children (3–12) $8

This family-run boat company offers three-hour sightseeing cruises over to **Shell Island** to observe creatures above and below the sea. There's also the chance to spot dolphins and collect shells.

Gulf World Marine Park

15412 Front Beach Road, **t** (850) 234 5271, **www.gulfworldmarinepark.com**
Open Daily 9–5 (earlier in winter). Dolphin Camp: (8.30–3)
Adm Adults $20.44, children $14.40 (5–11), plus tax, under 5s free. Dolphin Encounter: $150–$125, plus tax (depending on season). Dolphin Day Camp (ages 8–13 only): $55, plus tax (both Dolphin experience prices include admission)

The kids will love meeting the tropical birds and marine animals at this tourist attraction and dolphin rehabilitation centre. Attractions include dolphin and sea lion shows, sharks, alligators, sea turtles, penguins, an iguana, tortoises, flamingos, otters and a stingray petting pool. There are parrots, flamingos and turtles in the tropical gardens and the **Tropical Garden Theater**, which alternates magic shows with a Las Vegas rock tribute performance (events are individually priced, **t** (850) 234 5279 for information). Highlights for kids, however, will be seeing parrots, toucans, macaws, cockatoos in flight and the array of colours and pulsing water jets in the **Splash Magic Laser Show**. Best of all is the chance to swim and play with a dolphin on the encounter programme or attend a **Dolphin Day Camp** (minimum four children, maximum 14) where children aged 8–13 can take part in training sessions, learn about marine life and make arts and crafts items to take home. Campers get lunch and a free Gulf World Marine Park T-shirt.

Junior Museum of Bay County

1731 Jenks Avenue, **t** (850) 769 6128, **www.jrmuseum.org**
Open Mon–Fri 9–4.30, Sat 10–4
Adm Adults $3, children (2–14) $2

Hand-on science exhibits help kids to explore sound and weight, discover how the human body works and get up close to some fascinating reptiles. Then explore **nature trails**, a **train engine** and a 1800s **pioneer house** complete with smokehouse, log cabin, a barn and even a few chickens.

Museum of Man in the Sea

17314 Panama City Beach Parkway, **t** (850) 235 4101, **www.diveweb.com**
Getting there ¼ mile west of State Road 79 on Back Beach Road (US 98)
Open Daily 9–5; **Adm** Adults $5, children (6–16) $2.50

This unusual museum charts the development of diving from early experiments using animal bladders to the latest, deep-dive apparatus and includes items from shipwrecks, diving bells, submarines and remote operated submersibles. The museum also offers **educational activities** for children, including experiments that explain how undersea conditions arise, a saltwater touch pool, a diver's helmet that kids can try on and a hands-on computer station that showcases marine life in the St. Andrew Bay estuary. Outdoors there's a **climb-through submarine** and a **giant model of a killer whale** to explore.

Rock 'It Lanes Family Entertainment Center

513 Beckrich Road, **t** (850) 249 2696, **www.rockitlanes.com**
Open Daily 10–2am. Roller skating: Mon–Sat 10–late, Sun 12 noon–late

This non-smoking family fun centre offers **bowling**, **pool tables**, **roller skating** and **arcade games**. There are 24 bowling lanes with automatic pneumatic bumpers that can be raised to make it easier for kids to play. Teenagers might like to hang around until after 10pm for the **Ballistic Bowling** glow-in-the-dark and laser-lights experience.

St. Andrews State Park and Shell Island

4607 State Park Lane, **t** (850) 233 5140
Getting there 3 miles east of Panama City Beach off State Road 392 (Thomas Drive)
Open Shuttle Mar–Oct 10–4
Adm $5 per car, $3, per bike or pedestrian. Shell Island shuttle: Adults $9.50, children (6–12) $5.50

This former military reservation boasts fine white sands, blue-green waters and 1½ miles of beaches for swimming, snorkelling, scuba diving, kayaking, and canoeing. You can fish from the piers and a rock jetty or offshore via the boat ramp. Two **nature trails** lead through pine forests for bird watching and picnicking. There's also a **campsite** and snack bar for refreshments, souvenirs, and fishing gear. **Shell Island boat tours** for snorkelling and shell collecting trips are available during the spring and summer.

Sea Dragon Pirate Cruise

5325 North Lagoon Drive, Lighthouse Marina, t (850) 234 7400, www.piratecruise.net
Open Ticket booth: From 10am
Adm Adults $17, children $13, toddlers $7

Yo ho ho and a lot of fun is in store for all the family on this two-hour pirate cruise aboard the Sea Dragon – a striking red-and-black, 85-ft sailing ship. Kids can enjoy music and games, dragon tales and sword fights, plunder the treasure chest and have their faces painted. There's even a chance to spot dolphins. Refreshments, snacks and souvenirs are available.

Shipwreck Island

12201 Middle Beach Road, t (850) 234 3333, www.shipwreckisland.com
Open April–Sept 10.30–5.30, see website or call for seasonal variations
Adm $27 (over 50"), $22 (35–50")
Lockers, changing facilities, food outlets

This water park is in a lovely wooded setting, which thrill riders will most appreciate when plunging down the massive **Tree Top Drop** slide (minimum height 48"). There are two frothing **river rapid tube rides**, a sheer drop from a pipe and lots of family orientated water fun. There's a **lazy river** and a **wave pool** with waterfalls and a **floating island, zip wires, a shipwrecked boat**, **flumes** and **animal-themed slides** for younger kids. Lifeguards are on duty. No food, drinks or cool boxes are allowed in the park.

Super Speed Fun Park

9523 Front Beach Rd, t 850-234-1588, www.tcfb.com
Open 10– 12 midnight; **Adm** $4.75–$8 per ride

Dare you enter the haunted house with Captain Die? Rides include **dragster rally cars, bumper boats, laser tag**, **Skycoaster**,a skydiving/hang gliding experience, a **games arcade** and several go-kart tracks, including a one for younger riders (minimum height for drivers 42"), younger kids can ride with an adult.

ZooWorld Zoological and Botanical Park

9008 Front Beach Road, t (850) 230 4839, www.zoo-world.us
Open Daily 9–5.30 (seasonal variations)
Adm Adults $11.95, children (4–11) $7.95, plus tax, under 3s free
Gift shop

This 7½-acre zoo is home to about 300 endangered and exotic animals, including lions, jaguars, monkeys, orangutans, giraffes, tigers, bears, kangaroos and lemurs. The animals are spilt into **four zones**, South America, Australia, Africa and Asia within a botanical garden environment, which showcases 250 species of tree and plant life from around the world. There's a **petting zoo**, where kids can feed a giraffe, and an **infant nursery** for young animals in the zoo's care.

Shopping

Alvin's Island-Magic Mountain Store

12010 Front Beach Road, t (850) 234 3048, www.alvinsisland.com
Open Daily 8–12 midnight

This shopping emporium lies just across the street from all the amusements. Pop in for souvenirs, T-shirts, funky inflatables and tropical-style beachwear for all the family. Enjoy the **live shark and alligator feedings**, **parrots** and **aquariums** while you browse.

THE EMERALD COAST AND SOUTH WALTON COUNTY

A popular spot for spring breakers, the Emerald Coast encompasses **Fort Walton Beach**, the fishing village of **Destin** and **Okaloosa Island**. It attracts holidaymakers with scaled-down versions of the amusements in Panama City, family beach resorts and a variety of interesting attractions. The town's main source of industry comes from the **Eglin Air Force base**, which contains nature reserves but is off limits to the public apart from the **Air Force Armament Museum** just outside the gate. Coastal Highway 98,which links the two towns to Okaloosa Island, is one of the most picturesque road trips in Florida, continuing west it arrives at the lovely, sensitively developed beach communities of **South**

Walton County. **Grayton Beach's** 1920s cypress log cabins and award-winning sands are well worth a visit. Route 283 wends its way through this Bohemian enclave *en route* to another fashionable address – Seaside. Immortalized in the 1998 film *The Truman Show*, this model town was established in the 1980s and has proved particularly popular with families looking for a quiet but upscale, beachside community comprised of well-designed cottages and smart public facilities including, immaculate swimming pools, playgrounds, a post office, church, theatre, town centre buildings and parks. **Camp Seaside**, **t** (850) 231 2246, open Mon–Fri 8.30–2, is a summer programme for resort visitors offering sports and art and crafts activities. You can also tour the **Truman House**, browse the markets and the **Ruskin Beach** artist's colony. The townwebsite, **www**.seasidefl.com has information on events and accommodation.

Getting there

Tourist information

Emerald Coast Convention and Visitors Bureau, 1540 Miracle Strip Parkway, Fort Walton Beach, **t** (850) 651 7131, **www**.destin-fwb.com

South Walton Tourist Development Council, US 331 and Highway 98, Santa Rosa, Beach, **t** (850) 267 1216, **www**.beachesofsouthwalton.com

Things to see and do

Air Force Armament Museum

100 Museum Drive, Eglin Air Force Base, **t** (850) 882 4062
Open Daily 9.30–4.30 (except Federal Holidays)
Adm Free

The museum houses weaponry from antique flintlocks and western six shooters to huge bombs, rockets and air-to-air missiles, including the GBU-28 'bunker buster', used in Operation Desert Storm. There are indoor and outdoor aircraft exhibits from World War II to the Korean and Vietnam wars.

Big Kahuna's

1007 Highway 98 East, Destin, **t** (850) 837 4061, **www**.bigkahunas.com
Open May–Sept daily, Water park: 10–5, Adventure park: 11–10
Adm Water park: $33 (over 48"), $29 (under 48") under 2s free. Mini Golf: $5, Go-kart: $5.50, adrenaline rides: $15. Combined tickets available

Need to know

How to handle the Panhandle

Tourists may be aware that the black volcanic sands in parts of the Mediterranean absorb heat and make it impossible to walk on them without shoes, but may not know that the dazzlingly white sands of the Panhandle are equally tricky. Like snow, white sand magnifies the intensity of the sun and the glare can be unbearable and potentially damaging. Make sure everyone has wraparound sunglasses and uses high-factor sun lotion; bring legionnaires' hats for the kids. Families should also be aware of strong rip tide currents and avoid swimming in water that looks cloudy or choppy. It's extremely important to obey flag warnings on the beach, which vary from blue (calm waters) to yellow (exercise caution) and red (do not swim). Kids should stick to the paths when going to the beach and wear sturdy beach shoes to walk on the tough, crunchy quartz sands.

The water park offers over 40 rides of varying tempo, including body flumes, white water tubes and speed slides, as well as more gentle wave pools, lazy rivers, and **Pleasure Island** with its pools and giant squirting octopus that will be of particular appeal to the littlest members of the family. The Adventure Park has white-knuckle rides like **Cyclone** and **Sky Coaster**, but also offers the more sedate pleasures of mini golf and go-kart rides.

Eden Gardens State Park

Route 395, Point Washington, **t** (850) 231 4214
Getting there 1 mile north of Highway 98
Open Park: Daily 8-dusk, House Thu-Mon 10-3 guided tours available on the hour
Adm $2 per vehicle. Nominal extra charge for guided tours of the mansions

Once home to the lumber merchant Wesley family, this elegant **neo-classical manor house** and its gracious interior will evoke a sense of the plantation era. You'll not find it hard to imagine Scarlet O'Hara wafting through the rooms and fainting against the balustrades wearing a voluminous gown. The ornamental gardens are delightful, and there are numerous picnic sites. Get a **garden trail** guide from the fig leaf shop and explore the rose and butterfly gardens, enjoy the stunning azaleas and camellias, and gaze at the moss draped live oaks from the perspective of the reflection pool.

The Emerald Coast Science Center

139 Brooks Street, t (850) 664 1261, www.ecscience.org
Getting there Off Highway 98 west of the bridge to Okaloosa Island
Open Mon–Fri 10–4, Sat, Sun 11–4
Adm $3.50 per person

This enterprising centre houses 250 interactive science encounters to delight and fascinate the whole family. Try flying and attempting to land model aircraft in the wind tunnel, playing a laser harp, making giant bubbles that dwarf the kids or meet a tarantula and giant millipede in the nature discovery room.

Grayton Beach State Park

Getting there Route C–30A, 357 Main Park Road, Santa Rosa Beach, **t** (850) 231–4210, **www.floridastateparks.org**
Open daily 8-dusk
Adm $4 per car $1 per bike or pedestrian

Grayton Beach is one of the most beautiful and most highly rated beaches in the US. There's scope here for numerous active and passive outdoor pursuits; **canoeing** and **kayaking**, **hiking**, **swimming**, **cycling** and **bird watching**. Learn about the ecology of the area on the **nature trail**, which winds its way through an eerie, otherworldly coastal forest. The park has camping sites and modern cabins for overnight or weekly accommodation. Booking ahead is essential if you want to stay.

Gulfarium

1010 Highway 98 East, Fort Walton Beach, t (850) 244 5169, www.gulfarium.com
Open Tue–Sat mid-Aug–Apr: 9–6, Apr–May: 9–4. Jun–early-Aug 9–8. Shows throughout the day. Admissions close 2 hours before park closing
Adm Adults $17.50, children (4–11) $10.50, under 3s free with an adult. Dolphin encounters: $125 (advance booking of at least 24 hours is recommended)
Gift shop, snack bar

The world's oldest marine-show aquarium is home to baby dolphin Delilah, born April 21, 2005. Visitors can view the **dolphin habitats**, **shark pools**, **aquariums**, **touch tanks** and wander around the **lagoon** to spot heron and pelicans. There are also seals, sea lions, alligators, turtles, otters and penguins. **Live shows** feature bottlenose dolphins and Californian sea lions and scuba demonstrations with sea turtles, set against a backdrop of endless sea and sky. There is also a 40-minute interactive encounter (extra cost) with Kiwi and Daphne, pan-tropical spotted dolphins, which is unusual because most Florida dolphin encounters are with bottlenose species, and dolphin therapy for children with disabilities.

Henderson Beach State Park

17000 Emerald Coast Parkway, Destin, t (850) 837 7550, www.floridastateparks.org
Open Daily 8–dusk
Adm $4 per car, $3 per bike or pedestrian

Destin's main beach has excellent facilities for families, there's a **heated bathhouse**, **playground** and a **restaurant**, as well as toilets and outdoor showers. A complex of newly renovated boardwalks protect the fragile dunes from visitor damage and are great vantage points to spot dolphins frolicking in the sea at sunset.

Indian Temple Mound Museum

139 Miracle Strip Parkway, Okaloosa Island, Fort Walton Beach, t (850) 833 9595
Getting there Highway 98, just west of the bridge
Open Sept–May: Mon–Fri 10–4, Sat, Sun 9–4, Jun–Aug: Mon–Sat 9–4.30, Sun 12.30–4.30
Adm Adults $3, children (4–17) $1
Gift shop, educational tours

This huge prehistoric temple mound dates from between AD 800–1400. It's a remarkable feat of engineering and it is estimated its builders needed at least 500,000 baskets of earth to complete it. First investigated by the Smithsonian Institute in 1883, it has undergone nine more excavations and many of the finds are in the neighbouring **museum**. Native American Indian artefacts include stone and bone tools, clay and shell items and a quantity of finely wrought Fort Walton pottery. The museum also houses displays about the later history of the site, including exhibits about Civil War soldiers, Spanish explorers and pioneer settlers.

John Beasley Wayside Park

East of Fort Walton Beach on Highway 98 East
Picnic facilities, toilets, showers, lifeguards

This pleasant public access beach contrasts hilly dunes with powdery white sands against a background of impossibly pea-green sea.

Okaloosa Island Park

Highway 98, Fort Walton Beach

This network of boardwalks offers access to over six miles of amazingly white sands along the Gulf Island National Seashore. There are volleyball courts, a visitor centre, beach showers and playground, as well as shopping and dining facilities. The park also offers surfing, swimming and fishing from the Okaloosa Fishing Pier. Lifeguards are on duty.

Topsail Hill State Park

7525 West Scenic Highway 30A, Santa Rosa Beach, t (877) 232 2478, www.floridastateparks.org
Getting there Located in Santa Rosa Beach on Route 30A, one mile off US 98
Open daily 8–dusk. Tram service April–Sept from 9 to 20 minutes before sunset
Adm $2 per car $1 per bike or pedestrian

This scenic park offers more than three miles of undeveloped **beach** terrain with 25-ft sand dunes and three coastal **lakes** offering great opportunities for shoreline fishing, hiking, bike rides and sunbathing (boats are not allowed). Guided **tours** are available from the **visitor centre** and a tram service runs hourly to the beach and **campsite**. The fully serviced camping grounds include a swimming pool, tennis courts and a snack bar, as well bungalows and parking for mobile homes.

The Track Family Recreation Center

1125 Highway 98, Destin, t (850) 654 4668, www.destintrack.com
Open Daily, May–Sept 10–10, Sept–May call or check website for times
Adm Tickets for activities are sold in bulk, on average 2–3 tickets per ride

Wild Woody will keep big and little kids amused. this imaginative three-tier, three-storey, spiral go-kart track, offers single and two-seater karts. Other activities include bumper boats and cars, bungee jumping, sky flying, miniature golf, kiddy rides and video arcade games.

Snorkel Destin

392 South Shore Drive, Destin, t (850) 654-4655, www.snorkeldestin.com
Open May–Sept, Mon–Sat, Reef Runner tours: 8.30, 11.30 and 2.30
Adm Snorkel Adventure: $22 per person, Sunset Cruise: Adult $12, children $5, under-4s free

The Snorkel Adventure is a scenic boat cruise and snorkelling experience in one. All equipment and instruction is provided and you'll get the chance to see tropical fish, rays and sea creatures; you might even stumble across some forgotten pirate treasure. The Sunset Cruise departs two hours before dusk, so check for times when booking.

Shopping

Bayou Arts and Antiques

Hogtown Bayou Lane, Santa Rosa Beach, t (850) 267 1404
Getting there On Highway 393
Open Tue–Sat 10–4.30

This antiques shop has an unusual outdoor feature… a Wildlife Chapel where local kids can have their pets blessed or can create a memorial to the dearly departed in the grounds. The shop sells books, local landscape paintings, abstracts, jewellery and toy boats.

Silver Sands Outlet

10562 Emerald Coast Parkway, Destin, www.silversandsoutlet.com
Getting there 8 miles east of Destin on US Highway 98 just west of Sandestin Golf & Beach Resort, access is also available from the north across the Mid-Bay Bridge from State Road 20
Open Mon–Sat 10–9, Sun 10–6

This factory outlet centre, said to be the biggest in the US, has over 20 shops selling kids' clothing, including designer brands, many offering up to 75% off R.R.P.. Stores include **Banana Republic, Calvin Klein, Osh Kosh B'Gosh, Bose, Polo Ralph Lauren Factory Store, Vans, Tommy Hilfiger** and **Off 5th** (the Saks Fifth Avenue Outlet). There are plenty of places to get a bite to eat.

PENSACOLA

Pensacola and St. Augustine battle it out for the accolade of being Florida's oldest European city. St. Augustine, founded in 1565, is the first continual colonial settlement (*see* p.4) and Pensacola, first established in 1559 can claim to be the first attempted settlement. The history of this region is choppy, like the seas that pound its shores and the storms that have periodically shaped and reshaped its coast. Several incomplete Spanish invasions left it vulnerable between the attempts at settlement in 1559 and 1698, when France and Spain were fighting for control of its strategic deep port. The scramble for land between British, French and Spanish forces was the impetus for establishing a base in the Gulf of Mexico, which linked trade routes in the Caribbean with the American interior via the coastal rivers. It was not until British rule (1763–83), that the area became stable and Pensacola the capital of West Florida. The new state was a sizeable concern, stretching west as far as the Mississippi River. Spain soon clawed back the territory and established a new diocese in New Orleans covering Louisiana and the two Floridas. To this day, East Baton Rouge, East Feliciana, West Feliciana, Livingston, St. Helena, St. Tammany, Tangipahoa and Washington in Louisiana are known as the Florida Parishes.

Pensacola's historic **downtown district** and **Bay** reflect the eras of military occupation. Archaeological sites, restored colonial homes and Civil War forts all testify to the diversity of life there. **Perdido Key** is still under shared ownership with neighbouring Alabama, reminding visitors of Pensacola's location out on a limb from the rest of the state. Its historical treasures apart, Pensacola also provides access to the **Gulf National Seashore**. Hurricane Ivan (Sept 2004) damaged large portions of the coastal barrier islands between **Navarre beach** and **Perdido Key**. Check for restricted access (*see* p.73).

Getting there

By air Pensacola Regional Airport, 2430 Airport Blvd, **t** (850) 436 5000, **www**.flypensacola.com
American Airlines, Continental, Delta, Air Tran and US Airlines fly to Tampa, Orlando, Fort Lauderdale, Charlotte, Atlanta, Dallas, Chicago and New York, among other US destinations. There's a restaurant and passenger lounge and a newsagents stand. **Taxis** and **shuttle services** run from the airport, including **Pensacola Taxi**, **t** (850) 456 3000, **www**.pensacolataxi.com and **A+ Shuttle**, **t** (850) 803 1095, **www**.aplusshuttle.com
By bus Escambia County Area Transit, 1515 West Fairfield Drive, **t** (850) 595 3228, **www**.goecat.com – services include free **Tiki Beach Trolleys** from late May–Sept, which run every 20 minutes

Getting there

Greyhound Bus, 505 West Burgess Road, **t** (850) 476 4800, **www**.greyhound.com
By rail Amtrak, 980 East Heinberg Street, **t** (800) 872 7245, **www**.amtrak.com
By road From I–10, take Exit 4 off I–100 into the centre. Scenic Highway 90 snakes around the bay while Highway 98 sweeps in from the Panhandle

Tourist information

Pensacola Convention and Visitors Information Centre, 1401 East Gregory Street, **t** (850) 434 1234, **www**.visitpensacola.com

Things to see and do

Fort Barrancas

Pensacola Naval Air Station, 3822 Taylor Road, **t** (850) 455 5167
Getting there Off Route 292A on Blue Angel Parkway
Open Daily Mar–Oct 9.30–4.45, Oct–Mar 8.30–3.45. Tour: 2pm
Adm Free

A perfect picnic spot and a great place to explore. Cross the drawbridge, enter the sallyport and the parade ground, once home to 19 cannons. Explore the lower level scarp and counterscarp galleries and imagine defending these enormous 20-ft high, 4-ft wide walls during the Civil war.

The National Museum of Naval Aviation

Pensacola Naval Air Station, 1750 Radford Boulevard, **t** (850) 452 3604, **www**.navy.com/blueangels
Getting there off Route 292A on Blue Angel Parkway
Open Daily 9-5; check website for Blue Angel Q&A
Adm Museum and guided tours free. Simulator: $4 each, IMAX: Adult $6.75, children $6.25. Blue Angels practice sessions free

This fabulous museum has one of the world's largest aviation collections with over 140 restored aircraft. Even the café is an authentic recreation of the officers' club at Cubai point. See inside an aircraft carrier, walk the flight deck of **USS Cabot** and man an anti-aircraft gun; visit **Home Front USA** to gain a sense of American home life during World War II; sit inside the cockpit trainers of planes like the **Sea Cobra, Tiger or harrier** or experience flight up close in the **IMAX theatre**. In the **simulator** you'll experience the rolls, pitches and vertical climbs of a jet fighter. Watch the **Blue Angels** flight team practice (Tue and Wed 8.30am) and take part in scheduled autograph and Q&A sessions with the pilots.

Pensacola Historic Village

320 South Jefferson Street, Pensacola, **t** (850) 595 5985
Open Mon–Sat 10–4
Adm Adult $6 children (4–16) $2.50

Admission gives access to the places listed below, all within four blocks and, together, representing the diverse cultural influences of Pensacola's early years. **Guided tours** of **Lavalle House**, Old Christ Church and **Lear-Rocheblave House** are included and leave daily at 11 and 1 from the **Tivoli House**.

Tivoli House

205 East Zaragoza Street

Recreated in 1976, following the designs of the original Tivoli House, this building houses the **Historic Village gift shop** and **ticket office**. Built in 1805, it was formerly a boarding and gaming house, bordered by a large octagonal theatre and ballroom, which served as the local meeting house.

T. T. Wentworth Jr. Florida State Museum

Plaza Ferdinand

Built as Pensacola's city hall, this renaissance revival building houses the **Florida State Museum**. On the first floor is the T.T. Wentworth Collection, ranging from the mundane to the ridiculous, including stuffed bears, license plates, radio tubes, Coca Cola bottles and a petrified cat. The **Discovery galler** on the third floor is devoted to a hands-on children's museum, representing Pensacola past and present in scaled-down working exhibits like a post office, schoolhouse, city hall and hospital. The museum also hosts visiting exhibitions on the second floor.

The Museum of Industry

200 East Zaragoza Street

Exhibits represent the fishing, railroad, brick making and lumber industries, instrumental to Pensacola's economic success in the 19-century, including historic railroad cars and rolling stock.

The Museum of Commerce

201 East Zaragoza Street

The reconstruction of an entire street, complete with streetlamps, shops, including a historic toy store, and a collection of vintage horse-drawn carriages brings the 1890s commercial district to life.

The Weaver's Cottage

207 East Zaragoza Street

This traditional two-roomed, pioneer cottage, houses an exhibition about weaving and its importance to the local economy of the late 1800s.

Julee Cottage

210 East Zaragoza Street

Built in 1804, this cottage is dedicated to former owner Julee Panton, a free African-American woman. The collection relates to Julee and local black history.

Lavalle House

205 East Church Street

This fine example of French Creole colonial architecture is furnished in 1850s-style and provides a rare glimpse of the domestic reality of frontier life. It also contains a fine example of a colonial rope bed draped with cheesecloth, which was used as mosquito netting.

Lear-Rocheblave House

214 East Zaragoza Street

An example of Folk Victorian architecture. The maritime history of its occupants is told through displays in several of the spacious family rooms furnished with antiques from the late 1890–1900s.

Dorr House

311 South Adams Street

A grand example of Greek revival architecture, furnished throughout with fine Victorian antiques.

Quina House

204 South Alcaniz Street

This customised Creole Cottage houses the **Pensacola Historic Society** and exhibits household artefacts and furnishing displays from the society's collection.

The Barkley House

Florida Blanca Street

This French-Creole' high house' is one of the oldest masonry built houses in the state of Florida, and, for the region, is built in a very unusual style.

Tell us a tale

Bed bugs and ballyhoo

The saying, 'Sleep tight, don't let the bed bugs bite', may relate to the colonial rope bed. The support structure was a laced rope that crossed over and underneath. The rope was tightened by pulling slack out of the ropes exposed on either side of the bed frame. Very tight knots held the ropes in place at the headboard. The ropes slackened when they were slept on and were re-tightened every day by the children of the home, using a tool called a rope wrench. It was best to sleep on a supportive rope structure of tight, secure bindings, hence 'sleep tight.' 'Don't let the bed bugs bite', relates to the red insects, or 'chiggers' that often infested the Spanish Pensacola colony. They are found in the Spanish moss that hangs from trees in parts of Florida, particularly around Pensacola, which colonists used to stuff. They smoked or boiled the moss to kill the insects but some insects often survived and plagued the sleepers with a horribly itchy bite that lasted several weeks.

The Colonial Archaeological Trail

South Jefferson Street

Collect a trail map from Tivoli House. Each of the open-air archaeology exhibits on this trail has an explanatory metal marker and location map. Places include a **British fort** dating from 1778, including the garrison kitchen, **government house** and the partially reconstructed remains of **Fort George**.

Sam's Fun City

6709 Pensacola Boulevard, Pensacola, t (850) 505 0800, www.samsfuncity.com
Getting there Just south of I–10 on Route 29
Open Sun–Thu 12–8, Fri, Sat 10–11
Adm Multiple-ride wristbands available from $14.95–$29.95
Restaurant, snack bars

After all that learning let the kids let off steam in this fun amusement complex and water park. Attractions include a carousel, Ferris wheel, park train, 18-hole movie-themed miniature golf course, two go-kart tracks, electric and vintage vehicle tracks, numerous kiddie rides, including trucks, planes and a mini coaster and bumper boats. The adjacent **Surf City Water Park** boasts 15 water slides, a lazy river, spray jets, interactive play structures and toddler play pools.

Tours

Beach Boy Trolley

2237 W. Nine-Mile Road, t (850) 494 2270, www.beachboytrolley.com; Fares $10

Join a 50-minute narrated tour of the Downtown Historic District. Tours leave the Pensacola Visitor's Center Mon–Sat at 10.30, 11.30, 12.30 and 1.30. Or opt for an overhead view with **Santa Rosa Flightseeing**, fares $110 per person, a helicopter tour that includes a trolley service from your hotel to Pensacola Beach and a 25–30 minute flight over **Fort Pickens** and **Pensacola Pass** with views of historic Pensacola. Walking eco-tours, cruises, canoeing trips, ghost tours, museum visits and shuttle services are available, (airport shuttle pending), call or visit the website for details.

Shopping

Cordova Mall

5100 North 9th Avenue, t (850) 477 5563, www.simon.com
Getting there Intersection of North 9th Avenue and Bayou Boulevard.
Open Mon–Sat 10–9, Sun 12 noon–6.

Pensacola's largest mall has 140 speciality stores including **Zevo Urbanwear** for brands like Phat Farm, Baby Phat, Pepe Jeans and Timberland. There's a kids' **Footlocker** and a few other children's clothes and accessory shops, such as **Gymboree** and **Claire's Accessories**, plus two **Dillard's department stores** and a food court. There's also a **hair salon** and an **Aveda Spa**.

AROUND AND ABOUT

Buckets and spades

Please note

Owing to Hurricane Ivan (Sept 04) much of the Gulf National Seashore is undergoing reconstruction. Some beaches are reopening but their facilities may not all be up and running. Contact the tourist board or visit **www.nps.gov/guis** for updates,

Perdido Key Beach

Route 292/Johnson Beach Road, t (850) 934 2600

This lovely stretch of coastline was badly damaged by the hurricane and needs extensive remodelling and repairs. Visitor access will be resumed as soon as possible.

Santa Rosa (Opal Beach)

After considerable restoration in 1995 after Hurricane Opal, Santa Rose beach received another battering from Hurricane Ivan in 2004. The beach is closed awaiting repairs to Route 399.

Look at this!

Naval Live Oaks

East of the Three-Mile Bridge at 1801 Gulf Breeze Parkway, Gulf Breeze, t (850) 934 2600
Open Daily 8–5.30; **Adm** Free

This is the headquarters of the Gulf Islands National Seashore. Damage has been cleared and all trails are open unless notices have been posted.

The Zoo

5701 Gulf Breeze Parkway, Gulf Breeze, t (850) 932 2229, www.the-zoo.com

Getting there 10 miles east of Gulf Breeze on Highway 98
Open Daily 9–4. (summer 9–5)
Adm Adults $10.95, children (3–11) $7.95
Wildlife gift shop, snack bars

This 30-acre zoo houses over 700 animals in a lush botanical garden landscape. It has reopened following hurricane damage and now boasts a **Nile hippo exhibit**, the first stage of an African environment to include an African village, African Queen boat ride and enhanced chimpanzee and gorilla islands. At present, visitors can see bears, tigers, rhinos, zebras, monkeys, tropical birds and otters. They can also take a ride on the **Safari Line train** and visit the **petting zoo**. The zoo has a programme of seasonal events, see website for details.

Nature lovers

Big Lagoon State Park

12301 Gulf Beach Highway, **t** (850) 492 1595, **www.floridastateparks.org**
Getting there On County Road 292A, 10 miles southwest of Pensacola
Open Daily 8–dusk
Adm $3.25 per car, $1per bike or pedestrian

Due to hurricane damage at Big Lagoon, no rental facilities are available at time of going to press. The West Beach area is open but there are no bathroom facilities. Check the Florida State Parks website or call for details before setting out.

Fort Pickens National Park

1400 Fort Pickens Road, **t** (850) 934 2635, **www.floridastateparks.org**
Open Park: Daily 7–10

Access to the area is by boat only and visitors may access the beaches east of the Ranger Station. The Fort remains closed until further notice.

Perdido Key State Park

15301 Perdido Key Drive, **t** (850) 492 1595, **www.floridastateparks.org**
Getting there 15 miles southwest of Pensacola, off State Road 292
Open Daily 8–dusk; **Adm** $2 per car

This lovely stretch of coastline was badly damaged by Hurricane Ivan and needs extensive remodeling and repairs. Visitor access will be resumed as soon as possible.

WHERE TO EAT

Tallahassee

Andrew's Capital Grill and Bar

228 South Adams Street, **t** (850) 222 3444, **www.andrewsdowntown.com**
Open Mon–Sat for lunch and dinner; popular family brunch buffet Sun (11–2), under 5s eat free, (*moderate*)

Usual fare, salad bar and good value, high-quality sandwiches and snacks.

Barnacle Bill's Seafood Restaurant

1830 North Monroe Street, **t** (850) 385 8734, **www.barnaclebills.com** (*moderate*)

Local seafood, served either grilled, steamed, smoked or fried and a full American menu of burgers, dogs and fries. There's also a kids' menu.

Hopkins Eatery

1415 Market Street, Tallahassee, **t** (850) 668 0311, (Branch: 1700 North Monroe Street **t** (850) 386 4258) **www.hopkinseatery.com** (*inexpensive–moderate*)

Clean, no frills restaurant, ideal for takeaways or snack lunches, which offers healthy sandwich fillings, melts, salads and 20 cake varieties daily.

Nicholson Farmhouse Restaurant

200 Coca Cola Avenue, Havana, **t** (850) 539 5931, **www.nicholsonfarmhouse.com**
Getting there North of Tallahassee on US 27. Turn at the lights on to East 9th Avenue (SR 12), go west for about 3 miles, the restaurant is on the right
Open Tue–Sat 4–10 (*moderate–very expensive*)

Relaxed dining in a historic setting, offering steaks, grills, fish and seafood and homemade pies. The kids' menu includes grilled chicken, pizza and hot dogs. It has no licence so bring your own alcohol (over 21s only). Kids will love the **pony rides** and **Jimmy Lee Johnson's Mule wagon rides** (Fri– Sat nights).

Around and About

Apalachicola

Boss Oyster Restaurant

125 Water Street, Apalachicola, **t** (850) 653 9364, **www.apalachicolariverinn.com** (*moderate–expensive*)

One of the top 10 oyster bars in the US, Boss provides a relaxed and casual atmosphere with both indoor and outdoor dining. There's also a variety of fresh fish and seafood, plus steaks, chicken fingers and pizzas.

Nola's Grill at the Gibson Inn

51 Avenue C, Apalachicola, t (850) 653 2191, www.nolasgrill.com

Open Breakfast and lunch: Sat, Sun, Dinner: Wed–Sun (*expensive*)

For formal and prestigious Apalachicola dining, visit the main dining room of the Gibson Inn – a restored listed Victorian hotel with a tin roof and wraparound porches. Specials include Grouper Florentine and Filet Mignon topped with crabmeat. The lunchtime menu offers salads, soups and sandwiches.

Panama City

Captain Anderson's Restaurant & Waterfront Market

5551 North Lagoon Drive, Panama City Beach, t (850) 234 2225, www.captandersons.com

Open Dinner: Feb–Oct Mon–Sat (*moderate–very expensive*)

This restaurant is very popular with visitors and locals alike who come to sample its signature Gulf Coast dishes. There's an interesting kids' menu and you can eat outside. The market next door stocks oils, spices, sauces, cheeses, olives, pastries, Greek specialities, seafood, steaks, cookbooks, gifts and souvenirs.

Pineapple Willy's Beachside Restaurant and Sports Bar

9875 South Thomas Drive, Panama City Beach, t (850) 235 1225, www.pineapplewillys.com

(*inexpensive–expensive*)

Bar/grill fare served indoors in the air-con restaurant or outdoors on beachside tables. The kids' menu has hot dogs, chicken, shrimp, fish or peanut butter and jelly sandwiches. Main dishes include seafood and steaks, sandwiches and Jack Daniels BBQ ribs served in a souvenir bucket. Also features a Historic pier with views over the gulf, a 15-screen sports room and a gift shop.

The Treasure Ship

3605 Thomas Drive, Panama City Beach, t (850) 234 8881, www.thetreasureship.com

Open Mar–Oct Daily (*inexpensive–expensive*)

A restaurant that is a replica of Sir Francis Drake's Golden Hind? It could only happen on Panama beach. Kids can climb the decks and sight the cannons whilst waiting for the Pirate waiters to take their orders and entertain them with face painting and balloon animals. The main dining room serves seafood, fish, steaks and salads and is open for dinner only, but also on board is Captain Crabby's all-you-can-eat restaurant and Hooks Grill and Grog Bar for lunch and dinner. Full children's menus throughout and souvenir pirate glasses.

Uncle Ernie's Bayfront Grill and Brew House

1151 Bayview Avenue, t (850) 763 8427

(*moderate–expensive*)

A relaxed restaurant serving fresh breads, seafood, steaks, sandwiches and handmade desserts and beers, many charmingly named after the original owners Ernest and Jessie Morris. Uncle Ernie's boasts the best sunsets around and has a good claim to the best Bloody Mary in Bay County. With its waterfront location you can arrive by car or by boat!

The Emerald Coast

Mexico Beach

Halfshells Seafood Market and Steam Bar

3104 Highway 98, Mexico Beach, t (850) 648 2000, www.halfshells.com

Open Mon–Sat 11–9, Sun 11–8

(*inexpensive–moderate*)

No frills surroundings but good-value eating, whether staying in or taking away to cook yourself. Seafood raw or steamed, sandwiches, melts and hotdogs are all on offer.

Destin

AJ's Seafood and Oyster Bar

116 Highway 98 East, t (850) 837 1913, www.ajs-destin.com

Open daily from 11 (*moderate–expensive*)

This casual waterfront diner has a kids' menu of popcorn shrimp and burgers, cheese pizza, chicken or fish fingers. For adults, there is an oyster bar as well as a more sophisticated menu. AJ's also offers daily tours on a 73ft-passenger boat. The 1½ hour midday dolphin and beach cruise is best for families, adults $17, kids $8, under 4s free. Ring to reserve trips in advance.

Criolla's Restaurant

170 East Scenic Highway 30A, Santa Rosa Beach, **t** (850) 267 1267, **www.**criollas.com
Open Dinner Nov–Feb Tue–Sat; Mar–Oct Mon–Sat from 5.30 (*expensive*)

This high quality restaurant is a perfect choice for a family night out. Criolla's has an *à la carte* and a set menu for adults, while kids are treated to an imaginative and healthy menu without a fry in sight! The staff are very adaptable and will cater for almost all dietary requirements, from vegetarian and vegan to lactose and gluten intolerance. Reservations recommended and please state any dietary needs when booking.

Destin Chops

414 Harbor Boulevard (Highway 98 East, **t** (850) 654 4944 (*moderate–expensive*)

Sister restaurant to Marina Café (see below), offers innovative and traditional steakhouse fare. Reservations recommended.

Marina Café

404 Harbor Boulevard, (Highway 98 East), **t** (850) 837 7960, **www.**marinacafe.com (*moderate–expensive*)

Set in a spectacular location overlooking Destin Harbor, you can eat indoors or out. Specialities include sushi (menu on request), steak, rotisserie duck and gourmet pizzas. Try the peppercorn seared rare yellowfin tuna with spicy soy-citrus dipping sauce and wasabi oil, an epicurean treat. Inspired desserts, ice cream and sorbets. Reservations recommended.

Seaside

Bud & Alley's

Route 30A, **t** (850) 231 5900, **www.**budandalleys.com (*moderate–expensive*)

Enjoy waterfront dining at this charming colonial-style restaurant with gorgeous views over the Gulf of Mexico. The menu is a mixture of Southern and Mediterranean cuisine with oysters, blue crab, shrimp, scallops, fish and pasta, plus steaks, mixed grill and chicken dishes. The lunchtime menu has seafood and a variety of sandwiches and salads. Kids are welcome but there's no separate menu but plenty of healthy options, including vegetable dishes and sweet potato fries. The **Tarpon Bar** offers a kids' meal of macaroni with butter and cheese, served with either shrimp or chicken.

Pensacola

Jubilee Bushwacker's Café

400 Quietwater Beach Road, Pensacola Beach, **t** (850) 934 3108, **www.**jubileefun.com
Open Daily from 11 (*inexpensive–moderate*)

This is a great beachside café with an extensive menu of seafood meals, prime ribs and lobster and bar snacks. Under-12s can enjoy a meal for 99 cents and at weekends there are clowns.

Jubilee Topside Restaurant

400 Quietwater Beach Road, Pensacola Beach, **t** (850) 934 3108, **www.**jubileefun.com
Open Dinner: Mon–Sat 6–10, Sunday Brunch: 9–2 (*inexpensive–moderate*)

This prestigious five-star restaurant above the Bushwacker's Café offers amazing waterside views. There isn't a separate kids menu, although they will split entrées for smaller portions. On Sundays, Topside features a brunch menu, with complimentary champagne and muffin/biscuit basket.

McGuires Irish Pub

600 East Gregory Street (between the Bay bridge and the Civic Center), **t** (850) 433 6789, **www.**mcguiresirishpub.com (Branch: 33 Highway 98, Destin, **t** (850) 645 0567)
Open daily from 11 (*inexpensive*)

This family friendly, award-winning steak restaurant serves traditional pub fare. Tuck in to custom-made steak burgers, snow crab claws, baked oysters, sandwiches, salads and Cajun specialities in Irish themed rooms. Kids can choose from shrimp, chicken tenders, toasted cheese sandwiches or grouper nuggets served with fries in a sand pail. Sign a $1 bill and add it to the collection adorning the back bar ceiling and your arrival into the McGuire family will be accompanied with a fanfare of whistles and bells .

Peg Leg Pete's Oyster Bar

1010 Fort Pickens Road, Pensacola Beach, **t** (850) 932 4139, **www.**peglegpetes.com (*inexpensive–moderate*)

A real family-orientated restaurant serving seafood and Cajun dishes. The kids' menu includes frozen ice cream drinks; meals are served with fries and a soft drink in a beach bucket. There's also a playground and ship's store that sells a wide range of souvenirs from baby rompers to Pirate sauce and Peg Leg Pete's T-shirts, available in all sizes.

Quiz

1. Where can you find a reconstruction of an Apalachee Indian council house?

2. Where can you build, test and modify your own buildings, bridges and dams?

3. What is the name of the first Florida Governor?

4. Name three American Classic cars.

5. Where can you spot a gopher tortoise burrow?

6. What river is immortalized in the song 'Old Folks at Home'?

7. Where were many of the Tarzan movies filmed?

8. What two cities claim to be Florida's oldest European cities?

9. Where can you experience what it was like to fly a plane during World War Two?

10. What is the name of the hurricane that devastated much of the Gulf in 2004?

Northeast Florida

07

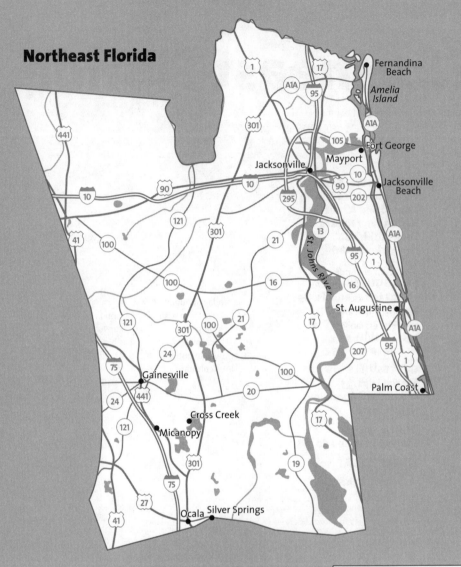

Northeast Florida

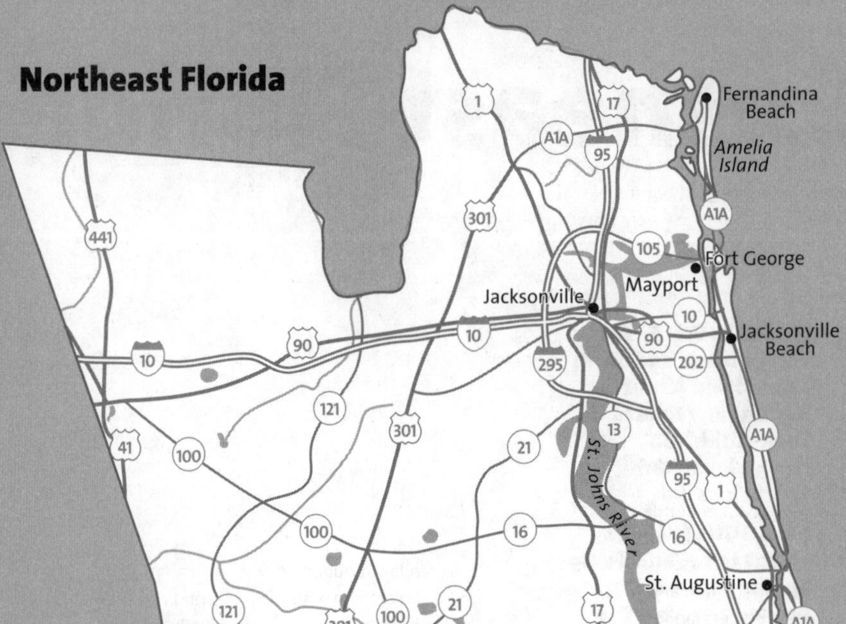

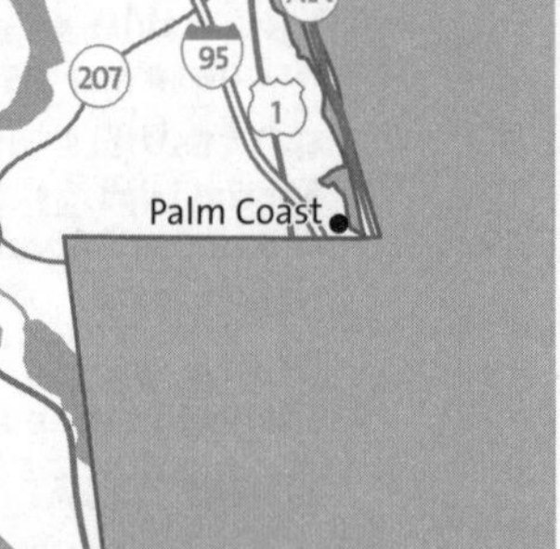

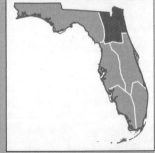

NORTHEAST FLORIDA

The northeast is known as Florida's First Coast as it was here that Juan Ponce de León claimed 'La Florida' on behalf of Spain in 1513. The native tribe of Timucuan Indians resisted but many succumbed to foreign disease and the rest were slowly wiped out by wave after wave of colonial intervention.

The Atlantic coast has certainly seen more than its fair share of frontiersmen. Spanish, British, French and, finally, US forces haved vie for power and to bring settlers in to occupy the territory. Between 1562–64 the French Huguenots came to challenge the Spanish claim. They sailed up the St. Johns River and established Fort Caroline near present-day Jacksonville. In 1565, the Spanish returned, determined to overthrow them and on 8 September, Pedro Menéndez de Aviles broke ground for the Spanish settlement of St. Augustine, which became the first continual colonial settlement on mainland America 55 years before the Pilgrim Fathers landed.

In the early 1700s, the British made a couple of attempts at invasion but they were repelled by St. Augustine's major fortification – the Spanish Castillo de San Marcos – constructed from a shell- and coral-based limestone called *coquina*, which absorbed their cannon fire. The British eventually received Florida from the Spanish in the late 18th century in a paper exchange for Havana, the capital of Spanish Cuba, which they had captured during The Seven Year's War (*see* History p.4).

British occupation lasted about 20 years but it had considerable impact. St. Augustine became the capital of a new territory called East Florida, which was divided from West Florida and its capital Pensacola. The British built roads, created plantations, extended regional boundaries north into Carolina and got rich from trading with native Indian tribes. They restored Florida to the Spanish in the Treaty of Paris in 1783 but, significantly, the two Floridas stayed separate. It was only when the Spanish finally ceded the territory to the US in 1821 and Tallahassee became the new capital in 1824 that the northeast ceased to be the main sphere of influence in the region. By 1845, when Florida became the 27th state in the Union, the seat of power had permanently moved west.

Today, St Augustine has a nostalgic air. It's a quaint colonial town with some of Florida's oldest buildings including a fascinating walk-in historic district.

Jacksonville, by contrast, is big, bustling and industrial but is gradually attracting more tourists to its cultural and entertainment centres. In addition to exploring the historic towns and sites, there are unassuming beaches, state parks, hardwood forests and salt marshes. The St. Johns River, with its 342 navigable miles of waterways, is Florida's longest river and offers plenty of scope for entertainment.

Travellers to the northeast will find that it is one of the few parts of Florida where they can experience four distinct seasons. The average annual temperature hovers just short of 70 degrees with a summer high in the 90s. Nights can be cooler so pack a few long-sleeved tops, especially if you're there in winter.

Highlights

Jacksonville Museum of Modern Art, p.81
Making science fun in the Museum of Science & History, Jacksonville, p.82
Taking the plunge at Adventure Landing, p.83
Talking to the animals in Jacksonville zoo, p.83
Quick march at Fort Clinch State Park, p.85
All aboard the Mayport Ferry, p.87
In with the old at The Oldest House National Historic Landmark, St. Augustine, p.90
Getting back to nature in Anastasia State Park, p.92
Hopping on and off the big red tourist train, St. Augustine, p.93
Sitting pretty at the Washington State Gardens, Palm Coast, p.94
Museum of Natural History, Gainesville, p.96
Riding out in a horse and carriage, Ocala, p.99

JACKSONVILLE

Jacksonville is the major gateway to the north-east of Florida. It is the 16th largest city in the US and Florida's largest and most industrial city. In terms of population. Its origins, however, could not have been humbler. The city was once called Cow Ford after the spot where cattlemen drove their herds to new pastures across the St. Johns River. In the 1820s, following the ceding of Florida to US forces, the name was changed to Jacksonville in

Special events

March

Annual Lighthouse Festival, St. Augustine, **t** (904) 829 0745, **www**.staugustinelighthouse.com

April

Annual Beaches Sandcastle Contest and Parade, Jacksonville Beach, **t** (904) 247 6236.

Last weekend in April.

May

Florida's First Coast Birding and Nature Festival, St. Augustine, **t** 800 653 2489, **www**.visitoldcity.com

Isle of Eight Flags Shrimp Festival, Fernandina Beach, **t** (904) 261 3248 or (904) 261 0203, **www**.shrimpfestival.com.

First weekend in May.

June

Drake's Raid. St. Augustine, **t** (407) 843 9967/ (904) 829 9792.

November

Nights of Lights. St. Augustine, **t** (904) 829 1711. Nov–early Feb.

December

Victorian Seaside Christmas, Amelia Island, **t** (904) 261 324

honour of Andrew Jackson who briefly became Governor of Florida but never actually set foot in the town that was to bear his name.

Jacksonville's major industries were lumber, cotton and shipping. World War II established the port of Jacksonville as one of three major bases in Florida and later, during the Gulf War (1991), it became the busiest naval port in the United States.

It was during the 1880s and early 1900s, though, that it was put on the tourist map, after Henry Flagler, an enterprising railway magnate, came to St. Augustine on his honeymoon in 1883 and, very disappointed by the lack of accommodation and transport links in the area, decided to build a string of hotels (including the now-demolished Atlantic Hotel on Atlantic Beach) and develop the East Coast Railroad.

The Great Fire of 1901, begun in a mattress-fibre factory, finished off what Flagler started and much of the downtown area was destroyed. During the early 1900s, Jacksonville was rebuilt as a winter tourist destination with beach communities to the north and south.

Two historic entertainment complexes, Dixieland on the south bank of the St. Johns River and the Florida Ostrich Farm on the north bank, drew in the crowds. These attractions are long gone but the two banks still vie for attention with the main leisure and shopping facilities situated to the north and a number of cultural establishments clustered together on the Southbank.

Getting there

By air Jacksonville International Airport **t** (904) 741-2000, **www**.jaa.aero/ is 12 miles or about 20 minutes from the city centre. There are indirect flights daily from Birmingham, Leeds, Luton and most London airports with connections in US cities (Atlanta, Chicago, Philadelphia etc).

By road Interstate 95 runs north/south through Jacksonville: Interstate 10 runs east/west through Jacksonville, I–75 is nearby and provides more interstate connections. Within Jacksonville, Highways 1 or 17 and I–95 are good out of peak time. Orlando is 135 miles away. Route A1A, the coast road, runs from Amelia Island north and connects to I–95, a more direct route for travellers heading north or south.

By rail Amtrak runs services from Jacksonville to Miami (9 hours), Orlando (3 hours) and Tampa (train to Orlando, then bus, 5 hours). **www**.amtrak.com.

Getting around

Jacksonville Transportation Authority, **t** (904) 743 3582, **www**.jtaonthemove.com

Provides a number of inter-connecting services for commuters and tourists:

The **Skyway monorail** runs six days a week to both sides of the St. Johns River and downtown district for a nominal fee. There are stations close to Jacksonville's major attractions and Kings Avenue station on the Southbank has ample parking. There are also three **free trolley services** operating between downtown with connections to the Skyway service. **Bus services** are also numerous and frequent, the R4 runs between Atlantic Beach and South Beach and there's the X2 Beaches Express from town to the beachfront.

Hornblower Marine Services, 4610 Ocean Street, **t** (904) 241 9969

The St. Johns River Ferry Service transports vehicle and pedestrian traffic across the St. Johns River from Mayport to Ft. George Island and back.

Runways, t (904) 741 6643, 800 578 6929 toll-free, www.rnwy.com
Scheduled mini-coach service between Jacksonville International Airport, local beaches and Gainesville. All vehicles seat up to nine passengers, or eight including a wheelchair.

Tourist information

Jacksonville and the Beaches Convention and Visitors Bureau, 550 Water Street, Suite 1000, **t** (904) 798 9111 or (800) 733 2668, **www.jaxcvb.com**

Things to see and do

The Northbank

Cummer Museum of Art and Gardens

829 Riverside Avenue, **t** (904) 356 6857, **www.cummer.org**
Open Tue and Thu 10–9, Wed, Fri and Sat 10–5, Sun 12 noon–5
Adm Adults $6, children $3, under 5s $1. Tue eve (4–9) free

Aside from a fascinating collection of paintings and inventive exhibitions depicting the history and changing landscape of Florida, the museum is also home to the interactive **Art Connections** area, which shouts 'do touch!' at visitors. Kids can walk through a painting, create patterns as they dance, make collages, listen to a noisy sculpture or paint with a virtual paintbrush. The website has fun things for kids to do. Relax in the gardens afterwards while the kids run about beside the river.

Kids' Kampus

410 Gator Bowl Boulevard, Metropolitan Park, **t** (904) 630 5437.
Open Spring/summer: Mon–Sat 8–8, Sun 10–8, autumn/winter Mon–Sat 8–6, Sun 10–6, Water park: May–Sept
Adm Free

This large children's play park should help kids let off steam. Bright, colourful tunnels and slides are designed to give hours of educational play. There's also a toddler splash pool with little slides and waterspouts, a sandpit with mechanical diggers and miniature reconstructions of local landmarks. **Metropolitan Park**, just next door, is a great place to catch a concert among the landscaped gardens. There's also a playground, picnic tables and riverfront walk with a boat landing. See website for a quiz and pictures for kids to colour in or send postcards to their friends.

The Jacksonville Fire Museum

1408 Gator Bowl Boulevard, **t** (904) 630 0618 (next door to Kids Kampus)
Open Mon–Fri 9–4; *Free parking is available*
Adm Free

The museum is housed in a beautifully preserved 1902 Fire Station and offers insight into Florida's firefighting history including accounts of the devastating fire of 1901. Among the artefacts are a hand pump (1806), a Steam Engine (1898) and an American LaFrance Fire Engine (1926).

Jacksonville Museum of Modern Art (JMOMA)

333 North Laura Street, **t** (904) 366 6911, **www.jmoma.org**
Getting there Adjacent to City Hall on Hemming Plaza
Open Tue, Fri 11–5, Wed–Thu 11–9, Sat 11–4, Sun 12 noon–4
Adm Adults $6, children $4, under 2s free, Sun free for families

The building that once housed the old Western Union Telegraph Company has been transformed into a state-of-the-art, six-floor facility containing **exhibition spaces, educational facilities**, a **theatre, museum shop** and a **café**. The museum holds a permanent collection of 20th-century art, plus travelling exhibitions with an emphasis on encouraging local talent. Films, workshops and lectures support the exhibitions.

On Sundays children and their accompanying adults visit free and can interact with exhibits in the **Art Explorium Loft**, in the fifth-floor Family Learning Centre. Families can participate in several events, including live performances, demonstrations and films. In addition, the education centre has regular Saturday drop-in sessions (most Sats call in advance) from 11–4 when visitors of all ages can engage in hands-on art activities for an additional $3 per person.

Museum of Southern History

4304 Herschel Street, Avondale, **t** (904) 388 3574
Open Tue–Sat 10–5
Adm Adults $2, children free

Florida's Confederate past is explored through museum displays and artefacts from the antebellum period, such as medicines, weapons, costumes and Civil War memorabilia. The research library contains 3,000 volumes on southern literature, history, art architecture, economy and government

Entertainment

Jacksonville Jaguars

Alltel Stadium, 1 Stadium Place, east of downtown, t (904) 633 2000
Tickets From $20–$90

Now immortalized as the 13th US city to host the Super Bowl, Jacksonville's stadium is home to the Jaguars from September to December. On 6 February 2005 all eyes were on the Alltel as the New England Patriots stormed to victory over the Philadelphia Eagles in a highly entertaining clash of the titans, winning 24-21.

Times-Union Center for the Performing Arts

300 W. Water Street, t (904) 630 3900. Box office (904) 354 5547 for symphony events; FCCJ Artist Series box office, (904) 632 3373; Coliseum box office (904) 6303900, www.ticketmaster.com

This prodigious performing arts centre is home to two theatres and the Jacksonville Symphony Orchestra, which hosts classical concerts, including family concerts with matinees at 3pm. The building has a pleasant riverside aspect and is adjacent to Jacksonville Landing for after-show dining.

The Southbank

The main museum district lies just over the river from Jacksonville Landing on the south bank of the river. The **RiverWalk** is a mile-long stretch of boardwalk great for relaxing and enjoying the fountains in **Friendship Park**. It's particularly pleasant in the evening when the fountains are lit by coloured lights. Water taxis cross between the two banks (fares $1–$2, under 3s free). *Toilets are available at the marina.*

Jacksonville Historical Center

Southbank Riverwalk, t (904) 665 0064
Open Mon–Sun 11–5; **Adm** free

Trace local history from the Timucuan Indians to the Civil War and the development of today's modern city. Children can try on costumes and handle objects related to the city's past.

Jacksonville Maritime Museum

Southbank Riverwalk, 1015 Museum Circle, t (904) 398 9011, www.jaxmarmus.com
Open Mon–Sat 10:30–3:30, Sun 1–5
Adm free (donation)

Come here for memorabilia, photographs, a 16-ft replica of the aircraft carrier *USS Saratoga*, which saw duty in the Gulf and in Bosnia and models of Jacksonville-built World War II ships and a German U-boat. Exhibits trace maritime history of the area from 1842 to the present day.

The Museum of Science & History (MOSH)

1025 Museum Circle, Southbank, t (904) 396 6674, www.themosh.org
Getting there Southbank, off Highway 1
Open Mon–Fri 10–5, Sat 10–6, Sun 1–6
Adm Adults $7, children $5, under 3s free

Lots of games and features here with interactive play zones for different ages. For young kids there's the soft play building structures, tree house and water table in **Kidscape**, while for older kids there are the latest gadgets and gizmos of the **Universe of Science**, which allows visitors to launch a hot air balloon, hear tones barely audible to the human ear and blow giant bubbles in the air.

With life-sized models of whales, dolphins and manatees, **Atlantic Tails** gives children a glimpse of Florida's amazing marine life before they experience real-life fish, alligators and snapping turtles among other species in **The Living World.** Visitors can also visit the Jacksonville **Jaguars Hall of Fame**, pilot an aircraft simulator, sort out scientific principles and walk with dinosaurs. On the upper level there are historical displays about the St. Johns River. There's a **nature courtyard** if you need a place to sit down and a **planetarium** for stargazers with regular cosmic concerts. Look out for special events and live demonstrations and be sure to leave time for the latest addition to the museum, **Florida Naturalist's Center**, which showcases over 60 indigenous species, such as American alligators, gopher tortoises, snakes and birds.

Tree Hill Nature Center

7152 Lone Star Road, t (904) 724 4646, www.treehill.org
Getting there off Arlington Road, ½ mile north of the Arlington Expressway between downtown Jacksonville and Regency Square Mall
Open Mon–Sat 8–4.30, tours Sat 10am
Adm Adults $2, children (under 18) $1

Don't let Tree Hill's suburban surroundings put you off. The site has been specifically designed to encourage urban communities to appreciate wildlife within this 50-acre preserve. Out of doors, visitors can explore hummingbird, butterfly, herb, and organic vegetable gardens or head along a shady forest path for a nature trail. There's a museum, plus exhibits on local endangered species, rainforests and solar power.

Jacksonville Zoo and Gardens

8605 Zoo Parkway, Heckscher Drive, **t** (904) 757 4462; **www.jaxzoo.org**
Getting there North of the city between 1–95 and 9A
Open Daily 9–5 (until 6 Sat/Sun and summer holidays)
Adm Adults $9.50, children $6.50 (3–12), under 2s, free. The train runs Mon–Fri 10–4.30, Sat–Sun 9–6. Fares: Adults $4, children $2, under 2s free
Gift shops, café

Begun in 1914 with a single red deer fawn, the zoo and gardens have grown to house over 1,000 rare and exotic animals and over 1,000 unique plant species. There are several distinct environments, such as **Wild Florida**, which includes black bears, Florida panthers and alligators among other native species and the latest exhibit, the **Range of the Jaguar**, home to animals native to the Central or South America rainforest, including tapirs, capybaras, otters, anteaters and, of course, jaguars. Other recent additions include an endangered bonobo, a koala and a baby white rhino and baby zebra born at the zoo. Regular events include sleepovers, zoo camps and feeding sessions.

Shopping

Jacksonville Landing

2 Independent Drive, situated off Highway 1, **www.jacksonvillelanding.com**
Open Mon–Thu 10–8, Fri–Sat 10–9, Sun 12 noon–5.

This shopping, dining and entertainment complex overlooks the river. There are gift shops, discount clothing stores, shoe shops, a toy store, an amusement arcade and food court, also a branch of the child-friendly **Hooters** restaurant chain, **Southend Brewery** for wood-baked pizzas, **The Ice Cream Churn** and **Coastal Cookie** for treats and the **An-Apple-A-Day** grocery and deli for healthy picnic essentials.

Hemming Plaza Farmers' Market

A few blocks down from Jacksonville Landing, between Hogan and Laura Street
Open Fridays 10–2 Fresh groceries, gourmet foodstuffs, flowers, herbs, fresh fish and handicrafts.

AROUND AND ABOUT

Route A1A hugs the coast from **Fernandina Beach and Amelia Island** to the north and **St. Augustine** to the south. Known as the **Bucaneer Trail**, it gives access to historical sights such as the **Kingsley Plantation** (see p.85) and **the Castillo de San Marcos** (see p.89), to state parks and shopping districts as well as surf and sand. Slower than Interstate 95, the A1A offers spectacular coastal views.

Buckets and spades

Jacksonville Beaches

Getting there

From Jacksonville, go east about 12 miles on the Arlington Expressway and take either Route 10 (Atlantic Blvd) or Highway 90 (Beach Blvd) or 9A (J. Turner Butler Blvd). The R4 bus runs between Atlantic Beach, Jacksonville and South Beach and the X2 Beaches Express runs from downtown Jacksonville to the beachfront.

Tourist Information

Beaches Visitor Center, 403 Beach Boulevard, **t** (904) 242 0024
Open Mon–Sat 10–6

Between the Intracoastal Waterway and the sandy beaches of the Atlantic, Jacksonville's beach resorts run north to south along Highway A1A. The 15-mile stretch of spectacular sands runs from **Atlantic Beach** and **Neptune Beach** south down to **Jacksonville Beach** and the more exclusive **Ponte Vedra Beach**. The former are quieter and good for surfing, while Jacksonville has sports and family entertainment.

Adventure Landing

1944 Beach Boulevard, **t** (904) 246 4386, **www.adventurelanding.com**
Open Waterpark: Mar–Oct. Other attractions Mon–Thu 12 noon–11, Fri 12 noon –1am, Sat 10–1am, Sun 10–11

Adm Water park: Adults $21.99, children $18.99 (under 42 inches 1.09m), Night Splash $14.99. Under 3s free. Other rides and attractions are individually priced

The **Shipwreck Island Water Park** offers wet and wild fun for all ages with a wave pool, water slides and rides. For big thrills try **The Rage,** a watercoaster, fly down the **Hydro Half Pipe** in a gush of water or swirl around in the **Eye of the Storm**. The **river ride** has family-sized tubes and there are plenty of water cannons and water play areas to keep younger kids happy. If you prefer to stay dry, have a go on the go-karts, play softball or hardball in the batting cages or try out two 18-hole miniature golf courses. There's a huge indoor arcade (including food) with 100 games including laser tag and the **MaxFlight Coast Simulator**, which promises more than the laws of gravity can allow on a normal roller coaster. Scary.

Amelia Island/ Fernandina Beach

Getting there 32 miles northeast of Jacksonville and 30 minutes from Jacksonville International Airport. From I–95 take exit 373 (old exit 129) East on A1A to Amelia Island (14 miles)

Tourist information

Amelia Island Chamber of Commerce, Old Railroad Depot Building, 102 Centre Street, **t** (904) 261 3248, **www.ameliaisland.org**

Amelia Island was originally called the Isle de Mai (Island of May) by the French explorer Jean Ribault in 1562. The Spanish reclaimed it soon afterwards, renaming it Santa Maria. During the British occupation it became Amelia Island, in honour of King George II's daughter. Mostly absentee English landlords set up huge plantations annexing northeast Florida into the Deep South. When Flagler's railroad came to the east coast, Amelia Island and its environs were spared, leaving **Fernandina Beach**'s Victorian district intact. This 50-block seaport has replica gas street lighting and many colonial homes from 1873–1900 and the Palace Saloon, one of the oldest bars in Florida. Several buildings are antique shops, boutiques, galleries and restaurants and some quaint old inns offer B&B (*see* p.34).

Fernandina Beach backs onto the salt marshes and the Amelia River, home to abundant bird life, including white pelicans, gannets and great blue herons. The sea is teeming with life. In winter, endangered Northern Right Whales travel down the Atlantic Coast from Canada to give birth in the warmer waters of Florida. Loggerhead turtles come to the beaches from May to October to lay their eggs. Watch out for areas cordoned off around turtle nests and be cautious when boating as manatees inhabit the creeks of the Intracoastal Waterway, also home to otters, dolphins and alligators.

Main Beach

Getting there At the intersection of Atlantic Avenue and North Fletcher Avenue.

Facilities include toilets, showers, arcade games, picnic tables, volleyball and a smart playground for toddlers, and a couple of snack bars and restaurants.

Eight Flags Water Slide

35 North Fletcher Avenue, **t** (904) 261 8212
Open late May–early Sept daily 10–7
Adm half hr $3, 1hr $5, all day $12

Grab yourself a coloured rubber mat and take a trip down this twisty but tame freshwater slide that guarantees a bit of a splash at the end.

Look at this!

Amelia Island Museum of History

233 South Third Street, Fernandina Beach, **t** (904) 261 7378
Getting there From Centre Street three blocks south on 3rd Street
Open Mon–Sat 10–4. Tours daily at 11 and 2. Closed Sun
Adm Adults $5, children $3. Walking tours: Adults $10, children $5

Set in the former county gaol, re-enactors to tell the story of the island's past at this innovative museum, Florida's only spoken history museum. Find out about the eight flags that formerly flew

Did you know?

Amelia Island is rife with the ghosts of its former inhabitants. Miss Nettie Thompson, though called 'a tease, not a terror,' switches items on dressing-table tops and rattles the beds in her former home. A gruesome foursome of headless soldiers are also said to patrol the grounds of Fort Clinch and the former bartender of the Palace Saloon, 'Uncle Charlie' apparently puts in an appearance from time to time in the massive mirror over the bar.

over the island as a host of nations battled it out for dominion. There are areas dedicated to Native American history, the Spanish Missions, the Civil War and land and marine archaeological artefacts depicting 4,000 years of island life. Children will enjoy the 'Mystery Box' in which they can discover shells, animal bones, and local plant specimens. Take a walking tour of the historic district (Sept–June Fri/ Sat at 3pm) or learn about ghostly goings-on at the island's cemetery (Sept–June Fri 6pm).

Fort Caroline National Memorial

12713 Fort Caroline Road, **t** (904) 641 7155
Getting there At the intersection of Monument Road and Fort Caroline Road, 14 miles east of downtown Jacksonville, 20 miles south of Jacksonville International Airport
Open Daily 9–5; **Adm** free

The Fort Caroline National Memorial was created to commemorate the 16th-century attempts to establish a permanent colony in Florida. The centrepiece, shaped like an arrowhead, is an almost full-sized replica of the fort. There's a visitor centre featuring a Native American dugout canoe and other artefacts from the Timucuan period and French occupation. There are nature trails and also the ranger-led Saltmarsh Programme, which includes a demonstration of seine net fishing. Call ahead for timings and bring a picnic.

Did you know?

The island's namesake, Princess Amelia, was in love with her cousin Frederick, Crown Prince of Prussia? Frederick (later Frederick the Great) was originally betrothed to Amelia and his sister Wilhelmina was promised to her brother the Prince of Wales. But, although Frederick and Amelia corresponded for years, they never married. Frederick's father, Frederick Wilhelm I openly disliked his son and his overbearing manner caused the young prince to flee to England. As punishment for unlawfully leaving the country, Frederick was imprisoned and one of his accomplices beheaded. Later, forced by his father, Frederick married to Elizabeth Christine von Braunschweig-Bevern in order to secure an alliance with Vienna. Following his marriage, he busied himself with military campaigns, including the War of Austrian Succession and the Seven Years' War. On succeeding the throne, Frederick lived separately from his wife and died without issue. Princess Amelia remained a spinster and lived to the age 76. On her deathbed in 1786, a tiny portrait of Frederick was discovered next to her heart. She died scarcely three months after he did.

Fort Clinch State Park

2601 Atlantic Avenue, Fernandina Beach, **t** (904) 277 7274
Getting there From I-95 take exit 373 (Old exit 129) east on A1A for 16 miles. At the intersection of 8th Street and Atlantic Avenue turn right on Atlantic Avenue for 2 miles, the park entrance is on the left
Open Daily 8–dusk (There are 75-min sunset candlelight tours from May–Sept on Fri/Sats)
Adm Park entrance: $5 per vehicle (max 8 people), $1 per extra passenger, cyclist, or pedestrian. Fort: $2 (ages 6 and up); candlelight tours: $3
Visitor centre, camping grounds, parking, picnic areas

The history of this Civil War Fort unravels as you explore the quarters of the soldiers, infirmary, forge, gaol and kitchens while re-enactors talk about the duties and privations of army life.There are candlelight tours and Civil war re-enactments with artillery demonstrations and marching drills on the first weekend of the month (all weekends May–Sept). The surrounding 1,086 acres comprise beaches and dunes, nature trails, ponds, salt marshes, camping grounds and a 1,500-ft fishing pier. On Saturday mornings there are guided walks along Willow Pond trail, exploring the flora and fauna of the coastal maritime hammocks and freshwater ponds.

Kingsley Plantation & Timucuan Preserve

Fort George Island, **t** (904) 221 5568
Getting there From I–95, exit on Heckscher Drive, follow Heckscher East to Florida 9A. Continue on Heckscher about 9 miles; after passing the Mayport Ferry landing on your right, turn left at the National Park Service sign onto Fort George Island. Follow the signs for parking
Open daily 9–5; **Adm** free (donation)

The original plantation was established in 1767 by an Englishman named J. Tucker who took ownership of Fort George Island as part of a settlement grant. In 1791 the island passed to John McQueen, who built the planter's house and operated a cotton slave plantation. Due to poor weather and flooding McQueen got into debt and had to rent out the property to Zephaniah Kingsley. By 1817, Kingsley was able to buy the plantation for

$7,000. Visitors can explore the finely preserved planter's house, the kitchen house, a barn, a reconstructed slave cabin and ruins of 25 original slave dwellings. The main buildings house exhibits about the lives of the plantation residents and how the plantation was run including details of the task system whereby slaves could tend their own gardens or participate in crafts once their duties were performed. Families can learn about Kingsley and his wife Anna, a former slave from Senegal, who became a free woman, slave owner and plantation manager in her own right. Kingsley moved his family to Haiti in 1837 along with 50 freed slaves to work as farm labourers, seeking to escape laws passed by the US government designed to subjugate free blacks. The plantation is part of the **Black Heritage Trail** showcasing over 200 sites of African–American interest. A book accompanies the trail; order it from the Florida State Department, www.dhr.dos.state.fl.us/services/trails/bht/

The surrounding 46,000 acre Timucuan Ecological and Historic Preserve maintains an area of unspoilt coastal wetlands including salt marshes, sand dunes and hardwood forests.

Nature lovers

Amelia Island Plantation's Nature Center

6800 First Coast Highway,
t (904) 261 6161 (888) 261 6161,
www.aipfl.com (*see* Sleep p.33).
Open daily 9–5:30.

Children of all ages can get up close to nature on these naturalist-led tours exploring the varied ecosystems of the Island. Habitats to discover include maritime hammocks, beaches and dunes, saltwater marshes, forests, estuaries and freshwater streams. Activities on offer range from crabbing to kayaking and bird watching to shark's tooth hunts.

Big Talbot Island State Park

Getting there 20 miles east of Jacksonville on A1A North. 12157 Heckscher Drive, **t** (904) 251 2320
Open Daily 8–dusk
Adm $1 per person to fish or enjoy the park, picnicking $2, boat launch $3

Canoes are available to rent from Long Island Outfitters, which has a $2 vehicle fee.

Visitors to the Talbot Islands State Parks can enjoy exploring one of the few remaining undeveloped sea-islands on the Atlantic coast. There are hiking and nature trails, which wind throughout the grounds, picnicking and boating facilities and a 40-site campground in the shade of a maritime forest. The shell-covered beaches are inaccessible in parts due to erosion but there are spectacular views to be had of the coastline and Nassau Sound. Beach access is available via a short five-minute trail from The Bluffs parking area. Visitors can also reach the beaches via Blackrock Trail or Big Pine Trail, located on the east side of A1A.

> ***Did you know?***
> ***Due to the nature of barrier islands where a combination of wave, wind, and tidal forces are constantly eroding and depositing sediments on the shorelines, the exact size of the islands varies from year to year. Since 2003, Big Talbot Island has actually been smaller than Little Talbot Island.***

Bird Emergency Aid and Kare Sanctuary

12084 Houston Avenue, Big Talbot Island,
t (904) 251 2473
Open Open Tue–Sun, call for times
Adm Free

BEAKS is dedicated to caring for and rehabilitating injured wildlife, especially Florida's wild birds, which can also be seen in abundance in the wild within the park. The sanctuary conducts tours for groups and individuals to view some of the resident 2,000 endangered and common species, which include owls, eagles, vultures, wood storks, blue jays and even an emu. There are lovely wooded trails to follow and lots of scenic spots, so bring along a picnic.

Huguenot Memorial Park

10980 Heckscher Drive, Fort George,
t (904) 251 3335
Open Summer 8–8, winter 8–6
Adm 50 cents per person, under 6s free

Located on Fort George Island on the opposite side to Mayport at the mouth of the St. Johns River, the park has good camping, fishing, surfing and boating facilities. Vehicles can drive on the beach but there is a 500-ft no-car zone if you're looking for a quiet spot to sunbathe. Since the inlet is calm it's a good place to swim and paddle in the shallows. Picnic shelters, toilets, and showers are available.

Kayak Amelia

13030 Heckscher Drive, Jacksonville
t (904) 251 0016 or (888) 30–KAYAK; www.kayakamelia.com
Half-day guided trips: $55, self-tour rentals: $25 for a single kayak or $40 for a double kayak or canoe.

The centre specializes in half-day (3-hr) environmentally friendly orientation trips in the marshes, sandbars and rivers led by guides. The trips include a half-hour preparatory session on land and about an hour's paddling back and forth. Children aged 5–12 are seated in double kayaks or with an adult and over 12 can have a go on their own in special child-sized craft. Visitors can also book yoga or night paddle trips.

Little Talbot Island State Park

South of Big Talbot Island, 12157 Heckscher Drive, t (904) 251 2320
Open Daily 8–dusk
Adm $4 per vehicle (8 passengers), $1 per extra passenger, cyclist, or pedestrian, camping $19 per day with all facilities, youth camping $4

Following construction of the paved Timucuan State and National Parks Multi-Use Trail visitors can now access a huge swathe of coastline from Hanna City Park all the way to Amelia Island State Park. The whole of Little Talbot Island is a protected environment consisting of beaches, dunes, hardwood hammocks and salt marshes. Visitors to the island should pay particular attention to signs, especially along the shoreline where sea turtles nest on summer nights.

Did you know?

The Florida Crackers were pioneers, mostly from Georgia and Carolina, who eked out a living in Florida in the 1800s driving their herds to pasture, hunting alligators and scraping out whatever kind of living they could make on the land. There are several theories for the origin of the name 'cracker'. One is thought to derive from the crack of the whips as they drove the cattle or from the noise of the corn biscuits as they ate, another relates to the practice of cracking corn to make liquor and another is that it refers to the English 'crack' – to boast. Since the Crackers are thought to be of Celtic origin it may also have links to the Irish word 'craic', which, like Cracker, indicates a fellow who can tell a good tale.

Biking, hiking, bird spotting, jogging, and roller blading are among the pastimes to enjoy along the trail. Junior Ranger activity sheets are available from the Ranger Station.

Mayport

Getting there On the A1A 15 miles east of Jacksonville at the mouth of the St. Johns River

Mayport remains a quiet fishing village despite its proximity to big city Jacksonville. The Naval Station is hard to miss, it's the fourth largest in the US with numerous big ships dominating the scene as shrimp and deep-sea fishing charters ply their trade nearby.

Kathryn Abbey Hanna Park

500 Wonderwood Drive, t (904) 249 4700
Getting there 17 miles east of Jacksonville, off Route A1A just south of Mayport Naval Station
Open Daily Apr–Oct 8–8, Nov–Mar 8–6
Adm $1, under 6s free

The park boasts 1.5 miles of sandy beaches that are ideal for swimming, sailing and fishing. The area known as The Poles is also popular for surfing. There are lifeguards in the summer. In addition, there's a 60-acre freshwater lake for kayaking, paddleboats, canoes and fishing. Younger visitors can also splash around in the adjacent water playground. If you want to make a day of it there are picnic tables and on site and scenic forest trails for cooling off. Camping is also available in the woods with facilities including power, laundry, toilets, showers and 24-hour security. The latest additions to the park are cabins for hire for $30 a day (minimum 2-days). The cabins sleep four and have air-conditioning and cooking facilities but not furniture, so bring your own bedding.

Mayport Ferry, St. Johns River Ferry

Hornblower Marine Services, t (904) 241 9969
The service runs daily on the hour and half-hour from 6.20–10 from Mayport and 6.10–10.15 from Fort George Island. Fares are $2.75 for cars, $2.50 for motorcycles and 50 cents per bike or foot passenger

The ferry runs across the St. Johns River to and from Mayport and Fort George Island. It's the only remaining public car ferry in Florida and is a popular way to reach Amelia Island following the Buccaneer Trail.

Mayport Naval Station

P. O. Box 280032, Naval Station Mayport, t (904) 270 5011/5266

Open Sat 10–4, Sun 1–4.30, closed to the public Mon–Fri. Call in advance for free weekend tours

Although not generally open to the public, the Station opens for occasional events. It houses frigates, destroyers and aircraft carriers. It is also home port to the USS John F. Kennedy. Visitors can view the Mayport Lighthouse and some of the craft from over the fence. Access to the Naval Station beach adjacent to Hanna Park (*see* p.87) is restricted.

Sporty kids

Putt Putt Golf

6 North Fletcher Avenue, Amelia Island, t (904) 261 4443

Try your putting skills on these two 18-hole miniature golf courses right beside the main beach.

Island Falls Adventure Golf

1550 Sadler Road, Amelia Island, t (904) 261 7881

Open summer daily 10–11, winter (Oct–Feb) Fri 2–10, Sat 10–10, Sun 11–9

Adm Adults $6.25, children (5–12) $5.25

This 18-hole miniature course spices up the golfing action with waterfalls, tunnels and meandering streams. Even the clubhouse is set on top of a 20-foot waterfall.

Amelia Island Charter Boat Association

1 South Front Street, Fernandina Harbour Marina, t (904) 261 2870, www.ameliaislandcharterboatassociation.com

Explore inshore and offshore waters on a guided fishing trip or go on a sightseeing cruise. Fishing licenses are available.

Kelly Sea Horse Ranch

7500 First Coast Highway, Amelia Island, t (904) 491 5166, www.kellyranchinc.com

Getting there From A1A South turn left into Amelia Island State Park

Open daily 8–6. One-hour guided rides available for ages 13 and up at 10, 12 noon, 2 and 4. $45 per person, by appointment only

Enjoy a gentle ride along the beach on well-trained horses. It's a great way to see marine and bird life and watch the sun go down over the ocean and marshes. Pony rides are available for toddlers.

ST. AUGUSTINE

St. Augustine's past is also its present. Being the oldest continuously occupied European settlement on the mainland US, it houses more than 60 themed attractions, including a plethora of museums, antique shops and a substantial historic district comprising 36 original colonial structures and 40 reconstructions of colonial dwellings. Wandering around the narrow streets with overhanging balconies, it's easy to imagine yourself in a 16th-century Mediterranean town. As you wander through the **Colonial Spanish Quarter**, don't be surprised to bump into someone dressed in authentic garb demonstrating some bygone craft. Imaginative **walking tours** recapture scenes from the past, increasing the feeling of times gone by, and re-enactors bring it back to life through creative storytelling. St. Augustine also bears the hallmarks of the railway age when Henry Flagler built three impressive hotels in the town at the junction of Cordova and King Street – The Alcazar now **The Lightner Museum** (*see* p.90), the **Casa Monica Hotel**, still a luxury resort, and the former Ponce de Le León Hotel, now **Flagler College** (*see* p.93), open daily for tours.

Getting there

38 miles from Jacksonville or 30 minutes from Jacksonville Beach via Route A1A south. The coastal Route 203 veers off the A1A past up-market Ponte Vedra Beach and then rejoins the A1A further on

Tourist information

St. Augustine, Ponte Vedra, and the Beaches Visitors and Convention Bureau. 88 Riberia Street, Suite 400, **t** (904) 829–1711 or (800) OLD-CITY; **www.visitoldcity.com**

Visitor Information Center

10 Castillo Drive, t (904) 825 1000

Adm Free. Colonial History Package (including the Spanish Colonial Quarter, the Government House Museum and 'Struggle to Survive' movie show) family ticket $16

Gift shop, snack bar, toilets

The centre is a one-stop shop for information, maps, accommodation, eating out, tickets and the place to book sightseeing tours, including the **Old Town Trolley** and **Sightseeing Train**, which both stop outside the building. Get a feel for the nation's oldest city by browsing the displays and watching a

20-minute orientation video. The 'Struggle to Survive' movie, which shows how former inhabitants kept St. Augustine on the map, runs hourly.

Things to see and do

Castillo de San Marcos National Monument

1 South Castillo Drive, **t** (904) 829 6506, **www**.nps.gov/casa
Open Daily 8.45–4.45
Adm Adults $5, children (6–16) $2, under 6s free

The Spanish Castillo de San Marcos was built between 1672-1695 as a strategic military outpost on the Atlantic coast of Florida. Its primary purpose was to guard the settlement of St. Augustine and afford safe passage for treasure ships returning to Spain. The unique shell-based limestone rock that forms the fabric of the walls managed to withstand numerous sieges by absorbing canon fire like a sponge. During the 18th century, the Castillo went from Spanish control to British and back to the Spanish but it was all done by treaty, not by force. The park consists of the original historic **Castillo fortress** itself and 25 acres of grounds where **ranger programmes**, including **historic re-enactments**, canon firing and demonstrations, are offered year round on most weekends. Call for a detailed schedule or check at the entrance station. A short video telling the story of the Castillo is presented on request in one of the casemates. Children aged 6–12 are invited to join in the **Junior Ranger programme**, so be sure to ask for an activity book on arrival.

Colonial Spanish Quarter

53 St. George Street, **t** (904) 825 6830, **www**.historicstaugustine.com
Open Daily 9–5.30
Adm Adults $6.89, children (6–18) $4.24, family ticket $13.78
Visitor centre, museum store, parking

The Colonial Spanish Quarter is not just a visitor attraction it's a **living history museum** where costumed guides re-enact the lives of soldiers and their families in this former outpost of the Spanish Empire. Children are encouraged to get involved in **craft demonstrations** and seasonal events at the site (such as Drake's Raid, which takes place annually on 4 June). Demonstrations include artisans reconstructing farm buildings from the Colonial Spanish occupation in 1740 and practicing traditional methods of iron forging, carpentry, leatherworking, candle making and other trades.

Can you spot?
A sign with the word 'old' on it. See how many you can find.

Fountain of Youth National Archaeological Park

11 Magnolia Avenue,
t (904) 829 3168 or 800 356 8222
Open Daily 9–5
Adm Adults $6, children (6–12) $3, under 6s free

There is some dispute about the exact spot where Ponce de León first stepped ashore and founded the colony of St. Augustine but excavations have revealed that the foundations of the Indian village of Seloy and burial site are within the park.

As the story goes, Ponce de León and his men were received as guests in the village and remained there for five days. The Spanish were impressed by the physical stature and prowess of the natives and, when they asked the Timucua to tell them the source of their strength, the Indians gestured towards the spring. Thus continued the legend of the 'fountain of youth', whose healing waters were said to have been the impetus for de León's voyage.

The original fountain still remains, so kids can take a sip and then try their luck at arm-wrestling dad. Also in the grounds are statues and exhibits, a **Planetarium** and the **Explorer's Discovery Globe**, a vast domed theatre where visitors can learn more about the Spanish conquistadors during an eight-minute presentation.

Government House Museum

48 King Street, **t** (904) 825–5033
Open Daily 10–4
Adm Adults $2.50, children (6–18) $1

The former Government house saw service as a courthouse and a post office before becoming a museum. It now houses around 300 artefacts relating to the development of the city, including salvage from shipwrecked Spanish treasure ships and architectural tools. The building also contains the offices of the Historic St. Augustine Preservation Board.

Lightner Museum

75 King Street,**t** (904) 824 2874,
www.lightnermuseum.org
Open Daily 9–5
Adm Adults $8, under 12s free when accompanied by an adult
Café, museum shop

Formerly the Hotel Alcazar, built in 1887 for railway magnate Henry Flagler, this imposing museum displays objects from the private collection of Chicago publisher, Otto C. Lightner, who bought the building in 1946. Among the exhibits are some fine examples of European and American Victoriana, including Brilliant Period cut glass, Italian marble, writing desks and curio cabinets, as well as Tiffany lamps. The grounds are pretty. The café is housed in the former hotel pool.

Museum of Weapons and Early American History

81-C King Street, **t** (904) 829 3727,
www.museumofweapons.com
Open Daily 9.30–5
Adm Adults $4, children (6–12) $1, under 6s free
Museum shop

There's a mesmerizing collection of firepower and weapons, including displays of Civil War memorabilia and American Indian artefacts.

Old Florida Museum

254D San Marco Avenue, **t** 800 813 3208,
www.historicvillages.com
Open Daily 10–5
Adm Adults $5, children $4

This thoroughly hands-on museum dedicated to preserving the customs of old Florida from the Timucuan Indians to pioneer times will show kids how to pump water from a well, write with a quill and grind corn. Take a self-guided tour and try out some traditional tools and games to get a feel for what life was like for the Florida Crackers.

Oldest House National Historic Landmark

14 St. Francis Street, **t** (904) 824 2872
Open Daily 9–5
Adm Adults $6, children (6–18) $4, under 6s free

Originally an early 18th-century, flat-roofed, single-storey dwelling built by the Gonzáles-Alvarez family, the house was remodelled in the 19th and 20th centuries with additions such as a second storey and glass windows. Like many early buildings in St. Augustine, it is constructed of *coquina*, the shell-encrusted rock that made the Castillo so durable a structure. The **Manucy Museum** next door covers 400 years of history in St. Augustine and the **Tovar House** traces military history in the area from colonial days to the Gulf War. behind the museum, there are leafy gardens and a store that sells history books about Florida and St. Augustine.

Old St. Augustine Village

149 Cordova Street, **t** (904) 823 9722,
www.old-staug-village.com
Open Daily 9–5; **Adm** Adults $7, children $5

This collection of historic houses dates from 1790–1910 and owes its existence to former resident, Kenneth Worcester Dow. The first house Dow bought on the site was occupied for a short while by Prince Murat (nephew of Napoleon Bonaparte), which Dow later furnished with items connected to the family. By 1950, he had accumulated nine houses, which he maintained by renting them to locals. One house is now a visitor centre and five others contain exhibits and period furnishings.

There is a self-guided tour around the district and authentically costumed guides describe the city's progress and a host of colourful characters dating back to the 16th century.

Tell us a tale – Old Spice

The origin of the super hot datil pepper is shrouded in mystery but local legend has it that a group of indentured servants brought it from the Spanish island of Menorca in 1768. The Menorcans came to Florida to clear forests for a 20,000-acre indigo plantation on behalf of a London physician named Dr. Andrew Turnbull. The plantation, named New Smyrna, was doomed to failure. Its location on the aptly named Mosquito Inlet offers one possible clue as to why it was abandoned in 1777. Disease and inadequate rations coupled with poor administration resulted in mutinies and what was left of the original workforce settled in St. Augustine bringing their pepper seeds with them. Other sources say that the little yellowy/green chilli was probably discovered in Cuba since it is from the same species of capsicum as habanero chillies. Whatever its source, the datil is now hot stuff and is used in closely guarded recipes for Minorcan clam chowder or sausage pilau and passed on from generation to generation. Look out for bottled sauces, jellies and dried peppers in specialist local shops and delis.

Oldest Wooden Schoolhouse

14 St. George Street,
t (904) 824 0192 or (888) 653 7245
Open Daily 9–5 (later in summer)
School shop
Adm Adults $3, children (6 to 12) $2, under 6s free

You are greeted at the schoolhouse by an animatronic teacher and students who guide you through a typical 18th-century school day. There are lots of textbooks to browse and good children can receive honourary diplomas. But miscreants may end up wearing the dunce's cap. Outside, there's a well, a separate kitchen building designed to prevent fire and a collection of colonial-era cooking utensils.

Potter's Wax Museum

17 King Street, **t** (904) 829 9056, 800 584 4781
Open Sun–Thur 9–5, Fri, Sat 9–9, daily 9–9 from mid-June
Adm Adults $8.95, children (6-12) $5.75, under 5s free

Peer in wonder at over 170 hideously lifelike mannequins, including actors, authors, inventors, scientists, explorers and celebrities of note. There's also a theatre show and window display where kids can watch sculptors at work. Britney Spears is among the latest of the pop idols in the making.

Project S.W.I.N.G.

24 Cathedral Place, **t** (904) 825 1279
Getting there Between Orange and Cordova Street
Open Daily; **Adm** Free

This impressive play facility is the result of a huge community project instigated by St. John's County volunteers, and inspired by the vision of local children. Toddlers to teens and their adults can all enjoy the space with its purpose-built wooden play structures ranging from a jet plane, lighthouse, pirate ship and puppet theatre to a Spanish fortress.

Ripley's Believe It or Not!

19 San Marco Avenue, **t** (904) 824–1606, **www.ripleys.com**
Open Sun–Thur 9–7, Fri, Sat 9–8, end May–early Sept 9–8
Adm Adults $12.95, children (5–12) $7.95

Visitors to Blackpool in Lancashire may well be familiar with the famous Ripley's chain of attractions. This is the original museum with more than 800 exhibits housed in Castle Warden, an historic Moorish Revival-style mansion built in 1887.

Can you spot?
The huge anchor attached to the side of the schoolhouse? It was fastened to the building in 1937 when locals feared it might take off in a hurricane.

Designed as a winter home for Millionaire William Warden, Castle Warden later served as a fashionable hotel owned by Norton Baskin and his wife, Pulitzer prize-winning novelist, Marjorie Kinnan Rawlings, author of *The Yearling*, *Cross Creek* and *South Moon Under*. Since 1950 the building has been the original permanent location of Ripley's Believe It or Not! Museum.

A cartoonist and adventure traveller, Robert Ripley was a frequent visitor to the hotel and had commented on numerous occasions that Castle Warden would be an ideal location to showcase his collection of unbelievable curiosities. Mr. Ripley attempted to purchase the building several times, but was not successful in his lifetime. After his death in 1949, his heirs managed where he had failed and in December of 1950, the museum opened. This is one of three Ripley's in Florida (the others are in Orlando and Key West). Highlights here include the world's largest moving Meccano model, London Bridge built using 264,345 matchsticks and a six-legged cow, plus the usual shrunken heads and giant mannequins. Not for the faint-hearted. Visit the Cargo Hold shop for some curios and souvenirs from far flung destinations.

Anastasia Island

Getting there

Across the Bridge of Lions (A1A South) 11/2 miles from St. Augustine.

It's only a short hop away from the historic district but the island offers enough scenic beauty and attractions to warrant a full day out. You'll definitely want to linger long enough to watch the sun go down from the beach.

St. Augustine Alligator Farm and Zoological Park

999 Anastasia Boulevard, **t** (904) 824 3337
www.alligatorfarm.com
Open Daily 9–5 (6 in summer)
Adm Adults $15.95, children (5–11) $8.95, under 5s free

Meet the marvelous **Maximo** a 15-ft saltwater crocodile, the largest of all the crocodilians and the biggest croc in this pond. The park is also home to other endangered species of crocodile, alligators, gavail and caiman. **Underwater viewing windows** give greater access to these fascinating reptiles and there are feeding times and educational shows to give a greater understanding of the species. **Shows** take place daily in the reptile theatre with crocodilians, parrots, native Floridian animals and snake displays. Other threatened creatures that are here include Galapagos tortoises, Tamarins, marmosets, macaws and iguanas. The park encompasses a two-acre **swamp** where American alligators and several types of native turtle live in their natural habitat. Wading birds such as egrets, ibis, herons, spoonbills and wood storks are also frequent visitors to the swamp and can be seen from the boardwalks that run through the park.

St. Augustine Lighthouse and Museum

Old Beach Road, off Route A1A, 81 Lighthouse Avenue, t (904) 829 0745, www.staugustinelighthouse.com
Open **Daily 9–6 (7 in summer)**
Adm **Museum and grounds: Adult $5, children $3, under 4s free; museum and tower: Adults $7.50, children $5. Children must be at least 44 inches tall to climb the tower**

This striking colonial building boasts a bold 165-ft black-and-white striped lighthouse, which was completed in 1874. Take care when climbing the 219 steps to the top, the building is prone to sudden gusts of wind, so keep hold of smaller children and exercise caution at all times. Children too small to climb can play at the base of the tower and the museum can provide them with their own lighthouse colouring book. The museum houses artefacts from the rubbish tips of previous lighthouse incumbents, photographs and items from shipwrecks washed up along the shore. Look out for the **Lighthouse Festival** in March, when admission is free from 11–6 and there are living history displays, live entertainment, pony rides, children's games, crafts and refreshments.

Anastasia State Park

1340A A1A South, t (904) 461 2033, www.floridastateparks.org/anastasia
Open **Daily 8–dusk**
Adm **$5 per vehicle of eight persons or less, $1 per extra passenger, bike, or pedestrian**

The self-guided **nature trail** through the hardwood hammock offers opportunities to view butterflies in summer and numerous species of birds throughout the year. **Guides** to the local flora and fauna are available from the ranger station. Lifeguards are on duty during the summer and families with small children can enjoy a car-free zone south of the ramp. Do not swim as far as the rocks as there are strong currents and submerged objects in the water. Surfers can make use of the Salt Run area, which is off-limits for swimmers and has a number of rental outlets. There are three shaded picnic areas close to the beach with tables and grills. The beach picnic pavilion has drinks machines and toilets.

Fiesta Falls

818 A1A Beach Boulevard, t (904) 461 5571, www.lafiestainn.com
Open **Daily, call for hours**
Adm **Adults $6.95 for adults, children (4–12) $5.45**

This Spanish-style 18-hole miniature golf course has an interesting undulating layout with waterfalls, caves and a 65-ft Spanish galleon to look at. There are views of the ocean from the gazebo. The course is beside La Fiesta Ocean Inn, so you can play all day and into the evening under lights if you want and then tumble into bed next door.

Lighthouse Park

Off A1A, t (904) 471 6616
Open **Daily**

This park across from the lighthouse museum is good for picnics and letting the kids run about a bit. There's also a restaurant and a fishing pier.

Raging Water Sports

57 Comares Avenue, t (904) 829-5001, www.ragingwatersports.com
Open **Daily, call for reservations.**
Hire **Jet skis from $50 per 1/2hr, sail boats from $40 per hr, kayaks from $20 ($25 for a 2-seater) per hr.**

Pontoon boats, jet skis and sailboats for hire. Located in the Conch House Marina Resort, which has a seafood restaurant.

Whitebirds Family Fun Center

701 Anastasia Boulevard, t (904) 825 0101
Open **Daily, call for times**
Adm **Adults $5.95, children (under 12) $8**

Entry allows visitors to play all day on this 18-hole miniature course.

Tours

Flagler College Tours

74 King Street, tickets available from Flagler's Legacy, 59 St George Street, t (904) 823 3378
Open Shop: 9.30–3.30, tours: daily at 10 and 2
Adm Adults $6, children (under 12) $1 includes free Flagler College colouring and activity book

Take a tour of one of Flagler's trademark red-tile and turreted Moorish confections, complete with Tiffany interiors and plumbing and lighting courtesy of one Thomas Edison. The tour begins in the magnificent rotunda with murals by one George W. – Maynard, in this case – depicting the four elements and then continues to the great hall adorned with Tiffany stained-glass windows and the grand parlour with its glittering Tiffany chandeliers. Flagler's Legacy stocks a number of custom-made T-shirts and souvenirs relating to Flagler and the college.

Ghost tours of St. Augustine

P.O. Box 528, t (904) 461 1009, (888) 461 1009, www.aghostlyexperience.com
Tours: Daily 8pm and (Fri/Sat) 9.30pm
A Ghostly Experience Tour: $10, under 6s free. Book in advance

This spooky 1 1/2 hour walk starts at the water wheel on North St. George Street near the Oldest Wooden School House. Beware of things that go bump in the night as you wend your way by candlelight past the spooky Huguenot cemetery. Cower in terror as your guide dressed in period garb tells tales from the dungeons of the Castillo and dastardly doings in the inns of St. Augustine among other local haunts. Spooky sailing, sightseeing train and lighthouse tours are also available.

Helicopter Tours of St. Augustine

4900 US 1 North, St. Augustine Airport, t (904) 824 5506, www.OldCityHelicopters.com
Open daily 9–7.
Flights from $25 per person.

Helicopter tours over St. Augustine and the beaches including downtown tours and sunset trips. During the Festival of Light from November–January there are special early evening flights taking in the illuminations across the city.

Latigo Yacht Charters

16 Cherokee Court, East Palm Coast, t (386) 445 4000, www.latigo.net
Tickets: $980 for 2 people, $1380 for 4 people, additional passengers $200 per day

Splash out on an overnight family adventure cruise aboard a 60-ft motor yacht. Boats are available for hire along the Palm Coast, St. Augustine and Daytona Beach areas of northeast Florida. Guests can swim, kayak, fish, water-ski, wakeboard and take a dinghy out to explore islands and beaches.

St. Augustine Sightseeing Train

170 San Marco Avenue, St. Augustine, t (904) 829 6545 or 800 226 6545, www.redtrains.com
Tours From 8:30–5 every 15–20 minutes
Adm Adults $17 three-day pass, children (6–12) $4, under 6s free

Catch the bright red sightseeing train from the visitor centre for a hop-on, hop-off narrated tour of historic St. Augustine. The one-hour circuit passes all the major attractions including Ripley's Believe It Or Not! Museum, the Fountain of Youth Park, Old City Gates, Castillo De San Marcos, the Oldest House, Museum of Weapons, Old St Augustine Village, Flagler College and the Lightner Museum, the Spanish Quarter, Old Florida Museum and the Oldest Wooden Schoolhouse. Ask for information about packages to attractions.

Victory III Scenic Cruise

Municipal Marina, t (904) 824 1806, www.scenic-cruise.com
Tours Daily from 11am. Call for schedule, which is subject to change
Tickets: Adults $15, children (5–12) $6

This family-owned and -run cruise company first began to provide sightseeing trips in the early 1900s when wintering guests needed to diversions. The 75-minute narrated tours take in the Castillo, the Menendez landing site, the lighthouse and provide plenty of opportunities for wildlife spotting. Snacks and drinks are available on board.

Whetstone Chocolate Factory Tour

2 Coke Road, St. Augustine, t (904) 825 1700
Open Tours Mon–Sat 10–5, factory hours vary

Chocoholics can get a free tour of St. Augustine's own chocolate factory, where they can watch a film about modern sweet making, tour the moulding plant, packing room and speciality room and, of course, sample a piece of chocolate. It is also accessible from the Red Train sightseeing tour.

Shopping

St. George Street

A much-welcome pedetrianized zone in Florida's car culture. Here kids can find kites, toys and books and parents can enjoy browsing the boutiques and gift shops and tour the historic shopping village decked out with vintage signage.

Wolf's Books

48 San Marco Ave, **t** (904) 824-9357

Offers a good selection of children's titles.

King Street and Cordova Street

This is the place for art galleries and craft shops.

Antique Warehouse

6370 North US Highway 1, t (904) 826 1524, www.antqware.com

Rummage among the storerooms filled with British, French and a selection of American antique furniture.

The Ponce de León Mall

2121 US 1 South, t (904) 797 5324

Department stores, gift and clothes shops, a cinema, community theatre and restaurants.

Chelsea Premium Outlets Center

off Exit 318 of I-95

This is great for discount shopping with 95 stores including Gap and Oshkosh.

Picnics and snacks

For lunchtime staples there's **Schmagel's Bagels**, 69 Hypolita Street, **t** (904) 824 4444 and St. George Street has the **Bunnery Café**, **Dippin' Dots Ice Cream** and the **Mix and Match Candy Shop** if the kids' spirits are flagging after all that retail therapy.

Should you fancy a bit of the hot stuff head for **Minorcan Datil Pepper Products**, 5057 Silo Road, **t** (904) 522 0059 and spread some of their enticing range of mustards, salsa and sauces on your sarnies.

Special trips

The Dolphin Conservation Center at Marineland

9600 Ocean Shore Boulevard, t (904) 460 1275 or (888) 817 3283, www.marineland.net

Getting there About 18 miles south of St. Augustine on Route A1A

Open Check website for details

First opened in 1938, the centre has recently undergone extensive refurbishment with new dolphin habitats and an information kiosk. The centre was not open at time of going to press but general manager Bill Hurley has much enthusiasm for the project.

'Our desire is to create more than just a dolphin swim program; we want our guests to walk away with an appreciation for the fragility of the ocean's ecosystems by being immersed in interactive dolphin research. It won't be your standard encounter, that's for sure.' The 1½ million gallon facility has been developed as a research and education facility with a nursery for future dolphin calves. There are eleven dolphins at present, including two toddlers and the oldest living Atlantic bottlenose dolphins ever to have been in human care.

Washington Oaks State Gardens

6400 North Ocean Shore Boulevard, Palm Coast, t (386) 446–6780, www.floridastateparks.org/washingtonoaks

Getting there 2 miles south of Marineland off the A1A

Open 8–dusk. Park entrance is $3.25 per car, $1 per bike or foot passenger.

Adm $4 per car, $1 per bike or pedestrian.

Situated on land belonging to a former plantation called Bella Vista, the 389 acres of Washington Oaks State Gardens comprise hard-wood hammocks, formal gardens, rivers, dunes and beaches strewn with coquina rock boulders and dotted with rock pools where the sand has washed away. Visitors can enjoy picnicking, fishing and walking along the many paved trails through the park. There is evidence of Native American Indian occupation on the site where discarded shells have formed into middens. One of these man-made hills is now the site of the rose garden.

The dunes and coastal scrubland provide homes for endangered species such as sea turtles, scrub jays, Gopher tortoises and manatees, which feed in the shallows by the seawall. There is a covered pavilion with picnic tables and grills, a children's play area and toilets. Seasonal events including recreations of Timucuan villages and Civil War re-enactments take place in season.

AROUND AND ABOUT

Look at this!

Palatka

There are several reasons to make a detour to this unassuming town on the St. John's River, especially if you are an art lover as there are several interesting galleries.

Getting there

29 miles from St. Augustine on Route A1A south. Then follow Routes 206, 207 and 100 southwest

Tourist information

Putnam County Chamber of Commerce
1100 Reid Street, t (386) 328-1503, www.putnamcountychamber.org

Art tour

Visitors can follow the **Palatka Mural Tour** featuring 25 large murals designed to reflect the historic and cultural achievements of Putnam County. Then take time to explore some of the historic district's museums and art galleries, including **Larimer Arts Center**, 260 Reid Street, **t** (386) 328 8998, open Thu–Fri 1–5, Sat 10–2; **Florida School of The Arts Galleries**, 5001 St. Johns Avenue, **t** (386) 328 1571, open Mon–Fri 8.30–5, **Historic Tilghman House**, 324 River Street, **t** (386) 325-8750, open Fri, Sat 12 noon–4.

Bronson-Mulholland House

100 Madison Street, t (386) 329 0140
Open Tue, Thu, Sun 2–5
Adm Donations welcome

This 1854 antebellum plantation home was formerly the residence of Judge Isaac Johnson. Guided tours of the property describe the life and time of the house through the Civil War and beyond.

David Browning Railroad Museum

Reid Street, t (386) 328 0305, www.railsofpalatka.org
Open 1–4 (1st Sun and 3rd Sat of the month only, call for tours
Adm Donations welcome

Visitors can take a look at the old Union Station and view documents, photographs, maps, signs and other items of memorabilia relating to the railway age. In one room there's a model train layout depicting Palatka and its environs during the heyday of rail traffic in the late 1800s. There is also an HO scale model railroad called Railrodeo, built by Irvin P. Saylor, which used to tour the East Coast in 1975.

Putnam Historic Museum

100 Madison Street, t (386) 325 9825
Open Tue, Thu, Sun 2–5
Adm Donations welcome

The Putnam Historic Museum is run by the Putnam County Historical Society. The collection comprises artefacts from the early Spanish settlements through to the 20th century and there are also displays relating to the Seminole Wars, when the building was used as a military barracks.

Nature Lovers

Bulow Plantation Ruins State Historic Site

Plantation Road, off Old King's Road, Bunnel, t (386) 517 2084
Getting there West off Route A1A to Route 100 and turn south on Route 2001 – Old King's Road
Open Daily 9–5
Adm is $3 per car. Canoe rentals $4 per hour, $20 per day

Visitors can wander around the ruins of a former sugar mill and browse the displays in the interpretation centre, which gives insight into how the former plantation was run. Bulow was one of a number of plantations destroyed by American Indian raids during the Seminole Wars (*see* p.5). There are several trails to follow through the park but at time of writing, some paths had not been cleared of hurricane debris from 2004, so call in advance to check. You can picnic, fish, camp and take a canoe trip or just take a short stroll down paths shaded by magnificent live oaks.

Gamble Rogers Memorial State Recreation Area

3100 South A1A, Flagler Beach, t (386) 517 2086
Getting there 30 miles south of St. Augustine via the A1A. Exit 284 off the I–95
Open 8–dusk
Adm $4 per car, $1 per bike or foot passenger

From May–September, endangered Loggerhead, Leatherback and Green turtles all come to nest on the beaches of this park, which is sandwiched between the Atlantic Ocean and the Inter-coastal Waterway. It's a good spot for a picnic and a trip to the beach. There's also a boat ramp and facilities for bird watching, swimming and coastal camping.

Mike Roess Gold Head Branch State Park

6239 Route 21, Keystone Heights, **t** (352) 473 4701
Getting there Off Route 100, west of Palatka on State Road 21
Open 8–dusk
Adm $4 per car, $1 per bike or foot passenger

There are over 2,000 acres of parkland to enjoy, offering the chance to spot white-tailed deer, turkey, gopher tortoises, foxes, hawks, kestrels and eagles, plus numerous species of water and wading birds. Come for a picnic, hire a canoe, have a quiet fish or take to one of the four trails through the park past sand hills and crystal-clear streams. There's a children's playground by the picnic area. There's also a swimming area on Little Lake Johnson, close to the rental cabins, but parental supervision is necessary as there are no lifeguards on site. For overnight stays, there are 1930s cabins overlooking the lake from $50–$85 per night for up to 4 people, minimum stay two nights at peak times, and 74 family camping pitches all with picnic tables and grills $16 per night, contact **www.reserveamerica.com**.

Ravine Gardens State Park

1600 Twigg Street, Palatka, **t** (386) 329 3721
Getting there From Route 100 turn south onto Moseley Avenue then east onto Twigg Street
Open 8–dusk
Adm $4 per car, $1 per bike or foot passenger

Enjoy a quiet stroll in this 153-acre park set in a 100-ft ravine, whose meandering paths form part of the Great Florida Birding Trail. Cardinals, mockingbirds, woodpeckers, owls and hawks are among the birds you can spot; ruby-throated hummingbirds frequent the formal gardens in spring and summer, attracted by the exotic blooms. Near the amphitheatre, there are toilets, a children's playground and two pavilions, which can be rented for picnic barbeques. Other picnic sites can be found along the paved trail. Rangler-led tours by wagon are available for $40, book two weeks in advance, if possible. Watch out for the annual air potato rodeo in February, where there are prizes for the biggest and the most unusually shaped spud.

GAINESVILLE

Gainesville is home to the University of Florida and the Gators American football team, so don't be surprised to see college jocks wearing foam alligator heads drinking cans of Gatorade – the town's other claim to fame. Affordable accommodation and interesting museums and state parks make it well worth a diversion.

Getting there

73 miles from St. Augustine, 68 miles from Jacksonville. East of I–75 at Highway 441

Tourist information

Alachua County Visitors and Convention Bureau, 30 East University Avenue,
t (352) 374 5231 or (866) 778 5002,
www.visitGainesville.net

Things to see and do

Florida Museum of Natural History

Powell Hall, Southwest 34th Street and Hull Road, University of Florida Plaza, **t** (352) 846 2000,
www.flmnh.ufl.edu
Open Mon–Sat 10–5, Sun 12 noon–5
Adm Free, except for special exhibitions

Geological and anthropological exhibits focus on the beasts and beings that once walked on Florida soil. Highlights include a row of ancient shark jaws set against a mirrored background, so you can see which ones could swallow your head, a walk-through a Calusa Indian village and the recreation of several native habitats such as a mangrove swamp, limestone cave and a hardwood hammock. There's also a fossil plant garden and a shop featuring nature kits and books on Florida.

Matheson Museum

513 East University Avenue, **t** (352) 378–2280
Open Museum: Tue–Fri 9.30–1.30, Sun 1–5. House: open for tours first Sun of the month from 1–4
Adm Free. The Matheson Museum offers tours by appointment only to school groups and families. Please call to book, donations welcome.

If you want to get an idea how Gainesville and Alachua County has developed since the 1800s, then a visit to this museum complex is a must. Displays vary but include local history maps and personal artefacts and the library collection houses a huge stash of postcards of old Florida. behind the museum, **Sweetwater Park** has benches, children's playground and natural history display boards. The Matheson House displays show period furnishings and memorabilia relating to the Matheson family.

Morningside Living History Farm

3540 East University Avenue, **t** (352) 334 2170, **www**.natureoperations.org
Getting there 3 miles east of Gainesville on State Road 26
Open Daily 9–5; **Adm** Free

The farm is a recreation of a traditional 1840s settlement and is constructed using authentic barns and cabins that have been moved from other locations in Florida. The schoolhouse and blacksmith's forge are open for demonstrations and at 9am and 3pm you can see the rare breeds animals being fed. Every Saturday from September to May, visitors can watch **costumed guides** going about their chores. Children can sample cornbread and fresh biscuits and quiz staff about the various tasks and equipment used on the farm. There are also seven miles of **trails** through the pine and cypress backwoods to explore. There are picnic areas, toilets, information kiosks and wildlife displays along the way.

Samuel P. Harn Museum of Art

Southwest 34th Street and Hull Road, University of Florida Plaza, **t** (352) 392 9826
Open Tue–Fri 11–5, Sat 10–5, Sun 1–5. Closed Mon. Guided tours Sat, Sun 2 and 7.30
Adm Free, donations for children's events appreciated

The museum's vast collection includes East, West and Central African pottery, figurines, beaded jewellery, baskets and paintings, Mayan, Inca, Toltec and Aztec sculpture, Chinese, Thai and Vietnamese ceramics, Modernist and contemporary paintings and photography, as well as contemporary costumes and masks from Papua New Guinea. On the last Tuesday or first Friday of the month, accompanied children aged 2–5 are invited on a special **guided tour** of the museum with plenty of hands-on activities and games. There are also special **Harn Family Days** once a month, where families can have a go at themed activities linked to the museum collections. Call for more details. The museum store stocks games and puzzles, plus a few board books and art books for children.

Santa Fé Community College Teaching Zoo

3000 Northwest 83rd Street, **t** (352) 395 5604
Getting there Off North Road, on the northwest campus of Santa Fe Community College. Exit 390 off I–75 onto State Road 222, go east to northwest 91st Street and the zoo is first right after the road makes a sharp turn to the left
Open 9–2. Sat, Sun. Mon–Fri by appointment only
Adm Free

Learn more about 75 different species of animals living in a natural wooded environment on a weekend tour. Access is limited so that the animals can exist in semi-wild conditions. You will see bald eagles, monkeys, deer, Galapagos tortoises, otters and several species of reptiles and amphibians.

Special trips

Marjorie Kinnan Rawlings State Historic Park

18700 Route 325, Cross Creek, **t** (352) 466–3672
Getting there Route 325, 21 miles southeast of Gainesville
Open Grounds: daily 9–5. House: Thu–Sun tours 10, 11 and hourly 1–4pm, closed Aug–Sept
Adm Adults $3, children (6–12) $2, under 5s free

Get the kids in the mood by watching *The Yearling* or reading choice snippets from Marjorie Kinnan Rawlings' timeless story of life in the Florida backwoods. This is where the author came to write her novels in the midst of Florida's sprawling scrub country, part of which remains today as the Ocala National Forest. Rangers in 1930s period costumes take visitors on a tour of this humble single-storied homestead bringing Rawlings' stories to life. Queues for tours are likely so arrive early and take it in turns to wander through the citrus groves filled with the scent of oranges, tangerines and grapefruit. The surrounding parkland is made up of Florida farmland, marshland and hardwood hammock.

AROUND AND ABOUT

Nature lovers

Devil's Millhopper State Geological Park

4732 Millhopper Road, **t** (352) 955–2008
Getting there Exit 390 off I–75 onto State Road 222 and drive east 3.8 miles. At 43rd Street, turn left and left again at the traffic lights
Open Wed–Sun 9–5; ranger-led tours Sat 10am.
Adm $2 per car, $1 per bike or foot passenger

Encounter a 120-foot sinkhole, waterfalls, streams and lots of trees and ferns. There's a visitor centre, a 1½-mile nature trail along boardwalks at the top of the hole or down 232 steps to the bottom.

Kanapaha Botanical Gardens

4625 Southwest 63rd Boulevard t (352) 372 4981, **www.**kanapaha.org
Getting there Entrance on Southwest Archer Road (State Road 24), 1 mile west of I–75
Open Mon–Wed and Fri 9–5
Adm Adults: $5, children (6-13) $3, under 6s free
Picnic areas plant shop, gift shop, snack bar

This lovely 62-acre site features herb gardens, lily ponds, desert cactus and bamboo forests.

Paynes Prairie Preserve State Park

100 Savannah Boulevard, Micanopy, **t** (352) 466 3397
Getting there 10 miles south of Gainesville on Highway 441. From I–75 take Exit 374 to Route 234. Head east through Micanopy for 1.4 miles until you reach US 441 and left into the park
Open Daily 8–dusk. Visitor centre: 9–4
Adm $4 per car, $1 per bike or foot passenger

21,000 acres of wet prairie, pine flatwoods, ponds and hammocks with a visitor centre, a viewing tower and several trails for hikers, bikers and horse riding. The lakeside recreation area offers fishing, picnicking, canoeing and camping. There are ranger-led campfire trips, rambles and overnight backpacking are at weekends. Call **t** (352) 466 4100 for further details.

San Felasco Hammock State Preserve

12720 Northwest 109th Lane, Alachua, **t** (386) 462 7905
Getting there 4 miles northwest Gainesville. Exit 390 off I–75 onto State Road 222, drive west 2.9 miles to Route 241, turn right and drive 2 miles to 232
Open Daily 8–dusk; **Adm** $2 per car, $1 per bike or foot passenger. Horse riding $6

Ranger-led hikes, beginner's bike trails and horse-riding trips are a feature of this vast 6,900-acre park comprising hardwood hammocks, sand hills, limestone outcrops, sinkholes and swamp.

OCALA

With more than 45 different breeds of horses and 200 horse farms and training centres, Ocala certainly does live up to its name as horse capital of the world. Horse farms are the major industry in the area, with breeding, training and showing of unique breeds, such as the Missouri, Paso Fino, Foxtrotter and Arabian, providing thousands of jobs locally.

Getting there

36 miles south of Gainesville on Route 441 or I–75.

Tourist Information

Ocala–Marion County Chamber of Commerce, 110 East Silver Springs Boulevard, **t** (352) 629 8051, **www.ocalacc.com**

Things to see and do

Don Garlits Museum of Drag Racing

13700 Southwest 16th Avenue, **t** (352) 245 8661, **www.garlits.com**
Getting there 8 miles south of Ocala, exit 341 of I–75, east on County Road 484
Open Daily 9–5
Adm Adults $12, children (5–12) $3, under 5s free

The Classic Car Collection features gleaming and lovingly cherished motor vehicles from 1900–1970 with around 70 models including Mustangs, Chevvies and early Fords. The adjacent **Museum of Drag Racing** features hot rods, a hall of fame and a collection of speedway memorabilia. The gift shop stocks some cool souvenir T-shirts, hats and groovy die-cast models.

KP Hole Park

9435 SW 190 Avenue Road, Dunnellon, **t** (352) 489 3055
Getting there Exit I–75 at Route 40 west to Dunellon. Go 16 miles until the road merges with Routes 41 and 45 South and follow signs.

Open Daily, summer: 8–8, winter: 8–5

This section of the Rainbow River has a sandy beach, a protected swimming area and picnic tables. Visitors can hire tubes to ride down the river, which has an average temperature of 72–74 degrees.

Ocala Carriage Tours

Ocala Square (downtown), t 352 867 8717, www.ocalacarriage.com

Tours: Daily (call in advance), $95 for a six-seater carriage (4 adults, 2 children), trolleys for groups of ten, $22 per person, picnic lunches $14; visits to the New England Shire Centre are an additional $15 per person.

Enjoy an hour-long trip to Ocala's famous horse farms by horse-drawn carriage or trolley wagon. The tour passes through quiet country taking in Thoroughbred farms, as well as horses in fields. There are plenty of stops along the way for visitors to pat the horses and take in the scenery.

Ocala National Forest

Lake George Ranger District, 17147 East Highway 40, t (352) 625 2520

Seminole Ranger District, 40929 State Road 19, Umatilla, t (352) 669 3153

Ocklawaha Visitor Center, 3199 NE Highway 315, Silver Springs, t (352) 236 0288.

Salt Springs Visitor Center, 14100 N. State Highway 19, Salt Springs, t (352) 685 3070

Pittman Visitor Center, 45621 State Road 19, Altoona, t (352) 669 7495, www.fs.fed.us

Getting there From Ocala take Route 40 East

Open 8–8 daily. Visitor centres: 9–5 (except Seminole 7.30–4.30 and Lake George 7.30–4)

Adm $4 (under 5s free)

In terms of English national parks, the 383,573-acre Ocala National Forest is just a thousand acres shy of the entire Lake District – i.e. it's big. Natural springs feed clear, shallow streams perfect for splashing around in on a hot day. The Ocala terrain includes wetlands made up of swamps, coastal lowlands, rivers and streams. Cypress and gum trees alternate with sandy pinewoods as you reach the higher ground in the middle of the forest. There are specially **marked walking and hiking trails** where you can observe a sinkhole or wander through backwoods country and discover the settings for Majorie Kinnan Rawlings bestseller, *The Yearling*. There are picnic spots and toilets at regular intervals and camping spots are also plentiful.

Juniper Springs, Alexander Springs, Salt Springs and Silver Glen Springs are all good for swimming. Other activities include cycling, boating, fishing, canoeing, kayaking, horse riding and off-road driving.

If you want to sample a short break in the forest, **Camp Ocala** 4-H Center, 18533 NFS 535, Altoona, **t** (352) 759 2288 offers cabin accommodation, an indoor gym and activities such as hiking, canoeing, nature trails, campfires and tennis. Programmes can be made to suit groups of any size and age. Because the park is so vast it's essential to have a map to plan your trip. Trail maps are available from the forest website but check in at one of the five visitor centres (*see above*) for more information.

Rainbow Springs State Park

18185 SW 94th Street, Dunnellon, t (352) 489-5201, (352) 489-8503

Getting there From I–75, exit at the second Ocala exit onto State Road 40. Take State Road 40, west to US 41, turn left, the park entrance is on the left-hand side of the road

Open 8–dusk

Adm $1per person , under 6s free

This 600-acre state park features a 400-acre campsite, shaded paths and the headwaters of the Rainbow River fed by numerous springs issuing from vents in the limestone bedrock. The park is a popular destination to swim, snorkel, fish, picnic, hike through oaks and magnolias, or canoe past cypress trees draped in Spanish moss. **Canoes** and **kayaks** are available ($25 deposit, $5 per hour). There are picnic tables, grills and three covered picnic pavilions overlooking the main spring basin and swimming area. There are no lifeguards on duty so swimming and snorkelling are only allowed in the buoyed area. Camping fees are $19/night. The main campsite area has a playground.

Silver Springs

5656 East Silver Springs Boulevard, Silver Springs, t (352) 236–2121, www.silversprings.com

Getting there One mile east of Ocala on Route 40

Open Daily 10–5

Adm Adults $32.99, children (3–10) $23.99, under 3s free. Entrance fee includes boat, museums and themed attractions

Silver Springs is the largest artesian spring system, by water flow, in the world. Archaeological evidence suggests that early man enjoyed taking a bath in these temperate waters and tourists have been flocking here ever since.

Today, the 350-acre nature theme park offers glass-bottom boat tours – a park institution since 1870. The latest additions to the park include an 80-ft lighthouse-themed carousel and gondola ride offering spectacular view of the park, which are illuminated by light shows at night. The **Fort King River Cruise** is a 10,000-year history lesson with interactive sites including an archaeological dig, a Seminole village, an authentic Florida pioneer settlement and a movie set recalling Silver Spring's history as a film location.

Last but not least, there's a theatre-style water show featuring synchronized jets and spouts of water that jump, twist and twirl to 1950s big band sounds. Think Busby Berkeley without the gals.

Elsewhere visitors can view rare Florida Panthers, black bears, alligators, go on a Jeep safari, check out the riverboat-shaped kids' play space with crawl tunnels, nets and interactive games or see a reptile or bird show. More than enough for a great day out.

Wild Waters Water Park

At Silver Springs, t (352) 236 2121, www.wildwaterspark.com
Open **Mar–Sept 10–7**
Adm **Adults $23.99, children (under 48ins) $20.99, under 2s free**

Like many Florida theme parks, Silver Springs operates its own water park when the weather warms enough for Americans to consider dipping their toes. There are several flumes, in the dark, interminably twisting, fast-paced, all the kind the kids really love, plus a wave pool, kiddie pool and a kids' cove water playground with slides, spouts, levers to pull and canons to fire.

Youngs Paso Fino Ranch

8075 Northwest State Road 326, t (352) 867 5305, www.youngspasofino.com
Getting there **Take exit 326 west off I–75 for 3½ miles and follow the sign at the top of the hill at 80th Avenue. Take a right and look for the barn entrance on the left hand side.**
Adm **Mon–Sat (by appointment). Tours: 10–2 $7.50 per person, trail riding $30 per person.**

This establishment offers children age four and up a chance to learn to ride these steady, docile and extremely attractive horses descended from Spanish mounts. 1½ hour riding trails are also available. Ranch facilities include a covered viewing pavilion, training arena and plenty of lush pasture

WHERE TO EAT

Jacksonville

Billy's Boat House Grill

2321 Beach Blvd, Jacksonville Beach, t (904) 241 9771
Open **Tue–Thu 4–10, Fri 4–11, Sat 10am–11pm, Sun 10am–10pm (*moderate*)**

Casual family dining overlooking the water with lunch and dinner menus featuring fresh fish and seafood specials such as shrimp and scallops, peppercorn tuna and cashew crumb snapper. Smaller dishes include chowders, sandwiches and fish and fries. Breakfast is available at weekends.

Country Cabin Restaurant

3646 Blanding Boulevard t (904) 317 9887
Open **Mon–Thu and Sat–Sun 7 am–9pm, Fri 7am–10pm (*inexpensive*)**

This restaurant in the Cedar Hills area is a popular spot for locals and offers Southern-style country cooking in a laid back setting. Come for a hearty cooked breakfast or lunchtime sandwich and, or, dine on fried chicken or grilled ham steak served with freshly baked breads. There's a kids' menu (for under 12s) and delicious homemade pies.

Dave & Buster's

7025 Salisbury Road, t (904) 296 1525
Open **Mon–Tue 11.30pm –12am, Wed–Sat 11.3am–1am, Sun 11.30am–12 midnight (*moderate–expensive*)**

If you can tear the kids away from all the flashing lights and electronic bleeps of the amusement arcade for long enough they can have their fill of some good quality pasta and pizza dishes.

Lighthouse Grill

2600 Beach Blvd, t (904) 242 8899
Open **Sun–Thu 11–10, Fri, Sat 11–11 (*inexpensive–moderate*)**

Superior steaks, ribs and local seafood are crowd pullers at this smart and roomy restaurant overlooking the Intracoastal Waterway. There are also salads and sandwiches, plus a selection of light bites.

River City Brewing Co

835 Museum Circle, t (904) 398 2299
Open **Lunch: Mon–Sat 11–3, Dinner: Mon–Thu 5–10, Fri–Sat 5–11, Sun brunch 10.30–2.30, buffet 4.30–8.30 (*moderate–expensive*)**

This modern-style brewpub offers *al fresco* dining by the river and is close to all the Southbank museums. There are children's menus and Sunday brunch gives families the opportunity to graze among seafood, salads, carvery and cooked breakfast items.

Around and About

Amelia island/ Fernandina Beach

Beech Street Grill

801 Beech Street, t (904) 277 3662, www.beechstreetgrill.com

Open Open Mon–Sun Dinner: 6–10 (*expensive*)

This former sea captain's house offers dining over two floors in spacious and airy surroundings. Seafood and fish specials, plus authentic key lime pie and roast lamb with applesauce are the highlights of the menu, accompanied by fresh herbs and homemade sauces and chutneys.

The Conch House

57 Comares Ave, t (904) 829 8646

Open Mon–Thu 11–9, Fri, 11–10, Sat 8am–10pm, Sun breakfast 8am–10am (*moderate*)

The lunch menu includes fresh grouper, crab or prawn sandwiches, Minorcan burgers made from ground pork, chorizo and sirloin, plus pasta dishes and salads. The Everglades Dining area features a live alligator exhibit.

The Palace Saloon

117 Centre Street, t (904) 491 3332, **www.thepalacesaloon.com**

Open daily 11–2am (*inexpensive–moderate*)

Once the stomping ground of the Du Ponts and Vanderbilts, the Palace is now a place where, according to the menu – 'cooking is like love, it should be entered into with abandon or not at all'. As such the restaurant offers lots of mouthwatering choices from smoked ham or turkey sandwiches to Asian-influenced fish and seafood dishes. There's live entertainment weekdays and weekend evenings. Oh yes, it's apparently such a popular watering hole that the ghosts of pirates and lost souls still come back for more.

Atlantic Beach

First Street Grille

807 North First Street, t (904) 246 6555

Open Mon–Sun 11.30–5 (*moderate–expensive*)

Casual dining specializing in seafood and steak dishes. There's a children's menu, entertainment at weekends and nice views of the ocean.

Sticky Fingers

363–1 Atlantic Blvd, t 904 241 7427

Open Mon–Sun 11–10 (*inexpensive–moderate*)

This casual chain diner offers classic smokehouse fare including hickory-ribs, smoked chicken and hand-pulled pork. The kids' menu features burgers, hotdogs, ribs and chicken fingers. There's an enclosed patio for relaxed family dining.

Sundog Diner

207 Atlantic Boulevard, t (904) 241–8221

Open Lunch and dinner daily with brunch on Sat and Sun (*inexpensive–moderate*)

If you're looking for an authentic retro American diner with heaps of chrome trim and booth seating this is the place to come. It's an Atlantic Beach institution. There's a good kids' menu and the service is friendly. Food ranges from hot dogs and meatloaf with mash to grilled fish and crab cakes.

Ponte Vedra Beach

Aqua Grill

950 Sawgrass Village Drive t (904) 285 3017

Open Mon–Sat 11.30am–1am, Sun 12 noon-1am (*moderate–expensive*)

Dine indoors or out at this lovely waterside restaurant, which features water fountains and an organic herb garden. The kids will want to come to look at the colourful fish in the aquariums; is that Nemo in there? Parents, meanwhile, will be able to enjoy the first-rate service and melt-in-the-mouth dishes, which, of course, happen to include fish such as red snapper, swordfish, sea bass, plus more unusual types such as triggerfish and wahoo. You can also get fried green tomatoes here, live Maine lobster, aged steaks, crab claws, oysters, shrimp or dine on succulent seafood with pasta. Vegetarian dishes, a takeout menu and a children's menu are available.

Barbara Jean's

15 S. Roscoe Blvd, t (904) 280 7522, www.barbara-jeans.com

Open Summer: daily 11–10, Winter: Fri, Sat only (*moderate*)

This is one of four restaurants in the Barbara Jeans stable and one of two in Florida (the other, being on Gateway Boulevard in Amelia Island). The Ponte Vedra Beach restaurant is a family-run place with booths and tables and outdoor seating offering peaceful waterside views. The kids' menu is more inventive than most, featuring pot roasts, turkey and dressing, meatloaf and grilled cheese sandwiches, plus all dishes come with vegetables and not fries! The main menu has plenty of chicken dishes, salads and vegetable side orders. The crab cakes come highly recommended.

St. Augustine

95 Cordova and Cobalt Lounge

Casa Monica Hotel, 95 Cordova Street, **t** (904) 819 6018
Open Daily for breakfast, lunch and dinner, brunch on Sundays (*expensive*)

If you fancy a peek inside one of the remaining elegant resort hotels built by railway magnate Henry Flagler in the 1880s, then dinner here is a must. If you've a passion for seafood try the crab ravioli with shrimp and vodka lobster sauce or the seafood strudel. Meats lovers can feast on steak and chicken, chops and duckling with Morrocan and Asian influences. The Sunday brunch menu has a large selection of salads, freshly baked breads, cheeses and cooked meats. The children's menu has beef, chicken or cheese and ham sandwiches, burgers, plus healthy choices such as steamed vegetable and fruit plates. For pudding there's ice cream, cookies and brownies washed down by a selection of fresh juices.

A1A Ale Works

1 King Street, **t** (904) 829 2977
Open Sun–Thu 11–10.30, Fri–Sat 11am–12midnight. Lunch daily 11–5 (*moderate–expensive*)

Bright micro-pub with views of the Matanzas Bay and the Bridge of Lions serving new world seafood and fish dishes, sandwiches, salads and soups. There's a children's menu and seating is available outside.

Santa Maria Restaurant

135 Avenida Menendez, **t** (904) 829 6578
Open Daily for lunch and dinner, except Weds lunchtime. Hours are seasonal, so call in advance (*moderate*)

Scallops with linguini, Minorcan clam chowder and a good choice of salads and seafood platters are the main reasons for visiting this waterside eaterie. As far as the kids are concerned, the chance to feed catfish, mullet, needlefish in summer, and birds in winter through trapdoors in the tables, will have more appeal than anything else. Just do bear in mind that they may be able to feed the wildlife here but it is not something to encourage elsewhere, particularly if you are heading into nature reserves and national parks. The kids' menu includes seafood, fried or boiled fish, chicken nuggets, spaghetti, grilled cheese sandwiches and hamburgers.

Around and About

Palatka

Angel's Dining Car

209 Reid Street **t** (386) 325 3927
Open 24hrs (*inexpensive*)

For a nostalgic treat for the kids, bring them to this old-fashioned 1950s dining car; it's the oldest in Florida and offers plenty to look at from neon signage, chrome fixtures and eclectic 50s kitsch. The menu features breakfast staples, house special milkshakes, onion rings and burgers but the main event takes place on Saturdays when the vintage car collectors come to call.

Corkey Bell's

133 Crystal Cove Drive **t** (386) 325 1094, **www.themooringsatcrystalcove.com**
(*inexpensive*)

This casual restaurant on the St. Johns River is part of the Crystal Cove marina and Moorings Motel. The menu specializes in seafood and steaks and features a signature Floridian dish – the Swamp Platter. Outdoor dining on the patio deck is available.

Gainesville

Emiliano's Cafe

7 Southeast 1st Avenue, **t** (352) 375 7381
Open Tue–Thu 11–10, Fri–Sat 11–11
(*inexpensive–moderate*)

Delicious culinary surprises abound at this Puerto Rican restaurant and bakery. The menu has lots of choice including tapas, bean soup, fried plantains, empanadas and pork tenderloin. The kids will be equally happy eating flaky pastries either as a lunchtime takeaway snack or at the sidewalk café watching the world go by.

Harry's Seafood Bar & Grille

110 Southeast First Street, Gainesville,
t (352) 372 1555, **www.hookedonharrys.com**
Open Daily lunch and dinner. Branch: 24 SE Avenue, Ocala (352) 840 0900 (*inexpensive–moderate*)

Casual but quality New Orleans steak and seafood dishes are served up at this sidewalk diner that's popular with local families.

Jimmy John's

2220 SW Archer Road **t** (352) 271 7600,
www.jimmyjohns.com
Open Mon–Sun 10am–2am (*inexpensive*)

If you just want a sandwich and only a sandwich will do, Jimmy Johns will serve you up a gourmet French bread sub or wholewheat or French bread club sandwich with fillings such as roast beef and provolone cheese, turkey breast, bacon lettuce and tomato, plus veggie options. Soft drinks, home-made pickles, chocolate or raisin and oatmeal cookies and crisps are also available. Eat in or grab yourself a picnic to go. Even if you're not hungry, just check out their website, it's hilarious.

La Fiesta

7038 Northwest 10th Place **t** (352) 332 0878
Open Mon–Thu 11–9.30, Fri–Sat 11–10.30 (*inexpensive*)

If you're after some authentic Mexican food, this friendly establishment boasts a great selection of affordable dishes including burritos, enchiladas, chimichangas, fajitas, tacos and tostadas. Specials include stuffed poblano peppers, pork chop with rice and black beans or shrimp, fajitas. Free corn chips and mild and spicy salsa are delivered to your table on arrival. The kids' menu (for under 10s) offers a choice of beef taco, combi burrito or cheese enchilada with rice and beans or hot dog, chicken fingers or corn dog and fries. The dessert menu is also bound to be a big hit with the kids featuring ice cream or more exotic dishes such as Tres Leches – a rich sponge cake made up of three types of sweet milk and cheesecake chimichanga - filled with cream cheese, apple pieces and cinnamon.

Melting Pot

418 East University Avenue, **t** 352 372 5623
Open For dinner only (*inexpensive–moderate*)

Fondues are made for sharing, so what better way to end the day than gathering round the table in a family style and dipping bread in pots of bubbling meat, fish or cheese? The highlight for the kids, of course, will be the fruit and chocolate fondue dessert.

Mori

908 NW 69th Ave, **t** (352) 331 0069
Open Sun–Thu 11.30–10, Fri–Sat 11.30–11 (*inexpensive–moderate*)

Japanese Steakhouse and Sushi Bar where kids can get a free cookery course at the tableside *habachi* grill. Specials include soup, salad, vegetables, rice and a choice of either lobster, shrimp, steak or chicken.

Ocala

Harry's Seafood Bar & Grille

Lorito's Italian Kitchen

1801 East Silver Springs Boulevard,
t (352) 629-1383 (*inexpensive–moderate*)

If you miss the 14-ft soda bottle sign from US 40, hopefully the scents of garlic and oven baked pizza will draw you in to this affordable and friendly Italian restaurant.

Quiz

1. Which two European countries fought over Northeast Florida in the eighteenth century?

2. In which part of Jacksonville did the Great Fire of 1901 start?

3. What was the original name of Amelia Island?

4. Where can you see reenactments of the American Civil War?

5. Which fountain can give kids strength and help them with say, arm-wrestling?

6. What size if the largest of all crocodilians?

7. What is the colour of the sightseeing train in historic St Augustine?

8. In what war did American Indians raid an important number of plantations?

9. What is the name of the famous football team in Gainesville?

10. What is known as the horse capital of the world?

West Central Florida

08

West Central Florida

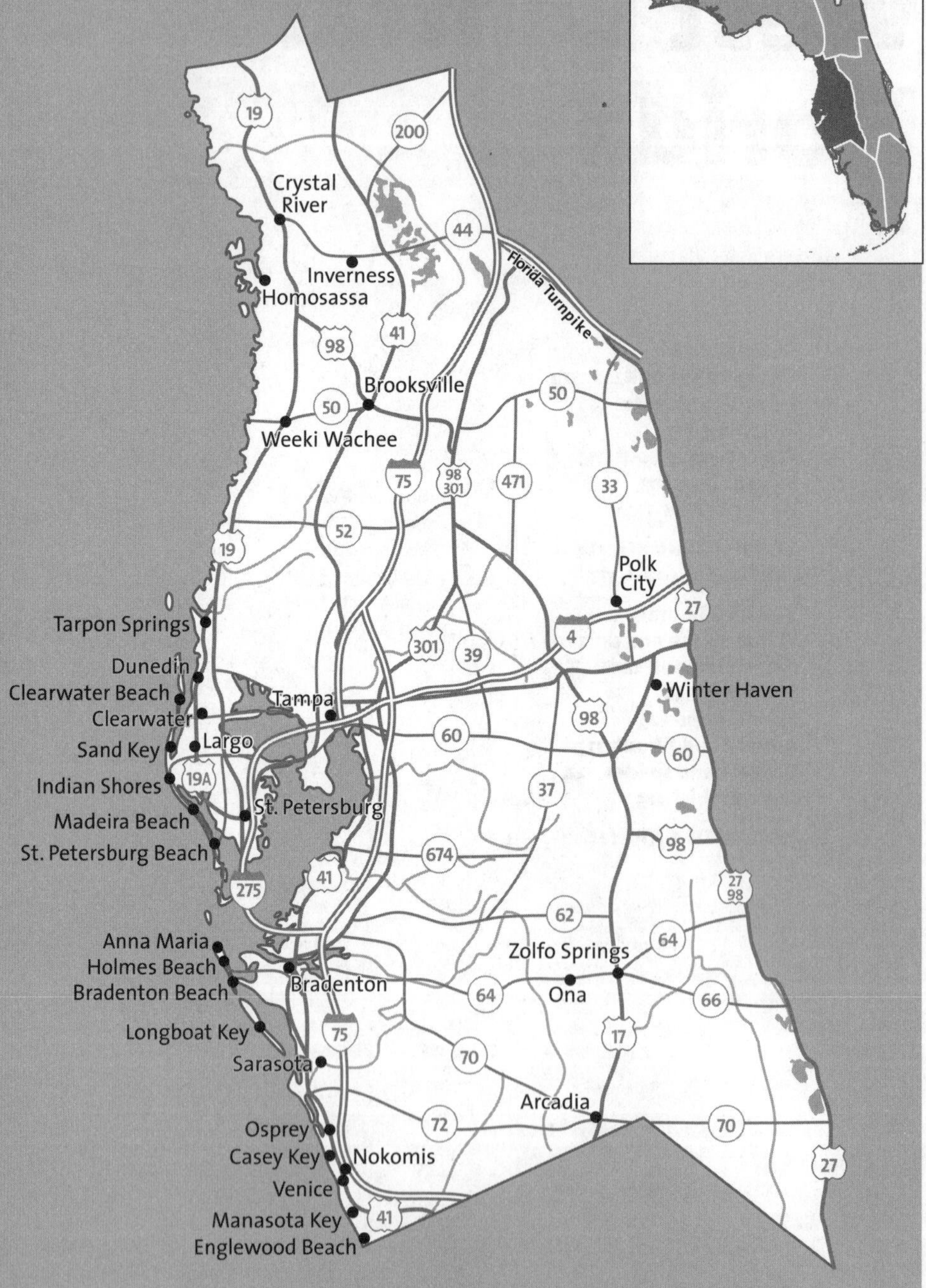

Crystal River
Inverness
Homosassa
Brooksville
Weeki Wachee
Polk City
Tarpon Springs
Dunedin
Clearwater Beach
Clearwater
Tampa
Winter Haven
Sand Key
Largo
Indian Shores
St. Petersburg
Madeira Beach
St. Petersburg Beach
Anna Maria
Holmes Beach
Bradenton Beach
Bradenton
Zolfo Springs
Ona
Longboat Key
Sarasota
Arcadia
Osprey
Casey Key
Nokomis
Venice
Manasota Key
Englewood Beach
Florida Turnpike
19
200
44
41
98
50
75
98 301
471
33
52
27
4
301
39
60
37
674
275
19A
27 98
62
64
66
17
70
72

WEST CENTRAL FLORIDA

Most international visitors see **Tampa** as a place they pass through on the way to somewhere else, such as Orlando or Fort Myers for a spot of sun and fun. The east coast doesn't even have the big city thrills to rival Miami either, so why go there? That's simple. Diversity. The stretch of coast from **Crystal River** to **Venice** offers the get-away-from-it-all locales of the **gulf islands**, award-winning beaches, one-of-a-kind family attractions and a whole variety of experiences from high-class resorts and *bijou* shopping in **Sarasota** to beatnik enclaves and powder sands around **St. Petersburg** and **Clearwater**. Where else in Florida can you walk in the trees, swim with the fishes in an aquarium or run away with the circus? **Busch Gardens** alone has an unparalleled range of attractions, from animal safaris to high-octane roller coasters – and still they're building. The nature coast to the north offers the chance to escape and encounter Florida's wild side, while the busy cities of Tampa and St. Petersburg offer enough museums, galleries, shops and restaurants, not to mention festivals and events, to keep any family occupied both night and day. It's this mix of hustle and utter calm that makes the region so special.

Don't be fooled by the maps, West Central Florida is vast and, unlike the Florida Keys, its outlying islands are not all linked by road, connected instead, by bridges to different parts of the mainland. So, if you want to see it all, there will be a fair bit of driving involved. Having said that, once you're in a city or beach community, the local bus system comes into its own and is cheap, efficient and extensive, if not always so frequent to the more outlying areas, so you can just park the hire car and go.

Early Spanish landings in the Tampa area by Pánfilo de Narvaés and Hernando de Soto (*see* History p.4) were unsuccessful and only served to antagonize the local tribesmen, so settlers did not arrive until most of the Native American Indian tribes were wiped out by either disease or war (*see* Seminole Wars, History p.5). Tampa became part of the United States in 1845 and a military outpost, Fort Brooke, was established in the downtown area. As with the East Coast, the West Coast had its own railway magnate, Henry B. Plant, who extended his railroad to the Hillsborough River in 1884 and later constructed a string of luxury hotels along the coast to attract wintering tourists. During the Spanish-American War, Tampa Bay became a strategic military post. Colonel Teddy Roosevelt set up the headquarters for his Rough Riders at Plant's lovely new Tampa Bay Hotel in 1898 and the town became the embarkation point for 30,000 American troops on their way to Cuba.

The Tampa region's traditional industries of phosphate mining and sponge diving in **Tarpon Springs** (plus formerly cigar manufacture in **Ybor City**) are now supplemented by trade in seafood and cruise liners frequenting the busy port of Tampa Bay.

The weather here is bright and sunny, though it doesn't always feel so warm. In the winter, especially along the coast, winds can be strong and chilly. In the northern reaches of the region, the average year-round temperature is 70 degrees. Winter temperatures average 60.1 degrees, and summer temperatures 82.4 degrees. Bring insect repellent in summer, layers of clothing in winter and suntan lotion all year round.

Highlights

Being licked by a giraffe in Busch Gardens, Tampa, p.110
Swimming with the fishes, Florida Aquarium, Tampa, p.110
Playing house at Kid City, Tampa, p.111
Staring into space at the Imax Dome, Museum of Science & Industry, Tampa, p.112
Making science work at Great Explorations, the Hands-On Museum, St. Petersburg, p.115
Thinking arty thoughts at the Salvador Dali Museum, St. Petersburg, p.115
Watching otters at play in Clearwater Aquarium, p.117
Just hitting the beach, Caladesi Island State Park, Dunedin, p.118
Party time, Pier 60 Park, Clearwater Beach, p.118
Doing a bit of shell searching, Pass-a-Grille Beach, p.119
Seeing life through the eyes of a shark, Mote Marine Aquarium, Sarasota, p.121
Walking in the trees, Myakka State Park, Sarasota, p.123
Dozing in the sun, Siesta Key County Beach, Siesta Key, p.124
Sifting for shark's teeth on Venice Beach, p.124

Annual Events

January

Black Heritage Festival, Tampa Bay, **t** (888) 224 1733), **www**.tampablackheritage.org
Epiphany, Tarpon Springs, **t** (727) 937 3540, **www**.ci.tarpon-springs.fl.us
Florida State Fair, Tampa, **t** (813) 621 7821, **www**.floridastatefair.com
Gasparilla Festival, Tampa **t** (813) 353 8108, **www**.gasparillapiratefest.com
Arts Day, Sarasota, **t** (941) 365 5118, **www**.sarasota-arts.org
Circus Spectacular, Ringling Museum of Art, Sarasota, **t** (941) 359 5700, **www**.ringling.org

March

Manatee Heritage Days, Bradenton, **t** (941) 741 4070, **www**.bradenton.com
Medieval Fair, Sarasota, **t** (888) 303 FAIR (3247), **www**.sarasotamedievalfair.com
Cracker Heritage Festival, Wauchula, **t** (863) 767 0330, **www**.florida-secrets.com

March–April

PAL Sailor Circus, Sarasota, **t** (941) 361 6350, **www**.sailorcircus.org
Festival of States, St. Petersburg, **t** (727) 898 3654, **www**.festivalofstates.com

April

Family EarthFest and Arbor Day, Gulf Coast Museum of Art, Largo, **t** (727) 518 6833, **www**.gulfcoastmuseum.org
Sharks' Tooth and Seafood Festival, Venice, **t** (800) 940 7427, **www**.venice-florida.com
Annual Highland Games, Dunedin, **t** (727) 733 6240

May

Watermelon Festival, DeSoto Park, **t** (863) 494 4033
Tarpon Springs Sponge Festival, **t** (727) 937 6109, **www**.tarponsprings.com

June

Suncoast Offshore Grand Prix Boat Race, Sarasota, **t** (941) 371 2827, **www**.sarasotafl.org

October

Guavaween Family Fun Fest, Ybor City, Tampa, **t** (813) 248 3712, **www**.ybor.org
John's Pass Seafood Festival, Madeira Beach, **t** (727) 398 5994

December

Victorian Christmas Stroll, Plant Museum, Tampa, **t** (813) 258 7302, **www**.plantmuseum.com
Santa Parade and Snow Fest, St. Petersburg, **t** (813) 274 8615
Lights in Bloom, Marie Selby Gardens, Sarasota, **t** (941) 366 5731, **www**.selby.org

TAMPA

Having invested heavily in its transport system, Tampa is now an easy place to get around without having to rely totally on a car. Its bright yellow streetcars (trams) have revitalized the up-and-coming Channelside waterfront district, which connects to **Ybor City Historic District**. Indeed, the humble cigar has done much for the development of this vibrant city. When Vicente Martinez Ybor decided to move his manufacturing business from Key West to Tampa in 1885 to escape labour unrest, the city began to take shape around the industry, drawing migrant workers from Cuba and Europe.

The museum in Ybor City brings the essence of the manufacturing district back to life as you wander among the restored cigar-workers houses (*casitas*) and watch cigars being hand-rolled in the shop. Afterwards browse the shops and restaurants of this lively **Latin Quarter**. Also offset by the glass and steel new buildings downtown are the beautifully preserved **Tampa Theatre** and Plant's grand old **Tampa Bay Hotel**, now part of the University of Florida, which houses the **Henry B. Plant museum**.

Visitors can easily spend a few days sightseeing before heading out to the Gulf beaches for a beach holiday. There's a good **zoo**, a major **theme park**, a **science centre**, an **aquarium** and **children's museum** along with outdoor attractions and sporting venues.

Beyond the city, opportunities for contemplating nature abound, from prowling the **Big Cat Rescue Preserve** to canoeing on the Hillsborough River.

Getting there

By air Tampa International Airport, 5507 Spruce Street, t (813) 870 8770, www.tampaairport.com is unusually central for a major city departure point and is ranked number one in the US for customer service. There are spacious and attractive seating areas, a shopping arcade featuring Florida gifts and a well-stocked bookshop, among other stores, plus restaurants and snack bars. Art displays brighten up many of the public areas and the Tampa

Gallery of Photographic Art is in the main terminal building on level 3. The airport is 20 minutes away from 35 miles of white-sand beaches, three of which are among the most highly regarded in the country.
By road Interstates 75, 275 run north to south both of which connect to I–4, the east-west coast road that links Tampa Bay to Orlando. I–275 runs through the centre of Tampa and crosses over to St. Petersburg, via the Howard Frankland Bridge.
By rail Amtrak, 601 Nebraska Avenue North, **t** (813) 221 7600 or, **t** (800) 872 7245, **www**.amtrak.com
Tampa's Amtrak Station offers connections to Jacksonville, Orlando, St. Petersburg and Miami (*see also* Northeast and Southeast pp.77 and 189). The **Greyhound bus** station is a few blocks away for connections to Fort Myers and beyond. Amtrak's **AutoTrain** offers daily service to passengers and vehicles travelling to Orlando. Amtrak is in down town Tampa at historic Tampa Union Station, also the main terminus for local bus and taxi services.
By bus Greyhound, 610 Polk Street, **t** (813) 229 2174, **www**.greyhound.com
Bus services run west from Tampa to St. Pete's (*see* p.114) or south to Nokomis, near Venice (*see* p.124), and to Fort Myers and Naples (*see* p.166 and p.179).

Getting around

By bus HARTline, **t** (813) 254 4278, **www**.hartline.org
It provides local and express bus services in Tampa. The no. 30 bus runs from the airport to Tampa Union Station (for Amtrak connections) and downtown's **Marion Transit Center** for bus connections. Service 200 runs from Tampa to Clearwater and buses no: 5 and 18 run to Busch Gardens. In addition, the **In-Town Trolley** connects downtown hotels to the Tampa Convention Center, Old Hyde Park Village Shopping District and the **TECO Line Streetcar System**.
TECO Line Streetcar, **t** (813) 254–HART, **www**.tecolinestreetcar.org
One-way fares $1.50 for adults, under 17s travelling with an adult ride free. You can't miss the snazzy bright yellow livery of Tampa's electric streetcars as they tootle down the 2.4-mile track calling at 10 stops between downtown, Channelside and Ybor City. The city has invested a considerable sum of money to resurrect this service, with replica trolleys just like the ones they used in 1946.

Tourist information

Tampa/Hillsborough Convention and Visitors Association, 400 North Tampa Street, Suite 2800, **t** (813) 223 1111, **www**.visittampabay.com

Things to see and do

Adventure Island

4500 Bougainvillea Avenue, **t** (813) 987 5600, **www**.adventureisland.com
Open Mar–Oct, hours vary call in advance for times. Weekends only mid-March and mid-Sept–Oct
Adm Adults $31.95, children (3–9) $29, plus tax. Combination tickets: Busch Gardens and Adventure Island ticket $65.95 and $56.95, plus tax, for one day at each. Parking: $5

Busch Gardens' (*see* below) sister park is located next door should you fancy a dip while in the area. There's an **Endless Surf wave pool**, a lagoon with diving platforms, zip wire, crawl nets and slides, plus two toddler pool areas – one with a beach and one with slides and water spouts. Older kids will love the many ways you can get wet in **Splash Attack** from the bucket-drop to the water cannon and beyond.

The rides are pretty amazing, especially the **Wahoo Run** (as in 'wahoo, here we go!') which plunges you along dark tunnels with plenty of twists and turns, down drops and through water curtains with only a raft for company. There are dizzying flumes, wicked water slides and a lazy river. Visitors who prefer to stay dry can head for the volleyball court, have a bite to eat at one of the two on-site cafés or soak up the sun on the beach. Picnic facilities, toilets, changing rooms, a gift shop and lockers are all available. Lifeguards are present throughout the day and the pools are heated seasonally.

Big Cat Rescue

12802 Easy Street, **t** (813) 920 4130, **www**.BigCatRescue.org
Getting there I–275 from Tampa take Busch Blvd exit and go west 9 miles until the road becomes Gunn Highway, follow signs or call for more directions
Open Tours: Mon–Fri 9 and 3, Sat 9.30, 11.30 and 3 (ages 10 and up only); Kids' Tours: Sat at 9am (suitable for under 10s and parents/carers), book in advance, call Kathryn on **t** (813) 323 3265 or email: Kids@BigCatRescue.org
Tour prices $20, Kids' tour $10 per person

The big cats at this 42-acre wildlife sanctuary may be living on Easy Street now, but that wasn't always the case. Several are on the endangered species list and many have been abandoned or kept in unsuitable conditions. The rescue centre is home to 200 animals, including snow leopards, bobcats, tigers, servals, lynx and Florida Panthers. Guided tours of the entire park last 1½ hours and allow visitors to learn more about individual inhabitants. Children's tours last an hour and are designed specifically for under-10s wishing to learn about these wild animals.

Busch Gardens

3000 Busch Boulevard, t (813) 987 5082, www.buschgardens.com
Getting there From Orlando it's 1 hour; go westbound on I–4, exit north on I–75, take Fowler Ave exit 265 and follow signs
Open Daily, hours vary call in advance for times
Adm Adults $53.95, children (3–9) $44.95, plus tax. Parking: $7. Combined attraction tickets (a good deal with Adventure Island, *see* p.143) are available.

If you like your park rides big, bold and up-to-the-minute then you'll not have a dull moment. Part-safari park, part-roller-coaster mega-park, Busch Gardens features several African-inspired regions such as Morocco, Egypt, Congo, Nairobi and Timbuktu. Plan a two-day visit minimum to make the most of it.

Start with a cable car ride or scoot around the outskirts of this vast 335-acre park on the **Transveldt Railroad** to orientate you or head straight for the number-one ride you've located on your map. The **Rhino rally off-road safari**, with water ride thrown in for good measure, is a giggle and very popular so get here early to avoid mind-boggling queues. The big guns among the highly respected roller coasters here are **Montu** with seven inversions, the duelling twister **Gwasi** and the mighty **SheiKra**, the first dive coaster in the US, featuring two 90-degree loops, one from a height of 200ft at 70mph, and another plunging 138ft into an underground tunnel. There's a nice water feature too, just to cool you down from the cold sweat of abject fear. Less daring coaster lovers can enjoy the **Scorpion** and **Cheetah Chase**, along with some absolutely drenching water rides.

Save time in the afternoon to take a tour – there are various options for ages 5 years up, **t** (813) 984 4043, or visit the website, some of which include express passes to the major coasters and water rides.

Among the wildlife encounters is **Serengeti Safari**, a low-key jeep trip that takes you away from the crowds to meet the park's resident animals and feed giraffe and African antelope. The journey is non-invasive, out of respect for the animals, and you leave knowing more about these creatures having got up close and personal. Bring a swimsuit to get the most from the **Land of the Dragons**, in Stanleyville, which is suitable from babies upwards and boasts water fountains, cannon and splash pools. Once dry, you can get to grips with the towering play structures and net bridges some 20ft (at least) up in the air. You can try saying 'please come down' – it doesn't work, you just have to gird your loins and get up there too. Safely back on *terra firma*, take a break in the **Stanleyville Smokehouse** before wandering back towards the park entrance to watch **Katonga**, a thrilling theatre show exploring tales from African folklore through storytelling, acrobatics and puppetry with lots of singing and dancing. Sit kids near the front for a chance to pop bubbles and catch fluttering butterflies. There are too many things to do here to list individually and a programme of daily events and shows only adds to the overwhelmingly good experience on offer.

Florida Aquarium

701 Channelside Drive, t (813) 273 4000, www.flaquarium.org
Open Daily 9.30–5
Adm Adults $17.95, children (3–12) $11.95, under 2s free. Parking $4. DolphinQuest: Adults $18.95, children $13.95

This thoroughly engrossing marine experience follows the course of water droplets forming underground through their journey through many environments and out to the open sea. Our journey takes us above and below the water level, along the shoreline, into the touch tank, through the wetlands and beyond to gaze out at the bay. There are lots of exhibits to handle, all at age-appropriate heights with hands-on information suitable for children aged 4–13. Outside, parents can sip a sneaky cocktail while the kids wage maritime warfare on each other from a pirate galleon. There are crawl nets and an 8-ft wave to dash about in. Bring swimwear so that your captain and his/her crew can have fun wasting a few landlubbers with the water cannon. The aquarium has several informative programmes about marine species. **Swim with the fishes** is suitable for ages 6 and up and allows you to swim in the coral reef tank among rainbow parrotfish, angelfish and moray eels, wearing special scuba gear. Certified divers over 15 can also dive with sharks (book ahead) **t** (813) 367 4005. **DolphinQuest** eco-tours take place in the bay aboard a 64-ft catamaran. Families can spot some dolphins and learn more about marine environments along the way. A full, fun and especially educational day out is guaranteed.

Henry B. Plant Museum

401 West Kennedy Boulevard, t (813) 254 1891, www.plantmuseum.com

Getting there From the north or south in Tampa on I–275, take exit 44, (Ashley Street, downtown) and proceed to Kennedy Boulevard, turn right and the entrance is just over a mile on the right

Open Tue–Sat 10–4, Sun 12 noon–4. Guided tours Tue–Sat at 1

Adm (suggested donation) Adults $5, children (under 12) $2

This former luxury hotel is bound to appeal to *Aladdin* fans with its silvery minarets and lofty domes. It now houses the University of Tampa and a museum dedicated to the man who dreamed up this Moorish masterpiece, the railway magnate Henry Plant. Period reconstructions of his Grand Salon and several lavishly furnished guest rooms recall a bygone age. Self-guided tours begin with a 14-minute introductory video – 'The Tampa Bay Hotel: Florida's First Magic Kingdom'. There are also guided tours on Tue–Sat afternoons and a shop with appealing educational toys and books

Hillsborough River State Park

15402 Highway 301 North, Thonotosassa, t (813) 987 6771

Getting there From Tampa I–75 Northbound to Fowler Avenue, exit 265 east to Highway 301, travel north for 9 miles, and the park will be on your left-hand side

Open Daily 8–dusk

Adm $4 per car, $1 per bike or pedestrian.

Café, gift shop and canoe rentals

This 3,950-acre park, only 10 minutes' away from Busch Gardens (*see* p.110), offers lovely nature trails, some swooping through the trees along high walkways, others sweeping down through valleys to the rapids. There are also swimming, camping and picnicking facilities. **Canoe Escape**, 9335 East Fowler Avenue, **t** (813) 986 2067, **www.**canoeescape.com, can provide canoe or kayaks to rent as well as guided tours through cypress swamps spotting alligators and other wildlife along the way. Visitors can also explore **Fort Foster**, a replica of the original Second Seminole War military fort that was built on the site in 1836, and the bridge that it was constructed to defend. The fort is open for guided tours and hosts a re-enactment in February. The **Fort Foster Visitor Station**, over the road from the fort, houses documents and artefacts connected with the site.

Kid City

Next to Lowry Park, 7550 North Boulevard, t (813) 935 8441, www.flachildrensmuseum.com

Open Mon 9–2, Tue–Fri 9–5, Sat 10–5 and Sun 12 noon–5

Adm $5

Pre-school children can run riot in this mini-town with themed environments helping them to discover new worlds through role play and fun activities. For physical challenges try the **Under the Sea** and **By the Sea Shore** exhibits where kids can climb and crawl through aquatic environments or role-play their way through a fire station, bank, travel agent and a grocers. Civic buildings include a library, where children can practice reading and writing skills, a hospital, post office, city hall, courthouse, art gallery and a music school. There's even a drive-in fast food restaurant and a call-centre. Future exhibits include a look at pond life and a home life play space. Additional activities include **Saturday Afternoon Adventures** – storytelling at 2pm and **Budding Artists** on Sundays, also at 2pm, where kids engage in a range of arts and crafts. See website for special events and relocation plans.

Lowry Park Zoological Garden

7530 North Boulevard, t (813) 935 8552, www.lowryparkzoo.com

Getting there 5½ miles north of Tampa. From I–275. exit at Sligh (Exit 48) turn west 1 mile to entrance

Open Daily 9.30–5

Adm Adults $11.50, children (3–11) $7.95, individual rides cost extra

A modest-sized but mega-exciting zoo – stop off here before you head on to the more themed animal attractions in the Tampa area to see endangered local species such as manatees, alligators and Florida panthers, along with elephants, giraffe, zebra and tigers. To get your bearings in the park and save tired little legs, take the **Treetop Skyfari** for a bird's-eye view of the zoo. In the interative exhibit area, kids can feed biscuits to the giraffe and nectar for the lorikeets, fish food to the koi carp and meal to the goats. There are pony rides and a merry-go-round and a bright and imaginative play area with tunnels and slides. There's also a children's splash zone so bring a swimsuit for maximum fun. Kids can get up close to jewel-coloured frogs, lizards, and snakes in the discovery centre and feel free as a bird in the free-flight aviary. A jeep muster to herd up sheep, camel rides and a climbing wall are also available.

Museum of Science & Industry (MOSI)

4801 East Fowler Avenue, t (813) 987 6100, 800 995 MOSI, or 877 987 IMAX, www.mosi.org
Open Mon–Fri 9–5, Sat, Sun 9–7
Adm Adults $15.95, children (2–12) $11.95 (including one IMAX movie)

MOS combines exciting exhibition spaces with low-key activities, so you can pace yourselves. Highlights include crawl tunnels simulating aspects of the birth canal; a soft play area where kids can build space rockets and read books; and, best of all, an **Imax dome**. Strictly for footsore parents, there's an excellent (if noisy) foot-massage machine on the third floor. Tornadoes, weather, space, Florida's environment and archaeology are all covered. The fun, interactive '**O is for Oranges**' exhibit is popular so head here first thing or at lunchtime to avoid crowds. Outside explore a **butterfly garden**, experience a tornado or take a guided **three-mile trail** through the backwoods. The museum is expanding to include a '**Kids in Charge**' science facility due to open in June 2005.

Raymond James Stadium

3501 West Tampa Bay Boulevard, t (813) 673 4300, for Buccaneers tickets, t (813) 879 2827, www.raymondjames.com
Getting there I–275 north to Dale Mabry (Exit 23-A)
Tours: Tue–Thu

Home to American football's perennial losers, the Tampa Bay Buccaneers, who surprised everyone by winning the 2003 Super Bowl. Mediocre ever since, their stadium is possibly the best in the NFL. At one end there's a **replica fishing village** stuffed with shops and food stores. The centrepiece is a 103-ft **replica pirate ship** that blasts cannon fire, smoke and confetti when the Buccaneers score.

Ybor City

Chamber of Commerce, 1800 East Ninth Avenue, t (813) 248 3712, www.ybor.org
Getting there Take exit 1 off I–4 West

Have a cigar. Have another cigar. Following business initiatives in the late 1980s and its revival as a National Historic Landmark District in 1991, Ybor City has become a major tourist attraction and thriving centre of commerce. This is a **Latin Quarter** as unique as New Orleans with wrought-iron balconies, restaurants, Cuban bakeries, cafés, shops and clubs. There are quarterly arts and crafts events on Main Street. **Centro Ybor** housed in the Centro Espanol Social Club, is the main shopping and entertainment district with a cinema, museum, visitor centre and stores. **Centennial Park** across from the Museum and State Park hosts a lively farmers' market on Saturday mornings.

Ybor City State Museum

1818 East Ninth Avenue, t (813) 247 6323, www.ybormuseum.org
Open Daily 9–5
Adm $3 (includes a tour of La Casita House Museum and a one-hour historic town tour (Sat 10.30) or 90-minute tour conducted by a cigar-roller's daughter.)

The museum focuses on the social and political organizations that developed as a result of immigrant workers feeling isolated and seeking better living and working conditions, with exhibits on Vicente Martinez Ybor, the early history of Ybor City and the cigar industry. Take a look at the restored worker's cottages (*casitas*) built *c.* 1895, which were relocated in the 1970s along with the Ferlita Bakery. The Mediterranean-style garden has examples of native flora, including fragrant, tropical fruit trees.

Entertainment

Legends Field

4330 North Dale Mabry Highway, t (813) 879 2244.
Tickets From $3–$5.

A near-replica of the famous Yankee Stadium, this is home to New York's biggest team during March spring training and also hosts college, high-school and semi-professional baseball. Legends Field is a minor league ballpark that feels like a major league stadium.

Tampa Theatre

711 Franklin Street, t (813) 274 8981, www.tampatheatre.org
Tours: 11.30 Wed and Sat, suggested donation $5 each

This beautiful movie theatre opened in 1926. After considerable restoration, it now operates a diverse programme of art-house and classic films, concerts and special events. The 1½-hour tour is led by veteran employee Tara Schroeder who tells tales of ghostly goings-on and reveals snippets from the building's history. The tour also includes a demonstration of the Mighty Wurlitzer Theatre Organ.

Did you know?
The Tampa Theatre was the venue for the world premiere of Walt Disney's 101 Dalmatians" on January 25, 1961?

Shopping

The Channelside District has shops for browsing but serious shoppers should head to these venues:

International Plaza & Bay Street

2223 North West Shore Blvd, **t** (813) 342 3790, **www**.shopinternationalplaza.com
Open Mon–Sat 10–9, Sun 12 noon–6

There's a courtesy bus that runs from here to the nearby airport, in case you need some last-minute bargains. This vast indoor mall features 200 outlets, including **Diesel**, **Sisley**, **Quiksilver**, **Abercrombie & Fitch**, **Christian Dior** and **Louis Vuitton**. For kids shops include **Oilily**, **Gymboree**, **A Pea in the Pod**, **The Children's Place**, **Cheeky Baby & Kids**, **Strasburg Children** and **KB-Toys**. There are plenty of places for snacks, including the **Gelateria del Duomo**, alongside several fast-food outlets and restaurants.

Old Hyde Park Shopping District

Hyde Park Village, **t** (813) 251 3500, **www**.oldhydepark.com/
Getting there South of downtown in the historic Hyde Park district between Swann and Dakota Avenues. Take the I–275, I–75 or the Lee Roy Selmon Expressway
Open Mon–Sat 10–7, Sun 12 noon–5

In the heart of Old Tampa, this shopping complex has two art galleries and a seven-screen cinema that shows free family movies on Saturdays from 10am. Family shops include **April Cornell**, **t** (813) 251 3019, **www**.aprilcornell.com, full of lovely hand-printed dresses, some in mother-and-daughter styles, and handmade soft toys; **Brooks Brothers**, **t** (813) 251 4711, **www**.brooksbrothers.com, sells sportswear, suits and tailored outfits for men, women and boys. There's **Pottery Barn Kids**, **t** (813) 253 0964 for imaginative toys, gifts and furniture and there's a branch of the paint-your-own-ceramics studio **Color Me Mine**, **t** (813) 258 8368, **www**.colormeminetampa.com. **Nature's Table Café**, **t** (813) 254 9288 or the **Blackhawk Coffee Café**, **t** (813) 258 1600 are recommended for snacks.

University Mall

2200 East Fowler Avenue, **t** (813) 971 3465, **www**.universitymalltampa.com
Getting there From Tampa, take I–275 North, exit on Fowler Avenue and go east 1 mile.
Open Mon–Sat 10–9, Sun 12 noon–6.

Only a mile from Busch Gardens with 170 shops, including Dillard's department store and kids' fashion, a cinema and restaurants.

AROUND AND ABOUT

Look at this!

Crystal River Archaeological State Park

3400 North Museum Point, **t** (352) 795 3817
Getting there North of Crystal River off Highway 19
Open Daily 8–dusk. Museum: 9–5
Adm $2 per car, $1per bike or pedestrian

At this park-within-a-park (the Crystal River Preserve State Park surrounds the site), there are 30-ft burial mounds, temple mounds and a plaza. The area is being excavated, so you can see the history of this ancient Native American burial site unfold before your eyes. Fishing, bird watching and manatee-spotting are available elsewhere in the park and there are boat tours on Fridays.

Dinosaur World

5145 Harvey Tew Road, Plant City, **t** (813) 717 9865, **www**.dinoworld.net
Getting there Exit 17 from I–4 between Tampa and Orlando. Turn north onto Branch Forbes Road, first left to entrance
Open Daily 9–6
Adm Adults $9.75, children (3–12) $7.75

Creeping Cretacious! Leaping lizards! There are dinosaurs on the loose. Dinosaur World has at least one dinosaur for every letter from A–V. These towering creations are made by artists using up-to-date scientific data. Model makers then create 3-D sculptures using Styrofoam, which are used to make fibreglass moulds. These amazing models are arranged chronologically in various settings. Flail in the jaws of a meat-eater, dig for bones, assemble a dino puzzle or, if you dare, enter the creepy caves or tickle the belly of a T-Rex!

Fantasy of Flight

1400 Boulevard, Polk City, **t** (863) 984 3500, **www**.fantasyofflight.com
Getting there Exit 21 off I–4 between Tampa and Orlando
Open Daily 9–5
Adm Adults $24.95, children (5–12) $13.95, under 5s free

Reach for the skies at this aviation-themed attraction where you can explore man's fascination with flight from early experiments through World Wars I and II until now. The museum is designed to reflect the heyday of air travel with 1930s Art Deco touches including a vintage-style American diner. The hangars house about 50 aircraft, including a Flying Fortress, a Sunderland flying boat and the Ford Tri-Motor plane featured in *Indiana Jones and the Temple of Doom*. Balloon and bi-plane rides are available, at extra cost, height restrictions may apply.

Rogers' Christmas House & Village

103 Saxon Avenue, Brooksville, t (352) 796 2415 or (877) 312 5046
Getting there Between Liberty and Saxon Avenue. North of Tampa take Route 44 southeast to Highway 41. Brooksville is at the intersection of Highways 41 and 98
Open Daily 9.30–5; **Adm** Free

Christmas is here all year, even in the heat of July and August; just be sure not to ring the sleigh bells on Christmas Day. Roger's village comprises five cosy cottages bestrewn with tinsel and bedecked with baubles – though you wouldn't know it from the outside. Explore the rest of this historic town afterwards, nestled among the hills – an unlikely sight in Florida. The **Withacoochee State Forest** is also nearby on Broad Street, **t** (352) 754 6777 or (352) 754 6896 offering nature trails, canoe trips and plenty of hilly paths for mountain bikers.

Nature lovers

Homosassa Springs Wildlife State Park

4150 South Suncoast Boulevard, t (352) 628–5343
Getting there Between Brooksville and Crystal River on Highway 19
Open Daily 9–5.30 (last adm 4)
Adm Adults $9, children (2–12) $5, plus tax

Observe manatee and other marine life from a floating glass observatory, take a walk on the wild side along a 1,600-ft boardwalk through the park among habitats for otters, alligators, bears, bobcats and cougars. There's also an animal encounter exhibit, a children's education centre with hands-on nature activities, two gift shops and a café. Visitors can explore the park between the visitor centre on US 19 and the west entrance by either tram or boat. **Alligator Bob's Ecotours**, **t** (813) 986 3008, are available for family groups ($135 for 2 adults and one child, $45 for individuals) and offer interpretative walks and canoe trips through wetland and coastal hammock environments.

Weeki Wachee Springs Waterpark

6131 Commercial Way, Spring Hill, t (352) 596–2062, www.weekiwachee.com
Getting there 15m south of Homosassa between Highway 19 and Route 50
Open Daily 10–4, later in summer. Buccaneer Bay: Spring holidays and summer only
Adm Adults $13.95–$21.95, children (3–10) $10.95–$15.95, plus tax depending on the season

This eclectic collection of attractions centres around a 72-degree hot spring, which houses an **underwater theatre** where 'mermaids' perform twice daily. The main family attraction is the **Buccaneer Bay water park**, complete with wobbly raft, beach area, slides, boat rides, lazy river, volleyball court, kids' pool and lots of warm water to splash about in. Other attractions include snorkel and canoe trips, a wilderness riverboat ride, reptile and parrot shows and a petting zoo with deer, sheep and goats.

ST. PETERSBURG

Most attractions in downtown St. Petersburg are clustered within walking distance of the pier, with the exception of the **Dali Museum**, which lies south of town, (rumoured to be moving to the Bayfront area in a couple of years), and **Great Explorations** and the **Sunken Gardens**, which are about the same distance to the north. There's a pleasant holiday feel both in and out of town in the tourist hot spots. Locals and holidaying Americans alike are friendly and helpful and the atmosphere is generally pretty relaxed. **Williams Park** is where the main bus interchange is but is also a magnet for vagrants. If you're in doubt as to where to wait for your bus, ask a driver and stand with other groups of tourists.

Getting there 21 miles west of Tampa. From downtown take US 92 across Gandy Bridge or I–275 across Howard Franklin Bridge. From St. Pete's Beach, head east on Pinellas Bayway/Route 682 (toll) to I–275
Getting around The buses and trolleys of the impressive **Pinellas Suncoast Transit Authority**, **t** (727) 530 9911, **www**.PSTA.net run the length and breadth of the coast and downtown St. Petersburg. Services include the No. 4 bus, which runs between Sunken Gardens and the Dali Museum, and No. 35 which accesses the Pier and Baywalk shopping area.

Tourist information

St. Petersburg/Clearwater Area Convention and Visitors Bureau, 14450 46th Street, Suite 108, Clearwater 33762, **t** (727) 464 7200 or (877) 352 3224, **www**.floridasbeach.com

Boyd Hill Nature Park

1101 Country Club Way South, **t** (727) 893 7326.
Getting there From I-275, take Exit 17. Turn east onto 54th Avenue South, then left on Dr. Martin Luther King Jr. Street South, entrance four blocks on left
Open Tue–Thu 9–8, Fri, Sat 9–6, Sun 11–6. Trails close ½ hour before dusk
Adm Adults $2, children (3–16) $1, tram tour: $1 plus adm, daily 1pm; guided tours and camping available

This 245-acre park features nature trails and boardwalks passing through five different ecosystems comprising hardwood hammocks, pine flatwoods, sand scrub, willow marsh and lakeshore. There's a **bird of prey aviary**, picnic areas, a tree-house playground and a gift shop. The park is part of the **Great Florida Birding Trail** for bird-watching enthusiasts and its latest exhibit – **Ripple Effect** – explores how the distinct ecosystems impact on each other, featuring aquatic and animal displays found in and around Lake Maggiore and an interactive crawl-through mole tunnel for children. Children can attend 1–1½ hour **activity tours** (Tue–Fri and Sun at 1, Sat 10 and 1) to learn about alligators, birds, gopher tortoises and wild flowers. Pre-school kids (3–5) can enjoy **Jungle Boogie nature sessions** (Wed 11.15) and babies and toddlers can go on a **Stroller Strut** through the woods (Fri 11.15) learning about safety, toxic plants and animals to avoid, as well as enjoying the fresh air and natural surroundings.

Great Explorations, The Hands-On Museum

1925 4th Street North, **t** (727) 821 8992, **www**.great-explorations.org
Open Mon–Sat 10–4.30, Sun 12 noon–4.30
Adm Adults $8, children (3–11) $7, under 2s free

This interactive science museum offers kids and eager parents the chance to sample stop animation, river estuaries, models that explore cause and effect, such as pulleys and levers, or to wear themselves out learning the logistics of a climbing wall. There's a separate section for the under-6s with soft play, dressing-up clothes and construction bricks. Pick up free leaflets offering interesting facts about Florida manatees, sea-grass beds and estuaries from the display counter upstairs.

The Pier

800 2nd Avenue Northeast, **t** (727) 821 6443, **www**.stpete-pier.com
Open Mon–Thu 10–9, Fri–Sat 10–10, Sun 11–7
Aquarium: Mon–Sat 10–8. Sun 12 noon–6
Adm Free. Parking $3, free Pier trolley service from the Dolphin and Pelican Parking Lots. Aquarium: Adults $2, children free

Despite offering a few shops, an art gallery and a nice little aquarium, this pier, as so often happens, inculcates a sense of hubris. This inelegant, upturned pyramid, built in 1973, replaced the romantic but badly deteriorated Million Dollar Pier, dating from 1926. Still, it's a nice spot to let kids run around outside or watch fishermen cast their lines. Littl'uns (2–6) can join the **Pier Pals Kids' Club** (second Saturday of the month 10.30–12 noon) for games with a popular cartoon or storybook character. You can also hire 2–6-seater cycles here or take a tour in a solar-powered boat or go on a dolphin cruise. Tourist information is on the ground floor. **BayWalk** (*see* p.116) is within walking or trolley distance.

Salvador Dali Museum

1000 3rd Street South, **t** (727) 823 3767, **www**.salvadordalimuseum.org
Getting there Exit 9 off I–275
Open Mon–Sat 9.30–5.30 (Thu to 8) Sun 12 noon–5.30
Adm Adults $13, children (5–9) $3, under 5s free. (Thu from 5, adm $5); Children's tours: $20 for two family members, $10 per extra person

Trace Dali's development from early landscapes and self-portraits through Cubism to Surrealism. The collection includes six vast Masterworks as well as smaller drawings, photographs and sculpture. Kids aged 6–12 can have **Breakfast with Dali** (second Saturday of the month, 9–11) and look at examples of his work with interactive activities and breakfast. Numbers are limited so book ahead.

Science Center

7701 22nd Avenue North, **t** (727) 384 0027
Open Mon–Fri 9–4, Sat 10–4
Adm $5 including laser and planetarium shows, touch tanks and other programmes. Sat: $1 for self-guided tours, $5 for super Saturday events

This 45-year-old science museum houses a 600-gallon marine **touch tank**, a **planetarium**, **laser theatre** and an **observatory**. Displays focus on social and environmental, as well as physical science from snakes and insects in the Animal Room to a history of the achievements of African American inventors.

Outside, visitors can explore a 16th-century **Native American Indian village** with mounds and temples, a cook hut, an Indian garden and replica excavation of a *midden* (rubbish dump). Video message boxes guide you through different aspects of the village.

St. Petersburg Historic Sunken Gardens

1825 4th Street North, **t** (727) 551 3100,
www.stpete.org/sunken
Open Mon–Sat 10–4.30, Sun 12 noon–4.30
Adm Adults $8, children (3–16) $4

An oasis of calm, this characteristic Florida sinkhole includes a Japanese garden, cactus garden and a butterfly garden with a walk-through encounter. The gardens, begun in 1903, are home to over 500 tropical and sub-tropical plants, including native species, aquatic plants and fruit trees. There are fountains, bird displays and pond areas. Tours are offered and festivals, including orchid and butterfly displays and springtime festivities, are hosted. Children must be accompanied at all times.

St. Petersburg Museum of History

335 2nd Avenue Northeast, **t** (727) 894 1052,
www.stpetemuseumofhistory.org
Open Mon–Sat 10–5, Sun 1–5
Adm Adults $5, children (7–17) $2, under 7s free

This small museum takes a fascinating look at the city and the people who shaped it. Highlights include a working replica of the Benoist Airboat, which flew the first scheduled passenger service on January 1, 1914, when pilot Tony Jannua flew Abe Pheil from St. Petersburg to Tampa for $400. Other displays look at the development of the city from its Native American roots and include an Indian dugout and a quilt bearing the names of local families.

Did you know?
Sunshine is such a given in St. Petersburg that in 1910, newspaper owner Lew Brown dubbed it 'The Sunshine City' and distributed free copies of his St. Petersburg Evening Independent every time the city had no sun for an entire day. Since St. Pete's averages 361 days of sunshine a year and holds the Guinness World Record for the most consecutive days of sunshine (768), it was a pretty safe bet. In 40 years, only a handful of copies were given away a year. Sadly, the paper went bust in 1987, but not due to inclement weather, as sister paper the St. Petersburg Times is keen to point out. The Times is not free but is full of local information and makes a good shade when you're enjoying the sun on the beach. Visit online at www.sptimes.com

The Weedon Island Preserve Cultural and Natural History Center

1800 Weedon Island Drive, **t** (727) 453 6500,
www.pinellascounty.org
Getting there From St. Petersburg take the I-275 north, exit 694 (Gandy Bridge Blvd) and go south 3 miles to San Martin Blvd, the park entrance is 1 mile from the intersection with Gandy Bridge Blvd heading east (left)
Open Wed–Sun 10–4. Park: daily 7–dusk.
Tours By reservation only, **t** (727) 453 6506

The centre has two observation decks, an art gallery and exhibits relating to early Native American Indian settlements and offers free, monthy guided hikes and twice-monthly canoe trips through mangroves. The Preserve has self-guided nature and paddle trails, a fishing pier, picnic areas and you can see manatees, dolphins and even sharks from its backwater areas. The saltwater ponds are home to wading birds.

Entertainment

Tropicana Field

One Tropicana Drive, **t** (727) 825 3250,
www.devilrays.com
Adm Season tickets: $1–$195, spring training tickets: $3–$12. Parking $10

Home to major league baseball's newest team, the **Tampa Bay Devil Rays** (Apr–Sept). The stadium is air conditioned and there's a play area and climbing wall for the kids. Spring training games are played in March at nearby Al Lang Stadium (822 2nd Avenue, **t** 727 893 7490).

Shopping

BayWalk

153 2nd Avenue North, **t** (727) 895 9277,
www.baywalkstpete.com
Getting there Corner of 2nd Avenue North and 2nd Street North
Open Mon–Thu 9–9, Fri–Sat 9–11, Sun 12 noon–6

A spacious collection of boutiques, restaurants and cafés. Shop for Birkenstock kids' shoes, at **Happy Feet Plus**, **t** (727) 894 9633, browse the jewellery and clothing stores and pop to **EB Games** for the latest releases on PlayStation et al. There's also a

20-screen cinema with a kids' playroom operated on a first-come first-served basis, so parents can watch the latest thrillers. Live bands perform on Friday and Saturday nights and BayWalk hosts the **ArtWalk Festival**, the first weekend of the month, with booths lined up selling paintings, sculpture and crafts.

Pinellas Suncoast

The beach and metropolitan communities of **St. Petersburg** (*see* p.114), **Tarpon Springs**, **Dunedin** and **Clearwater** all fall under the umbrella (or is that the beach *cabana*?) of the **Pinellas Suncoast**. It's where you'll find some of the best and cleanest beaches in the state. Cyclists, boarders, skaters and super-fit joggers can take to the 37-mile paved **Pinellas Trail**, **t** (727) 464 4751, which runs through parks, suburbs and coastal areas between Tarpon Springs and St. Petersburg along a disused railway route, with refreshment (and Trolley) stops on the way.

Getting there From Tampa Airport: For **Clearwater** follow signs to Route 60 West/Clearwater, go west across Courtney Campbell to US 19, which then links to Alt Highway 19. For **Tarpon Springs** take Route 584 (Hillsborough Avenue/Tampa Road) to US 19 then Alt Highway 19. Alt Highway 19 runs along the coast between Tarpon Springs, **Dunedin** and Clearwater before heading inland towards Largo. Clearwater down to Pass-a-Grille is linked by Route 699

Getting around PSTA (see St. Petersburg, above) The **Suncoast Beach Trolley** runs from Pass-a-Grille and St. Pete's Beach to downtown Clearwater. Look out for the big yellow sun signs along the road. It takes a good 1½ hours to go the 12 miles from St. Pete's up to Clearwater but it's a fun way to travel and great for spotting mansions and luxury cruise boats. Drivers will tell you where to get off for attractions *en route* or where to connect with other services. No. 66 links Clearwater with Tarpon Springs going north and Indian Rocks going south.

Tourist information

St. Petersburg/Clearwater Area Convention and Visitors Bureau, 14450 46th Street, Suite 108, Clearwater, **t** (727) 464 7200 or (877) 352 3224, **www**.floridasbeach.com

Tampa Bay Beaches Chamber of Commerce, 6990 Gulf Boulevard, St. Pete Beach 33706, **t** (727) 360 6957 or (800) 944 1847; **www**.tampabaybeaches.com

Clearwater/Clearwater Beach

Getting there 4 miles south of Dunedin on Alt Highway 19. To get to Clearwater Beach, turn west on Route 60

Getting around Jolley Trolley, Clearwater Beach, **t** (727) 445 1200. Pick-ups every 30 mins daily. Fare $1 This yellow trolley bus runs between Clearwater Beach and Pier 60 (*see* p.118) and downtown Clearwater. Make sure when boarding that you're going in the right direction, since some of the bus drivers are not as 'easy-going' as the name suggests. Services connect with the Suncoast Beach Trolley from South Gulfview Boulevard/Coronado Drive.

Clearwater is a largely suburban district with a downtown district at one end and Clearwater Beach's barrier island at the other. The beach is wide and pleasant with lovely sand offering lots of scope for kite flying, building sandcastles and digging. The big city buzz seems a million miles away when you're looking out across the beach at the calm waters of the gulf. Stay for the sunset, it's worth it.

Captain Memo's Pirate Cruise

Clearwater Marina, 25 Causeway Boulevard, Slip 3, Clearwater Beach, **t** (727) 446 2587, **www**.pirateflorida.com

Open Daily 10 and 2 (not Sun). Sunset Champagne cruises: Apr–Aug 4.30 and 7pm, Nov–Feb 5pm, Sept, Oct and Mar 6pm

Adm Adults $32, children (3–12) $20 (plus tax, includes drinks). Evening cruise: Adults $35, children $20

Right, you landlubbers! it's time to sail aboard the good ship Ransom, the best pirate galleon to sail the seven seas... You can see how easy it is to get carried away! Kids wear moustaches, don pirate hats and engage in water-pistol battles before lining up for the limbo dancing. If you're no good, you walk the plank! Nearby pleasure craft are considered hostile and fired upon at will. Don't forget to load up with pirate booty afterwards from the captain's stash of pirate water pistols, bandanas and Jolly Roger flags.

Clearwater Marine Aquarium

249 Windward Passage, Clearwater, **t** (727) 447 1790, **www**.cmaquarium.org

Getting there Turn right off Memorial Causeway onto Island Way at Island Estates and follow signs

Open Mon–Fri 9–5, Sat 9–4, Sun 11–4

Adm Adults $9, children (3–12) $6.50. Two-hour boat tours: Adults $14.75, children (3–12) $9.50

Meet local and tropical fish, sea turtles, dolphins and river otters at this quiet aquarium complex, which is essentially a research and rehab centre for marine animals unable to survive in the wild, many of which are dependent on humans for treatment and care. Families can watch the daily programme of sessions, which include otter feedings and dolphin displays; they can also feel rays in the touch tank. Marine biologists guide its daily dolphin-spotting **Sea Life Safari Cruises, t** (888) 239 9414, from the aquarium at 11, 1.30 and 4 and Clearwater Beach Marina boat slip at 11.15, 1.45 and 4.25.

Pier 60 Park

Getting there Intersection of Causeway and Gulfview Boulevards, **t** (727) 462 6466
Parking: $1 per hour

This is Clearwater Beach's social centre where everyone converges for the nightly sunset celebration, live entertainment and craft stalls. There are two covered **playgrounds** with nets, twisting slides and bridges, one for under-5s and the other for older kids, both with benches for parents. Pier 60 is also a good spot for **fishing** and **volleyball**. Lifeguards patrol the swimming areas in season. The attractive, landscaped three-acre **park** also incorporates a pavilion, pedestrian boardwalks, showers and bike racks. There are cafés, food shops, beach supplies and water-sports rentals conveniently located nearby.

Sand Key

Getting there Just south of Clearwater Beach on Route 699
Watersport rental, changing rooms, showers, lifeguards all year

Sand Key State Park is sandwiched between the bustling marinas on the outskirts of Clearwater and the exclusive beach homes of Belleair (no gaudy bus signs here!). A stunning emerald-green and dusty-white peninsula jutting into the gulf, Sand Key is a lovely spot. The 90-acre park, also offers fishing, picnic shelters, a playground, toilets and fountains.

Dunedin

Getting there South of Tarpon Springs on Alt 19

Of Scottish origin, this long-established community celebrates its heritage with an annual **Highland Games**. Take a 15-block walking tour through Dunedin's historic buildings, some now antique shops and galleries. There's an enterprising **Fine Art and Children's Art Museum**, 1143 Michigan Blvd, **t** (727) 298-3322, **www**.dfac.org, which offers family programmes and workshops in its imaginative gallery space or take a trip out to **Caladesi State Park** from **Honeymoon Island State Park**, North of Dunedin, 1 Causeway Boulevard, **t** (727) 469 5942, **t** (727) 734 1501 for ferry schedule. Ferries leave for Caladesi Island every hour (30 mins in summer) from 10. Round-trip: Adults $8, children (4–12) $4.50. Kids can play Crusoe to their hearts' content on this lovely island fringed with fine white sand, featuring a nature trail, concessions and picnic area.

Indian shores

Indian Rocks Beach and neighbouring Indian Shores are smart, quiet residential beach communities. Indian Rocks saw development in the 1920s during the Florida land boom when it became a weekend destination for wealthy Tampa folk. It has almost three miles of sandy beaches, which are great for building sandcastles and sunbathing, surfing, snorkelling and also fishing from the pier.

Indian Shores has over two miles of attractive beaches made famous by the **Pelican Man Bird Sanctuary**. There's plenty to do here from swimming and renting Jet Skis to volleyball and fishing. There are two parks offering shady areas for picnics, nature trails, and places to swim and camp.

Pinewood Culture Park

12211 Walsingham Road, t (727) 518 6833, www.gulfcoastmuseum.org
Getting there 2.5 miles east of Indian Rocks Beach, travel east along Route 688, Walsingham Road and follow signs
Open Art museum: Tue–Sat 10–4, (Thu 10–7), Sun 12 noon–4, Botanical Gardens (t (727) 582 2100, www.flbg.org) 7–7, Heritage Garden and Museum Pen Tue–Sat 10–4, Sun 1–4, t (727) 582 2123, free, Welcome Centre Mon–Fri 8–5, Sun 12 noon–4
Adm Adults $5, children (under-10s) free, Sat (10–12 noon) adm free

This 182-acre park is home to some thoroughly engaging attractions. Pack a picnic and stay the day.

The **Art and Sculpture Gallery**, set in the tranquil botanical gardens, focusses on American fine crafts and works by Florida artists from 1960 onwards and offers activites such as monthly **Family Classic Film screenings** and family-orientated festivals.

The **Botanical Gardens** are stunning with palm, rose, tropical fruit and aromatic herb gardens, an

English cottage and an aquatic habitat. Visit the **Welcome Centre** for wildlife tours and encounters with otters, heron, butterflies and eagles, while the 21-acre **Heritage Village** is West Florida's showcase village for architectural styles from the mid-late 18th century. It has 28 structures, including a sugar mill and a church built in 1905, a school, railroad depot and engine, a 1920s store, bandstand and barns full of tools and carriages, as well as houses ranging from a simple log cabin – the oldest structure in the county – to the seven-room **Plant Sumner House**, which had all mod cons, including electricity, running water and indoor plumbing. The museum traces the history of Pinellas County from the Indian-Spanish period to the present. Costumed tour guides bring it all to life.

Suncoast Seabird Sanctuary

18328 Gulf Boulevard, Indian Shores, t (727) 391 6211
Open Daily 9–sunset. One hour tours Wed at 2 and 2nd, 3rd and 4th Sun of the month. Occasional free educational talks on 1st Sun of the month, also at 2
Adm Free (donations appreciated)

The sanctuary entrance is watched over by a large wooden pelican and when you go to the beach, you'll see lots of them looking for a free meal. Many species of bird are cared for here, including woodpeckers, cormorants, owls, hawks, songbirds and, of course, pelicans. Roughly 25–30 injured wild birds are admitted daily and all are cared for. The centre has also successfully mated injured brown pelicans, a captive breeding programme that has been of benefit to wildlife refuges the world over.

Madeira Beach

Getting there

John's Pass Village and Boardwalk

150 John's Pass Boardwalk, Madeira Beach, t (727) 394 0756

Between the relatively calm sands of family-friendly Madeira Beach and the clapboard houses and boardwalks of St. John's Pass Village you can hit the shops for some quality surf gear and chow down at the **Friendly Fisherman Restaurant** in a former lighthouse (*see* Where to Eat, p.127). **Hubbard's Sea Adventures**, Hubbard Marina, **t** (727) 393 1947, **www**.hubbardsmarina.com run deep-sea fishing trips lasting either 5 or 10 hours or overnight. Take your catch to the restaurant afterwards and they'll cook it for you. Families can also opt for a dolphin-watching, sunset or shelling cruise. Costs for excursions are adults $11.95–$19.95, children (2–12) $6–$9.95, plus tax. *See also*, Fort DeSoto Park, p.120.

Tarpon Springs

Getting there Alt Highway 19, off Highway 19 north of St. Petersburg

When Key West lost its sponge business to red tides in the 1880s, Greek divers, aided by deep-sea dive suits, built a successful sponge industry here. You can still see sponges drying on the docks among cafés, shops and bakeries. Visit the **aquarium**, **t** (727) 938 5378, to view sharks, living coral, sponges and over 30 fish species. The **National Historic District** downtown has a fine Greek Orthodox church, a City Hall that provides a programme of arts and entertainment, along with galleries, antique shops, private homes and an assortment of B&Bs.

The Brooker Creek Preserve Environmental Education Center

3940 Keystone Road, Tarpon Springs, t (727) 453 6800; for free guided wilderness hikes (Sat) t (727) 453 6910, www.friendsofbrookercreekpreserve.org
Getting there On Route 582, follow parking signs and walk the boardwalk to the entrance
Open Wed 9–8.30, Thu–Sun 9–4; **Adm** Free

The Environmental Center at this wildlife preserve opened in 2004 with a **3-D theatre**, **herbarium** and 22 fascinating **discovery experiences**, including a tunnel through a gopher tortoise burrow, which you can climb into to see how animals share habitats. There are self-guided **nature trails** along a 1½-mile boardwalk with an observation platform.

St. Pete Beach

Getting there South of Sand Key and Treasure Island along Route 699

This beach and neighbouring Treasure Island is where you'll find most family-friendly resort hotels with entertainment programmes and kids' clubs, along with shopping boutiques and restaurants. **Sunset beach**, in between, has quiet beach bungalows for a more laid-back kind of break. *See* Sleep p.37.

Pass-a-Grille Beach

Getting there Gulf Way between 1st and 21st Avenues

At the southern end of St. Pete's Beach, this is a nice, undeveloped spot for swimming but has few other amenities on the beach, except for a café nearby and toilets on the pier. It's hard to miss the pink paradise of the **Don Cesar Beach Resort**, built in 1928 and now part of the Loews Hotel group (*see* Sleep, p.31). Catch the **Shell Key Shuttle**, 801 Passe-a-Grille Way, **t** (727) 360 1348, **www**.shellkeyshuttle.com (adults $14, children under 12 $7, plus tax) from the pier for a dolphin eco-tour on unspoiled **Shell Key**, a small barrier island where families can enjoy shelling, bird watching and sunbathing. Sunset cruises by reservation.

Tierra Verde

Fort DeSoto Park

3500 Pinellas Bayway South, Tierra Verde,
t (727) 866 2484, www.fortdesoto.com
Open 8–dusk; **Adm** Free

Fort DeSoto Park has two beaches with picnic, play and designated swimming areas, which visitors should adhere to due to strong currents. The fort retains four of its original 12-inch mortars and six-inch rapid-fire rifle guns, and the museum, housed in a former guardhouse, gives information about the fortifications here and at Fort Dade on Egmont Key (see below). There is a 90-minute guided tour (Sat at 10) and seasonal nature walks and events.

Fort Dade is also a wildlife refuge and bird sanctuary (accessible from here on a Hubbard's tour – *see* p.119). Originally the larger of the two forts, it is gradually eroding and has fewer buildings. Elsewhere on **Egmont Key** there is a good shelling beach, a lighthouse and nature trails through gopher tortoise and rattlesnake territory. Don't allow children to wander from the path or kick at sand mounds that might contain tortoise eggs. Bring a picnic. There are no facilities on the island. Toilets are at Fort DeSoto Park or on the ferry.

SARASOTA

The trip from St. Petersburg to Sarasota on I–275 crosses the Sunshine Skyway Bridge, an amazing feat of engineering that at night looks like a spider's web strung across the black water. The old bridge it replaces has been turned into two piers, one (on the Tampa side) 1½ miles long, the other ¾ mile.

This side of the bridge, the mood changes as you leave the business district and head into the leafy suburbs of Bradenton and Sarasota. The barrier islands to the west are very attractive from the crown of beaches around **Anna Maria Island** down to not-so-sleepy **Siesta Key**. Sarasota is pretty, with characteristic low-rise neighbourhoods shrouded in luxuriant foliage. It is best known for its circus history when ringmaster John Ringling brought his troop to town in 1927. He bought his first property in Sarasota in 1911 and over the years established a winter estate (*see* p.121) with a priceless art collection, which is now home to the **State Art Museum of Florida** and the **Circus Museum**.

Getting there 37 miles from St. Petersburg. Take I–275 south and either take US 41 via Bradenton or I–75 to Sarasota Exit 210. Both routes link Tampa in the north to Naples in the south. I–75 is faster but if you're not in a hurry take the more scenic US 41, which takes in parts of the coast.

Getting around SCAT, **t** (941) 861 1234 links north and south Sarasota with the downtown area. Bus No.11 runs to Siesta Key, No. 28 goes to Longboat Key and No. 4 to Lido Key. Buses do not run on Sundays.

Tourist information

Sarasota Convention and Visitors Bureau,
655 North Tamiami Trail, **t** (941) 957 1877 or (800) 522 9799, **www**.sarasotafl.org

Things to see and do

Bayfront Plaza

Bayfront Drive (US 41), downtown Sarasota

This is the place to catch a sightseeing cruise or just wander looking at fancy boats. **Enterprise Sailing Charters**, **t** (941) 951 1833, **www**.sarasota-sailing.com offer **Home of the Stars** trips combined with dolphin watching, daily from 8am–sunset. For deep-sea fishing try **Flying Fish Fleet**, **t** (941) 366 3373, **www**.flyingfishfleet.com who run 4-, 6- or 8-hour trips from 7am–9pm daily.

G. Wiz

Blivas Science and Technology Center, 1001 Blvd of the Arts, **t** (941) 906 1851, **www**.gwiz.org
Getting there Off US 41, just north of Bayfront Plaza, turn left at Blvd of the Arts
Open Tue–Sat 10–5, Sun 1–5
Adm Adults $7, children (2–18) $5, free adm first Wed of the month from 5–8

At the **Gulfcoast Wonder** and **Imagination Zone** (GWIZ) get ready for the appliance of science. This well laid out science centre is housed in the futuristic pyramid-topped Blivas building, itself a working example of scientific endevour. Interactive areas include an **EnergyZone** exploring light, sound, electricity and magnetism, a build-it-yourself **TechZone** and a **WaveZone**, a sort of hands-on music lab. Kids can also meet bees, fish, snakes and turtles, dig for fossils, play with lasers and get use the sprint track in the **BodyZone**. There's an area for toddlers with giant soap bubbles and a funky science-themed play area with wind chimes and a suspension bridge.

John and Mabel Ringling Estate

Ringling Estate, 5401 Bay Shore Road,
t (941) 351 1660, www.ringling.org
Open Daily 10–5.30.
Adm Adults $15, under 12s free. Art museum: Free Sat

This value-for-money attraction is becoming increasingly family-friendly with several new additions planned to open in 2006. Of these, the **Tibbals Learning Center** is likely to have the most appeal for kids with a 16-inch replica circus complete with parade, railway cars, sideshows and a 4-ft-high big top, lovingly handcrafted with over a million pieces.

In the meantime, the **Circus Museum** contains costumes, circus wagons, human cannons, clown regalia and props for kids to dress up.

There's also John Ringling's opulent palazzo **Cà D'Zan** ('House of John' in Venetian dialect), a 32-room, 4-storey fusion of Gothic, Italian Renaissance and Baroque architectural styles, rescued by a $16-million restoration project. Think Great Hall meets the Medicis with a hint of Louis XIV and you're on track. The gardens of this 66-acre estate offer several lakes, a rose garden, fountains and statuaryr. Book guided tours of the house in advance, **t** (941) 358 3180.

The **Art Museum**'s vast collection of Old Masters includes several floor-to-ceiling Rubens tapestry cartoons and works by Hals, Van Dyck and Guercino. To pace the day make use of the two gift shops and the **Banyan Café** for pit-stops between attractions.

Marie Selby Botanical Gardens

811 South Palm Avenue, t (941) 366 5731,
www.selby.org
Getting there South of Bayfront Plaza off US 41
Open Daily 10–5; **Adm** Adults $12, children (6–11) $6
Café, plant shop

Walk the paved paths of these delightfully shady gardens, browse the **Tree Lab** and the **Tropical House** with its stunning orchids, palm- and mangroves and botanical art exhibitions. Kids will love watching the Poison Dart frogs and Koi carp, as well as exploring the shoreline habitat and butterfly garden. From mid- to end-December the gardens are decorated with illuminated rainforest creatures and there are other seasonal activities. Call for details of this and other special events.

Mote Marine Laboratory and Aquarium

1600 Ken Thompson Parkway, t (941) 388 2451 or
(800) 691–MOTE, www.mote.org
Open Daily 10–5. Boat tours, **t** (941) 388 4200, daily at 11, 1.30 and 4. Book in advance
Adm Adults $12, children (4–12) $8, under 3s free
Boat tours: Adults $24, children (4–12) $20
Aquarium and boat tour: Adults $30, children $24

This is a great for getting a clear picture of Florida's diverse marine life. It began with shark research and has become a scientific lab and rehabilitation centre for fish, dolphins, sea turtles, manatees as well. Highlights are the giant squid in formaldehyde, the ocean-going eco-tour where you can analyze a catch at sea and study the different species you find and the brilliant 12-minute film *Shark Attack*, which puts you in the driver's seat as the ocean's most efficient predator – the mum-to-be shark.

Sarasota Bay Explorers run by the aquarium offers daily boat tours, between City Island and Siesta Key led by a marine biologist, kids can see manatees and bottlenose dolphins and pelican and egret nests on the outlying islands. The trip also includes a nature walk and the chance to look at sea creatures, including stone crabs, puffer fish and seahorses scooped right out of the sea. Kayak tours are also available. See also the next-door bird sanctuary (*see* below).

Pelican Man's Bird Sanctuary

1708 Ken Thompson Parkway, t (941) 388 4444,
www.pelicanman.org
Open Daily 10–5
Adm Adults $6, children (5–13) $2, under 4s free

Next door to the Mote (*see* above), spare time to meet the 270-odd residents of this sanctuary where brown and white pelicans, woodpeckers, owls, hawks, gulls, sandpipers, geese, heron, ibis and many other species recuperate from injuries.

The sanctuary cares for the birds in a natural habitat while also teaching visitors about the importance of protecting wild birds from fishing lines and other sporting hazards. The sanctuary also runs **boat tours** from the Holiday Inn Marina, 7150 North Tamiami Trail, to view shorebirds and sea birds and other marine life. Call for morning and lunchtime weekly trips.

Sarasota Classic Car Museum

5500 North Tamiami Trail, t (941) 355 6228, www.sarasotacarmuseum.org
Open Daily 9–6
Adm Adults $8.50, children (13–17) $5.75, (6–12) $4, under 6s free
Collectables shop, limo service

This purpose-built 1950s museum showroom has so many cars they've even had to park one on the roof! The main building features a timeline from the late 1880s to now. See John Ringling's collection of Rolls Royces and 'Cars of the Stars', including John Lennon's Mercedes Roadster and Paul McCartney's Mini Cooper. There's also a vintage gaming arcade and camera and photography displays.

Sarasota Jungle Gardens

3701 Bay Shore Road, t (941) 355 5305, www.sarasotajunglegardens.com
Open Daily 9–5; **Adm** Adults $11, children (3–12) $7
Café, gift shop, shell museum

Another place to relax, this time with bird, critter and reptile shows, as well as nature trails, streams and lakes set within 16-acres of tropical gardens. There's a kiddie jungle, bird of prey exhibit and meet the keeper sessions at 1 and 4pm.

Sarasota Ski-A-Rees Show

City Island, behind Mote Marine, t (941) 388 1666, www.skiarees.com
Open Feb–May Sun at 2 and select holiday dates
Adm Free.

Fab and free formation water-ski show from behind the aquarium. Yes, it's real!

Entertainment

Van Wezel Performing Arts Hall

777 North Tamiami Trail, t (941) 953 3366, www.vanwezel.org
Backstage tour 1st Tue of the month, Oct–May 10am, $5 per person

The purple clamshell right on the bay is Sarasota's other thoroughly modern landmark, built in 1968 by the Frank Lloyd Wright Foundation. Apart from a regular programme of concerts (classical, jazz and pop), dance and Broadway shows, it also hosts family productions including circus acts and musicals. Visitors can ook in on free pre- and post-theatre discussions, which are open to all (although age-specific restrictions may apply).

Shopping

Head downtown every Saturday (7–12 noon) for the **farmers' market** between Lemon Avenue and Main Street and art lovers will find plenty at **Towles Court Artist Colony**, 1950 Adams Lane, **t** (941) 365 8683, **www**.towlescourt.com (open Tue–Sat 11–4), which is an entire block of artists' homes, studios, and galleries, grouped around an Art Centre.

Prime Outlets at Ellenton

5461 Factory Shop Boulevard, Ellenton, t (941) 723 1150, www.primeoutlets.com
Getting there North of Bradenton. From I–75 take exit 224. Turn left then go left ¼ mile onto 60th Avenue and the entrance is ¼ mile on the left
Open Mon–Sat 10–9, Sun 11–6

Okay, so it's a fair way out of town but this is the major outlet mall in the area, and is the best place to do discount label shopping on a grand scale. Just remember to leave yourselves some spare cash for Sarasota's lovely boutique shops as well. Active kids are particularly well catered for with **Gap**,**Big Dog Sportswear**, **Quiksilver** and **Swim Mart**, plus **Nike** and **Reebok Factory Stores**. For adults, there are the likes of **DKNY**, **Polo Ralph Lauren**, **Tommy Hilfiger** and **Versace**. There's a food court plus restaurants, a children's playground and an ATM. The Customer Service Centre has free strollers, a lost and found department and tourist information point.

St. Armand's Circle

300 Madison Drive, t (941) 388 1554, www.starmandscircleassoc.com
Getting there From Sarasota head west and follow signs to St. Armand's Key. Cross Ringling Causeway Bridge and Sarasota Bay to St. Armand's Circle
Open Nov–Apr 10–9, May–Oct 10–6

This arrangement of 140 boutiques and restaurants set out like a Ludo board amidst lush tropical landscaping, courtyards and patios is a classy joint, akin to Windsor or Wilmslow in Cheshire. Try **Ladies Tee** for golf gear, **Breezin' Up** for beachwear, **Oh My Gauze** for floaty cotton and gorgeous jewellery and **Brighton Collectibles** for accessories. Our favourites were: **Little Bo-Tique** for girl's frocks and playwear, **Dream Weaver** for American 'artwear' and **Foxy Lady West** for those dressed-to-kill occasions. The four ice cream parlours will, no doubt, appeal to the kids. Finish off at **Circle Books**, 478 John Ringling Blvd, **t** (941) 388 2850, **www**.circlebooks.net, which stocks children's books, fiction and books on Florida.

Special trips

Myakka River State Park

13207 Route 72, Sarasota, t (941) 361 6511 for park information, t (941) 365 0100 for tours

Getting there 9 miles southeast of Sarasota on Route 72

Open Daily 8–dusk

Adm $5 per car, $2 single passenger, $1 per bike or pedestrian. One-hr boat and tram tours: Adults $8, children (6–12) $4

The Myakka River State Park is a 35,000-acre tract of land cut in two by Route 72, a lake in each part. There are **airboat rides** on the upper lake and **tram safaris** to take you through the different habitats from shady hammocks and pine flatwoods to wetlands and, a unique feature of the area, dry open prairies. There are also **hiking trails** but, owing to the exposed nature of the terrain, some are more suitable for experienced hikers than families. If the kids don't mind heights, let them walk an 85ft-long **boardwalk**, 25ft up in the air, originally built for researching into treetop environments. It's an exhilarating, and yet totally secure, experience and offers magnificent views. There are mesh side panels and sturdy railing planks to guide you. Ranger-led walks are on Saturday mornings. **Camping, fishing, bird watching** and **canoeing** are also available.

AROUND AND ABOUT

Anna Maria Island

Just 40 minutes' from Sarasota, Anna Maria is an old-fashioned beach retreat where one of the most pleasant pastimes is to stroll along the 700-ft **City Pier**, at the northeast end of the island. Built in 1910, it offers spectacular views over the bay and the **Sunshine Skyway** and you can stop for a bite to eat in the restaurant or fish for your own supper. If you're looking to avoid the crowds, the **Bayfront Park** is a peaceful spot, also offering toilets and picnic facilities. Bring a picnic or hop on the trolley to another beach for lunch.

Getting there US 41 north to Bradenton then Route 64 west over the Anna Maria Island Causeway

Getting around Manatee Trolley, **t** (941) 749 7116. Free trolley rides round the island depart every 20 mins and connect with other Bradenton services

Tourist information

Anna Maria Island Chamber of Commerce, 5313 Gulf Drive North, Holmes Beach, **t** (941) 778 1541, **www.annamariaislandchamber.org**

Anna Maria Island Historical Society Museum

402 Pine Avenue, **t** (941) 778 0492

Open Tue–Thu and Sat only; May–Sept 10–12.30, Oct–Apr 10–3

Adm Free (donations appreciated)

Step inside a former 1920s icehouse for a potted history of the island. Listen to video archives made by residents, browse photographs, books and old island maps, as well as viewing the shell collections and island artefacts. There's also a gift shop.

Coquina Beach

At the southernmost point of the island, off Gulf Drive

Coquina Beach's wide white sands are only interrupted here and there by a few amenities such as swing sets and modest play equipment for the kids, shady picnic areas, toilets and showers. Lifeguards are on duty and there's a pleasant nature trails to follow.

Manatee Beach

40th Street and Gulf Drive, Holmes Beach

This is the business end of the island where you find the most facilities including lifeguards, a children's playground, toilets and showers, picnic tables, café and a fishing pier.

Bradenton

A prosperous region full of sugar plantations in the 1800s, Bradenton boasts a historic waterfront district on the banks of the Manatee River. It is home to the South Florida Museum and is a popular spot for fishing with freshwater and pier fishing facilities, as well as deep-sea charters. It's also the easiest place to access the lovely beaches of Anna Maria Island via SR 64.

Getting there 40 miles south of Tampa, follow I–75 south for 5 miles from the I–275 intersection. Follow Route 70 from Arcadia, then take Exit 43 off I–75 north to Bradenton

Tourist information

Bradenton Area Convention and Visitors Bureau. P.O. Box 1000, Bradenton, **t** (941) 729 9177, **www.flagulfbeaches.com**

DeSoto National Memorial Park

75th Street Northwest, Bradenton,
t (941) 792 0458, www.nps.gov/deso/
Open Daily 9–5; **Adm** Free

The park commemorates Hernando DeSoto's arrival on Florida soil in 1539 and his subsequent march across the American southeast. Visitors can wander around a re-created Indian village and follow an audio or nature trail through the park. Kids can try on a piece of armour or pick up a Junior Ranger Booklet from the Visitor Centre and answer questions to obtain a free badge. From Dec to mid-April park rangers dress up as 16th-century explorers and American Indian tribesmen to perform demonstrations and give talks about DeSoto's controversial expedition (*see* History p.4).

Manatee Village Historical Park

604 15th Street East, Bradenton, t (941) 741 7165
Getting there 15th Street East and 6th Avenue East, 1 block south of Route 64
Open Mon–Fri 9–4.30, Sun 1.30–4.30 (closed Sun July–Aug); **Adm** Free

There are nine buildings of local historical significance in the park, all built between 1860 and 1918. There's a general store with staff dressed as pioneers and hands-on activity areas for kids, a Cracker farmhouse, a school, smokehouse, boat-works, church and a courthouse. There are nice areas for picnicking under the trees.

South Florida Museum

201 10th Street West, Bradenton, t (941) 746 4131, www.southfloridamuseum.org
Open Tue–Sat 10–5, Sun 12 noon–5
Adm Adults $9.50, children (5–12) $5, under 5s free with a paying adult

The museum traces Southwest Florida's development from prehistoric times through to now. A hunt diorama covers extinct species such as Mastodons, sabre-toothed cats and bison. Families can also view fossil, bird, and shell collections and marvel at the size of an 11-ft prehistoric shark's jaw. In the **aquarium** kids can also meet Snooty the manatee who has lived here since 1949 and his most recent house guests, rescued manatees that the museum looks after until they can be released into the wild. There are manatee programmes daily at 10.30, 12.30, 2 and 3.30. The museum also boasts a state-of-the-art **planetarium**, with stadium-style seating, a 180-degree projection dome and surround sound.

Buckets and spades

Longboat Key

A pretty, upmarket enclave popular with golfers and the tennis set. You're best off staying in a resort on the island if you want to make use of its lovely quiet beaches where visitors can sift for sand dollars or ride the 12-mile-long paved bike path.

The northern end is the least exclusive area offering public beach access along Gulf of Mexico Drive at Broadway Street, Atlas Street and Gulfside Road. There are no facilities available on the beach.

Getting there

Route 789 spans the tiny pass from Anna Maria Island to Longboat Key

Tourist information

Longboat Key Chamber of Commerce, Whitney Beach Plaza, 6854 Gulf of Mexico Drive, t (941) 383 2466, **www.**longboatkeychamber.com

Siesta Key

Midnight Pass Road at Beach Way Drive, Siesta Key
Getting there South of downtown Sarasota, via Route 72 to Siesta Key

Along the wide sands you'll find covered picnic areas, volleyball nets, tennis courts, toilets, showers, lifeguards on duty and gift shops. Behind the beach there's a good playground and playing fields. Its popular but there's lots of room and if you stay in a beach bungalows (*see* Sleep p.37) you can watch the sun rise. Get here early to park.

Venice

Venice is the West Coasts' answer to Lyme Regis, only here you will pick up fossilized shark's teeth rather than dinosaur bones. The local shops sell sieves for panning for 'black gold' on the beaches, which are replenished from a sharks' graveyard on an offshore reef. **Caspersen Beach** is sharks' tooth central and has toilets, boardwalks, picnic areas and nature trails. At **Manasota Beach**, a mile on, there are lifeguards, volleyball courts and other facilities. **North Jetty Beach** is good for surfing and fishing and popular with families for picnicking. Work is currently underway to improve access for families between the parkland and the beach.

Getting there

18 miles south of Sarasota on Highway 41

Tourist Information

Venice Area Chamber of Commerce, 597 Tamiami Trail South, Venice, **t** (941) 488 2236, **www**.venicechamber.com

Look at this!

Gamble Plantation Historic State Park

3708 Patten Avenue, Ellenton, **t** (941) 723 4536, **www**.floridastateparks.org/gambleplantation
Getting there From I–75 take exit 43 and then go west on US 301
Open: Park: 8–dusk, Visitor centre: Thu–Mon 8–4.30 (closed 11.45–12.45) Tours: 9.30 and 10.30 and 1, 2, 3 and 4
Adm Visitor center: Free, Mansion: Adults $5, children (6–12) $3

This is a genuine South Florida Plantation home built by slaves in the late 1840s within the grounds of Major Robert Gamble's 3,400-acre sugar plantation. He left in 1856 when crop losses and a fall in the price of sugar left him in severe debt. After that the site was largely neglected until the Civil War, when Union Troops burned the sugar mills believing the site to be a strategic post for the Confederates. The mansion, although in disrepair, was unharmed. The site and mansion were restored in 1925.

Historic Spanish Point

500 North Tamiami Trail, Osprey, **t** (941) 966 5214, **www**.historicspanishpoint.org
Open Mon–Sat 9–5, Sun 12 noon–5. Living History Performances: Jan–Apr on Sunday afternoons
Adm Adults $7, children (6–12) $3

This spot on Little Sarasota Bay is where early man once crafted his tools, discarded the remains of his shellfish dinner and sat back to watch the sunset. Some several thousand or so years after these first settlers, the Webb family decided it would make a good place to start a farm and they cultivated the land for citrus crops for about 40 years. In 1911, the property was sold to a Mrs Potter Palmer, a wealthy widow who had the foresight (and indeed the cash) to preserve the ancient Indian burial mound and shell middens, as well as a number of important pioneer buildings alongside her own designs for peaceful landscaped gardens.

Oscar Scherer State Park

1843 South Tamiami Trail, Osprey, **t** (941) 483 5956
Getting there Off US 41, two miles south of Osprey and six miles south of Sarasota
Open 8–dusk
Adm $4 per car, $1 per bike or pedestrian

Just south of Sarasota, this is a nice place to spend a quiet hour or two communing with nature. The park's pine and shrubby flatwoods provide an important environment for the threatened Florida scrub jay. There are bird walks on Thursday mornings to spot these and other birds, such as bald eagles, warblers and woodpeckers. On Wednesday mornings you can join ranger-led canoe trips out on South Creek in the hope of seeing wading birds, otters and alligators; on Friday and Sunday mornings take a guided nature trail. In addition there are fishing, picnicking and swimming areas on Lake Osprey. *See also* Historic Spanish Point.

Solomon's Castle

4533 Solomon Road, Ona, **t** (863) 494–6077, **www**.solomonscastle.com
Getting there Take Exit 42 off I–75, turn left on Route 64 and go east, turn right to Route 665 and go south, turn left and then bear right on Solomon Road
Open 2 Oct–Jun Tue–Sun 11–4
Adm Adults $10, children (under 12) $4

If you think your eyes are deceiving you, look again. Yes, it's a castle and no, you haven't been transported to Mountfitchet near Stanstead, England – you're still in Florida and, yes, it is a real castle, albeit a castle made from recycled materials. Howard Solomon is the man behind the mirage, a sculptor who lives and works on the premises and built the moat, drawbridge and the castle within the grounds of his oak- and palmetto-shaded kingdom. The façade of this shiny stronghold is made up of discarded newspaper offset plates and has a tower and all the usual crenellations you'd expect to see, plus around 80 interpretive stained glass windows featuring mythical and real flora and fauna. Wander inside to see more examples of Howard's work with found objects and don't forget to pay a visit to **The Boat in The Moat**, a replica 16th-century Spanish galleon that houses the Castle's restaurant. There's a lovely nature trail, a gift shop featuring some of Howard's wares and overnight accommodation is available to all you fairytale princesses out there.

Tampa

The Loading Dock Sandwich Pub

100 Madison Street, Tampa, **t** (813) 223 6905
Open Breakfast and lunch daily (*inexpensive*)

This friendly restaurant is very popular with locals and serves up a mean grouper sandwich. Kids are well catered for with fresh juices, deli sandwiches and salads.

Romanos Macaroni Grill

17641 Bruce B Downs Blvd, **t** (813) 977 7798
(Branch: 14904 North Dale Mabry Highway, **t** (813) 264 6676)
Open lunch and dinner (*inexpensive–moderate*)

Part of a chain of family-friendly restaurants that serve an extensive Italian fare, this branch is close to Busch Gardens and other attractions northeast of Tampa. The kids' menu includes wood-fired pizza, pesto ravioli or chicken with steamed broccoli, or kids might like to choose from the 'create your own' pasta from the main menu. The restaurant also does family meals to go for groups of 8–10.

Ybor City

Columbia Restaurant

2117 East 7th Avenue, **t** (813) 248 4961
(*expensive–very expensive*)

A Tampa institution, Columbia is as much a place to go for the atmosphere as a place to eat. Now 100 years old, the restaurant has branches in **Sarasota**, **St. Petersburg**, **Clearwater Beach**, **Celebration**, **West Palm Beach** and **St. Augustine**. There are 11 dining rooms (seating a staggering 1,600 guests), including a courtyard and a central stage area offering live jazz (Thu–Sat nights) and flamenco dancers who tour the restaurant (Mon–Sat). The menu is Spanish/Cuban featuring the restaurant's own signature salad, chicken with rice and unbeatable paella. Children can choose from steak, Cuban sandwich or chicken and fries or graze from the extensive Tapas menu that is made for sharing.

Dish

1600 East 8th Avenue, **t** (813) 241 8300
(*inexpensive*)

Choosy children will like being able to pick whatever they like from the extensive Asian-influenced menu. Grab a palette with a sauce bowl and main meal bowl fill it with fresh vegetables, pasta, and stir-fried meats, fish and seafood from the Teppenyaki grill. Rice and tortillas are served at your table and vegetarian meals are cooked separately. The more trips you make the more you pay; a simple concept that makes these restaurants highly popular of an evening.

Around and About

Homosassa

Riverside Crab House

Homosassa Riverside Resort, 5297 South Cherokee Way, **t** (352) 628 2474 (*inexpensive–moderate*)

The place to come to get crabs, steamed and ready to crack open with a mallet. If you're not keen on doing it all yourself, opt for the garlic crabs, which have been pre-cracked, or try some tasty crab cakes. Family crab platters are also available if you're not sure what to try. The clams, mussels and crayfish aren't half bad. The kids' menu offers spaghetti marinara, fish or chicken fingers, hot dogs or burgers, all served with dessert and a 'river side' dish of rice, potatoes, vegetables or salad. It costs $2.95–$4.95, for kids under 10 only.

St. Petersburg

Captain Al's Waterfront Restaurant

The Pier, 800 2nd Avenue Northeast, **t** (727) 898 5800
(*inexpensive–moderate*)

The Little Mate's menu is for children under 10 and includes hamburger, fish fingers, chicken and hot dog and fries or spaghetti marinara. The main menu features crab cakes, snow crab, Florida lobster tail, oysters, scallops, plus sandwiches and burgers. There's ample seating indoors and out overlooking the bay.

Dish

197 2nd Avenue North, **t** (727) 894 5700
(*inexpensive*)

Another in this popular Asian chain. *See* Ybor City.

Dockside Eatery

800 2nd Avenue Northeast, **t** (727) 895 4460
(*inexpensive*)

This food court inside the Pier complex has outlets offering pizza, burgers, sandwiches, Chinese dishes and ice cream.

Skyway Jacks

2795 34th Street South, t (727) 866 3217
Open Breakfast and lunch (*inexpensive*)

No frills motorway caf-style diner with southern specialities such as sausage gravy over biscuits, meatloaf and grits. You can have your eggs fried or scrambled but definitely not poached. The kids will like the Southern French toast, Belgian waffles and pancakes.

Around and About

Clearwater

Frenchy's Rockaway Grill

7 Rockaway Street off Gulfview Boulevard, Clearwater Beach, t (727) 446 4844
(*inexpensive–moderate*)

If you fancy some fresh grilled grouper or a seafood salad, pop in for lunch at this casual café right on the beach.

Island Way Grill

20 Island Way, t (727) 461 6617, www.islandwaygrill.com
Open Mon–Thu 4–10, Fri, Sat 4–11, Sun Champagne Brunch: 11–3, dinner 4–10 (*inexpensive–expensive*)

This is a great option for Sunday brunch where the buffet table is loaded with everything from fresh salad, pasta, hot and cold meats, fish and seafood to cheeses, breads, pastries, cakes and desserts. The crab salad is sublime; they do a nice range of wines and it's good value for money. There's spacious indoor seating and a large, sunny waterside deck. They cater for large parties, so get there early for Sunday lunch or opt to eat early between 4 and 5pm.

Dunedin

Kelly's

319 Main Street, t (727) 736 5284
Open Breakfast, lunch and dinner
(*inexpensive–moderate*)

'For Just About Anything', is their motto and it's not wrong. The kids will rave about this place -they can actually get peanut butter and jelly sandwiches served with fries! The lunchtime and afternoon menus are mostly sandwiches and snacks, but parents can dine on anything and everything from mussels, ahi tuna salsa, smoked fish spread or seafood chowder for starters, and apple chipotle pork loin, ginger chili smoked shrimp and seafood cakes among many other tasty mains. So now you know what the 'just about anything' refers to.

Indian Rocks Beach

Crabby Bill's

401 Gulf Boulevard, Indian Rocks Beach, t (727) 595 4825 (*inexpensive–moderate*)

Family-friendly casual dining specializing in crack 'em and eat 'em blue, Alaskan, snow, and stone crab claws, plus fish and shrimp dishes.

The Lobster Pot

17814 Redington Shores, t (727) 391 8592
Open Mon–Thu 4.30–10, Fri, Sat 4.30–11, Sun 4–10 (*moderate–very expensive*)

Lobster lovers will be well served at this casual restaurant that's popular with both locals and visitors. Maine lobsters, lobster tails, stuffed lobsters, Alaskan king crab, Florida stone crab and tuna are among the selections at this high quality establishment. The children's menu offers lobster and mini filet mignon among other choices.

Madeira Beach

Friendly Fisherman Seafood Restaurant

150 John's Pass Boardwalk, Madeira Beach, t (727) 391 6025
Open Breakfast, lunch and dinner (*moderate*)

You can't miss the lighthouse and the big red fish sign pointing out the Friendly Fisherman to passers-by. Stop in for fresh seafood and fish (or bring your own to have cooked). The kids' menu features pancakes and toast for early risers and hot dog, pasta, shrimp served with a side of sweet or baked potato, fries or coleslaw for lunch or dinner. Watch the fishing boats ply their trade and keep a keen eye out for dolphins in the bay.

Tarpon Springs

Hellas Restaurant & Bakery

785 Dodecanese Boulevard, t (727) 934 8400
(*inexpensive–moderate*)

This family style restaurant features traditional Greek fare such as moussaka, keftedes, shish ke bobs, Greek salad or dolmades, all served with rice, potatoes, bread and fruit. Children can choose from

Greek-style spaghetti, moussaka, pastitsio, burger or hot dogs. There is ample outdoor seating and the bakery is good for sticky pastries, cakes and other picnic items.

Pappas Riverside Restaurant

10 West Dodecanese Boulevard, t (727) 937 5101 (*moderate–expensive*)

Pappas Restaurants are famous in this neck of the woods, having served the area since the 1920s. The present eatery overlooks the Anclote River and serves Greek platters, seafood dishes such as Peperi Garethes (peel and eat shrimp in a citrus vermouth sauce), soups and Pappas famous salad. The children's menu features spaghetti, shrimp, ribs or port souvelakia and comes with a drink and ice cream for $6.95.

St. Pete's Beach

Bermudas

Tradewinds Island Grand, 5500 Gulf Boulevard, t (727) 367 6461

Open Dinner only from 5pm (*moderate–expensive*)

This steak-and-seafood resort restaurant offers spacious family dining and attentive service. They don't mind if your kids aren't up to a full meal and will gladly adapt dishes for younger taste, plus give you a box for a carry out. The surf and turf and the tuna appetizers are particularly memorable.

Captain Al's Waterfront Restaurant

9555 Blind Pass Marina, St. Pete's Beach, t (727) 367 5010 (*inexpensive–moderate*)

Another in the chain. *See* St. Petersburg p.126.

Sea Critters Café

2007 Pass-a-Grille Way, t (727) 360 3706, www.seacritters.com (*moderate*)

This cheery waterfront restaurant offers steak, seafood and chicken dishes, salads and sandwiches. Kids can admire the under-the-sea décor or sit out on the dockside watching the catfish. Children have their own colour-in menu, or you can opt for a seafood combo platter to share. Specialities include crab cakes, cedar planked salmon and lobster roll (*moderate*).

Wharf Seafood Restaurant

2001 Pass-A-Grille Way, t (727) 367 9469 (*inexpensive–moderate*)

Great casual spot for dining, serving up peel and eat shrimp, crab claws and fish.

Woody's Waterfront

7308 Sunset Way, t (727) 360 9165 (*moderate*)

Prop up your surfboard and meet with the locals at this casual waterfront restaurant. There's a beach bar and entertainment, plus a menu offering seafood, chicken, fish and burgers.

Sarasota

Marina Jack

2 Marina Plaza, Bayfront, t (941) 365 4232, www.marinajacks.com

Open Daily for lunch and dinner, Sunday brunch from 12 noon (*moderate–expensive*)

This smart waterfront restaurant has a casual downstairs area where families can sit in comfort and gaze out at the boats in the bay. The food is mainly seafood and fish dishes, including spot-on surf and turf, plus sandwiches, soups and salads. The wine is excellent too. Upstairs is more formal but there are spectacular views of Sarasota and the waterfront. The very adventurous might like to opt for lunch out at sea on the Marina Jack II, call for details.

Old Salty Dog

1601 Ken Thompson Parkway, City Island, t (941) 388 4311 (*inexpensive–moderate*)

Tuck in to beer battered hot dogs and fried grouper sandwiches served by friendly staff at this comfortable diner that's right on the water and close to the Mote Aquarium.

Vernona

The Ritz-Carlton, 1111 Ritz-Carlton Drive, t (941) 309 2043 (*expensive–very expensive*)

Spoil the little darlings with lunch at the Ritz (*see also* Sleep, p.37). Dine indoors or out on the terrace (reservations recommended) at this very smart and amenable restaurant. The circus-themed kids' menu offers healthy options such as chicken noodle soup, fruit plate, chicken fingers with celery and carrot sticks, followed by naughty but nice desserts including brownie sundaes or strawberries and marshmallows dipped in chocolate. Parents can choose from the largely organically grown ingredients including osso bucco, salmon and farm-reared chicken.

Around and About

Anna Maria Island

Café on the Beach

4000 Gulf Drive, Holmes Beach, t (941) 778 0784
(*inexpensive*)

All-you-can-eat pancakes, served up right on the beach.

Rotten Ralph's

902 South Bay Boulevard, t (941) 778 3953
(*inexpensive–expensive)*

Eat fish and chips indoors or out with great views of the bay.

The Sandbar

100 Spring Avenue, t (941) 778 0444
(*moderate–expensive*)

Sit on out on the sand or on the deck and enjoy some fine seafood accompanied by live music. Mains include wasabi encrusted tuna or salmon, crab pasta salad or chicken and rice.

Longboat Key

The Colony Dining Room

1620 Gulf of Mexico Drive, t (941) 383 6464, www.colonybeachresort.com
(*moderate–very expensive*)

Smart dining is available at this gulf-side resort restaurant that is famous for its tennis. The menu features lobster, caviar, duck or veal topped with shrimp, all beautifully fresh and perfectly presented with fresh vegetable accompaniments. Children can have chicken planks, hamburgers, a kids' salad (which makes a very pleasant change from most kids' menus), steak, pizza or pasta. There's also the Monkey Room for indoor and outdoor dining with your little monkeys where they do an excellent tuna nicoise salad.

Mar Vista

760 Broadway Street, t (941) 383 2391
(*moderate–expensive*)

Dine indoors or out on the deck at this sister restaurant to the Sandbar (see above). Some of the recipes are shared between the restaurants but here you can try some conch and vegetable fritters, scallops with bacon in ginger plum sauce, clam or mussel pots, oysters or stuffed snapper.

Siesta Key

The Broken Egg

210 Avenida Madera, t (941) 346 2750
Open Daily 7am–3 (*inexpensive*)

Quite the loveliest American breakfast café you can imagine, this Sarasota gem offers egg-shaped menus, friendly waitresses and eggs any way you like them, plus fruit platters for the healthy and buttermilk pancakes for the indulgent. What a way to start the day.

Coasters

1500 Stickney Point Road, t (941) 925 0300
(*inexpensive–expensive*)

Coasters offers casual waterfront dining and spectacular views, especially at night, book ahead for a good booth table. The main menu features delectable oysters, shrimp, seafood wraps, swordfish and open-pit grilled steaks, among others. Kids can colour-in their sea-themed menus and eat grilled cheese sandwiches, hamburgers, fish or chicken fingers, all served with fries and a soft drink. Buy a kids' T-shirt and you get the meal free.

Old Salty Dog

5023 Ocean Boulevard, Siesta Key, t (941) 349 0158, www.theoldsaltydog.com (*inexpensive–moderate*)

Another in the chain. *See* Sarasota, p.128.

Venice

Sharky's on the Pier

1600 South Harbor Drive, Venice, t (941) 488 1456
(*moderate*)

Poised on the pier over pristine waters, Sharky's offers relaxed surroundings and seafood specials, including shrimp stuffed with Florida blue crab and grilled grouper or lobster tail in garlic butter, served with rice or potatoes and vegetables. Sandwiches, ribs and steaks are also on offer.

Quiz

1. Name one product that has made a major contribution to the development of Tampa?
2. Which African countries have inspired some of the scenery at Busch Gardens?
3. Where can you swim with the fishes?
4. Where can kids become Budding Artists?
5. Where can you tickle the belly of a T-Rex?
6. Which Surreal Spanish artist has a whole museum devoted to him in St Petersburg?
7. What happens if you're no good at limbo dancing at Captain Memo's Pirate Cruise?
8. What can you see drying on the docks at Tarpon Springs?
9. What looks like a spider's web strung across black water?
10. What can you see on the roof of the Sarasota Classic Car Museum?

East Central Florida

09

East Central Florida

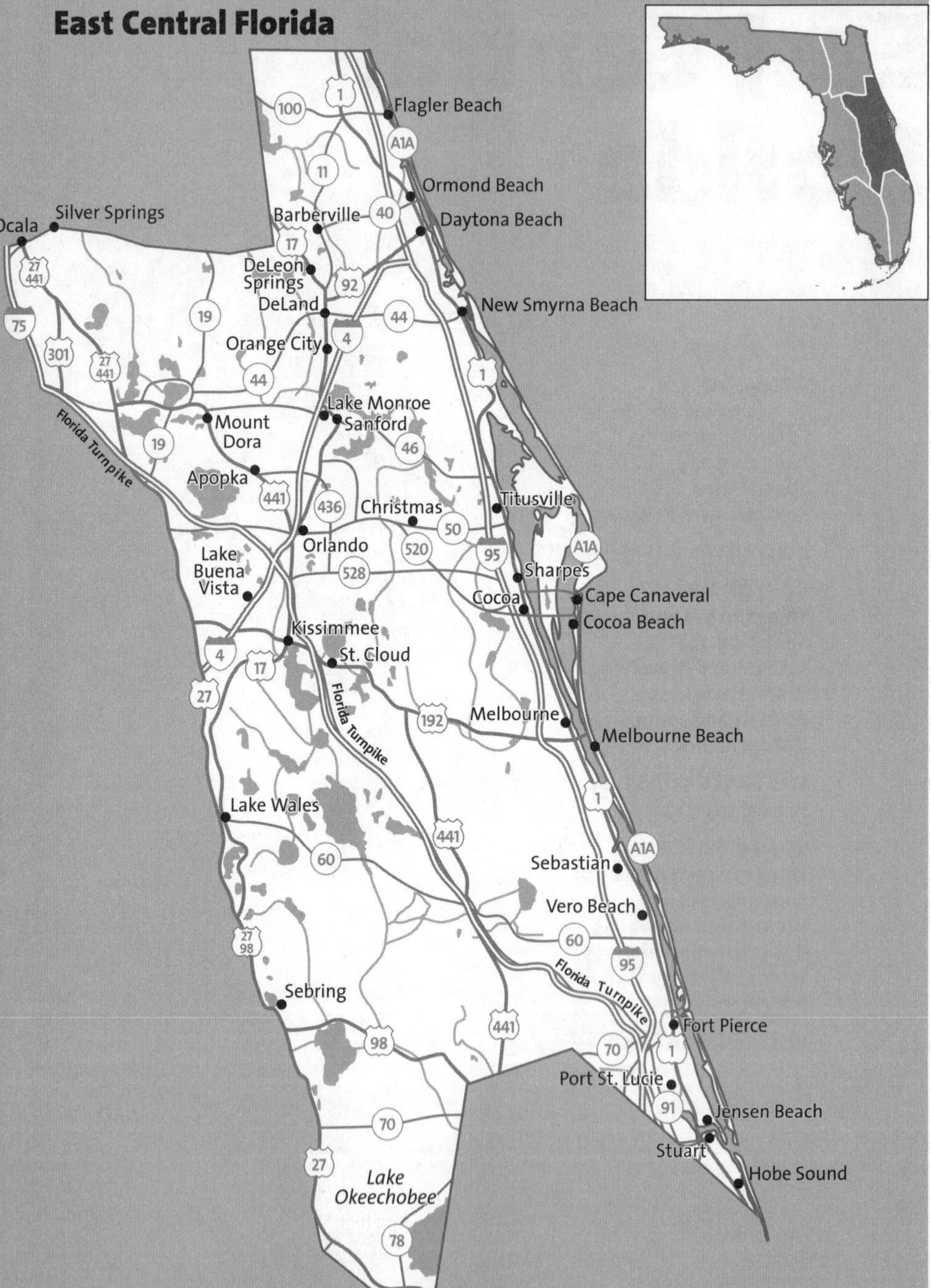

EAST CENTRAL FLORIDA

For Walt Disney World® Resort see Chapter 12, p.225

Orlando is the gateway to Disney and you will soon find, if you are travelling with kids, that you are one of a tribe, a "Disney mom" (or dad). This chapter, however, is dedicated to everything the East coast of Florida can offer – minus the mouse. It has many charms, from space exploration and fast cars to dolphin discoveries and gravity-defying flumes

East Central Florida has come a long way since the 1840s when the area first saw major development. A visitor arriving before then would have had considerable trouble getting about since the only transport was a steamboat from Jacksonville (*see* p.79) down the St. John's River and then either going by horse or on foot. Despite its proximity to St. Augustine (*see* p.88), which the Spanish had settled in 1565, this part of Florida remained pretty rural, divided between the Spanish and British settlers and the Indian tribes until the Seminole Wars in the mid-1800s (*see* History p.5.) brought a series of defensive forts to protect what, by then, had become US territory. **Fort Mellon** (Sanford) and **Fort Gatlin** (Orlando) were strategic outposts along with **Fort Maitland** on the west shore of Lake Maitland and **Fort Ann** in Titusville. East Florida was regarded at the time as a particular threat owing to the proliferation of slaves escaping from over the border in Georgia and South Carolina, as well as illegal goods trading, both of which contravened the laws of the US government.

When the Indian wars ended in 1858, the forts were torn down and the pine forests cleared for citrus groves. The abundance of natural spring water in the area attracted farmers and the development of the railroad between Jacksonville and Maitland in 1880 and Daytona in 1889 meant they could explore wider markets for their produce. After devastating frosts blighted the citrus crops in 1894 and 1895, many of the grove owners sold up, ushering in a new phase of development. By 1892 Flagler's railroad was pushing southwards towards **Miami** (*see* Southeast p.191) consolidating plantation settlements along the coast, such as **New Smyrna** and **Titusville**, as well as bringing tourists to the east coast's beaches. The area remained largely a farming district with satellite beach towns benefiting from the 1920s land boom.

After that not much happened until after World War II, when the space race brought **NASA** into town. **Disney** followed in 1971 and the die was cast for a whole load of fun and the highly developed tourist attraction belt that you can see today.

The average temperature ranges from 60–90 degrees with an average of 230 days of sunshine a year, making the area attractive year-round. The best times to head to Orlando are between October and November or at Christmas or in February. However, if you've got your heart set on a summer holiday or a springtime break, bring buckets of high-factor sun block and long-sleeved, light cotton tops and take some time out in the pool or on the beach to offset the days spent standing in line for theme-park thrills.

Highlights

Taking a dip with the dolphins at Discovery Cove, Orlando, p.135
Being lab rats in the Orlando Science Center, Orlando, p.137
Diving and dining with sharks, SeaWorld Adventure Park, Orlando, p.137
Camping out with the cowboys Lake Kissimmee State Park, Lake Wales, p.142
Dining like royalty, Medieval Times Dinner & Tournament, Kissimmee, p.142
Getting a real good soaking, Water Mania, Kissimmee, p.143
Making a scene at Universal Studios, Orlando, p.143
Comic book capers at Universal's Islands of Adventure, Orlando, p.144
Car culture: Daytona International Speedway/Daytona USA, Daytona Beach, p.146
Museum of Arts and Sciences, Daytona Beach, p.147
Merritt Island National Wildlife Refuge, Titusville, p.151
Rocket power, Kennedy Space Center, p.151
Exploring Florida's ancient past, Brevard Museum of History & Science, Cocoa Beach, p.153
Golden Sands County Park, Vero Beach, p.155
Stuart Beach, Stuart, p.155
Fort Pierce Inlet State Park, Fort Pierce, p.157
Hobe Sound National Wildlife Refuge, Hobe Sound, p.157

Special events

January

Blue Spring Manatee Festival, Blue Spring State Park, Orange City, **t** (386) 775 3663

February

Orlando Wetlands Festival, Christmas, **t** (407) 568 1706, **www**.cityoforlando.net

Daytona 500 NASCAR Stock Car Races, Daytona Beach, **t** (386) 253 7223, **www**.daytonainternationalspeedway.com

March

Tico Warbird Airshow, Valiant Air Command and Museum, Titusville, **t** (321) 268 1941

Kissimmee Bluegrass Festival, Osceola County Historical Museum and Pioneer Center, Kissimmee, **t** (813) 783 7205, **www**.originalbluegrass.com

Seafest, Cocoa Beach, **t** (321) 459 2200, **www**.seafest.com/

Easter Surfing Festival, Cocoa Beach Pier, **t** (321) 783 7549, **www**.ronjons.com http://eastersurffest.com/

Pelican Island Wildlife Festival, Sebastian, **t** (772) 564 0540, **www**.pelicanislandfriends.org

April

Rajuncajun Crawfish Festival, Isle of Pine's South Beach, **t** (407) 737 9049, **www**.crawfishcoofcentralflainc.com/

May

Family Fest at Daytona USA, Daytona International Speedway, Daytona Beach, **t** (386) 947 6800, **www**.daytonausa.com

Beach Fest, Cocoa Beach Pier, **t** (321) 783 7549, **www**.cocoabeachpier.com

October

Halloween Horror Nights at Universal Studios, Orlando, **t** (407) 363 8000

November

Space Coast Birding and Wildlife Festival, Titusville, **t** (321) 268 5224, **www**.nbbd.com/fly

ORLANDO

Before you go anywhere, log on to the tourist board website www.orlandoinfo.com for information about shopping discounts cards for visitors – it'll save you a lot on purchases and eating out.

Orlando is undoubtedly the fun time capital of the Sunshine state. Home to the big names in entertainment – **Disney** (*see* pp.225–268), **Universal**, **SeaWorld** (*see* p.137 and p.143), it also has a dozen or so smaller parks and attractions. There's certainly no shortage of things to do. When you've finished turning every which way on the rides, there are water parks to float about in, shopping malls to browse and lots of restaurants, diners and cafés for a spot of refuelling in between. At first sight, it's bewildering but if you follow the signposts, try to balance your time each day between all the must-see attractions with some time out to catch your breath and come back to earth, you'll have the best of holidays here. One of the nicest ways to negotiate the area is to rent a house and divide your time between following a carefully planned schedule of park visits with time out by the pool and cooking on the barbecue. A few days and nights in will also be a bit easier on the wallet and give the kids a chance to wind down properly rather than spending every night in the theme park villages. Orlando's major attractions and resorts are southwest of downtown a long International Drive and I–4. If you want to see more than theme parks visit the **Church Street Station district** and the **museums** and other attractions that once held sway here. Whether you're a roller-coaster veteran or making your first inroads into amusement-park territory, Orlando will still take you by surprise and you won't have laughed so much in years.

Getting there

By air There are two airports for Orlando, Orlando International Airport and Sanford Airport Authority.

Orlando International Airport , 1 Airport Boulevard (Greater Orlando Aviation Authority), **t** (407) 825 2001, **www**.orlandoairports.net, is sprawling but, thankfully, has a **monorail** system (which gives great views) to take you to the main terminal building, where you will find most shops and services, including outlets for the major attractions from SeaWorld and The Kennedy Space Center to Universal and Disney. There's a food court that also has a saltwater aquarium, which'll entertain the kids. There's even a 'departure spa' for a last-minute hair-do and massage. The airport is currently undergoing a $1.2 billion expansion programme with plans to double its capacity and build a fourth runway. There are direct scheduled services from London airports and select cities in the UK, *see* Travel p.13 for flight details.

Many hotels offer free **shuttle buses** from the airport, check the website or pre-arrange with your hotel. Buses are available on Level 1 of the Main Terminal, A-side. **Lynx buses** (*see* below) depart every 30 minutes to downtown Orlando and International Drive, from 5.30am–11.30pm (less frequent services on Sundays). Services downtown take approx 40 minutes; **International Drive** takes about an hour. Several **taxi** companies service the airport; expect to pay about $39 for a one-way trip to International Drive. **Mears Transportation** is an airport and attraction shuttle service, reserve ahead **t** (407) 423 5566, **www.**mearstransportation.com

Sanford Airport Authority, 1 Red Cleveland Blvd, Suite 1200, Sanford, **t** (407) 585 4000, **www.**orlandosanfordairport.com, is 18 miles north of Orlando and the city's other airport. It gets direct charter flights from London Gatwick and select UK cities. To get there, take exit 98 from I–4 and turn east on to Lake Mary Boulevard.

Shopping facilities include a newsagents and travel games store; restaurants are limited. There's also a games arcade on site. Numerous **taxi** and **shuttle** services access the airport, see website.

By road Orlando is 86 miles from Tampa, 231 miles from Miami, the city lies at the junction of I–4 and US 91 (the Florida Turnpike). The main artery for attractions is International Drive or the I-Drive, which snakes alongside I–4 between Walt Disney World in the south and Universal Studios to the north.

By rail Amtrak, **t** (800) 872 7245, **www.**amtrak.com, runs between Orlando and Tampa (2 hours), Miami (5–7 hours) and Jacksonville (3–3½ hours), (service runs out of New York).

By bus Greyhound, 555 North John Young Parkway, **t** (407) 292 3440, **www.**greyhound.com

Getting around

By bus Lynx Bus Service, **t** (407) 841 2279/LYNX, **www.**golynx.com. Daily services cover nine travel zones with destinations, including Sanford to the north of Orlando; Disney World, downtown Orlando, Orlando International Airport, SeaWorld, Kissimmee and St Cloud. Fare: one-way $1.50, single-day pass $3.50, 7-day pass $12.

I-Ride Trolley, **t** (407) 248 9590, **www.**iridetrolley.com There's a **daily shuttle** service that departs around every 20 minutes from Vineland Road and Major Boulevard, just north of Universal Studios, and runs down International Drive from Belz Factory Outlet World to Sea World and south International Drive to Orlando Premium Outlets. **Green Line** services run along Universal Boulevard ending at SeaWorld, arriving approximately every 30 minutes. Fares: 75 cents, three-day pass $5, five-day pass $7 (under 12s free). See website for maps and details.

Tourist information

Orlando/Orange County, Official Visitor Center, 8723 International Drive, Suite 101, **t** (407) 363 5872, **www.**orlandoinfo.com

Things to see and do

Discovery Cove

6000 Discovery Cove Way, **t** (877) 4–DISCOVERY, **www.**discoverycove.com

Getting there Exit 71 off I–4

Open Daily 9–5.30

Adm All-inclusive with dolphin encounter: $229–$259 per person (over 6s only), plus tax. Non-dolphin encounters (suitable for ages 3–5) $129–$159. *See* Universal Theme Parks, p.143, for **Orlando Flexticket** Admission includes unlimited access to all areas, a dolphin swim and complimentary photograph, mask, snorkel, swim vest, towel, locker, sunscreen and other facilities plus seven-day admission to either SeaWorld Orlando (*see* p.137) or Busch Gardens Tampa Bay (*see* p.110)

This spin-off to SeaWorld gives guests the use of a private beach, pool and lagoon area and a chance to swim and interact with dolphins (children must be at least six). You may baulk at the price but, when you tot up the cost of the seven-day pass to either SeaWorld or Busch Gardens that is included, it's very good value and they limit the number of people within the park to 1,000, which buys you some peace and quiet. Groups are limited to eight and visitors watch a brief video presentation on safety and how to listen to and communicate with dolphins. A play session lasts for 30 minutes and includes holding and kissing a dolphin and a one-on-one swim together. Trainer-for-a-day and sleepover packages are also available, see website or call for details. Elsewhere in the park, families can view more than 30 species of birds in a free-flight aviary and encounter giant rays and tropical fish in the ray lagoon. At the beach indulge in some peaceful sunbathing or swim through underwater caves and under waterfalls. It's a lovely, gentle escape from the crowds.

Gatorland

14501 South Orange Blossom Trail, t (407) 855 5496, www.gatorland.com
Getting there I–4 West, exit 72, head east and take Orange Blossom Trail (S R 441). Go right at the lights and south for 5 miles, Gatorland is to the left
Open Daily 9–6
Adm Adults $19.95, children (3–12) $9.95, plus tax

You walk through the giant head of an alligator to enter this long-standing Florida attraction. Once inside, steer kids past the gift emporium, there will be time to buy rubber 'gators and glow-in-the-dark snakes later on, and make a beeline for the **train**. Start your day with a tour around the park, through the **saltwater crocodile** area, the 10-acre **alligator breeding marsh** and **bird rookery**, where anhingas, egrets, heron, grackals and other birds nest. There's an observation boardwalk for viewing up close. Get back on the train to explore the south end of the park where the 800-seat **alligator-wrestling stadium** entertains visitors with 20-minute 'gator wrangling shows and commentaries.

Other shows involve Florida snakes and critters, crocodile presentations and alligators jumping 4–5ft into the air. Kids can stop at the train station for **face painting**, to visit the **lorikeet aviary** and **baby-animal petting zoo**, or to let off some steam in the **play area** with its water jets, waterfalls and jungle gym. For refuelling between events, **Pearl's Smokehouse** serves delicacies such as smoked 'gator ribs, 'gator nuggets, as well as burgers and hot dogs. There's also a cypress **boardwalk trail** and **Snakes of Florida** exhibit featuring Eastern Diamondback rattlesnakes, Rat Snakes and Cottonmouth Moccasins.

Holy Land Experience

4655 Vineland Road, t (407) 367 2065, www.holylandexperience.com
Getting there Exit 78 off I–4
Open From 12 noon on Sun, other times vary, call or see website for details. Thu 7.30 free Bible study public service
Adm Adults $29.99, children (6–12) $19.99

A strange concept, perhaps,but somehow, amidst all the showbiz razzmatazz of Orlando, this park manages to be quite a contemplative place. This is a living, biblical history museum that recreates Jerusalem as it might have looked between 1450 BC and AD 66 (through the Old and New Testaments, from *Genesis* to *Revelations*). Visitors pass through the gates into the ancient walled city where they encounter a lively street market. Here craftsmen and musicians go about their business (alongside the themed souvenir and gift shops)

The 15-acre park has a lake with fountains and several authentic recreations of historic sites, including the **Garden Tomb** where Jesus was buried, the **Qumran Dead Sea Caves** where the Dead Sea Scrolls were discovered and the **Plaza of the Nations**. Two other buildings of particular note are a scaled-down version of the **Temple of the Great King**, a replica of the six-storey edifice that stood on Mount Moriah in first-century Jerusalem, where Jesus first spoke with the Pharisees, and **The Wilderness Tabernacle**. Both show interesting multimedia presentations. Throughout the day there are also musical and theatrical events detailing Jesus' life, death and resurrection. **The Scriptorium: Center for Biblical Antiquities** contains texts written in ancient cuneiform, as well as scrolls, manuscripts and a collection of rare Bibles. Stop off for some delicious Middle-Eastern food at the **Oasis Palms Café**. There's also a new exhibit called 'A Day in the Life of a Monk', which explores the humble and unassuming service to God – it could be habit forming.

Orange County Regional History Center

65 East Central Boulevard, t (407) 836 8500, www.thehistorycenter.org
Getting there From I–4 Exit 82C/Anderson St. turn left on Magnolia Ave and right on Central Blvd
Open Mon–Sat 10–5, Sun 12 noon–5. Saturday Pastimes (monthly) 10–3
Adm Adults $7, children (3–12) $3.50

This imaginative museum covers 12,000 years of local and statewide history from ancient American Indian tribes to the building of Walt Disney World. Once a month, during **Saturday Pastimes** sessions, actors and guest speakers involve visitors in hands-on activities exploring different aspects of Florida life and customs from a bygone age. **Guided tours** are available every Saturday and family events focussing on aspects of the museum's collection are scheduled every second Saturday in the month. Bring swimming gear or a change of clothes to let kids frolic in the pop-up fountains in **Heritage Square** where there are also occasional events and concerts.

Orlando Museum of Art

2416 North Mills Avenue, t (407) 896 4231, www.omart.org

Getting there From I–4 take the Princeton Street Exit 85, go east to Mills Avenue, turn left on Mills Avenue, left on Rollins Street and first left into Loch Haven Park
Open Tue–Fri 10–5, Sat, Sun 12 noon–5
Adm Adults $8, children (6–8) $5
Giftshop

The museum's permanent collection includes work by **Andy Warhol**, **Roy Lichtenstein**, **Georgia O'Keeffe** and **Ansel Adams**, among others, as well as displays of **African and ancient American art**. Younger visitors can take part in activities at various discovery centres within the galleries or borrow a fun-filled tote bag to help them find their way around. There are drop-in sessions (Thursday afternoons) for visitors to try out different art techniques and a stimulating programme of touring exhibitions that looks at the work of famous artists, illustrators and objects, among other subjects. There's also a **Folk Museum** and pleasant grounds to enjoy in this peaceful cultural park.

Orlando Science Center

777 East Princeton Street, **t** (407) 514 2000, **www.**osc.org
Getting there Exit 43 off I–4.
Open Mon–Thurs 9–5, Fri, Sat 9–9, Sun 12 noon–5. Observatory: Fri 7–9, Sat 6–9
Adm Adults $14.95, children (3–11) $9.95, under 2s free; after 6pm: $9.95, children $4.95; Parking: $3.50
Giftshop, café, nappy-changing facilities, free strollers

Head here for a little mental stimulation where kids can take part in experiments using computers, aided by instructors, inside **Dr Dare's Laboratory**, and explore the history of flight through replica aircraft models. They can also design and navigate crafts using interactive displays and simulators. There's a section on Florida's strategic role in the development of air travel and a hands-on area where they can test paper airplanes and operate a mock airport terminal and flight cabin. **Lasers**, **robotics**, the **solar system** and **human biology** are among other zones with an interactive element, as well as **ShowBiz Science**, which opens kids' eye to a gamut of special effects.

Then take a trip to **Science City** to explore mathematical principles, electricity and the laws of physics before touring **NatureWorks** for a closer look at Florida's ecosystems. If they've any energy left, kids can climb, crawl and create while learning about science along the way. A **dinosaur dig** completes the line-up of must-touch attractions for school-age kids. **Planetarium shows** look at the stars and Orlando by night and there are also touring nature and discovery films.

SeaWorld Adventure Park

7007 Sea World Drive, **t** (407) 351 3600; Tours **t** 800 406 2244 for reservations, **www.**seaworld.com
Getting there Exit 71 or 72 off I–4, intersection of Interstate 4 and FL 528 (Bee Line Expressway), 10 mins south of downtown Orlando and 15 mins from Orlando International Airport
Open Daily 9–times vary
Adm Adults $59.75, children (3–9) $48; Tours: Adventure Express Adults $89, children (3–9) $79 (Discovery Cove admission policies or SeaWorld Passports do not apply); Behind-the-scenes Adults $16, children (3–9) $12. Adult Scuba: $150, Adult Snorkel $125 (both for over 10s only). *See Universal Studios* p.143 for **Orlando Flexticket** options and Discovery Cove, p.143, for special deals. Parking: $7

You may have come here to see the celebrated sea creatures but a visit to this beautifully landscaped 200-acre marine park will also reap other, less expected benefits. On arrival, look out for characters like **Shamu the Killer Whale** and check the notice boards for feeding times and shows. Apart from the killer whales, dolphins, sharks, and sea lions, you'll also encounter some killer rides such as **Kraken**, a legs-free looping coaster, **Journey to Atlantis** a multi-sensory flume ride and **Wild Arctic**, a helicopter simulator ride into a land of ice inhabited by polar bears and penguins. Arrive early to beat the queues and start with the rides, or opt for an **Adventure Express tour**, which allows visitors to reserve seating for a couple of shows, receive preferential access on the rides, feed dolphins, sea lions and sting rays and have a penguin encounter, all as part of a six-hour tour. Lunch is provided but the price of the tour is in addition to admission. If you want to be more flexible or need to budget, take a one-hour **Behind-the-scenes** tour to explore environments where either penguins, sharks or manatees and sea turtles live with a chance to meet some creatures or feed the birds afterwards. So on with the shows. It's a good idea to arrive early for most shows in order to find a decent seat and some, such as the sea lion and otter presentation, reward early arrivals with a pre-show performance. Pride of the park is **Shamu – the Killer Whale show** where these majestic mammals display their power and beauty accompanied by video footage. Other shows include **Odyssea**, an underwater acrobatic spectacle involving penguins and people and **Pets Ahoy**, where agile domestic animals and performing rodents rock the house. The *pièce-de-resistance* is **Blue Horizons** , which has awesome sets, costumes and acrobatics, set to an original orchestral score. Picture the scene – a huge sun rises over a pool of bubbles where bungee acrobats and aerialists swoop overhead on cloud swings and dolphins and false Killer Whales dazzle with faultless aquatic aplomb.

Find time between shows, if you can, to let the kids run about in **Shamu's Happy Harbor**, a three-acre play area complete with a four-storey net and climb-and-crawl tunnels, plus a water feature that includes slides and a water mazes. Kids should also check out the **interactive workstations and computers** located throughout the park that help them to interpret the exhibits. Children aged 10 and over can take part in special programmes like **Shark Deep Dive**, a two-hour experience in which you put on a wetsuit and either snorkel or scuba dive (proof of scuba certification required on day of programme) in an authentic shark cage. About 50 sharks inhabit the 125-ft long enclosure and the cage allows you to be in close proximity to tiger sharks, nurse sharks and thousands of fish. The programme includes a T-shirt, Shark Information booklet and snorkel but does not include admission.

Round the day off at a waterfront restaurant where entertainers roam and families can dine *al fresco* on pizza, fajitas, sandwiches, seafood or smokehouse fare. Or dine with the fish at **Sharks Underwater Grill**. Don't leave before SeaWorld has had a chance to **Mistify** you with its popular closing show on the centre lake. Here 60-ft mist screens, towering fountains, flames on water and dazzling fireworks combine for a fin-tastic finale (sorry).

Skull Kingdom

5933 American Way, t (407) 354 1564, www.skullkingdom.com
Getting there Off International Drive, opposite Wet 'n' Wild
Open Daily: day show: 10–5, night show: 5–12 midnight (hours are extended weekends and upon demand)
Adm Day show: $8.99, evening: $14.95. Skull Kingdom and magic show: Adults $28.25, children $24.45

You'll not be surprised to find a castle in this city of fantastic constructions, but beware, because this one is haunted. Welcome to Skull Kingdom where live actors lead the unsuspecting along spooky corridors bristling with things that go bump in the night. Children are given torches and daytime shows are geared more towards humour than big frights. Still, nervous children might not be up to the air of suspense. Evening shows are more intense, as eerie costumed guides usher you through ghoulish halls on a white-knuckle walk-through where skeletons, severed heads and horned beasts lurk in the dark. There's a **magic show** to help laugh off your cares afterwards with all-you-can-eat pizza and a constant stream of drinks. Or should that be scream?

Wet 'n' Wild

6200 International Drive, t (407) 351 9453 or (800) 992 9453, www.wetnwildorlando.com
Getting there Exit 75A off I–4
Open Daily; hours vary
Adm Adults $33.95, children (3–9) $27.95. Parking: $6, a combined locker, towel and tube rental costs $9 with a $4 deposit
Locker, tube, towel rental, beachwear shop, fast-food outlets, café, toilets, changing rooms, showers

If you like your excitement on the frothy side, this large water park has lots of thrilling slides and rides for all the family. The big spills include the **Blast** – a raft adventure ride that leads you through tunnels and underneath broken ducts gushing gallons of water in your direction at high speed; **The Storm** – get in a spin with its manic whirlpool action; **The Black Hole** – a towering inferno of tubes in the dark and the latest ride; and **Disco H2O** – a 70s-themed thrill ride that's sure to rock the boat. Add to this a **surf pool**, children's thrill rides for school-age kids and a **water playground** for toddlers, two large **sundecks** and a revamped **lazy river** that meanders under rope bridges and waterfalls, and you've fun to last till bedtime. The pools are heated in winter, some rides close Oct–March, check for details. Lifeguards are on duty throughout the park and life vests are provided at no extra charge.

Wonderworks

Pointe Orlando, 9067 International Drive, t (407) 351 8800, www.wonderworksonline.com
Getting there Exit 74A off I–4, across from the Orange County Convention Center
Open Daily 9–12 midnight. Dinner magic shows: 6 and 8, reservations recommended
Adm Adults $17.95 ($20.95 with laser tag, $34.95 with dinner magic show), children (4–12) $12.95

($15.95 with laser tag, $25.95 with dinner magic show). Laser tag: $4.95 per person. Dinner magic show: Adults $19.95, children $14.95

Just when you're beginning to get your bearings, suddenly someone comes along and turns everything on its head. This upside-down world features fun exhibits purely designed to disorientate and befuddle you and make your mind boggle. You enter through a hole in the roof and that's when the topsy-turvy tricks begin as you test the effects of a **hurricane**, stand up to an **earthquake**, climb the walls and have a hair-raising time, among many other hands-on activities. Visitors with guts of steel can also design and ride their own roller coaster on a **state-of-the-art simulator**. End the day with an **Outta Control Magic Show** that's packed with laughs, pizza and a liberal application of cold alcoholic and non-alcoholic drinks.

Entertainment

Dolly Parton's Dixie Stampede

8251 Vineland Avenue, **t** (866) 443 4943, **www**.dixiestampede.com
Getting there Exit 68 off I-4
Open Shows: 6.30 and 8.30, see website for schedule, advance reservations required
Adm Adults $46.99, children (4–11) $19.99, plus tax

This dinner experience offers good ole Southern hospitality with a gracious welcome from a beautiful belle and pre-show entertainment courtesy of a cowboy crooner on horseback, a juggling duo or some other exciting performance. Arrive about an hour-and-a-half before the show to have a look in the **open-air stables** to see Quarter Horse, Paint, Appaloosa and Palomino breeds. During the main show tuck into Southern-style cooking, including rotisserie chicken, barbecued pork loin (lasagne and fruit options for vegetarians), vegetable soup, corn on the cob, baked potato and dessert, accompanied by beer, wine, coke, tea or coffee. Expect stunts and audience participation in this fun and lively family show. There's an extra special show for Christmas.

Pirate's Dinner Adventure

6400 Carrier Drive, off International Drive, **t** (407) 248 0590, **www**.piratesdinneradventure.com
Getting there Exits 75A or 74A off I-4
Open Shows: 6.15 and 8.30 or 8 depending on season, book places in advance
Adm Dinner and show: Adults $49.95, children (3–11) $29.95, plus tax

First it's ghosts and magicians in Skull Kingdom (*see* p.138) and now its pirates. This **dinner-theatre show** is designed to dovetail with when the theme parks close for the night, offering food and entertainment in one easy package. So swash your buckles and shiver your timbers as fearsome brigands battle it out with swords and perform daring stunts on a floating ship-shaped stage. There's even an on-site **pirate's museum** full of treasures to get you in the mood for a night of skullduggery. Audience participation is encouraged and children, in particular, are asked to set sail upon the indoor lagoon for a night of fun on the high seas. There are pre-show games and a salad buffet before the main show and meal, so hungry kids need not wait to eat. Dinner features bread, chicken, beef or shrimp dishes, Caribbean rice, vegetables and desserts, plus free drinks, including coke, beer and wine. Children's meals are available on request. Join the pirates afterwards for a **buccaneer's boogie**.

Shopping

Shopping in Orlando is like visiting an attraction; it's busy, bright, brash and fun. Thankfully most malls have entertainment zones as well, so the kids can watch a movie or play a round of golf while one of you sets out on a serious spending spree.

Festival Bay Mall at International Drive

5250 International Drive, **t** (407) 352 7718, **www**.belz.com
Open Mon–Sat 10–9, Sun 11–7

If you only have time for one shopping trip you'll be happy to spend all day at this vast mega-mall. There's a range of entertainments including mini **glow-in-the-dark golf**, **arcade games**, a Vans **skate park**, a children's **carousel** and a **20-screen cinema**. You'll also find lots of speciality stores like **Charlotte Russe** and **Urban Planet** for dressing trendy girls and **Little Princess** for their younger siblings. Kids will feel cool hanging out in **Big Dog Sportswear**, the **Ron Jon Surf Shop** (www.ronjons.com) or getting kitted out for the pool at **Swim Smart**. If they need a pit stop there's the **Cold Stone Creamery** for ice cream or **Smoothy Bee** for yummy fruit smoothies. Visit the **Belz Designer Outlet Center** for **OFF 5th,** the Saks Fifth Avenue Outlet, **Calvin Klein**, **Polo Ralph Lauren Factory Store**, **DKNY** and more. The Belz

Factory World is a huge emporium with lots of choice in kids' clothing, including **Oshkosh B'gosh**, **Birkenstock**, **The Gap Outlet**, several toy shops, a **Universal Studios Outlet**, **Samsonite**, **Sunglasses Hut** and the widest range of shoe shops in town from **Vans** to **Footlocker**.

Belz Designer Outlet Center

5211 International Drive, t (407) 352 3632 (branch: Belz Factory Outlet World, 5401 West Oakridge Road, t (407) 352 9611

Don't miss this designer outlet store on the same road as the Festival Bay Mall.

The Florida Mall

8001 South Orange Blossom Trail, t (407) 851 6255, www.simon.com

Open Mon–Sat 10–9, Sun 12 noon–6

Anchored by no less than seven department stores – **Burdines**, **Dillard's**, **JCPenney**, **Saks Fifth Avenue**, **Sears**, **Nordstrom** and **Lord & Taylor** – and with 250 speciality stores, you're unlikely to be at a loss here. Kids and their parents should make a beeline for **Abercrombie & Fitch** for preppy jackets, T-shirts, jeans and underwear. Other casual wear outlets are **PacSun** for beach gear and **Banana Republic** for smartening up mums and dads. Pick up *frou frou* cosmetics and accessories at **Claire's Boutique** or **Club Libby Lu**, which specializes in fluffy ephemera. Reward good children with a visit to the **Playmobil Fun Park** and stop off for a healthy bite at **Salad Creations** or **Harry & David's Gourmet Foods**. For flagging spirits pop to **Teavanna** for a restorative cuppa.

The Mercado

8445 International Drive, t (407) 345 9337, www.themercado.com

Open Daily 10–late

An eclectic gift shop mall with **live entertainment** daily from 7.30pm, featuring jazz, rock and pop, reggae, blues and country tunes performed by up-and-coming artists. **Titanic – The Exhibition** (**t** (407) 248 1166, open daily 10–10, Adults $17.95, children (6–12) $12.95, plus tax, under 5s free), has costumed guides and full-scale sets that relive the life and times of the fateful voyage. Shops include **Good Luck Rice** for unusual jewellery, puppet and magic trick stores, hair plaiting and wraps. There's an **International Food Court** and the opportunity to have your picture taken with some parrots.

Orlando Premium Outlets

8200 Vineland Avenue, t (407) 238 7787, www.simon.com

Getting there I–4, exit 68

Open Mon–Sat 10–10, Sun 10–9

Village-style arcades with 110 outlet stores, such as **Disney's Character Premiere**, **Universal Studios Outlet Store**, **Tommy Kids** and **Oilily** among other kids' toy and fashion stores. There's also **Barneys New York**, **Coach**, **Fendi**, **Armani**, **Kenneth Cole**, **Polo Ralph Lauren**, **Salvatore Ferragamo**, **Versace** for up-market men and women's wear, also a **Levi's Outlet** and **Nike Factory Store**.

Special trips

Cypress Gardens Adventure Park

6000 Cypress Gardens Boulevard, Winter Haven, t (863) 324 2111, www.cypressgardens.com

Getting there Exit 55 (Highway 27 South) off I–4 west, turn right off Highway 27 at State Road 540/Cypress Gardens Boulevard

Open From 10, closing times vary

Adm Adults $34.95, children (3–9) $29.95, plus tax, under 2s free, 2nd day free (within six days of visit)

Toilets, showers, changing area, rental lockers

More than $45 million is being spent on revitalizing this, one of Florida's oldest tourist attractions. Famed for its 1930s water-ski shows and graceful Southern belles, the old Cypress Gardens was a place to wander and wonder at the beauty of the surroundings and artistry of the performers. Its new incarnation boasts five roller coasters, numerous thrill and family rides, shops, restaurants and a water park, as well as choreographed figure skating in the **Royal Palm Theater** and signature **water-ski shows** out on Lake Eloise and high jinx on the high seas in **Mango Bay**, when the 'Pirates of Cypress Cove' stage show sets sail. Thrill-seekers can take on the big rides, including the steel coaster **Okeechobee Rampage**, the **Triple Hurricane** wooden coaster with its negative Gs, **Swamp Thing**, a suspended coaster ride and vertical-drop tower and **Storm Surge**, the world's tallest spinning rapids ride, which twists and turns through 60 feet of white water. There are gentler pursuits for young children, including a **mini train, plane** or **dinosaur ride**. Narrated **train** and **ferry trips** recalling the park in its heyday when even Elvis came to learn to water-ski are fun for everyone. In the landscaped gardens ladies in crinolines transport you back to a time of plantation homes, as they glide across the lawns. Hundreds of butterflies in the **Wings of Wonder** exhibition add to the colourful display. There's even an **old-style shopping village** where you can press your nose against windows to ogle old-fashioned sweets, see artisans working or watch the toy trains running on tracks in the model shop. There's a year-round **Christmas shop** and **Aunt Julie's Country Kitchen** offers chicken and dumplings and other Southern specialities; **Backwater Bill's Barbecue** is the place for smokehouse treats.

The latest attraction is **Splash Island**, a Polynesian-themed water park. Littl'uns will enjoy the slides, water jets and geysers in the **Tikki Garden**. Older ones can brave the **Polynesian Adventure** with its slides and rope ladders, 42-ft-high water dump-bucket and water cannons. There's also a 20,000sq-ft wave pool with inner tubes, a not-so-lazy river and a 40-ft tube-slide. Splash Island has two restaurants, **Volcano Jim's Snack Shack** and **Tikki Bar**, serving refreshing drinks, hamburgers, fries, pizza and snacks.

Historic Bok Sanctuary

1151 Tower Boulevard, t (863) 676 1408, www.boktower.org

Getting there **Exit 55 (Highway 27 South) off I–4 west, continue for approx 23 miles to Eagle Ridge Mall, turn left on Mountain Lake Cut Off Road and turn right (south) onto County Road 17. Proceed on CR 17 for ¾ miles. Turn left (east) onto Burns Avenue for 1.3 miles until you see the entrance on your left**

Open **Daily 8–6 (last adm 5). Pinewood Estate tour: Mon–Sat 11.30 and 1.30, Sun 1.30**

Adm **Adults $8, children (5–12) $3, under 5s free. Pinewood Estate tour: Adults $5, children $3**

Visitor centre, free strollers (limited number)

The 205-ft tower within the park is more like York Minster than sub-tropical Florida, which is all the more reason to head for these hills (the only ones you'll find in Florida) on a scenic driving detour. This pretty **bird sanctuary** is the perfect place to escape the bright lights and attractions of the East Coast. Wildlife scampers and over 100 species of bird twitter among the oaks, palm and pine trees. The image of the Gothic and art-deco tower ripples in the **reflection pool** and camellias, magnolias and azaleas thrive. The **57-bell carillon tower** (listed on the National Register of Historic Places) is closed to the public but has a programme of recitals. Dutch-born magazine editor and Pulizer-prizewinning novelist Edward W. Bok masterminded this sanctuary as his gift to the American people and commissioned landscape gardener Frederick Law Olmsted, Jr., to plant the gardens that wind along tree-canopied paths throughout the estate. Bring a picnic and head for the western edge of **Iron Mountain**, the hill on which the sanctuary stands (there are seats and benches and the '**window by the pond**', an indoor overlook for watching wildlife). On deposit of a driver's license, families can borrow a free **Reading Basket** from the Visitor Centre, containing books, puppets and a blanket. The Visitor Centre also contains a **museum** focussing on the Bok family history, a gallery of paintings of Florida's flora and fauna, a courtyard café and a gift shop. Also in the grounds is **Pinewood Estate**, a 1930s Mediterranean Revival manor, which is open for tours.

Can you spot?

A slithering snake? Find the sundial on the south side of the tower and you'll see that the dial support is in the shape of a coiled serpent – the ancient symbol of time. The 12 signs of the zodiac mark the hours and the inscription recalls the speech made by President Calvin Coolidge in which he dedicated the park to be 'for the visitation of the American people'.

AROUND AND ABOUT

Kissimmee and Lake Buena Vista

Kissimmee's cow town days may be long gone as theme parks and resort accommodations have ploughed southwards, but there are still some old-style things to do, including **rodeo shows** and **farm visits**. Along East Irlo-Bronson Memorial Highway (US 192) you'll find a cluster of amusements, including mini golf, go-karting, water parks and gift emporiums.

Getting there

Exit 64A off I–4 East on US 192 (Irlo-Bronson Memorial Highway)

Tourist Information

Kissimmee–St. Cloud Convention and Visitors Bureau, 1925 E. Irlo Bronson Memorial Highway, t (407) 847 5000, www.floridakiss.com

Green Meadows Farm

1368 South Poinciana Boulevard, **t** (407) 846 0770, **www**.greenmeadowsfarm.com
Getting there 5 miles south of Highway 192
Open Daily 9.30–5.30. Tours every two hours until 4
Adm $19, under 2s free
Picnic area, snack bar, gift shop, play area

Children can experience life on the farm at this gentle attraction where the emphasis is on being at one with nature. The two-hour tour gives kids the opportunity to hold a baby chick, milk a cow, ride a pony and learn about and pet the resident goats, sheep, turkeys, geese, pigs and donkeys. There are also tractor and train rides.

Horse World

3705 South Poinciana Boulevard, Kissimmee, **t** (407) 847 4343, **www**.horseworldstables.com
Getting there 12 miles south of Highway 192
Open Daily from 9. Rides: one-hour nature trail $39, under 5s riding double with a parent $16.95. Other rides minimum age 10. Reservations advised

Here young riders can enjoy a guided walking trail through the woods.

Kissimmee Rodeo

Kissimmee Sports Arena, 958 South Hoagland Boulevard, (407) 933 0020, **www**.ksarodeo.com
Shows: Fri at 8
Adm Adults $18, children (under 12) $9
Food outlets, souvenir stalls, bar

This authentic cowboy experience features calf-roping, bareback riding, barrel racing, bull-riding and a calf scramble.

Lakefront Park

250 Lakeshore Boulevard, **t** (407) 518 2501, **www**.kissimmeeparksandrec.com

If you're looking for somewhere to stretch your legs, this is a great place for a stroll or to take a boat out on the lake. There's a playground, a picnic area with barbecue grills, horseshoe tossing pits, a volleyball court and lots of room to run about in.

Lake Kissimmee State Park

14248 Camp Mack Road, **t** (863) 696 1112
Getting there 15 miles east of Lake Wales on Route 60
Open 8–dusk. Cow camp: Sat, Sun and school holidays 9.30–4.30. Canoe/kayak tours: call in advance
Adm $4 per car, $1 per bike or pedestrian

This historic park was used to raise cows for the Confederates during the Civil War (1861–65) and at weekends and in school holidays, a recreation cow camp (dating from *c*.1876) recalls the pioneer days with scrub cattle in pens and cowboys at their cookout. Children can even partake of a cowboy's cup of coffee. This 5,900-acre park offers picnic areas, 13 miles of **trails**, three **fishing** lakes and **camping** under the stars. Wildlife spotters may chance upon white-tailed deer, bobcats, bald eagles or sandhill cranes. There are **guided canoe and kayak trips** to view birds and wildlife but you will need to rent a boat elsewhere, as there are no rental facilities in the park.

Medieval Times Dinner & Tournament

4510 West Irlo-Bronson Memorial Highway, **t** (407) 396 2900, **www**.medievaltimes.com
Open Show times vary
Adm Medieval village and dinner: Adults $48.95, children (3–11) $32.95, plus tax

Knightly entertainment is available at this snowy white castle where guests don paper crowns and wave banners while using their fingers to feast on ribs and roast chicken (though you might want a spoon for the vegetable soup). Tables are arranged on all sides of the torch-lit arena so everyone has a good view of the tournament, which begins with a display of jousting that features contrasting Andalusian white stallions and a single black Friesian. Thereafter, there follows hand-to-hand fighting, unexpected twists, the clash of steel on steel and deft horsemanship, as daring noblemen battle to become the new champion and win the hand of one fair lady. If, beforehand, you would like to tour the village where medieval artisans weave cloth, make pots and pound anvils, get here an hour or so early.

Old Town

5770 West Irlo-Bronson Memorial Highway, **t** (407) 396 4888, **www**.old-town.com
Open Daily 10–11
Adm 22 tickets for $20 or 35 tickets for $30, rides cost one or more tickets each. Separate admission for other attractions. Family Sundays: all-you-can-ride wristband special, $12

More than just an attraction, this 1950s–60s district offers shopping, dining and an entertainment zone. There's a 60-ft **Ferris Wheel**, a **haunted house**, **carousel**, **go-kart track** and kiddie rides, as well as the **Hollywood Wax Museum** and the **Tower of London Experience**. There are also weekly **classic car cruises** (Fri or Sat) and **motorbike cruises** (Thu).

Osceola County Historical Museum and Pioneer Center

750 North Bass Road, **t** (407) 396 8644
Open Thurs, Fri times vary, Sat 10–4, Sun 1–4
Adm Adult $2, child $1 (suggested donation)

Visitors can drift back to the pioneer days with a tour of this Cracker homestead and general store. There are nature trails and the Bluegrass Festival every March is a good excuse for a family picnic.

Water Mania

6073 West Irlo-Bronson Memorial Highway, **t** (407) 396 2626, **www**.watermania-florida.com
Open Mar–early Sept daily 10–5, mid–end Sept Mon–Fri 11–5, Sat, Sun 10–5, Oct call for times
Adm Adults $29.95, children (3–9) $26.95, plus tax, under 3s free. Parking: $6
Locker, towel and tube rental, free children's life vests

There's a wide range of exciting rides from cresting an endless wave on the surf simulator to challenging your mates on the duelling slides. Several steep and twisting flumes, tube rides, a lazy river and a wave pool only add to the fun. Children are well catered for with a pirate boat and a play train. Families can take a break from the sun in the shaded picnic area (no glass or alcohol allowed), volleyball court and a playground. Lifeguards and slide attendants are on duty throughout the park.

UNIVERSAL THEME PARKS

Universal Studios Orlando

1000 Universal Studios Plaza, **t** (407) 363 8000, **www**.universalorlando.com
Getting there Both parks and CityWalk: Exits 75A or 74B off I-4
Open Both parks from 9am, closing times vary, **Citywalk**: 11am–2am. Seasonal special events include Halloween, Christmas and Easter specials
Adm One-day pass to each park: Adults $59.75, children (3–9) $48. There are money-saving passes that allow access to both parks and there are also seasonal web discounts. The **two-day/two-park** ticket gives access to both Universal Studios and Universal's Islands of Adventure (adult $104.95, children (3–9) $94.95). The **Orlando Flexticket** (four-park: Adults $184.95, children (3–9) $150.95, five-park: Adults $224.95, children (3–9) $189.95) offers unlimited admission to **Universal Studios, Universal's Islands of Adventure, SeaWorld, Wet 'n' Wild** for 14 consecutive days (five-park also with admission Busch Gardens in Tampa, *see* p.110). CityWalk: Free. Parking: $8 (up to 6pm)
Getting around Universal Studios and Universal's Islands of Adventure are both easy to negotiate on foot, although they are spacious and you will have tired feet by the end of the day. there are stroller/pushchair and wheelchair rentals at the entrance to both parks and to the left of it. Rental fees are approx $10 for a single and $16 for a double stroller. Your name is displayed on the stroller but they all look the same so customize yours with a scarf or ribbon. It's not wise to leave handbags or shopping in the strollers while on the rides but the odd drinks carton or snack box won't hurt. Strollers are sturdy, easy to manoeuvre and large enough to let children lie down. They come with sunshades that keep your kid's eyes out of the glare but not much else. Wear hats, comfortable shoes and reapply sun block at regularly – it's easy to get burnt just waiting in line.

> ***Need to know***
> **Express Pass**
> ***The Universal Express system makes it possible to pre-book a time slot on the most popular attractions, and, although you may still have to wait you won't be there for hours getting hot and frustrated. Only one Express Pass per person can be booked at a time. Resort guests have all-day priority access.***

Having only just hit town in 1990, this Johnny-come-lately of themed attractions has benefited from the development of coaster technology and is planning to become one of the most exciting places in town – especially for teenagers. Universal Studios is based around rides with a technicolour movie twist. To make the most of your time and to try to avoid the inevitable queues, the best line of approach is to head for the back of the park first. Here you can deal with hot attractions in the **World Expo**, such as *Men in Black* (an alien-style shoot 'em up ride) and *Back to the Future* (a simulator ride set to images of boiling volcanoes, ice caves and a fear-some T-Rex), then swing round towards San **Francisco/Amity** for the mid-range thrills of *Jaws* and *Earthquake*, which are more likely to raise a giggle than a scream these days. Thereafter, head over to **New York** where it seems that the more recent the film, the better the ride as the *Revenge of the Mummy* proves with its blasts of hot air, scurrying scarabs and false ending. Then get in a spin at *Twister*, which has unnecessarily long queues but once you get in the effects of meeting a freak storm are quite effective. Younger visitors will be happier to visit **Production Central** where the wonders of OgreVision see **Shrek**, **Princess Fiona** and **Donkey** off on another whirlwind adventure in 3-D plus sensory effects as well. Here the dynamic trio is just setting off on honeymoon, only to be quite rudely confronted by Lord Farquaad's ghost. It's a pretty long adventure and very funny show, which gives you enough time to relax and has the odd smell, and bit of spray to keep kids on their toes. Queues are long, so opt for an early lunch and head here armed with juice, as you're not allowed to drink inside the theatre. Nearby is **Jimmy Neutron's Nicktoon Blast**, a combination of film and motion ride in which you help Jimmy fight the evil Oublar with the help of Nickelodeon stablemates **SpongeBob Squarepants**, The **Rugrats** and the **Fairly Odd Parents**. There's also much to attract pre-schoolers in **Woody Woodpecker Kidzone** where they can cool off in **Curious George**'s water playground, complete with water cannons, paddling pools, drop bucket and waterfall. Remember to bring a swimsuit. **Fievel's Playland** is a fun diversion with mouse-sized scramble nets, rope bridges, slides and a nice little dinghy ride. **Woody Woodpecker's Nuthouse Coaster** also draws the crowds but looks much faster than it is and, at only 90 seconds long, is a good place to start your child's theme-park education. After that go on a bike ride with **E.T.** over the rooftops to save his dying Green Planet. If you pace the day hitting the big rides first and leaving the afternoon for shows or a trip to the water playground, you should be able to do it all in a day. Leave the clever trickery of *Terminator 2* to the end and go out in a blaze of glory. Then buy some glow-in-the-dark Terminator souvenirs to light your way home.

Universal's Islands of Adventure

See Universal Studios for getting there, opening times and admission.

Why do one when you can have both? Built in 1999, the Islands of Adventure is the new kid on the block when it comes to Orlando's theme parks and it has a star prize that is well worth the price of admission on its own – **The Amazing Adventures of Spider-Man** – quite possibly the most exciting ride in town. Don't dream of going anywhere else first, go straight to **Marvel Super Hero Island** and get in line, if you go early enough you won't have to queue. The fun starts with some well-designed waiting areas and a peek into Peter Parker's office and darkroom, then it's on to the newsroom where all hell is breaking loose and your mission (and the ride) begins. Combining 3–D vision, movie footage and sensory drop simulator effects that, at one point, leave you reeling from a 40-storey tumble, you follow Spider-man on a quest to crush the bad guys. Meanwhile they're sending missiles at you from all directions, which hover menacingly right before your eyes. The likes of Doc Oc and his gang are none too pretty, so be prepared to cover small eyes from time to time. Most kids over five will love it. Next, it's time for the older members of your party to tackle the ride that dominates the park visually, the **Incredible Hulk Coaster**. This giant, green, gut-wrenching machine has a trick start that zooms you from 0–40 mph in just two seconds into a series of corkscrew spins. Things then start getting scary! It's an exhilarating experience but could leave younger kids looking as green as the Hulk himself.

Following on in an anti-clockwise direction, it's time to get wet, wet, wet in **Toon Lagoon**. If you're wondering why everyone else on the **Bilge-Rat Barges** are putting their shoes in the central console and donning their kagoules, it's because you're in for a real shoe-squelching soaking. If you try going for the driest seats you can bet you'll be the ones going backwards over the rapids and under most of the waterfalls on this thrilling, white-water, circular raft ride. Watch everyone else coming out dripping wet, then, it's your turn. It'll have you laughing all the way to the changing room. Hold your fire, however, if you're going to follow on with **Dudley Do-Right's Ripsaw Falls** because they're

Where to eat

There are lots of options available within these well-designed parks, so you can have anything from sushi to bangers and mash. You can also opt to go for lunch just outside the park gates in CityWalk; just ask to have your hand stamped for re-entry. Remember that the parks sometimes close around dinnertime, so it might be an idea to book your evening meal at CityWalk in advance. Call, t (407) 224 3663 for reservations, www. citywalkorlando.com. _See_ p.159 for restaurants

Need to know

Practicalities

Child/Baby Swap Areas

Not as sinister as it sounds, this allows parents to avoid the queues and go on a ride while the other waits in a designated area with their small child. When the ride has finished the parents swap places, again without queuing, so everyone has a turn. Ask attendants to help you with this scheme, which is invaluable if you've got toddlers.

First Aid

At **Universal Studios Orlando**, there's a first aid station in Family Services, near the Studio Audience Center. There's also a Health Services station on Canal Street between New York and San Francisco, opposite Beetlejuice's Graveyard Revue. At **Universal's Islands of Adventure**, there's a first aid point in the Guest Services Lobby and another in Sinbad's Village within The Lost Continent.

Height restrictions

Signs outside all the attractions display specific height requirements and warnings for certain medical conditions, where necessary. Children under 48" (1.22 metres) must be accompanied by an adult at all times.

Lockers

Guests will find lockers at the entrance to both parks, rental costs approx $8 for a standard locker. **Universal Studios** also has family-sized lockers for approx $10 with unlimited access all day. At **Universal's Islands of Adventure**, lockers are available at the entrance to the three biggest shake-em-up rides: Incredible Hulk Coaster, Dueling Dragons and Jurassic Park River Adventure. There is a nominal fee of $2 per hour (max $14).

Lost Children

Should your child be lost in the park, report to the Guest Services Office immediately or contact the nearest attendant.

Postal Services

There are US stamp machines and post boxes near the lockers and main exit in **Universal Studios Orlando**. There's also a stamp machine in the Trading Company Gift Shop at **Universal's Islands of Adventure**.

Telephones

There are several telephone points in both parks; you'll find them near the toilets and at the main entrance and exits. At **Universal CityWalk** there are telephones by the main toilets, near to the Guest Services Window.

Toilets

Toilets, including disabled facilities, are clearly sign-posted and are available throughout Universal theme parks. Baby-changing facilities are available in both male and female toilets. Nursing rooms and companion toilets are also available in Family Services at **Universal Studios Orlando**. At **Universal's Islands of Adventure**, both first aid points also have toilets.

Safety

No outside food or drinks may be brought in and coolers are prohibited, as are oversized bags or umbrellas and folding chairs. Shoes and shirts must be worn at all times. All bags and backpacks will be inspected before entry.

Smoking

Restaurants and bars that serve food are now designated smoke-free zones in the US. Smoking is permitted only where you see a smoking sign.

likely to leave you high and not a bit dry. The queues are almost as dizzying as the experience itself, so get an **Express Pass** (*see* above) and, even then, prepare to sit it out. This is the steepest water ride and you begin to see why about halfway along when you've gone round and up and up again a few times. There are a few mock drops and then it's the biggie and after all that anticipation, you'll be glad to know that it is, terrifyingly, worth it. Leave younger kids safely on *terra firma* for this one. They can have fun climbing aboard the **Good Ship Olive** with its climbing nets and soft play shapes. It's a big boat so keep an eye on them as they tumble about with other shipmates. **Jurassic Park** is around the corner, so try and get there before lunch for another lunging drop, courtesy of the **Jurassic River Adventure**. There are dinosaurs on the loose and you're adrift in the primeval park where raptors lurk, there are perilous hazards around every corner and a massive T-Rex looms up from the gloom to swallow you. Finally, you plunge 84 feet down into a watery grave and a photo finish where everyone has vertical hair. Fantastic. Take a break afterwards in **Camp Jurassic** exploring in the amber mines and climbing the crawl nets or head to the **Jurassic Park Discovery Center** for some interactive and informative Dino doings. The **Pteranodon Flyers** are here too, offering a prehistoric bird's eye view of the park. There's a certain feeling of vulnerability when you climb aboard these ancient chair swings and go soaring above the heads of other visitors with your arms and legs dangling. It's actually not so very scary and gives a bit of a thrill, providing you've a head for heights. The **Lost Continent** boasts the world's first catch-me-if-you-can dual racing roller coasters, which are pretty zippy, plus a couple of show-style attractions featuring **Sinbad** and **Poseidon** that are good for younger kids and a fast but clunky unicorn-themed coaster. Keep your powder dry though, for the zany delights of **Seuss Landing** where kids can run around the interactive water play area, ride a fish through cooling fountain jets and take a trip on a couch through the crazy world of the *Cat In The Hat*. Great fun for hot days and for taking a bit of time out from the action.

DAYTONA BEACH

If you want time at the beach to your theme-park holiday, Daytona is one of the nearest resorts and has an amazing 23 miles of sands, even if the speed is restricted to 10mph (there are restrictions during the turtle nesting season May–Oct). Beachfront parks with amenities for families include **Bicentennial Park**, 1800 North Oceanshore Boulevard, **t** (386) 756 5953, which has basketball courts, softball fields, a fishing dock, picnic area and playground, toilets, and boardwalks and trails for scenic views of the Halifax River. **Sun Splash Park**, 611 South Atlantic Avenue, **t** (386) 736 5953, has a water playground with climbing equipment and families can have a picnic or a game of volleyball. Daytona's downtown **historic district** lies on the other side of the Intracoastal Waterway at Highway 92 (International Speedway Boulevard), which links to the **Daytona race track**.

Getting there

55 miles north of Orlando off I–4, on Highway A1A

Tourist information

Daytona Beach Area Convention and Visitors Bureau, 126 East Orange Avenue, **t** (386) 255 0415, www.daytonabeach.com

Things to see and do

Atlantic Race Park

2122–28 South Atlantic Avenue, Daytona Beach Shores, **t** (386) 226 8777
Open Daily 10am–11pm
Adm Call for prices

Exercise your own need for speed on the hairpin turns at this track. Double and single go-karts are available.

Daytona Beach Boardwalk and Main Street Pier

Ocean Avenue, **t** (386) 253 1212 for pier information
Getting there Off Route A1A, behind Ocean Avenue between Main Street and Auditorium Boulevard
Open Pier: Daily 6am–11pm (later in summer), restaurant: 11–10
Adm Fishing pier: Adults $3.50 ($9.50 with equipment rental), children (under 12) $2 ($5 with equipment rental), spectators $1. Sky Lift: $4, Space Needle: $4, ($6 for both)

Nostalgic seaside attractions line the boardwalk and 100-ft fishing pier. Highlights are the **Speeding through Time** racing exhibit dedicated to Daytona's automotive past, a gondola-style **chair lift** that travels the length of the pier, a revolving 180-ft **Space Needle observation tower**, and **helicopter rides**.

Daytona Ghost Walks

Main Street & Peninsula Drive, **t** (386) 253 6034, **www.hauntsofdaytona.com**
Tours: Riverfront Park: Thurs and Sun 7.30
Adm $8. under 6s free, reservations required

Discover the spooky side of Daytona Beach with a certified ghost hunter on a 1½-hour walking tour that takes in the spooky sights of Daytona Beach including Pinewood Cemetery and explains the history of hauntings in the area, including spirits that are still at large today. Call for more details.

Daytona International Speedway and Daytona USA

1801 West International Speedway Boulevard, **t** (386) 254 2700 (speedway) or (386) 947 6800 (Daytona USA), **www.daytonainternational speedway.com**, **www.daytonausa.com**
Getting there From Daytona Beach take A1A and cross one of the bridges to US 1. Continue onto Mason Avenue West then take Clyde Morris Blvd and go north to Lot 7 for free parking and shuttle

Track tours: Daily 9.30–5. Daytona USA: Daily 9–7 (later during race events). IMAX screenings: 9.30, 11, 12.30, 2, 3.30 and 5.45
Adm Speedway tours: $7.50, under 6s free. Daytona USA: Adults $21.50 children (6–12) $15.50, plus tax, under 6s free. Some activities incur an additional fee
Gift shop, restaurant, Welcome Centre

Home to both the **Daytona 500**, which debuted here in February 1959 and the **Independence weekend Pepsi 400**, this famous track also hosts regular speedway, super bike, classic car shows and go-kart events. Thanks to a multi-million dollar project, the venue is undergoing an infield renovation that will allow fans access to a state-of-the-art infield Fan Zone and pre-race entertainment areas.

Daytona USA is a purpose-built entertainment centre where visitors can have the drive of their life on a **NASCAR simulator**, experience a real race in a 32-seater simulator, play up-to-the-minute **racing car video games**, try their luck as a sports reporter or get hands-on in the pit lane. There are also **exhibitions** about classic races with memorabilia harking back to the first speed trials on Daytona Beach in 1902, including a series of vehicles that have shaped racing as we know it. At the **Pepsi IMAX Theater**, catch the 14-minute film, *The Daytona 500: The Movie*, in which drivers prepare for the big race, and *NASCAR 3D: The IMAX Experience*, a 45-minute film with on-track and behind-the-scenes footage.

Daytona Lagoon at Ocean Walk Village

601 Earl Street, **t** (386) 254 5020,
www.daytonalagoon.com
Open Times vary, call for details
Adm Activities are individually priced. High Ballocity: $4.99 per day or evening session. Water park: $19.99 (over 48”), $16.99

This family water park has had a major facelift. It now boats 10 giant looping waterslide rides, a wave pool, multi-level children's play island with waterfalls and drop buckets, a lazy river, go-kart track, laser tag, climbing wall and mini golf, plus a state-of-the-art video arcade, sports bar and grill and a two-storey children's ball pool play area.

Halifax Historical Museum

252 South Beach Street, **t** (386) 255 6976,
www.halifaxhistorical.org
Getting there From I–95 or US 1 take International Speedway Boulevard (US 92) east to Beach Street, turn right just before Orange Avenue
Open Tue–Fri 10–4, Sat 10–12 noon
Adm Adults $4, children (under 12) $1 (free on Sat)

This delightful museum is in the Merchant Bank Building and is stuffed to the gills with curios and artefacts in neat wooden cabinets. There are exhibits on early plantation owners and pioneer families, dolls and antique costumes, Native American tribes, Victorian homes, Florida in wartime from the Civil War to World War II, as well as beach auto-racing memorabilia. There's a video theatre that screens historical documentaries about the area. Note that the museum store is full of glass and collectibles, so keep a tight rein on small children.

Lighthouse Point County Park

5000 South Atlantic Avenue, Ponce Inlet,
t (386) 756 7488
Open 8am–9pm; **Adm** $3.50 per car

The tranquil 55-acre park surrounding the lighthouse is a good bet if you have young children who want to escape the noise of beach traffic. There are calm waters for swimming, picnic areas, an observation deck and tower and nature trails to observe wildlife, including shore birds, raccoons and possums. The park also houses the **Marine Science Center**.

Marine Science Center

100 Lighthouse Drive, Ponce Inlet, **t** (386) 304 5545,
www.marinesciencecenter.com
Open Tue–Sat 10–4, Sun 12 noon–4
Adm Adults $3, children (5–12) $1

Although primarily a rehabilitation centre for sea turtles and sick and injured birds, the centre also contains conservation exhibits, an artificial reef aquarium, boardwalks and nature trails, a gift shop and an observation tower. Visitors can view turtles that are recovering in the seven outdoor hospital pools and take part in seasonal events such as nature talks and seaside story time sessions.

Museum of Arts and Sciences

1040 Museum Boulevard, **t** (386) 255 0285,
www.moas.org
Open Tue–Fri 9–4, Sat, Sun 12 noon–5. Planetarium shows: Tue–Fri at 2, Sat, Sun at 1 and 3
Adm Adults $8, children $4, under 5s free. Planetarium shows: Adults $3, children $2

It makes a nice change to find a science museum in Florida that is more about looking than doing. The intriguing collection features some impressive fossils, including an ancient ground sloth, armadillo and several types of elephant, all of which once roamed on Florida soil. The **American collection**, meanwhile, comprises oil paintings, watercolours and drawings, as well as furniture, silverware and glass. The **Cuban Museum** holds a fascinating and rare array of maps, documents, sculpture, paintings and ceramics from the 18th- to early 20th-century. The **Chinese Collection** features gemstones, pottery and documents, the **African Collection**, sculpture, masks, vessels and religious objects. The museum also has displays on the development of African-American culture in Florida and the US. However, kids will best like the collection of over 800 **teddy bears** dressed to represent historical eras or cultural events. The bears were donated by the Root family, who also bequeathed a selection of glass bottles representing their personal history of packaging and distributing of Coca-Cola. The **Planetarium** shows explore the wonders of nature and space.

Ponce de León Inlet Lighthouse

4931 South Peninsula Drive, Ponce Inlet, t (386) 761 1821, www.ponceinlet.org
Getting there From A1A Atlantic Avenue go south for 6 miles and turn right at the lights onto Beach Street. At the next lights turn left (south) on Peninsula Drive. The entrance to the lighthouse is two blocks down on your left
Open Daily 10–5 (10–9 in summer)
Adm Adults $5, children (under 11) $1.50

This charming red lighthouse was built in 1887. Formerly the Mosquito Inlet Lighthouse, its name was changed in 1927 to honour the Spanish explorer who first set foot on this coast in 1513 (*see* History p.4). It was restored in the 1980s. Its reinforced metal spiral staircase is very sturdy and has safety guards. Climb the 203 steps to the top, a staggering 175-ft in the air, for magnificent panoramic views of the coast down to New Smyrna Beach. There's a cluster of historic buildings at the bottom, one of which houses a gift shop and another a display of Fresnel lenses. The museum building features exhibitions about shipwrecks, the history of Daytona Beach and of the lighthouse keepers and their families. There's also a gift shop.

Shenandoah Stables

1759 Tomoka Farms Road, t (386) 257 1444
Rides: Adults $20 per hour, children (under 7) $3 when riding with an adult

Both beginners and experienced riders are welcome at this equestrian establishment, which has picnic areas and offers hay rides, pony trails and riding lessons.

Speed Park Motorsports

201 Fentress Boulevard, t (386) 253 3278, www.speedparkdaytona.com
Open Mon–Thurs 10–10, Fri, Sat 10–12 midnight
Adm Call for prices

This three-track go-kart park, opposite Daytona International Speedway, offers vehicles for children from 4ft 2" tall and zippy dragsters that go from 0–75 mph for more ambitious family members. There's also a well-stocked video games arcade.

Trolley Boats

406 Walker Street, Holly Hill, t (386) 238 3499, www.trolleyboattours.com
Tours: Daily, times vary. Departing from Ocean Walk Village, see above
Adm Adults $19.70, children (5–12) $14

For an alternative view of Daytona Beach, take the narrated **splash cruise**, which plunges you into the Halifax River. The 1¼-hour amphibious bus tour takes in the elegant homes and yachts of Volusia County's elite. Sites include the historic **Halifax Marina**, the **Riverfront Shops** and **Market place** and a ride along the **World's Most Famous Beach**.

Shopping

Ocean Walk Shoppes at Ocean Walk Village

250 North Atlantic Avenue, t (877) 845 9255, www.oceanwalkshoppes.com

Shop for surf gear, Harley Davidson apparel and accessories and pay a visit to **Bath Junkie** for robes, towels, body washes and things that put bubbles in your tub. There's also a **10-screen cinema**. Dining options include the **Bubba Gump Shrimp Company**, a **Johnny Rockets' diner**, and the **Cold Stone Creamery** and **Planet Smoothie** for kids' treats. *See* **Trolley Boats** above, for sightseeing tours that depart from the shopping village.

Riverfront Marketplace

300 South–300 North Beach Street, t (386) 671 3272, www.riverfrontmarketplace.com

This is downtown Daytona Beach's main shopping drag where you'll find antique shops, art galleries, gift shops and boutiques as well as restaurants and entertainment venues. It's home to the **Angell & Phelps Chocolate Factory**, 154 South Beach Street, **t** (386) 252 6531, **www**.angell andphelps.com, open Mon–Fri 9.30–5.30, Sat 9–5, where families can indulge in a free 30-minute guided tour of this traditional chocolatier, which features a chocolate conveyor belt and a chocolate waterfall for coating nuts. Next door is the **restaurant** and **wine bar**, which serves a variety of deli sandwiches, as well as kids' favourites such as peanut butter and jelly or grilled cheese, and salads and soups. That is, before pigging out on hand-made sweets for afters. On Saturdays, there's also the **City Island Farmers' Market**, 111 West International Speedway Boulevard, **t** (386) 671 3272, 7–12 noon, for plants and fresh fruit and vegetables.

Volusia Mall

1700 West International Speedway Boulevard, **t** (386) 253 6783, **www.volusiamall.net**
Getting there On US 92, across from the race track
Open Mon–Sat 10–9, Sun 12 noon–5.30. Free parking

This shopping mall features department stores such as **Burdines-Macy's**, **Dillard's**, **JCPenney** and **Sears**, as well as specialist retailers including **Abercrombie & Fitch**, **Gap**, **American Eagle Outfitters**, **Victoria's Secret Express** and **Bath & Body Works**. Kit the kids out with clothes, shoes, toys and books from the likes of **Footlocker**, **Waldenbooks**, **Gymboree**, **KB Toys**, **Anime House** and **Limited Too**. There's also a food court and several restaurants.

AROUND AND ABOUT

Animal magic

Barnyard Friends Animal Farm

505 North Samsula Drive, New Smyrna Beach, **t** (386) 428 0983
Getting there 10 mins' drive from Port Orange, 15–20 mins from Daytona Beach. From US 92 West take the I–95 south to SR 421 exit 256 toward Port Orange turn left onto Airport Road, turn right onto Pioneer Trail CR 4118 turn left to entrance
Open Tours: Fri 10, Sat 10, 12 noon and 2, Sun 12 noon and 2
Adm $5, under 2s is free

There's lots to see and learn at this working farm in **New Smyrna Beach**. A 1½–2-hour farm tour introduces kids to over 200 farm animals including goats, sheep, pigs, chickens, ducks, geese, turkeys, cows, ponies and donkeys. Hands-on activities include feeding white tail deer, goats, sheep and cows, holding baby rabbits, chicks and ducklings, milking a goat and having fun on a pony or hayride.

Central Florida Zoological Park

3755 Northwest Highway 17/92, Lake Monroe, **t** (407) 323 4450, **www.centralfloridazoo.org**
Getting there Exit 104 off I–4, travel east to Exit 104. Exit right onto Orange Avenue, turn left at the lights on Lake Monroe Road (County Road 15) continue over railroad tracks and right on Highway 17–92, zoo entrance ⅛ mile on the right
Open Daily 9–5
Adm Adults $8.95, children (3–12) $4.95. Thu 9–10 half price

This innovative 116-acre zoo park features about 145 species many of which are endangered. Kids can follow a **nature walk**, visit the **children's zoo**, ride on a **carousel or train** and learn about amphibians in the **Herpetarium**. There are **feeding sessions** and demonstrations (Sat–Sun) and two special behind-the-scenes events: the **Cheetah Encounter** (Sat 2.45) where kids can get a closer look at the world's fastest land mammal and the **Elephant Encounter** (Sun 2.15) a tour of the Asian elephant enclosure with a feeding session.

At the moment, the park is expanding. The latest additions are an **Australia exhibit** with kangaroos and emus and the **ZooLab** teaching laboratory, which houses an exhibition gallery and animal holding areas. Plans are underway for a **Woodland Park** where visitors can have a taste of pioneer life and a **Swamp Stomp Water Play Zone** for kids. The **Swamp Forest** exhibit will be a haven for Sumatran tigers and orangutans and will emphasise the fragility of wetland environments. There will also be **Grassland** and **Wild Florida** exhibits.

Buckets and spades

Watch out for signs warning about 'sea lice' along this stretch of coast. These itchy jellyfish larvae are common Mar–Aug with highest levels occurring from Apr–July. In the water, the larvae resemble dots of black pepper. As a precaution, women are better off wearing two-piece swimming costumes and all swimming gear should be removed directly after bathing and the skin showered thoroughly.

New Smyrna Beach

Getting there Off I–95, exit 84A
Open 8–dusk. Visitor centre: 7611 South Atlantic Avenue, New Smyrna Beach, **t** (386) 428 3384
Adm $5 per car

There are two beach areas to choose from, New Smyrna Beach being modelled on Daytona Beach with a **nine-mile car track** and **water sports** rentals offering anything from Jet Skis to sailboats and windsurf boards. It's also a popular spot for surfing and fishing. Families will prefer the quieter reaches of **Apollo Beach** where rocks out at sea protect the coast from strong undercurrents making it an ideal area for swimming. There's great shelling here, too, and the chance to see loggerhead turtles leaving their nests in the dunes from May–Sept as well as a wide variety of shore birds, year round. There are also **nature trails** and toilets. The **Canaveral National Seashore** is to the south along the A1A. **Playalinda Beach** is popular with families but only has basic facilities. Its beach walkovers protect the nests of loggerhead, leatherback, and green turtles.

Nature lovers

Blue Spring State Park

2100 West French Avenue, Orange City, t (386) 775 3663
Getting there **Exit 114 off I–4, follow signs. South off US 17–92 to Orange City and two miles west to entrance**
Open **8–dusk**
Adm **$5 per car, $1 per bike or pedestrian. Nature tours: Daily 10 and 1. Additional tours: Dec–Apr 3.30 and sunset cruises May–Jun Thu–Sun at 5. Tours: Adults $16, children (3–12) $10, plus tax)**

The temperate waters of the natural spring attract large numbers of manatees from November–March and Blue Spring has been designated a **Manatee Refuge** due to its growing population. The Native American Indians were drawn here, too, for the 72-degree waters and the abundance of fish. The river is still popular today for fishing, canoeing, boating and swimming but there are strict guidelines against swimming or boating near the manatees. Please adhere to signs throughout the park. The **Blue Spring Manatee Festival** every January brings entertainment and stalls with an emphasis on raising awareness about the endangered manatee population. Manatee educational programmes are scheduled mid-November–mid-March. Two-hour boat tours for viewing manatees, alligators, birds and deer are also available, for reservations, call **St. Johns River Cruises, t** (386) 917 0724/(407) 330 1612, **www**.sjrivercruises.com.

Sugar Mill Botanical Gardens

950 Old Sugar Mill Road, Port Orange, t (386) 767 1735
Getting there **I–95, take the Port Orange exit ramp (exit 85), go east on Route 421 to Route 5–A and onto Herbert Street and follow the signs**
Open **Apr–Oct 8am–7pm, Nov–March 8–6**
Adm **Free. Guided tours: Free, call, t (386) 767 0996**

The ruins of this abandoned sugar mill have been left to crumble and rust quietly along with a clutch of concrete dinosaurs from a now defunct theme park. There's something organic about the place on account of all this decay, which contrasts nicely with the lustrous Botanical blooms.

THE SPACE COAST

Whereas Orlando's big date was in 1971 when Disney took up residence, Titusville came alive with the roar of rocket launches back in 1950. A glance at the population increase between 1860 and 1960 – a staggering leap from 246 people to 6,410 – indicates just how big an impact the space race and its attendant tourist industry has made. Apart from the **Kennedy Space Center**, the town has a **theatre** and two **local history museums**.

Tourist Information

Titusville Area Chamber of Commerce, 200 South Washington Avenue, **t** (321) 267 3036, **www**.spacecityflusa.com

Getting there

40 miles from Orlando and 46 from Daytona Beach. If you're in a hurry take Highway 1 or for a more scenic route, Route A1A hugs the shore along the Space Coast and further south to the Treasure Coast. At Fort Pierce Route 707 runs between the two and is a better choice if you want to see the sights.

Things to see and do

American Police Hall of Fame and Museum

6350 Horizon Drive, t (321) 264 0911, www.aphf.org

Here, visitors can view cells, an electric chair (a rather sobering exhibit) and other instruments of law enforcement. The Hall of Fame also commemorates all the members of America's police force who have lost their lives in duty.

Kennedy Space Center

Kennedy Space Center on Route 405, t (321) 449 4444, ATX Programme: t (321) 449–4400, www.KennedySpaceCenter.com
Getting there 45 mins' drive from Orlando. Travel east on SR 50 turn right (east) onto SR 405 after the I–95 underpass and follow signs for Kennedy Space Center (approx 11 miles) the visitor complex is on your right. From Daytona Beach take exit 215 off I–95 and turn left (east) onto SR 50, then follow directions as above
Open Daily 9–6 (closing hours vary). Astronauts Hall of Fame: 9–7, check with, **www**.ksc.nasa.gov for launch schedule details and, **www**.ksctickets.com for tickets in advance. Kennedy Space Center bus tours: daily 10–2.50 (every 15 mins)
Adm Standard with Kennedy Space Center tour: Adults $30, children (3–11) $20, plus tax; Astronaut Hall of Fame: Adults $17, children (3–11) $13, plus tax; Maximum Access Admission: (includes the Space Center tour, IMAX® space movies and all exhibits and shows, plus Astronaut Hall of Fame and its space-flight simulators) Adults $35, children (3–11) $25, plus tax. ATX Programme $225 per person. Tours: Up-Close tour or Cape Canaveral Then and Now: Adults $22, children (3–11) $16

Housed on its very own island, the Kennedy Space Center occupies a territory larger than Manhattan; hence you need to bus it to get about and should plan to spend the whole day. From this site all the hardware for the space shuttle flights is prepared, tested and constructed, crews are trained and equipped and rockets and parts for the International Space Station are assembled. In the **Visitor Center Complex** kids can visit Mars from the comfort of their seat with Professor Pruvitt and his futuristic space team. Hands-on fun, live action, 3-D computer animation and special effects combine to put the audience of space cadets through their paces. In the **Rocket Garden** outside, you can climb inside the astronauts' cramped living quarters on a **Mercury** and **Gemini** spacecraft. There are free tours daily at 10.30 and 4.30. There's even an opportunity to tour the inside of a full-size shuttle **Explorer** in **Space Shuttle Plaza**, take a look at the history of space travel and quiz a real astronaut. The information centre has audio guides, hires strollers and will provide information on toilet facilities and restaurants. The standard 2–2½-hour **Kennedy Space Center bus tour** takes visitors inside a recreation of the **Apollo/Saturn V Center** where man's mission to travel to the moon began. View the multi-media presentation and marvel as you pass beneath the staggeringly huge, full-size replica of a **Saturn V Rocket**. It also includes visiting two **IMAX theatre**s, where kids will find out about exciting space initiatives, such as the construction of the International Space Station and the Space Shuttle Program (subject to seasonal change). There's also a chance to view the **launch pads** and the **Vehicle Assembly Building** from the LC 39 Observation Gantry where a theatre presentation and hands-on exhibits give insight into what goes into a NASA Space Shuttle launch. A **NASA Up Close Tour** gives z and the International **Space Station Center** where there's a full-scale mock-up of the astronauts' sleeping quarters and you can see components for the International Space Station in the making. A **Maximum Access Pass** also includes entry to the **Astronaut Hall of Fame**, where there are interactive exhibits and training simulators, including the **G-Force Trainer** and a **Space Shuttle experience**. It also celebrates the achievements of American astronauts, including the latest inductees who have experienced un-tethered space exploration and houses the world's largest collection of **astronaut memorabilia**. For a personal exploration of space training, try the **ATX Astronaut Training Experience**. This is usually only available to children aged 14+ but once a month, there are **family ATX sessions** that allow accompanied children to be in tests and training sessions to see if they've got what it takes to become an astronaut. You'll explore weightlessness and the forces of gravity in state-of-the-art **space shuttle simulators**, man a full-scale simulated Space Shuttle Mission and get to grips with Mission Control. The full-day experience also gives access to parts of the Space Centre that are off-limits to other tours. Finish with a trip to the Space Shop to buy flight suits for all the family, even toddlers (babies must make do with a space romper), before boldly going on your way.

Merritt Island National Wildlife Refuge

Visitor Centre on Route 402, t (321) 861 0667
Getting there 3½ miles East of Titusville on Route 402
Open Daily, Visitor Centre Mon–Fri 8–4.30, Sat–Sun 9–5 (Sun Nov–Mar only)
Adm Free

This 140,000-acre wildlife preserve borders the Canaveral National Seashore to the north of the Kennedy Space Center. The refuge is home to migratory birds, wading birds, shorebirds, and other native species of plants and wildlife including endangered species such as the Florida scrub jays, bald eagle, wood stork, manatee and loggerhead turtle. **Hiking trails** vary from ¼-mile to 5 miles and details of the four routes can be obtained at the visitor centre. There's also a **manatee observation deck** and an **observation tower** for views across this magnificent landscape that takes in coastal dunes, marshes, estuaries, pine forests and flatwoods, scrub oaks and palm hammocks. The seven-mile drive along **Black Point Wildlife Drive** is best early in the morning or late afternoon. Fishing, boating and canoeing are permitted although walking is the best way to appreciate this haven for Florida's amazing array of flora and fauna.

North Brevard Historical Museum

301 South Washington Avenue, Titusville, **t** (321) 269 3658
Getting there Highway 1 North, corner of Main Street
Open Tue–Sat 10–3
Adm Free (donations welcome)

This downtown museum has an impressive costume collection dating from the late 19th century, including a hand-stitched maternity dress, wedding dress, bathing suits, accessories, under garments and nightwear. The Seminole Indian display also includes clothing, tools, baskets and pottery, along with displays on Seminole village life. There's also a large collection of photographs relating to local history, which naturally covers the areas' strategic role in space exploration and the development of the coast.

The Titusville Playhouse

Emma Parrish Theater, 301 Julia Street, **t** (321) 268 1125

Seasonal children's shows and is housed in a former silent movie auditorium.

Valiant Air Command and Museum

6600 Tico Road, Titusville, **t** (321) 268 1941, **www.vacwarbirds.org**
Getting there Route 405
Open Daily 10–6
Adm Adults $9, children (under 12) $5

While in an air travel mood, pay a visit to the **Space Center Executive Airport** in Titusville, to view displays of lovingly restored and preserved air craft. The collection showcases the best of the world's Air Force planes and memorabilia from World War I to the present. See some of the museum's craft in action at the annual **Tico Warbird Show** in March.

Special trips

Christmas

Getting there Off State Road 50, 20 miles east of Orlando

It's Christmas all year round in Christmas, Florida, which is worth a stop-off *en route* to the Kennedy Space Center if only to send a postcard to the folks back home.

Fort Christmas

1300 Fort Christmas Road, **t** (407) 568 4149
Open 8–8 (8–6 in winter). Museum: Tue–Sat 10–5, Sun 1–5. Tours: 11–3
Adm Free
Picnic area, playground, gift shop

This is a replica of the fort that was built near here on December 25, 1837 as part of the Second Seminole War defences. There's a video and exhibits relating to the Indian Wars and seven restored Cracker homes that display pioneer life from the 1870s until the 1930s. Guided tours focus on the homesteads and the ways in which the inhabitants made their living, which ranged from raising cattle and growing citrus fruits to hunting, fishing and trapping. The shop sells Native American toys, books and sweets.

COCOA BEACH

As the crow flies this is the nearest beach to Orlando and since it's only 10 minutes' away from the Kennedy Space Center, it is adequately geared up for family trips with lots of affordable resort accommodation and a few seaside attractions. South of Cocoa Beach, Route A1A joins resort towns together like a string of pearls starting with Melbourne Beach all the way down the coast to Hobe Sound and Jupiter.

Getting there

46 miles (45mins) from Orlando and 20 mins south of Titusville on Highway 1

Getting around

Space Coast Area Transit (SCAT) 231 633 1878 runs a trolley bus beach service from Port Canaveral to South 13th Street Mon–Sat, 7–9, Sun 8–5. There are also services to Titusville and Melbourne Beach

Tourist information

Cocoa Beach Area Chamber of Commerce, 400 Fortenberry Road, Merritt Island, **t** (321) 459 2200, **www.visitcocoabeach.com**

Things to see and do

Ace of Hearts Ranch

7400 Bridal Path Lane, **t** (321) 638 0104
Getting there From Route 528 go east to 407 (Titusville exit) turn right on Shepard Drive and one mile to the traffic lights, turn right on Grissom, go two miles south to Ranch Road, turn right go one mile to entrance on the right
Adm Eco tours: $25 or a full day on the ranch, including lunch $125. Call ahead for reservations

Visit this peaceful country ranch for an hour-long eco-tour along wooded bridalways or the beach. The ranch also offers barbecues and hayrides.

Alan Shepard Park

Getting there Off State Road 520
Open Daily; Parking $3

Just south of the pier, this lovely, natural expanse of beach boasts excellent water quality and good amenities. Just one block from the famous Ron Jon Surf Shop, the beach is a regular venue for surfing competitions and affords visitors great views of the space shuttle launches. Bike and beach rentals are available and the park offers showers, toilets, picnic areas with barbecue grills and a bathhouse.

Andretti Thrill Park

3960 South Babcock Street, Melbourne, **t** (321) 956 6706, **www.andrettithrillpark.com**
Getting there Take A1A to Route 192 and go west over the Melbourne Causeway to Babcock Street. Then turn left and head south two miles, the park entrance is on your right
Open Mon–Fri 10–11, Sat, Sun 10–1am, some weeks from 12 noon, call or see website for variations
Adm Wristbands: 3 hours of unlimited attractions $23.95, 4 hours $27.95, chidren 36–48" $17.95

A family park where children from age four can take a spin on the **Junior Safari track** while their older siblings battle it out on the **F1 Extreme track** with its sweeping turns or the **Junior Indie Track** with sharp banking. The figure of eight **Super Speedway Track** also features two-seater cars for children and adults to ride together. There are paddle boats, batting cages, kiddie rides, laser tag, a games room, mini golf and an indoor playground.

Brevard Museum of Art and Science Center

1520 Highland Avenue, Melbourne, **t** (321) 254 7782
Getting there From US 1, turn east onto Eau Gallie Boulevard, go two blocks to Highland Avenue, turn left; museum entrance is on the right
Open Tue–Sat 10–5, Sun 1–5
Adm Adults $5, children $2, under 2s free

This museum and art gallery resides in the lovely historic district of Eau Gallie, one of Brevard County's best-preserved locales, one block from the Indian River. There's a children's **science centre** where kids can learn about space, the earth, the weather, physics and Florida using touch screens, microscopes and about 30 interactive exhibits. The **Art museum** houses contemporary works by American artists, including a large collection of works by Florida artists. There are also examples of Japanese, Egyptian, African and Chinese decorative arts, including Tibetan costumes and Burmese tribal masks. Afterwards, cross the street to **Pineapple Park** for a picnic and a run in the playground.

Brevard Museum of History and Natural Science

2201 Michigan Avenue, **t** (321) 632 1830, **www.brevardmuseum.com**
Getting there From I–95 take SR 524 exit east 3 miles to Clearlake Rd. ¼ mile south and turn west (right) at the traffic lights onto Michigan Avenue
Open Mon–Sat 10–4, Sun 12 noon–4
Adm Adults $5.50, children (5–16) $3.50, under 5s free
Gift shop

Here visitors can travel 8,000 years back to the time when the Windover Pond burial ground was in use. This amazing site was only discovered in 1984 but it has yielded much information about the development of early man in North America. The rich peat deposits have even preserved portions of ancient human brains. Also on site are dioramas exploring the county's natural habitats of swamp, marsh and coastal reef. Outside, you can walk the corresponding trails of the 22-acre nature reserve.

Brevard Zoo

8225 North Wickham Road, Melbourne, **t** (321) 254 9453, **www.brevardzoo.org**
Getting there Exit 191 off I–95
Open Daily 9.30–5 (last adm 4.15)

Adm Adults $9, children (2–12) $6. Train ride: $3. Guided kayak trips: $3–$5. Eco-tours: $10

This interesting zoo is divided up into zones, each with unique opportunities for encountering the wildlife. In **Expedition Africa**, kids can feed the giraffe from the boardwalk overlook or take a **guided kayak trip** through the rhino and giraffe habitat where there's also the chance to view gazelle, antelope and primates. **Native Florida** offers up red wolves, white tailed deer and plenty of alligators. The recent addition of the **Wetlands Outpost** opens up guided kayak tours through the zone, which also conducts four-hour eco-tours for dolphin and manatee spotting on the Indian River Lagoon. The **Austral–Asia zone** features a free-flying aviary with lorikeets, fruit bats and parrots and the jungle environs of **La Selva** house monkeys, tapirs, llamas and more. There are alligator and crocodile demonstrations (3.30 Wed, Fri and Sun) and River Otter Feedings (Tue and Sat at 2). A 10-minute **train journey** takes visitors past the Australian aviary and around Lemur Island.

Kids all enjoy the **Paws On Animal Study Zone**, a multi-level interactive playground where they can troop around with their families and encounter smaller animals in the hands-on petting zoo. Stroller rentals are also available.

Cocoa Beach Pier

401 Meade Avenue, Cocoa Beach, t (321) 783 7549, www.cocoabeachpier.com
Adm Fishing: spectators 50 cents, Adults $3.50, children (under 12) $3; Parking $5

This 800-ft fishing pier is the focal (and social) point in Cocoa Beach. Along its length you'll find seafood restaurants and bars, an ice cream parlour, games arcade, beachwear and nautical gift shops and a beach rental concession. It's also popular for concerts, local events and annual festivals, including the BeachFest in May and Surf Contest at Easter.

Cocoa Beach Recreation Complex

Cocoa Beach Country Club, Tom Warriner Boulevard (west end of Minutemen Causeway), **t** (321) 868 3314
Open Pool: May–Sept Mon–Fri 9–6, Sat 10–4, Sun 11–5, Oct–April Mon, Wed, Fri 10–5, Tue Thurs 10–6, Sat, Sun 11–4
Adm May–Sept Adults $2.50, children $1.50, Oct–Apr Adults $3, children $2
Lockers, showers, toilets, changing rooms, restaurant, concession stands

The 212-acre park contains a public outdoor **heated swimming pool** at the Cocoa Beach Country Club. It is open for swimming lessons and recreational swimming. There's also a jumbo water slide and children's play pool with a shower umbrella and water sprays. The grounds are also open for **golf**, **tennis**, **volleyball soccer** and **fishing**.

Jetty Park

400 East Jetty Road, Cape Canaveral, t (321) 783 7111
Open Daily to 9pm; **Parking** $1

This is a good spot for watching the rocket launches and viewing the cruise ships on their way to Port Canaveral. The park has plenty of facilities, including a general store, toilets and showers, picnic areas, barbecue grills, playground, bike path and lifeguards in summer. The refurbished boardwalk along the jetty is a good spot for fishing.

Sidney Fischer Park

2100 Route A1A
Open Daily; **Parking** $3

This 10-acre oceanfront park offers playgrounds, refurbished toilets and changing facilities, picnic areas, shops and rental concessions. It's also a popular swimming spot for families.

TRAXX at Jungle Village Family Fun Center

8801 Astronaut Boulevard, Cape Canaveral, t (321) 783 0595
Getting there South of Route 528 on Route A1A
Open Sun–Thurs 10– 12 midnight, Fri, Sat 10–1am
Adm Per activity

This family fun centre boasts bright animal sculptures, go-kart tracks suitable for both adults and children, a mini golf course, a large games arcade, laser tag and batting cages.

Shopping

Old Cocoa Village, which lies inland along the banks of the Indian River Lagoon, boasts historic architecture and shopping boutiques, as well as casual dining and restaurants. **Atlantic Avenue** is the main shopping area and here you'll find the **Ron Jon Surf Shop**, 4151 North Atlantic Avenue, **t** (321) 799 8820, **www**.ronjons.com, which claims to be the biggest surf shop in the world and will sort out cool swimwear for the whole family, as well as beach accessories, sun lotion and beach toys. Once you've bought your surfing essentials, you can get kitted out with the hardwear at **Ocean**

Sports World, 3220 South Atlantic Avenue, **t** (321) 783 4088, **www**.oceansportsworld.com, where you can rent paddleboards, surfboards, one–three man kayaks and surf kayaks. Lessons are also available. Pop into **The Dinosaur Store**, 299 West Cocoa Beach Causeway, **t** (321) 783 7300, **www**.dinosaurstore.com, for a retail experience with some natural science thrown in, as you gaze at the vast array of fossils, minerals and meteorites on display. There's amber jewellery, dinosaur T-shirts, shark's teeth and shark teeth necklaces, dinosaur casts, as well as children's educational books and toys.

Merritt Square Mall

777 East Merritt Island Causeway, Merritt Island,
t (321) 452 3272, www.MerrittSquareMall.com
Getting there SR 520 Causeway, across the Banana River from Cocoa Beach

This is the biggest shopping centre in the area with four sizeable department stores (**Dillards**, **JCPenney**, **Macy's** and **Sears**), which stock children's toys and clothing. Elsewhere kids can browse around at **EB Games**, **Footlocker**, **Claire's**, **Books-a-Million** and **Hot Topic** for funky gifts and streetwear. There are also plenty of gift shops, ice cream parlours, cafés and restaurants to keep everyone amused.

AROUND AND ABOUT

Buckets and spades

Along the lovely shores of the **Treasure Coast barrier islands**, you'll find plenty of family parks and beaches, some with full amenities and others in a more natural state. Route A1A south of Sebastian Inlet passes through **Indian River Shores** with a host of well-equipped family sands. There's **Round Island Park** (A1A south, west side close to the Indian River), with picnic areas and an observation tower, **Jaycee Park** (Ocean Drive and A1A) with ocean boardwalks, shaded picnic tables and grills, and **Sebastian Inlet State Park** (*see* below), which is known as a surfers' paradise. **Treasure Shores Park** and **Golden Sands County Park** are good for swimming with lifeguards on duty and playgrounds, among other facilities. **Vero Beach**, in the heart of citrus country, is great for outdoor activities and there are interesting restaurants, shops, museums and arts establishments clustered here and on the mainland. Further south towards **Fort Pierce** and **Hutchinson Island**, you come to **Jensen Beach**, which has avoided being dominated by high-rise developments. The best family beach here is **Sea Turtle Beach** with its dune-backed swathe of sand, lifeguards, volleyball, restaurant, toilet and shower facilities. Just south along Route A1A is the popular **Stuart Beach**, with its well-equipped facilities, including picnic tables and grills, volleyball and basketball courts, lifeguards, an outdoor café and a playground. The New York Mets, Los Angeles Dodgers and new Washington Nationals (formerly the Montreal Expos) all play pre-season spring training games each March within a short drive of the historic town of Stuart. For coastal attractions, *see* below.

Look at this!

Elliott Museum

825 North Ocean Boulevard, Jensen Beach,
t (772) 225 1961
Open Mon–Sat 10–4, Sun 1–4
Adm Adults $6, children (6–12) $2

This eclectic collection includes the timesaving inventions of Sterling Elliott, including his knot-tying and automated addressing machine, American antiques and decorative arts, vintage cars, dolls, local history displays, store interiors, including a blacksmith's forge, ice cream parlour and a barber's shop, as well as an exhibition of baseball memorabilia.

Florida Oceanographic Coastal Center

890 Northeast Ocean Boulevard, Jensen Beach,
t (772) 225 0505, www.floridaoceanographic.org
Getting there Exit 101 off I-95
Open Mon–Sat 10–5, Sun 12 noon–4
Adm Adults $6, children (3–12) $3

This interpretative centre offers the chance to learn more about the local marine environment by exploring the nature trails through coastal hardwood hammocks and mangrove forest. There's a children's activity pavilion with hands-on science displays, a visitor centre, touch tanks and aquariums, and a daily schedule of nature walks and stingray feeding sessions, call for eco-tour reservations.

Harbor Branch Oceanographic Institution

5600 US Highway 1 North, Fort Pierce,
t (772) 465 2400, www.hboi.edu

Getting there Exit 138 off I–95 to Route 614 (Indrio Road) head east 3.5 miles to US 1, turn left (north) and drive one mile to Harbor Branch, entrance on your right
Open Boat tours: Mon–Sat at 10, 1 and 3
Adm Free. Boat tours: Adults $12, children (6–12) $6
Gift shop

This museum, teaching and research facility houses over 450,000 specimens of marine animals and plants from around the world, including localities in South Florida and the Caribbean Islands. They aren't all on display but a 90-minute tour bus and tram tour of the campus explores aquariums, research submersibles and marine exploration vessels. Kids can clamber aboard the model of a deep-sea submersible beside the visitor centre.

Heritage Center and Citrus Museum

2145 14th Avenue, Vero Beach, t (772) 770 2263
Getting there Off Route 60 (Beachland Boulevard)
Open Tue–Fri 10–4; **Adm** (donations welcome)
Gift shop

Learn everything you ever wanted to know about citrus farming at this museum dedicated to the county's production of zesty fruits. The life of pioneers who threw in their lot against the elements to make their living from citrus crops is played out through photo displays, artefacts and memorabilia, including packaging, labels and models of packing plants. Book in advance for free guided tours of the groves, which highlight present day production.

Indian River County Historical Society

2336 14th Avenue, Vero Beach, t (772) 778 3435
Open Mon 10–1, Tue–Sat 10–4
Adm Free (donations welcome)

Discover the importance of the East Coast Railway to the citrus industry along this stretch of coast through exhibitions that chart the development of the area. Book in advance for downtown **Vero Beach historical walking tours** (Weds 11–1 in season).

Did you know?
The water trough in the grounds of the St. Lucie County Historical Museum once stood in the winter home of Edwin Binney, the creator of Crayola crayons? Binney's schoolteacher wife, Alice, is said to have made up the name Crayola by merging the French word 'craie' chalk with 'ola', pertaining to oil or wax.

McLarty Treasure Museum

Sebastian Inlet State Park (*see* p.157), 13180 Route A1A, Vero Beach, t (772) 589 2147
Open Daily 10–4.30 (last film showing 3.15–4)
Adm $1, under 6s free

In 1715, a hurricane stranded 1,000 Spanish sailors along this coast and committed 700 of their fellows, along with their cargo of gold and silver, to the deep. Thus the area became known as the Treasure Coast. Displays include ships' fittings, jewellery and religious artefacts, gold buckles and coin, ingots, nails and fine porcelain. The museum stands on the site of the Spanish salvagers' camp but some of the most fabulous items from the inventory are said to be still in the watery depths.

Mel Fisher's Treasure Museum

1322 US Highway 1, Sebastian, t (772) 589 9875, www.melfisher.com
Open Mon–Sat 10–5, Sun 12 noon–5
Adm Adults $6.50, child $2

The 1715 shipwreck was the original inspiration for the late Mel Fisher and his crew and the partial success they had here, spurred the team on to discover the cargo of the Atocha in Key West (*see* Southeast p.218). Mel's salvagers are still searching for the main treasures lost in the 1715 hurricane. Although some sources maintain that all the treasure has been recovered, the Mel Fisher website holds a fascinating story about what still might lie buried beneath the waves of the Treasure Coast.

St. Lucie County Historical Museum

414 Seaway Drive, Fort Pierce, t (772) 462 1795
Open Tue–Sat 10–4, Sun 12 noon–4
Adm Adults $4, children (6–12) $1.50, plus tax, under 6s free

This modest museum contains a round up of all that the east coast is famous for, bar the rockets. There are pioneer home exhibits, fixtures and fittings from a general store built in the late 1800s, Native American Indian displays, railroad and citrus farming memorabilia, a forts exhibit and a fire engine (1919).

UDT-SEAL Museum

3300 North Route A1A, North Hutchinson Island, Fort Pierce, t (772) 595 5845
Open Tue–Sat 10–4, Sun 12 noon–4
Adm Adults $5, children (6–12) $2

If watching re-runs of Demi Moore hitting pay dirt while undergoing Navy Seal training in *G.I. Jane* has inspired your kids, then this museum should sort the wheat from the chaff. Think Royal Marines with suntans, as you tour the exhibits dedicated to Naval heroes. The main focus is on the training of US Navy frogmen for the 1943 D-Day invasion. There are also displays that look like an Aladdin's cave of Action Man accessories, for air, land and sea missions. Outside you can see a couple of boats (one nattily decorated with shark's teeth), submersibles and other exhibits. The museum stands in the grounds of Pepper Park where families can swim on the beach, which is supervised by lifeguards or have a picnic and a game of tennis.

Nature lovers

Fort Pierce Inlet State Park

905 Shore Winds Drive, **t** (772) 468 3985
Getting there Southernmost end of North Hutchinson Island
Open Daily 8–dusk
Adm $5 per car, $1 per bike or pedestrian

This park did sustain damage due to the 2004 hurricanes but is now up and running. The storms have deposited more sand in some places making it even more fun for digging and castle building than before. **Dynamite Point**, previously a World War II Navy training ground (*see* UDT-SEAL Museum p.156), is now a popular spot for bird watching. There are picnic areas, a playground and you can surf from the beach or collect shells. The south end of the park attracts fishermen. The best swimming beach is on the Oceanside at **Jetty Park** where lifeguards are present. **Jack Island Preserve**, one mile to the north, has hiking, bike and nature trails.

Hobe Sound National Wildlife Refuge

13640 Southeast Federal Highway, **t** (772) 546 2067
Getting there Visitor centre: on the mainland on US Highway 1, two miles south of Bridge Road (State Road 708)
Open Refuge 8–dusk; Visitor centre: Mon–Fri 9–3
Adm Free

This nearly 1,000-acre refuge comprises 232 acres of pine-scrub oak forest, which is inhabited by endangered scrub jays and other rare birds, and 735 acres of coastal dune and mangrove swamp. At the visitor centre, children can walk a short waterfront nature trail and view interpretative nature displays. The beach here is a key site for nesting sea turtles and sea turtles walks take place from June–July.

Jonathan Dickinson State Park

16450 Southeast Federal Highway (Highway 1), **t** (772) 546–2771
Open Daily 8–dusk
Adm $4 per car, $1per bike or pedestrian

In 1696, a Quaker merchant called Jonathan Dickinson was shipwrecked off the coast in the area of Hobe Sound. Along with his wife and baby, he encountered the local tribe, the Ais, and made an account of their culture in his journal, along with observations about the Spanish settlers he encountered. The shipwrecked survivors then set off on a long and difficult journey up the coast to St. Augustine. All but two of the party survived the trip, Dickinson's family were among the fortunate. Hire a cabin and walk the trails through the park to imagine the wilderness that Dickinson first laid eyes on. Loxahatchee River Adventures, **t** (561) 746 1466. Tours: 9, 11, 1 and 3 daily. Adults $12, children (6–12) $7. Take a narrated tour through the park to hear more about Dickinson and his crew and also about a lone pioneer named Trapper Nelson, who made his home near the scenic Loxahatchee River in 1930. Visitors can explore his homestead and environs.

Sebastian Inlet State Park

9700 South Route A1A, Melbourne Beach, **t** (321) 984 4852, camping (561) 589 9659
Open Daily 24 hours
Adm $3.25 per vehicle

If you're wondering where everybody's gone surfing in the USA, well, it's probably here, at least while you're in Florida. The park hosts several surfing contests every year. The restored north jetty of Sebastian Inlet, which sustained hurricane damage, is now fully open and is about as good as it gets for surf breaks. In addition, you can catch a mean wave out at Monster Hole, which lies 1.3 mile from the beach. A man made swimming area behind the jetty provides safe swimming for young children. The three miles of sands provide further opportunities for swimming, as well as scuba diving, snorkelling and shelling. Fishing and catching shellfish are also popular pursuits and there are facilities for canoeing and kayaking in the Indian River Lagoon. There are ranger-led tour cruises to neighbouring Pelican Island. In summer, there are also night-time walks to observe nesting turtles.

Orlando

Of the multitude of restaurant signs you see along almost every street, **Denney's** is good for breakfast and **Red Lobster** serves good seafood and steaks. **Hooters** do a kids' breakfast for about $1, though later in the day they cater for a more adult crowd. One of the main restaurant drags is off I–4 (exit 74A) along **Sand Lake Road**, where you can sample sushi and seafood or visit one of the largest **McDonald's** in the world. Most hotels will be able to point out the good restaurants nearby, reservations and requests for driving information are highly recommended.

Bonefish Grill

7830 Sand Lake Road, t (407) 355 7707, www.bonefishgrill.com (*moderate*)

Good, fresh seafood from this Florida-founded chain, which is now being rolled out nationwide, as part of the Outback Steaks enterprise. Wood-grilled fish dishes include rainbow trout, sea bass, tuna and snapper, as well as steak and chicken dishes, pork chops and pasta marinara. Side dishes include steamed vegetables and island rice.

Café Tu Tu Tango

8625 International Drive, t (407) 248 2222, www.cafetututango.com (*moderate–expensive*)

(*See* also Coconut Grove, Southeast p.220.) The brightly coloured walls match the diversity and flavours of the food at this art-inspired restaurant. Kids will enjoy creating their own masterpiece on a pizza from the children's menu or they can pick and choose from the tapas-style main menu, which includes a variety of chips and dips, skewers, ribs and wings, quesadillas, empanadas and other finger-friendly foods.

Dan Marino's Town Tavern

9101 International Drive, t (407) 363 1013, www.danmarinostowntavern.com (*expensive–very expensive*)

This sports-bar restaurant is part of a chain dreamed up by Miami Dolphin football quarterback Dan Marino. As such, you can catch a football (American, that is) game while tucking in to good quality food. There's a children's menu and the usual sports bar fare is spiced up with dishes such as chicken quesadilla, barbecue salmon, seared tuna, meatloaf and steaks.

Flipper's Pizzeria

7480 Universal Boulevard, t (407) 351 5643 (*inexpensive*)

Good quality, homemade pizza, plus salads and desserts. Takeout and delivery services are available.

McDonald's

6875 Sand Lake Road, t (407) 351 2185
Open 7am–3am. Breakfast Mon–Fri 7–10.30, Sat, Sun 7–11 (*inexpensive*)

Bigger than your average McDonald's this fun factory boasts an upstairs **PlayPlace** filled with bright, colourful twisting tubes and slides, including a 60-ft super slide. There are also about 60 arcade games to keep older kids busy and families can find out about attraction tickets, transportation, reservations and daily theme park information at the McDonald's Hospitality Center. The Bistro Gourmet menu features meatballs, shrimp and chicken dishes, create your own pasta, deli sandwiches, panini and pizzas. Desserts are suitably exotic too, ranging from carrot cake to crème brulee cheesecake.

Ming Court

9188 International Drive, t (407) 351 9988, www.ming-court.com (*expensive*)

Food is not just something that you put in your stomach here; it's an art form.

This award-winning gourmet restaurant serves handmade dim sum, sushi and innovative Oriental dishes such as, filet mignon in Szechwan sauce, Eight Treasure Duck with scallops, shrimp and other delights, plus seafood and steaks. The Ming Court kids' menu offers a choice of crispy chicken, barbecue pork or beef or golden tempura shrimp, all served with shrimp chips, fries, vegetable noodles, rice, dipping sauce and a fortune cookie. Sit outside in the walled courtyard or indoors overlooking the fishpond.

Sweet Tomatoes

6877 South Kirkman Road (at International Drive), t (407) 869 5550 (*inexpensive*)

If you're craving something green in this fast-food universe, these buffet chain restaurants feature massive salad bars, a bread bar, a pasta bar, a fruit bar, and a dessert bar, so that kids can choose what they want from each. The salads are fresh and it's a cheap family option, too.

Ruth's Chris Steak House

7501 Sand Lake Road, **t** 407 226 3900, **www.**ruthschris.com

Open Mon–Sat 5–10, Sun 5–9 (*moderate*)

A variety of steak dishes, plus chicken and veal chops, are served up here with vegetable sides, including steamed broccoli au gratin, spinach sautéed in butter, asparagus and grilled tomatoes. The lunch menu also includes sandwiches, specialities and mixed grills.

Universal Theme Parks

Universal Studios
Best for snacks

Louie's Italian Restaurant/Starbucks, New York – pizza, pasta and ice cream.

Beverly Hills Boulangerie, The Front Lot – for pastries, coffee and sandwiches.

Best for a quick bite

Mel's Drive-In, Hollywood – gets very busy so head there early for ultra-fast food (burgers, hot dogs, fries and shakes) in this popular 1950s-style diner.

Café La Bamba, Hollywood – burgers and salads, plus fruit salads for healthy lunches.

Best for family meals

Finnegan's Grill, New York – nice long bar for drinks with TV screens showing sports games, as well as a large restaurant serving UK dishes, such as bangers and mash, fish and chips and Irish stew, plus sandwiches; it's also within earshot of the Blues Brothers shows.

Lombard's Seafood Grille, San Francisco/Amity – in the corner of the park where there are quite a few restaurants, this large establishment gets very busy, so plan for an early lunch. Quality steak, fish and seafood dishes are on the menu and diners can enjoy pleasant waterside views.

Universal Islands of Adventure
Best for snacks

Croissant Moon Bakery, Port of Entry – Grab a wholesome sandwich and a cookie at this nice little spot near the entrance.

Hop on Pop Ice cream Shop, Seuss Landing – Sweet somethings for your little ones.

Best for a quick bite

Circus McGurkus Café Stoopendous, Seuss Landing – if your kids like to be entertained while they eat, then head to this goofy establishment for pasta and pizza fare accompanied by big top décor and strange mechanical contraptions that pass by from time to time.

Captain America Diner, Marvel Super Hero Island – burgers, sandwiches, fries and salads for building up future defenders of the earth.

Best for family meals

Mythos Restaurant, The Lost Continent – there's a children's menu, crayons and the food is inventive and healthy with fresh tuna salads, Asian influenced pasta dishes as well as chicken and burgers. Kids will like the rock formation walls and the great views.

Confisco Grille and Backwater Bar. Watch out for the tricky waiters whose sleights of hand are legendary in this thieves' den. If the light-fingered crew has misplaced your cutlery, let the manager know and he'll soon mend their larcenous ways. Keep a close eye on your dinner, be it a burger, chicken salad, plate of ribs, pasta or a pad Thai, because they might take a shine to that next. Character lunches and priority seating are available, pre-book at the Port of Entry Dining Cart.

Universal CityWalk
Best for snacks

Cinnabon – Hot cinnamon rolls, coffee and ice cream.

Best for a quick bite

Latin Quarter Express – Tamales, nachos and Cuban sandwiches to go.

Best for family meals

Hard Rock Café, **t** (407) 351 7625, **www.**hardrock.com **(*moderate*)**

This branch of the famous Hard Rock chain has walls crammed with 'rockabilia' and a huge pink Cadillac suspended over the bar. Families can enjoy smokehouse specials, including barbecue ribs, chicken or a pulled pork sandwich. There are burgers, steaks, fries, meatloaf, and pasta and salad dishes for those wanting a lighter bite. There's also a Hard Rock Live 3,000-seater concert venue for when you want to rock till dawn.

Latin Quarter (*moderate–expensive*) – this friendly restaurant has live entertainment nightly and serves Mexican and South American dishes. Portions are huge and families can start with nachos and dips and graduate to the chicken, pork, fish and beef dishes with Latin American and Caribbean influences. There's a kids' menu offering chicken and rice, as well as burgers, pasta and grilled cheese sandwiches. It gets lively after 9pm when there are live DJs, so dine early if you have young kids or ask if there's any seating available on the patio.

Daytona Beach

Cruisin' Cafe Bar & Grill

2 South Atlantic Ave t (386) 253 5522.
Open Daily 11am–2.30am. (*inexpensive–moderate*)

Diners at this café/motor museum sit in real race-car booths and can choose from American fare such as burgers and steaks or sandwiches (on marble rye, wheat, pumpernickel or homemade white bread), plus soups, seafood and salads.

Gene's Steak House

3674 West International Speedway,
t (386) 255 2059 (*inexpensive–moderate*)

Get your motor running at this great family run steakhouse that also serves up fresh seafood. Reservations suggested.

Lighthouse Landing

4940 South Peninsula Drive, Ponce Inlet,
t (386) 761 9271 (*inexpensive–expensive*)

Enjoy some fresh seafood or the house special, 'fish in foil' cooked with white wine, lemon and garlic, at this nautical waterfront diner by the lighthouse. Kids can have fish and chips or sandwiches.

Ocean Deck

127 South Ocean Avenue, t (386) 253 5224,
www.oceandeck.com (*moderate*)

There's plenty of choice when it comes to where to sit at this casual beach restaurant. Upstairs it's air-conditioned and offers great views of the ocean action, while below reggae beats keep the clientele on a laid-back vibe. The latest addition is large enclosed deck that looks a bit like an overgrown treehouse and as such should prove a hit with the children. Kids will love their menu, which features peanut butter and jellyfish sandwiches, chicken bites or wings, hot dog, hamburger, cheese sticks, a ham, turkey or beef sub, fish sandwich or shrimp bucket, all served with fries in a frsibee that they can take home afterwards. The main menu features shrimp, crab legs, clams and fresh fish dishes, plus sandwiches and salads.

The Space Coast

Titusville

Dixie Crossroads

1475 Garden Street, t (321) 268 5000
(*inexpensive–moderate*)

For fresh fish to cook at home try their outlet: Wild Ocean Seafood Market, 688 South Park Avenue, Titusville, t (321) 383 8885. Shrimp, stone crab, fish dishes and lobster are the order of the day here. If you're very hungry between launchings, try the Cape Canaveral Special, which festures one dozen boat run shrimp, 2 dozen rock shrimp and a ¼lb scallops for $20.99 or with lobster for $31.99. Children under 12 can opt for the $2.99 kids' menu and choose from hamburgers, clams, fish, shrimp or chicken nuggets served with fritters, fries, a drink and chocolate pudding. There's live music on Saturday afternoons.

Cocoa Beach

Bernard's Surf

2 South Atlantic Avenue t (321) 783 2401
(*moderate–expensive*)

A family institution, Bernard's serves up quality steak and seafood, including their signature baked oyster starter and specials such as roast duck with pecan maple glaze and red snapper in seafood béchamel sauce. Children under 10 can have pasta marinara, fried clams, shrimp or flounder, hamburger or chicken fingers, plus a free ice cream.

Marlins Bar & Grill

Cocoa Beach Pier, 401 Meade Avenue, Cocoa Beach,
t (321) 783 7549 (*inexpensive–moderate*)

Enjoy snacks, sandwiches, homemade soups, chicken wings, burgers, seafood and desserts in a relaxed atmosphere overlooking the ocean. There's indoor and outdoor seating and a kids' menu is also available.

Roberto's Little Havana Restaurant

26 North Orlando Avenue (A1A), Cocoa Beach,
t (321) 784 1868 (*moderate*)

This offers authentic Cuban cuisine served in relaxed and very family-friendly surroundings.

Around and about

Fort Pierce

Mangrove Mattie's

1640 Seaway Drive (Hutchinson Island), **t** (772) 466 1044 (*moderate–expensive*)

Dine in casual family style on the waterfront terrace for great views over Fort Pierce Inlet. Seafood specials, plus chicken and pasta dishes.

Jensen Beach

Conchy Joe's

3945 Northeast Indian River Drive, **t** (772) 334 1130 (*moderate–expensive*)

Kids will like the Caribbean style décor where swordfish and parrots observe them tucking in to their burgers and fries or fish, hot dog and spaghetti dinners. Casual seafood fare is on offer at this unfussy restaurant overlooking the Indian River. There's live entertainment Thurs–Sun nights.

Kissimmee

Azteca's

809 North Main Street, **t** (407) 933 8155 (*inexpensive–moderate*)

This rustic, family-owned eatery serves up wholesome Mexican cuisine. Dine in cosy nooks indoors or out on the patio. Dishes include enchiladas, pollo con mole (chicken with spicy chocolate sauce), plus steak and fish dishes.

Magic Mining Steaks and Seafood Co.

7763 West Irlo-Bronson Highway, Kissimmee, **t** (407) 396 1950

Open Daily 5.30–10 (*moderate*)

Beneath two three-storey golf courses you'll find this Wild West themed restaurant complete with mineshaft interior and faux-mountain range walls. So, pretty much your average Orlando eatery, then. For a handful of change you can set the steam train on its way in and out of the building or save your pennies for the arcade games. Kids will love the waterfalls and kitsch décor while parents will appreciate the chance to sit outdoors and enjoy quality steak and seafood dishes including lobster tail, crab claws and grilled shrimp.

Pacino's Italian Restaurant

5795 West Highway 192, **t** (407) 396 8022, **www.pacinos.com**

Open Daily 4–10 (*inexpensive–moderate*)

This family-friendly Italian restaurant offers a variety of pasta and pizza dishes, as well as veal, lamb, seafood, salads and steaks. Diners can choose to eat indoors under the fibre-optic lights out in the courtyard in true Tuscan fashion.

Port Canaveral

Grills Seafood Deck & Tiki Bar

Sunrise Marina, 505 Glen Cheek Drive, **t** (321) 868 2226, **www.visitgrills.com**

Open Daily 6am–11pm (*inexpensive*)

Perfect for watching the ships coming in and going out. Whether you need a hearty breakfast for a fishing trip or a bite to eat before boarding your cruise ship, this casual restaurant is ready for business. Omletes, buttermilk pancakes, fish breakfasts or fruit bowls are ready to help you start the day. Or pop in later for some fresh shrimp, sushi or their range of tempting chowders and sandwiches.

Stuart

Prawnbroker Grill

Harbour Bay Plaza, 3754 Southeast Ocean Boulevard, **t** (772) 288 1222, **www.prawnbroker.com** (*expensive*)

This recently refurbished English pub-style restaurant is highly regarded for its menu of nightly specials that include fresh seafood and steak dishes. There's a children's menu and chicken, pasta, salads and sandwiches are also available.

Vero Beach

Ocean Grill

1050 Sexton Plaza, **t** (772) 231 5409, **www.ocean-grill.com**

Open Lunch: Mon–Fri 11.30–2.30, dinner daily 5–10 (*expensive–very expensive*)

This 1930s beachside restaurant offers casual dining with either spectacular views of the ocean or equally fascinating walls indoors, adorned with pictures of pirates. Seafood and steak specials, ribs or roast duckling, served with steamed vegetables, plus tasty soups, hot crab dip and salads. Children's menu available.

Quiz

1. What is known as the fun time capital of the Sunshine state?

2. What do you have to walk through to enter Gatorland?

3. Where do things go bump in the night?

4. Where can you jump on rides with a technicolour movie twist?

5. Where can you ride a fish through cooling fountain jets?

6. What is the world's fastest land mammal?

7. What animals leave their nests in the dunes from May to September?

8. Where did man's mission to travel to the moon begin?

9. What 8,000-year old site was discovered in 1984?

10. Where is it Christmas all year around?

Southwest Florida

10

Southwest Florida

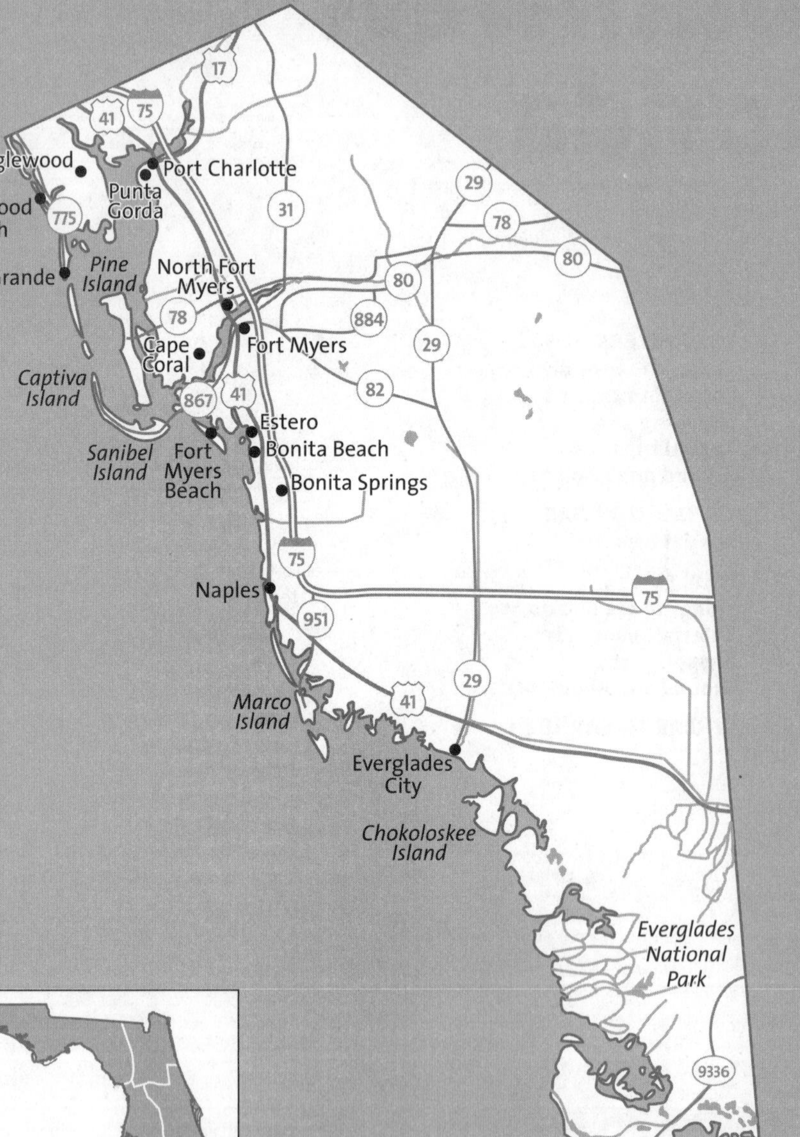

SOUTHWEST FLORIDA

Southwest Florida has not been opened up to tourism in the same way as other parts of the state. Henry Plant's railroad reached Fort Myers in 1904, only reached Bonita Springs 20 years later, finally arriving in Naples in 1927, by which time the service was part of the Atlantic Coast Line. The discovery of phosphate on the Peace River and establishment of clam canning plants in Marco Island were strategic to the development of the railroad, along with the influx of rich northerners building their winter homes in the area. Passenger trains ceased running in 1972 but freight trains and day excursions run on parts of the line. There are few roads to disturb the the region, so if you want to go in any direction other than North-South there's likely to be back-tracking involved. I–75 and Route 41 link the coastal areas before veering sharply east, leaving the Everglades and Ten Thousand Islands in peace. There are lots of golfing resorts around the exclusive neighbourhood of Naples, which has been dubbed the Palm Beach of the West Coast. Most resorts are on outlying islands, some of which have been carefully planned to maintain a healthy balance between the residential and the natural landscape. Fort Myers Beach on Estero Island is the busiest with the widest range of places to stay, including family resort hotels; Sanibel and Captiva are also popular but most accommodation is low-key and quite pricey. As this is where people from other parts of the state also come for their holidays, advance planning, booking and careful budgeting are essential. If you can book months in advance and stay for at least a week or two there are good deals to be found.

In August 2004, Hurricane Charley swept across the Southwest causing widespread damage, mainly to heavily forested areas and coastal islands. Many people were reported missing and thousands left homeless by the disaster in Charlotte County, to the north of Fort Myers, where the rows of temporary housing testify to the might of the natural forces that have historically reshaped Florida. In Fort Myers, flood damage was so severe that piles of white goods were stacked along the beaches for months while the costly process of drying out possessions and property took place. Of the 100 or so out islands around Fort Myers, many resorts have updated their facilities, as well as making repairs after the storm. Conditions were bad on Sanibel and Captiva Islands where locals had no power for several weeks and the Australian pines that used to shade the roadways alongside J. N 'Ding' Darling National Wildlife Reserve, came crashing down. Plans to replant with native, more hurricane-resistant species are underway. Visitors to the area will not see much evidence now of hurricane damage – a testament to the resilience and resourcefulness of the local people. The redevelopment of Southwest Florida International Airport, which began in 2003 has just been completed with a new terminal building and state-of-the-art security features that may result in direct flights being available from the UK.

The climate is temperate all through the winter averaging at about 70 degrees. Summers are hot and sultry with short bursts of rain just to clear the air. The islands are breezier but it's a warm breeze and the waters are fabulously warm.

Highlights

All aboard! Daytime Excursion Trains, Fort Myers, p167
Exploring man's inventions at the Edison and Ford Winter Estates, Fort Myers, p.167
Taking a walk on the wild side, Calusa Nature Center and Planetarium, Fort Myers, p.167
Stormy weather and calm waters at Imaginarium: Hands-on Museum and Aquarium, Fort Myers, p.168
Stepping back in time, Punta Gorda, p.171
Shelling out at Bailey-Matthews Shell Museum, Sanibel Island, p.174
Letting sleeping 'gators lie, J. N. 'Ding' Darling National Wildlife Refuge, Sanibel Island, p.175
Perfecting the Sanibel stoop, Lighthouse Beach, Sanibel Island, p.175
Watching dolphins at play, Captiva, p.176
Getting sand between your toes, Barefoot Beach Preserve, Bonita Beach, p.178
Up the creek with a paddle, The Great Calusa Blueway, Fort Myers Beach, p.178
Admiring the view, Lover's Key State Park, p.179
Catching fish or having a swim, Delnor-Wiggins State Park, p.180
Discovering animal habits, Naples Nature Center, Naples, p.180
Taking turns, Corkscrew Swamp Sanctuary, Naples, p.180
Going on a wet walk with Orchids & Egrets (Naples), Everglades National Park, p.181

Annual Events

January

Medieval Faire, Lakes Regional Park, South Fort Myers, **t** (239) 432 2000, **www**.leeparks.org

Creepy Crawlie Fair, Calusa Nature Center, Fort Myers, **t** (239) 275 3435, **www**.calusanature.com

February

Everglades Seafood Festival, Everglades City, **t** (239) 695 4100, **www**.evergladesseafoodfestival.com

Edison Festival of Light, Fort Myers, **t** (239) 334 2999, **www**.edisonfestival.org

Native American & Pioneer Heritage Days, Collier-Seminole State Park, Naples, **t** (239) 394 3397

Southwest Florida and Lee County Fair, Lee Civic Center, Fort Myers, **t** (239) 543 8368, **www**.leeciviccenter.com

March

Sanibel Shell Fair & Show, Sanibel Island, **t** (239) 472 2155

Fort Myers Beach Shrimp Festival, Fort Myers Beach, **t** (239) 463 6986

April

Lee Island Pirate Days Festival, Centennial Park, Fort Myers, **t** (239) 481 7231, **www**.LeePirateFest.com

Taste of the Islands, Gulfside City Park, Sanibel Island, **t** (239) 472 3644

October

Ding Darling Days, Ding Darling National Wildlife Refuge, Sanibel Island, **t** (239) 472 1100, **www**.dingdarlingdays.com

Haunted Walk, Calusa Nature Center, Fort Myers, **t** (239) 275 3435

November

Old Florida Festival, Naples, **t** (239) 774 8476

Bear Fair, Naples, **t** (239) 598 2711

Sandsculpting Festival, Fort Myers Beach, **t** (239) 454 7500, **www**.fmbchamber.com

Big Arts Annual Art Fair, Sanibel Island, **t** (239) 395 0900, **www**.bigarts.org

December

Old Tyme Holiday Festival, Koreshan State Historic Site, Estero, **t** (941) 992 0311

FORT MYERS

Until the onset of the Seminole Wars (*see* History p.5) the area around Fort Myers was largely Indian territory, belonging to the Calusa Tribe. Contact with European diseases soon wiped them out and new groups of Indians, the Seminoles, came to the area. They were forced to fight against the US government for the right to remain here. The government built a military base at Fort Dulany, on the banks of the Caloosahatchee River, to quell the Indian forces. After a storm destroyed the fort in 1841, the base was moved inland and reopened as Fort Harvie, only to be renamed Fort Myers in 1950.

The fort was occupied on and off until after the Civil War (1861–65), when it was abandoned and its timber used to build homes for settlers. By 1885, the town had two general stores, a school, and several homesteads where cattle, citrus farming and logging were the major industries. The mild climate attracted wealthy businessmen, such as Thomas Edison, in the mid to late 1800s, who came to escape the harsh northern winters. The population in Fort Myers grew from 349 to 943 citizens between 1885 and 1900. The 1920s building boom never really died out here, despite the Depression Years, and there are still many fine examples of Mediterranean-style architecture in the city. Fort Myers now preserves its historic downtown buildings and ensures that new constructions are in keeping with the overall style.

Fort Myers is an attractive spot for a family holiday with a cluster of resort hotels, excellent sports facilities, especially golf, and a wide range of entertainment and attractions. It's also within striking distance of several fine white-sand beaches and excellent ecological parks and refuges.

Getting there

By air Southwest Florida International Airport, 16000 Chamberlin Parkway, t (239) 768 1000, www.flylcpa.com/ is conveniently located just a mile or so from I–75 (exit 131). The airport has recently upgraded with a new terminal building featuring state-of-the-art facilities, tourist information, 11 more gates, (making 28), across-the-street car rental outlets (visitors used to have to take a shuttle to the rental base) and a 15-unit shopping area with about 15 restaurants including cafés and fast-food outlets. Pleasingly decorated too, the development is highly likely to attract direct services to Fort Myers from the UK. There are already direct flights from Germany, so other European cities are bound to follow suit. Watch this space.

By bus Greyhound bus services, t (800) 231 2222, **www**.greyhound.com connect with Tampa (3½–4 hours), Miami (4½–5½ hours) and other parts of Florida. Fort Myers to Naples takes an hour.
By road Fort Myers is 77 miles south of Sarasota. I–75 and US 41 broadly follow the coast until I–75 turns 45-degrees east near Naples to run straight through the Everglades and on to Fort Lauderdale. Highway 41, also known as Tamiami Trail, calls in at all the towns on the west coast before swinging down through the Everglades south of I–75 *en route* to Miami. Park and ride facilities are available at Summerlin Square, *see* bus services below.

Getting around

By bus LeeTran, t (239) 275 8726, **www**.rideleetran.com Operates connecting bus and trolley services between downtown Fort Myers, the main shopping districts and Pine Island and Estero Island. Buses run Mon–Sat 5am–9.45.
Trolleys: 6.30am–9.25. There's a limited service on Sunday. There is no public transport to Sanibel and Captiva Islands but adventure tours are available, *see* p.175.

Tourist information

Greater Fort Myers Chamber of Commerce, 2310 Edwards Drive, **t** (239) 332 3624, **www**.fortmyers.org

Things to see and do

Calusa Nature Center and Planetarium

3450 Ortiz Avenue, **t** (239) 275 3435, **www**.calusanature.com
Getting there I–75 to Exit 136 (22), west on Colonial Blvd to traffic light, go right on Ortiz Avenue
Open Mon–Sat 9–5, Sun 11–5. Planetarium: Wed–Sun
Adm Adults $8, children (3–12) $5

The rough boardwalk trails in this museum and centre lead through cypress swamp and allow you to see a wide range of native species in the wild. The museum has manatee-viewing decks, snakes, birds of prey and butterfly aviaries, a sugar mill, an Indian village and an environmental education centre. There are guided walks (Tue and Fri 9.30), plus daily talks, demonstrations and feeding sessions that allow kids to get close to alligators, birds of prey, snakes and butterflies. The planetarium shows range from laser displays and moon studies to space storytelling sessions, daily at 1.30 and 3.

Can you spot?
A banyan tree? The massive specimen near the car park in the grounds of Edison's home has a 40-ft root circumference and is reputedly the biggest one in the world.

Castle Miniature Golf

7400 Gladiolus Drive, **t** (239) 489 1999
Open Daily 10–11pm
Adm Adults $7.75, children (under 12) $6.75

When visiting Lakes Regional Park (*see* p.168) stop here for a round of mini-golf on this 18-hole course.

Centennial Park

2100 Edwards Drive

This 10-acre park gives access to two fishing piers and pleasant walks by the Caloosahatchee River. There's a playground, picnic facilities, a fitness trail and a pool with fountains and statuary depicting Edison, Ford and Harvey Firestone, plus models of native flora and fauna such as alligators and manatees. There's a **farmers' market** on Thursdays and it's a popular spot for concerts and events.

Daytime Excursion Trains

Seminole Gulf Railway, Metro Mall Station, 4110 Center Pointe Drive, **t** (239) 275 8487, **www**.semgulf. com
Open Dec–Sept Wed and Sat 10, 12.15, Sun 12.15. Closed on some public holidays.
Adm Adults: $19.95, children (3–12) $11.95, family ticket (2 adults, 2 children) $39.95, all plus tax. Book in advance for special excursion tickets, including Christmas, on selected dates from mid-Nov.

Learn about Southwest Florida's transport, wildlife and history on a 1¾-hour narrated train trip through Fort Myers and across the Caloosahatchee Trestle and Drawbridge to Bayshore.

Edison-Ford Winter Estates

2350–2400 McGregor Boulevard, **t** (239) 334 3614, **www**.edison-ford.estate.com
Tours Mon–Sat 9–5.30, Sun 12 noon–5.30. Electric boat tour: daily 9–3
Adm Adults $14, children (6–12) $7.50, family ticket $20 (2 adults, 2 children; Electric boat tour 0 $5.50
Picnic tables, gift shop, garden centre

Set in the peaceful, charming homes of inventor friends, Thomas Edison and Henry Ford, this is a shrine to Edison's 1,000 or so patents, ranging from making cement and kid's furniture to the phonograph and movie camera. You can also see garages full of early Ford models and Edison's garden, home to 6,000 rare and tropical plants, many of which he gathered while abroad searching for an economical way to make rubber. In the lab, you can see his (largely unsuccessful) vulcanization techniques.

You can also take a narrated river cruise in the Reliance II, a replica of the battery-powered boat bought by Edison in 1903 for his estate guests.

Fort Myers Skatium

2250 Broadway, **t** (239) 461 3145,
www.fmskatium.com
Open Daily. Public skating: Fri 7.30–10pm, Sat 1–3.15 and 7.30–10, Sun 1–3.15
Adm Adults $5, children (under 12) $4. Skate rental: $2

State-of-the-art skating facilities and home to youth and adult ice hockey teams and figure-skating clubs, there are also indoor soccer and volleyball courts, laser tag, bumper cars, practice and warm-up areas and a video games room.

Imaginarium: Hands-On Museum and Aquarium

Dr. Martin Luther King Jr. Boulevard and Cranford Avenue, **t** (239) 337 3332
Getting there From I–75 exit 23, travel west on Dr. Martin Luther King Blvd to the centre and turn left
Open Mon–Sat 10–5, Sun 12 noon–5
Adm Adults $7, children (3–12) $5

Over 60 exhibits and hands-on activities fire up the imagination and allow kids to get to grips with marine biology, anatomy, meteorology, physics and the economy. There are 3-D slide shows and videos, touch tanks, a wetlands zone with aquariums, a weather studio and a hurricane experience. Outside, there's a butterfly garden, reptiles and fish, alligators, turtles, snakes and swans. For younger kids a play-boat, a house, a puppet theatre with extra-large puppets to play with and a crawl-through maze are fun. There's also a dinosaur-bone dig and daily live animal programmes and interactive shows.

Lakes Regional Park

7330 Gladiolus Drive, **t** (239) 432 2000.
Marina: **t** (239) 432 2017; train: **t** (239) 267 1905
Getting there From US 41 south for 2 miles, park entrance is on the right
Open Daily 8–6. Train: Tue–Fri 10–2, Sat 10–4, Sun 12 noon–5; Fares $2.50, under 5s 50 cents

This family-friendly park offers freshwater lakes for fishing, canoeing, kayaking or paddleboat rentals. There's also a 2½-mile trail through the woods with picnic spots, an amphitheatre, playgrounds, a miniature railroad, village and a fragrance garden. *See also* p.167 Castle Miniature Golf.

Manatee Park

10901 Route 80, **t** (239) 694 3537
Getting there I–75 to Exit 25, then east on Route 80 for 1 mile. The entrance to the park is on the right
Open Apr–Sept 8–8, Oct–Mar 8–5
Visitor centre (9–4), gift shop (summer only)

Yes, this is a good place for manatee spotting! In the winter (Nov–Mar) they migrate here to the warm waters. There are observation areas and lovely picnic spots. The park has several nature habitats, including a butterfly garden. Guided tours are available. The park also has facilities for hiking and fishing year round, as well as kayaking and canoeing on the Orange River on summer weekends.

Southwest Florida Museum of History

2300 Peck Street, off Jackson Street,
t (239) 332 5955
Open Tue–Sat 10–5, Sun 12 noon–4. Historic walking tour (2 hours): Wed and Sat at 10, call for reservations
Adm Adults $9.50 children (3–12), $4.
Tours : Adults $5, children $3

Housed in a former depot of the Atlantic Coast Railroad, this enterprising museum explores the history of the region from prehistoric times to the post-war period. Exhibits focus on the Calusa and Seminole Indians, a furnished pioneer home, a fort and a riverfront wharf and kids can climb aboard a 1930s pullman railcar, a fire truck and see a vintage fighter plane.

Entertainment

Broadway Palm Dinner Theater

1380 Colonial Boulevard, **t** (239) 278 4422,
www.BroadwayPalm.com
Dinner theatre shows Various dates and times (including some matinees), call for details
Children's shows Selected dates in May, July and December from 12 noon
Dinner theatre shows Adults $39–$46, children (under 12) $19, show only $22
Children's shows $14 per person (including buffet)

For a unique experience head to this charming dinner theatre for a matinée family show, which include popular classics such as Cinderella and Aladdin and include a buffet with kids' dishes.

City of Palms Park

2201 Edison Avenue, t (239) 334 4700, www.redsox.com, www.cityofpalmspark.com
Getting there Off Broadway in the centre of Fort Myers. From north Exit 22, from south Exit 27 off I–75
Adm Box seats $24, reserved $21, bleachers $13, standing room $10

Home to the 2004 World Series champion Boston Red Sox's spring training between March and April every year, City of Palms Park is a pleasant, 7000-capacity stadium with a good range of food and merchandise stores. Tickets go on sale in December.

Lee County Sports Complex

14100 Six Mile Cypress Road
Twins tickets:, t (941) 768 4270, Miracle:, t (941) 768 4210
Getting there Just off I–75, south of Fort Myers
Adm Twins: $9–$12, Miracle $3–$4.

Major League Baseball's Minnesota Twins play spring training games here. The rest of the year, it is home to Twins' minor league feeder clubs, chiefly the Miracle, who play in the Class A Florida State League.

Shopping

Royal Palm Square is the place to head for some boutique shopping and a chance to browse art galleries and antique shops and dine out at a sidewalk café or restaurant.

Edison Mall

4125 Cleveland Avenue, t (239) 939 5464
Open Mon–Sat 10–9, Sun 11.30–5.30

The largest shopping centre in the area with several department stores and children's clothing outlets, games and toy stores and places to eat.

Bell Tower Shops

13499 Belltower Drive, Daniels Parkway (and US 41), t 239 489 1221
Open Mon–Sat 10–9, Sun 12 noon–5

Apart from the usual Saks Fifth Avenue, Victoria's Secret and other mall regulars, the Bell Tower has a few lesser-known retailers. Pick up some casual beachwear at **Echosurf** and **Trader Rick's** or find sun- safe items or sporty outfits at **Wallaby Trading**, which stocks trendy bags and accessories, plus magic T-shirts that change from black and white to colour when you go out in the sun. Kids will also like the educational and unique playthings at **Cheshire Cat Toys** and the souvenir-worthy glass and collectibles at **The Mole Hole**. The venue also houses a **multi-screen cinema**, **t** (239) 437 2020, info line: (239) 590 9696, and a number of places to eat including an ice cream shop, Italian and American-style restaurants, a **TGI Fridays**, a decent Mexican, **Cantina Laredo**, and **Mimi's Café**, open for breakfast, lunch and dinner, which offers family-friendly surroundings, baby-changing facilities in both male and female toilets and a kids' menu.

Fleamasters Fleamall

Dr. Martin Luther King Blvd (Route 82), t (239) 334 7001 www.fleamall.com
Getting there 1¼ miles west of I–75 (exit 138)
Open Daily 8–4

Don't let the name put you off. This mega marketplace has 900 stores offering everything from kids T-shirts and luggage to fresh vegetables and shampoo. There are even second-hand outlets for searchign out old Americana. There's plenty of food too – sandwich- and snack bars and outlets selling ice cream, pizza, Mexican dishes or Chinese food. Where else can you get your jewellery cleaned, find some flip-flops, have your palm read and design your own appliqué shirt – and all under one roof? If you're touring or self-catering it's a good all-rounder.

Special trips

Cape Coral Historical Museum

544 Cultural Park Boulevard, Cape Coral, t (239) 772 7037
Getting there Off Northeast Pine Island Road, *see* below, Children's Science Center
Open Sept–June Wed, Thu and Sun 1–4
Adm Adults $1 (donation)

Read Carl Hiaasen's excellent novel *Hoot* and then come to see the Florida burrowing owl exhibit here. There's also a burrowing owl festival in February (call for details). The museum also has a collection of Cape Coral memorabilia, maps, photos, shells, fossils and local history displays.

Did you know?
You are more likely to see the rare Florida Burrowing Owl, if you look in fields and on fence posts in the early morning or late afternoon.

Children's Science Center

2915 Northeast Pine Island Road, Cape Coral,
t (941) 997 0012, **www**.childrenssciencecenter.org
Getting there ½ mile west of US 41 on Pine Island Road, (SR 78)
Open Mon–Fri 9.30–4.30, Sat, Sun 12 noon–5
Adm Adults $5, children (3–11) $3, under-3s free

Children are free to explore this science-inspired environment by themselves but if they get stuck there are lots of assistants to answer questions or explain concepts from holograms to paleontology. The centre also deals with more usual subjects such as mathematics, electricity and astronomy. There are oversized construction bricks and big bubbles to play with, magnets and optical illusions, NASA space displays, puzzles, rocks and minerals and a Calusa Indian feature showing modern and ancient tools. There's also an outdoor area offering nature walks, whisper dishes and a giant maze.

ECHO Farm

17391 Durrance Road, North Fort Myers,
t (239) 543 3246
Getting there 1 mile east of I–75 (exit 143) follow signs on Bayshore Road to Durrance Road
Open Mon–Sat 9–12 noon. Tours: Jan–Mar Tue–Sat at 10, Apr–Dec: Tue, Fri and Sat at 10
Bookstore and plant nursery

This innovative education centre is dedicated to finding practical solutions to world hunger. The nursery at ECHO (Educational Concerns for Hunger Organization) began in 1981 and now has over 100 species of trees, shrubs, vines, herbs and perennial vegetables, over 30 varieties of bananas and about 50 varieties of citrus. Although a showcase for a unique plant collection, its main work is to provide ideas, information, agricultural training and seeds for sustainable living. Visitors can have a free tour of the 47-acre demonstration farm and Global Village where students learn about growing plants in challenging environments, such as hillsides, flood plains, urban rooftops, and dry regions. The bookstore sells cookery books, as well as gardening and science books for children.

Shell Factory

2787 North Tamiami Trail, North Fort Myers,
t (239) 995 2141, **www**.shellfactory.com
Getting there 4 miles north of Fort Myers, from I–75 take exit 143 and turn left onto State Road 78, then 5 miles to US 41, turn right and go 1½ miles north
Open Daily 9–9. Nature park: Mon–Fri 10–6, Sat, Sun 9–5. Fun park: Mon–Thu 11–7, Fri–Sun 11–8
Adm Free. Bumper boats $5, mini-golf $5, batting cage $1. Nature park and zoo: Adults $6, children (4–12) $4

This all-under-one-roof attraction is mainly a shell factory outlet but has attractions thrown in. There's a **nature park** with a botanical trail and gardens; a **petting zoo** (including llamas); an **environmental education centre** showcasing different ecosystems with baby alligators, iguanas, bees, a skunk and a hedgehog; and an **eco lab** where kids can participate in eco-friendly tasks. The **fun park** offers video games, bumper boats, miniature golf and a bridge from which you can feed the ducks and tortoises (food is available in the gazebo). If you like shells, don't miss out on the many treasures from under the sea displayed in the shell factory and shell-inspired gifts in the shop.

Sun Splash Family Waterpark

400 Santa Barbara Boulevard, Cape Coral,
t (239) 574 0557, **www**.sunsplashwaterpark.com
Getting there South off Pine Island Road, exit 136 (Colonial Boulevard) off I–75
Open Mid-May–Aug 10–6 (Thu, Sat 10–9), mid-Mar–mid-May and late Aug–Sept 11–5, see website or call for more details
Adm (over 48in) $11.95 (under 48in) $9.95, under 2s $2.95, plus tax
Picnic tables, giftshop, icecream shop, café

This family fun water park doesn't have too many fearsome rides but it has got a couple of fun flumes and drop slides, a large lazy river tube ride leading to a lagoon complete with water spouts, rain tree and fountains. Young adventurers can cross the lily pads using a crawl net, if they dare, or check out the 'gator and brave the rapids in the children's tot spot. There's also a volleyball court and a games arcade. Facilities include toilets, changing rooms and lockers. However, note that you are not allowed to eat food that has not been bought on the premises.

AROUND AND ABOUT

Punta Gorda

Sandwiched between Sarasota and Fort Myers and reaching south to the boundary of North Fort Myers, is the old cattle town of Punta Gorda. The town occupies a sheltered nook within Charlotte Harbor at the mouth of the Peace River offering waterfront parks and recreation facilities along Retta Esplanade. Live Oak Point in Charlotte Harbour is the supposed landing site of Hernando de Soto expedition in 1539 but Tampa Bay and Pine Island are also possible landing spots. The area is dotted with landmarks regarding Spanish expeditions but no clear evidence remains as to the exact locations of where the forces came ashore. The city was officially founded in 1885 when most of the dwellings and civic buildings in the historic district were erected. The historic district lies between the County Courthouse and Marion, Olympia, Virginia and Charlotte Avenues. The city is bounded by the harbour on one side and by citrus and cattle farms on the other with the small community of Fisherman's Village at its southernmost point. Visitors should be aware that Charlotte County was badly affected by Hurricane Charley in late 2004 and are advised to call to check on the progress of repairs.

Getting there

31 miles north of Fort Myers, Punta Gorda is near to exit 29 off I–75

Tourist information

326 West Marion Avenue, Suite 112, Punta Gorda, t (941) 639 2222
2702 Tamiami Trail, Port Charlotte, t (941) 627 2222, www.charlottecountychamber.org

Babcock Wilderness Adventures

8000 State Road 31, t (800) 500 5583, www.babcockwilderness.com
Getting there I–75 exit 164 (29) to Highway 17 North, one mile to State Road 74 East, 15 miles to State Road 31 South Entrance is 6 miles on left
Open Tours: Nov–May 9–3, Jun–Oct mornings only, call in advance all tours are by reservation only
Adm Adults $17.95, children (3–12) $10.95

This vast wilderness area encompasses 90,000 acres of cypress swamp, farmland and wetlands. Narrated swamp buggy tours explore aspects of the ranch and **Telegraph Cypress Swamp**, so named because they had to route the telegraph poles around it rather than through it. Visitors have the chance to see deer, alligators, turkeys and pigs in the wild, as well as Cracker cattle, bison and Florida panthers on the ranch. Three-hour bike tours along a nine-mile, off-road path are also available, including equipment. The natural history museum was once used as a location for the Warner Brothers film *Just Cause*, starring Sean Connery. The Country Store has ranch and wilderness tour souvenirs and the **Gator Shack café** is open for snacks, sandwiches, hot dogs and drinks, in season.

Capt. Don Cerbone Memorial Skate Park

6905 Florida Street, t (941) 627 1074
Open Thu, Fri 3–dusk, Sat, Sun 1–dusk

Safe and supervised skate park for skaters, skate-boarders and BMX riders with a street course and 3 half bowls. Protective gear must be worn, rentals available.

Charlotte County Speedway

8655 Piper Road, t (941) 575 RACE, www.charlottecountyspeedway.net
Getting there Off I–75, exit 161 eastbound on Jones Loop Road ½ mile, turn left onto Piper Road and the speedway is half a mile on the left
Open Mid-Sept–Jun Sat at 7, plus additional special events, see website
Adm Adults $15, children (6-11) $5, under 5s free

This 3/8-mile semi-banked asphalt track sees regular speedway action on Saturday nights along with special events throughout the year. Children's and teens' stock car races are a regular feature in the new four-cylinder Front Wheel Drive class.

Charlotte Harbor Environmental Center

10941 Burnt Store Road, t (941) 575 5435, www.checflorida.org

A 20-acre nature centre offering environmental education tours (in season), programmes and recreation with over five miles of trails intersecting a variety of native ecosystems, including hammocks, pine flatlands and marshes inhabited by alligator, snakes, bobcats and wading birds.

Fishermen's Village

1200 West Retta Esplanade, office: t (941) 639 8721/(800) 639 0020. Boat charters: t (941) 639 0969, www.kingfisherfleet.com
Fares: Adults $7.50–$21.95, under 12s half price
www.fishville.com

This busy waterfront mall and marina sustained considerable damage during Hurricane Charley but most services will be operational by Sept/Oct 2005. This is the place for fishing charters, sightseeing cruises (nature tours, sunset trips and harbour tours) or to hire a boat. In addition there are clothing boutiques and gift shops and the **military history and aviation museum** to explore, **t** (941) 575 9002, open daily. The village also has several waterfront restaurants and cafés, plus a programme of live entertainment and special events.

Peace River Wildlife Center

3400 West Marion Avenue, **t** (941) 637 3830
Open Wed–Mon 8–4. Tours: 10–3.30
Gift shop

Next to Ponce de León Historical Park, this active wildlife rehabilitation centre cares for native birds and animals and teaches visitors to respect their local environment and wildlife.

Ponce de León Historical Park

4000 West Marion Avenue, **t** (941) 575 3324

This 10-acre park has a monument dedicated to the memory of Ponce de León's search for the fountain of youth in 1513, which he may or may not have begun from here. There's a raised boardwalk through a wetland habitat, a boat ramp, beach, playground and picnic area.

Englewood

This is a bit of a diversion being, strictly speaking, south of Venice but since it's in Charlotte County it's listed here and makes a nice beach diversion from the Punta Gorda area. County Road 776 takes you to the beach on the border of Charlotte and Sarasota Counties. Port Charlotte Beach State Park to the southcan be accessed by boat, jet ski or on foot.

Getting there 50 miles north of Fort Myers. From I–75, exit 34 and head west (left) on River Road for 13⅓ miles. River Road will turn into Dearborn Street

Englewood Beach

2100 North Beach Road, **t** (941) 473 1081,
www.charlottecountyfl.com
Open Daily 6am–11pm

Sand dunes and parkland flank a wide beachfront area with fishing and picnic facilities, barbecue grills, toilets and showers, a playground, boardwalk, as well as volleyball and basketball courts.

Grande Tours

12575 Placida Road, **t** (941) 697 8825,
www.grandetours.com
Rentals Kayak from $20 for two hours. Ecotour: $45 for three-hour kayak tour; Treasure hunt: $20 "per buccaneer"

Naturalist-interpreted deck boat and kayaking excursions tour the Myakka River and Charlotte Harbour Aquatic Preserve. Sea Life Excursion features seine net pulling to collect and study marine life. The Back Country Adventure combines boat and kayak touring. The staff specializes in fishing trips for the kids. Twice a week, treasure hunt with Red Beard and the Pirates of Placida takes kids in search of booty.

Island Jet Ski Tours and Rentals

1450 Beach Road, **t** (941) 474 1168

Hire a Jet Ski for a unique one-hour jaunt along the coast, guided tours, deep-sea and bayside fishing trips are also available.

Pelican Pete's Playland

3101 S. McCall Road, **t** (941) 475 2008

Head to Pete's for a spot of mini golf, batting cages, go karts, a miniature train, arcade games and food outlets.

LEE ISLAND COAST

Tourist information

Lee Island Coast Visitor and Convention Bureau, 2180 West First Street, **t** (239) 338 3500 or (888) 231 6933, www.leeislandcoast.com
Lee Island Coast VCB covers tourist information for the set of islands the coast south of Englewood starting with Gasparilla Island (**Boca Grande**) **Pine Island, Sanibel and Captiva Islands**, as well as **Fort Myers Beach** on Estero Island. It also covers **North Fort Myers, Fort Myers, Cape Coral, Bonita Beach** and **Bonita Springs** on the mainland.

Boca Grande

For a taste of old (and monied) Florida take a peek at upmarket Gasparilla along a seven-mile bike path from Gasparilla Pass to the Island State Park, along the railway that once brought phosphate from Boca Grande's harbour and wintering Vanderbilts to The Gasparilla Inn. The railway stopped in the late 1950s and the depot was vacant until the 1970s when it became home to boutique shops and restaurants.

Getting there

23 miles southwest of Punta Gorda. From Englewood, follow Route 776 to Route 775 (Pine Street) and west to Gasparilla Island on Route 771.

Tourist information

Boca Grande Chamber of Commerce, P.O. Box 704, Boca Grande, **t** 33921; (941) 964–0568; **www.bocagrandechamber.com**
Information centre at Courtyard Plaza at the island's north end.

Things to see and do

Boca Grande Lighthouse Museum and Gasparilla Island State Park

Gulf Boulevard, t (941) 964 0060, www.barrierislandparkssociety.org
Getting there South end of Gasparilla Island via the Boca Grande Causeway (private toll road) at County Road 775 and Placida
Open Park 8–dusk. Lighthouse museum: Nov–May daily 10–4, Jun–Oct Wed–Sun 10–4
Adm $2 per car, $1 per bike or pedestrian, Lighthouse: $1 suggested donation

The lighthouse , which was built in 1890, is the oldest structure on the island. It houses artefacts covering the occupation of the island, including early American Indian settlers, Spanish adventurers, the Tarpon-fishing industry, the phosphate railroad and Port Boca Grande. The lighthouse itself, which was saved from falling into the sea by the local community, is still operational and has dramatic views of the Gulf of Mexico and Charlotte Harbor. The surrounding parkland is good for shelling in the winter months, hiking, fishing, bike rides, canoeing and kayaking. There are picnic and parking areas, showers and swimming beaches on the gulf side of the island.

Island Bike 'N Beach

333 Park Avenue, Boca Grande, t (941) 964 0711
Open daily. Rates range from $7/hour to $49 a week

Shop here for beach essentials (dash board hula dolls anybody?). You can also rent bikes or golf carts for island fun.

Pine Island

This 17-mile chunk of land lies between Cape Coral and the barrier islands of Sanibel, Captiva and Cayo Costa. Not a beach destination due to its position, but there are lovely rural retreats among the fruit farms and waterfront developments with not a high-rise in sight. There are great opportunities for viewing bald eagles, brown and white pelicans, woodpeckers, ibis, osprey, heron, roseate spoonbills, endangered wood storks and other bird species. Dolphins, manatees, sea otters and sea turtles enjoy the waters of Pine Island and short boat trips take you to the wilds of **Caya Costa State Park, North Captiva Island** and **Little Pine Island**. The **Charlotte Harbor Aquatic & State Buffer Preserves, t** (239) 575 5861, offers recommended guided trail walks.

Pine island itself retains evidence of Indian settlement dating back some 6,000 years. For history tours and educational programmes contact the **Randell Research Center, t** (239) 283 2062, next to the Post Office at Pineland. The **Calusa Heritage Trail**, next-door, explores the life of the Calusa Indians through text and artworks positioned beside shell mounds, an ancient canal and other archaeological features.

Getting there

From I–75 take exit 143 (old 26) onto State Road SR78, west (Bayshore Road) to US 41 and Pine Island Road. Right (north) on Route 767 takes you to Pineland and Bokeelia, or left (south) takes you to St. James City

Things to see and do

Gulf Coast Kayak

4530 Pine Island Road, Matlacha, t (239) 283 1125, www.gulfcoastkayak.com
Rentals From $30 for a half-day single or canoe, $45 for a double kayak
Tours: $30–40 per person, reservations required

Offers sheltered kayaking opportunities in the Matlacha Pass Aquatic Preserve in safe and sturdy sea kayaks. Daily three-hour mangrove guided tours are available, as well as seasonal manatee trips and sunset birding tours (Tue–Sun) $30.

Museum of the Islands

5728 Sesame Drive, Pine Island Center, t (239) 283 1525
Open Nov–Apr Tue–Sat 11–3. Sun 1–4, May–Oct Tue, Thurs, Sat 11–3
Adm Adults $2, children $1

Vintage household objects, wildlife and fishing displays, Calusa Indian pottery and tools discovered in Pine Island shell mounds and an impressive local shell collection tell the island's history.

Tropic Star Cruises

Pineland Marina, 13921 Waterfront Drive, Pineland, t (239) 283 0015, www.tropicstarcruises.com
Departs Ferry: 9.30, 11 and 2. Cruise: 9.30–4.30.
Trips Day: Adults $20, under 7s $15; Overnight Adults $25, under 7s $15; Two-island nature cruise: Adults $25, under 7s $15

Ferry trips to Caya Costa also offer additional kayaking or bike riding on this remote island. There are no facilities, so bring a picnic and lots of insect repellent. Narrated sightseeing and nature cruises are on offer to outlying islands such as Cabbage Key, Cayo Costa, Boca Grande, North Captiva and Useppa.

Sanibel Island

Sanibel and Captiva islands lie close together and, although accommodation isn't cheap, there are ample opportunities for families wishing to take it easy so plan a couple of days here. The islands' 16 miles of beaches, bordered with grassy vegetation, are great for shelling, so good that the pose adopted by shell hunters is known here as the 'Sanibel stoop'. The remote **Bowman's Beach** at the northwest end is best for sunsets and offers great shelling. The quiet waters of **Tarpon Bay** are best for swimming. There are also bike paths, wild nature refuges, cruise boats and kayaks, beach restaurants and arty shopping experiences along Periwinkle Way. Note that neither island has street or traffic lights and there are few paths or crossing points so warn children to take care, especially after dusk.

Getting there

From Highway 41 or I–75's exit 131 (21), head west on Daniels Parkway and follow signs to Sanibel/Captiva. After crossing the Sanibel Causeway ($6 toll) turn right onto Periwinkle Way.

Tourist information

Sanibel–Captiva Islands Chamber of Commerce, 1159 Causeway Road, Sanibel Island, t (239) 472 1080, www.sanibel-captiva.org

Things to see and do

Bailey-Matthews Shell Museum

3075 Sanibel-Captiva Road, t (239) 395 2233, www.shellmuseum.org
Open Daily 10–4
Adm Adults $6, children (5–16) $3, under 5s free

Due to their unique east/west geographic location, the coastlines surrounding Fort Myers, particularly the Sanibel, Captiva and Pine Islands, boast some of the best shelling in the world. After a morning

A story to tell: Gasparilla

According to legend, the coast around Fort Myers was once the kingdom of Gasparilla, a fearsome pirate. A dastardly rogue, he was once a gentleman, born one José Gaspar near Seville in Spain in 1756. Like many a tyrant, he was small of stature but also stocky, well mannered and gallant. He took to the high seas after he was caught kidnapping and ransoming a young girl – it was gaol or joining the Spanish navy. Naturally, he chose the navy and was successful in military matters.But, sadly his affairs with the ladies were imprudent and his enemies framed him as a thief causing him to flee in a stolen ship thus beginning his life of piracy. He established a base in Pine Island Sound and, renaming himself Gasparilla, set about the ruin of the Spanish fleet. He flourished as a pirate with the sacking of 400 ships and became known for either slaughtering his helpless victims or, if they were beautiful and female, holding them to ransom on Captiva Island (thus giving the island its name). When Florida came under American control, it became harder to outrun the law and Gasparilla decided to give up piracy. But, lured by the booty of an English vessel, he set out to plunder one last time. A mistake – the boat was the USS Enterprise in disguise and the pirate was trapped. Rather than surrender, Gasparilla went down with his ship, drowning himself from the anchor. Some say that his treasure hoard still lies buried on Gasparilla Island, others that his men buried the loot along the banks of the Peace River, where it has lain forgotten in the swamps. Shrouded in mystery, Gasparilla's life is largely viewed as a work of fiction but the Gasparilla Festival in Tampa (*see* p.108), having moved the pirates' base further up the Gulf coast, has been celebrating his deeds since 1904, so who are we to fly against tradition?

sifting through specimens at the beach, come here to measure up your finds with the museum's fine exhibits from around the world – big, small, rough, shiny and in all colours from bright yellow to purple. Learn how shells have been used to cure ills and pay for goods and services. There's also a hands-on area where kids can handle soft sea shapes, view native species in the touch tank, play with floor puzzles and read books. The shop has children's guides to Florida, colouring books and free leaflets so you can identify your finds.

J. N. 'Ding' Darling National Wildlife Refuge

1 Wildlife Drive, **t** (239) 472 1100
Getting there The visitor centre is roughly in the middle of the refuge, off Periwinkle Way, opposite Rabbit Road
Open 8–dusk, Visitor Centre May–Oct 9–4, Nov–Apr 9–5. (Wildlife drive closed Fri)
Adm $5 per car, $1 per bike or pedestrian

Occupying almost a third of the island, this refuge, named after Pulitzer prizewinning cartoonist and conservationist Jay Norwood Darling, offers 6,000 acres of protected lands comprising sea grass beds, mangrove islands, mud flats, **beaches**, freshwater habitats and hardwood hammocks. Five-mile car tours and **tram trips** (*see below*) are popular but the best way to see wildlife is to walk one of the ⅓–2-mile foot trails, bike along the paths or take to the water in a canoe or kayak. This is a great place to enjoy peace and some quiet and see nature at its best. Take hats and plenty of water as there's not much shade. Alligator sightings along the river are pretty frequent so take care with smaller children as the paths are narrow and the 'gators are quite big. Other animals include raccoons, manatees and loggerhead turtles and, among the many birds, herons, ducks, ibis, ospreys and the rare roseate spoonbill. The **visitor centre** sells bottled water and contains exhibits on mangroves and wildlife in the park. Please note that picnicking is not permitted within the refuge. There are picnic spots outside close to Shell Mound Trail and Dixie Beach Boulevard.

Lighthouse Beach

Southernmost point of Periwinkle Way, **t** (239) 472 9075
Getting there Left off Sanibel Causeway

Here you'll find a fishing pier, hiking and bike trails, toilets, picnic areas, a boat ramp and an historic lighthouse (1884), now a wildlife refuge.

Sanibel-Captiva Conservation Foundation

3333 Sanibel-Captiva Road, **t** (239) 472 2329, **www.sccf.org**
Open Oct–Jun Mon–Fri 8.30–5 (Nov–Jun Sat 10–3), Jun–Oct 8.30–4
Adm Adults $3, under 12s free. Tours: Adults $3, Butterfly House Tours: $1

Here you'll find natural history displays about the islands, touch tanks, wildlife exhibits, a butterfly house and nature trails. There are guided walks looking at different habitats (Jan–Apr Mon–Fri at 10 and 2, May–Dec Tue, Wed and Fri at 9) and butterfly house tours looking at the lifecycle and behaviour of butterflies (Tue at 10).

Sanibel Historical Village and Museum

950 Dunlop Road, Sanibel Island, **t** (239) 472 4648
Open Wed–Sat Nov–May 10–4, Jun–mid-Aug 10–1
Adm Adult $3 (suggested donation)

This collection of early 20th-century buildings invites you to imagine Sanibel in the days of the early pioneers when families set out to live off the land. The museum is housed in a 1913 Cracker home, complete with a country kitchen and wide verandahs. There's also a general store, 1926 post office, a model-T Ford van, a 1925 pre-fab cottage, a restored 1930s tearoom offering light refreshments and the oldest house on the island – a beach cottage built in 1898, which contains memorabilia connected to Sanibel's oldest structure – the lighthouse (*see* above).

Tours

Adventures in Paradise

Port Sanibel Marina, **t** (239) 472 8443, **www.adventureinparadiseinc.com**
Tours Adults $18–$55, children $12–$35, under 3s free

Trolley and boating excursions to discover the eco-heritage of the Fort Myers and Sanibel area. Trips include backwater fishing, sea-life encounter excursions, tropical sunset cruises, dolphin watching, history and nature trolley tours, as well as boats and kayaks to rent. Free trolley pick-ups from hotels on Sanibel are available.

Tarpon Bay Explorers

900 Tarpon Bay Road, **t** (239) 472 8900, **www.tarponbayexplorers.com**

Open Daily 8–6 (last rental at 4). Call ahead for tram times
Rentals $30 double canoe/kayak for 2 hours; Bike rentals: from $12–$27 full-day
Tram tour: Adults $10, children (under 12) $7. Nature cruise: Adults $20, children $12
Gift and Nature shop

You can rent canoes and kayaks or trips through 'Ding' Darling Refuge (*see* p.175). Narrated **tram tours** last 1½ hours and introduce families to the history of the island and offer unique opportunities for wildlife viewing. **Guided canoe** and **kayak eco-tours** are also available, the first leads visitors through red mangroves and back bays and is suitable for all ages, the second is a sunset trip to a rookery to watch the birds come in for the night. In addition, eco-friendly electric boat cruises offer visitors the chance to view birds, dolphins, manatees, and alligators in Tarpon Bay and sea creatures up close in the **aquarium** and **touch tank**. Alternatively, hire your own pontoon boat and guide for a personal family tour. This enterprising company also offers free naturalist-led beach walks and deck talks daily from 12.30–1, departing from Tarpon Bay and Everglades exploration trips with airboat and swamp buggy trips. **www.evergladesexplorers.com**

Touring rentals

Billy's Rentals

1470 Periwinkle Way, t (239) 472–5248,/(800) 575 8717 www.billysrentals.com

Visitors can hire bikes by the hour, day or for two weeks to explore Sanibel's 22-miles of **paved trails**. There are models to suit everyone, including a tandem for ages 4–8 and surrey bikes. Other equipment includes single or double jogging strollers, beach chairs and umbrellas, kayaks, wind-surf boards and sail boats. Billy's also offers beach rental service to the West Wind Inn and Casa Ybel.

Finnimore's Cycle

2353 Periwinkle Way, t (239) 472 5577, www.finnimores.com

Provides free child helmets, locks and child seats, mountain or road bikes, bikes with child seats, tandems, trail-a-bikes and 2–4 person surreys for hourly, daily or weekly rates. Beach equipment, fishing rods, skim or boogie boards, in-line skates and other services are also available.

Captiva Island

The rows of Australian pines that shaded Captiva's roads were mostly wiped out by Hurricane Charley (Aug 14, 2004), which did considerable damage to the wildlife refuge on Sanibel and to property and vegetation here. Islanders have restored their homes and businesses and are replanting forest areas with native plants. Pop over to walk on the **beach** in Captiva and have a bite to eat at one of the eclectic cafés or restaurants here that offer live music daily. For lovely jewellery, unique souvenirs and a spot of fun head to **Jungle Drums Gallery, t** (239) 395 2266, **www**.jungledrumsgallery.com

Getting there

Go right on Periwinkle Way at Sanibel, then right on Tarpon Bay Road and left on Sanibel-Captiva Road

Tours

Adventure One Charters

McCarthy's Marina, 420 Lighthouse Way, t (239) 472 4875

Boat charters for up to six people offering family-friendly shelling, sightseeing, fishing and lunch cruises with some local history and nature.

Captiva Cruises

South Seas Resort Marina, t (239) 472 5300, www.captivacruises.com
Cruises Adults $17.50–$35, children (under 12s) $10–$17.50

Offers a variety of cruise options including wildlife, beach and shelling trips, out islands excursions or sunset cruises. Also lunch cruises to Useppa, Cabbage Key and Boca Grande. For a true eco-tour take the new **Lessons from the Eye of Hurricane Charley**, which focuses on how hurricanes impact on wildlife, communities and vegetation. Book in advance.

New Moon

'Tween Waters Marina, Captiva Drive, t (239) 395 1782 or (888) 472 7245, www.newmoonsailing.com

Full-day or three-hour sailing trips to the out islands with lunch, shelling and swim stops. Also sailing lessons (adult and over 8s) and extended overnight or weekly Keys sailing trips. Book in advance.

Seawave Boat Rentals, Inc.

South Seas Resort, Bayside Marina, t (239) 472 1744, www.captivaboatrental.com

Day rental: 8.30–4.30, from $300 (full-day), $210 (half-day)

Powerboat rentals, water taxis to out islands, plus guided snorkel, dive, fishing and shelling trips.

Estero Island

Best known for **Fort Myers Beach**, Estero island offers plenty of other attractions as well.

Getting there

From Sanibel Island, follow Summerlin Road (Route 867) to San Carlos Boulevard and turn right (west) and cross the bridge to Estero Boulevard (Route 865)

Tourist information

Greater Fort Myers Beach Chamber of Commerce, 17200 San Carlos Boulevard, t (239) 454 7500, www.fmbchamber.com

Things to see and do

Bay Oaks Recreational Center and Playworks

Oak and School Street, t (239) 765 4222

Open Mon–Fri 10–9, Sat 10–6

This wooden play park enjoys a quiet, natural setting. There are climbing towers, swings and slides, benches and picnic tables in the shade. Sports facilities include tennis, baseball and soccer, indoor basketball and a gym. At the 56-acre **Matanzas Pass Wilderness Preserve** nearby on Bay Road, families can take a boardwalk trail through the mangrove swamp for views of **Estero Bay Aquatic Preserve**.

Bowditch Point Regional Park

50 Estero Boulevard, t (239) 463 1116

Open 8–dusk

There are delightful beach, estuarine and upland habitats at the north end of the island. Take a walk along the mangrove-lined beach for views of wading and nesting birds, tortoises, turtles and raccoons. The park has a playground, picnic tables and grills.

Fort Myers Beach

This family-friendly destination offers amusements from jet ski excursions and parasailing to adventure golf and beach volleyball. There are lots of resort hotels, some with more family options and character than others, (*see* Sleep p.44). Popular with Spring Break college kids, it is a lively spot around Easter but later in the year things quieten down.

Lynn Hall Memorial Park and Pier

Old San Carlos Road and Estero Boulevard, t (239) 463 1116

Open 24hours

Squint and you're in Brighton! this family-friendly beach, beside the Fort Myers Beach Sky Bridge, offers good fishing from the 560-ft pier, as long as the pelicans don't get there first. The beach is also good for shelling, sunbathing and swimming, has outside showers, toilets, a children's playground, covered picnic areas and a nature kiosk. Shopping malls and restaurants are close by.

Smuggler's Cove Adventure Golf

17450 San Carlos Blvd, t (239) 466 5855

Open Daily 9am–11pm

Adm Adults $8.99, children (under 12) $7.99, plus tax

Miniature golf course with water features, caves and rocky outcrops, where visitors can view live alligators. Do not feed them as this encourages children to feed alligators in the wild. There's a stall for ice creams and drinks.

Tours

Beours Inc.

4765 Estero Boulevard, Snook Bight Marina, t (239) 443 7456

Depart: 9 and 12.30, plus sunset trips, times vary, book in advance

Tours: Adults $25, children $10

Take a three-hour dolphin/eco tour of the Estero River where you can see river otters, egrets, pelicans, dolphins and alligators. Trips include a visit to the uninhabited island of **Mound Key** and its archaeological treasures. Or join a three-hour dolphin/shelling tour to **Lover's Key State Park** (*see* p.179). Toilets, drinks and binoculars are provided. Sunset cruises are also available.

Getaway Deep Sea Fishing

18400 San Carlos Boulevard, Getaway Marina, t (239) 466 3600

Trips Half-day (9–3): Adults $40, children (under 12) $30; Full-day (8–4.30): $65, book in advance. Night snapper trip (Tue and Fri, 6pm–1am): Adults $60, children $40

Escorted half or full-day fishing trips are available for a chance to catch grouper, snapper, mackerel and shark, which the crew will happily fillet for you to take home. Night snapper trips are for more seasoned sailors but children are welcome, as long as they're not afraid to pitch in. Private charters, seasonal lunch and dinner cruises are also available.

Tours rental

Fish-Tale Marina

7225 Estero Boulevard, t (239) 463 4448, www.getawaymarina.com
Open Daily 8–5
Rental From $95 (half-day), $200 (full-day) including fishing tackle. Costs and tax extra.

Rent a power boat for a family fishing trip out in the backwaters.

Mid Island Watersports

5550 Estero Boulevard, t (239) 765 0965

Hire a Jet Ski for an exhilarating coastal trip or opt for a dolphin watching tour. Parasailing is also available; choose to fly triple, double or go solo.

Special trips

Barefoot Beach Preserve

2 Barefoot Beach Boulevard, Bonita Springs, t (239) 353 0404
Getting there From I–75 take exit 116 (Bonita Beach Road) and go 5.6 miles to Leley Boulevard (park entrance road), turn left and go through residential development to the preserve
Open 8–dusk

For a quiet beach experience head to this island preserve where lovely beaches give way to rolling sand dunes and mangrove forests. The one-mile self-guided nature trail offers the chance to explore coastal habitats populated by shore birds. Ranger-led nature walks are also a good way to learn more about this fragile environment where gopher tortoises and loggerhead turtles nest. There are toilets and showers on site, plus food concessions and picnic areas. Around the corner is the lively public beach, which offers water sports, swimming, picnic areas and lifeguards on duty.

Everglades Wonder Gardens

27180 Old U.S. 41, Bonita Springs, t (239) 992 2591
Getting there 18 miles south of Fort Myers. Exit 116 off I–75 and west to Old US 41
Open Daily 9–5 (last tour 4.15)

This showcase for native Florida species opened in 1936 as a refuge for injured animals. Within the **botanical gardens** you'll find crocodiles, Florida panthers, trained otters and tame deer, alligators, flamingos, snakes, birds and bears. There's also a quirky **natural history museum** and a wobbly bridge over alligator-infested waters. Guided tours include 'gator feedings and otter displays.

The Great Calusa Blueway

Tourist information: For more information contact the Lee County Visitor & Convention Bureau, **t** (800) 237 6444, **www.**greatcalusablueway.com

This clearly marked **paddle trail** opens up 75 miles of waterways passing through sheltered back bays, aquatic preserves, creeks, rivers and estuaries. Many courses follow ancient Indian canoe routes and offer the chance to see dolphins, manatees and rare birds in the wild. The Blueway runs from **Bunchie Beach** above Matanzas Pass through **Estero Bay** and on past Lover's Key to **Bonita Springs** and the Imperial River. Clear signage lets paddlers know where they are and there are kayak and canoe rental outlets along the way. If you're planning a family trip, bring plenty of insect repellent and arrange overnight stops in advance.

Key West Excursions

Salty Sam's Marina 2500 Main Street, Fort Myers Beach, t (239) 463 5733, bookings, t (888) 539 2628/ (239) 394 9700, www.seakeywestexpress.com www.keywestshuttle.com
Getting there From I–75 take exit 131 and follow Daniels Parkway West to Summerlin Road, then turn left. Turn left on San Carlos Boulevard to the big bridge, left again on Main Street and right at end of road for parking
Open Two departures daily: Fort Myers: 8am, arrive Key West 12 noon. Depart Key West 5pm, arrive Fort Myers 8.30 or 9am, arrive 1pm, depart 6, arrive 9.30
Fares Round trip: Adults $129 plus $6 security fee, children (6–12) $109 plus $6 security fee, under 5s $3 with full-fare adult. One-way fare: $73 per person. Additional departures from Marco Island run from Nov–May

If you really want a day out with a difference, hop on the Big Cat or the swish new Atlanticat for a tour of Key West. Day trips take around 3–3½ hours and give you plenty of time to explore the island – or opt for a one-way fare and an extended stay. While on board, you can bask in the sun on deck, view fantastic sunsets over the gulf from the huge cabin windows or watch movies on the plasma TV screens. Most seating on the vessel is in contoured seating with built-in headrests, but there are also plush couches with tables and a bar and refreshment area serving food, drinks and snacks.

Koreshan State Historic Site and Mound Key State Architectural Site

Corkscrew Road, **t** (239) 992 0311
Getting there Go 2½ miles west on Corkscrew Rd. and cross US 41, entrance on the right, boat or canoe access only
Open Daily 8–dusk
Adm $4 per car, $1 per bike or pedestrian

This historic site is both famous for its associations with a religious cult and as a ceremonial centre for the Calusa Indians. The Koreshan Unity settlement established a commune on the island in 1894. Koreshans held utopian beliefs based around theories that the earth lies inside a sphere with the cosmos in the middle. Believers practiced self-sufficiency, equality and were interested in the arts and horticulture. The ambition for the sect was to reach 10 million members but it hovered around 250 before finally disbanding in 1961. The last cult members thoughtfully bequeathed the lands to the State. Visitors can camp in the grounds and explore eight of the original buildings, including a bakery, meeting hall and home of their leader, one Cyrus Reed Teed. The original tropical gardens are also well worth a look. Among the exhibits at Mound Key are information panels depicting the history of the Calusa Indians in Estero Bay.

Lover's Key State Park

8700 Estero Boulevard, **t** (239) 463 4588
Getting there South of Estero Island on Route 865 over the Big Carlos Pass drawbridge
Open Daily 8–dusk
Adm $4 per car, $2 per bike or pedestrian

Pack a picnic and plenty of drinks and set off to explore the barrier islands (Lover's Key, Inner Key, Long Key and Black Island) in this 712-acre park. Trams from the parking zones run to the beach where there are picnic facilities, food outlets, outdoor showers and toilets. The boat ramp on the Estero Bay side of the park allows access to the **Estero Bay Aquatic Preserve**. Canoe and kayak trails are the best ways to explore the islands or head inland to the freshwater lagoons; bike and kayak rentals available.

NAPLES

Be prepared to move a few notches up the social scale as you head further south. The cultural charms of cosmopolitan Naples are enough to attract families and are neatly juxtaposed with the surrounding areas of stunning natural beauty. Naples is a place on the up with designer boutiques, beachfront condo communities and fine dining restaurants. A stay here will require careful budgeting but it's definitely day-trip worthy if you're staying in the Fort Myers area.

Getting there

36 miles south of Fort Myers on Highway 41

Tourist information

Chamber Centre, 2390 Tamiami Trail North, t (239) 262 6376, **Visitors & Information Centre**, 895 5th Avenue South, **t** (239) 262 6141, **www.napleschamber.org**
Greyhound Bus Service, 2669 Davis Blvd, **t** (239) 774 5660

Things to see and do

Aviary of Naples and Park Zoo

9824 Immokalee Road, **t** (941) 353 2215
www.aviaryofnaples.com
Getting there Exit 111 off I–75
Open Sat–Wed 10–4; **Adm** Adults $8, children $4

Although primarily a place to come and learn about owning a parrot or macaw, the on-site zoo features around 200 exotic birds and animals including camels, miniature donkeys, miniature horses, wallabies, Galapagos tortoises and emus.

Collier County Museum

3301 Tamiami Trail East, **t** (239) 774 8476.
Open Mon–Fri 9–5. Sat 9–4.
Adm Free (donations welcome)

Review Southwest Florida history and pre-history at this five-acre historical park where displays cover 10,000 years from when mastodons, giant sloths and fierce sabre-toothed cats roamed through to human settlement of the area. Exhibits include a Seminole Indian Village, pioneer homesteads and a logging station. There is also a botanical gardens, which includes a native plant exhibit and orchid house.

The Conservancy of Southwest Florida Nature Center

1450 Merrihue Drive, t (239) 262 0304, www.conservancynaturecenter.org
Getting there From I–75; take exit 107 (Naples, Golden Gate). Head west towards Naples and turn left onto Goodlette-Frank Road, follow signs at 14th Avenue North and turn left at the lights
Open Mon–Sat 9–4.30 all year, Nov–Apr also Sun 12–4. Cruises: Dec–Apr Mon–Sat
Adm Adults $7.50, children (3–12) $2, free 1st sat of month; Canoe rental: from $15. Cruises: Adults $25, children $12.50

The **Museum of Natural History** offers **interactive exhibits** where children can learn more about the geology and biology of the local area and includes snakes, baby alligators, coral shrimp and loggerhead turtles. The centre also houses an **animal hospital**, not open to the public, but you can see recovered owls, hawks, pelicans and a bald eagle outside that cannot be released into the wild. There are **walking trails** and a free electric **boat ride**, which takes you on an eco-tour of mangrove and river environments to spot herons and egrets and learn about local ecology. There are also daily **nature talks**, **demonstrations** and **guided tours**. On the first Saturday of the month, there are kid's activities such as crafts, colouring contests, storytelling and face painting. In April, there's the annual **Earth Day environmental celebration**. **Good Fortune Cruises** also run from December to April (Mon–Sat), where visitors can get a closer look at nature on a **Key Island Shelling Expedition** or a **Sunset Bird-Watching Tour** led by professional naturalists.

Corkscrew Swamp Sanctuary

375 Sanctuary Road, t (239) 348 9151
Getting there 21 miles east of Highway 41, off Immokalee Road
Open Daily 7–7; **Adm** Adults $10, children (6–18) $4

Managed by the National Audubon Society, the park encompasses 11,000 acres, the largest virgin bald cypress forest in North America where cavity-nesting birds such as barred owls, screech owls, wood ducks, raccoons and woodpeckers thrive. A 2½-mile raised boardwalk takes you through pine upland, cypress forest, prairie and marsh habitats. Families can pick up a field guide and children's activity book from the Blair Audubon Center admissions desk for a self-guided tour. There are shelters and benches at regular intervals and naturalists at various points to answer questions. You cannot eat outside but there's a tearoom in the **Blair Center** (items must be eaten on the premises) and a nature store.

Delnor-Wiggins State Park

11100 Gulf Shore Drive North, Naples Park, t (239) 597 6196
Getting there Off I–75, six miles west of Exit 111 (17) on Route 846
Open Daily 8–dusk; **Adm** $5 per car, $3 single passenger, $1 per bike or pedestrian

Head out early in the holiday season to avoid traffic jams for this highly favoured beach area where snorkelling, sunbathing, shelling, kayaking and swimming are popular. Or fish in the swimmer-free waters of **Wiggins Pass**. There are picnic facilities, showers and toilets, kayak rentals, food outlets and ample parking. The observation tower at the north end of the island offers great views across this tranquil coastal habitat.

Florida Sports Park

Rattlesnake Hammond Road t (239) 774 2701 or (800) 897 2701, www.swampbuggy.com
Getting there Route 951, 3½ miles south of I–75 exit 101 (15)
Adm Adults $17, children (6–12) $7

Get a taste of Florida's more eccentric side at the annual Swamp Buggy races (held Jan, Mar, Oct), using amazing hi-tech vehicles. The swamp buggy queen gets dunked in the mud at the end.

King Richard's Medieval Family Fun Park

6780 North Airport Road, t (239) 598 2042, www.kingrichardspark.net
Open Sun–Thurs 11–9, Fri, Sat 11–10. Merlin's Moat: summer only 12 noon–6, ring for details
Adm Individual rides: $5 each, value package: 6 tickets $28.50. All day pass (3–adult): $25.95

Ride knightly go-carts, play laser tag, ride bumper boats, have a ball in batting cages or on a miniature golf course. There's also a dragon-themed roller coaster, a dungeon vertical-drop tower and a family water play area called Merlin's Moat.

Lowdermilk Park

Gulf Shore Boulevard and Banyan Boulevard
Open 8–dusk

This lovely beachfront park is within striking distance of the shops along 3rd Street and 5th Avenue. Facilities include picnic tables, a volleyball court, children's playground, and a duck pond. Toilets and showers are also available.

Naples Fishing Pier

12th Avenue South, off Gulf Shore Boulevard, t (239) 213 3062
Open 9–dusk
Adm Free

Take a walk on the pier to view dolphins and pelicans or enjoy free fishing courtesy of the city. There's a bait shop and snack bar, about halfway down and toilets and showers are at the beach end.

Naples Museum of Art

5833 Pelican Bay Boulevard, t (239) 597 1900
See **Philharmonic Center of Arts, p.181**

Shy Wolf Sanctuary, Education and Experience Center

1161 Southwest 27th Street, t (239) 455 1698
Open By arrangement only
Adm Free (donations welcome)

This non-profit-making refuge cares for several wolves and other injured or neglected animals. It is now home to a jaguar-leopard cross, wolves and wolf-dogs, cougars, coyotes, fennec foxes and prairie dogs. Although mainly a teaching facility for schools, small pre-booked groups are welcome to visit.

Teddy Bear Museum of Naples

2511 Pine Ridge Road, t (239) 598 2711, www.teddymuseum.com
Getting there I–75 (Exit 107) at the corner of Pine Ridge and Airport-Pulling Road
Open Tue–Sat 10–5, Storytime and bear-stuffing classes: Sat 10.30–11
Adm Adults $8, children (4–12) $3. Bear stuffing class: $35 (includes bear)

The late Frances Pew Haye started this amazing bear collection in 1984, when her grandson gave her a teddy for Christmas. The museum now houses over 5,000 teddy bears by artists and manufacturers from all over the world. There are 800 bear books in the library, including stories from British authors about characters such as Paddington Bear, Winnie the Pooh and Rupert Bear. From rare bears to Care Bears there's something here to suit all young children. They can visit the home of the Three Bears, attend a bear wedding, go on a teddy parade or head outside for a teddy bears' picnic.

> ***Did you know?***
> ***A teddy-bear enthusiast is called an arctophile?***

The Zoo at Caribbean Gardens

1590 Goodlette Road, (239) 262 5409, www.napleszoo.com
Open Daily 9.30–5.30 (lat adm 4.30)
Adm Adults $15.95, children (4–15) $9.95, plus tax, includes presentations and cruise

Set in a lovely **botanical park**,this well-planned zoo is home to tigers, sloths and clouded leopards, amongst other species, and has recently introduced some new kangaroos. There is a special exhibit about the ecology of Madagascar. A trip here includes Meet the Keeper sessions, a boat ride to view lemurs, apes and monkeys living the high life on their own island paradises and a programme of animal demonstrations with live action and video footage. The zoo received the Champion Award (top place) for "Place to Take Kids" in the 2005 Southwest Florida Choice Awards.

Entertainment

Philharmonic Center for the Arts

5833 Pelican Bay Boulevard, t (239) 597 1900
Getting there 5 miles off Pine Ridge Road, turn right at US Highway 41 and then left
Open Various; Art Museum: Sept–Oct and May–Jul Mon–Sat 10–4, Sun 12 noon–4, Nov–May Mon–Sat 10–5, Sun 12 noon–5
Tickets Various

Visit the Phil for concerts and shows, ballet and theatre. Also on site is the **Naples Museum of Art** with 15 galleries and a stunning glass-domed conservatory hung with chandelier sculptures.

Tours

Authentic Nature Tours by Orchids & Egrets

238 Silverado Drive, t (941) 352 8586, www.naturetour.com
Tours $350/day (max 4 adults or 2 adults and 4 children (6–12) including transport to from hotels in the Naples/Marco Island area.

Half and full-day Everglades tours include a 1½-hour cruise through the **Ten Thousand Islands National Wildlife Refuge**, followed by lunch and a wet or dry eco-walk. There are also naturalist-led tours that include dolphin or manatee swims, wildlife and bird watching, hiking and biking trips, kayaking and snorkelling and visiting the Florida Keys.

Naples Trolley Tours and Everglades Excursions

Old Naples General Store, 1010 6th Avenue South; t (941) 262 7300 (Trolley) www.naplestrolleytours.com; t (941) 262 1914 (Everglades) www.everglades-excursions.com
Tours Everglade Excursions: price varies according to tour

Hop on and off the trolley on a two-hour history and shopping tour around Naples taking in 100 points of local interest. **Everglades Excursions** offer half-day and full-day tours on a Safari wagon. The full-day tour includes an airboat ride through the **Ten Thousand Islands** and a jungle cruise through the Everglades National Park, with lunch provided. Visitors conclude with a trip to Everglades City (*see* p.183).

Shopping

Shopping experiences in Naples tend towards the one-off with bijou boutiques lining the leafy shopping districts of **3rd Street South** with its charming Cracker cottages and **5th Avenue South**, which is where you'll also find several art galleries and sidewalk cafés. Along **North Tamiami Trail** there are department stores such as **Dillards and Burdines/Macy's**, clothes for young children are available at **Rock A By Baby**, 4751 North Tamiami Trail, **t** (239) 649 5150, and the **Waterside Shops** at Pelican Bay, 5415 North Tamiami Trail, **t** (239) 598 1605, **www**.watersideshops.net, stock designer labels such as Gucci and Burberry, as well as books, kids' clothes and gifts.

The Village on Venetian Bay

4200 Gulf Shore Boulevard, t (239) 261 6100
Getting there I–75, take Exit 107 onto Pine Ridge Road and travel west to US 41 (Tamiami Trail), turn south to Park Shore Drive and right on to Gulf Shore Boulevard

An upmarket collection of 60 shops and art galleries arranged in a crescent around suburban homes and flanked by waterfront restaurants. Shop here for shoes, outdoor and sports wear, matching mother-and-daughter frocks, designer clothes, handmade gifts, watches, jewellery, fine art and ceramics.

AROUND AND ABOUT

Marco Island

Despite being part of the Everglades' Ten Thousand Islands, Marco Island has not escaped development as a resort hotel destination. In fact, its proximity to the Everglades has sealed its fate as a springboard for exploring the surrounding areas of natural beauty. The northeast end still retains the feel of a quiet fishing village, if you're looking for an escape route from all the golfing communities .

Getting there

From I–75 take Exit 101 (Marco Island), heading south on Collier Boulevard (formerly County Road 951) for 20 miles

Tourist information

Marco Island Area Chamber of Commerce, 1102 North Collier Boulevard, t (239) 394 7549, www.marcoislandchamber.org

Captain's John and Pam Stop

Calusa Island Marina, Goodland, t (239) 394 8000, www.stopsmarinecharters.com
Tours Start at $45 per person ($40 under 10s) for a three-hour shared fishing charter

Small, family-riendly eco tours, sunset cruises, shelling expeditions or fishing trips are all on offer at this long-established environmentally aware establishment.

Key Marco Museum

Area Board of Realtors Building, 140 Waterway Drive, corner of Bald Eagle Drive, t (239) 394 5616.
Open Mon–Fri 9–4; Adm Free

This new facility traces the development of Marco from a fishing community to a busy resort town, focussing on the archaeological excavations carried out here in 1896 by Frank Cushing. Exhibits include a replica of the Key Marco Cat, Calusa Indian tools, fishing nets and ceremonial masks.

Marco Island Trolley

Collier Boulevard, t (239) 394 1600
Adm Adults $16, children (under 12) $7

Start with an entertaining hop-on hop-off narrated tour of the island which gives you the history of Marco Island, takes you past some lovely old Florida homes and fills you in on where to shop and eat while you are here.

Tigertail Beach

Hernando Drive (take Tigertail Court north off Collier Boulevard, entrance at intersection of Spinnaker Drive and Hernando Drive)

Open 8–dusk

On the north section of the island this public beach features a developing sandbar and a shallow lagoon. Beach equipment and water sports rentals on site, plus picnic facilities, toilets and showers, an extensive children's playground, butterfly garden and boardwalks, volleyball nets and snack stalls.

Shopping

Head to **North Collier Boulevard** to, browse the speciality shops and restaurants in Esplanade, 740 North Collier Blvd, or **Island Plaza**, corner of North Collier Boulevard and Bald Eagle Drive, where you'll find surf gear, gift shops, ice cream parlours and restaurants. **Marco Town Center Mall**, also on the corner of North Collier Boulevard and Bald Eagle Drive, is the largest shopping centre on the island. Among the 40 shops in this village-style set-up, you'll find health food cafés, restaurants and boutiques selling everything from beachwear to ball gowns. **Kid N' Around**, 1089 North Collier Boulevard, **t** (239) 389 0966, stocks children's clothes, toys and accessories. There's free live entertainment on Tuesday and Thursday nights from 6–8.

Everglades City and Chokoloskee Island

East of Marco Island, Everglades City is the nerve-centre for visitors wishing to explore the Everglades and Ten Thousand Islands. It is also home to the Wilderness Waterway, the back-country paddle route that links Everglades City to Flamingo. From here you can set off on a fishing trip, rent canoes or kayaks or explore the state.

Getting there

From Goodland, take Route 92 off the island to Highway 41. Turn right. Take Route 29 from Highway 41 to reach Everglades City

Tourist Information

Everglades Area Chamber of Commerce, Corner of Highway 41 and Route 29, **t** (239) 695 3941 or 800 914 6355

Collier-Seminole State Park

20200 East Tamiami Trail at Route 92, **t** (239) 394 3397

Getting there I–75 south to SR 951 south to US 41. Take US 41 approximately 14 miles to the park entrance, located just east of the junction with CR 92

Open 8–dusk

Adm $4 per car, $1 per bike or pedestrian

Leave all your cares behind as you enter Florida's great wilderness comprising 6,500 acres of cypress swamp, salt marshes and tropical hammocks. There are hiking and bike trails, plus canoe rentals and **fishing** on the Blackwater River. Camp overnight or just stay for a picnic to get a real sense of the remoteness of this spot. The park has a snack shop, playground, **nature trails** and narrated **boat tours** are available, **t** (239) 642 8898. Just don't forget the insect repellent.

Everglades National Park Boat Tours

National Park Ranger Station, Chokoloskee Causeway, **t** (239) 695 2591

Getting there From Naples take US 41 east and turn south on Route 29, then follow signs

Tours depart daily 9–4.30 every 30mins

Adm Adults $16, children (6–12) $8.

Canoe rentals: $25.44 a day

Discover the Ten Thousand Islands of the Gulf Coast on a 1½-hour narrated tour led by a naturalist. Explore this watery region, keeping your eyes skinned for dolphins, ospreys and wading birds. Half-day **ranger-led canoe trips** allow you to explore the mangroves and learn about the park's natural and cultural history. The centre also conducts seasonal **bike and hiking tours**, call for details.

Ted Smallwood's Store and Museum

360 Mamie Street, Chokoloskee Island, **t** (239) 695 2989

Open Daily Dec–Apr 10–5, May–Nov 11–5

Adm Adults $2.50, accompanied children (under 12s) free

This authentic 1906 store was reopened in 1989 as a tourist attraction and old fashioned gift shop. Step back in time to the old frontier days when trappers traded their furs for goods in the store, marvel at the old packaging and foodstuffs and peer among the old photographs depicting pioneer life in the Everglades.

Fort Myers

La Casita

15185 McGregor Boulevard, t (239) 415 1050
Open Lunch and dinner daily, breakfast at weekends (*inexpensive*)

Fresh, authentic Mexican cuisine served in cheery surroundings with colourful décor and friendly staff. There's a kids' menu and dishes include shrimp and corn soup, basil chicken and hot apple pie.

Mel's Diner

4820 South Cleveland Avenue, t (239) 275 7850, www.melsdiners.com
Open Breakfast, lunch and dinner (*inexpensive*)

Part of the popular Mel's chain of diners, this 1950s-style restaurant offers comfy booth seating and an activity sheet children's menu. Kids can have pancakes, scrambled eggs or French toast in the morning and turkey platters for lunch or dinner, plus the usual burgers and fries fare. Parents can opt for a deli sandwich or one of Mel's salads; they do a mean chili taco variety here.

University Grill

7790 Cypress Lake Drive, t (239) 437 4377, www.prawnbroker.com (*moderate*)

If you want some tasty fish or seafood, look no further. Horseradish encrusted grouper or Yellowtail Snapper with lemon caper sauce are among the offerings at this spacious restaurant, which also serves salads, burgers, sandwiches and pasta. Families can sit out on the porch to watch heron trying to snag their own meal from the ornamental pond with its fluttering fountains, outside.

Around and About

Punta Gorda

Harpoon Harry's

Fishermen's Village, 1200 West Retta Esplanade, t (941) 637 1177, www.harpoonharrys.com (*inexpensive–moderate*)

This roomy waterfront restaurant has a raw bar for oysters, clams, shrimps and crab legs and also offers salads, soups, sandwiches, plus seafood fried baskets and steam pots. Kid's plates include chicken or fish sticks, grilled cheese sandwiches or fried shrimps.

Cape Coral

Iguana Mia

1027 Cape Coral Parkway, **t** (239) 945 7755 (*inexpensive–moderate*)

This small chain serving Mexican food is fun and worth a visit. Choose from chimichangas, fajitas, enchiladas and other staple dishes or opt for a seasonal special such as Chile Rellenos or Blue Crab and Shrimp Tacquitos. The 'Little Juan's Menu' (under 12s, $4.75) offers cheese, chicken or beef enchiladas, beef or chicken tacos, beef, chicken or bean burrito or pizza, chicken tenders, mini corn dogs and the all-American peanut butter and jelly sandwich. All kids' meals are served with rice, pinto beans, corn on the cob, black beans, fruit or vegetables, plus drink and dessert.

Tony's Italian Grill

1341 Del Prado Boulevard, t (239) 573 8669
Open Tue–Sun 4–9 (*inexpensive–moderate*)

Come here for casual family style dining with great homemade pizzas, soups, breads and coffee. There's a children's menu available and they serve delicious ice cream desserts.

Lee Island Coast

Boca Grande

Dolphin Cove Café

421 Park Avenue, **t** (941) 964 0109 (*inexpensive*)

A good stopping place for light bites, ice creams and takeout sandwiches and salads.

Jam's Italian-American Restaurant

480 East Railroad Avenue, **t** (941) 964 2002, www.jamsrestaurant.com (*inexpensive–moderate*)

If you're hankering for homemade pizza, stromboli and calzone, this is the place. Sandwiches, salads and traditional Italian meat and fish dishes are also available. Dine indoors or out. Another branch on the mainland is in nearby Placida.

Loons on a Limb

Corner of 3rd Street and East Railroad, **t** (941) 964 0155
Open 7.30–11.30 and 6–9 (*inexpensive*)

This is an excellent spot for a hearty, home-cooked breakfast or brunch. Enjoy eggs benedict, bacon and eggs, omelets, corned beef hash, bagels and fresh fruit.

Loose Caboose

433 West 4th Street, **t** (941) 964 0440
Open Breakfast snacks, 11–4.30 daily, Fri–Sat 6–9 (*inexpensive–moderate*)

This café in the old Railroad Depot offers sandwiches, soups, burgers, hand-cut fries, shakes and great ice creams. Eat in the railway waiting room or on the patio.

PJ's Seagrille

321 Park Avenue, **t** (941) 964-0806
Open Mon–Sat Lunch: 11.30–2.30, Dinner: 5.30–9.30 (*inexpensive–expensive*)

A former theatre with 1920s décor and an aquarium for the kids, the Seagrille offers a fine-dining experience in a laid-back atmosphere with fresh daily seafood specials. Reservations recommended. Lighter fare is on offer in the lounge.

South Beach

777 Gulf Boulevard, **t** (941) 964 0765, **www.southbeachgrille.com** (*moderate–expensive*)

This relaxed beachside restaurant offers seafood, steak and chicken dishes. There's a kids' menu of pasta, burgers, chicken and hot dogs and 'all you can eat' specials on Wednesday and Friday nights.

Pine Island

Cabbage Key Inn

Cabbage Key, accessible only by boat, **t** (239) 283 2278.
Open for breakfast, lunch and dinner (*moderate–very expensive*)

You can only reach this historic inn, built as a hideout for novelist Mary Roberts Rinehart in the 1930s, by boat. The walls of the main dining room and bar are lined with signed dollar bills – the kids can find one signed by someone with your surname or add their own. Dishes include salmon with peppercorns, seafood strudel, fresh shrimp and lobster. There are stone tables and benches under shady trees outside, if you'd like sit out by the water.

Waterfront Restaurant

2131 Oleander Street, St. James City, **t** (239) 283 0592, **www.waterfrontrestaurant.com** (*inexpensive–moderate*)

Eat overlooking the boats bobbing in the marina. They do a cracking clam chowder here, plus any way you like grouper, spicy shrimp, devilled crab, seafood casserole, salad and sandwiches.

Sanibel Island

Hungry Heron Restaurant

2330 Palm Ridge Road, Sanibel, **t** (239) 395 2300
Open Lunch daily and dinner. Breakfast on weekends (*moderate*)

The kids won't mind a bit of a wait for their food because this family friendly restaurant has TV screens showing cartoons and a live magician doing tricks. There's lots for kids to choose from, for mostly between $2.99–$4.99, including ham and cheese melts, burgers, pizzas, popcorn shrimp, macaroni and cheese or turkey sandwiches. Adults should go for the steam bucket packed with delicious seafood, corn, red potatoes and onions.

The Lighthouse Café

362 Periwinkle Way, Sanibel, **t** (239) 472 0303
Open Breakfast daily 7–3. Lunch 11–3. Dinner Jan–Mar only (*inexpensive–moderate*)

Enjoy farm fresh eggs any way you like them or tuck into a plate of delicious wholewheat pancakes with or without fruit. Fresh juices and omelettes are also available. For lunch choose from salads, sandwiches and steaks.

McT's Shrimp House & Tavern

1523 Periwinkle Way, Sanibel Island, **t** 239 472 3161
Open Dinner daily 4.45–10 (*inexpensive–moderate*)

Pop in to this casual spot for the all-you-can-eat shrimp and crab dishes, ribs, pasta, steaks and delicious homemade desserts.

Captiva Island

The Bubble Room

15001 Captiva Drive, Captiva, **t** (239) 472 5558 (*expensive*)

Head over early if you want to avoid the queues both at lunchtime and in the evening. Visitors and locals alike flock here for the kitsch décor as much as for the food, which tends to be pricey but worth it. Choose from pork loin chops with garlic and key lime sauce, beer-battered shrimp, chicken with cornbread stuffing, roast duck, poached grouper or chargrilled tuna among other dinner delights. Their famous desserts are huge – share one or ask for a goody bag and have it later. Kids will enjoy roaming around the rooms looking at the collection of cartoon character memorabilia, the eternal Christmas scene and watching the little train chugging its way through the main dining area.

Mucky Duck

11546 Andy Rosse Lane, Captiva, **t** (239) 472 3434, **www.muckyduck.com**

Open Lunch: daily 11–3, Dinner: Mon–Sat 5–9.30 (*inexpensive–moderate*)

This English-run pub offers snacks and meals, though service is a bit slow, so order straight away. Lunchtime dishes include breaded duck fingers with raspberry sauce and coleslaw, meatloaf, steamed mussels or black bean burgers. Kids can opt for pasta, beer-battered shrimp or ducky-fried chicken among other choices. You can then sit awhile on the beach sipping a grape-based Bloody Mary watching the kids play in the sand. The sunsets are gorgeous and if you're lucky you might spot a dolphin or two. Sounds nice huh? We saw three.

RC Otters

Captiva Island Inn, 11509 Andy Rosse Lane, Captiva, **t** (239) 395 1142

Open for breakfast lunch and dinner (*inexpensive–moderate*)

This friendly and casual restaurant has live music, plenty of outdoor seating and a tempting kids' menu, which features dishes such as omelettes and scrambled eggs accompanied by fresh fruit. Freshly squeezed juices, enormous salads, lobster pots, vegetarian pasta and a delightful range of fish and seafood dishes complete the experience.

Englewood

Fort Myers Beach

There are lots of seafood restaurants right by the beach here and most establishments are willing to do kids' meals for children up to 15.

Iguana Mia

4329 S Cleveland Avenue, Fort (*inexpensive–moderate*)

Another in this small chain. *See* p.184, Cape Coral.

Island Pancake House

2801 Estero Boulevard, **t** (941) 463 0033 (*inexpensive*)

Friendly local place with great big pancakes.

Snug Harbor

645 San Carlos Boulevard, **t** (239) 463 4343, **www.snugharborrestaurant.com** (*inexpensive–moderate*)

Smart waterfront dining indoors or out with great dolphin spotting opportunities. The menu specializes in seafood, plus slow-roasted ribs, pasta, chicken and steaks, there's also a separate kids' menu with crayons.

Matanzas Inn Restaurant

416 Crescent Street, **t** (239) 463 3838, **www.matanzasrestaurant.com** (*inexpensive–moderate*)

This huge waterfront restaurant has great views from the upstairs deck over the Matanzas Pass. Sit under parasols outside or in the air-conditioned restaurant. They serve lots of seafood, including lobster, steamed clams and sautéed scallops. Sandwiches, chicken dishes and steaks are also available. There's live music most days.

Bonita Beach

Anthony's Trattoria

8951 Bonita Beach Road (Springs Plaza), **t** (239) 947 2202

Open Lunch: Mon–Sat; dinner daily (*inexpensive–moderate*)

Good friendly place to come for traditional Italian fare made with fresh ingredients.

Doc's Beach House

27980 Hickory Boulevard, **t** (239) 992 6444

Open Daily breakfast, lunch, and dinner (*inexpensive*)

Casual beachfront hang-out serving pizza, burgers, hotdogs and seafood with outdoor seating downstairs and air-conditioning and beach views above. They also do sports and beach equipment rentals.

Iguana Mia

28051 South Tamiami Trail, Bonita Springs, **t** (239) 949 1999 (*inexpensive–moderate*)

Another in this small chain of Mexican restaurants. *See* p.184, Cape Coral.

Naples

Aurelio's Pizzeria

590 North Tamiami Trail, **t** (941) 403 8882 (*inexpensive*)

Local family friendly favourite pizzeria featuring Chicago style meat toppings ranging from taco to barbecue flavour. They also serve a variety of pastas, chicken dishes, sandwiches and salads.

Bha! Bha!

847 Vanderbilt Beach Road (Pavilion Shopping Centre), **t** (941) 594 5557 (*moderate*)

Give the kids a taste of something a bit different at this Persian Bistro where you can dine beneath exotic tapestries on spicy garlic green shell mussels or fish, garlic eggplant chicken and shellfish simmered with saffron and served with couscous. The menu also features kebabs, lamb, duck and rice dishes for children who prefer plainer meals. If you visit on Sunday, you can sample a bit of everything from the brunch buffet.

Chops City Grill

837 5th Avenue, **t** (239) 262 4677
Open Mon–Thur 5–10, Fri–Sun 5–11
(*moderate–very expensive*)

Traditional and high-quality grill house fare, plus tempting sushi, Thai curries, seafood and salads served indoors or out.

Riverwalk Fish & Ale House

Tin City, 1200 5th Avenue South, **t** (239) 263 2734
(*moderate*)

This is the place to go for casual, open-air waterfront dining, specializing in fresh seafood, steaks, salad and sandwiches with a separate kids' menu.

Whistle Stop Steakhouse

Waterloo Station, 200 Goodlette Road South,
t (239) 262 1167 (*moderate*)

The name kind of gives it away but that shouldn't stop the kids from enjoying this railroad themed restaurant serving steak, ribs chops and seafood, plus a kids' menu and lunchtime salad bar.

Around and About

Marco Island

Olde Marco Restaurant

Olde Marco Island Inn, 100 Palm Street
t (239) 394 3131, **www.oldmarcorestaurant.com**
(*moderate–very expensive*)

This hotel restaurant offers outdoor dining overlooking the pool and gardens and has a children's menu for under-12s with pasta dishes and chicken fingers etc. The hotel also houses **Captain Collier's Steak Room** for more intimate dining.

Snook Inn

1215 Bald Eagle Drive, **t** (239) 394 3313
(*moderate–expensive*)

Dine indoors or outside at this family-friendly waterside restaurant. Seafood specials, steaks, salads, sandwiches, pork chops and baked grouper are among the many fresh dishes on offer. Or bring your own catch and they'll cook it for you.

Stan's Idle Hour Seafood Restaurant

221 West Goodland Drive, Goodland,
t (239) 394 3041 (*moderate*)

Home to the Goodland Mullet Festival, Stan's is the place to come to soak up the old island atmosphere. Eat fresh seafood and enjoy live music at weekends including the famous Stan singing songs and doing his own dance known locally as the Buzzard Lope on Sundays from 12 noon–6.

Everglades City

Ivey House Restaurant

107 Camellia Street, **t** (239) 695 3299
(*inexpensive–expensive*)

This friendly bed and breakfast establishment is fast growing a reputation for quality Southern-style cuisine such as sautéed frogs' legs and 'gator chowder and hearty breakfasts.

Joanie's Blue Crab Café

39395 Tamiami Trail, Ochopee, **t** (239) 695 2682
Getting there on the Tamiami Trail (US 41), just east of SR 29 (*inexpensive–moderate*)

It specializes in fresh blue crab dishes caught by staff and cooked on the back porch every day. They also serve oysters, shrimp, grouper sandwiches, conch fritters, 'gator nuggets and black beans and rice .

Rod & Gun Club

200 Riverside Drive, Everglades City,
t (239) 695 2101 (*inexpensive–expensive*)

This famous hunters lair is decorated with their trophies, so if you've got sensitive children eat out on the porch overlooking the river. Here you'll find typical Everglades fare such as swamp and turf (frogs' legs and steak) peanut butter pie and stone crab claws.

The Oyster House Restaurant

901 Copeland Avenue, Chokoloskee Causeway,
Highway 29 South, **t** (239) 695 2073,
www.oysterhouserestaurant.com
(*inexpensive–moderate*)

Dine overlooking the beauty of the Ten Thousand Islands on seafood baskets, chicken wings, numerous crab dishes and steams. The kids' menu features clam or chicken strips, hotdogs or burgers.

Quiz

1. What were the names of the American Indians who lived in the area around Fort Myers?

2. What finally reached Fort Myers in 1904?

3. Who invented the phonograph and the movie camera?

4. Where can you experience a hurricane?

5. What is the name of the fearsome pirate who roamed the coast around Fort Myers?

6. What sort of town was Punta Gorda originally?

7. What hurricane damaged wildlife and destroyed vegetation in Captiva Island?

8. Where can you visit an animal hospital?

9. Where can you attend a bear wedding or go on a teddy parade?

10. Where can kids climb aboard a 1930s Pullman railcar?

Southeast Florida

11

Southeast Florida

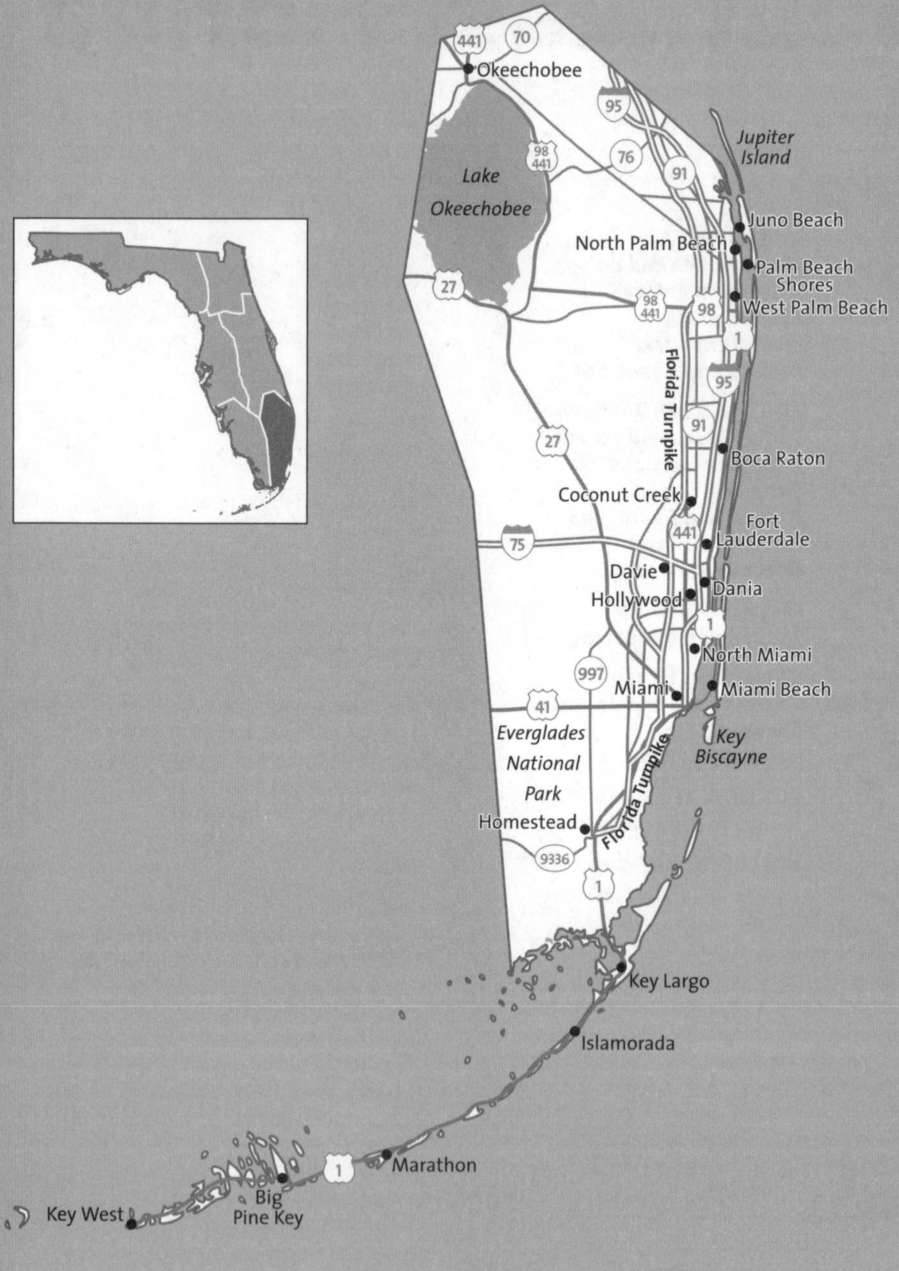

SOUTHEAST FLORIDA

When the kids are done in the Magic Kingdom® (*see* p.245) what every self-respecting parent needs is to spend a couple of days and nights living it up in the Magic City, preferably topped off by a week lounging around in the **Florida Keys**. Take the kids, certainly, but don't forget to enjoy yourself as well. The main reason for visiting Miami is still the same now as it was in the early 1900s – fabulous beaches and year-round good weather attracts people in droves. Property buyers still vie for their condos in the sun much as the early landowners saw the potential for growth in Miami some 200 years ago.

Following the frosts of 1894–5 when most of Florida's citrus crop was wiped out, an enterprising Cleveland widow named Julia Tuttle lured Henry Flagler's railway to town by sending him orange blossoms blooming in midwinter signalling that there were lands that had been untouched by the big freeze in south Florida and they were ripe for development. Flagler took the bait. Tuttle and fellow Cleveland landowner, William Brickell, granted Flagler the territory to extend his railroad along with a large chunk of Miami real estate. Flagler repaid them by building several resort hotels, an impressive transport system and the foundations of today's city. The first passenger train arrived in April 1896 and soon Irish Catholic, Jewish, Caribbean and African settlers arrived. By 1912, just a year before his death, Flagler's railroad reached as far as **Key West**. No doubt inspired by Flagler's enterprise, men such as John Collins, Carl Fisher and the Lummus Brothers built bridges, drained the mosquito-infested swamps along the coast and dredged Biscayne Bay to create **Miami Beach**. The first land boom came in the early 1920s but the onset of the Great Depression and the hurricanes of 1926 and 1935 took their toll on land sales. The mid-30s Art Deco movement helped revive the area by attracting tourists to a string of chic new hotels on **South Beach** (now designated the Miami Beach Architectural Historic District, *see* p.194). Another boom followed World War II when Frank Sinatra, Jackie Gleason, Bob Hope and the like played to packed audiences in the Miami Beach Auditorium (now the **Jackie Gleason Theater**) and neighbouring hotels. Crash followed boom in swift succession throughout the decade with organized crime groups descending on the area in the '50s and '80s before Miami improved its act in the late '90s and a much needed infusion of capital ensured the return of tourist money.

The city's appeal today is reflected in hotel prices by the beach but if you shop around, book well in advance and travel out of high season there are deals to be had. North of Miami Beach the price tags even out towards family-friendly **Fort Lauderdale** and then soar again as you head into exclusive **Palm Beach**. Still, you don't have to venture too far if you're looking for a quiet bolthole along this stretch of coast. **Lake Okeechobee** and the **Loxahatchee National Wildlife Refuge** lie to the west of Palm Beach and both Fort Lauderdale and Miami are 30 minutes' drive from the Everglades. Highway 1 will take you down to the Florida Keys, where the cares of everyday life dissolve with each passing mile down to mile marker 0 in far out **Key West**.

The southwest's frost-free climate brings an average temperature of 77 degrees year-round. January and February are coldest with lows around 66 degrees but highs can reach the mid-80s. In

Highlights

Becoming a fireman, policeman, a bank teller or a dentist at Miami Children's Museum, p.194
Learning about art deco architecture on a South Beach walking tour, Miami, p.194
Taking the plunge at the Venetian Pool, Coral Gables, p.196
Touring Miami Metrozoo on a safari cycle, p.197
Anyone for tennis? Crandon Park, Key Biscayne, p.198
Camping out in a chickee in the Everglades National Park, p.199
Seeing under the sea on a Glass Bottom Boat Ride, Biscayne National Underwater Park, p.199
Careering around at Wanadoo City, Sawgrass Mills, p.206
Taking to the water at John D. MacArthur State Park, North Palm Beach, p.212
Meeting Flipper's descendants at the Dolphin Research Center, Grassy Key, p.215
Discovering your own island paradise at Bahia Honda State Park, Bahia Honda Key, p.216
Spotting the little dears in the Key Deer National Wildlife Refuge, Big Pine Key, p.216
Petting the six-toed cats at the Hemingway House, Key West, p.217
Stargazing from the deck of the Schooner Western Union, Key West, p.218

Special events

January

Children's Theater Festival, Miami, **t** (305) 444 9293

Old Island Days, Key West, **t** (305) 294 9501.

Carnaval Miami, Miami, **t** (305) 644 8888.

February

Coconut Grove Arts Festival, t (305) 447 0401.

Taste of the Beach, Lauderdale-By-The-Sea, **t** (954) 776 1000, **www**.lbts.com

April

Independence Celebration, Key West (Conch Republic), **t** (305) 294 2298, **www**.conchrepublic.com

April–May

SunFest, West Palm Beach, **t** (561) 659 6980.

Sugar Festival, Clewiston, **t** (863) 983 7979

June

Bahamian Goombay Festival, Coconut Grove, **t** (305) 372 9966, **www**.goombayfestival.com

September/October

Viva Broward! Hispanic Heritage Month, Fort Lauderdale, **t** (954) 527 0627, **www**.fiestafortlauderdale.com

October

Fantasy Fest, Key West (305) 296 1817, **www**.fla-keys.com

Junior Orange Bowl International Youth Festival, Coral Gables, **t** (305) 662 1210

December

King Mango Strut Parade, Coconut Grove, **t** (305) 401-1171 **www**.kingmangostrut.org

Miccosukee Indian Arts Festival, Miccosukee Indian Village, **t** (305) 223 8380

Winterfest, Fort Lauderdale, **t** (954) 767 0686, **www**.winterfestparade.com

August and September temperatures can reach the mid-90s. Take care in this region as ocean breezes can make it feel much cooler than it is and you can easily get wind-burnt strolling along the beach. Children and adults should apply high factor sun lotion at regular intervals to ensure a stress-free holiday, especially when venturing toward the Keys.

MIAMI

Miami's long history of immigration makes for a heady cultural combination with Cubans, Haitians, Nicaraguans, Colombians, Puerto Ricans, Bahamians, Jamaicans, Venezuelans and Mexicans among other groups adding their own style, music and cuisine to the mix and creating distinct communities such as Little Havana and Little Haiti.

Miami's crime scene has had considerable exposure on our TV screens but there is another side to this teeming metropolis that deserves closer observation. As with any big city, it's unwise to wander around at night and visitors should take care with personal possessions at all times. Having said that, there are an increasing number of family-friendly attractions to explore and the shopping streets of **Bayside** and **Lincoln Road** offer well-lit and populated areas in which to browse even after the sun goes down. Downtown Miami's urban sprawl is offset by a prolific, if not entirely logical inner-city transport system that provides access to shopping districts, entertainment complexes and the busy **Port of Miami** where the cruise ships dock on their way to the Caribbean. A series of bridges connect the beaches to the mainland.

The thriving **South Beach** Art Deco district is the first place to head for a stroll. The area was created out of drained swampland following the failure of a large coconut plantation in the late 1800s but by the 1970s the area had deteriorated with dubious business practices and dilapidated buildings. Now, thanks to the vision of the Miami Design Preservation League, many of South Beach's 800 remaining art-deco gems have been renovated for local and tourist accommodation. SoBe, as it has been dubbed, is certainly glamourous. From **Lincoln Road Mall**'s Mediterranean-style shopping streets to the restaurants and hotels of sand-fringed **Ocean Drive**, there are stunning views, strolling players and plenty of opportunities for people watching from cafés. Towards the northern end of South Beach and Middle Beach you'll find the busy resort behemoths with their swimming pools and beach frontage but choose carefully as the ratio of rooms to sun loungers can prove a bit of a problem (*see* Sleep p.48). Up past **Middle Beach** is the up-and-coming **North Beach** area (NoBe) flanked by the exclusive designer boutiques of **Bal Harbor** (*see* p.199).

Getting there

By air Direct flights run daily from all London airports and other UK cities including Aberdeen, Birmingham, Bristol, Edinburgh, Glasgow, Leeds, Manchester and Newcastle. Although **Miami airport** attracts about 30 million visitors a year, it is uninspiring places to wait around in. The best facilities are strung out along the eight concourses before you go through to the departure gates but even these are thin on the ground. There are hardly any shops but if you want to eat there's a nice Cuban restaurant called **La Carreta** (Concourse D), otherwise you'll find the same old newsstands and not much else. The **MIA Hotel**, **www**.miahotel.com (Concourse E, Level 2) has a fitness centre and a rooftop sundeck and pool that are open to non-residents but these are closed until November 2005. The first floor bar and sushi bar remain open along with the 7th floor **Top of the Port Checkrooms** are located in Terminal E, Level 2, open 5–11 and Terminal G, Level 1, open 9–9.

SuperShuttle, t (305) 871 2000 operate a service between the airport and Miami with fares ranging between $9–$14 per person. **Taxis** cost around $30 flat rate to the beaches and can be picked up right outside the terminal building.

By rail Amtrak runs services between Miami and Jacksonville (9 hours), (service runs out of New York) with stops in Fort Lauderdale, West Palm Beach, Okeechobee and other local station stops. Miami to Tampa and Miami to Orlando both take around 6 hours. **www**.amtrak.com

By road Route A1A and Highway 1 battle it out for supremacy down the far south coast. I–95 and the Florida Turnpike are less busy approach roads, especially during rush hour.

Getting around

There are lots of options for car-free travel and connecting between services is either free or a nominal fee (for example, if you have a tri-rail ticket then metrorail services are free) **www**.miamidade.gov/transit/

Metrorail – this elevated rail system covers 21 miles from Hialeah to Kendall serving downtown and popular tourist destinations such as Coconut Grove and Vizcaya.

Metromover – free motorized shuttle service covering the downtown area, including attractions like the Bayside shopping mall and Miami Arena. Kids love riding in the front pretending they are driving and enjoying great views of the city.

Metrobus services also connect to rail services. There are frequent buses from downtown to the beaches.

Tri-rail – commuter rail service between Dade County, Broward and Palm Beach with stops in Boca Raton, Fort Lauderdale and West Palm Beach. **www**.tri-rail.com/

Tourist information

Greater Miami Convention and Visitors Bureau, 701 Brickell Avenue, Suite 2700, Miami 33131, **t** (305) 539 3000 or (888) 766 4264; **www**.miamiandbeaches.com

Things to see and do

Miami Beach

Enchanted Forest Elaine Gordon Park

1725 Northeast 135th Street, North Miami,
t (305) 895 1119
Getting there From I-95, take exit 14, towards NW 135th Street/Opa-locka Blvd. Stay straight to go onto NW 6th Avenue, then turn left onto Opa-locka Blvd. Turn left onto NW 19th Avenue, left again onto 135th Street
Open 8–dusk
Adm Free (activities individually priced)

This 22-acre oasis is located in North Miami's Arch Creek district. Enjoy a quiet picnic, ride or hike the nature trail, admire the swans or take a pony ride. Non-riders can feed the ponies and look around the stable. There are two playgrounds and lots of space to unwind in after a few days in the city.

Haulover Park

10800 Collins Avenue, North of Miami Beach,
t (305) 947 3525
All-day parking $4

This 180-acre park offers plenty of scope for active kids. You can hire bikes and kites, play golf or tennis, follow a hiking trail or rent a boat for a fishing trip. There's also a restaurant, an ice cream shop and picnic shelters with grills. An underground path leads to the attractive two-mile beach area.

Holocaust Memorial

1933–1945 Meridian Avenue, Miami Beach,
t (305) 538 1663, **www**.holocaustmmb.org
Getting there Between Meridian Avenue and Dade Boulevard
Open 9–9. daily; **Adm** free

The Holocaust Memorial was devised by architect and sculptor Kenneth Treister and first opened to the public in February 1990. A hand reaches skywards from a mass of human figures representing the six million Jewish victims of The Holocaust. The list of names carved in black granite on the Memorial Wall are tributes to the loved ones of Miami Beach's Jewish community – one of the largest communities of Holocaust survivors in the world.

South Beach

Art Deco District Welcome Center

1001 Ocean Drive, Miami Beach, t (305) 531 3484. www.mdpl.org
Walking tours **Sat 10.30, Thu 6.30, Adults $20, child $15, under 5s free. Self-guided (tape) tour Adults $15, children/students $10 . Available daily 11–4.**
Giftshop

This fascinating tour of South Beach's Architectural Historic District focuses on the history, influences and design features of the Art Deco movement. The 90-minute tour is not taxing for children because there is plenty of stopping-off to nose around in hotel lobbies and have a brief sit-down. Highlights include the Tides and Essex House hotels and a trip to the post office.

Flamingo Park

11 Street & Jefferson Avenue, t (305) 673 7730

This central park is within striking distance of Lincoln Road Mall and features basketball and tennis courts, play space and children's playground, plus a water play area.

Lummus Park Beach

8th Street and Ocean Drive, t (305) 673 7730

Head here for a picnic, stroll along the beach or hire sports equipment including bikes, boats and in-line skates. There are regular sporting events to watch like volleyball contests and kids can climb around in the children's playgrounds.

Miami Children's Museum

980 MacArthur Causeway, t (305) 373 5437
Getting there **I-395 (MacArthur Causeway). Exit at Watson Island and follow road to the museum. Museum and parking on left**
Open **Daily 10–6;** **Adm** **Adults and children $10**
Shop, café, outdoor picnic area

The museum is just across the way from Parrot Jungle Island but annoyingly only accessible by road via an underpass, so you need a car if you want to visit both in one day. Once inside, however, you can relax knowing that the kids will have the time of their lives trying on costumes and role-playing in a hospital, bank or supermarket and manning a police bike, fire engine or cargo dock. There's a nice outdoor playground with tubes, tunnels and ropes and an interactive water play area designed to look like a ship heading to sea complete with fishing poles. Tiny tots have their own book and soft play corner stuffed with spongy sea creatures and treasure chests. Imaginative, informative fun for all ages. There are free evenings (3rd Fri of the month 6.30–8.30) and storytime/craft sessions (Wed 3pm). Fancy a souvenir? Sing your own version of popular karaoke hits in the studio and record it to take home on CD! The museum shop also has lots of colourful books and imaginative gifts.

Miami Duck Tours

1661 James Avenue, t (305) 913 1365/(786) 276 8300, www.DuckToursMiami.com
Tours **Daily on the hour between 10–6**
Adults $24, children $17, under 3s free

These land- and sea-worthy amphibious vehicle tours are already popular with visitors to London and Liverpool. In Miami they offer tourists the chance to drive straight into Biscayne Bay and gawp at the expensive homes on Star Island. The 90-minute narrated tour takes in Ocean Drive and the Art Deco district, Collins and Washington Avenues, the Lincoln Road Mall, Port of Miami and other nautical landmarks in the downtown area. Tickets are also available from the Art Deco Welcome Center.

Parrot Jungle Island

1111 Parrot Jungle Trail, t (305) 258 6453, www.parrotjungle.com
Getting there **Off I–395 (MacArthur Causeway), between downtown Miami and South Beach**
Open **daily 10–6**
Adm **Adults $23.95, plus tax, child (3–10) $18.95, under 3s free**
Lakeside café, gift shops

Birds of a feather sure do flock together at this parrot-tastic experience. Parrot Jungle Island offers trained **bird shows** and feeding encounters, a free-flying aviary, **animal nursery**, serpentarium, tortoise exhibit and an **Everglades habitat** plus wild animal presentations in the **Jungle Theater**. If you don't mind waiting and paying extra, the kids can have their picture taken after the show with an exotic animal like a baby tiger. Flamingo Lake features lots of its pink namesakes and is housed in a large, shady park where it's not unusual to see keepers taking baby limas and monkeys for a stroll. There's also a rare plant nursery, petting barn and playground.

Downtown Miami

Miami-Dade Culture Center

101 West Flagler Street, t (305) 375 3000, www.miamiartmuseum.org/
Getting there NW 1st Street, accessible from Government Center Station.

Miami Art Museum

Open Tue–Fri 10–5, Sat, Sun 12 noon–5
Adm Adults $5, under 12s free
Snack bar and shop

MAM combines a programme of touring exhibitions with displays from the South Florida community and the Americas. Families go free on the second Saturday of the month and can take part in activity sessions, including live music, dance, storytelling, games and tours. The Plaza Level and Upper Level galleries are stocked with art books, videos and hands-on areas where children can let loose their own creative ideas in fashion, art and crafts.

Historical Museum of Southern Florida

t (305) 375 1492, www.historical-museum.org
Open Mon–Sat 10–5 (10–9 on third Thu of the month), Sun 12 noon–5
Adm Adults $5, child (6–12) $2. Tours twice monthly on Sats $39–$20, book in advance

Join historian Dr Paul George for a fascinating boat ride or a walking tour exploring the history of the area and the many communities that make Miami such an interesting place. In addition, there are regular family fun days (Sat from 10–12 noon) where you can take part in art and drama activities inspired by the museum's collections. Kids can also view museum's interactive displays and the changing exhibitions focussing on both the natural and social development of South Florida.

Little Havana

Miami's Cuban district lies between Downtown Miami and Coral Gables between W Flagler and SW 22nd Street. The main street, the **Calle Ocho** is on Southwest 8th Street (Highway 41). If you don't time to take a guided tour with the Historical Museum, just take a stroll along here and stop off for some local cake and coffee or watch the old boys playing dominoes in **Maximo Gomez Park**.

Key Biscayne

Getting there South of downtown and east off Highway 1 onto Rickenbacker Causeway (toll $1)

South of Miami the landscape gets leafier as you head toward Key Biscayne. There are lots of quiet amusements here and lovely parks so pack a picnic and make a day of it. Stop on the causeway at **Hobie Beach** to watch the windsurfers and rent sports equipment if you feel like a sail or a boat tour.

Bill Baggs Cape Florida State Park

1200 South Crandon Boulevard, Key Biscayne, t (305) 361 5811, www.floridastateparks.org
Open 8–dusk
Adm $5 per vehicle with up to eight passengers, $1 per bike or foot passenger. Lighthouse tours: Thu–Mon at 10 and 1 in groups of 20, register at the gate. Children must be 8 or older to climb the tower

Climb the 109 steps to top of this historic lighthouse, built in 1825, and enjoy spectacular views of the beach, Miami and Biscayne Bay. There's a movie and a tour of the **Keeper's Quarters** while you catch your breath. Bring a picnic or eat in **Boater's Grill**, a Cuban-influenced seafood restaurant (open daily 9–9) overlooking No Name Harbor. The park also has **watersports, nature trails, beaches** and **bike paths**.

Crandon Park

4000 Crandon Boulevard, Key Biscayne, t (305) 361 5421
Open 8–dusk
Parking $4

Tourists and locals alike enjoy spending the day strolling along the pristine sands of this three-mile long lagoon. The water is calm, there are several lifeguard posts and picnic areas with tables and grills. In the **Family Amusement Center** children can catch a ride on the restored carrousel, take a spin round the roller rink, splash about in the fountains or take a hayride. In addition the park offers playgrounds, a golf course, tennis courts, baseball and soccer pitches, shower facilities, toilets and shelters. There's also a nature centre, self-guided trails, tram tours, kayaks and a mangrove boardwalk that leads to a fossilized reef overlook.

Miami Seaquarium

4400 Rickenbacker Causeway, Key Biscayne, t (305) 361 5705, www.miamiseaquarium.com
Open Daily 9.30–6
Adm Adults $24.95 plus tax, child (3–9) $19.95 plus tax. Last admission 4.30. A swim with the dolphins costs $140 per swimmer and $32 for observers and includes an aquarium tour (swimmers must be 52 inches or taller); **Parking** $4

You can virtually hop straight from one show to the next at this end-of-the-pier style entertainment complex. Salty the sea lion goofs it up with his clown friends, Flipper the dolphin and pals do star turns with a bunch of smiling beach babes and Lolita the killer whale makes a big splash in the arena. The killer whale show is a fittingly awesome finale but just watch where you sit if you don't want to end up being doused in seawater. The alligator area, reef aquarium, underwater manatee observation pool and rain forest habitat are good to stroll around at the end of the day when the crowds disperse.

Coral Gables

Getting there South of Highway 41 and east of Route 959 (Southwest 57th Street)

This delightful suburb of Miami features fine 1920s Mediterranean-Revival style buildings, parks and gardens, theatres and galleries, golf courses, a spring-fed grotto swimming pool, bike paths, walking trails and old-fashioned trolley buses that stop off at all the major landmarks listed below. Visit the galleries on the first Friday of the month when they throw open their doors in the evening.

Venetian Pool

2701 DeSoto Boulevard, t (305) 460 5356
Open Apr–Jun and Aug–Oct, Tue–Fri 11–5.30 (mid-Jun–mid-Aug 11–7.30), Nov–Mar and Sat–Sun all year 10–4.30
Adm (April-Oct) Adults $9, children (3–12), $5; (Nov-Mar) Adults $5.50, children (3–12) $2.50

Dubbed 'the world's most beautiful swimming hole', this sumptuous 820,000-gallon bathing pool was carved from a coral rock quarry in 1923 and is listed on the National Register of Historic Places. The pool is fed with invigorating spring water, which is now recycled back into the aquifer, and is surrounded by two waterfalls, coral caves, loggias, porticos, stone bridges and grottos.

Coconut Grove

Getting there South of Miami Avenue at the end of Bayshore Drive. There are Metrobus connections to Coconut Grove and a Metrorail station in Vizcaya

The air of refinement continues as you travel east of Coral Gables to the waterfront parks of verdant Coconut Grove. There are great views of the bay with plenty of vantage points for watching manatees and sailboats. The main thoroughfare is **Grand Avenue**, where you'll find two shopping centres: **CocoWalk piazza** with branches of Gap, Banana Republic and Victoria's Secret, several bistros and cafés, plus a 16-screen cinema and **Mayfair in the Grove** with its bookstores, beauty boutiques, gift shops, clothing stores, bars, restaurants and outdoor cafés. At night the area comes alive with jazz, salsa and reggae beats. There are art gallery open days every second Friday of the month.

Barnacle Historic State Park

3485 Main Highway, off McFarlane Road, t (305) 442 6866
Open Fri–Mon 9–4. Tours 10, 11.30, 1 and 2.30
Adm $1 (under 6s free)

Tour the former home of Coconut Grove's founding father, Ralph Middleton Munroe, a New York yacht designer. Munroe and his family had tuberculosis and in 1851 were advised to move south to recuperate. Sadly, his wife, sister and baby died *en route* and he was forced to continue alone. Built in 1891 as a one-storey bungalow, the house was extended to give more room for Ralph's second family in 1908. It is the oldest home in the county that isstill in its original location and the grounds contain a lovely hardwood forest. Ralph's home and boathouse reflect his work as a yacht designer, wrecker and community developer. Open-air film screenings, concerts and dances are regularly held in the park.

Larry and Penny Thompson Park

12451 SW 184th Street, t (305) 232 1049, adjacent to the Metrozoo, *see* p.197
Open 8–dusk
Adm Waterslide and beach: Adults $4, children (3–17) $3. Individuals must be at least 4ft tall to ride the slide. Beach only: Adults $3, children $2. Camping: $22 daily (inc tent), $135 a week; tent sites $10 nightly. Call in advance for reservations

The park comprises 270 acres of natural South Florida woodland with bridle trails and hiking paths among wildflowers, palmettos and rock pinelands.

The main family attraction is the large lake with its own beach and an impressive series of water slides carved into the rock, which are open seasonally and are manned by lifeguards. The large **campground** offers 240 pitches with full electrical and water hook-ups, toilet and laundry facilities, hot showers, camp store, picnic shelters and a playground.

Matheson Hammock Park

9610 Old Cutler Road, t (305) 665 5475
Open 8–dusk; **Parking** $4

This lovely scenic park is unique because it has a man-made pool that is washed regularly by the tide from Biscayne Bay. The beach is particularly popular with families who enjoy its warm, safe waters and services, which include lifeguards, picnic areas, dressing rooms, nature trails and a snack bar.

Miami Metrozoo

12400 Southwest 152nd Street, t (305) 251 0400, www.miamimetrozoo.com
Getting there From Coconut Grove and I-95 (South) take South Dixie Highway (US 1) to 152 Street (Coral Reef Drive). Turn right and proceed west for 3 miles. Zoo entrance is on the left at SW 124 Avenue. From the Metrorail Dadeland South Station catch the Coral Reef Max bus. It's a 20-minute bus ride
Open Daily 9.30–5.30 (last admission 4)
Adm Adults $12, children (3–12) $7

The best way to tour this 300-acre open habitat parkland is on a family-sized safari cycle. Younger kids sit up front while you pedal, affording everyone great views of the 400 resident species. Among the separate Asian, Australian and African enclosures you'll find lions, tigers and bears, elephants, Komodo dragons, otters, leopards, giraffe, lemurs, hippos and hyenas. There are food and drink outlets, gift shops, stroller rentals and a children's zoo area with a water play area, carousel and petting pen. Keeper talks and ecology and wildlife shows take place each day.

Miami Museum of Science and Planetarium

3280 South Miami Avenue, south of Rickenbacker Causeway, t (305) 646 4200, www.miamisci.org
Getting there Just north of Coconut Grove, across from Vizcaya Museum and Gardens
Open Daily 10–6
Adm Adults $10, children (3–12) $6, under 3s $2; one-hour planetarium laser shows are presented on the first Friday of the month. Adults $7, children $4

One of the most recent permanent displays in the museum is a collaborative exhibit created by the Smithsonian's National Museum of Natural History Miami Museum of Science and Planetarium. It includes early Latin American and Caribbean artefacts including pottery, temples and figurines. You can join a virtual expedition following scientists through the decades as they travelled to remote regions exploring desolate shores, tropical jungles, archaeological ruins and a Mayan king's tomb.

Children can view archaeological videos, peer at botanical specimens through microscopes, examine crates and pull-drawers packed with archaeological curiosities and sift through sand for artefacts in a recreated dig.

The museum is also home to robotic dinosaurs, numerous native animal species, including reptiles and it houses a rehabilitation centre for birds of prey. In the planetarium children can watch astronomy and laser shows and there are free viewing sessions using the observatory's telescopes on Friday nights from 8–10.

Monkey Jungle

14805 Southwest 216th Street, off Highway 1, t (305) 235 1611, www.monkeyjungle.com
Open Daily 9.30–5
Adm Adults $17.95 plus tax, children (3–9) $11.95

'Where the humans are caged and the monkeys run wild' runs the slogan and with 400 primates swinging around in a 30-acre preserve you're bound to spot something. Visitors can observe gibbons, spider monkeys, tamarins, colobus and orangutans from screened-in walkways. The first residents were Java monkeys and there are now about 80 of them. Javas are skilled divers and feeding times demonstrate their amazing water skills as they dive into a pool to retrieve fruit. There are also regular daily Orangutan training sessions and gorilla encounters.

The Gold Coast Railway Museum

12450 SW 152nd Street, t (305) 253 0063, www.goldcoast-railroad.org
Getting there Adjacent to the Metrozoo, *see* p.197
Open Mon–Fri 10–4, Sat, Sun 11–4
Adm Free, donations appreciated; Train rides (Sat–Sun at 1pm and 3pm, $2

This not-for-profit organization is dedicated to preserving historic railroad equipment, including vintage trains from the East Florida Railroad Company. In addition to the engines, railcars and rolling stock, visitors can view coach liveries and see engines demonstrations. Kids like walking among the model railways and building their own layouts using wooden train sets with both free-wheeled and motorized vehicles. Train rides on the 2-ft gauge-track 'Edwin Link Children's Railroad' lasts 20 minutes. Cab and diesel rides are also available, call ahead for these and for details of the museum's **Junior Trainman Programme**. Seasonal events include the popular 'Day Out with Thomas' weekends where kids get to ride aboard the Tank Engine and meet some of his friends.

Vizcaya Museum and Gardens

3251 South Miami Avenue, t (305) 250 9133, www.vizcayamuseum.com
Open 9.30–5.30, (house closes at 5)
Adm Adults $12, children (6–12) $5, under 5s free; Moonlight Garden tours (once a month) 7.30pm, $5, call for details
Shop, cafe

This Italian-Renaissance style mansion, built in 1916, was the winter home of American industrialist James Deering. Today, the extraordinary European-inspired estate includes a house filled with art and furnishings representing 400 years of European history, 10 acres of gardens overlooking Biscayne Bay, a hardwood forest and an historic village that is under reconstruction. Regular house tours focus on the 'Gilded Age' of American innovation.

Wings Over Miami Museum

14710 Southwest 128th Street, in Tamiami Airport, t (305) 233 5197, www.wingsovermiami.com
Open Thu–Sun 10–5.30
Adm Adults $9.95, children $5.95

Visitors can watch formation flying displays every Saturday (weather permitting) and can view an extensive display of classic and military aircraft in the museum hangar.

Entertainment

Actors' Playhouse at the Miracle Theater

280 Miracle Mile, Coral Gables, t (305) 444–9293, www.actorsplayhouse.org
Children's theatre performances Sats at 2
Tickets Adults $12,children $10

This beautifully restored Art-Deco theatre hosts a season of award-winning children's plays and musical theatre throughout the year and a family festival weekend in March-April as part of the National Children's Festival.

American Airlines Arena

601 Biscayne Boulevard, downtown Miami, t (786) 777 1000, www.heat.com; Adm Tickets $9–165

Since the Heat traded Shaquille O'Neal from the LA Lakers they've gone on to fulfill their potential as one of the NBA's elite teams with a host of promising young players in the bag. The state-of-the-art arena is visible from Bayside Marketplace and is linked by a bridge.

Miami Arena

701 Arena Boulevard, North Miami Avenue, downtown Miami, t (305) 530 4400, www.miamiarena.com/
Box office open Mon–Fri 10–4
Adm Ticket prices vary according to events

Features scheduled events including concerts, family theatre shows, circus acts and ice dancing, as well as sporting events. It is easily accessible from the Metromover system and is close to Bayside Marketplace.

Miami Jai-Alai

3500 Northwest 37th Avenue, downtown Miami, t (305) 633 6400; Adm $1

This fast-paced intriguing sport shares similarities with handball and lacrosse. Originating in the Basque region of Spain it came to Miami via Cuba. Spectators can witness both the game itself and the fierce betting process that goes along with it.

The Tennis Center at Crandon Park

7300 Crandon Boulevard, Key Biscayne, t (305) 365 2300
Open Daily; court fees $3–10 per person

Home to the NASDAQ 100 in March, the centre has a 14,000-seat stadium court, 12 competition courts and six practice courts. It is open to the public and is also home to four European red clay, four American green clay courts and two grass courts.

Pro Player Stadium

2269 Dan Marino Boulevard, Northwest 199th Street, Miami Beach, t (305) 626 7400; for Marlin tickets t (305) 7000 www.flamarlins.com; for Dolphin tickets t (305) 620 2578, for Dolphin information t (305) 623 6200, www.miamidolphins.com
Adm Marlin tickets $9–$55, Dolphin tickets, $20–$48; Parking $9–$25.

The Florida Marlins and the Miami Dolphins share this stadium. The Marlins baseball team is in residence from April–October and the Dolphins kick off August–December.

Shopping

Bal Harbour Shops

9700 Collins Avenue, **t** (305) 866 0311

Getting there North Miami Beach, directly opposite the Sheraton Bal Harbour Beach Resort at Collins Avenue and 96th Street

An airy, lush location with **Chanel**, **Dior**, **Armani**, **Gucci**, **Prada** and **Ralph Lauren** to name a few. Kids love the extravagant toys in **Neiman Marcus**. Try **Lea's Tea Room** for a restorative cup of coffee and cake.

Bayside Marketplace

401 Biscayne Boulevard, **t** (305) 577 3344, **www**.baysidemarketplace.com

Getting there Take I–95 North or South to Biscayne Boulevard (exit 3), head north to Port Boulevard and follow signs for parking

Open Mon–Thu 10–10. Fri–San 10–11, Sun 11–9 (extended hours at some restaurants and bars). A parking ramp charges $2 to $2.50 per hour, $10 max

Shops include **Sketchers**, **Footlocker** and **Nike** shops for shoes and sportswear, **Gap** and **Gap kids**, a **Disney Store**, plus lots of gift, homeware and entertainment stores. There's good market that sells Cuban, Chinese, Italian and Japanese cuisine as well as seafood. It gets busy but it's worth a wait. There's also a **Hard Rock Café** and a few seafood restaurants. **Lombardi's Ristoranti** offers *al fresco* dining by the marina, where you can take a 'homes of the stars' boat tour daily from 11am. For tall ship tours contact the **Island Queen**, **t** (305) 379 5119, **www**.islandqueen cruises.com or **Heritage of Miami**, **t** (305) 442 9697.

Genius Jones

1661 Michigan Ave, **t** (305) 534 7622, **www**.geniusjones.com

Open Tue–Thu, Sun 12 noon–8, Fri–Sat 12 noon–10

If you want to indulge the little darlings, make a beeline for this design store exclusively for hip kids and their attendant hangers-on. It sells toys, accessories, clothing, books, furniture, strollers and gifts.

Lincoln Road Mall

Getting there South Beach, west of Washington Ave and between 16th and 17th Street

This pedestrianized shopping district has one-off fashion boutiques and art galleries, as well as big stores such as **Burdines-Macy's**. It's also handy for *al fresco* dining, **theatre** or **cinemas** and is close to the **Collins Avenue Shopping District's designer outlets** (Armani, Kenneth Cole, Polo Sport, Tommy Hilfiger and Versace) for you to shop till you drop.

Special trips

Biscayne National Underwater Park

9710 Southwest 328th Street/Route 9336; Homestead, **t** (305) 230–1100 tours, (305) 230–PARK for park information, **www**.nps.gov/bisc

Getting there 9 miles east of Homestead take US 1 or Florida Turnpike to North Canal Road.

Open Daily 8.30–5

Tours Family snorkelling tour daily, 1.30pm; tour lasts 3 hours, $35 per person, plus tax. Three-hour glass-bottomed boat tour daily, 10am; adults $24.45, children $16.45; Island camping transport $25.95 round-trip; camping fee $10

Rentals Canoes $9 per hour, kayaks $16

Diving trips Sat–Sun 8.30–1; $54. Reserve ahead

A crystal-clear watery playground with a rocky shoreline, mangrove outcrops and living coral reefs. About 95 per cent of the 181-acre park is underwater, which attracts private boats as well as canoeists and kayakers. On the first Sunday of the month (Jan–May) the park hosts **Family Fun Fest**, three hours' that guarantee families have a splashing time. Kids can follow the activities in the **Junior Ranger Program** as they explore the different habitats within **Biscayne National Park**, **Big Cypress National Preserve** and the **Everglades**. The **Dante Fascell Visitor Center** at Convoy Point has information on events. Fishing, diving and snorkelling are popular or, if you prefer to stay dry, take a glass-bottom boat tour. Bring a picnic and end the day with a barbeque or camp overnight off the mainland on **Boca Chita Key** or **Elliott Key**.

Everglades National Park

40001 State Road 9336, **t** (305) 242 7700, **www**.nps.gov/ever/

Getting there From Miami take the Florida Turnpike (Route 821) south until it ends, merging

How to be an environmental helper

1. Learn about on the status of plants and wildlife in your area
2. Do not purchase products that exploit endangered or threatened plants or wildlife
3. Report people who are seen to be harming endangered or threatened plants and wildlife
4. Support conservation legislation

The Everglades

As you enter the deep south you should remember that the Everglades once extended from the flood plains below Lake Okeechobee across the whole of the lower part of Florida in a mass of vegetation and wildlife. Today about 30% of this unique subtropical habitat has been lost to roads, canals, dykes and drainage for farming. The debate continues about the future of this environment. Developers would like to push the boundary further inland but the fragile distance between construction and nature is already alarming. From the air you can see rows and rows of houses that seem to march towards the wilderness, protected only by a narrow canal and a ribbon of road clogged with traffic – the hedgerows littered with the debris of human habitation. Moving away from Highway 1, the buildings disappear and give way to uniquely shaped pieces of land, some heart-shaped, some fringed with bright clumps of grass or topped by outcrops of trees – all flanked by muddy or dark blue water. There are sawgrass prairies, pinelands and hardwood hammocks, mangrove and cypress swamps and marine and estuarine environments.

The South Florida Research Center is actively monitoring how changes beyond the outer limits of the park affect the species and environment in it . At the centre, structures are in place to help restore the ecosystem through scientific research, monitoring of field conditions and educating the public about the need for change.

Legislation such as the Endangered Species Act (1973) has given the wildlife some protection. As a result several birds and animals are now on the endangered or threatened list, which means they require protection to avoid further decline.

with US 1 at Florida City. Turn right at the first traffic light onto Palm Drive (State Road 9336/SW 344th St.) The main entrance is 15 miles southwest of Homestead on Route 9336. **Greyhound buses** run to Homestead, but there is no public transport from there either to the park entrance or inside the park. You can rent canoes, bikes or kayaks to get round or opt for a boat tour. In summer, cover the kids liberally with insect repellent and bring plenty of water
Open Main Visitor Centre: daily 9–5
Adm $10 per car, $5 per bike or pedestrian, valid 7 days

Start with the **Ernest F. Coe Visitor Center** at the main entrance where you can watch a film inspired by Marjory Stoneman Douglas' book *The Everglades: River of Grass* (1947), an award-winning description of the area that still draws visitors today. SD was a driving force in the classification of the Everglades and was highly influential in the development of the National Park. The centre has maps and guides and a brilliant display of Glades flora and fauna.

There are several trails – start 4 miles from the entrance at the **Royal Palm Visitors Center**, where you can also buy refreshments. The **Anhinga Trail** is best for spotting wildlife along the boardwalk; **Gumbo Limbo** explores the tropical forest of these characteristic red trees while **West Lake Trail** leads through dense mahogany jungle. At **Pahayokee Overlook observation tower**, 13 miles inside the park, you can look across the sawgrass marshes, punctuated by cypress islands, while **Eco Pond** on Flamingo Road is best for bird watching.

One of the best ways to explore is by canoe on the **Nine-Mile Pond** or **Turner River trail**. From the water, you are amid slithering, chirruping, basking and crawling, teeming with life and have the chance to see alligators, crocodiles, snakes, turtles, river otters, frogs, manatees and hundreds of species of fish and bird, such as the great blue heron, roseate spoonbill, wood stork and a variety of egrets.

The Flamingo Visitors' Center and Marina has a restaurant and shop and can provide information on camping, sightseeing cruises, fishing trips, canoe, bike or boat rentals. You can take a boat tour from Everglades City or Flamingo to see pelicans, terns, cormorants, osprey, and possibly dolphins, manatees or crocodiles. In the winter, there are ranger-led walks, campfire programmes, and family bike trips. *See also*, **Shark Valley**, p.201.

Everglades Alligator Farm

40351 Southwest 192nd Avenue, Florida City,
t (305) 247 2628, www.everglades.com
Open Daily 9–6
Adm Adults $11.50, children (4–11) $6.50. Entry, plus airboat ride Adult $17, children $10

This working alligator farm is the oldest one in South Florida and currently home to about 2,000 alligators as well as crocodiles, caimans, and native Florida wildlife such as black bears, local snakes, cougars, bobcats and exotic species of snakes from around the world. Informative **wildlife shows** are presented hourly with snake shows at 10, 1 and 4,

Did you know?
Some animals and plants in the Everglades are extremely rare. Get a wildlife observation card from one of the visitor centres but if you spot any of these creatures do not approach them – they are not tame and can be dangerous.

- ***Florida panther***
- ***West Indian manatee***
- ***American crocodile***
- ***Green turtle***
- ***Atlantic leatherback turtle***
- ***Atlantic hawksbill turtle***
- ***Atlantic Ridley turtle***
- ***Cape Sable seaside sparrow***
- ***Snail kite***
- ***Red-cockaded woodpecker***

alligator shows at 11, 2 and 5 and alligator feeding at 12 noon and 3. Children can handle a baby 'gator during the show. The 30-minute **airboat tours** allow you to experience Florida's river of grass up close and spot alligators in their natural habitat along with roseate spoonbills, hawks, ospreys and herons.

Miccosukee Indian Village

Across the road about ½ mile from the Shark Valley Information Center (*see* below), MM 70, US 41 Tamiami Trail, **t** (305) 223 8380
Open Daily 9–5
Adm Adults $5, children (5–12) $3.50 for children, under 5s free. Airboat tours $10 per person

Begin by touring the **museum** to see photos, clothing, paintings and artefacts from the tribe and to watch a short film on its history and relation to other Native American Indian groups.

There are also woodcraft, doll-making, basket weaving and alligator wrestling **demonstrations** and fabulous crafts, from Miccosukee patchwork and beadwork to Cherokee moccasins and Navajo silver, are on sale. The village also conducts 30-minute **airboat tours** to traditional Indian settlements. The restaurant serves up fried bread with frogs' legs or alligator tail, along with more usual fare.

Shark Valley

Tamiami Trail, **t** (305) 221 8455
Getting there From Miami take the Florida Turnpike to the exit for SW 8th Street (also known as US 41 and Tamiami Trail). Go 25 miles west on US 41 to signs for Shark Valley. From Homestead, follow Krome Avenue (Route 997) 20 miles north to Tamiami Trail and head west for about 20 miles.
Open Daily 8.30–6, visitor centre: 8.30–4.45
Adm $10 per car. Bike rentals are available from 8.30–3 for $5.50 per hour.
Tram tour: Adults $12.75, children $7.75 call in advance for reservations.

This part of the Park is the best place to experience the 'river of grass' – the unique ecosystem of the sawgrass marshes and tree islands. Take a two-hour **narrated tram tour** or rent a bike, hike short trails and parts of the 15-mile loop road into **Shark Valley Slough**. The winding path to the observation tower is fun and the views spectacular. Look out for egrets, heron, roseate spoonbills, marsh rabbits, possums, river otters, Florida panthers, alligators and bobcats.

AROUND AND ABOUT

Dania and Hollywood

No relation to its glamorous namesake, this is the ninth largest city in Florida with a population of 130,000 inhabitants whose current demographics are said to best represent those of the US in 2020.

How to get there

Off A1A between Miami and Fort Lauderdale

Tourest Information

Greater Hollywood Chamber of Commerce, 330 North Federal Highway, Hollywood 33020, **t** (954) 923 4000, **www.**hollywoodchamber.org

Anne Kolb Nature Center and Marina

751 Sheridan Street, Hollywood, **t** (954) 926 2410
Getting there between Highway 1 and Route A1A
Open Daily 8–dusk. Exhibit hall: daily 9–5
Adm Free, West entrance: $1 weekends and holidays Exhibit hall: $1. Boat tour: Adults $4, children $2

1,500 acres of mangroves with a new forest to attract herons and ibises. There are also hiking and biking trails, canoe and kayak rentals, pier fishing and picnic spots. There are **narrated boat tours** and a five-storey **observation tower**.

Brian Piccolo Park

9501 Sheridan Street, Cooper City, **t** (954) 437 2626
Getting there From I-95 take Sheridan Street west. The park's entrance is on the right between Douglas Road and Palm Avenue
Open 8–dusk

Adm Skate park: $7 for two hours, Velodrome: Adults $2, children $2, $4 evenings
Park entrance fee weekends only

If you've a need for speed, pack a picnic and head out for a spin around the park's purpose-built velodrome, which has both 500-m and 800-m track loops. The skate park features a 4-ft-high mini ramp, small and large street courses, a spine ramp and vert ramp. In the park you can rent bikes, skates, and skateboards, lessons are available for an extra fee.

C.B. Smith Park

Pembroke Pines, 900 North Flamingo Road, **t** (954) 437 2650
Open Daily 8–6 (7.30 in summer), waterslides and beach: Apr–Sept 9.30–5.30, Sept–Mar weekends only
Adm $7 per person, $4 after 3pm

The addition of the **Paradise Cove aquatics complex** has made the park the new place to be. There are two new large water playgrounds, one specifically designed for toddlers, and a meandering rushing water tube ride, in addition to the two original 350ft-long slides. The park also offers tennis/racquetball, golf, batting practice, basketball, biking, volleyball, fishing, canoes and paddleboats, playgrounds, picnicking and a man-made beach.

IGFA Fishing Hall of Fame and Museum

300 Gulf Stream Way, Dania Beach, **t** (954) 922 4212, **www.igfa.org**
Getting there Take I-95 to Griffin Road Exit 23, west on Griffin to first light (Anglers Avenue), south to Gulf Stream Way, left at Sportsman's Park
Open Daily 10–6; **Adm** Adults $6, children (3–16) $5

The kids will have a *reel* good time (pardon the pun) at this interactive museum dedicated to the art of angling. Marvel at the mega-sized catch suspended from the roof, view the fishing medals, records and tales of daring or explore fish habitats, models and play virtual reality fishing games. Under 7s can play with puzzles and dress up as boatmen to ride the seas from the safety of a sofa. Outside there's a wetlands trail and marina with historic craft and models of big fish to pose beside.

John U. Lloyd State Park

6503 North Ocean Drive, Dania Beach, **t** (954) 923 2833
Open 8–dusk
Adm $4 per car, $1 per bike or pedestrian

Despite damage caused to areas of the beach and jetty by Hurricane Charlie, this 251-acre park is open for business with picnic facilities overlooking the shipping route to Port Everglades. Visitors can also go fishing, kayaking or canoeing among the barrier islands. The south end of the beach is quieter and offers a self-guided trail through a subtropical hardwood hammock.

T.Y. (Topeekeegee Yugnee) Park

3300 North Park Road, **t** (954) 985 1980
Open Daily 9–5. Castaway Island Apr–Sept daily 9–5, Sept–Mar weekends only
Adm $5 including lagoon and Castaway Island session, additional sessions $3

The park has facilities for picnicking, volleyball, camping and boat rentals. The lagoon next to Castaway Island is a man-made lake with a sandy beach. The Castaway Island water playground complex has one large water playground for the whole family and a small play pool for toddlers.

FORT LAUDERDALE

Once the most popular spot for college kids on spring break, Fort Lauderdale has refined its image as a family-friendly destination with resort hotels and arts establishments. As with Miami, Henry Flagler's railroad lifted the area from swampy obscurity and the land rush followed, spurred on in the early 1900s by Governor Napoleon Bonaparte Broward's ill-conceived legislation to drain the Everglades for real estate. Inspired by the grace and grandeur of Venice in Italy, local landowner Charles Rodes set out to reclaim land from the swamps by creating narrow strips of landfill alternating with channels of water, known as 'finger islands' linked by canals. He set to work on his plan in 1922, which has largely shaped the development of the area as a pleasure ground for boaters ever since. During the 1980s the number of college kids partying got out of hand and local businessmen got together and the ensuing purge closed a host of tacky attractions to be replaced by swanky shops and restaurants. The addition of an attractive wavy wall and neatly paved path to south beach and a series of boardwalks along the riverfront have allowed better access to the water for parents with pushchairs, as well as bikers and in-line skaters. **Las Olas Boulevard** and **Riverwalk** on the New River are where you'll now find most of the crowds but the people and their pastimes are now much more sedate.

Getting there

By air Fort Lauderdale/Hollywood International Airport, 320 Terminal Drive, **t** (954) 359 1200. Although not the first choice from the UK, this airport provides a nonstop service to over 30 US destinations, including Key West, plus daily flights to Canada and the Caribbean. **Taxi** stands are centrally located. Fares are $3 for the first mile, then $2 per mile and $0.25 per minute of waiting time. **Yellow Cab/Checker** can be reached at, **t** (954) 777 7777. **USA Transportation** provides private car services to and from airports and seaports, plus larger van and mini-buses, **t** (954) 457 4141.

By rail *See* Miami p.193 for Amtrak services and Miami's Tri-rail system, which has direct connections with Fort Lauderdale airport and with bus services such as the Tri-rail shuttle call (954) 728 8512 for schedules.

By road About 26 miles north of Miami along Route A1A or Highway 41.

Getting around

Travelling by **boat** is the best and most exciting way to get about in Fort Lauderdale. If you don't have one, jump aboard the **Water Taxi** to reach shopping, restaurants, and other attractions. Book ahead or wait (up to 30 mins) at a scheduled stop. **Water Taxi**, 651 Seabreeze Boulevard, **t** (954) 467 6677.

Broward County Transit runs 250 on 40 routes throughout the county. Rider information, **t** (954) 357 8400.

Downtown A&E Trolley Line. This new free weekend service runs between the Riverwalk arts and entertainment district and Las Olas Boulevard. Services depart from the Arts and Entertainment Garage (opposite the Broward Center for the Performing Arts) through Old Fort Lauderdale Village, Las Olas Boulevard, The Museum of Art, Stranahan House and points in between. Fri 5–11, Sat 12 noon-11.

Tourist information

Greater Fort Lauderdale Convention and Visitors Bureau, 100 East Broward Boulevard, Suite 200, **t** (954) 765–4466, **www**.sunny.org

Cultural Information Center (CIC), 100 South Andrews Avenue, **t** (954) 357 7979. Located on the first floor of the Broward County Main Library, the CIC is a one-stop shop for information, maps and leaflets. There's also a gift shop, online ticketing system and a café.

Things to see and do

Bonnet House Museum & Gardens

900 North Birch Road, **t** (954) 563 5393, **www**.bonnethouse.org

Getting there South of Sunrise Boulevard

Open Dec–April Tue–Sat, 10–4, last tour at 2.30, May–Nov Wed–Fri 10–3, Sun 12 noon–4, last tour 2.30

Adm Adults $10, children $8, $6 grounds only, under 5s free

This wonderful establishment is worth setting aside time for. Built in 1920 to an original design by artist Frederick Bartlett, the house echoes the plantation era and has several interiors created by the artist, later assisted his third wife, Evelyn. After the death of first wife, Frederick married the daughter of Hugh Taylor Birch who gifted them a plot of land for the house. From 1920–25, the Birch-Bartletts wintered there with Birch lending a hand to his son-in-law's construction plans. Frederick built a music room for his wife Helen, an accomplished pianist, and an art studio for himself. Helen tragically died of cancer in 1925 but her father remained a close companion. The paintings the couple had collected together now hang in The Art Institute of Chicago as a memorial to Helen Birch Bartlett. They include Picasso, Matisse, Seurat, Gauguin and Van Gogh. Frederick married again in 1931 . A 75-minute tour takes you through the loggias and family rooms embellished with the Bartlett's own paintings. The grounds include saltwater wetlands, anorchard with mango, avocado, guava and citrus trees and a dense mangrove jungle where manatees, land and fiddler crabs, fish and wading birds thrive. There's also a small lake with swans, a curious shell museum, an orchid house and the Bartlett's bar and boathouse. In April, the house hosts the **Bonnet House Jazzfest**. Browse in the shop for posters, reproduction paintings, handmade crafts, collectibles, antiques, clothing and jewellery.

Hugh Taylor Birch State Park

Getting there Off Ocean Boulevard 3109 East Sunrise Boulevard, **t** (954) 564 4521

Open Daily 8–dusk. Beach gate open 9–5

Adm $4 per car, $1 per bike or pedestrian

In 1893, a Chicago attorney called Hugh Taylor Birch reputedly set sail in a boat loaned to him by Henry Flagler in search of a quiet corner to call home. He was blown ashore in Lake Mabel (Port Everglades)

and settled in the village of Fort Lauderdale, which, at the time, comprised of a few houses, a store (run by Charles Rodes) and a disused army post. Birch called his 180-acre oceanfront estate Terramar, 'land to sea', and, wishing to preserve its beauty for future generations, bequeathed it, on his death, as a public park. Vistors can explore Birch's former home with its art-deco and Spanish architecture, now used as a visitor centre. Call or check at the park entrance for special tours and seasonal ranger-led walks. From the visitor centre, you can rent a canoe to paddle on the freshwater lagoon, set off on a bike ride or take a self-guided nature trail through the hammock, looking out for medicinal and exotic plants. There are several picnic areas with playgrounds. Ducks, turtles, wading birds, hawks, raccoons, marsh rabbits and snakes can all be seen within the park. There's also a safe underground pathway beneath A1A that leads to the beach.

Museum of Art

1 East Las Olas Boulevard, t (954) 525 5500, www.moafl.org

This beautiful facility, designed by Edward Larrabee Barnes, attracts a range of touring exhibitions, as well as housing a permanent collection of American and European modern and contemporary art. Ceramics by Picasso and contemporary Cuban art are among the highlights. The museum also has a large collection of works by American impressionist William Glackens, as well as one of the country's largest collections of works by the Northern European artists who collectively make up the movement known as CoBrA (named for the cities of Copenhagen, Brussels, and Amsterdam).

Museum of Discovery and Science

401 Southwest 2nd Street, t (954) 467 6637, www.mods.org

Getting there Take I-95 north (from Miami) or south (from Palm Beach) to Broward Boulevard. Drive east to SW 5th Avenue (Commodore Brook Avenue). Turn right. The Museum will be on the left with the Arts and Sciences parking garage on your right

Open Mon–Sat 10–5, Sun 12 noon–6. IMAX extended hours

Adm Adults $14 for adults, children (3–12) $12 (includes one IMAX film)

On arrival you'll be awed by the museum's 52-feet tall, Great Gravity Clock, surrounded by bubbling fountains. It's the biggest kinetic energy sculpture in Florida and the adventure does not stop there. Within these walls you can learn how to launch a space vehicle, get close to the sun, observe the polar aurora, take a trip to Mars or float through space to repair a satellite. Elsewhere visitors can examine the world's largest captive Atlantic coral reef and see sharks, spiders and snakes, sea turtles and alligators.

The museum is also home to **Living in the Everglades** exhibit, designed to raise public awareness about the restoration efforts surrounding the Greater Everglades Ecosystem. Using interactive kiosks, kids can gauge the effect of human development on the Everglades and the scope of the Restoration Project and follow a trail through Florida's fragile ecosystems. After all that contemplation, they can then let loose in the **Discovery Center** where they can climb, build and run off excess energy or visit **Gizmo City Lift** to programme a robot or play virtual volleyball. **Ecofloat boat tours** explore the barrier islands, mangrove swamps, beaches and sinkholes off the coast in summer. The **3-D IMAX Theater** shows an impressive array of science and wildlife movies. Call in at the **Explore Store** for science kits that help you make your own kaleidoscope or instant snow and card games featuring mummies, space travel and dinosaurs. There's an on-site café, plus vending machines and a selection of snacks and drinks available in the store or you can pop across the street for a picnic.

Riverfront Marina

420 Southwest 3rd Avenue, t (954) 527 1829

If you want to head out on the water, the marina offers boat rentals, servicing and supplies.

Riverwalk Park

20 North New River Drive, t (954) 828 5346

The pride of the city, this smart new park, between the banks of the New River down to Las Olas Boulevard, with its walkways and picnic benches is a great place to wander. There are educational stations and native plant exhibits along the way. On Sundays the area is popular with jazz enthusiasts.

South Beach Park

Getting there South of the Route A1A (Southeast 17th Street) Causeway

Here you'll find less development and some of the prettiest beaches. There are picnic tables, lifeguards on duty and a children's playground. Across busy A1A there are lots of beachfront shops and restaurants to complete your day by the sea.

Entertainment

Broward Center for the Performing Arts

201 Southwest 5th Avenue, t (954) 462 0222, www.browardcenter.org

This multiple theatre waterfront complex is home to Broadway in Fort Lauderdale, touring shows, Florida Grand Opera, Florida Philharmonic, the Concert Association and Miami City Ballet.

Fort Lauderdale Children's Theater

640 North Andrews Avenue, t (954) 763 6882, advance tickets (954) 763 6701. www.flct.org
Adm Tickets from $4–$18
Getting there Between Broward and Sunrise Boulevards, north of downtown

This not-for-profit education centre provides summer camps and workshops for local communities culminating in productions of historic dramas and children's classics, held at the **Dillard Center for the Arts Theater** (*see* below).

Fort Lauderdale Stadium

1301 Northwest 55th Street, off Commercial Boulevard, t (954) 776 1921
Adm Tickets $6–$14

Major league baseball comes to Fort Lauderdale here every March when the Baltimore Orioles hold their spring training in a series of pre-season games against other MLB teams.

International Swimming Hall of Fame

501 Seabreeze Boulevard, t (954) 462–6536, Aquatic complex 954-828-4580
Getting there South of Las Olas Blvd on A1A
Open Mon–Fri 9–7, Sat–Sun 9–5; public swimming Mon–Fri 8–4 and 6–7.30, Sat–Sun 8–2. Diving daily 11–1
Adm Adults $3, family $5, under 12s free. Swim: Adults $4, children $3

The walls of the Hall of Fame, which honours outstanding athletes in swimming, diving, water polo and synchronized swimming, are bristling with medals. Among the notables are Olympic swimmer and Tarzan, Johnny Weissmuller, Mark Spitz and Presidents Reagan and John F. Kennedy. Housed in a wave-shaped building, the museum features 40 exhibits and displays illustrating the history of water sports. You can watch videos of the Olympics in The **Huizenga Theater**, use interactive computers and browse educational displays on water safety, health and fitness. Sculpture and artworks by LeRoy Neiman, Norman Rockwell, Ken Danby, Joseph Brown, R. Tait McKenzie and Odouardo Tabbacchi are also on display. The open-air **ISHOF Aquatic Complex** has two 50-m pools, a diving well and swimming flume.

Old Dillard Museum

1009 Northwest 4th Street, t (954) 765 6952
Open Sun–Tue 11–4, Wed 11–8; **Adm** Free

Opened in 1924, this building was the first African American school in Fort Lauderdale and was the only high school for black students in Broward County. It was named after Dr. James Hardy Dillard, a philanthropist and educator who spent his life improving conditions for black students in rural schools and houses displays on black history. It also runs educational programmes on the artistic, cultural and historic legacy of people of African descent. Exhibits include tribal masks, a replica of a 1920s classroom and musical instruments from all over the world.

Stranahan House

335 Southeast 6th Avenue at Las Olas Boulevard, t (954) 524 4736, www.stranahanhouse.com
Open Wed–Sat 10–4. Sun 1–4, tours hourly to 3pm
Adm Adults $6, children $3

Formerly a Seminole Indian trading post dating back to 1901, the house evolved into a post office, community centre and town hall, as well as being the home of pioneer Frank Stranahan. It is a fine example of Florida vernacular with dark pine interiors and antiques. The life of the house is brought to life through knowledgeable guides and seasonal events such as ghost tours and festive storytelling.

Story Theater Productions at Parker Playhouse

707 Northeast 8th Street; off Highway 1, t (954) 763 8813
Adm Tickets $10

Performances of favourite children's works run daily from October to April.

Shopping

The Gallery At Beach Place

17 South Fort Lauderdale Beach Boulevard, t (954) 764 3460

Right on the beach, there are cafés and restaurants with great ocean views as well as upmarket stores selling swimwear, beach accessories and children's toys. There's live music most evenings and seasonal beachfront events.

Las Olas Riverfront

300 Southwest 1st Avenue, t (954) 522 6556

This multistorey entertainment and retail centre has designer stores and outdoor and indoor casual dining. **Sunrise Cinemas, t** (954) 761 9400, **www**.sunrisecinemas.com) is on the second floor and there's **live music** in the riverfront gazebo from 7pm (Fri and Sat). If you wish to take to the water, there are daily, narrated **river tours** of the inland waterways and Port Everglades, clocking up the homes of the rich and famous on the way. Tours last 1½ hours (Mon–Sun 10.30, Thu–Sun 12.30, 2.30, 4.30, 6.30 and 8.30) For more information, call, **t** (954) 527 0075, **www**.anticipation.com

AROUND AND ABOUT

Lauderdale-by-the-Sea

This smart little town beckons with its charming fishing pier, **unusual shops** and boutiques in Pelican Square, and peaceful, clean **beach**, which gives access for diving and snorkelling the coral reefs from the shore. There are several small hotels, apartments and villas and some good fish restaurants.

Getting there

Just across the bridge over the Intracoastal Waterway from the northern end of Fort Lauderdale.

Tourist Information

Chamber of Commerce, 4201 Ocean Drive, Lauderdale-By-The-Sea, **t** (954) 776-1000, **www**.lbts.com

Look at this!

Sawgrass Recreation Park

Getting there 2 miles north of I–75 at 5400 North Highway 27, **t** (954) 389 0202

Open Mon–Fri 7–6, Sat, Sun 6.30–6 winter, (8–5 summer)

Adm Adults $19.50, children 4–12 $10, plus tax for 30-minute airboat tour and exhibits

The main attractions here are the 18th-century **Indian Village**, **airboat tours** and **fishing trips**. There are alligator and reptile shows, birds of prey, a gift shop, picnic tables and a barbecue cookhouse. You can also camp overnight.

Wannado City, Sawgrass Mills Mall

12801 West Sunrise Blvd, Sunrise, t (954) 838 7100, Mall, t (954) 846 2300, www.wannadocity.com

Getting there 2 miles north of Interstates 75 and 595, just off the Sawgrass Expressway interchange. From I–95 or I–75 exit on Flamingo Road. At Sunrise Boulevard, make a left, going west. At Purple Parrot Way, make a right, and enter Sawgrass Mills Mall directly to Wannado City

Open Daily from 10, seasonal closing hours vary from 5–8 or 10–3 and 4–9. Mall open Mon–Sat 10–9.30, Sun 11–8

Adm Children (3–14) $24.95, $15.95 (14+), under 3s free. Admission is limited based on available capacity

Parking at Sawgrass Mills Mall is free

Wannado City takes off where Miami Children's Museum (*see* p.194) began. America's only role-playing theme park for kids, it offers them the chance to explore different jobs and lifestyles in a purpose-built environment.

The entertainment park features fire and police stations, a hospital, bank, flight training centre, a circus, theatre, television studio, radio station, fashion house, dance club and newspaper office – the trick is deciding what you 'wannado' first. The city even has its own official currency, which children gain by working. They can then invest it or spend it in the leisure sectors of the park. Once a child runs out of readies, they select a new career to earn more. Everybody wears locator wristbands and kids can't leave the site without their designated adult family member. Children over 8 can explore the city unaccompanied. Adults can watch, join in, relax in one of several restaurants on site or in the parents' lounge or hit the adjacent mega-shopping complex.

Young at Art Children's Museum

11584 West State Road 84, Davie, t (954) 424 0085, www.youngatartmuseum.org

Getting there South of I–595 at the Plaza, on SR84 between Hiatus and Flamingo Rd

Open Mon–Sat 10–5. Sun 12 noon–5

Adm $5, under 2s free

Kids can unleash their creative talents on the **Global Village**, where they can have a go at making music, dig for artefacts, write a story and learn about other cultures along the way. There's also a colourful art display and touring exhibitions to explore. Toddlers need not feel left out as they can ride a recycling truck and get as messy as they like making artworks in their very own playspace.

Nature lovers

Billie Swamp Safari and Camping Village

12261 Southwest 251st Street, Princeton, t (800) 949–6101, www.seminoletribe.com
Getting there 19 miles north of I–75 off exit 14
Open Daily 9.30–2 for day package, gift shop 8.30–6. Tours from: Adults $20, children (4–12) $10

Experience Seminole life on a daily tour into reservation wetlands, hardwood hammocks and sloughs for sightings of deer, water buffalo, bison, wild hogs, hawks, eagles Florida panthers and alligators. At the **Swamp Water Café**, sample Seminole specialties such as 'gator nuggets, frog legs, catfish and fry bread with honey. Swamp critter, alligator and snake educational shows, guided hikes and night buggie tours are all available. Overnight accommodation in a native-style chickee hut must be booked in advance.

The village is part of the **Big Cypress Reservation**, which also houses the **Ah-Tah-Thi-Ki Museum** (open Tue–Sun 9–5), **t** (954) 965 2424, which shows the lives of the Seminoles in south Florida in the late 1800s (*see* History p.5) with artefacts relating to hunting, cooking, transport, weddings, folklore and religion. Exhibits include moccasins and leggings, turtle shell rattles, bracelets and beaded sashes, and medicine baskets, Seminole war-period swords and firearms, beaded shoulder bags, and Seminole patchwork.

The gallery includes a **theatre** showcasing Seminole traditions and there are interactive computers to learn more. The museum is set in 1½ miles of boardwalk nature trails and there are signs explaining how the Seminole used plants.

Flamingo Gardens and Arboretum

3750 South Flamingo Road, Davie, t (954) 473–2955, www.flamingogardens.org
Getting there 3 miles south of I–595, I–95 or Florida Turnpike to I–595, west to Flamingo Road, then south 2.5 miles, Exit 1B
Open Daily 9.30–5.30. Closed Mon Jun–Sept
Adm Adults $12, children (4–11) $6. Tram tour and wildlife encounter: Adults $8.50, children $6 tour only $4 and $3

Gift shop, gourmet food store

This lovely botanical garden and wildlife sanctuary features a free-flight aviary, wildlife encounters, a narrated tram tour, hammocks and citrus groves and habitats for flamingos, alligators, river otters, hummingbirds and bobcats.

BOCA RATON

Back on the coast, Boca Raton offers an air of refinement through its high quality resorts (*see* Sleep p.46), beautifully landscaped parks, spacious beaches, top-notch shopping malls and wholesome family attractions.

Getting there

Getting there Take Route 802 east to I–95

Tourist Information

Greater Boca Raton Chamber of Commerce, 1800 North Dixie Highway, Boca Raton 33432 1892, **t** (561) 395 4433; **www.bocaratonchamber.com**

Things to see and do

Boomer's Family Recreation Center

3100 Airport Road, t (561) 347 1888, www.boomersparks.com
Open Indoor play: Mon–Thu 12 noon–11, Fri–Sat 10–1am, Sun 10–11. Outdoor play Mon–Thu 1–10, Fri, Sat 10–12 midnight, Sun 10–10 (open earlier in summer)
Adm Various prices, tokens available. Family packages: 6 attractions and 20 game room tokens $40, 10 attractions and 40 tokens $65 per family

This branch of the popular amusement centre will have them up all hours with batting cages, bumper boats, state-of-the-art games, go-karts, a play park, laser tag, miniature golf and a climbing wall.

Butterfly World

Tradewinds Park, 3600 West Sample Road, Coconut Creek, t (954) 977 4400
Open Mon–Sat 9–5, Sun 1–5
Adm Adults $16.95, children (4–12) $11.95

This fascinating park is home to over 80 species of butterfly flying free in the gardens and among the waterfalls. The peaceful grounds are also home to insects, fish and birds, but kids will be fascinated to see rare butterflies on the wing and learn about the lifecycle and how to attract them to your garden.

Children's Museum

498 Crawford Boulevard, t (561) 368–6875
Open Tue–Sat 12 noon–4; Adm $3

This well-designed museum teaches children about local history through themed exhibits and activities inside a 1912 pioneer home. Many of the rooms have an old-fashioned appeal with vintage props, so children can imagine what it was like to cook meals or run a grocery store in pioneer times. Elsewhere the **Space Place** helps them to grasp early ideas about magnetism, space travel and gravity while **Change This Art** allows children to create new art from old. There's also a bank vault, post office and a back porch where kids can sift for fossils and finds. Call for details of the annual **KidsFest** in April, as well as seasonal story times and events.

Children's Science Explorium

Sugar Sand Park, 300 South Military Trail, t (561) 347 3913.
Getting there **Exit I–95 to Palmetto Park Road, head west (right) to Military Trail, go south (left) on Military Trail, park entrance is on the left**
Open Mon–Fri 9–6, Sat, Sun 10–5; **Adm** Free

This enterprising science centre features hands-on interactive exhibits that focus on the physical sciences. Among many educational activities, kids can mess with pulleys and levers, turn a crank to run an electric train, get all steamed up in a fog chamber or operate a Mars robot. You can also view the **Explorium**'s reconstruction of Flagler's railroad from Jacksonville to Key West which was completed in 1912 (*see also* p.80).

Gumbo Limbo Nature Center

1801 North Ocean Boulevard (Route A1A), Red Reef Park, t (561) 338 1473
Open Mon–Sat 9–4. Sun 12 noon–4
Adm Free (suggested donation $2)

This nature centre benefits greatly from its position within Red Reef Park on a barrier island between the Atlantic Ocean and the Intracoastal Waterway. Rare and **endangered species,** such as the manatee, the brown pelican, the osprey and sea turtles are often seen in this coastal hammock environment. **Shell middens** from the Pre-Columbian Indians and remnants from shipwrecked vessels add to the sense of maritime history. Seawater is pumped directly into **outdoor aquariums** filled with local fish, tidal pool sea creatures and baby loggerhead turtles. The centre also houses interpretive and visual displays, touch tanks, a butterfly garden, a 40-foot high observation tower and a raised board-walk through the hammock. There are seasonal programmes, which are suitable for all ages. Call in advance for details .

South Beach Park

400 North Ocean Blvd (Route A1A), t (561) 393 7973
Open 8–dusk
Parking **$17 weekends and holidays, $15 weekdays**

There are no picnic facilities but there are showers and lifeguards. Swimming is allowed in designated areas and there's a separate area for fishing.

Entertainment

Little Palm Family Theater

154 Northwest 16th Street, t (561) 394–0206, www.littlepalm.org
Box office Mon–Thu 10–6, Fri 10–4
Adm Tickets $10–$20

Local children and their adults get to have their hour upon the stage producing a range of theatrical and musical shows for all ages.

Shopping

Mizner Park

433 Plaza Real, t 561 362 0606
Open Mon–Thu 10–6, Fri–Sat 10–9, Sun 12 noon–6

More than just a shopping centre, this is an entire entertainment complex with restaurants, cafés, a **multiplex cinema** and an **amphitheatre** within a Mediterranean-style courtyard, which features seasonal children's shows. The most recent additions include an **outdoor cinema, La Maison du Soleil** for home accessories and gifts, **La Botegga di MammaRo** for Italian kitchenware, **Les Bijoux and Stelios Galgadas** for jewellery, **Z Gallerie** for unique accessories for the home and office, and **Robb & Stucky's** home furnishings store. There's also the **Femme Coiffure day spa** and salon and **Douglas Cosmetics. Mark's in the Park, GiGi's** and **Pranzo**, to name a few, are places to find the best of gourmet delights, as well as wines and desserts. Meanwhile, children with a sweet tooth will be right at home at **Sloan's**.

Town Center Mall

6000 Glades Road, t (561) 368 6000
Open Mon–Sat 10–9, Sun 12 noon–6

With more than 180 stores including **Bloomingdale's, Burdines, Lord & Taylor, Nordstrom, Saks Fifth Avenue, Sears** and over 220 speciality stores.

AROUND AND ABOUT

Delray Beach

Atlantic Avenue is in the heart of this charming oceanfront community with over 250 restaurants, galleries and boutiques. **Old School Square** on the corner of Atlantic Avenue and Swinton Avenue houses the **Old School Square Cultural Arts Center** and **Cornell Museum.** The beautiful **Old School Square Entertainment Pavilion** hosts festivals, concerts and events through the year. On **Municiple Beach**, there are designated areas for swimming, volleyball, sailing, wind surfing, snorkelling and surfing, plus two recreational areas for beach games and kites. There are also several parks, including the **Delray Beach Tennis Center**, 201 West Atlantic Avenue, **t** (561) 243 7360,and the **Delray Swim** and **Tennis Center**, 2350 Jaeger Drive **t** (561) 243 7058. The **Lakeview Golf Course t** (540) 434 8937 **www.**lake viewgolf.net, has youth golf (ages 8–14), and **Knowles Park**, 1001 South Federal Highway **t** (561) 243 7250, has a playground, a boat ramp and picnic facilities.

Getting there

North of Boca Raton on I–95 or Route A1A

Tourist information

City of Delray Beach, 100 Northwest 1st Avenue, **t** (561) 243 7000, **www.**mydelraybeach.com

Cornell Museum

51 North Swinton Avenue, **t** (561) 243 7922, **www.**oldschool.org

Open May–Sept Tue–Sat 10.30–4.30, Oct–April also open Sun 1–4.30

Adm Adults $6, under 13s free

Tearoom, gift shop

The museum has four galleries and a two-storey atrium exhibition space, which has a changing programme, reflecting national and international talent, as well as artist showcases and demonstrations (Tue 2.30–3.30).

On the second floor, the **Delray Beach Historical Society** houses archives and hosts special exhibits. There are two on-going education programmes for families (first Thu of the month, 3.30–4.30. Call ext 317 to register). Ages 9–11 explore the works of major artists and the history of art through creative activities. Meanwhile children aged 4–8 go on a grand tour to explore different countries learning facts and making masks or crafts along the way.

The Morikami Museum and Japanese Gardens

4000 Morikami Park Road, **t** (561) 495 0233

Getting there I–95 south to Linton Blvd, travel west for 4 miles to Jog Road, turn south (left), 3/4 miles, museum entrance is just past the traffic lights on Morikami Park Road

Open Tue–Sun 10–5; **Adm** Adults $9, children $6

Museum store, café

The museum is dedicated to George Morikami, a pineapple farmer who bequeathed his land to the state in the memory of his Japanese pioneer countrymen. Recently expanded, the museum includes a library, classrooms, 230-seat auditorium, authentic tea house, lakeside terrace and interactive computer screens. Within the museum, there are exhibits relating to Japanese culture from tea ceremonies to samurai armour. Additional displays describe the history of the Yamoto Colony, a Japanese farming community in South Florida that eked out a living 100 years ago. The colony did not thrive and by the 1920s only George Morikami (who became a fruit wholesaler) remained. Enjoy the peace and beauty of six traditional Japanese gardens. Call for details of family (Sat) and seasonal events.

Museum of Lifestyle & Fashion History

241 Northeast 2nd Avenue, **t** (561) 243 2662, **www.**MLFHMuseum.org

Getting there From Swinton Avenue go 4 blocks to Northeast 4th Street, turn right (east), go one block to Northeast 2nd Avenue/Pineapple Grove Way to Pineapple Grove Shops plaza

Open Sept–May, Tue–Sat 10–5, Sun 1–5, Jun–Aug Tue–Sat 12 noon–5, Sun 1–5

Adm Adults $5, children (6–12) $3

This museum, located, appropriately enough, in a shopping mall, offers changing displays from the permanent collection and touring shows focussing on lifestyle, history, cultures, people, places, fashion trends, architecture, furnishings, locomotives and toys. Vintage toy exhibits include Barbie dolls and teddy bears and women, men's and children's fashion from the 1900s. Guided tours, lectures and children's arts and crafts sessions are also available.

Sandoway House Nature Center

142 South Ocean Boulevard (A1A), **t** (561) 274 7263, **www.**sandowayhouse.com

Open Tue–Sat 10–4.30, Sun 12 noon–4.30

Adm $2. Events $3

This 1930s beachfront home now houses a non-profit-making marine and coastal life museum. It has an impressive shell collection, a microscope lab, Delray beach history room and marine and fresh-water environments. Regular events include shark feedings and seasonal nature walks and talks.

Entertainment

Crest Theater

Old School Square, **t** (561) 243 7922

Open Box Office: Mon–Fri 10–1 and 2–4, Nov–Apr also open Sat 10–3. Performances: Fri 8, Saturday, 2 and 8, Sun 2 and 7, unless otherwise noted

Adm Tickets prices vary. Main stage events matinee: $34, evening $36

This lovingly created, state-of-the-art, 323-seat theatre is in the restored 1925 Delray High School, which also houses six restored classrooms and two art studios. The venue presents a variety of theatre, music, dance and national tours as well as Broadway Cabaret and community performances and events, including children's shows and family films.

PALM BEACH

Sandwiched between the Atlantic, the Everglades and Lake Okeechobee, Palm Beach County boasts 47 miles (75 km) of pristine sands from Boca Raton to Jupiter Sound, and offers great outdoor pursuits, (including several quality golf courses, tennis courts and parks) over 40 cultural venues, five shopping malls and dozens of restaurants. The average temperature is a comfortable 78° F (25° C). The luxury does not come cheap but, with over 200 hotels, you can find accommodation to suit any budget.

Getting there

By air Two miles from downtown West Palm Beach is Palm Beach International Airport, 1000 Turnage Boulevard, **t** (561) 471 7420, **www**.pbia.org.
16 domestic and international airlines serve the airport. Flights to major US cities have UK connections. The terminal building has snack outlets and stores selling kids' toys, clothing, games and gifts. Ground transportation services is on Level One.
Tri-Rail, **t** (954) 788 7936. *See* Miami p193. A feeder bus service can be found outside the Terminal building Level One, on the outer curb, to Airport Station, on Mercer Avenue.
Amtrak, **t** (800) 872 7245. *See* Miami p.193.
Palm Beach Transportation, **t** (561) 684 9900.
Taxi and limousine service is available at the transportation desks.
By road I–95 and Florida's Turnpike, both run the length of the county with exits to all the major streets. State Roads 441 and 7, US Highway 1 and Coastal Highway A1A also run through. Head south on Highway 1 or take scenic Flagler Drive for about 10 minutes to West Palm Beach. Cross the Route A1A bridge (Royal Palm Way).

Getting around

Palm Tran, **t** (561) 841 4200. Local bus services run throughout the county including services to the airport, Boca Raton and Delray Beach.
Palm Beach Water Taxi, **t** (561) 683 TAXI, **watertaxi**.homestead.com
Daily at 11, 1, 3 and 5 (5pm is one-way only). 90-minute narrated sightseeing, nature, sunset and moonlight cruises are offered from Palm Harbor to downtown West Palm Beach's Clematis Street district, Singer Island, Palm Beach Gardens, Peanut and Munyon Islands and waterfront restaurants and bars.

Tourist information

Palm Beach County Convention and Visitors Bureau, 1555 Palm Beach Lakes Boulevard, Suite 800, **t** (561) 471 3995, **www**.palmbeachfl.com

Things to see and do

Flagler Museum

1 Whitehall Way at Cocoanut Row, Palm Beach, **t** (561) 655 2833, **www**.flagler.org

Open Tue–Sat 10–5, Sun 12 noon–5

Adm Adults $10, children (6–12) $3

Naturally the home of the railway magnate Henry Flagler is just as, if not more, opulent than the resort confections he dreamed up. His palatial home was built in 1901 as a present for his third wife. It has a staggering 55 rooms decorated in period styles, including Louis XIV, Louis XV, Louis XVI and the Italian Renaissance. From the marble hall with its double staircase, you proceed through the grand public rooms on the first floor to the guestrooms and servants quarters above. Among the collections are fine porcelain, glass and silver, as well as articles relating to the East Coast Railroad. Don't miss Flagler's private railroad car on the south lawn.

Palm Beach Maritime Museum

4512 North Flagler Drive, **t** (561) 540 5147, **www**.pbmm.org

Getting there I-95 to Exit 71, Palm Beach Lakes Blvd, east to North Flagler Drive (on Intracoastal Waterway), then north ½ mile to 2400 N. Flagler Dr. Free parking on the street or in the parking lot

Open Mon and Wed 10–1, Tue and Thu 3–5, Sat 9–1, Sun 11–4

The museum comprises a marine science field office and dock on the Intracoastal Waterway, an educational centre, preview building and ferry dock at Currie Park. The docks are open for boaters and there are facilities for swimming and camping. Boat tours are currently suspended due to damage from Hurricane Frances, call for updates.

West Palm Beach

Downtown West Palm Beach offers happening haunts for the discerning and stylish, especially along **Clematis Street** with its art and interior design galleries. The centrepiece is **Centennial Square**, which offers plenty of outdoor dining and a series of open-air concerts. West Palm Beach is also undoubtedly where the action is when it comes to family entertainments and attractions.

Museum at Ragtops

2119 South Dixie Highway, **t** (561) 655 2836, **www**.ragtopsmotorcars.com

Getting there Off I–95 between Okeechobee Blvd and Belvedere Rd

Open Mon–Sat 10–5

Adm Adults $5, children (8–12) $3, under 8s free

Shop, soda bar, Classic car salesroom

This unique and ever-expanding facility houses memorabilia, a drive-in theatre, pedal cars, vintage station wagons, a 1954 silver diner and a gas station.

Palm Beach Zoo

1301 Summit Boulevard, **t** (561) 547 9453, **www**.palmbeachzoo.org

Getting there between Southern and Forest Hills Boulevards. From I-95 northbound take Exit 66 Forest Hill Blvd, go east (left) to Parker Ave, left again on to Summit Blvd

Open Daily 9–5

Adm Adults $9.50, children (3–12) $5.50

Gift shop, café

Children can learn about native Florida species, explore Asian and Australasian environments and meet black bears and reptiles. There's a petting zoo, carousel and an interactive water fountain play area with changing huts. The recent **Tropics of the Americas** showcases animals from South America, such as jaguars, bush dogs, tapirs and monkeys, in among replicas of Mayan temples and caves. There are regular animal encounter sessions and story-time sessions (Sat 10am).

Pine Jog Environmental Education Center

6301 Summit Boulevard, **t** (561) 686 6600, **www**.pinejog.org

Open Mon–Sat 9–5; **Adm** Free

This centre actively educates children to care for the planet and the animals and plants that live in it through pre-school nature walks, talks, environment days and campouts during the year. Some Saturday events need pre-registration but otherwise families are free to walk around. Check the website or call for more details. The **Wakodahatchee Wetlands**, 13026 Jog Road, **t** (561) 493 6000, **www**.pbcwater.com and **Okeeheelee Nature Center**, 7715 Forest Hill Boulevard, **t** (561) 233 1400 are also nearby.

Rapids Water Park

6566 North Military Trail, **t** (561) 842 8756/(561) 848 6272

Getting there One mile west of I–95 on Military between 45th Street (exit 74) and Blue Heron Blvd. (exit 76)

Open Mid-Mar–Mid Oct daily 10–7

Adm $28 plus tax, under 2s free

Older kids can have fun among the 16 different tubes, flumes and water slides or float down the lazy river or surf the wave pool. There's a lagoon area with slide for parents and toddlers, crawl nets above 'alligator-infested waters' and a 'tadpool' with water animals to climb on and tree trunk slides.

South Florida Science Museum

4801 Dreher Trail North, Dreher Park, **t** (561) 832 1988, **www**.sfsm.org

Getting there West on Summit Blvd. (½ mile) to Dreher Trail

Open Mon–Fri 10–5, Sat 10–6, Sun 12 noon–6

Adm Adults $7, children (3–17) $5. Planetarium: $2, laser matinee $4, galaxy golf $2 extra per person

Kids can ride a sky cycle, construct their own plumbing and explore principles of light and colour among many activities. Exhibits include an **Egypt Gallery** and **Space Hall** along with some fascinating aquarium displays. Outdoors there are science-inspired games to play and trails to follow. A purpose-built facility with an airport tower, theatre and planetarium and hand-on science centre is due to open 2006–2007, see website for further details.

Shopping

CityPlace

700 South Rosemary Avenue, West Palm Beach t (561) 366 1000
Getting there I–95 to exit 70, 1 mile east on Okeechobee Boulevard
Open Mon–Thu 10–9, Fri, Sat 10–10, Sun 12 noon–6

You can easily spend a whole day at this shopping, entertainment and residential complex complete with plazas, fountains and outdoor terraces. In Palladium Plaza **synchronized fountains and light shows** are fun, there are **Jazz brunches**(Sun) and the **performing arts centre** offers theatre, concerts, art exhibits and events. There's also a **20-screen cinema** complex, branches of **Macy's** and **Barnes & Noble**, **Gap Kids**, **Oilily** and more than 17 places to eat from pizza parlours to seafood restaurants.

The Mall at Wellington Green

10300 West Forest Hill Boulevard, Palm Beach, t (561) 227 6900, www.shopwellingtongreen.com
Open Mon–Sat 10–9, Sun 11–6

This latest addition to the Palm Beach retail scene boasts Mediterranean-style landscaping, signature skylighting, cappuccino court and a play area. Huge department stores **Nordstrom's**, **Lord & Taylor**, **Dillards**, **Burdines** and **JCPenney** sit alongside unique family stores, such as **Cheeky Kids**, **t** (561) 296 0309, which sells clothing for ages 0–12. There are also shoe stores, a couple of maternity wear shops and **Toys 4 U Gifts 4 U**, **t** (561) 790 2848, which specializes in puzzles, wooden toys and unusual gifts. Among the restaurants and cafés, there are a couple of good steakhouses, a create-your-own sandwich bar and two ice-cream shops. Discount passports for international visitors are available from the information desk (proof of ID needed).

Worth Avenue

Royal Palm Way and South Ocean Boulevard (A1A), Palm Beach, t (561) 659 6909, www.worth-avenue.com

The world-famous 'Rodeo Drive of the East Coast' runs between South Ocean Boulevard across South County Road and Hibiscus Avenue down to Coconut Row. The blocks in between are embellished with Italianate names – the Via Roma, Via Parigi and Via Bice among them – set among tropical plants and Romanesque décor. Over 200 exclusive boutiques sell clothes, scent and eye-popping jewellery. Kit out the kids at in chic French style at **Bonpoint** or browse the departments in **Neiman Marcus**. **Chanel**, **Van Cleef & Arpels**, **Tiffany**, **Gucci**, **Ralph Lauren** and **Salvatore Ferragamo** are some of the names that make this street world-class. It draws celebrities, multi-millionaires and visitors alike, who sit cheek by jowl at one of the Avenue's many fine-dining locales including **Bice**, **Renato's** and **Ta-Boo**.

Special trips

Hoffman's Chocolate Shoppe

5190 Lake Worth Road (Route 802), Greenacres, t (561) 967 2213
Getting there South of Highway 98 via Highway 441
Open Mon–Sat 9–8, Sun 9–6
Adm Free

This is the place to appeal to one's children on an instinctive level – in a word, chocolate. The Hoffmans have been crafting exotic confections for generations. You can taste free samples and watch as mouth-watering goodies are made in the kitchen. The factory is surrounded by lush gardens dotted with ponds and waterfalls. A model train toots its way through the grounds, which are enhanced (mid-Oct–New Year) with a glittering display of lights, music and glistening winter vistas.

John D. MacArthur Beach State Park

10900 State Road 703, North Palm Beach, t (561) 624 6950
Getting there Take I–95 to SR 786 East exit 79AB (PGA Boulevard) continue 3 miles to US1, cross over and PGA Boulevard becomes State Road 703. Continue east 2 miles to entrance on left
Open 8–dusk. Nature centre: Daily 9–5
Adm $4 per car, $1 per bike or pedestrian

This state park encompasses 760 acres at the north end of Singer Island and includes the area's most naturally intact **beach**, which runs for 8,000 feet. The **nature centre** has wildlife exhibits, aquariums, video and historic displays. There's a 1,600-ft-long board-walk (tram service available) for amazing views over **Lake Worth Cove**. **Nature walks** take place through the year (Wed–Sun mornings) and **nocturnal turtle walks** from May–July. **Guided kayak tours** are on offer daily from the beach to the estuary, looking out for roseate spoonbills, herons, ibis, terns, gulls and fish and nature rides exploring native Florida habitats. Snorkellers can also bring their gear (Sat Jun–Aug) and explore the rock reef with an expert guide.

Lion Country Safari

2003 Lion Country Safari Road, Loxahatchee, t (561) 793 1084, www.lioncountrysafari.com
Getting there Off Southern Boulevard (Highway 441/98), 20 miles west of Highway 1 about 20
Open Daily 9.30–5.30 (last admission 4.30).
Adm Adults $17.95 plus tax, children (3–9) $13.95.
Restaurant, snack bar, fast food outlets, picnic facilities available, gift shops

Part fairground, part wildlife conservation centre, this drive-in park features fairground rides, paddle-boats, a miniature train ride, crazy golf, a safari maze and a petting zoo. In the safari park you'll find giraffes, gazelle, lions, rhinoceroses, moneys, bison, elephants, wildebeest and many more African species. The park is undergoing expansion to include a wet play area, feeding exhibits and volley- and softball fields. Special events run all year, including the chance to spend Christmas with the chimps.

Loxahatchee National Wildlife Refuge

10216 Lee Road, Boynton Beach, **t** (561) 734 8303
Open Park: Daily 8–dusk. Refuge: Mon–Fri 9–4, Sat, Sun 9–4.30 (closed Mon, Tue May–Oct)
Adm $5 per car

Located in Boynton Beach just west of Lion Country Safari, this 147,000-acre refuge lets you explore the last remaining area of the northern Everglades. A guided tour is the best way to explore the vast, untamed areas of marsh wetlands, along with pine flatwoods and a 400-acre cypress swamp. You can also explore along boardwalk trails, or a canoe and bike trail. The park also has boat ramps, a fishing platform, observation towers, a butterfly garden and a visitor centre that shows videos on ecology and offers children (aged 4–8 and 9–14) the chance to join a **Junior Refuge Manager program** and take part in fun activities on a nature theme.

Lake Okeechobee

Lake Okeechobee or the big 'O' is a vast 730 square -mile body of water with an average depth of 9–17 ft. It is the second-largest freshwater lake on the US mainland, second only to Lake Michigan. Like Lake Michigan you cannot see right across it, (partly because of the **Hoover Dike** and partly because of its size) and hence it is also known as 'Florida's Inland Sea'. Following a series of devastating hurricanes in the 1920s, the lake overflowed causing awful floods and the loss of thousands of lives. More hurricanes in the late 1940s, along with periods of drought and building projects led to the construction of a 30-ft earthen wall around part of the lake. The Okeechobee Waterway connects the lake to the sea via two man-made waterways – to the Gulf of Mexico in the west via the Caloosahatchee River and to the Atlantic Ocean in the east via the St. Lucie Canal. The 152-mile boating channel is popular and anglers have plenty of sport fishing for largemouth bass, speckled perch, catfish and blue gills. Bald eagles, blue herons, ospreys, pelicans, egrets, white ibis, owls alligators and bobcat are among the species on or near the lake. Start in one of the towns listed below for boat rides and leaflets to make the most of your visit.

Clewiston, on its southwest shore holds its annual **Sugar Festival** in April, which harks back to the days when sugar boils were a part of Cracker life.

Places of Interest

Okeechobee Battlefield Site, US Highway 441, **t** (863) 763 3959
Okeechobee Historical Museum, Highway 98 North, **t** (863) 763 3959
Lake Okeechobee Scenic Trail, Herbert Hoover Dyke, **t** (863) 983 8101. The trail runs for 110 miles along the top of the Hoover Dike and is open to cyclists and hikers
Okeechobee Airboat Rides
Between Routes 441 and 78, 220 Highway 78, **t** (863) 763 2700. Airboat or pontoon tours and rentals available.
Eagle Nest Airboat Tours, Belle Glade, **t** (561) 996 5357. Travel into the marsh flats of Lake Okeechobee on an airboat and see Florida wildlife in its natural environment.

Getting there

West on Highway 98/441. Turn north on Highway 98 to reach the town of Okeechobee on Lake Okeechobee's north shore, or north on Highway 27 to get to Clewiston on the south shore.

Tourist Information

Okeechobee County Chamber of Commerce, 55 South Parrott Avenue, **t** (863) 763 6464; **Clewiston Chamber of Commerce**, 544 West Sugarland Highway, **t** (863) 983 7979, **www.clewiston.org**

FLORIDA KEYS

Getting there

By air If your budget can stretch to it, the best way is to fly. There are airports in both Key West and Marathon serviced by Continental, US Airlines and Delta. For flights call **Marathon airport**, **t** (305) 289 6060 and for **Key West**, **t** (305) 296 5439.

By road South of Miami, the traffic is turgid along Highway 1 *en route* to the Upper Keys. Expect single-lane snarls offset by the occasional passing place but it's best to set out early or late to avoid delays and try not to travel on Fridays when locals head south for the weekend. The road becomes the **Overseas Highway** when you hit the Keys, which are numbered by mile markers (MM) down to MM 0 in Key West. Therefore, if an attraction is at MM 40 then you know it is 40 miles from Key West. There are 42 bridges along the way, including Flagler's masterpiece, the Seven Mile Bridge.

The **Keys Shuttle** offers a door-to-door service from Fort Lauderdale and Miami International Airports to numerous points in the Keys, including Marathon Airport. Call 24-hours ahead, **t** (305) 289 9997.

Greyhound bus services, **t** (305) 296 9072/(800) 231 2222, **www**.greyhound.com

Services run from Miami to Key West and take about 5½ hours depending on traffic conditions. If you're on a budget, this is the best bet and you can always stop off *en route* to Key West for a couple of days to break the journey. If you let the driver know which mile marker you want to get off at, they'll stop in between scheduled stopping points. There's a stop for refreshments and toilets in Islamorada.

Things to see and do

Upper Keys

The Florida Keys may not be as remote as they were before the age of the motorcar danced a highway down their spine but they still retain characteristics that set them apart from the mainland. It's easy to forget these are islands until you stand on their southernmost edge and gaze out at nothing but sea. Vast tracts of land given over to nature reserves where Key deer thrive. You can hire a bike or take a hike, go sea-fishing or simply meander and watch lovely sunsets at Key West. The idea is not so much to find lots of things to do but just to make time to just sit back, relax and enjoy the view.

If you're handy with a rod or just want to try your hand there are bonefish, tarpon, grouper, marlin, sailfish and dolphinfish to catch. You'll find fishing charters at most large resorts and marinas. Expect to pay around $550 per day for four to six persons.

Getting there

About 45 minutes south of Homestead along Highway 1

Tourist Information

Key Largo Chamber of Commerce, 106000 Overseas Highway, Key Largo 33037, **t** (305) 451 1414, **www**.keylargo.org; **The Florida Keys and Key West**, **t** (800) FLA–KEYS, **www**.**fla-keys.com**

John Pennekamp Coral Reef State Park

Getting there MM 102.5, Key Largo 33037, **t** (305) 451 1202 for park information, **t** (305) 451 6300 for tour reservations, **www**.**pennekamppark.com**

Open 8–dusk. Visitor centre: 8–5

Adm $5 per car, $1.50 per bike or. Glass-bottom boat tour: Adults $20, children $12

Among a sea of boat outfitters and gaudy motel signage in the Upper Keys, this park comes as a quiet and welcome relief. Besides snorkelling, sailing, fishing and diving trips, you can also hire motor-boats, canoes and kayaks to explore this fascinating 25-mile locale comprising mangrove swamps, seagrass beds and coral reefs. Among the varieties of soft and hard corals there are sponges, turtles, crabs, eels and lobsters. At **Key Largo Dry Rocks** you can also view the submerged 9-ft tall bronze statue of the *Christ of the Deep* but if you don't want to get your feet wet there's a replica near the main entrance. Families can also opt to head for the beach for a swim, have a picnic, walk along wildlife trails, visit the playground or go camping. The marina is where you'll find the boat rental and diving facilities and two observation towers for views over **Largo Sound**. At the visitor centre children can browse natural history exhibits, such as a saltwater aquarium and watch nature videos in the theatre.

Long Key State Park

Getting there MM 67.5, 67500 Overseas Highway, Long Key, **t** (305) 664 4815

Open Daily 8–dusk

Adm $3.50 single passenger car, $6 for two passengers, 50 cents for each additional passenger. Camping fees are $31.49, tax included, per night

The park sits on the site of a former luxury fishing resort that was destroyed by the same 1935 hurricane that put Flagler's railway out of action. Today the area is rich in tropical plants and trees including the gumbo limbo, mahogany and Jamaican dogwood. Visitors can enjoy snorkelling, fishing, birding, canoeing and can walk along nature trails, swim and camp by the beach.

Theater of the Sea

MM 84.5, Islamorada, **t** (305) 664 2431,
www.theaterofthesea.com
Getting there take US1 to MM84.5, oceanside
Shows Daily from 9.30–4
Adm Adults $23.95, children (3–12) $15.95. Swim programmes $150 (ages 5 and up)
Restaurant, gift shop, private beach and lagoon

This long-established marine animal park includes dolphin, sea lion, and parrot shows, a guided tour of marine life exhibits, a lagoon-side beach, and the bottomless boat ride. You can see sea turtles, tropical and game fish, sharks, crocodiles, alligators, parrots and birds-of-prey. The theatre also offers encounters, including dolphin, ray and sea lion swims, dolphin wades from the beach (suitable for from age 3) and 4-hour snorkel cruises to **Lignumvitae Key** and **Indian Key Historic State Park**.

Marathon

Locals call Marathon the 'heart of the Keys' because it is right in the middle. It is a charming, former fishing village with plenty of shopping, a small airport and resort accomodation. Most marine activities centre around Boot Harbor.

Getting there

About a half hour south of Long Key on Highway 1

Tourist Information

Greater Marathon Chamber of Commerce,
12222 Overseas Highway, **t** (305) 743 5417,
www.floridakeysmarathon.com

Crane Point Nature Center and Children's Museum

Getting there MM50, bayside 5550 Overseas Highway, **t** (305) 743 9100, **www.cranepoint.org**
Open Mon–Sat 9–5, Sun 12 noon–5
Adm Adults $7.50, children $4, under 6s free

The trick here is deciding what to do first. There's a **Natural History Museum**, **Children's Museum**, **Adderley Town Historic Site**, **Marathon Wild Bird Center** and **tropical forest habitat**. The nature trails to **Florida Bay** offer interesting information about creatures and plants that you might see here. The Natural History Museum has dioramas featuring stuffed Keys fauna, displays about shipwrecks and Flagler's ill-fated railroad and a simulated coral reef habitat. At the Children's Museum kids can dress up as pirates, sail a play galleon, view the shell collection and interact with sea creatures in the touch tanks. Kayak and trolley tours are also available.

Dolphin Research Center

Getting there MM 59, 58901 Overseas Highway, Grassy Key, **t** (305) 289 1121, Swim reservations, **t** (305) 289 0002, **www.dolphins.org**
Open daily 9–4
Adm Adults $17.50, children (4–12) $11.50, under 3s free. Prices $50–$165, call ahead for reservations

This not-for-profit organization provides a home for marine mammals and conducts research into their care, most of which takes place within view of the visitor. The centre has a daily programme of events, including **dolphin swims**, **dolphin splash**, play and even **paint sessions** where the dolphin creates a T-shirt for you. The dolphins will call for your attention as you walk into this friendly facility, which also houses sea lions. There is staff on hand to answer questions and trainers explain what they are doing during research sessions. There are also opportunities to adopt or sponsor a dolphin and to support the organization's work rescuing injured manatees. It's very popular so plan your day ahead. There's a gift shop and a restaurant next door.

Hawk's Cay Resort and Dolphin Connection

Getting there MM 61, north of Marathon, 61 Hawk's Key Boulevard, Duck Key, **t** (305) 743 7000, **www.hawkscay.com**, **www.dolphinconnection.com**
Open Various times, book in advance **t** (888) 814 9154
Encounters: $100 (non-residents $110 per person, Dockside $45 (non-resident $55)

Primarily a resort (*see* Sleep p.52), Hawk's Cay runs dockside viewings and dolphin encounters from submerged platforms. You spend 20 mins learning

Did you know?
The Grassy Key Dolphin Research Center used to be a movie set? The original Flipper film was shot here in 1963. Descendants of one of the dolphin stars still swims around and poses for celebrity shots.

about dolphins before heading to the saltwater lagoon. The water is not always warm so opt for a wetsuit and make sure children do what they are told. Participants do not swim but there are plenty of opportunities for touching and interacting with the dolphins, including giving a cuddle and a kiss on the nose. There's also a **sailing school** open Mon–Fri 8.30–5.30, **www**.offshore-sailing.com

Pigeon Key

Getting there MM 47, 1 Knight's Key Boulevard, oceanside right before the Seven Mile Bridge, Marathon, **t** (305) 743 5999, **www**.pigeonkey.org
Open Daily 9–4. Tours: hourly 10–3
Adm including tram: Adults $8:50, children (6–13) $5, under 6s free

The tour includes a self-guided walk around the buildings that once housed the men who built and operated the **Old Seven Mile Bridge**. Cross the bridge in an open tram for fantastic views of the bay. The museum was the assistant bridge tender's house (1912) and memorabilia from the site, which was also once used as a fishing camp, marine research station and an outpost for Flagler's navvies.

Lower Keys

For a real taste of island life amid peaceful back-waters where you can fish, snorkel, dive and kayak, it's really worth making the journey down to the lower reaches of the Florida Keys. State parks and wildlife preserves abound and tiny islands reach out into the turquoise waters of this tropical paradise. The wild old ways of way out Key West await at mile marker 0, where the kids can let loose on an eclectic mix of museums and attractions and families can mark the moment when the setting sun sinks into the ocean from the southernmost point of the United States.

Getting there

Continue south along Highway 1.

Tourist Information

MM 31, **Big Pine and Lower Keys Chamber of Commerce**, 31020 Overseas Highway, **t** (305) 872 2411, **www**.lowerkeyschamber.com

Bahia Honda State Park

Getting there MM 37, south of the Seven Mile Bridge, north of Big Pine Key, 36850 Overseas Highway, Big Pine Key, **t** (305) 872 2353, Snorkelling reservations, **t** (305) 872 3210, **www**.bahiahondapark.com
Open 8–dusk
Adm 1–2 Adults $2.50/$5.00; children (over 6) 50 cents, $1.50 per bike or pedestrian

Beach lovers are spoilt for choice at Bahia Honda's two lovely sands, one on the Atlantic shore another in Florida Bay. There's a gift shop, snack bar and kayak, snorkel trip concession outlets, toilets, changing room and showers on the bayside, which is where the waters are calm enough for family swims. Camping facilities are also available, call for details.

Big Pine Kayak Adventures

Big Pine Key, **t** (305) 872 9860, **www**.keyskayaktours.com
Getting there MM 30.2, turn right and bear right to Wilder Road at the stop sign head left to No Name Key, road heads right to No Name Pub then proceed ⅛ mile to yellow kayak sign
Open Daily, call to schedule kayaking trips

Offers half- and full-day kayaking nature tours, kayak rentals, skiff eco-tours, backcountry sailing catamaran cruises and fishing trips .

National Key Deer Refuge

Getting there MM 30.5, entrance on Key Deer Blvd (Route 940), off Route A1A, **t** (305) 872 2239
Open Park 8–dusk, Visitor centre: Mon–Fri 8–4
Adm Free

The diminutive Key deer are the stars of the show here but the refuge is also home to alligators, turtles, fish and a rich variety of plant-life, including slash pine, silver palms and orchids. Central on **Big Pine Key** is an old quarry, called the **Blue Hole**, which has visitor facilities, including an information booth staffed by volunteers, and an observation platform. North of here there are two interpretive **nature trails**, one exploring the hardwood hammock, the other passing through pine rocklands to a freshwater wetland slough. Visit early or late for the best chance to see the deer.

Reflections Nature Tours

Getting there Big Pine Key, **t** (305) 872 4668, **www**.floridakeyskayaktours.com
Open daily
Cost $50 per person for three-hour guided tour

Mobile service offering safe and stable sea kayaks for exploring the Keys and Everglades. Offers half- and full-day tours and rentals, plus backcountry transport.

Underseas Inc.

Getting there Oceanside at mile marker 30.5, Big Pine Key, **t** (305) 872 2700
Open Daily
Cost Snorkelling charter $29.95 per person, including gear, diving from $45, dive courses from $125

The friendly and professional service sets this establishment apart. Snorkelling and scuba charters are available including instruction and equipment.

Key West

The sunsets are remarkable, the locals are affable and laid-back, the tours are memorable and there's so much to do, you need at least a week. One-time home of Hemingway and self-proclaimed Republic, Key West is about as interesting as you'd expect a city perched right at the end of the mainland US to be. Just don't expect to do things in a hurry. The main drag is **Duval Street** where you'll find restaurants and shops as you head towards the **Historic Seaport**, studded with resort hotels, bars, cruise boats and sailing ships. This is the place to stay for easy access to the main attractions and make the most of day and nighttime entertainments.

Getting there

At the southernmost end of Highway 1.

Tourist Information

Greater Key West Chamber of Commerce, 402 Wall Street, **t** (305) 294–2587
'Passports' to Key West's main attractions offer discounts on tours, shopping discounts, plus money off admission to museums and historic buildings. Call, **t** (305) 292 8978, **www.keywestpassports.com**

Ernest Hemingway Home and Museum

907 Whitehead Street, **t** (305) 294 1575
Getting there The Old Town Trolley stops just across the road
Open Daily 9–5
Adm Adults $11, children $6, under 5s free

Although primarily a treat for the adults, Hemingway's former home is populated with the descendants of his curious polydactyl (six-toed) cats, named after famous people and latterly after hurricanes (the kittens Charlene, Frances and Ivan). Ask a guide which ones like to be stroked and do not pick them up or you'll have a few extra scratches for your trouble. The tour takes in the modest quarters where Hemingway and his second wife Pauline lived from 1931 until their divorce in 1939 when Hemingway wented to Cuba. Pauline stayed in the house until her death in 1951. There are lovely shady gardens, complete with Pauline's $20,000 swimming pool, an unusual 'drinking trough' for the cats and the highlight of the trip for any lover of words, Hemingway's studio where he wrote many of his world-famous works, including *A Farewell To Arms*, *For Whom The Bell Tolls* and *To Have and Have Not*, the latter inspired by characters Hemingway met in Key West.

> ***Can you spot?***
> ***Hemingway's last penny? Under a small square of Perspex on the patio beside the swimming pool you can just about make out a greenish bronze penny that belonged to Hemingway. The story goes that when he found out how much his wife had spent on the pool he dug in his pocket and remarked laconically that she should have his last penny as well since she had spent everything else.***

Fort Jefferson

Garden Key, Dry Tortugas
Yankee Freedom II, t (305) 294 7009, **www.**yankeefreedom.com, **adm** adults $134, children (4–16) $89
Sunny Days Catamarans, t (305) 292 6100, **www.**drytortugasferry.com, **adm** adults $110, children (under 16) $80
Seaplanes of Key West, t (305) 294 0709, **www.**seaplanesofkeywest.com, **adm** half-day adults $179, children (6–12) $129 (3–6) $99, under 2s free. Full–day $305, $225 and $170

If you're in a hurry, take a seaplane for a spin – here are half-day and full-day trips as well as camping stop-overs. You pay more but it is truly exhilarating. Both boat services provide free breakfast and lunch. All include a guided tour of the fort.

Plan to spend a whole day and pack lots of water on hot days for the 70-mile trip out to **Dry Tortugas**. Take a tour around the massive fortifications of **Fort Jefferson** where Dr. Mudd, the infamous doctor who tended the broken leg of Lincoln's assassin, John Wilkes Booth, was imprisoned. Controversy over Mudd's guilt continued until 1869 when he was pardoned and the family named cleared in 1970. But the saying 'his name is mud' still continues.

Fort Zachary Taylor State Historic Park

End of Southard Street on Truman Annex, t (305) 292 6713
Open 8–dusk
Adm $5 per car, $3 single passenger, $1 per bike or pedestrian, plus a 50 cent surcharge per person aged over 6

Down at the beachy end of Key West this former Union stronghold offers daily tours but the main reason to come is to swim, snorkel, have a picnic, go on a nature trail or make the most of the lovely sands, which aren't so plentiful in Key West.

Historic Seaport

Come here to sail in a sailing ship or catamaran. **The Western Union**, **t** (305) 587 2715, runs sunset and atmospheric stargazing trips where children can learn about the constellations and fill in activity sheets afterwards. If you want to view under the sea, take a glass-bottomed boat out to the coral reef on the look out for parrotfish, barracuda and nurse sharks. **Discovery**, **t** (305) 293 0099, combine narrated reef viewings with a champagne sunset celebration. Boats for the **Dry Tortugas National Park** (*see* p.217) also depart from here.

Key West Aquarium

1 Whitehead Street, off Mallory Square, t (305) 296 2051
Open Tours Daily 11, 1, 3 and 4.30
Adm Adults $9, children (4–12) $4.50 for a two-day pass

Built in 1938, this was the original Key West attraction, showing interesting fish in attractive displays as well as tanks housing sharks, sea turtles and larger species of fish outside. It'll not take more than a morning but kids will like the touch tank and feeding sessions, which include a chance to have a close encounter with a baby nurse shark.

Key West Lighthouse Museum

938 Whitehead Street, t (305) 294 0012, www.kwahs.com
Open Daily 9.30–4.30.
Adm Adults $8, children $4, under 6s free.

The present lighthouse dates from 1847, after the original was swept away in a hurricane. Climb the 88-step circular iron stairway for stunning views. The fully restored and recreated house and verandah displays instruments, maps, photos and historic artefacts belonging to the lighthouse keepers, including the ill-fated, yet resilient Mabrity family.

Key West Shipwreck Historeum

Across the street from the Aquarium at 1 Whitehead Street, t (305) 292 8990, www.shipwreckhistoreum.com
Open Guided tours Daily every half hour 9.15–4.45
Adm Adults $9, children (4–12) $4.50

A highly entertaining museum with actors. If you have strong legs and stomachs, climb the 64-ft lookout tower for staggering views over the town and docks. Don't forget to ring the bell on the way back down. The lower level houses artefacts from ships wrecked offshore and upstairs visitors can peer in the windows of a model of a typical wrecker's home and watch videos about this lucrative industry that was so influential on Key West's development.

Mel Fisher's Maritime Museum

200 Greene Street, t (305) 294 2633, www.melfisher.org
Open Daily 9.30–5; **Adm** Adults $10, children $6

In this town where many fortunes were made from salvaging goods from wrecked vessels, Mel Fisher planned the biggest recovery mission of them all – the search for the lost Spanish treasure ships *Nuestra Senora de Atocha* and *Santa Margarita*, sunk off the coast of the Keys in 1622. It took Mel and his team over 15 years to recover the ships and almost another 10 to restore the artefacts and display them in this former Naval Station. Watch your kids' eyes bulge with delight as they gawk at silver and gold bars, chests filled with silver coins, beautifully crafted silverware and jewellery set with precious stones; gold chains, pottery and bronze cannons. The museum store sells replica jewels and gold doubloons.

Did you know?

That Key West is also known as the Conch (pronounced konk) Republic? During the 1980s the islanders got fed up with US Border Patrols stopping everyone at roadblocks in Florida City and causing massive traffic jams to the Keys. In protest they decided that if the US government were going to treat them like foreigners then foreigners they would be. In April 1982, they seceded from the Union and declared themselves independent, even going so far as to throw stale bread. Minutes later the rebels surrendered and demanded war relief and foreign aid amounting to 1 billion US dollars. They are still waiting...

Pirate Soul

524 Front Street, t (305) 292 1113, www.piratesoul.com
Open Daily 9–7.
Adm Adults $12.95, children: $6.95

Well shiver me timbers and hoist the Jolly Roger, this latest Key West attraction looks just like Port Royal, Jamaica, did in 1690, when scurvy dogs and pestilent pirates ran amok in the town. Feel the terror, smell the unwashed crew, hear the brothel keeper's curse and see into the black heart of a pirate's soul. This celebration of all things piratical includes authentic pirate possessions, as well as period artefacts, video footage and props that invoke the spirit of the times. Check out the talking severed head of Blackbeard or the treasure chest belonging to Captain Thomas Tew and enter the Captain's quarters for a Depp-a-like photo in front of an original Jolly Roger flag with Captain Johnny O. Kids will also love the computers, which have puzzles for them to solve and a level of interactivity that leaves most national museums standing. Some younger children may not like the below-deck sequence where you sit on benches in pitch blackness listening to eerie sounds of rats scuttling and dastardly pirates whispering in your ear, but most children over four should enjoy it. Explore at your leisure to make sure you take it all in from the details of the hanging of Captain Kidd to lift-the-flap boxes for kids to nose inside. The shop stocks an array of plastic swords, pirate hats and flags for staging mock battles on the beach afterwards. Children's activity sheets are provided.

Reef World

201 William Street, t (305) 294 3100, www.reefrelief.org
Open Mon–Fri 9–5
Adm Free

If your kids are keen on conservation stop here to see the displays, artworks and a video about the ocoral reef ecosystem. The gift shop has a coral reef colouring book for kids and coral reef posters, DVDs and postcards for sale.

Tours

Bone Island Shuttle

Departs Mallory Square, t (305) 293 8710, www.boneislandshuttle.com
Open Shuttle service daily 9am–11pm
Adm Adults $8, under 12s free

The shuttle makes an even wider loop than the trolley taking in the new town side of the island towards the airport and is open late, so you can head out for and catch the shuttle back to your hotel afterwards.

Conch Tour Train

Departs from station at 303 Front Street, t (305) 294 5161, www.conchtourtrain.com
Open Tours depart daily 9–4.30
Adm Adults $22, children (4–12) $11
Adults $34, children $17 combination ticket includes admission to the Key West Aquarium and Shipwreck Historeum

The Conch Tour Train features a 90-minute tour, so you're unlikely to do this and the Old Town Trolley, (*see* below), especially since elements of the commentary do overlap. The train is more frequent, so you're more sure of a seat and it's popular with small children who like to hear the clang of the bell as you depart. The train only stops once at Flagler Station on Caroline Street, so if you'd rather get on and off frequently, you're better off with the trolley.

Old Town Trolley

Depart from Mallory Square, (just opposite the aquarium, ticket booth on the right), t (305) 296 6688, www.trolleytours.com
Open Tours depart daily 9.30–4.30, every 30 minutes
Adm Adults $22, children (4–12) $11

These 90-minute tours allow passengers to get off at any stop, although to do so interrupts the flow of the commentary, so you are advised to rejoin the tour at the point at which you left. The often laconic, always helpful tour guide-cum-driver is happy to rattle off historical facts about the passing streets and structures, interlaced with amusing anecdotes and enticing legends. On your tour you'll also find out where to dine, go shopping, hit the best beaches and where all the key attractions are, so make this the first port of call on your journey. The stops, which loop around a fair chunk of the island, are as follows: (1) Mallory Square, (2) Historic Key West Seaport, (3) Simonton Row, Simonton and Greene St, (4) La Concha Crowne Plaza, (5) Bahama Village Market, (6) Key West Welcome Center, (7) Wyndham Casa Marina Resort, (8) Southernmost Trolley Stop, (9) Truman Ave. & Duval St. (10) Angela and Duval Streets.

Miami

Bal Harbour

Carpaccio

Bal Harbour Shops, first level, **t** (305) 867 7777
Open 11.30–11 (*inexpensive*)

Among the choices at Bal Harbour this has the edge offering indoor and café style outdoor dining. The menu features fresh salads, carpaccios and a variety of homemade pastas. Linguini with lobster in a spicy tomato sauce is a favourite.

North Beach

Café Prima Pasta

414 71 Street, **t** (305) 867 0106
(*inexpensive–moderate*)

If you sit outside you're right on the road but there are nice twinkly lights at night. Inside it's roomy and airy with lots of dark corners for lounging family style. They're happy to serve pasta with butter dishes and tone down sauces a little for younger tastes. The filet mignon carpaccio and the hand-made pastas are superb.

Panna Café

7305 Collins Avenue, **t** (305) 866 0677
(*inexpensive–moderate*)

The main reasons to visit are to let the kids loose on the amazing collection of chocolate desserts and to sit outside enjoying some live music of an evening in the courtyard out back. Italian dishes such as sea bass, snapper and veal are among the lighter choices and there's plenty of pasta for the kids. If they won't eat, bribe them with cake.

South Beach

Cafe Nuvo Y Mojitos

410 Espanola Way, **t** 305 486 1490
(*inexpensive–moderate*)

Not as expensive as some of the restaurants you'll find along this busy tourist street and thankfully, they don't go in for the usual menu waving antics either. The food is good Italian staples with big portions of pasta and the kids' menu features scaled-down versions. The best aspect of this place, however, is sitting outside, ensconced in upholstered armchairs and banquettes strewn with cushions, in the style of Imperial Rome .

Joe's Stone Crab Restaurant

11 Washington Avenue, **t** (305) 673 0365, takeout, **t** (305) 673 4611, **www.joesstonecrab.com**
Open Lunch: mid-Oct–Apr, Tue–Sat 11.30–2. Dinner: Mon–Thu 5–10, Fri, Sat 5–11, Sun 4–10 (*expensive*)

A Miami institution, Joe's, offers scintillating and yet unfussy crab, fish, seafood and steak dishes, accompanied by fresh vegetables and served either inside the rather elegant restaurant or in the shady courtyard outside. There's a no reservation policy, so be prepared to wait. If you're impatient or hungry on Sunday lunchtime do not be discouraged. Joe's takeout next door will do you a lovely platter (shrimp, crab claws, oysters and lobster) or crab dinners to take away along with tasty bread rolls, plastic knives and forks and even, if you wish, a bottle of chilled white wine (*expensive*).

News Café

800 Ocean Drive, **t** (305) 538 6397
Open 24-hours (*inexpensive–moderate*)

It's always busy, which is a good sign but head over by 12 noon if you're serious about lunch because there do not take reservations here. It's excellent for people- (and car-) watching on Ocean Drive and the waiting staff are efficient if not effusive. Main meals are on the large side but they do all-day breakfast items and don't bat an eye if all your kids want is a snack and a drink. There's a shop that sells T-shirts, swimwear and sun tan lotion if you want to head straight over the road to the beach afterwards.

Little Havana

Ayestaran

706 SW 27th Avenue, **t** (305) 649 4982 (*inexpensive*)

This vast establishment offers Cuban staples like chicken and rice and shredded beef sandwiches, plus specials like turkey fricassee, all washed down with the obligatory café con leche. Try the kids out on fried plantain (tell them it's a bit like banana with lemon and honey) and pumpkin flan.

Coconut Grove

Café Med

CocoWalk, 3015 Grand Avenue, **t** (305) 443 1770
Open Mon–Wed 11–10, Thu-Sun 11am–12am
(*inexpensive–moderate*)

This pleasant casual restaurant serves really good wood oven pizzas, crisp salads and plentiful pasta, in a friendly, relaxed atmosphere. Kids' menu spaghetti and pizzas available.

Café Tu Tu Tango

CocoWalk, 3015 Grand Avenue, t (305) 529 2222 (*inexpensive–expensive*)

This is the original bohemian café (branch on International Drive, Orlando) where local artists display their works. Main dishes include empanadas, quesadillas, Asian- and Spanish-influenced dishes, including chips with a variety of dips, tapas, pizzas and intriguing combinations such as lobster tails in chipotle oil with black bean salsa. Kids' menu offers spaghetti and build your own pizza options, plus usual hot dog, chicken fingers options.

Key Biscayne

Sundays on the Bay

5420 Crandon Boulevard, t (305) 361 6777
Open lunch and dinner daily, Sunday brunch 10.30–3, call for reservations (*moderate–expensive*)

This is a cheery spot to watch the sun go down while feasting on salads, soups, fish and seafood. Eat indoors amid colourful surroundings and tropical fish tanks or outside for great views of the dockside.

Fort Lauderdale

There are lots of outdoor dining cafés along **Las Olas Boulevard** including creperies, pizzerias and bistros. **Stork's Café**, 1109 East Las Olas Boulevard, **t** (954) 522 4670, is open daily for breakfast pastries and coffee, lunchtime snacks, sandwiches, as well as a huge selection of fancy cakes and pies.

Cap's Place

2765 Northeast 28th Ct., Lighthouse Point, t (954) 941 0418
Getting there Lighthouse Point Yacht Basin & Marina (8 miles north of Fort Lauderdale) turn east two blocks north of Copans Road, at US–1 and northeast 24 Street, follow the double lines and signs to the Yacht Basin/Marina.
Open daily from 5.30. Reservations recommended, call after 4.30 (*inexpensive–moderate*)

Children will love the fact that they have to catch a boat to get to this restaurant, which is situated on an island off Lighthouse Point. This is Broward County's oldest restaurant and a national monument, where movie stars and famous characters have come to dine, Winston Churchill and Franklin D. Roosevelt, among them. The menu includes dolphinfish, crab claws, lobster and other seafood specials.

Mai-Kai

3599 North Federal Highway, t (954) 563 3272
Open Sun Thu 5–10.30, Fri, Sat 5–11.30. Reservations required. Shows: Sun–Thu, 7 and 9.30, Fri, Sat, 7 and 10. Show: $9.95 per person, under-12s free (*moderate–expensive*)

For something completely different, try this Polynesian restaurant where there's after-dinner music and dancing. The owners devise a new show every year with two performances nightly. There are special shows put on by Polynesian children on Sunday evenings (Jun–Sept) where attending children are given a *lei* and a colouring book. The food is a mixture of Chinese, Thai and Hawaiian wok dinners, plus divine duck specials, followed by tropical fruit. The children's men features beef, chicken, ribs or shrimp, accompanied by rice and with ice cream to follow.

Boca Raton

Crab House Seafood Restaurant

6909 Southwest 18th Street, t (561) 750 0498 (*moderate–expensive*)

Outdoor waterfront dining is available at this friendly restaurant that draws locals and tourists with its signature crab specials. The menu also has steaks, oysters, scallops, clams and other seafood delicacies, all served with steamed vegetables.

Delray Beach

32 East

32 East Atlantic Avenue, t (561) 276 7868
Open Sun–Thu 5.30–10, Fri, Sat 5.30–11 (*moderate–expensive*)

On Delray's main restaurant drag, 32 East serves up imaginative and beautifully crafted food using fresh ingredients daily. Whether you opt for spaghetti with rocket or tuna with wasabi salad the result is the same – satisfaction guaranteed. Children love the wood oven pizzas and fresh fish dishes. Sister restaurant **Sol Kitchen**, 4 Atlantic Avenue, **t** (561) 921 0201, is just down the road and serves steaks and seafood dishes with Latin leanings.

Palm Beach

South County Road is restaurant central and if you don't want a sit down meal you can visit **Sandwiches by the Sea**, 363 South County Road, **t** (561) 655 7911 or **Sunrise Natural Foods**, 279 Royal Poinciana Way, **t** (561) 659 1140 for takeaway sandwiches and meals.

Chuck & Harold's

207 Royal Poinciana Way, t (561) 659 1440
(*moderate–expensive*)

Families can enjoy indoor or outdoor sidewalk dining with jazz music of an evening and dancing beneath the garden room's retractable roof. Lunch features small seafood and steak plates along with sandwiches and interesting soups and salads. For dinner start with mussels, clams, oysters or crab cakes followed by mains including fresh fish or veal meatloaf. Reservations recommended.

Hamburger Heaven

314 South County Road, t (561) 655 5277
(*inexpensive*)

Casual dining spot that is popular with the locals who come for the great burgers served with tasty toppings. If you're looking for something without a bun, there are vegetarian meals, soups, sandwiches and delectable homemade pies.

West Palm Beach

Aleyda's Tex-Mex Restaurant

1890 Okeechobee Boulevard, t (561) 688 9033
Open Mon–Thu 11–10, Fri 11–11. Sat 5–11, Sun 5–9. Buffet lunches Mon–Fri (*inexpensive–moderate*)

This is Mexican heaven with fajitas, tamales, chili rellenos, tostados and Quesadilla including vegetarian version or with beef, chicken, shrimp or crab, among many other delicious specialities. Children under 12 can choose from beef tacos, burgers, burritos, hot dogs, enchiladas or chicken fingers served with fries or beans and rice.

Sailfish Marina Restaurant

98 Lake Drive, t (561) 881 8936
(*moderate–expensive*)

The dinner menu features yellowtail snapper, grouper, shrimp, dolphinfish, lobster and seafood pasta dishes. Breakfasts include waffles, pancakes and eggs done just about any way you like and at lunchtime there are wraps and other deli treats. Brunch buffet Sat and Sun from 8–1.

Hollywood

Le Tub

1100 North Ocean Drive, Hollywood, t (954) 921 9425 (*inexpensive*)

This unusual diner is decorated outdoors with antique, painted bathtubs and lavatories cunningly disguised as planters. Kids can have fun choosing which of the baths they'd prefer to have a soak in. The menu features seafood and fish, chilli, great burgers and ribs.

Clewiston

Clewiston Inn

108 Royal Palm Avenue, Clewiston, t (863) 983 8151
(*inexpensive–moderate*)

Don't be put off by the air of grandeur of this country hotel; it's not as formal as it looks. The Colonial dining room is elegant yet inviting serving steak, seafood and pasta dishes. Pay a visit to the Everglades lounge while you're here to view the fantastic 360-degree mural depicting native flora and fauna.

Florida Keys

Upper Keys

Crack'd Conch

MM 105, Key Largo, t (305) 451 0732
(*inexpensive–moderate*)

This friendly sprawling restaurant specializes in seafood dishes such as fish and shrimp, cracked conch, lobster, scallops and oysters. The colour-in activity kids' menu offers fried chicken, shrimp or fish, burgers or grilled cheese served with honey biscuits and fries.

Islamorada Fish Company

MM 81.5, Islamorada, **t** (305) 664 9271 (*moderate–expensive*)

Eat fresh fish, Florida lobster, stone crab and shrimp at this waterside restaurant overlooking the bay. There are sandwiches and salads, plus ice cream sundaes if your kids aren't big on seafood.There's also a branch on Dania Beach.

Manny and Isa's

MM 81.6, Islamorada, **t** (305) 664 5019
Open Late Nov–mid-Oct, Wed–Mon lunch and dinner (*inexpensive–moderate*)

Cuban and Spanish home cooking including lobster enchiladas and palomino steak served by friendly waitresses in a laid-back setting. It's popular and therefore gets busy on weekends but if you call in advance you can get a takeout. Here is where you go to get your Key Lime pie.

Marathon

Seven Mile Grill

MM 47, Marathon, **t** (305) 743 4481 (*inexpensive*)

This 1950s institution is open for breakfast, lunch and dinner and is situated just north of The Seven Mile Bridges. The restaurant's casual, relaxed atmosphere sits well with the unfussy menu of homemade soups, sandwiches, shrimp in beer, blackened fish and omelettes.

Big Pine Key

Mangrove Mama's

MM 20, Sugarloaf Key, **t** (305) 745 3030 (*moderate–expensive*)

Stop for a typically Conch special, good vegetarian choice and healthy Floribbean fare .

Key West

Grazing in the bars around the **Historic Seaport** is perfectly acceptable as you wait for the sun to go down or to board your vessel out to sea. Most vessels don't even mind if you take a carry-out on board (though ask first).

Alonzo's Oyster Bar

700 Front Street, **t** (305) 294 5880 (*inexpensive–moderate*)

There's a downstairs casual bar-style setup with ¾ wraparound outdoor seating overlooking the marina or an upstairs restaurant. Either way the food is excellent with succulent dolphinfish sandwiches, tasty conch chowder and spicy mussels. Children can opt for simple pasta dishes followed star-quality chocolate cake.

Crabby Dicks

712 Duval Street, **t** (305) 294 7229 (*inexpensive–moderate*)

This upstairs casual restaurant has a wide verandah overlooking the eclectic hubbub along Duval Street where incredibly friendly waiting staff attend to you like you're old friends.

El Meson de Pepe

410 Wall Street, **t** (305) 295 2620 (*inexpensive–moderate*)

This indoor-outdoor traditional Cuban restaurant offers friendly service in pleasant, spacious surroundings. There are tasty appetizer platters for starters, as well as gorgeous classic dishes such as black bean soup, fried plantains and a piquant ropa vieja (shredded beef in spicy sauce) that is out of this world. Kids will be happy with melted cheese wraps and salad.

Shula's on the Beach

Wyndham beach Resort, 1435 Simonton Street, **t** (305) 296 6144 (*expensive–very expensive*)
Open Sun–Thu 5.30–10.30, Fri–Sat 5.30–11.
Reservations recommended

The setting and the food vie for supremacy at this romantic beach restaurant where you can hear the gentle lapping of the waves as you devour mouthwatering surf and turf. The portions are big, so don't over order on side dishes. The kids' menu does not stint on quality either. Perfect for a last night of the holiday blowout treat.

Sloppy Joe's

201 Duval Street, **t** (305) 294 5717 (*inexpensive–moderate*)

This Cheers-style pub is chock-a-block with Hemingway photos and memorabilia as a tribute to the original hostelry that the writer frequented when he was in town. There's live music and often-livelier clientele but the food is good and the waiting staff are highly attentive. Dishes range from American staples like pizza and burgers to Tex Mex and shrimp.

Quiz

1. Where can kids try manning a police bike, fire engine or cargo dock?
2. Where can kids have their picture taken with a baby tiger?
3. What mammal can make a big splash in the water?
4. Where can you join scientists in exploration adventures to remote regions?
5. What is the 'river of grass'?
6. What do Johnny Weissmuller, Mark Spitz, President Reagan and John F. Kennedy have in common?
7. Where can you taste free samples of chocolate?
8. What is the big 'O'?
9. What are you supposed to do on the way back down from the lookout tower at Key West Shipwreck Historeum?
10. How long did it take to recover the lost Spanish treasure that sunk off the Keys in 1622?

Walt Disney World® Resort – Need to Know

12

DISNEY NEED TO KNOW

Welcome to the house of mouse. Walt Disney World Resort® in Florida was Walt's dream vacation-land, first envisaged in the 1960s and opened to the public in 1971. Today it remains high on the list of dream destination for families; offering an incredible, action-packed, 47-square-mile entertainment zone that will beguile and entertain everyone from little tots to great grandparents. The sheer scale of the complex is staggering and it's impossible to get from one park to the next without the aid of a motorized vehicle of some kind or another – thankfully Disney buses are there to whisk you to and fro, not to mention a host of other modes of transport that are attractions in themselves both inside and around the parks. If you imagine Disneyland Paris® being contained inside a snow globe that is then shattered and its pieces scattered to the four winds, then you have something of an idea of the scale of the place. Walt Disney World® Resort sits resplendent in around 30,000-acres, only a quarter of which is taken up with resort and theme-park structures, another quarter is a designated wilderness reserve. Around 27,000 trees blew down in Disney parks during the 2004 hurricane season, but you wouldn't even notice it now. The open spaces and forests around Disney's properties are undergoing renewal, albeit in a less showy way than the amusements around them.

The key attractions of Walt Disney World® Resort are its four very unique theme parks, **Magic Kingdom®, Epcot®, Disney-MGM Studios** and **Disney's Animal Kingdom®**, where spectacular shows, thrill rides, family attractions and beautiful scenery offer a full-on day of fun. When the kids get hot and bothered there are two refreshing water adventure parks, **Blizzard Beach®** and **Typhoon Lagoon®**, to explore and, for fun and games, there are 99 holes of golf on six courses, the **Disney's Wide World of Sports Complex** and **Downtown Disney**, an entertainment-shopping and dining complex encompassing the Marketplace, Pleasure Island and Disney's West Side. This well-oiled machine requires approximately 51,000 cast members to keep the wheels of fun turning for you, with resort attractions open daily, year-round. When it's time to hit the hay, Walt Disney World® Resort also boasts 32 resort hotels (22 owned and operated by Walt Disney World®) to guarantee you a really good night's sleep (*see* pp.237–241).

BARGAIN HOLIDAYS

Most tour operators are reliable, but if you are in any doubt as to which operator to use, check for the IATA and ATOL symbols, which guarantee that your money is safe should a company go out of business. For cheap package deals to Orlando, see below, *see* p.14 for a complete list of tour operators to Florida. British Airways allows customers the chance to choose between flight prices quickly and easily so you can see how much you are paying for each leg of your flight and adjust dates to get the best prices available, **www**.britishairways.com

Check newspapers for flight bargains. Although these tend to be for certain dates only, you can save a lot if you travel out of the school holidays. Last-minute bargains are possible, especially if you source accommodation and flights separately. The best bargains are often through tour operators, those booked well in advance of your travel dates.

Bargain Holidays, t 0871 230 0653, **www**.bargainholidays.com
Bon Voyage, t 0800 316 3012, **www**.bon-voyage.co.uk
Broadway Travel, t 0871 855 0680, **www**.broadwaytravel.com
Best@Travel, t 0870 709 3020, **www**.bestattravel.co.uk
Cosmos, t 0870 44 35 285, **www**.cosmos.co.uk
Going Places, t UK 0870 400 1288, **www**.going-places.co.uk
Kenwood Travel, t 08000 11 22 11, **www**.kenwoodtravel.com

See also Travel and Preparation p.14

Useful websites

In UK: **www**.disneyworld.co.uk
In Florida: **www**.disneyworld.com
Flights plus add-ons Airline Network, **www**.airline-network.co.uk
British Airways, www.britishairways.com
Flightline, www.flightline.co.uk
Expedia, www.expedia.co.uk
Ebookers, www.ebookers.co.uk
Last Minute, www.lastminute.com
Teletext, www.ukaway.co.uk
www.teletextholidays.co.uk
Virgin Atlantic, www.virgin-atlantic.com

Portland Direct, **t** 0870 241 3172, **www**.portland-direct.co.uk
Travel Shop USA, **t** 0870 444 1918, **www**.travelshopusa.co.uk
Travelplanners, **t** 0800 0350 359, **www**.travelplanners.co.uk
Vacations Group, **t** 01582 469661, **www**.vacationsgroup.co.uk

Attractions tickets

Attraction Tickets Direct, **t** 0845 130 3876, **www**.attractionticketsdirect.com

For Disney theme park saver tickets and discounted passes to attractions in Orlando and beyond.

Meridian Line Travel, **t** 0845 6121 747, **www**.onlineflorida.co.uk

Offers Disney park tickets and other Orlando attractions, plus Kennedy Space Center.

BUYING TICKETS IN ADVANCE

Visitors to Walt Disney World® can purchase multi-day tickets online and take advantage of excellent offers and bargains at, **www**.disneyworld.co.uk

The ticket savings are included when guests buy select Walt Disney World® vacation packages before leaving home. See website for prices, which are subject to change.

If you'd rather wait until you arrive in Florida, you can also book tickets on **t** (407) 934 7639, at participating Disney Stores or at your Walt Disney World® resort hotel.

Magic Your Way Tickets

These are customized tickets that allow you to choose the park and number days that you want. You can select from ticket options that include:

Park Hopper Option – allows access to all four theme parks.

Magic Plus Pack Option – For admission to Disney's Blizzard Beach water park, Disney's Typhoon Lagoon water park, DisneyQuest, Downtown Disney Pleasure Island or Disney's Wide World of Sports Complex.

No Expiration Option – For guests who don't want a time limit on when they can use their base ticket (useful if you're planning a two-centre holiday).

Magic Your Way Premium Ticket – Access all areas with this ticket, which combines the benefits of Park Hopper and Magic Plus Pack options.

The top ten shows and parades

1. Mickey's Philharmagic (Magic Kingdom®)
2. The Enchanted Tiki Room Under New Management (Magic Kingdom®)
3. Mickey's Jammin' Jungle Parade (Animal Kingdom®)
4. Festival of the Lion King (Animal Kingdom®)
5. Flights of Wonder (Animal Kingdom®)
6. Fantasmic! (Disney-MGM Studios)
7. Lights, Motors, Action! ™ (Disney-MGM Studios)
8. Indiana Jones Epic Stunt Spectacular! (Disney-MGM Studios)
9. Jim Henson's Muppet*Vision 3-D (Disney-MGM Studios)
10. The American Adventure (EPCOT®)

Disney's Ultimate Tickets

Advance purchase savings are also available for Ultimate Tickets, *see* website.

Tickets are available for 14 or 21 days exclusively for UK visitors (prices are in UK sterling):

21 day pass: Adults £199, children £169

14-day pass: Adults £181, children £156

Disney's **Ultimate Tickets** provide unlimited admission to all four theme parks, Magic Kingdom Park®, Epcot®, Disney-MGM Studios, Disney's Animal Kingdom® Theme Park, two themed water parks, Typhoon Lagoon and Blizzard Beach, and other attractions including DisneyQuest® Indoor Interactive Theme Park, Downtown Disney Pleasure Island and Disney's Wide World of Sports Complex. Disney's Ultimate Tickets are valid for 14 or 21 days from first use based on duration of ticket purchased.

Disney's Premium Tickets

Disney also offers 7- and 5-day Premium Tickets, which expire 14 days from first use.

7-day pass: Adults £167, children £143

This give unlimited admission to Magic Kingdom Park®, Epcot®, Disney-MGM Studios and Disney's Animal Kingdom® Theme Park, plus five admissions in total to Typhoon Lagoon, Blizzard Beach, DisneyQuest®, Downtown Disney Pleasure Island and Disney's Wide World of Sports Complex.

5-day pass: Adults £165, children £142)

This gives unlimited admission to Magic Kingdom Park®, Epcot®, Disney-MGM Studios and Disney's Animal Kingdom® Theme Park, plus three admissions in total to Typhoon Lagoon, Blizzard Beach, DisneyQuest®, Downtown Disney Pleasure Island and Disney's Wide World of Sports Complex.

TRAVEL

Getting there

By air, rail and bus Please see Orlando travel section p.134, for information.

By road Walt Disney World® Resort is located at Lake Buena Vista, 20 miles southwest of Orlando. Exits 27, 26, and 25 off I-4.

Getting around

Disney's fleet of coaches transport resort guests around Walt Disney World® with a shuttle service running between the parks, dining, shopping, entertainment and resort hotels. Non-resort pay a nominal fee. Monorail trains, ferryboats and launches are also available. **www.**disney world.co.uk or **www.**disneyworld.com

Tourist information

Walt Disney World® Guest Information, P.O. Box 10040, Lake Buena Vista, **t** (407) 824 4321 or visit **www.**disneyworld.co.uk or **www.**disneyworld.com

Park opening hours

Opening and closing times vary at all the Disney parks. It's a good idea to call, check online or pick up a list of times at the park entrance to be sure of any seasonal changes. These are approximate times:

Magic Kingdom®	9–10 (later in peak season)
Disney–MGM Studios	9–8.30 (up to 10 in season)
EPCOT®	Future World: 9–9, World Showcase: 11–9
Animal Kingdom®	9–5 (6–8 in season)

Admission prices

One-day one-park ticket: Adults $59.75, children (3–9) $48 (prices subject to change).

Blizzard Beach, Typhoon Lagoon and DisneyQuest: Adults $36.21, children (3–9) $29.82. (per attraction) For saver tickets and advance booking *see* Buying tickets in advance, p.227.

TOP TIPS

Choose your time!

Late August/early September and October half-term are great times for a Disney break and you'll find shorter queues than in the height of summer. Early to mid-November is good for parents with pre-school age children. If you can go a week or so before Christmas or for New Year and the first week of January, you will find it much quieter than in the Christmas week. August is very hot, so if you're planning on a summer trip, bring lots of sun lotion, water, sun shades, hats and try to spend at least some time inside watching the shows or at a water park cooling off in between visit to the theme parks. *See* p.23 for a full list of US Federal Holidays, as these tend to be the busiest times in the theme parks. February half term often coincides with Presidents' Week (from third Mon in Feb), which is right in the heart of the high season, so you'll find it hard to find accommodation and it will be more expensive. Easter can also be busy and expensive because it's high season and Spring Break draws the college crowds. Memorial Day falls at the end of May during the spring half term, so again it's likely to be busy. Obviously holiday times like summer and Christmas are very popular with American tourists, so you may find it better to avoid these busy times.

FastPass – beat the queues

Use a **FastPass**, which gives you with a pre-booked one-hour time slot, so you can join a much shorter queue for the rides. Go to your favourite ride first and if it's busy, get your first FastPass and move on to the next thing on your list. If your first choice of ride is looking quiet, get a FastPass for the next ride on your list while you experience ride number one. And so on. A FastPass drastically reduces wait time. They are available from machines outside all FastPass attractions. *See* individual parks for details of rides with FastPass options. Some FastPass queues for the top-flight attractions may still be quite long but they usually save at least half an hour more than waiting in the standard lines. FastPasses are free, just put your park ticket into the slot to obtain one. One pass is issued per park ticket.

Eat at different times

Stagger your lunch and dinner times. If you can go on the rides when everyone else has stopped for a bite to eat (roughly 12 noon–2 and 5–7) then you'll find much shorter queues. Pack a few light snacks for eating while waiting in line should the kids get peckish.

The top ten rides for fun

1. Test Track (EPCOT®)
2. Maelstrom (EPCOT®)
3. Buzz Lightyear's Space Ranger Spin (Magic Kingdom®)
4. Tomorrowland Indy Speedway Spin (Magic Kingdom®)
5. Pirates of the Caribbean (Magic Kingdom®)
6. Peter Pan's Flight (Magic Kingdom®)
7. Kali River Rapids (Animal Kingdom®)
8. Kilimanjaro Safaris (Animal Kingdom®)
9. Primeval Whirl (Animal Kingdom®)
10. The Great Movie Ride (Disney-MGM Studios)

First in, last out

Get there early and stay as late as possible. Unless there's a late night show on, the crowds start to thin out around 6 or 7pm when people are thinking of finding somewhere for dinner. Or, if you're not bothered about seeing the shows, you find the rides much quieter while they are on. Check for daily show times. Approximate opening times for the theme parks are given on page 228, but all are subject to seasonal variation. Certain days of the week are better for some parks than others, see below for when to go and when not to go.

Magic Kingdom®	**Go:** Tue, Wed, Fri, Sun, **Avoid:** Mon, Thurs, Sat **Open:** 9–10
EPCOT®	**Go:** every day except Tue and Fri morning **Open:** 9–9
Disney-MGM Studios	**Go:**Fri–Tue, **Avoid:** Sun, Wed, Thu **Open:** 9–9
Animal Kingdom®	**Go:** Thu–Sun **Avoid:** Mon–Wed **Open:** 8–7

Watching parades

For an alternative view of the parade, head to some of the rides along the route about half an hour before it's due to begin. Some of the rides can provide you with better views of the procession than you might get on the ground. As the parade goes past you might also find some queues are shorter for the attractions on its path, so make a beeline for the most popular rides once the floats have passed on by.

Money savers

- Leave the rental car behind or, better still, if you're just spending the week at Disney, don't bother to hire a car at all. There really is no need to bring a car with the abundance of reliable free transport laid on.
- Bring your own bottled water and fruit for snacks. No coolers are allowed in the parks and snacks should be kept within reason.
- Buy refillable drinking mugs for unlimited refreshments in the park, be aware however, that some may be for fizzy drinks only.
- Decide on which photo to keep on merit. If someone in your family has their eyes shut or their hair covering their face on a ride it may not be worth buying a copy. Pre-choose which ride to have the photo on, tie hair back and try and get everyone to be smiling and ready for the photo finish.
- Restrict access to arcade games within the parks. Remind children that you came for the rides rather than amusements that require using up more cash. Epcot® has a great range of hands-on activities that do not cost any extra to play.

Inside track

For the ultimate little helper on your Disney visit, you can even buy a **Pal Mickey interactive Mickey Mouse toy**. He'll let you know when the key events and parades are going to start. He'll recommend attractions and impart interesting snippets of information as you tour all four of the parks and he'll also tell you where to go to meet the

The top ten rides for thrill seekers

1. Space Mountain (Magic Kingdom®)
2. Splash Mountain (Magic Kingdom®)
3. Mission Space (EPCOT®)
4. Tower of Terror (Disney-MGM Studios)
5. Rock 'n' Roller Coaster starring Aerosmith (Disney-MGM Studios)
6. Star Tours (Disney-MGM Studios)
7. Dinosaur® (Animal Kingdom®)
8. Expedition Everest (Animal Kingdom®)
9. Humunga Kowabunga (Typhoon Lagoon)
10. Summit Plummet (Blizzard Beach)

characters. Mickey is both a novel companion while you're in the parks and a cuddly friend for your child to take home afterwards. Pal Mickey is available in English or Spanish for $56.33 plus tax. You can find him at all the Disney theme parks and select Disney hotels.

Shopping

Try and make an early visit to **Downtown Disney** to see what toys are on offer before you visit the parks and make a note of which toys your children really like. Then tour the parks and see if the merchandise varies at all. If they spot something that's affordable and not sold in the downtown area, then buy it in the park. Otherwise, wait until the end of your trip and ask each member of your family to choose the thing they liked best in Downtown Disney and buy it as a souvenir of your trip. Package pickup is available at no extra charge at all Disney theme parks, simply make your purchase and pick it up later from the guests' pickup station near the front entrance of the park. Hotel delivery is also available at no charge at all Disney theme parks for guests staying at Walt Disney World® Resort hotels. Purchases made prior to 7pm will be delivered to the your room by 12 noon the following day. If there's something you've forgotten to buy that the kids just can't live without, visitors can also call, **t** (407) 363 6200 and describe what they saw and where it was located and the **Attractions Merchandise Guest Services Department** can find the gift on their computers and arrange to buy and ship the item for you.

Shopping hours within the parks and Downtown Disney vary, call, **t** (407) 824 4321 for more information.

Can you spot?

A mouse? Disney Imagineers have been having fun for years devising and designing, inventing and secreting lots of hidden Mickey-Mouse heads all over the parks and hotels that make up Walt Disney World® Resort. You might want to look out for them on bed covers, on curtains, fence posts, in fountains, topiary, landscaping, swimming pools, flower beds, on pavements and carpets, even bubbles painted on a wall or a wedding pavilion's fretwork, a pizza menu or a mural might contain the image of the mighty mouse, even on golf courses. You'll probably find them anywhere you might have to queue, which is convenient because it gives you a challenge to amuse the kids with while you wait. Mickey branded merchandise such as napkins, plates and waffles don't really count because they are hardly hidden but silhouettes on crockery or room keys, on covers for glasses or table arrangements do. Happy hunting.

Guided tours

A number of tour options are available, some of which are suitable for family groups. To book call, **t** (407) 939 8687. Tours that children might enjoy include:

Disney's Family Magic Tour

This two hour daily tour is designed for first time visitors to Magic Kingdom®. Suitable for all ages, $25 per person (plus park admission).

Mickey's Magical Milestones Tour

Take a more in-depth look at the history and ideas that went into the creation of the Magic Kingdom® and learn some fascinating facts to impress your friends with. Two-hour tours take place on Mon, Wed and Fri. Suitable for ages 10 and up, $25 per person (plus park admission).

The Magic Behind Our Steam Trains

All aboard for a behind-the-scenes tour of the Magic Kingdom® marvellous steam trains as they are readied for use. Three-hour tours take place Mon, Tue, Thu and Sat. Suitable for ages 10 and up, $40 per person (plus park admission).

Dolphins in Depth at Epcot

This tour gives kids the chance to interact with these wonderful marine animals in knee-deep water. Three-hour tours take place Mon–Fri and are suitable for ages 13 and up, $150 per person, no theme park admission required. Younger children might like to go on an **Epcot Seas Aqua Tour** in the Living Seas Pavilion. These 2½-hour tours take place daily and are suitable for children with some previous snorkelling experience. Children from age 8–16 can participate and receive refreshments, a group photo and T-shirt. $100 per person, no theme park admission required.

DISNEY KNOW-HOW

Baby care centres

Family facilities are available in all of the theme parks and water parks. Baby care centres include baby-changing units (also available in all toilets), plus nursing rooms with microwaves and high-chairs. If your child is lost, report it to the nearest member of staff and head for the baby care centre. Baby supplies are available for a small fee.

Babysitting

See under Disney hotel benefits p.241 or Practical A–Z p.20 for Orlando babysitting services.

Car parks

All Walt Disney World® Resort attractions have car parks, which are on a first come, first served basis. Where possible, use the Disney transport provided.

Cash

ATMs are located throughout Walt Disney World® Resort, you'll usually find them near the lockers, which are at the front entrance just after you pass through the turnstiles in most of the parks.

Childcare centres

Available at various locations in Walt Disney World®, call, **t** (407) 824 2421, for details see under Disney hotel benefits p.241.

Credit cards

Visa Cards, Traveller's cheques, JCB, Diners Club Card®, Discover®, MasterCard®, American Express® and The Disney Credit Card are all accepted.

Dress codes

Avoid loose clothing that may flap about on the rides. Shirts and shoes must be worn at all times. Crop tops and boob tubes are not advisable and swimwear is prohibited, except in the water parks (no exposed rivets or metal fastenings allowed). Kids' swimsuits are also allowed for the fountains in Downtown Disney's Marketplace. Bring sun block or lotion wherever you go. It's also advisable to bring hats for all the family and lightweight kagoules or cotton cover-ups in the event of rain or fierce heat. Avoid dressing kids in theme-park T-shirts while you are there, they are hard to recognise in a crowd.

FAQs

You'll find these on the Disney websites or call, **t** (407) 939 6244, for more information.

First aid centres

All the theme parks offer first aid facilities. In addition, Disney resort guests can call the Front Desk from their room phone for medical services. Complimentary transport to Florida Care Walk-In Centres can be arranged throughout Walt Disney World®, call, **t** (407) 239 6463.

Guest services

Disney resort hotels all have their own Guest Services at the reception desks. In the theme parks, guest services are clearly signposted and are generally located near the entrance.

Lockers

Lockers can be found at the front entrance just after you pass through the turnstiles in most of the parks, fort an additional fee. Further lockers are available near the more energetic rides for personal possessions such as handbags etc that might otherwise be lost in space!

Lost children

See Baby care centres (above). Show your child what cast members look like and point out their distinctive clothing and name tags. Tell them that should they be lost they should look for who looks exactly the same as this.

Lost property

Report missing items to Guest Services, where possible, use lockers to keep personal items safe while in the parks, especially if you're planning on going on the big rides or in the water parks where lockers are really essential.

Parent swap

Families with young children need not miss out on the fun. You queue as normal and when it is your turn, tell the Cast Member operating the ride that one of the adults is going to wait for a parent swap (also called baby swap). Everyone else goes on the ride and, once it is over, the adult who missed out gets to ride and the kids who are old enough can have another go! If you can plan this for your baby or toddler's nap, the waiting parent gets a break too.

Photography

Film and batteries are available at stores throughout Walt Disney World®. Disney photographers are also on hand in the parks should you wish to have a souvenir picture of your family group or child, in the park. You can also drop off your films at PHOTO EXPRESS points and they'll be ready for collection in two hours. All parks have photo collection points and at least one ride where you'll want to look your best (or scariest) for the photo opportunity.

Post

The following places will accept packages for posting.

Magic Kingdom®	Package Pick-Up, Main Street U.S.A.
Epcot®	Package Pick-Up at the Entrance Plaza and International Gateway Entrance.
Disney-MGM Studios	Package Pick-Up to the left of the front gates beside the exit.
Disney's Animal Kingdom®	Package Pick-Up, located at Garden Gate Gifts.

Pushchair/stroller hire

Available in all theme parks but you can't take them with you from one park to another. The charge is $8 per day per park and $1 refundable deposit with receipt, available on a first come first served basis. They all look the same so drape a coloured scarf on yours to save you peering at the labels. Guests can also use their own pushchairs in the parks.

Smoking

Allowed in designated areas within Walt Disney World® Resort parks, restaurants and hotels. Smoking is not allowed on any rides or attractions. The best place to light up is in a bar area where they do not allow children.

Special needs

Disabled access to shops, attractions and restaurants and toilet facilities is available throughout the theme parks. Wheelchairs and motorized vehicles are available for hire. For assistance and specific information, please call, **t** (407) 939 7807, or visit (in UK) **www.**disneyworld.co.uk on (in Florida): **www.**disneyworld.com

Toilets

Available at various locations in Walt Disney World®, all toilets have bayb-changing units and disabled facilities.

Telephones

Available at various locations in Walt Disney World®.

DOWNTOWN DISNEY®

After your day in the theme park there's no need for the fun to end straight away. The downtown district is open from 7pm–2am (some shops are open 7–1am!), so you can unwind over a meal, sit out over the water with a quiet drink, listen to music, see a show or shop and play the night away. There's so much here you'll need at least another week to see and do it all. Here's a guide to what's on offer:

Downtown Disney Marketplace

Best for fun

Lego® Imagination Center

One of the most fun destinations for kids (and parents) is this huge multi-coloured temple to the humble Lego® brick. There are starter packs, kits for building movie studios, racing cars, pirate ships and castles, plus a pick-a-brick section, just in case you want to design something that requires more of one colour. Several tables keep the children busy making model cars, houses or towers, which seem to be a favourite edifice among Lego® enthusiasts, leaving you free to shop for presents. There are beat-the-clock challenges, an outdoor Lego® playground and Lego® models, including dragons, a roaring T-Rex and giant Lego® people to marvel at both indoors and out. They even do Lego® Christmas decorations that make perfect stocking fillers.

Once Upon a Toy

This huge toy store features exclusive new toys, games and Disney collectibles, including a special Disney-themed MR. POTATO HEAD and a Disney theme-park version of MONOPOLY® by Hasbro.

Best for babies

Pooh Corner

Snuggle your little ones in soft, adorable Winnie the Pooh and Friends outfits. The shop also stocks accessories and cuddly toys for babies and toddlers.

World of Disney

The Bird Room features children's and toddler's outfits and accessories, including the new Disney Baby line. The Snow White Room also contains sleepwear, infant outfits and accessories.

Best for dressing up

World of Disney

The Princess room is the place to go for dressing up clothes for all ages.

Best for sportswear

Team Mickey

Golf and character sportswear and accessories, including athletic shoes and socks, Nike trainers and sports gear, golf accessories, college-themed sweatshirts and tennis balls, beachwear and casual clothing.

Super souvenirs

Disney's Days of Christmas

Here you'll find hundreds of hand-crafted baubles, handmade cards, Disney stockings and traditional holiday decorations available 365 days a year.

Disney's Wonderful World of Memories

Preserve your memories with scrapbooks, autograph and photo albums, stationery, stickers and pens.

Yummy treats

Ghirardelli Soda Fountain

Pop in for a milkshake, a sundae or a chocolate roll.

Downtown Disney West Side

Best for fun

DisneyQuest

Downtown Disney West Side, **t** (407) 828 4600, **www.disneyquest.com**
Open Sun–Thu 11.30–11, Fri–Sat 11.30–12 midnight
Adm Adults $36.21, children (3–9) $29.82. Children under 48" must be accompanied by an adult. No smoking or strollers are allowed on the premises

Five floors of interactive fun with virtual reality experiences, state-of-the-art computer games and journeys in 3-D – all vying for your attention. Your quest begins at the entrance portal, **Ventureport**, accessed through a space capsule (lift). You can then access four entertainment zones: **The Explore Zone**, which elaborates on some of the attractions from the Magic Kingdom's Adventureland, including **Pirates of the Caribbean – Battle for Buccaneer Gold**, a game for four players involving strategy, team building and, of course, virtual swashbuckling skills. The **Score Zone** is definitely one for competitive dads, on the **Ride the Comix** game and even the odds against cyber foe in a city full of superheroes. In the **Create Zone**, wannabe pop stars (and, dare we say it, future Disney cast members and Imagineers!) can learn the tricks of the trade as an animator or add their own lyrics in a virtual recording studio. Last is the **Replay Zone** – one for the whole family, where old meets new in a futuristic moonscape setting on board **Buzz Lightyear's Astroblasters**. These next-generation bumper cars are very advanced but they're also out of control and you're facing an onslaught from far, far away... Can you make it? Only Disney could carry it off. Other DQ highlights include: **CyberSpace Mountain** where you design your own white-knuckle thrill ride and then hop in the 360° simulator to see how your personal super coaster performs and the **Virtual Jungle Cruise** a prehistoric white-water ride (it may be virtual but you'll feel immersed in it by the end). **Aladdin's Magic Carpet Ride**, meanwhile, offers an alternative Agrabah that's all inside your head and the **Mighty Ducks Pinball Slam** rounds off the day as you enter the game as a life-size pinball bouncing off the walls and off bumpers too, to score points and prove, once and for all, that you're the Mightiest Duck in the pond.

Cirque Du Soleil: La Noubia

Downtown Disney® West Side, **t** (407) 939 7719
Open Shows Tue–Sat at 6 and 9
Adm Adults $87–$53, children (3–9) $65–$44, plus tax

This French Canadian airborne circus troupe may be familiar. Their sell-out shows are legendary, so families will be delighted to know that their current show is exclusive to Walt Disney World® Resort. The 90-minute performance combines acrobatics with circus skills, choreography, modern ballet and a unique twist of high drama that only Cirque Du Soleil can convey. The kids will be amazed.

Magic Masters®

They've some tricks up their sleeves here and plenty of mesmerising gifts to dazzle your family and friends with.

Starabilias

As much a place to gaze around in wonder as a retail outlet, this shop is choc-a-bloc with nostalgic memorabilia, including autographed photos, signed celebrity posters, jukeboxes and Coca-Cola machines.

Best for babies

Mickey's Groove

If it's got Mickey on it, you'll find it here from clothing to accessories, toys and souvenirs.

Best for groovy gear

DisneyQuest® Emporium

Shop here for snazzy sweatshirts, T-shirts and accessories with exclusive DisneyQuest logos, plus toys, collectibles, jewellery and sweets.

Best for sportswear

Sunglass Icon

Cool shades for hot, hot days.

Super souvenirs

Hoypoloi

If you want to take something home that's out of the ordinary, here you'll find 3-D artworks

Yummy treats

Candy Cauldron

This is sure to meet your confectionery needs.

Pleasure Island

Best for fun

Superstar Studios®

Become your very own pop idol at this recording studio where you can buy copies of your very own hit single on CD, DVD or VHS. Now that *will* impress your friends.

Best for groovy gear

Changing Attitudes

Stocks brand name streetwear for cool kids with discreet Disney logo, plus trendy backpacks and cool accessories.

DTV

Here you'll find a range of themed clothing for all the family reflecting the holiday atmosphere of Disney's Pleasure Island.

Best for sportswear

Mouse House

Dedicated to golf gear and accessories. Maybe there's some Goofy golf gear to be had?

Super souvenirs

Reel Finds

Home to movie memorabilia, classic films and TV programmes, plus cinematic souvenirs and toys.

Best for sport

Disney's Wide World of Sports

P.O. Box 10000, Lake Buena Vista, t (407) 828 3267, www.disneyworldsports.com

Getting there I–4 between Osceola Parkway and US 192

If you can bat it, kick it or smash it you'll find it at this hallowed ground of sport. There are 220-acres of sports facilities in this complex, which caters for sports events and festivities, recreational fitness activities and training at competition level.

The complex is home to the **Atlanta Braves Major League Baseball** team, who use the 7,500-seat stadium for spring training from mid-February to April. The Braves' presence is felt throughout the year though, with their minor league feeder club playing there from June–September. The complex has proved lucky for its other home team, American football's **Tampa Bay Buccaneers**, who set up their first NFL training camp here in 2002 and went on to victory in the Super Bowl. The team has been returning for spring training ever since.

Visitors can also have a bite to eat in the **All Star Cafe** sports-themed restaurant with widescreen TVs and booth seating in giant baseball mitts. Families can enjoy the facilities in the **Sports Experience** interactive playground area, which is suitable for all ages and abilities. Test your skills in football, basketball, baseball and soccer challenges; there's a play area for younger kids. The complex has locker rooms, athletic tracks and equipment, weight-training equipment and is the base for most sporting events held at Walt Disney World® Resort. The annual Disney Endurance Series uses the ground as its headquarters for events, including the Walt Disney World® Marathon, Half Marathon and Inline Marathon, plus other races and running events.

WHERE TO EAT

Once inside the park it's not really feasible to leave to find something to eat, so pre-plan where you're going to dine and, preferably, book ahead. If you want a **character breakfast**, book it through yourtravel agent before you leave the UK if you can. For meal reservations in any of the parks, including Downtown Disney, call, **t** (407) 939 3463 – reservations must be made at least 24-hours in advance on this number. All restaurants listed below can be booked through this service; additional numbers and websites are given for the main restaurants only. If you've not booked lunch or dinner at the park, try to eat brunch before 11am or lunch after 2.30pm and dine after 6–8pm to avoid the crush. If you've already seen the parade, eat while it is on when the restaurants ought to be less busy. There are lots of fast-food outlets, so, even if you haven't booked, you won't go hungry. However, if you want a sit-down meal away from the crowds, advance booking is strongly recommended. During peak holiday season, book every meal in advance to avoid disappointment. Children's menus are available in many Disney restaurants, as are bottle-warmers. Booster seats and high chairs for babies and toddlers are available in all table service restaurants. All Walt Disney World® dining locations are non-smoking. For places to eat in the theme parks *see* individual park entries, pp.243–268.

Downtown Disney Marketplace

Cap'n Jack's Oyster Bar

Open: all day (*inexpensive–expensive*)

Casual lakeside restaurant serving seafood, fish and chicken dishes. The kids' menu features macaroni cheese, chicken breast and hotdogs.

McDonald's Ronald's Fun House

Open: all day (*inexpensive*)

McDonald's burgers, fries, milkshakes and Mc-breakfasts available all day.

Rainforest Café

t (407) 827 8500, **www.rainforestcafe.com**

Open: Sun–Thurs 11.30–11, Fri, Sat 11.30–12 midnight (*expensive*)

Like its sister restaurant just outside the gates of the Animal Kingdom®, this restaurant features animatronic animals, birds and beasties all making a ruckus in the mock tropical foliage draped from floor to ceiling. The kids' menu features chicken, and seafood dishes, salads, pizzas, pasta, sandwiches and burgers. Ask about the restaurant's Educational Programme, which includes a safari through the café to learn about fish and endangered species.

Wolfgang Puck Express

Open Daily 8.30am–10.30pm (*inexpensive*)

Quick service deli items, pizzas and mains from the Wolfgang Puck restaurant menu, *see* below.

Downtown Disney West Side

Wolfgang Puck

t (407) 938 9653, **www.wolfgangpuck.com**

Open Sushi bar: 11.30–11, dining room: 6–10.30pm (*expensive–very expensive*)

Smart waterfront dining offering a separate sushi menu, main menu and kids' menu. Lunchtime dishes include fresh-made soups, sandwiches, fish, salads, and the signature Wolfgang Puck pizza. Dinner is an elegant affair with many Asian-American fusion dishes and nouvelle cuisine. Main meals range from steak-and-horseradish mash to Florida grouper with fruit-chipotle relish or salmon with miso broth.

Downtown Disney Pleasure Island

Bongos Cuban Café

t (407) 828 0999

Open Mon–Thu 4–11, Fri–Sat 11–12 midnight. Sun 11–11 (*moderate–expensive*)

Gloria and Emilio Estefan's flagship restaurant features Cuban cuisine served in a lively Latin atmosphere. Black bean or chicken soup, fried plantains, tropical fruit platters, Cuban style steaks, Creole seafood or chicken with yellow rice are among the many authentic dishes on offer. The kids' menu has steak and rice, chicken nuggets or cheeseburger served with fries. The lunch menu has various Cuban sandwiches available. Live music is available in the bar area Fri, Sat 9pm–2am.

Fulton's Crab House

t (407) 934 2628
Open: Lunch and dinner, daily
(*expensive–very expensive*)

This busy seafood restaurant on board a replica paddle steamer offers bar appetizer and cocktails before seating you upstairs in the waterfront dining room. Starters are huge ranging from melt-in-the-mouth oysters and perfectly seasoned mussels to clam chowder and their speciality crab claws. Mains include lobster and crab platters for two, steaks or filet served with or without seafood, scallop pasta and roast chicken. Service is excellent and attentive within the central dining room. There is a separate children's menu featuring spaghetti with tomato sauce, plus shrimp, chicken breast or tenders, hamburger, fish fingers or hotdog served with fries. Children's cocktails and fruit lemonades are also available.

House of Blues Orlando

t (407) 934 2583, **www.**hob.com
Open: Lunch and dinner, daily
Live blues: Thu–Sat at 11pm (*moderate–expensive*)

The menu might just have to play second fiddle to the music at this popular entertainment venue, but if you've a hankering for file gumbo or oven roasted pizza, meatloaf and cornbread you'll find it here. Visit on a Sunday for Gospel Sunday Brunch with some good ole New Orleans cooking followed by a rousing chorus. Outdoor dining areas and a children's menu are available.

Best for...

Desserts	Planet Hollywood, Portobello Yacht Club
Fish & Chips	Fulton's Crab House
Hamburger & Fries	McDonald's Ronald's Fun House, Planet Hollywood
Pasta	Portobello Yacht Club
Sandwiches	Bongos Cuban Café
Seafood	Fulton's Crab House
Steaks	Wolfgang Puck
Tex-Mex	Planet Hollywood

Planet Hollywood

t (407) 827 7827, **www.**planethollywood.com
Open: 11am–1am
(*moderate–expensive*)

It's hard to miss this neon fireball at the entrance to Pleasure Island and once the kids spot it, you've no chance of going anywhere else, at least not on the first night. The menu features American greats, such as the Cobb salad, club sandwiches, burgers and ribs. There are also steaks, tortillas, fajitas and mouthwatering desserts and ice creams on offer.

Portobello Yacht Club

t (407) 934 8888,
Open: Lunch and dinner, daily
(*expensive–very expensive*)

Popular Italian restaurant featuring lunchtime pizzas, salads and chicken, fish and steak dishes. Dinner is a more leisurely affair with starters including wood roasted shrimp and mussels, handmade wild mushroom ravioli and tomato and mozzarella salad. Next comes the meat course with veal, lamb, chicken, beef or even lobster followed by pasta and rounded off (you will be with traditional Italian desserts).

Character meals

Kids can meet their favourite characters for a bite of breakfast, a working lunch or a leisurely dinner at a variety of locations within Walt Disney World® Resort. Character meals tend to be buffet style for convenience and every character visits each table, so don't feel the need to dash across the room and drag characters to your child's table. Do bear in mind that character meals are also available in select resort hotels, *see* below, or that you can still meet and greet characters within the parks and eat your meals elsewhere. For priority seating at any of the restaurants, call, **t** (407) 939 3463.

In the theme parks

Please note all character meals in Disney theme parks require park admission.

Disney's Animal Kingdom®

Donald's Breakfastosaurus at Restaurantosaurus in DinoLand U.S.A., buffet with Donald Duck and friends from park opening until 10.30am daily, adults $17.99, children (3–11) $9.99.

Epcot®

Chip 'n' Dale's Harvest Feast at Garden Grill in The Land with Mickey and his critters, serving lunch from noon to 3 p.m., $20.99, $10.99 ages 3-11; dinner from 5-8 p.m., $22.99, $10.99 ages 3-11.

Princess Storybook Dining at Restaurant Akershus in the Norway pavilion with all the girls: Belle, Jasmine, Snow White, Sleeping Beauty, Mary Poppins, Pocahontas and Mulan. Offering family-style breakfast from 8.30–11.40 daily, adults $21.99, children (3–11) $11.99.

Magic Kingdom®

Once Upon a Time Breakfast at Cinderella's Royal Table in Cinderella Castle with Cinderella and her entourage, daily 8–11, adults $21.99, children (3–11) $11.99.

A Buffet With Character at The Crystal Palace features Pooh and friends from the Hundred Acre Wood, breakfast 8–10.30, adults $17.99, children (3–11) $9.99; lunch 11.30–3, adults $18.99, children (3–11) $10.99; dinner from 4–closing, adults $22.99, children (3–11) $10.99.

Goofy's Liberate Your Appetite Character Dinner at Liberty Tree Tavern in Liberty Square with Goofy, Minnie, Pluto and friends of the free, daily from 4pm, adults $22.99, children (3–11) $10.99.

Character dining in the resort hotels

Beach Club Buffet at Disney's Beach Club Resort with Goofy and friends catching a wave, daily at Cape May Café from 7:30–11, adults $17.99, children (3–11) $9.99.

Chef Mickey's Fun Time Buffet daily at Disney's Contemporary Resort with Mickey and pals cooking up a storm with breakfast from 7–11.30, adults $17.99, children (3–11) $9.99, dinner from 5–9.30, adults $26.99, children (3–11) $11.99.

Just a spoonful of sugar should make the **Supercalifragilistic Breakfast** go down a treat at 1900 Park Fare at Disney's Grand Floridian Resort & Spa, with Mary Poppins and friends, daily from 8–11.10, adults $17.99, children (3–11) $10.99.

Have a ball at **Cinderella's Gala Feast** at 1900 Park Fare at Disney's Grand Floridian Resort & Spa, dinner buffet with Cinderella and courtiers from 4.30–8.20 daily, adults $27.99, children (3–11) $12.99.

Ohana Character Breakfast at Disney's Polynesian Resort, family-style breakfast 7.30–11 with Mickey and friends, adults $17.99, children (3–11) $9.99.

Special occasions

Celebration cakes are available at Disney restaurants for an additional charge and should be ordered 48 hours in advance.

WHERE TO SLEEP

Variety is the spice of life at Walt Disney World® resorts, which vary from the remote and natural to the zany and fabulous. Like the parks, many accommodations are themed so if you like sports or movies or have a penchant for 70s disco or long for the peace of a Caribbean island, you can fulfil your desires. See pp.240–241 for a list of privileges exclusive to Disney resort guests. Booking

Heroes...

1. Ariel (*The Little Mermaid*)
2. Belle (*Beauty and the Beast*)
3. Bob Parr (*The Incredibles*)
4. Buzz Lightyear (*Toy Story*)
5. Flik (*A Bug's Life*)
6. Genie (*Aladdin*)
7. Marlin and Dory (*Finding Nemo*)
8. Merlin (*The Sword in the Stone*)
9. Simba, Timon and Pumba (*The Lion King*)
10. Tinker Bell (*Peter Pan*)
11. Will Turner (*Pirates of the Caribbean*)
12. Woody (*Toy Story*)

and Villains...

1. Amos Slade (*Fox and the Hound*)
2. Aunt Sarah, Si and Am (*Lady and the Tramp*)
3. Captain Hook (*Peter Pan*)
4. Cruella De Vil (*101 Dalmatians*)
5. Edgar (*The Aristocats*)
6. Gaston (*Beauty and the Beast*)
7. Hades (*Hercules*)
8. Jafar (*Aladdin*)
9. Lady Tremaine, Anastasia and Drizella (*Cinderella*)
10. Madame Medusa (*The Rescuers*)
11. Prince John (*Robin Hood*)
12. Ursula (*The Little Mermaid*)

accommodation in resort through Disney can also end up being a lot cheaper than through your tour operator or travel agent – always compare before you buy. Children under 18 stay free in a room when sharing with their parents. For reservations call, **t** (407) 934 7639 or visit, **www**.disneyworld.com

Disney accommodation

Prices are subject to change and are per room per night. Driving directions are available when booking, or call the parks direct. Disney transport links all of the resorts to the parks and recreation areas. Please note: Disney Vacation Club and other investor properties have not been listed here.

Magic Kingdom® Area

Disney's Contemporary Resort

4600 North World Drive, Lake Buena Vista, t (407) 824 1000 (*very expensive*)

1,008 rooms and suites are on offer in this 14-storey deluxe resort. Dining options include the **California Grill**, **Concourse Steakhouse** and **Chef Mickey's**, two lounges, two snack bars and room service. Additional amenities include six tennis courts, jogging track, volleyball court, parasailing, water skiing, boats, playground, childcare centre and two swimming pools. Facilities include boutique shops, games room, laundry service, a beauty shop and health club.

Disney's Fort Wilderness Resort and Campground

4510 North Fort Wilderness Trail, Lake Buena Vista, t (407) 824 2900 (*moderate–very expensive*)

Families will feel a bit more down to earth at this rustic setting, which features 784 campsites, 409 wilderness cabins set in 700-acres of parkland. Campsites are flat, paved spaces with heating lighting and toilet hook-ups, charcoal grills and picnic tables. All campsites have close access to air-conditioned comfort stations with private showers, laundry facilities, vending machines and telephones. Cabins sleep six and are fully air-conditioned with furnished kitchens, bathrooms, TV, VCR, barbecue grills, picnic tables and a private patio deck. Cabin room amenities include hairdryers and foldaway cots. Amenities include tennis courts, water sports craft, beach, fishing, two heated swimming pools and arcade games room. **Meadow** and **Settlement Trading Posts** are on hand for grocery staples and all-day meals are available at **Trail's End Restaurant**. The resort also features nightly campfire and marshmallow roasts with Disney characters and a Disney movie, plus a nightly dinner show at **Pioneer Hall's Hoop-Dee-Doo Musical Revue**.

Disney's Grand Floridian Resort & Spa

4401 Grand Floridian Way, Lake Buena Vista, t (407) 824 3000 (*very expensive*)

867 rooms and suites designed to invoke the golden age of high Victoriana Dining is available at **Citricos**, **Victoria & Albert's**, the **Gasparilla Grill**, **Grand Floridian Café**, **1900 Park Fare**, **Narcoossee's** and in three lounges. Recreation and amenities include boat rentals, swimming, a playground, childcare facility, games room, a health club and laundry facilities.

Disney's Polynesian Resort

1600 Seven Seas Drive, Lake Buena Vista, t (407) 824 2000 (*very expensive*)

This palm-fringed resort has 847 rooms and suites reflecting the laid-back atmosphere of the South Pacific. Dining options include **Ohana**, **Kona Café**, **Captain Cook's**, the **Spirit of Aloha** dinner show, snack bars, two lounges and room service. Resort features include the **Seven Seas Lagoon** and beach area, swimming, boating, jogging, playground, Peter Pan-themed childcare centre, games room, shopping and laundry facilities.

Disney's Wilderness Lodge

901 Timberline Drive, Lake Buena Vista, t (407) 824 3200 (*very expensive*)

Get away from it all in this National Park experience setting where 728 guestrooms and 27 suites let nature back into your life, albeit with all the comforts of a high-class hotel. The centerpiece is the six-storey lobby decked out with teepee-shaped chandeliers, totem poles and an 82-foot-tall stone fireplace, not to mention the bubbling hot spring that cascades through the building and out into the swimming pool (with hot and cold spas). Guest amenities include bike and boat rentals, laundry, games room, children's playground and on-site childcare. Guests have the choice of two full-service restaurants, a snack bar, lounge bar, pool bar and room service.

Epcot® Area

Disney's Caribbean Beach Resort

900 Cayman Way, Lake Buena Vista, t (407) 934 3400 (*very expensive*)

Cast yourself away to the Caribbean at one of these three, bright resort villages located on 200-acres of lakeside property. Most of the 2,112 rooms have water views and feature mini bars and coffee makers. The lake offers plenty of scope for water enthusiasts with boat rentals, swimming. beach, children's playground and themed slides, games room, cycle paths, nature walks, jogging track, laundry facilities and shopping. Children can take part in relaxing evening activities including a spa experiences for ages 10 –14. Well you may as well start them early. Dining options include the **Old Port Royale food court** and **The Captain's Tavern** full-service restaurant.

Disney's Pop Century Resort

1050 Century Drive, Lake Buena Vista, t (407) 934 7639 (*moderate*)

Try not to arrive very early in the morning or too late at night because despite the fact that the doors are still welcomingly open, you will not be able to get your head around this place and will imagine, therefore, that you must be dreaming. You're not. This is the latest hotel in the Disney stable and, as such, it is a melting pot of Imagineering genius with more than a tinge of wacky thrown in for good measure. The buildings of this pastel-hued complex are accessed by covered walkways offering great views of the surrounding environs. There are 2,880 rooms on offer furnished in 1950s, '60s, '70s, '80s and '90s style. Huge fashion icons from each decade dominate the scene from an oversized mobile (cellphone) to a four-storey Rubik's Cube and a towering platform shoe. Recreation includes three pools, a children's pool and themed play areas. Guests can eat throughout the day at the **Everything Pop food court** area or enjoy an evening in the **Classic Concoctions lounge** or **Petals Pool Bar**. The resort is close to Disney's Wide World of Sports Complex (*see* p.234).

Walt Disney World® Swan and Walt Disney World® Dolphin

1200–1500 Epcot Resorts Boulevard, Lake Buena Vista, t (407) 943 3000/4000 (*very expensive*)

These Sheraton-run swan-shaped and dolphin-crested hotels feature 2,267 luxury rooms, 17 restaurants and lounges, four swimming pools, two health clubs and a wide area of recreational activities between them. The hotels are in easy reach of Epcot and Disney-MGM Studios via ferry services and walkways.

Disney's Yacht Club and Beach Club Resorts

1800 Epcot Resorts Boulevard, Lake Buena Vista, t (407) 934 8000 (*very expensive*)

Nautical themed lakeside resorts featuring 621 accommodations in the Yacht Club and a further 576 rooms and suites in the Beach Club. Room feature hardwood floors and balconies or patios with weathered clapboard exteriors invoking Florida's beach retreats. Dine in waterfront style at the **Yacht Club Galley**, **Yachtsman's Steakhouse** or the **Crew's Cup Lounge** or at the beach **Club's Cape May Café** and **Martha's Vineyard Lounge**. Kids will love the old-fashioned ices at **Beaches and Cream**. They'll also having a go at croquet on the lawn, checking out the marina lighthouse or splashing about in **Stormalong Bay** with its three lagoons, spray jets and water slides. **The Ship Shape Health Club** offers a full range of spa and exercise facilities.

Disney's Animal Kingdom® Area

Disney's All-Star Movies Resort

1901 West Buena Vista Drive, Lake Buena Vista, t (407) 939 7333 (*inexpensive–moderate*)

As with its neighbours, the Movies Resort has 1,920 rooms resort and all the usual facilities. Younger kids will love this one all the more though because its kitted out with scenes from their favourite Disney movies such as *101 Dalmatians*, *Toy Story*, and *Fantasia*. There are also two pools, one shaped like the hockey rink in *The Mighty Ducks* and the other from the Sorcerer's Apprentice section of *Fantasia* featuring a Mickey fountain.

Disney's All-Star Music Resort

1801 West Buena Vista Drive, Lake Buena Vista, t (407) 939 6000 (*inexpensive–moderate*)

Much the same as the above, including the mysterious number of 1,920 rooms and the same amenities, this complex of affordable accommodation is bedecked with the trappings of musicals, rock, jazz, calypso, and country music including a towering chorus line and mega jukebox. The on-site pools are also themed – one's a piano and the other's a guitar.

Disney's All-Star Sports Resort

1701 West Buena Vista Drive, Lake Buena Vista, t (407) 939 5000 (*inexpensive–moderate*)

Good value accommodation on a sporty theme with 1,920 rooms featuring vast replicas of recreational objects such as surfboards, basketballs and a baseball-inspired pool. Amenities include a food court, shop, games room, two sports-themed swimming pools and a kiddie pool.

Disney's Animal Kingdom Lodge

2901 Osceola Parkway, t (407) 938 3000 (*expensive*)

If your children are yearning to be close to animals, then a stay at this beautifully designed African-themed lodge, to the west of the Animal Kingdom park, will certainly satisfy their needs. The comfortably furnished rooms offer views of the poolside area and some look out over an area of parkland where zebras, giraffes and several species of African antelope roam free. The 1,293-room, six-storey resort is styled in a horseshoe shape reminiscent of an African *kraal*. The best times to view animals in the adjacent 33-acre savannah is early morning, at dusk or during designated feeding times, which are posted in the reception area. Children's events, a kids' club and lovely pool complete the facilities at this superior lodging. There are two full-service restaurants, including the imaginative and first class buffet style restaurant **Boma**, plus a mezzanine lounge and a quick-service café with poolside dining.

Disney's Coronado Springs Resort

1000 West Buena Vista Drive, Lake Buena Vista, t (407) 939 1000 (*expensive*)

Mexican and Southwest US influences combine at this mid-range 1,921-room resort situated beside a 15-acre lagoon. A five-storey Mayan pyramid dominates a series of pools featuring secluded bathing spots and a family-sized fun pool with a water slide. The on-site restaurant, the **Maya Grill**, features authentic Mexican specialities cooked over a wood fire. There's also a food court for satisfying even the fussiest tastes, a lounge, poolside bar and light room service for other dining options. The resort also features the **La Vida Health Club**, a salon, bike and water sports rentals, arcade games, beach volleyball court and children's playground.

Downtown Disney® Area

Disney's Port Orleans Resort-French Quarter

2201 Port of Orleans Drive, Lake Buena Vista, t (407) 934 5000 (*moderate*)

Feel the magical rhythm of the French Quarter-style at these 1,008 mid-priced accommodations situated between Epcot and the Downtown Disney Marketplace. The resort is adjacent to Disney's Port Orleans Resort-Riverside and commands a lovely 325-acre stretch of woodland with boat rentals and a lagoon pool with a sea serpent slide. Guests can dine at the **Sassagoula Floatworks food court**, which offers pizza, bakery goods, burgers and Creole specialities.There are on-site lounges, a games room and retail shops but the highlight of a stay here has to be the chance to catch the riverboat over to the Marketplace and Downtown Disney Pleasure Island for shopping, dining and fun.

Disney's Port Orleans Resort-Riverside

t (407) 934 6000 (*expensive*)

If you want to spend a night on the bayou this resort has 2,048 riverside rooms in southern-style mansions and low-level rustic accommodations. Of the many pools on-site, Ol' Man Island, is the best for kids, with slides, rope swings and playgrounds surrounding a swimming hole. There are also quiet pools, a marina with boat rentals, games room, lounges and a gift shop. Dining options include a food court, restaurant and pizza delivery service but families can also opt to use the riverboat service and hop across the water to Downtown Disney for their tea.

Hotel benefits

Extra Magic Hour

Each day, Disney resort guests get to enter one of the parks an hour before they open to the general public and up to three hours after they close. Do you need any other reason to book yourself a room?

Convenient transportation

Free shuttle buses, boats and monorails transport Disney resort guests directly to any area in Walt Disney World®, allowing guests to explore the parks and attractions their way.

Guest services

The guest services team at the reservations desk in each of the resorts can arrange park tickets, dining reservations and golf, as well as advice on other activities.

Guaranteed entry

The parking areas may be full but resort guests using Disney transportation are guaranteed entry to all Walt Disney World® theme parks and water parks.

Character dining

Avoid the rush for tickets to dine with characters in the theme parks, Disney's Beach Club Resort, Disney's Polynesian Resort, Disney's Grand Floridian Resort & Spa and Disney's Contemporary Resort feature daily character breakfasts.

Central billing

Your resort ID card issued at check-in can be used as a charge card for food and shopping throughout Walt Disney World®.

Babysitting

In-room babysitting can be arranged in your resort hotel through Kids Nite Out, **t** (407) 828 0920, at extra cost. Make sure you book at least 24 hours in advance.

Childcare

Resort childcare facilities are available to guests at additional cost. Children aged 4–12 (must be fully toilet trained) can enjoy fun and games at the **Neverland Club** at Disney's Polynesian Resort or watch classic Disney movies, play video games or with toys at **Disney's Sandcastle Club** at Disney's Beach Club Resort. The **Mouseketeer Clubhouses** at Disney's Contemporary Resort and Disney's Grand Floridian Resort & Spa, Cub's Den at Disney's Wilderness Lodge and **Simba's Cubhouse** at Disney's Animal Kingdom Lodge also offer childcare facilities.

Sports and recreation

In-resort sports range from tennis, swimming, boating, gyms and golf. Other activities available to resort guests include water skiing, fishing, canoeing, surfing, parasailing, riding, carriage rides, playgrounds, croquet and shuffleboard.

Themed dinner shows

At Disney's Polynesian Resort, guests can enjoy the sounds of the South Seas with **Disney's Spirit of Aloha Dinner Show** or have a hoedown and wild-west cookout at the **Hoop-Dee-Doo Musical Revue** at Disney's Fort Wilderness Resort and Campground.

Non-Disney hotels

These hotels are all within the Walt Disney World® Resort.

Best Western Lake Buena Vista

2000 Hotel Plaza Boulevard, Lake Buena Vista, t (407) 828 2424, www.orlandoresorthotel.com (*expensive*)

This 325-room resort offers family sized rooms with king size beds and separate sofa beds. Families can also choose to stay in a suite, which features a separate living room area, balcony and oversized bathroom. Amenities include casual restaurants, lounges, a grocery store, Disney Gift Shop, heated swimming pools, coffee maker and hair dryer and TV with pay-per-view movies and Nintendo games. There's also an on-site video games room, babysitting service and over-18s nightclub. Courtesy buses run to Disney parks and other Walt Disney World® Resort attractions.

Doubletree Guest Suites Resort

2305 Hotel Plaza Boulevard, Lake Buena Vista, FL 32830, t (407) 934 1000, www.doubletreeguestsuites.com (*expensive*)

Surrounded by leafy foliage, this 229-room resort is great for families since accommodation is all suites with their own living room including a sofa bed and separate bedroom area, which can either be a twin or king-size bedroom. Rooms come equipped with three TVs (Disney Channel is free), a microwave, fridge and coffee maker, plus a supply of chocolate chip cookies, so you needn't eat out every night. Resort amenities include a swimming pool and kiddie pool, an exercise centre and jogging paths, games room and video arcade, children's check-in desk, kids' theatre and tennis courts. Casual dining is on offer at **Streamers Restaurant** and the on-site market offers, food, snacks and breakfast items, along with gifts, stamps and necessities. Services include a courtesy bus to all the Disney parks, plus guaranteed access and priority seating at Disney restaurants.

Grosvenor Resort Hotel

1850 Hotel Plaza Boulevard, Lake Buena Vista, t (407) 828 4444, www.grosvenorresort.com (*expensive*)

This attractive 626-room lakeside resort features **Children's Suites** with separate accommodation for the kids in a partition room with bunk beds and a TV. Amenities in the main room include a TV with video games and pay per view movies, hair dryer and refrigerator, plus tea and coffee making facilities. The hotel also has two heated swimming pools, a playground, thermal spa, volleyball and tennis courts, games room, shuffleboard, a casual poolside restaurant and cafés with a Disney character breakfast three days a week. The hotel also offers transport, childcare facilities and a range of Disney benefits.

The Hilton

1751 Hotel Plaza Boulevard, Lake Buena Vista, t (407) 827 4000, www.hilton.com (*expensive*)

814-room resort with family suites and non-smoking rooms throughout. Facilities include a coffee maker, minibar, in-room movies, a range of casual dining restaurants and lounges with children's menus, two swimming pools, fitness centre and tropical outdoor spa. For families there's a babysitting service, cots and highchairs, plus kids movies and games are available in your room. Disney services include an on-site Character Breakfast and Extra Magic Hours at Disney theme parks.

Hotel Royal Plaza

1905 Hotel Plaza Boulevard, Lake Buena Vista, t (407) 828 2828, www.royalplaza.com (*expensive*)

Due to hurricane damage in 2004, the hotel is undergoing landscaping renovation and has chosen to update hotel facilities in the process. As a result a new-look Royal Plaza is due to reopen in September 2005. Highlights will include new interior décor with flamboyant draperies, sumptuous carpeting and new 'Royal Beds'. Additional guest room amenities will include internet access, a hair dryer, refreshment centre, TVs and step-out balconies or patios. See website for updates.

Wyndham Palace Resort & Spa

1900 Buena Vista Drive, Lake Buena Vista, t (407) 827 2727, www.wyndham.com (*expensive*)

This well-appointed hotel has the advantage of being the best of both worlds – it's in the Walt Disney World® Resort but also is minutes away from Orlando's other attractions such as Seaworld® and Universal Stuidos®. Set on a pretty lake, the 27-storey hotel has 1,014 rooms and suites offering spectacular views over the world of Disney from its upper floors. Amenities include a spa, sauna, three heated swimming pools, a beauty salon, fitness centre, marina with boat rental, plus tennis and volleyball courts. Guests can also make use of free transport to the Disney Resorts, book dinner at Disney restaurants and enjoy a character breakfast in the **Watercress Café**. The hotel has several restaurants and lounges, which range from casual pasta and steakhouse fare to fine dining, Kids can make use of the playground and games room.

Walt Disney World® Resort – The Parks

13

Disney's Magic Kingdom®

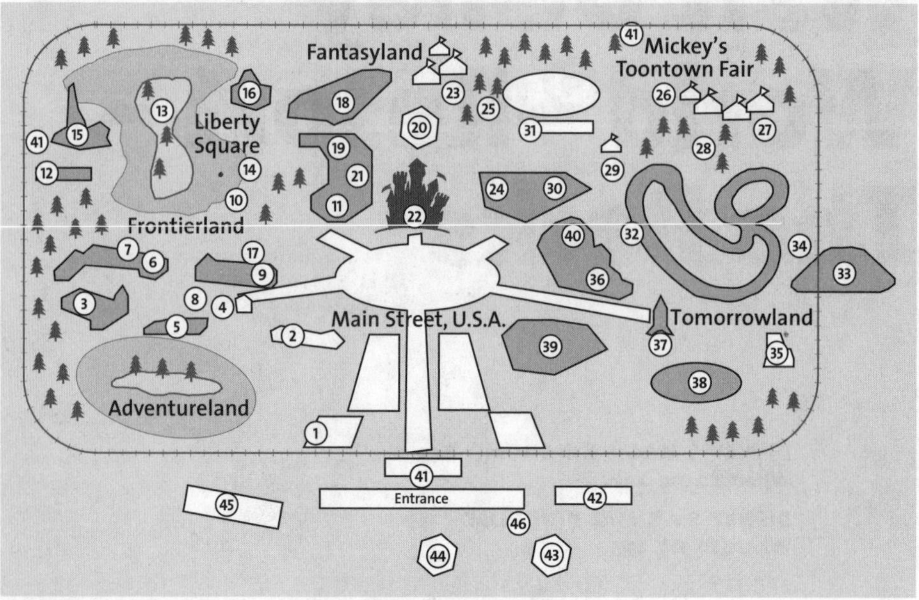

Map © Econoguide Travel Books www.econoguide.com

1 City Hall
2 First Aid
3 Pirates of the Caribbean
4 Swiss Family Treehouse
5 Jungle Cruise
6 Enchanted Tiki Room
7 Country Bear Jamboree
8 The Magic Carpets of Aladdin
9 Diamond Horseshoe Saloon Revue
10 Liberty Square Riverboat
11 The Hall of Presidents
12 Splash Mountain
13 Tom Sawyer Island
14 Mike Fink Keelboats
15 Big Thunder Mountain Railroad
16 The Haunted Mansion
17 Frontierland Shootin' Arcade
18 It's a Small World
19 Peter Pan's Flight
20 Cinderella's Golden Carousel
21 *Mickey's PhilharMagic*
22 Cinderella Castle
23 Dumbo the Flying Elephant
24 Snow White's Scary Adventures
25 Ariel's Grotto
26 Toontown Hall of Fame
27 Mickey's and Minnie's Country Houses
28 The Barnstormer at Goofy's Wiseacre Farm
29 Mad Tea Party
30 The Many Adventures of Winnie the Pooh
31 Fantasyland Character Festival
32 Tomorrowland Indy Speedway
33 Space Mountain
34 Tomorrowland Transit Authority
35 Tomorrowland Stage
36 Stitch's Great Escape
37 Astro Orbiter
38 Carousel of Progress
39 *The Timekeeper*
40 Buzz Lightyear's Space Ranger Spin
41 Walt Disney World Railroad station
42 Magic Kingdom bus transportation
43 Ferryboat to Parking
44 Boats to Discovery Island and Fort Wilderness
45 Monorail station
46 Stroller rental

DISNEY'S MAGIC KINGDOM®

Depending on the day you arrive, this should really be your first port of call. (Sun, Tues, Wed and Fri are the best days to visit and Sat is by far the busiest). Get there early and allow a full day; you can always mop up what you missed later in the week, if you've bought a **5 or 7-day theme park pass** (*see* p.227). The great thing about the Magic Kingdom® is that it's not just about the rides, it's also about pace. The parades, shows and smaller attractions, even the park transport all contribute to the fun, so go with the flow and alternate excitement with a chance to just soak up the atmosphere. If you've been to Paris, comparisons are inevitable but the beauty of Disney is that no two rides are exactly the same. You can even go on the same ride in the same park and, depending on where you sit, you'll have a different experience from one day to the next. Being the first Magic Kingdom®, Florida's maiden amusement park has had to keep adding to its line-up to remain up-to-date but it is big enough to take it. As one Disney bus driver pointed out – the Magic Kingdom®'s car park alone could house the whole of Disneyland® and all its car parks, and still have room for cars. The Magic Kingdom® is vast, so it has room to evolve as well as to hold on to its vintage attractions. A good example of this is the **Carousel of Progress** in Tomorrowland®. It's a classic. And as for the future, look no further than **Stitch's Great Escape**; it's right around the corner.

Main Street U.S.A.®

Main attractions

Walt Disney World® Railroad

If you want to get an overview of the park and skip round to the big thrills of **Frontierland®** or see who's hanging out round at Mickey's house in **Mickey's Toontown® Fair**, hop aboard the steam train.

City Hall

This is the place to make reservations for lunch and dinner, if you haven't done so already. They'll also answer any queries you may have about attractions, shows, shopping and anything and everything to help you make the most of your day. Check the notice board as well for show and waiting times.

Tomorrowland®

Main attractions

Space Mountain® (FastPass)

The front car is definitely the best and scariest. Before you is darkness, behind you other screaming riders. That disembodied strangled wail is you! Children who don't like being disorientated or plunging down steep tracks in the pitch dark will not enjoy it. Daredevil school kids will love it. Minimum height 44".

Tomorrowland Indy Speedway

This is hugely popular so get here early or late in the day. It looks more complicated than it actually is because the cars are fixed to the twisty track, so there's no way you can crash but you can zip along at a fair pace. The struggle will be working out who's going to drive but if your child is too small to reach the accelerator, you can put your foot down and let them steer thus satisfying everyone's need for speed. Minimum height to ride alone 52".

Buzz Lightyear's Space Ranger Spin (FastPass)

And now its time to zap 'em all as you board your personal Star Cruiser and ride the galaxy with Buzz, aiming your laser at the weird and wonderful aliens that you pass. The ability to spin your car adds to the fun as you lock sights with your target only to be whizzed around in another direction by your co-rider before you've even fired a round. Of course, if you're travelling solo you can clock up as many points as you want and the more you get the higher your space ranking at the end. It's fun for younger kids because there's nothing scary and they like being able to move the cars around and it's seriously addictive for adults who fancy themselves as something of a hot shot.

Stitch's Great Escape (FastPass)

You're here to witness the naughty antics of one Experiment 626 – a.k.a. Stitch – captured by the Galactic Federation and brought to a processing centre for neutralization. Guests are roped in to ensure there's no funny business but it's soon clear that there's no holding this little critter. Stitch, held in a traction beam in the centre of the room, is determined to get out using any means. He proceeds to show you exactly what a six-legged alien is made of (DNA and all) with funny, amazing and erm, smelly results. Along with Stitch,there are several other characters from the film, including **Captain Gantu** and **Agent Pleakley**, who are voiced by the original actors.

Other fun

Astro Orbiter

If you've a head for heights this spacecraft ride is top of the bill. It's a gentle ride for young kids and offers great views over the park even if you are a little windswept afterwards.

The Timekeeper

Disney's eternal quest to bring you new adventures in film is the idea behind this **Circle-Vision 360°** presentation where viewers join **Jules Verne** and **H.G. Wells** on a time travelling voyage to Paris future and Paris past. Kids will love trying to keep up with all the images flying by and seeing a city transformed before their eyes. (Seasonal operation).

Walt Disney's Carousel of Progress

See 100 years pass before your eyes as a series of mannequins equipped with audio-animatronics lead you through man's major advancements using a series of dioramas. A nice diversion if you have the time. (Seasonal operation).

Tomorrowland Transit Authority

If your kids love monorails (and most of them do) then this elevated train ride through the inner workings of **Space Mountain®** will be a fun diversion if they need a little time out.

Mickey's Toontown® Fair

Main attractions

Minnie's Country House and Mickey's Country House

Come and nose around the two mouse houses. Well, you don't expect them to live together, do you? Come and gawp at their bright interior décors and see if **Minnie** is any good with a hammer or if **Mickey** ever pushes a broom around. You'll be pleased to know they both pass muster. There are even some interactive elements. Head for the gazebo to say 'hi' to Minnie and the Judge's Tent to meet 'the Mickster'.

Did you know?
Mickey has about 175 different outfits while Minnie has 200? That's a lot of wardrobe space. Perhaps these are just their weekend cottages after all.

Toontown Hall of Fame

Pluto, Goofy, Daisy and **Donald, Chip** and **Dale, Prince John, Pooh, Eeyore** and **Tigger** are all regulars here. There are usually three lines for meeting them and you're never sure who'll be waiting behind the door. If your kids are nervous about certain characters or impatient to meet their favourites, ask a cast member to let you know which line is for which character or pop round the back and ask people coming out. That way you'll not have waited in vain and may be able to steer the kids past the merchandise before they know what's hit them.

The Barnstormer at Goofy's Wiseacre Farm

Kids can make a bit of an entrance into the world of coaster fun on this short family-orientated ride. You're piloting a crop-dusting plane through the barnyard when, in typical Goofy fashion, the plane dips and dives along its track and you end up in the chicken coop. Minimum height to ride 35".

Other fun

Donald's Boat

Let the kids clamber aboard **Donald's** craft and cool off in the spray jets. A spare T-shirt might be handy.

Fantasyland®

Main attractions

Peter Pan's Flight (FastPass)

Another huge crowd-puller where the queues are phenomenal by mid afternoon. If it is a must-see, put it at the top of your list and wield that FastPass to fly in a pirate ship over London at night and on to Neverland where Peter must take on the fearsome Hook. The sets and characters are brilliant and it's a nice gentle experience for young riders.

Mickey's Philharmagic (FastPass)

This 3-D theatre show is the best in the park full of trademark Disney surprises, a superb musical score and lots of antics courtesy of one **Donald Duck**. Mr Duck has taken it upon himself to wear Mickey's magic hat and conduct the band. Naturally, with the meddlesome drake at the helm the music is likely to be somewhat improvised and soon Donald realizes that there's more to being in charge of an orchestra than simply waving a baton. It's a great show that takes you through movie clips galore and finishes with a suitably big surprise.

The Many Adventures of Winnie the Pooh (FastPass)

In which we enter **Pooh's** honey-drenched world for a gentle respite from the big thrills. It's a very blustery day in the Hundred Acre Wood and **Kanga** is trying to stop **Roo** from flying like a kite and the pages of Pooh's storybook are blowing hither and thither. There are darker bits with **Heffalumps** and **Woozles** lurking but it's a really sweet ride where the highlights are getting to travel in a honey pot and to bounce along with the one and only **Tigger**.

Snow White's Scary Adventures

Or not so scary, depending on whether your kids are made of sterner stuff. Riding in one of the **Seven Dwarves**' mine carts, you proceed through a series of tableaux showing how the lovely princess is tricked by the wicked queen. The evil old crone pops up from time to time but she's not so horrendous off screen as on. To offset the frights, there are more moments with our lovely heroine and her forest friends, plus the inevitable happy ending. Hurrah!

Dumbo the Flying Elephant

For another good view of the park, fly high with **Dumbo** and co. There are 16 moveable Pachyderms, which are really best appreciated later in the day when the air freshens and the crowds thin. You get great views of all the lights across the park as well.

Other fun

Cinderella's Golden Carousel

This is a lovely old-fashioned carousel ride that has three different-sized, hand-carved wooden horses to choose from and lap straps so that parents of very young children can take them for a gentle spin.

"It's a small world"

Diminutive dolls from around the world and plinky, plinky music. Toddlers love it so, hard cheese, there's no escape.

Liberty Square

Main attractions

The Haunted Mansion (FastPass)

Get into the grave with this spooktacular attraction that combines visual trickery, special effects and a little bit of otherworldly 'matter'. Like the eponymous 2003 film, this is much more of a hoot than a howl. Pre-school children with lively imaginations might find it a bit much but older kids will think it tame.

Other fun

The Hall of Presidents

This cast of old statesmen is truly impressive, especially for children with an interest in American

Speed coasting

Here's a quick route through the park for avoiding the crowds and pacing your visit to suit everyone's tastes. Moving in an anti-clockwise direction from **Main Street**, head straight for **Tomorrowland®** and pick up a **FastPass** for **Space Mountain** before joining the queue for the Tomorrowland **Indy Speedway**. After this, clock up **Buzz Lightyear's Space Ranger Spin**, get a **FastPass** for **Stitch's Great Escape**. Try to accomplish this and the **Astro Orbiter** before lunch. Take a quick dip through **Mickey's Toontown® Fair** where you can get another **Fastpass** for **Peter Pan's Flight** and something to eat between attractions. Then it's on to **Frontierland®** for another **Fastpass** to either **Big Thunder Mountain Railroad** or **Splash Mountain®** (depending on which has the longer queue) before catching a ride to **Tom Sawyer's Island**. The kids can let off steam on rope ladders and in the caves, though hang on to your toddlers who may be easily misplaced along the twisty paths and in the dark caverns. It's a breath of fresh air and, if you time it right, you can watch the **parade** from across the water. If you bring binoculars or a video camera you'll be able to see the whole show from the rather special vantage point of the island's fort. After a snack while waiting for the return ferry, it's time to head back and take in **Adventureland®'s** top draws – **Pirates of the Caribbean, The Jungle Cruise** and **Aladdin's Flying Carpets** before boarding the train back to **Fantasyland®** for a nice sit down while you enjoy **Mickey's Philharmagic**.

politics. The show consists of film footage related to the history of the American Presidency and the constitution combined with 3-D animatronics and sound that bring several former presidents to life. Hear **Abraham Lincoln's** thoughts on the rights of man and specially recorded contributions from **George Bush** and **Bill Clinton**, recorded from the White House Oval Room. It's stirring stuff.

Liberty Square Riverboat

Circumnavigate **Tom Sawyer's** Island on this replica paddleboat. It's very popular for views over the park and is a nice treat for families with young kids.

Frontierland®

Main attractions

Splash Mountain® (FastPass)

This is the other big thrill in the park, where you start out laughing dryly and end up with a gushing guffaw. Riding the waves in a hollow log on the trail of **Brer Rabbit**, you'll see guitar-strummin' crocs and fluffy ducks, plus a model of the **Liberty Square Riverboat**. There are good views over the park on this 10-minute ride, giving you ample opportunity to take in what's in store for you on the **Big Thunder Mountain Railroad** next door. And so it goes on through caves and over two or three smallish drops before cranking you up just a little bit higher for the big splash. Minimum height to ride 40".

Big Thunder Mountain Railroad (FastPass)

Not as mad and bad as its Parisian cousin but nonetheless a good old giggle. The best time to ride is at night when the track feels a little bit faster and the queues are on the wane. It's a quick trip but if you're get seats in the front or back it's a wild ride. Minimum height to ride 40". Stick with the train theme and take a trip on the Walt Disney World® Railroad before or afterwards (*see* p.245).

Other fun

Tom Sawyer Island

Take some time out at this tropical isle, accessed only by ferry, where the kids can run riot and play king of the castle. Stop for a picnic lunch and quench your thirst at the water fountains before heading back to the mainland and the mayhem.

Country Bear Jamboree

Have a rootin' tootin' hoedown at Grizzly Hall. Kids can try out their line dancing moves and shake a tail with ole Wendell and his banjo pickin' bruins.

Adventureland®

Main attractions

Pirates of the Caribbean

Well shiver me timbers there's a horrible horde of pirates at large. You're on board ship, surrounded by rogues, bloodcurdling shouts, a clash of steel and the roar of cannon fire echoing in the gloom. A clutch of skeletons are an ominous warning. Witness the lives of the hapless sailors who braved these treacherous seas in search of the fabled treasure that's said to be buried about these parts. See the feckless travellers being sold into slavery and tortured for their gold and the mad captain, drunk amid his booty, who will never reach the shore. It's a desperate quest for an elusive prize, so landlubbers need not apply. There are comic vignettes at every turn and superbly crafted moving models keep the kids alert. The only addition they could possibly make to improve the proceedings is to bring in Johnny Depp. Yeaharrh!

Jungle Cruise (FastPass)

This jolly boat ride floats past elephants taking a shower and hippos hungry for a bite of fresh tourist. The jokes come thick and fast, as does the parade of fauna, including giraffes, zebras and lions. It's lush and convincing but not as much fun as seeing the real thing in Disney's Animal Kingdom® (*see* p.250). A nice jaunt, especially for young children.

The Magic Carpets of Aladdin

This mild but fun ride has you sitting on a flying carpet dodging the spitting camels.

Other fun

Swiss Family Treehouse

For a bird's eye view of the park climb up to check out the Swiss Family's chalet-style hideout, which has lots of handy gadgets.

The Enchanted Tiki Room Under New Management

Meet **Iago** the irrepressible sidekick from *Aladdin* and long-suffering **Zazu** from *The Lion King* at the

Tiki Room where they're taking over the show by whipping the chorus into shape and adding some high-flying numbers. This quirky indoor attraction involves numerous robotic flappers and tweeters (birds) who either crack jokes or sing along parrot fashion (sorry, couldn't resist making at least one corny wisecrack in this palace of puns).

Where to shop

It's more a case of where not to, as every corner has a stall and every stall has something that will catch someone's eye. *See* **Disney Need to Know**, p.230, for shopping survival tips. The best toys are found in areas with a strong theme like **Mickey's Star Traders** in Tomorrowland® where you can pick up Sci-Fi themed articles or, in Fantasyland®, **Pooh's Thotful Spot** for Pooh memorabilia and **Tinker Bell's Treasures**, which has all things fairy as well as soft toys. The other places to pick up souvenirs are in the **Pirates** and **Agrrabah Bazaars** and in the clothing and collectibles stores along **Main Street**.

Where to eat

It's predominantly a fast-food small world, after all, but improvements such as sugar-free desserts and more salad items are beginning to appear. In general, a sit-down restaurant is likely to have more choice and a wider range of healthy options than a counter service diner. For Character meals, *see* **Disney Need to know** p.236. The main dining area is around **Main Street U.S.A.®**. For more information about Walt Disney World® dining, call, **t** (407) 939 3463.

Main Street U.S.A.®

Best for snacks

Main Street Bakery Cookies, pastries and coffee for that early morning energy boost.

Plaza Ice cream Parlour Old-fashioned ices to cool kids down on a sunny day.

Best for a quick bite

The Plaza Restaurant Deli sandwiches and burgers, plus sundaes. Outdoor seating is available.

Best for family meals

Tony's Town Square Restaurant This friendly Italian is styled after the restaurant where Lady and the Tramp go *tête-a-tête* over a bowl of pasta. Offers steak dishes, chicken, salads, as well as pizza and pasta. Reservations recommended.

The Crystal Palace Buffet meals with character dining featuring Pooh, Tigger, Eeyore and friends.

Tomorrowland®

Best for snacks

Auntie Gravity's Galactic Goodies Smoothies, ice cream, hot and cold drinks.

Best for a quick bite

Cosmic Ray's Starlight Cafe Fresh salads, burgers, roasted chicken, soups and sandwiches, plus juice, water and soft drinks. There's an automated crooner in one section for added entertainment.

Best for family meals

Tomorrowland Terrace Noodle Station

There's lots of outdoor seating and views of Cinderella's Castle from the terrace. The kid's menu offers chicken with rice or noodles, a drink, jelly and a fortune cookie. Adult fare includes Shrimp Pad Thai, salads and chicken or vegetable noodle dishes.

Mickey's Toontown® Fair

Best for snacks

Toontown Farmers' Market Handy if the kids are flagging while queuing to meet the characters.

Fantasyland®

Best for snacks

Mrs Potts' Cupboard Soft drinks, milkshakes, sundaes and ice cream.

Enchanted Grove Coffees, fruit 'Slushies' and juices.

Best for a quick bite

The Pinocchio Village Haus Burgers, hot dogs, fries, sandwiches and salads made to order.

Best for family meals

Cinderella's Royal Table Reserve a table in the home of the ultimate royal, Cinderella. Buffet breakfasts include fruit, pastries, eggs, cereal and toast; buffet lunches have a choice of five main dishes plus salad and soup to start, and dessert. The dinner menu offers inventive American cooking, including rib of beef, chicken breast and baked salmon dishes. Children will love the flag-waving, medieval décor and walking up the winding staircase to their table (a lift is available). Dress to impress. Advance booking is strongly recommended, especially for character breakfast and lunches (up to 90 days in advance!).

Liberty Square

Best for snacks

Sleepy Hollow Cake, snacks and hot and cold drinks. There's also a fruit and vegetable wagon near the Columbia Harbor House (see below).

Best for a quick bite

Columbia Harbor House Clam chowder, fish or chicken baskets, sandwiches and vegetarian chilli are among the choices at this counter service restaurant. Children can have either macaroni cheese or chicken strips served with grapes, a drink and cheese biscuits for around $3.99.

Best for family meals

Liberty Tree Tavern Dine colonial-style with Disney characters.The buffet dinner is carvery-style with roast beef, pork loin and turkey. At lunchtime there are no special guests and the menu is à la carte with beef, chicken and fish dishes, plus vegetarian options and salads. Kids can have burgers, hot dogs or chicken strips with fries or macaroni and cheese with fruit. Reservations recommended.

Frontierland®

Best for snacks

Frontierland Fries McDonald's drinks and snacks, well there had to be one around here somewhere.

Best for a quick bite

Pecos Bill Cafe Saloon style diner with burgers, hot dogs, wrap sandwiches and a chicken salad that's served with distinctive house coleslaw.

Adventureland®

Best for snacks

Aloha Isle Fresh fruit and juices (making a nice change from all the fizzy stuff), desserts and coffee.

Agrabah Bazaar Graze your way through the stall selling fruits and exotic sweets.

Best for a quick bite

Sunshine Tree Terrace Ice creams, fruit 'Slushies', frozen yoghurts, hot and cold drinks and snacks.

El Pirata y el Perico Restaurante Mexican fast fare including nachos, salad, tacos and empanadas. Kids get tacos with cookies and a drink.

DISNEY'S ANIMAL KINGDOM®

There's a gentle pace to Disney's Animal Kingdom®, which sprawls across more Florida acres than any other Disney park and features lots of leafy trails and open-air eateries. The park is around five times the size of the Magic Kingdom®, although much of it is a reserve where the animals run free.

Tots and younger school children will love to see all the animals. The **Jungle Parade** is among the best of all the parks but, if it's big thrills you're after, you'll have to wait for **Expedition Everest™** to open in 2006. Pick a **Kids' Discovery Club Guide** at the entrance to the first trail you visit and answer a few questions to receive a stamp. Collect all six and you'll get a special Rafiki stamp confirming that your child is a friend of the animals.

The park is especially nice when it rains and steam rising from the paths and dripping foliage make you feel as if you are in a tropical rainforest.

That is, until you are confronted by the odd, end-of-the-pier attractions in **DinoLand**. This mish-mash of extinct creatures and even more ancient roller coasters is still a big hit with the kids who will want to ride the **TriceraTop Spin and Primeval Whirl**. The big attraction is **DINOSAUR®** a bone-rattling journey through a primeval swamp where kindly leaf-eaters and fearsome carnivores lurk in the murk. A couple of exciting new crowd-pullers are planned for the **Happiest Celebration on Earth**. The first will certainly enliven the proceedings at DinoLand as **Lucky**, the free-roaming audio-animatronics dinosaur plods into view. He's a marvel of cutting-edge technology and tours the park with his trainer doing the meet-and-greet rounds. Later in the celebration year, the 200-ft structure looming over the park will transform into **Expedition Everest™**; a snow-packed runaway train ride involving a close encounter with a yeti.

Camp Minnie-Mickey

Main attractions

Festival of the Lion King

This rip-roaring show takes places in a 1,375-seat theatre and involves acrobatics, stilt-walking, dramatic storytelling, sing-along songs, fire

Disney's Animal Kingdom®

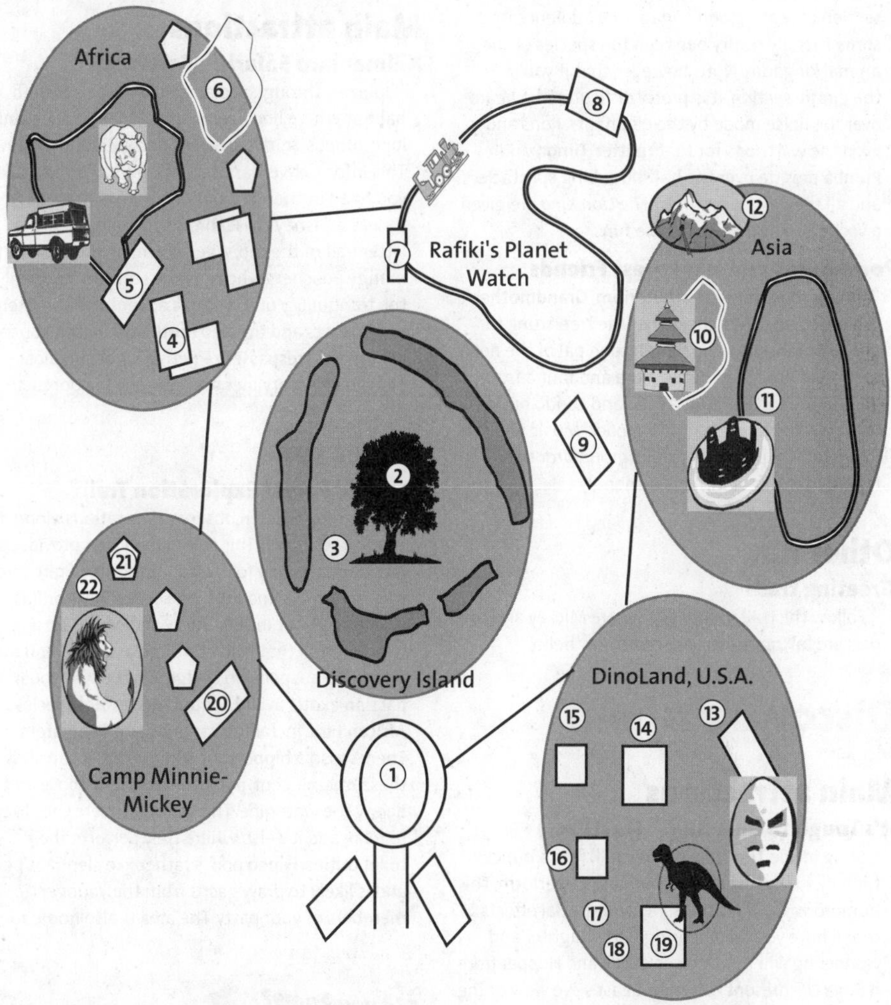

Map © Econoguide Travel Books www.econoguide.com

1 The Oasis
2 The *Tree of Life*
3 *It's Tough to Be a Bug!*
4 Harambe
5 Kilimanjaro Safaris
6 Pangani Forest Exploration Trail
7 Wildlife Express Train
8 Conservation Station
9 *Flights of Wonder*
10 Maharjah Jungle Trek
11 Kali River Rapids
12 Expedition Forest
13 *Tarzan Rocks!*
14 Fossil Preparation Lab
15 The Boneyard
16 Cretaceous Trail
17 Primeval Whirl
18 TriceraTop Spin
19 Dinosaur
20 *Pocahontas and Her Forest Friends*
21 Character greeting area
22 *Festival of the Lion King*

juggling, dancing and high wire acts. The four quadrants of the stage are topped by enormous animal puppets that each preside over a different section of seating and engage the audience in some friendly rivalry between the species of the animal kingdom. Note, however, that if you're in the giraffe section, it is pretty difficult to be heard over the noise made by the elephants, lions and even the warthogs for that matter. **Timon** and **Pumba** preside over the half-hour long spectacle and all the best songs from *The Lion King* are given a vociferous airing. Join in the fun.

Pocahontas and Her Forest Friends

At this more modest auditorium, **Grandmother Willow** speaks from inside her the tree-trunk to advise **Pocahontas** and her raccoon pal of the need to protect America's native flora and fauna from destructive forces. Florida road and condo builders beware – the forest is fighting back. Music and sets from the film provide the background for the telling of this 12-minute eco-friendly tale.

Other fun

Greeting trails

Follow the trail to find out where Mickey and his pals are taking some time out to say hello.

Discovery Island

Main attractions

It's Tough to be a Bug!® (FastPass)

Snug inside **The Tree of Life** you'll find a bunch of friendly, funny insects just bursting to perform. This humorous show features 3-D and special effects that'll have your kids roaring with laughter and wondering where to look next. **Flik** and **Hopper** from *A Bug's Life* present this mini-beast's eye view of the meaning of life. Very young children might not like-some of the noises and effects but most will love the puppet techniques and 3-D film tricks.

Other fun

Discovery Island® Trails

Take a walk around the Tree of Life to discover tortoises, lemurs and tamarins. Look for the insects buzzing among the flowers and hiding in the grass.

Africa

Main attractions

Kilimanjaro Safaris® (FastPass)

Journey through 100 acres of African-inspired habitat where lions, zebra, crocodiles, giraffes, antelope, hippos, rhinos, gazelles and elephants roam. This informative, narrated, off-road safari trip takes you to an authentic wildlife preserve. Naturally, there's a Disney twist thrown in to spice up the latter half of the trip, when you're on the lookout for mangy poachers who must be stopped. Suddenly the tranquillity of the scenic adventure is shattered by gunshots and the jeep hurtles off into the bushes to stop the trespassers – perhaps not the most plausible of storylines and possibly in poor taste.

Other fun

Pangani Forest Exploration Trail®

From rough-hewn observation stations along a shady forest path, this self-guided tour provides a great opportunity for a close-up study of rare birds, fish, mammals and reptiles. See mighty **gorillas** lounging about in their rocky enclosures on a winding trail that leads through a canyon and over a swaying suspension bridge. On the way you'll pass an exotic aviary containing several species of **African** bird, including canaries and bee-eaters. There's also a **hippo pool** where visitors can view these magnificent, portly beasts from above and below the waterline. The water is where they like to relax and it's also where they perform their toilet duties. Hippo poo is rather like elephant poo and is likely to draw gasps from the younger members of your party. The area is also home to

Did you know?
If you stay at the Animal Kingdom Lodge you can get close up to giraffe, kudu, flamingos, zebra, from vantage points within the hotel. So if your children can't get enough of the creatures in the Animal Kingdom® then a stayover in the breathtakingly beautiful Lodge will do the trick. The Lodge also is home to Boma, quite possibly the best Disney resort restaurant, if not the best place to eat at any Disney property in Florida.

Speed coasting

The best idea here is to slow down and just go with the flow. The different areas of the park radiate like spokes on a wheel from the central hub of the **Tree of Life** on **Discovery Island®**. Access to the attractions lies off the central path around the island – just think of it as a pedestrian version of the M25, complete with stroller traffic. If you've got young children, you'll have to bite the bullet and hire one as well – this park is too much of a stretch for little legs. The secret of mastering the Animal Kingdom® is undisputedly timing. As with most animal parks, it's best to arrive early when the creatures are most active, especially since the park closes earlier than the others. Then arrange your day carefully around the shows and attractions, allowing time to get from zone to zone. Start with a **Kilimanjaro Safari®** over in **Africa** where there's the largest concentration of animals. From here you can hop on the **Wildlife Express Train** to **Rafiki's Planet Watch** for a tour of the **Conservation Station®** and then pet the animals in the children's zoo. Then track back to **Discovery Island®** and grab a **FastPass** for the edge-of-your-seat show, **It's Tough to be a Bug!®** and, while you wait for your slot, watch one of the **Camp Minnie-Mickey** shows. Next cross to **DinoLand**, grab a **FastPass** for **Dinosaur®** and finish off in **Asia** with a nice cooling ride on the **Kali River Rapids®**. If there's time, you can end the day by mopping up any trails you missed earlier in the day.

naked mole rats and diminutive antelope called **gerenuk**, which can be spotted hiding out in the knee-high grass. Stop off at the research centre to look at the interactive displays and earn yourself another stamp in your discovery guide. There's a guide on duty here who is happy to talk to guests about the importance of their studies in global animal conservation.

The **African village** beside the reserve features trading posts, stalls, places to eat and, best of all, a set of African drums where kids can just sit an amuse themselves playing their own natural rhythms. This is a good place to view **Mickey's Jammin' Jungle Parade** passing by. Grab yourself a seat outside the **Dawa Bar** to watch all your favourite Disney characters heading off on their own safari through Africa and along by Discovery Island.

Rafiki's Planet Watch

Main attractions

Wildlife Express Train

Half the fun here is taking a trip aboard a puffing steam train past the animals of Africa over to this conservation facility. On the way, you'll learn all about how the facilities have been designed to protect and care for the animals in the park.

Conservation Station®

To enter this animal encounter experience you pass through the **Hall of Animals** where there are large animal murals on the walls. The next room is filled with cut-outs of wild creatures, such as the tiger, rhino, elephant and gorilla. There is information about the animals on the reverse side of each cutout. From there, visitors enter the main arena to watch **nature presentations** with rare or endangered animals, such as boa constrictors, spectacled owls, tarantulas or fennec foxes, and to find out about areas of extreme importance to the conservation effort and places where animals are at risk. You can also see conservation in practice and ask questions. At the **Animal Cam**, you can find out about different species using four sets of computer screens. There are also veterinary laboratories and animal nurseries with incubators and video observation points for viewing creatures in recovery. At the **sound-graph posts**, you can compare your voice patterns with those of animals and learn how animal-tracking devices can be used to monitor animal behaviour and habitat. There's even a **food preparation area** where kids can learn more about the diets that the animals need.

Guests can also access the **Eco Web** computer near the centre of Rafiki's Planet Watch to discover what conservation efforts are underway in their own hometowns and around the world.

The Affection Section

It may sound more like sleazy DJ patter than a theme-park attraction but this is actually a **petting zoo** for kids who are probably dying to get their hands on some furry, fluffy and cuddly creatures. Children can stroke goats, sheep and donkeys and see live demonstrations featuring llama, porcupines, owls and anteaters. They can also wander inside the pens to feed some of their favourite farmyard friends.

Other fun

Habitat Habit!

There's an informative trail leading from the train station to the **Conservation Station®** with educational signposting and colourful animal portraits. Helpful exhibits point out how kids can make wildlife habitats at home.

Asia

Main attractions

Expedition Everest™ (FastPass)

Although not due to open until 2006, this is set to be the best thrill ride in Disney's Animal Kingdom®. As legend has it, there's a fearsome, hirsute beast at large on the treacherous path up to the Himalayas' highest peak. Only a trainload of impetuous fools would breach the boundaries of his realm... Disney's latest white-knuckle experience takes visitors 200ft in the air, through forests and past thundering waterfalls on board an old mountain train bound for the foot of Mount Everest. But, suddenly, something goes wrong and the train hurtles among the glaciers and canyons towards the lair of the fabled yeti. Through the snow flurries a figure looms into view – is it the abominable snowman? Do you want to wait to find out or is it time to hot foot it out of here before big foot makes his move? Let's just wait and see. Minimum height tbc.

Kali River Rapids® (FastPass)

This wet n' wild ride comes with an environmental message. As you plunge down the Chakarandi River you're meant to observe how this precarious jungle habitat is being threatened by illegal logging. The circular boat passes through jasmine-scented hills and climbs towards a blazing forest fire, which is laying waste to this pristine environment. As the raft twists and spins through the rapids, you are confronted by a barren landscape of charred stumps. The water churns and the boat tumbles, twisting and turning down a rocky drop, with a big splash at the end. If you find yourself going backwards, brace yourself for a thorough drenching. For kids though, the educational message may be lost in the fun of getting a good soaking on this rumbustious river ride. Put your shoes and carry-ons in the central storage area, so they don't end up lost as well. Minimum height 38".

Flights of Wonder

Trained ibis, hawks, macaws, toucans and other feathered friends pop out to soar over the heads of the rapt crowd at this outdoor amphitheatre show. They have been trained to show their natural abilities rather than to do tricks – but they do have some delightful habits that will amuse young children.

Other fun

Maharajah Jungle Trek®

Look to the trees on this walking tour through the mythical realm of the Anandapur Royal Forest where gibbons gambol through temple ruins and tigers prowl about a crumbling palace. See if you can spot komodo dragons, fruit bats and lots of different birds.

DinoLand U.S.A.®

Main attractions

DINOSAUR® (FastPass)

It makes a difference where you sit on this roller coaster as the seats on the outside are vulnerable to snapping jaws and ferocious roars, so tuck smaller kids in the middle to muffle their screams. This is a dark and jolty ride through a primeval world where only the biggest of the terrible lizards survive. It starts gently with a short film, narrated by Bill Nye, about how a meteor smashed into Earth and destroyed all of dino kind. Then, scientists impart the amazing news that we can travel back in time to before the big collision. So it's off to the **Time Rovers**, which accelerate through a time tunnel with flashing lights to bring you deep within a prehistoric forest where the vegetation is so dense it blocks out the light. The dinosaur food chain begins with plant-eaters and moves through several species, to the fierce carnivores, ready to lunge at anything. The audio-animatronic models are very convincing and the show leaves you feeling pretty exhilarated, especially if you're on the left, where most of the big frights seem to happen. Minimum Height 40".

Primeval Whirl (FastPass)

Your Wurlizer-style car bobs, weaves, twists and plunges around a track that resembles a strand of Medusa's hair. It's fast, it's furious, it's extremely popular and is all over far too quickly, so grab a FastPass to avoid the lines. Minimum Height 40".

TriceraTop Spin

This is a favourite with little kids who like to fly gently up and down. The queues are minimal so kids can even go round again.

The Boneyard

A prehistoric play area where kids can slide, climb, clamber over rope bridges, run along walkways and dig for bones.

Tarzan™ Rocks!

The lord of the jungle turns lord of rock with this high-energy 30-minute musical spectacular. **Tarzan**, **Jane** and **Terk** lead a troupe of dancers, singers, aerialists, gymnasts and in-line skaters, not all human, but certainly all whipped up into a frenzy by the power of this operatic odyssey. **One World, One Family** is the theme bringing animals and human together for a celebration of the common thread that links us all – life. Be ready for extreme stunts, spectacular costumes and very loud music.

Fossil Fun Games

Here you'll find a bunch of fairground try-your-luck games with a dinosaur twist.

Where to shop

Pick up last-minute film in **Duka la Filimu** before joining your safari in Africa; browse the **Ziwani Traders** and **Mombasa Marketplace** for wood-carvings, animal gifts and safari gear. At **Island Mercantile** stop in for hair braiding and Disney character gifts. The **Rainforest Café** (*see* below) also has a gift shop that toys, souvenirs and clothing.

Where to eat

The Africa section of the park is where you'll find fresh fruit stalls and places to sit and sip cocktails in the sun. There's not a lot of choice for dining in the Animal Kingdom®, so book dinner at your hotel or in **Downtown** Disney (*see* p.240) before you set out.

Best for snacks

Kusafiri Coffee Shop and Bakery (Africa) Stop by for a coffee, milk, fresh juice or a refreshing bowl of yogurt and fruit, muffins, cakes, cookies and pastries.

Dawa Bar (Africa) This cocktail lounge has outdoor seating and offers long cool drinks, accompanied by African tunes. There are non-alcoholic drinks for the kids and bar snacks.

Tamu Tamu (Africa) Sample a fresh fruit smoothie or an ice cream sundae.

Best for a quick bite

Flame Tree Barbecue (Discovery Island) Pop in for a quick sandwich or sit outdoors and enjoy ribs or chicken served with cheese fries and salad.

Tusker House Restaurant (Africa) Vegetarian sandwiches, rotisserie chicken and salads are available for pre- or post-safari pit stops.

Best for family dining

Rainforest Café (outside the Entrance Plaza) Alongside the food, the Rainforest Café has a active 'volcano' and live and animated wildlife encounters. The menu is veggie-friendly with lots of salads, meat-free pasta and pizzas, wraps, seafood and fish dishes, as well as chicken, pork and beef dishes. Call in to reserve on arrival and make sure you have your hand stamped for re-entry to the park.

Restaurantosaurus (DinoLand U.S.A.®) McDonald's burgers, hot dogs, fries and nuggets with a pre-historic spin. Check out the Turkey Wraptor Sandwich. For the kids there's the usual Happy Meal (including toy) for $3.49. Donald's The Breakfastasaurus character dining with Donald, Mickey and friends features an all-you-can-eat buffet of morning goods, including eggs, cereals, pancakes, sausages, muffins, juice, coffee and milk.

EPCOT®

Epcot® (Experimental Prototype Community of Tomorrow) was designed to be a kind of Olympic village for Disney employees but then Celebration was built instead and Florida got another theme park. Younger children especially enjoy the hands-on zones of **Future World** at the front of the park but these tend to clog up mid-morning, so arrive early or leave time for them later on in the day. The larger portion of this vast 260-acre park (it's twice the size of the Magic Kingdom®) contains the **World Showcase**, which is more of a model village than a theme park but it does allow you to shop, eat or sightsee your way around several countries in one fell swoop. The best time to visit is in October when the annual Food and Drink Festival is in full swing. It's all the more exciting to be browsing in Petit France or sauntering through a

Epcot®

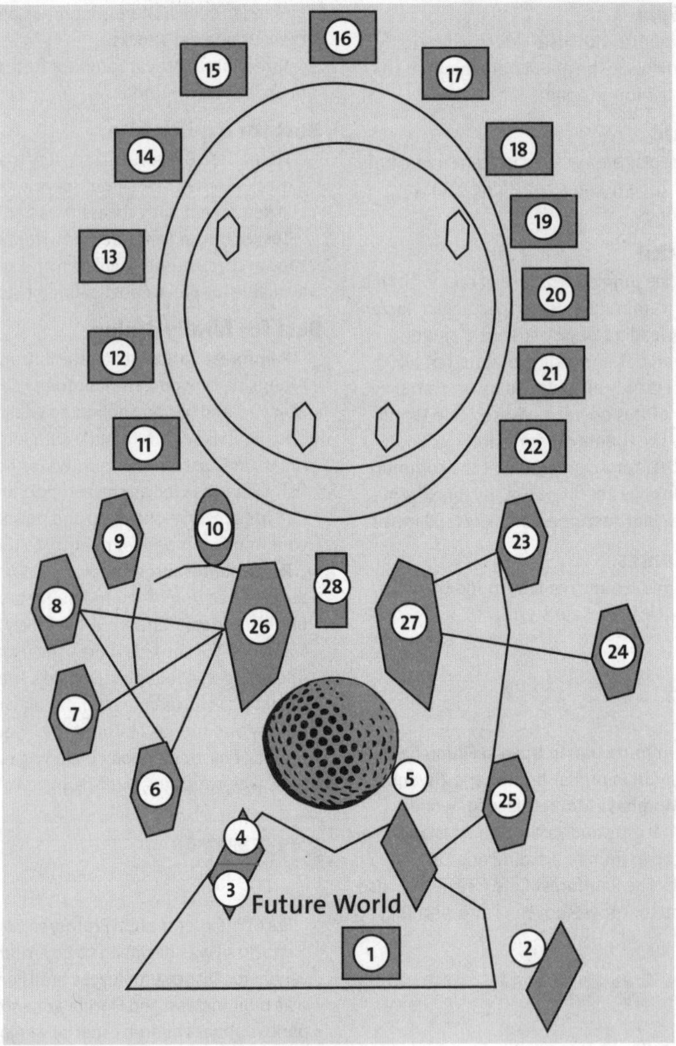

Map © Econoguide Travel Books www.econoguide.com

1 Monorail Station
2 Bus terminal
3 Banking
4 Strollers
5 Spaceship Earth
6 Universe of Energy
7 Wonders of Life
8 Mission: SPACE
9 Test Track
10 Special events
11 Mexico
12 Norway
13 China
14 Germany
15 Italy
16 United States
17 Japan
18 Morocco
19 France
20 International Gateway ferry terminal to Epcot resorts
21 United Kingdom
22 Canada
23 Imagination!
24 The Land
25 The Living Seas
26 Innovations East
27 Innovations West
28 Fountain of Nations

mini St Marks Square while grazing on scoops of *gelato* and sipping Champagne. Many attractions have been spruced up or given additional elements as part of the **Happiest Celebration on Earth**.

Future World Pavilions

Main attractions

Mission: SPACE (FastPass)

If you ever wondered whether you could hack it out there in the cosmos now's your time to try. After a brief orientation video in the **International Space Training Centre's Ready Room**, you're split into groups of four. Your mission: to be one of the first crews to make a successful landing on Mars. Once inside your capsule, it is a mistake to point out the sick bag to your children. It may have been placed there as a visual gag by the Imagineers but don't underestimate the power of prop to a child's imagination. As simulator rides go, this is an amazing experience that is highly unlikely to make anyone unwell Having said that, it is disorientating and anyone who gets claustrophobic in lifts or dislikes being confined in a small space might be better off giving this ride a miss. Inside the space-craft each team member is assigned a role, so, when it's your turn to press buttons and operate the gear stick, you need to react straight away. The only problem being, that since you're in space and are coping with the effects of weightlessness and still recovering from the Gs you pulled at liftoff, you don't quite feel as mentally alert as usual. Don't panic, if you miss a command the computer will take over, which takes the sting out of the experience for kids. It's more fun to tough it out rather than resort to the autopilot. It's a simulator, yes, but the enormous satisfaction you get from mastering the art of space travel is very real. Minimum height 44".

Play the **Space Race** game outside afterwards to see how you'd fare on the return trip from Mars or let the kids send their friends a space email to help them come back down to earth. There's a parent/swap play area for little kids as well.

Test Track (FastPass)

Test Track allows visitors to feel the thrill of speeding round a track in a rally car and is the best all-round family fun to be had in the park. It's good fun whether you're seated in the front or back of the vehicle (they each seat six) but children might want to sit up front for a better view (where it's also less windy), so consider using the single rider line if you feel they're old enough to ride solo. The queues are fun in themselves as you pass a series

Speed coasting

Since this park stays open until 9pm most nights, you can easily combine a trip to one of the water parks (which close at 5pm) with a stroll around Epcot®'s World Showcase. At Epcot shopping, eating and sightseeing all come rolled into one, so make sure you've pre-booked lunch or dinner and plan your day around these. A lot of dining places tend to sell out early in the day here due to the range of live entertainment on offer. If you're not bothered about being serenaded while you eat, there are still lots of good-quality counter service restaurants in the park and the views from the public benches are great. To experience all the rides, set aside a full day and set out as early as possible. You'll have to make a sharp left inside the entrance (and drag the kids kicking and screaming past the first two or three structures in Future World with all their interactive lures) to pick up a FastPass for Test Track before joining the queue for Mission: SPACE, if you want a chance to ride the big two in the same visit. These really are great rides, among Disney's best so make sure you get to experience them both. Afterwards, you're free to take in the Universe of Energy, Journey into Imagination with Figment, check out the latest *Finding Nemo* attractions over in the Living Seas and then dip into the World Showcase as you please. Epcot® has two entrances, so if you're staying at any of the Epcot® resort area hotels (Disney's Yacht Club Resort, Disney's Beach Club Resort, Disney's BoardWalk, Walt Disney World® Swan and Walt Disney World® Dolphin) you needn't queue up at the main entrance with everyone else and can access the park at the World Showcase between the UK and France. The main entrance, which leads into Future World, has a 162-acre parking area and links with the Epcot® monorail station for easy access to the Magic Kingdom®, so if the lines are too busy, go visit the magic for a while and pop back later in the day.

of vehicles and test dummies being put through their paces in sadistic fashion; slamming into walls, being crushed, twisted and generally manhandled. Then it's your turn to take one of the zippy little cars for a spin. Each of the six riders has a separate seatbelt (there's no wheel or accelerator pedal), and once everyone's in place, you embark on a high banking speed chase along the track that lasts for an invigorating 5 minutes. It's guaranteed to leave all occupants grinning their heads off, even if just from the G-force. Minimum height 40". The simulator games outside are fun but if the queues are long there are better things to see elsewhere.

The Living Seas

Only in a Disney park would you get to experience roller coaster rides, space simulators, take a jaunt around the world's markets AND view sharks, tropical fish and dolphins in an underwater research facility. There's a 12-minute look at the power of our oceans to create and sustain life, followed by a short ride through marine environments to wonder at the exotic creatures that reside beneath the waves. There's a diving experience that's strictly for adults but kids can see the coral reef world that the divers are submerged in, through an observation window.

Turtle Talk With Crush

The main reason for a visit to this zone is to witness genius in the making as Disney unleashes Turtle Talk With Crush, an innovative experience where visitor interact with the loveable turtle from Pixar's *Finding Nemo* (voiced by director Andrew Stanton for those you who like to be in the know). From his digital undersea world, Crush tells jokes and engages guests in playful conversation. He's solicitous about who you are and where you've been and he personalizes his comments to individuals by name. The mind-boggling technology behind this experience utilizes digital projection and sophisticated, voice-activated animation to create a unique experience between the animated and the human world. Families can also pose for photographs in **Bruce's Shark World**, an interactive area where kids can learn all kinds of shark facts and immortalize the moment with a picture of their face beside Bruce's trademark toothy grin.

Also on-site is the **Coral Reef Restaurant** where kids can get a tank-side seat and enjoy looking at all the exotic tropical fish swimming by the 8-ft aquarium wall during lunch or dinner. Just remember that they may never forgive you for ordering the seafood special. There are vegetarian options available and kids' can have pizza, chicken or pasta marinara.

Wonders of Life

Body Wars

Visitors to London's ill-fated Millennium Dome will be familiar with the idea of using a human artery as a vessel for exploration (Sci-Fi fans might recall the film *Fantastic Voyage* (1966) in which Raquel Welch heads up a team of miniature surgeons let loose inside a body on a mission to heal its ailing brain). Here Disney uses a body probe as the mode of transport and the drama is sustained by a killer attack of the white blood cell that sends visitors careering through the heart, lungs and brain. Don't worry; the body fights back!

Cranium Command

Now we get to be 12 (again!). Which is great for older folk but even more exciting if you're only eight or nine. It's fun to try and keep up with the stream of thoughts and emotions that you feel when you're young. Buzzy, an audio-animatronics 'brain pilot' is at the helm to try and take control of body parts that seem to have developed minds of their own, albeit very comedic ones.

The Making of Me

This explores human reproduction through the cartoon medium. It sure beats talking about the birds and the bees. Try the Pure and Simple canteen for some healthy snacks along the way.

The Land

Soarin'

This is a new addition in celebration of 50 years of Disney parks. The journey starts in the departure area where panoramic photographs showcase the most stunning environments on Earth; in all the colours of the rainbow. You then embark on a trip up and away across the different landscapes of California. The simulated filmic fly-by takes in the Golden Gate Bridge, Napa Valley, Palm Springs, the Yosemite National Park, San Diego and many other famous locales. The scents, sounds and even the feel of the breeze will delight visitors as they jump ship from various aircraft, including helicopters, hang gliders, jets and hot air balloons.

It's a good ride and is certainly appropriate to a theme park that takes you anyplace but where you actually are. The only consideration is that perhaps a sweep over the Everglades and through the Florida Keys would make more of an impression here.

The other area to have undergone a makeover is the **Land's Sunshine Season Food Fair** where you can dine at the grill shop for wood-fired rotisserie chicken, beef or salmon served with flatbreads and autumn vegetables. There's also a noodle bar spiced up for summer, a sandwich shop that uses winter ingredients and a soup and salad counter inspired by the zest of spring; together they reflect the different seasons of the year.

Other fun

Spaceship Earth

Climb inside this great golf ball in the sky for a history lesson that leads through man's efforts at civilization, developments in writing and understanding of the world around him through to how we might communicate and interact in the future. The ride spirals round and up and at the top you're faced with a ceiling full of stars where you pause to contemplate how tiny we are when compared with the universe around us. The backwards ride down the steep track to the exit may cause some discomfort to small children. Once back on the ground they can experiment with video phones and voice recognition machines in the Global Neighbourhood.

Imagination!

Journey Into Imagination with Figment

Explore your five senses with Eric Idle as the voice of Dr Channing explaining the whys and wherefores of sight, sound etc accompanied by his assistant Figment, a rather independently minded purple dragon (imagine Barney, with attitude). Thus, as the good professor leads us through and out of our minds, Figment plays around a little in the labs with hilarious results. Watch out for the smell section, it's likely to cause a bit of a stink.

Honey, I Shrunk the Audience (FastPass)

Professor Wayne Szalinski is at it again and this time you're the one who gets shrunk. This interactive adventure goes beyond 3-D with incredible special effects and awesome surprises. Be ready to be nice to mice, face the fangs of a python and duck when a dog has a very itchy nose. You might feel small, but your laughs will be big.

Innoventions

Here you can see the all the latest gadgets and gizmos at work from computer technology to new modes of transport, discoveries in medicine and the toys of the future. It's very hands-on and every kid's dream. Invigorate your own grey matter afterwards with free samples of Coca Cola at Ice Station Cool.

Universe of Energy

Join Ellen DeGeneres on a voyage back to the land of the dinosaurs when fossil fuels were just a twinkle in the eye of these giant land lizards. There are dark sequences that might bother young children but otherwise it's a fun and informative lesson about conserving our natural resources. The solar panels on the outside of the building and topiary triceratops only add to the level of instruction.

World Showcase Pavilions

Before you start your international odyssey pick up a passport for the kids and check in at all the Kidcot stations to get your stamps. It's hard to say how other nations feel about how they're represented here but being summed up by English pubs and ye olde thatched cottage is a bit of an embarrassment. Still, if you're after a swift pint then you've probably come to the right place.

Mexico Pavilion

Take a boat ride through Mexico's Mayan past and the resort attractions that draw international visitors today. Visit the **Plaza de los Amigos** for baskets, pottery and brightly coloured blankets, hammocks, carvings and clothing. Try **La Cantina De San Angel** for delicious Mexican snacks such as tortillas, nachos, burritos and sweet churros or opt to dine in the **San Angel Inn** where strolling mariachi and percussionist enliven the scene.

China Pavilion

Disney's CircleVision 360° artistry sets *Reflections of China* apart from other films as we take a closer-than-usual journey along the Great Wall, through the Gobi Desert and on to the mountains. It's a breathtaking trip that leaves you feeling like you've really been somewhere special. It's an all-standing auditorium, so kids will need a piggyback to take it all in. Relax afterwards in a temple garden and browse among shops selling authentic Chinese silks, paintings and toys. Acrobatic and musical performances complete the experience. Try the **Lotus Blossom Café** for fried rice, vegetable and chicken dishes. **The Nine Dragons Restaurant** has a more extensive menu, including hot and sour soup, spring rolls, duck, pork, chicken and seafood dishes.

USA Pavilion

The American Adventure

This colourful, star-spangled performance takes visitors on a half-hour potted history of the American nation. Part film, part audio-animatronic presentation, the show is co-hosted by writer Mark Twain and scientist and statesman, Benjamin Franklin. The scene opens with the Pilgrim Fathers landing on Plymouth Rock and moves on to celebrate the great and good souls who have shaped the country. Walt Disney is among the notables and the list manages an even balance of male and female luminaries, as well as celebrating the achievements of Native and African Americans. The Colonial-style building is also bedecked with flags and the inside walls are lined with inspirational quotes. Take a stroll through the American Gardens afterwards to enjoy the rousing sounds of the Spirit of America Fife & Drums Corp.

Echoes of Africa

This exhibition combines the works of contemporary African-American artists with historical pieces from the Walt Disney-Tishman African Art Collection. The collection encompasses works from all the regions of Africa, which will be represented through a rotating display of 15–20 pieces, together with the works of a dozen or so modern artists.

Germany Pavilion

Bavarian towers and a medieval castle flank the cobblestone square of this German-inspired village, with its displays of dancing and chiming clock tower. Shops include *Der Bücherwurm*, for hand-painted eggs and pottery; *Der Teddybar*, for wooden toys, puppets and, of course, bears; *Die Weihnachts Ecke* for traditional German Christmas decorations and *Kunstarbeit in Kristall*, for some sparkly jewellery. Then clank your steins together at the *Oktoberfest Musikanten* in the **Biergarten**, or sample some wine at the **Weinkeller**. German pastries are also on offer at the **Sussigkeiten** or visit the **Sommerfest** for some *schnizel* and *sauerkraut*.

Italy Pavilion

Squint and you're in Venice surrounded by bridges, gondolas and bustling market stalls. The pavilion contains a stunningly accurate replica of the Campanile (bell tower) of St. Mark's Square, minus the pigeons. Stroll around looking at the statuary and see if you can spot the entertainer, Imaginum, who is posing as a piece of sculpture. Shop for leather goods, crystal ware and porcelain figurines at **Il Bel Cristallo** and graze along the stalls of **Delizie Italiane** for sweet-toothed treats. **La Bottega Italiana** offers an assortment of deli items pastries, wines, oils, vinegars and speciality coffees. For something more substantial book **L'Originale Alfredo di Roma Ristorante**, which serves up pasta, salads and delicious Italian desserts. If you want to see the strolling performers, ask to be seated near the front.

Japan Pavilion

Here you'll find a perfect fusion of the old and the new. Inside the **Mitsukoshi Department Store** visitors can shop for kimonos and lacquer screens as well as the latest 'Hello Kitty' hair accessories and stationery. Outside face the elements of earth, water, air and fire as you take a walk through the rock gardens, past koi-filled pools and streams and on to the lively **Mitsukoshi Teppanyaki Dining Room** where chefs cook up a feast on a flaming grill before your eyes. Follow lunch with a look at the dramatic displays of taiko drumming and don't miss the collection of tin toys in the **Bijutsu-kan Gallery**. For light bites pop into the **Yakitori House** for some skewers of beef or chicken or try some saki and sushi in **The Matsu No Ma Lounge**.

France Pavilion

Disney's petite Paris features all the flourishes, fine fragrances, wines, pastries, chocolates and even a miniature version of the Eiffel tower (sadly not topped by an observation tower). Nip into the cinema for the epic wraparound movie *Impressions de France*, which hovers over French hotspots and lingers on images of the lovely countryside, accompanied by stirring concertos by famous French composers such as Debussy and, Disney favourite, Saint-Säens. French art and mime artists await onlookers in the arcades and there's a good choice of places to eat. Complete the picture with dinner at the **Bistro de Paris**, a peaceful upstairs restaurant where guests can dine on duck, seafood, snails, foie gras, scallops and filet mignon among other choices. Children can enjoy pasta with chicken, beef in a bun or fish with fries. For a fine dining experience try **Les Chefs de France**, which is open for lunch and dinner. Here you can sample lobster bisque or French onion soup, chicken, seafood, lamb, fish and steaks. The children's menu is the same for the Bistro.

Canada Pavilion

Rocky mountains, landmark hotels, rushing waterfalls and glorious gardens – Canada's got it all. Experience a coast-to-coast tour courtesy of another CircleVison 360° film *O Canada!*, which will leave you hungry for vast open spaces where bears and bobcats roam. If you're feeling peckish, tuck in to a sizzling slab of meat at **Le Cellier Steakhouse**, where Celtic rock n' roll band, Off Kilter, are throwing some mean guitar licks. Shop at the **Northwest Mercantile** for trader type goods and **La Boutique des Provinces**, for French Canadian folk art and cuddly toys.

United Kingdom Pavilion

So here we are back in Blighty watching a mock Beatles tribute performance beside the bandstand in 70-degree weather. And if that's not bizarre enough for you, take in the view of Merry Olde England where thatched cottages and canals nestle beside a country pub and a pretend stately home styled on Hampton Court. Pick up some true Brit souvenirs at **The Toy Soldier**, grab a natty sweater at the **Sportsman Shoppe** or fill the air with the scents of English tea-rose perfume and handmade soaps from the **Queen's Table**. There's a **Harry Ramsden** fish and chip stand and the **The Rose and Crown** serves up traditional pub grub, such as bangers and mash and steak and kidney pie, which can all be washed down with a pint or two of real ale while waiting for the sing-along to begin. The kids will like running about in the **Tigger maze** afterwards.

Morocco Pavilion

And now for something completely different and step into the old-meets-new world of Morocco, where street vendors entice you to buy their wares and dancers and folk musicians join the throng. Shops hold a mesmerizing array of colours, textures and scents packed with everything from Rabat carpets and leather sandals to traditional fez and sheepskin wallets. For a more contemporary view-point visit the **National Tourist Office** for a slide show of Moroccan natural treasures, such as the Atlas Mountains. Walk through the **Royal Gallery** and **Gallery of Arts and History** for a closer look at North African costume, arts and crafts. Snack on tabbouleh and hummus at the **Tangierine Café** or try the sticky, sweet treats and refreshing mint teas at the **Moorish Café and Pastry Shop**. At the **Restaurant Marrakesh**, watch agile belly dancers, while sampling couscous served with vegetables, lamb or chicken or share a plate of spicy mezze.

Norway Pavilion

There's still time for one last ride, **Maelstrom (FastPass)**, and this one is a total hoot with grumpy old trolls, rampaging Vikings and snarling polar bears menacing you on an adventure-packed voyage across the stormy North Sea.

Elsewhere browse among streets recalling ancient Norse settlements and troll around the shops for ... erm ..., Norwegian trolls, Danish Lego® and Swedish sweaters.

Living with the Land (FastPass)

Take a boat ride through the history of agriculture, through rainforest, grassland and desert environments, looking at advancements in crop production, fishing and farming.

Where to shop

Imagine a kind of supermarket sweep through the boutiques and gift shops of the world's major cities and you're halfway to envisaging what shopping at Epcot® feels like. It's a curious fusion of kitsch and couture with showy Armani-crafted Seven Dwarf figurines swanning around in the Italy pavilion; robust beer steins in the Germany pavilion and delicate Guerlain perfumes wafting through the air in the France pavilion. See individual countries in the World Showcase for more information.

Where to eat

The World Showcase is a virtual smorgasbord of eateries, so you can either snack your way through the service counters or make a lunch or dinner reservation at one of the restaurants that, between them, reflect 11 different national cuisines.

Disney–MGM Studios

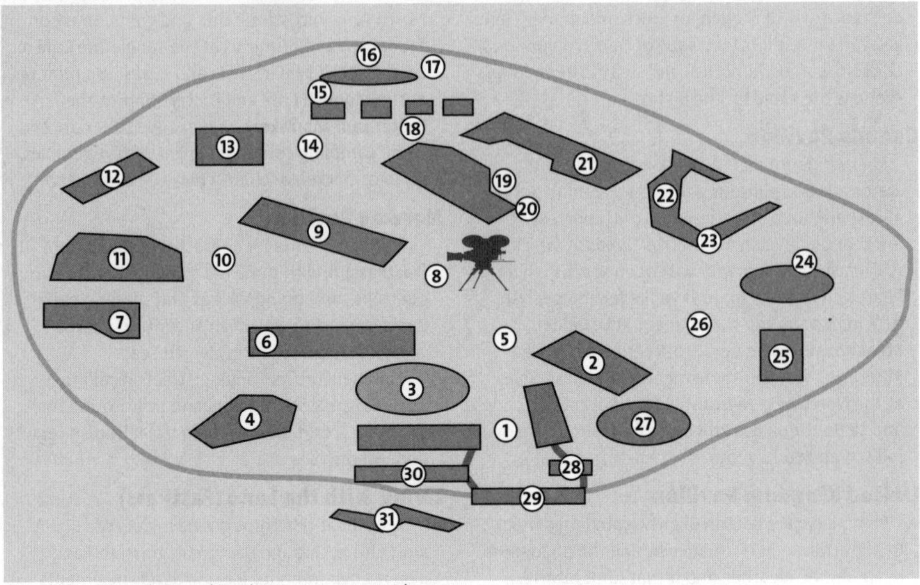

Map © Econoguide Travel Books www.econoguide.com

1 Hollywood Boulevard
2 *Beauty and the Beast – Live on Stage*
3 Echo Lake
4 *Indiana Jones Epic Stunt Spectacular*
5 Plaza
6 ABC Sounds Studio: Sounds Dangerous
7 Star Tours
8 The Great Movie Ride
9 *Honey, I Shrunk the Kids* Movie Set Adventure
10 New York Street
11 Jim Henson's Muppet Vision 3D
12 *Hunchback of Notre Dame*
13 Lights, Motors, Action!
14 Disney–MGM Studios Backlot Tour
15 The Backlot
16 Catastrophe Canyon
17 Residential Street
18 Soundstage I
19 *Who Wants to Be a Millionaire – Play It!*
20 *Playhouse Disney – Live on Stage!*
21 Production Center
22 *Voyage of the Little Mermaid*
23 *The Magic of Disney Animation*
24 Rock 'n' Roller Coaster Starring Aerosmith
25 Twilight Zone Tower of Terror
26 Sunset Boulevard
27 *Fantastic!*
28 Lockers/strollers
29 Entrance Plaza
30 First Aid
31 Guest Relations

DISNEY–MGM STUDIOS

If the Magic Kingdom® is the magic then the Studios are what's behind the magic and, as such, are doubly good, offering a fine range of innovative attractions. Like it's sister park in Paris, the Disney-MGM Studios in Florida is spacious and well planned combining big-thrill rides like **The Twilight Zone Tower of Terror™** and the **Rock 'n' Roller Coaster®**, starring Aerosmith with hands-on activities and exciting live shows. The park is not divided into zones as they are in the other parks but each of the three main groups of rides and attractions is reached from a major thoroughfare – **Sunset Boulevard, Mickey Avenue** (incorporating The Animation Courtyard) and **Streets of America**. This is the best park for older kids and adults with plenty of all-round family entertainment. Since the elements of the park are so very different from each other, queues are much shorter for everything but the really big thrills and even these have FastPass entry, making the Studios a breeze in comparison to the Magic Kingdom®.

Sunset Boulevard

Main attractions

The Twilight Zone Tower of Terror™ (FastPass)

This is the big pull in this park, offering 13 floors of fear but it's a very quick trip lasting only 2 minutes of ride time. The deserted hotel has beautiful 1920s–30s' furnishings, some of which are authentic fittings from defunct resorts.The main excitement here is the fact that the computers are in control. The lifts run to a random sequence, so no matter how many times you go on, it will be different each time. Add some spine-tingling effects, lots of sparks and noise and the inevitable plunges are all the more gut wrenching. Ride it at night to increase your sense of disorientation. Minimum height 40".

Rock 'n' Roller Coaster® Starring Aerosmith (FastPass)

This is the other major-league ride in the park – the coaster cars shaped like luxury stretch limos, ready to whisk you off to the rock hall of fame. Listening to heavy metal music in the dark is always going to be a disquieting experience but add to this several lunging twists and turns and you've the formula for a really rollicking good theme park ride. Minimum height 48".

The Great Movie Ride

This brilliant road trip along Tinseltown's golden mile combines live action with vintage footage to recall cinema's most classic moments. It begins with some spectacular props from our favourite flicks, followed by a loop of marvelous movie trailers. From here you enter the cars for the narrated tour. A short way in to the 20-minute journey, a gangster or a cowboy hitches a ride on your jalopy. All of a sudden you're heading you off into the gun-totin' environs of 1920s' Chicago or the Wild West, where hoodlums are taking potshots from every available vantage point. After that excitement, things return to normal and a cast of models fitted with the latest audio-animatronics effects enhance our voyage through such epics of the silver screen as *The Wizard of Oz, Indiana Jones and the Raiders of the Lost Ark, Alien* and *Casablanca*.

Other fun

Beauty and the Beast – Live on Stage

The open-air **Theater of the Stars** is the venue for this popular Broadway-style show with songs and scenes from the film. The opening sequence with the dancing crockery is particularly effective.

Animation Courtyard and Mickey Avenue

Main attractions

Who Wants To Be A Millionaire – Play It! (FastPass)

This feels so very much like the show you'll swear you can hear Chris Tarrant snickering in the wings. Here the whole audience gets to watch and participate. Questions are read out and whoever gets the right sequence first is plucked from the aisles right into the hot seat. The replica set features the same dramatic lighting, glass floors and décor, not to mention the famous hot seat.

Instead of money, guests play for points, which win them Disney goodies. In order to win it big, contestants must answer the usual number of questions and have an ask-the-audience option, a 50/50 and an amusing twist on the phone-a-friend option – to phone a complete stranger in the park. Prizes range from Disney baseball caps to commemorative pins and if a contestant gets all the questions right they receive the big prize – a three-night Disney Cruise Line break for four people (prizes subject to change). So, get those digits flexing, it's time to play to win!

The Voyage of the Little Mermaid (FastPass)

This lovely indoor theatre show takes us under the sea with Ariel and friends. Based on scenes from the animated classic, *The Little Mermaid*, it features puppetry, special effects, film footage and live performers, plus a couple of surprise tricks to amuse the kids. The soundtrack is pretty loud and some of the effects are quite powerful, so reassure your toddlers on the way in that it's just a show.

Playhouse Disney – Live On Stage!

Preschoolers rejoice! This one is definitely for you. Cuddly, snuggly Bear (from *Bear in the Big Blue House*™) is your host on this stage adventure, which leads you through stories from popular Disney TV shows, such as **Rolie Poly Olie**, **Stanley** and **The Book of Pooh**. Kids deprived of a diet of digital and satellite TV may not be so familiar with all the characters in the show but they will recognize good old Pooh bear and his pals. Kids are encouraged to get up and dance about in the musical sequences and the story-time sessions work wonders on hyped- up kids. Don't be put off by the queues; it's a huge auditorium where you all sit together on the floor.

Disney-MGM Studios Backlot Tour

Peer behind the curtain to see the inner workings of the movie special effects, props and costume departments – the nerve-centre if you will – that combine to hold the magic together. There is a real working film studio back here as evidenced in the lighting rigs and building facades that litter the

Speed coasting

The trick here is to plan your day around the grand finale **Fantasmic! Show**, which takes place at about 7.30pm (seasonal variations may apply and since the show is outdoors it may be cancelled due to inclement weather). So, the first thing to do on arrival is book dinner at the Guest Relations window to the left of the entrance. You need to eat no later than 4.30pm, so that you can get a decent seat in the auditorium. Granted, there are in the region of 6,500 seats available but the gates open 90-minutes before the start of the show. If you leave it until the last minute, all seats will be occupied and 25 minutes is a long time for tired kids to stand while the show goes on. There are lots of disabled priority seats at the edges and, if these are not occupied, they can be used once the cast members have indicated that it is okay to do so. The **Sci-Fi Dine-In Theater Restaurant** on Commissary Lane, which is fairly central to the park is a nice place for a pre-show supper. Having made your dinner reservations, you'll be ready to explore the park. If you like your frights right after breakfast, turn right and make a beeline for the **Tower of Terror** first (you never know where you might end up and later in the day queues are prohibitive) and then hit the **Rock 'n' Roller Coaster**, if your stomach allows. Both attractions have **FastPass** entry so get a timed entry ticket for the one with the longest line. Then progress in an anti-clockwise direction (a good idea since it seems to be the route less travelled), through the **Animation Courtyard's** hands-on fun and shows to the **Backlot tour** for a glimpse inside the film industry's special effects box. Using your new knowledge of movie-making take in **Lights, Motors, Action!™**. By now you'll be ready to eat, and after you've done so there will still be lots of time for a leisurely stroll through **Jim Henson's Crazy Muppet Capers** while waiting for your **Star Tours FastPass** to mature. Then marvel at the macho prowess of **Indiana Jones** as he takes on the baddies amid flames aided by a few members of the audience. If you've not booked dinner, you'll still have time to graze along the stalls of **Sunset Boulevard** to tide the kids over until later in the evening. Then take your seat in the amphitheatre and get all hyped up for the **Fantasmic!** show by joining in on the Mexican waves that ripple back and forth through the audience. This spectacle of sound and lights is a fitting finale to a day of magic – and then some.

place, as well as several 'imagineered' experiences to keep the kids on the edge of their seats. It all starts out rather mildly with a lesson in special-effects techniques presented on the big screen. Then you enter an outdoor area that houses an effects tank for demonstrating how filmmakers recreate battles and storms at sea. There's an element of audience participation and some visual gags leaving the audience in good spirits. Then it's all aboard the shuttle buses, which guide 200 passengers through the backlot, past wardrobe and the scenic shop, on to **Catastrophe Canyon** where the bus breaks down. Depending on where you are sitting, you're then treated to spectacular sound and visual effects, including flaming explosions and torrents of water. If you want to get wet, sit on the left side of the vehicle. It's fun working out which props belong to which film. Visit the **American Film Institute Showcase** afterwards for themed movie exhibitions such as Disney villains.

Lights, Motors, Action!™

Skidding motorcycles, synchronized water raft, choreographed cars and spectacular stunt vehicles abound in this full-on show. The performance is inspired by the 'Moteurs...Action!' show from Disneyland Resort Paris®. We're on the set of a state- of-the-art spy thriller and the director wants the very best from his crew, especially his mechanical cast. Several major-league stunt scenes are shot with the director stopping and starting the action, seemingly at random. Without giving too much away, there are lots of surprises in store and some smashing special effects. After the event, the audience gets to watch the whole filmed sequence from start to finish, doubling the fun.

Other fun

The Magic of Disney Animation

Here families get a chance to test their own skills at drawing and animation at a sequence of interactive screens and workstations. There's an animation gallery, a showcase of Disney cartoons and an artists' studio where visitors can sketch along with a Disney animator. If you ask nicely at the end of the session, you are allowed to take the animator's drawing home with you.

Walt Disney: One Man's Dream

This exhibit traces the fascinating story of the man behind the mouse, from early experiments in cartoons through to the establishment of the Walt Disney Studios and beyond. Among the exhibits is an early map of the proposed Walt Disney World® site in Florida, along with some models where kids can push buttons and marvel at the intricacy of the set designs. The display and short film presentation charts a courageous journey that saw Disney fall in and out of fortune, but one which ultimately has a happy ending – resulting in the successful legacy we see today. Inspiring stuff.

Streets of America

Main attractions

Star Tours (FastPass)

This is one of the best rides at Disneyland Resort Paris® and it's equally as fun here, if not more so because **R2D2** and **C-3PO** are speaking in English and not French. It's a minor consideration but when you're trying to contain excitable kids while waiting in line, it really does help to have two robots chatting in a language they can understand. There's a video screen preamble advertising tour packages to various space destinations and then you're on board your spacecraft for a routine flight to Endor. The spaceship's trusty pilot **Rex (RX-24)** turns out to be a little bit rusty on the controls and after an encounter with a black hole and several meteorites, you're suddenly thrown into a pitched battle with an **Imperial Star Destroyer**. Can Rex save the day? Only the brave can tell you. The lurching simulator side of this experience is not recommended for toddlers who dislike being off-balance. Kids of five and above simply love it (and that includes big kids in their 30s and 40s too). Minimum height 40".

Indiana Jones Epic Stunt Spectacular! (FastPass)

Here you'll really feel in on the action, especially if you're lucky enough to be chosen as an extra. Several members of the audience are needed at each sitting to scream, gasp and run away at appropriate moments during the show. The 35-minute live spectacle takes place in a 2,000-seat amphitheatre, so your odds of being picked are not that great, but sit on the end of a row near the front and you never know your luck. The scene is the market square sequence from *Indiana Jones and the Raiders of the Lost Ark* where Indy is trying to rescue Marion from a horde of whip-wielding baddies. Great acrobatic displays, choreography and daring stunts, plus some amazing special effects involving a moving plane, all combine here to make for a very entertaining show.

Honey, I Shrunk the Kids Movie Set Adventure

Based on the hit film *Honey, I Shrunk the Kids*; this movie-set adventure playground features insect sounds, an ant the size of a pony, cereal hoops as big as cartwheels, 30-ft blades of grass and a snake-like garden hose (with water feature of course). Kids can have loads of fun climbing, jumping and generally making merry in this giant world. There's a designated zone for very young children within this out-sized play area but be careful not to lose sight of their slightly more adventurous and mobile siblings.

Jim Henson's Muppet*Vision 3-D

There are several capers all rolled into one at this 3-D stage show extravaganza. Firstly, we get to see excerpts from the *Muppet Show* back catalogue and pry into the Muppet band's suitcases, including the personal luggage of porcine Diva, **Miss Piggy**. Inside the theatre Jim Henson's famous crew are getting to work, including **Statler** and **Waldorf** in their (dis)royal box. **Kermit**, **Fozie** and Miss Piggy are directing the proceedings while an orchestra pit full of virtual penguins strike up a tune. The film itself involves some sing-along songs, special effects, floating bubbles, strobe lights and live action.

Sounds Dangerous – Starring Drew Carey

This audio tour takes place partially in total darkness, so warn little kids before you go in. The effect is compelling as your ears guide you through some of the sound effects that make movies so convincing. Experiment with noises in the interactive studio outside afterwards.

Hollywood Hill Amphitheater
Fantasmic!

And now for the finale – on a clear night you can see the stars above this vast lakeside amphitheatre where visitors amuse themselves by instigating Mexican waves across the 6,500 or so seats. It's nice to sit down and rest awhile in this big bowl surrounded by other Disney park attendees and chat about your day with family and friends. Before the show starts kids like to scan the rows for newlyweds (you can tell them by their top hats and white mouse ears plus veil) or play with the obligatory neon toys bought from the stalls lining the route to the theatre. The show itself combines film projection of Mickey standing on a central island conducting an orchestra of fountains, water jets, comets, fire and stars all beautifully bouncing in time with soaring crescendos. The music softens as favourite Disney characters float by along the lake, including the cast from *The Lion King*, plus **Cinderella**, **Ariel**, **Pocahontas** and **Jasmine** along with their paramours and other heroic folk. Various Disney villains then muscle in to knock the mouse Maestro from his perch but Mickey has a trick or two up his sleeve to counteract their wicked ways. Good eventually triumphs over evil and the show finishes with some super flourishes. Bring a coat to sit on as the seats are pretty hard.

Where to shop

Downtown Disney is by far the best shopping area within the Disney region but Disney-MGM Studios comes top within the parks. Movie buffs will have a field day at the likes of **Sid Cahuenga's One-of-a-Kind**, which stocks books, films, posters and ex-wardrobe items, such as jackets from tough-guy movies and a selection of autographed photos. They'll also feel the force of pester power at **Tatooine Traders**, where kids drool over collectibles and clothing featuring characters from *Star Wars* films. The Yoda T-shirts are superb. For those all-action moments try **Indiana Jones' Adventure Outpost** or prove you're tough enough for anything with a Twilight Zone Tower of Terror hat. There are several outlets in the park that sell Disney toys, clothes and souvenirs, plus the **Stage 1 Company Store**, which specializes in Muppets and Bear in the Big Blue House merchandise.

Where to eat

There's lots of choice for dining outdoors, American style, especially at the **Sunset Market Ranch** where you can get lunch staples, such as hamburgers, hot dogs, pizza, baked potatoes, turkey legs and beer. At the **Starring Rolls Café** you'll find pastries, salads and fresh coffee served on the patio or you can sit beside Echo Lake and enjoy some of the novel ices on offer at **Dinosaur Gertie's Ice Cream of Extinction**.

Best for snacks

Min & Bill's Dockside Diner Stock up on fruit, yogurt, drinks and snacks.

Anaheim Produce A fresh produce stand offering fruit, vegetables and beverages.

Best for a quick bite

50's Prime Time Cafe/Tune In Lounge The kids can pig out on peanut butter and jelly sandwiches and milkshakes, while you tuck in to some Southern specialities like fried chicken, meat loaf or chicken potpie.

ABC Commissary Snack your way across the continents with some vegetarian stir fry noodles, fish and chips or a bowl of Brazilian black bean stew.

Mama Melrose's Ristorante Italiano Gourmet pizza baked in wood-burning brick ovens, plus pasta and seafood dishes.

Best for family meals

Sci-Fi Dine-In Theater Restaurant You can't miss this restaurant on Commissary Lane as there is an old-fashioned convertible parked outside. It's hugely popular with kids and adults alike because you sit in car booths to have your dinner and can watch old black-and-white movies while you eat. Don't be surprised if you're asked to share your vehicle with strangers; they really do need to fill the cars up to ensure no one ends up stranded at the drive-in. It's a good idea to book early on in the day for a table here or a few days in advance if you can. The lunch menu features salads, burgers and sandwiches, while the dinner menu offers, steak, fish and seafood dishes. If you order one of the house Glowing Concoctions, which are all thoroughly alcoholic, the kids can take home the glow-in-the-dark cup afterwards. The children's menu includes Space Mush (macaroni and cheese), Meteor (grilled chicken breast served with roasted red potatoes and green beans) or several Mini choices including burgers and hot dogs with fries.

The Hollywood Brown Derby This beautiful replica of the famous 1930s' Hollywood restaurant features Art deco flourishes and a great menu, including the signature Cobb salad, plus steaks, seafood, fish and pasta specialities and a selection of wines. The kids' menu has salads and chicken noodle soup along with the more usual children's choices of macaroni cheese and hot dogs.

DISNEY WATER PARKS

Typhoon Lagoon

t (407) 560 4141
Open 10–6 (earlier and later in summer)
Adm Adults $36.21, children (3–9) $29.82, plus tax, under-3 free. Snorkelling with sharks: ????

After all that hot theme-park action, take some time out to relax and catch the odd wave. Here at Typhoon Lagoon there's plenty of fun to be had body surfing in the main pool with 6-ft waves crashing down at 90-second intervals. There are warning sounds when the surf is about to hit and every hour or so there are lulls between the big splashes for family swimming. The waves are extremely powerful, so do keep an eye on children while in the pool. There are quieter swimming areas around the edges. You'll find sun beds both right and left of the main pool but if you're visiting with toddlers head left and aim for the outer edge beyond the lazy river to **Ketchakiddee Creek**. This is where you'll find most of the slides, bubbling jets and water cannons for younger children, as well as individual and family **raft rides**. The **lazy river** has single and two-person tubes, so little ones need not miss out on the fun. Thrill-seekers will enjoy the **Storm Slides** – a series of fast body slides through caves, gushing waterfalls and under bridges – and the white-knuckle **Humunga Kowabunga** (minimum height 48"), which sends three brave souls racing down dark tunnels along 214-ft speed slides with a 51-ft drop. Was it dark all the way down or did you have your eyes shut? Typhoon Lagoon also offers 30-minutes snorkelling with sharks (ages 7 and up) inside a saltwater pool with nurse sharks and tropical fish. Non-swimmers can see the action through portholes in an observation tank. There are several food outlets in the park serving hot dogs, pizzas, burgers and hot snacks, as well as sandwiches, frozen drinks and ice cream. The on-site shop stocks beachwear, accessories and sun lotion.

Blizzard Beach

t (407) 560 3400
Open 10–5
Adm Adults $36.21, children (3–9) $29.82, plus tax, under-3 free

As theme-park themes go, this one beats the lot. A freak storm has landed a snow-capped mountain range right in the heart of sub-tropical Florida. The enterprising locals have seen an opportunity to cash in and have built an impromtu ski resort. They've even installed a **ski lift** to get you to the top of the slopes. But now the weather is hotting up and, although some parts of the park are still stuck in the deep freeze, the ice is starting to melt. What's to be done? Well, there's nothing for it but to go with the flow. So now there are wicked **bobsleigh runs**, **slides** and **flumes** cut through the drifts by the fast-flowing water and the ski resort has become a water park instead. As you enter, head sharp right after the main entrance for the children's **play pool** with its mini boat ride, slides and water fountains. Alternatively, if you're looking for a place in the sun, go over the bridge and head left. You'll find most of the sun loungers by the pool, which is set in a rocky inlet. It is a wave pool – and although it doesn't have really big waves like at Typhoon Lagoon, the surface is quite choppy and it's deep by the rocks – so young children will need to be accompanied. Grab a tube and slosh about in the bobbing waves together. Meanwhile, the big kids can get to grips with the range of exciting slides, flumes and chutes up above. The jaw dropper in this park is the **Summit Plummet**, a towering slide that looks like a ski jump but actually shoots 120 feet in a vertical drop and then heads on through a log cabin and down the hill for around another 300 feet (minimum height 48"). Running parallel to this is the **Slush Gusher** speed slide with its two humps, which may not be as high as its next-door-neighbour but still packs a quite a punch (minimum height 48). To the left of this is an eight-lane **toboggan run**, which is great for mat races against the family. Further over to the left you'll find the **Snow Stormer slalom mat slides**, plus the **Downhill Dipper racing slides** (minimum height 48"). The park is encircled by a long **lazy river** and even boasts a **pre-teen pool** with its own slides, aerial runway and a set of perilous iceberg steppingstones. There are several fast food huts offering light meals, drinks and snacks. There are also four shops in the park that sell souvenirs, beachwear, sunglasses, hats and sun lotion – if you've forgotten it, buy some! You'll definitely need it.

Good to know

Waterparks

Disney buses run to the water parks from around 8.30am. Opening hours for the park are 9am at the earliest, usually 10am. The queues do start to form before the gates open but waiting around for an hour is not really the best way to start your day. Check opening times, have breakfast before you set out and arrive at the water park half an hour before it opens. Bring some drinks, as there are no facilities outside the park and join the line. Once the gates open head straight for the sun loungers (see individual parks for details) and leave one member of the family with the bags while the rest go off to change, get lockers and hire towels (there's no need to bring your own). Without a base camp you'll feel pretty uncomfortable; but try not to use up too many beds. If the kids are going to be in the water most of the time then just get one or two beds for them to share between them. That way everyone gets to have a place in the sun. If you arrive in the afternoon, it's highly unlikely there will be any spaces left but the lockers are large enough to offload all your gear and you can always hit the lazy river for a cool down until the park empties a bit. If you're riding the flumes or hitting the wave pool, don't wear your sunglasses, or make sure that your expensive designer shades are firmly attached to a neck strap. Sun protective goggles are best for kids. One-piece swimsuits or closely fitting bikini tops and bottoms are recommended for riding the big slides. If the kids are getting hungry, they serve peanut butter and jelly sandwiches and a drink inside a handy children's bucket with a spade as well, so you needn't go out and buy one for the beach. Fruit cups and Caesar salads are also available for lean lunching. Typhoon Lagoon does not allow coolers but you can take a picnic into Blizzard Beach providing there are no glass containers or alcohol in your basket. Showers, lockers, toilets, towels and life vest hire are all available within Disney's water parks.

Reference

14

American English originally derives from the English of the British settlers who began to arrive in the late 16th century, settling successfully from the early 17th. Thus, in many ways, it is closer to Shakespearean English than to modern British English. Some phrases now regarded as American, such as 'fall' for 'autumn' and 'trash' meaning rubbish, are actually 16th-century English phrases that have fallen out of use. Some words, many of which are now accepted English words, such as 'tomato', 'canoe' and 'savanna' have their origins in indigenous Native American languages. Spanish has also been an influence, introducing words like 'canyon', 'mustang', 'ranch' and 'stampede' and to a lesser extent there have also been borrowings from French and West African dialects.

American English

There are various differences in both spoken and written British and American English, but with the exception of some vocabulary, you are unlikely not to understand what anyone is saying. The main differences between British and American English is in the spelling of some words and in the use of the present perfect tense, including with adverbs such as just, already and yet, prepositions and some past participles. Below is a short guide.

Grammar

Present Perfect tense

Where, in British English, you would use the present perfect tense to express an action that has occurred in the recent past and has an effect on the present, in American English, using the simple past tense is more usual. E.g.

British: I've missed my train. Where's the waiting room?
American: I missed my train. Where's the waiting lounge?

Using the past perfect and 'just', 'already' and 'yet'

British: I've just had breakfast
American: I just had breaksfast
British: I've already been there
American: I already went there.
British: Have you seen that film yet?
American: Did you see that film yet?

Prepositions

There are also a few differences in use of prepositions, including the following:

British: at the weekend
American: on the weekend
British: in a team
American: on a team
British: write to me soon
American: write me soon

Past verb tenses

Some past participles in British English can end in a 't' or an 'ed'. It is more usual in British English, to use the 't' ending, but in the US, the 'ed" ending is much more common. E.g.

British: She smelt it
American: She smelled it
British: He burnt his toast
American: He burned his toast
British: They learnt their verbs
American: They learned their verbs

Note too, the American use of the past participle 'gotten', where in British English, 'got' is used. E.g.

British: She's got a lot better at doing that
British: She's gotten a lot better at doing that

Spelling

Here are some general differences between British and American spellings. E,g.

- Words spelt 'our' in British English are spelt 'or' in American English. E.g:

British: colour, flavour, endeavour, humour, favourite
American: color, flavor, endeavor, humor, favorite

- Words ending in 'ise' in British English are spelt 'ize' in American English. E.g:

British: idealise, mechanise, recognise, organise
American: idealize, mechanize, recognize, organize

- Words ending in a vowel and a double 'l' in British English are spelt with one 'l' in American English. E.g:

British: travelled/travelling/traveller, modelling, snorkelling
American: traveled/traveling/traveler, modeling, snorkeling etc

• Words ending in 're' in British English are spelt 'er' in American English. E.g:
British: theatre, centre
American: theater, center

• Words ending in 'lyse' in British English are spelt 'lyze' in American English. E.g:
British: analyse
American: analyze

• Words using 'ae' or 'oe' in British English are spelt without the 'a' or 'o' in American English. E.g:
British: manoevre, archaeology
American: maneuver, archeology

• Words ending in 'ogue' in British English are spelt without the 'ue' in American English. E.g:
British: catalogue, dialogue
American: catalog, dialog
NB: 'Vogue' remains the same

• Some nouns ending in 'ence' in British English are spelt 'ense' in American English. E.g:
British: pretence, defence, offence, licence
American: pretense, defense, offense, license

Vocabulary

Some words in American English are just different, but beware of the ones that are familiar but means something else!

This happens quite a lot with driving vocabulary (see below) but more importantly perhaps, please note that a 'rubber' in British English, for rubbing out pencil marks (a word you may need when you have tots in tow), means 'condom' in American English!

American English	British English
antennae	aerial
apartment/condo	flat
auto teller (ATM)	cashpoint
Band Aid®	plaster
bangs	fringe
bar	pub
barrette	hair slide
bathroom/restroom	toilet
bill	banknote
broiled	grilled
buck	one dollar note
cab	taxi
call collect	reverse charges
can	tin
candy	sweets
cart	trolley
check	bill (in a restaurant)
chips	crisps
cleats	football boots
closet	wardrobe
cookie	biscuit
cot	camp bed
counterclockwise	anticlockwise
crib	cot
cup cake	fairy cake
diapers	nappies
dime	ten cent coin
drugstore	pharmacist-stationer, which may sell soft drinks and snacks
duplex	semi-detached house
eggplant	aubergine
elevator	lift
eraser	rubber (for rubbing out pencil marks)
fall	autumn
fanny pack	bumbag
faucet	tap
flashlight	torch
freeway	motorway
french fries	chips
gas station	garage
gas	petrol
grits	ground corn, usually boiled and served as a breakfast cereal or side dish
hood	car bonnet
ice cream soda	fizzy drink with ice cream in it
jello	jelly
jelly	jam
john	toilet/loo
jumper	pinafore dress
jungle gym	climbing frame
layer cake	sponge cake

American English	British English
line	queue
mailman	postman
mean	angry/bad-tempered
movie theatre	cinema
nickel	five cent coin
oatmeal	porridge
overpass	flyover
pacifier	dummy
panties	knickers
pants	trousers
penny	one cent coin
pharmacy	chemist
preserver/buoy	life buoy/belt
principal	headteacher
pumps	court shoes
quarter	twenty five cent coin
realtor	estate agent
rotary	roundabout
rubber boots	wellingtons
scallion	spring onion
sedan	saloon car
shrimp	prawn
sidewalk	pavement
ramp	slip road
sneakers	trainers
snow peas	mange tout
soda	fizzy drink
soda fountain	counter in a drug store where sodas, light snacks are served
soda jerk	person who dispenses soda etc in a drugstore
squash	marrow
station wagon	estate car
stick shif	gear stick
stroller	pushchair
sweater	jumper
tailboard	tailgate
teller	bank clerk
thongs	flip flops
tow truck	breakdown truck
trailer	caravan
training wheels	stabilisers (on child's bike)
trash/garbage	rubbish
truck	lorry
trunk	car boot
turn signal	indicator
vacation	holiday
vest	waistcoat
wind breaker®	wind cheater
wind shield	windscrees
zip	postcode
zipper	zip
zucchini	courgette

Quiz Answers

Chapter 6

1. The Mission San Luis Archaeological Historic Site.
2. MOAS, Mary Brogan Museum of Art and Science.
3. Andrew Jackson.
4. Cadillac, Corvette, Mustang. (Also Buick, Pontiac, T-Bird and De Lorean.) They can all be seen at the Talahasee Antique Car Museum.
5. The Talahasee Museum of History and Natural Science.
6. The Suwanee River.
7. Wakulla Springs State Park.
8. Penascola and St Augustine.
9. The IMAX theatre at the National Museum of Naval Aviation.
10. Ivan.

Chapter 7

1. Great Britain and Spain.
2. A mattress-fibre factory.
3. The Isle de Mai (French for 'the island of May').
4. Fort Clinch State Park.
5. The Fountain of Youth at St Augustine.
6. Maximo, a saltwater crocodile in Anastasia Island, is 15 foot long.
7. Bright red.
8. The Seminole Wars.
9. Gators American.
10. Ocala.

Chapter 8

1. The cigar.
2. Egypt, Morocco and the Congo.
3. Florida Aquarium.
4. Kid City next to Lowry Park.
5. Dinosaur World.
6. Salvador Dali.
7. You walk the plank.
8. Sponges.
9. The Sunshine Skyway Bridge at night.
10. A car parked on the roof. (There wasn't enough space inside the museum.)

Chapter 9

1. Orlando.
2. The giant head of an alligator.
3. Skull Kingdom in Orlando.
4. Universal Studios Orlando.
5. Seuss Landing at Universal's Islands of Adventure.
6. The cheetah. You can see one at Central Florida Zoological Park.
7. Loggerhead Turtles. They can be spotted a New Smyrna Beach.
8. The Apollo/Saturn V Centre. Visit its recreation at the Kennedy Space Center.
9. The Windover Pond burial ground at the Brevard Museum of History and Natural Science.
10. Fort Christmas, built on December 25, 1837, as part of the Second Seminole War defences.

Chapter 10

1. The Calusa tribe.
2. The railroad.
3. Thomas Edison.
4. The Imaginarium: Hands-On-Museum and Aquarium.
5. Gasparilla (originally named Jose Gaspar).
6. A cattle town.
7. Hurricane Charley.
8. The Conservancy of Southwest Florida Nature Center.
9. The Teddy Bear Museum of Naples.
10. Southwest Florida Museum of History.

Chapter 11

1. Miami's Children Museum.
2. Parrot Jungle Island.
3. A killer whale.
4. Miami's Museum of Science and Planetarium.
5. The unique ecosystem of the sawgrass marshes and tree islands in Everglades National Park.
6. They were all excellent swimmers.
7. Hoffman's Chocolate Shoppe.
8. Lake Okeechobee, the second-largest freshwater lake on the US mainland.
9. Ring the bell.
10. 15 years (and another 10 to restore the artifacts).

Index

Main page references are in **bold**.

take the kids
Florida touring atlas

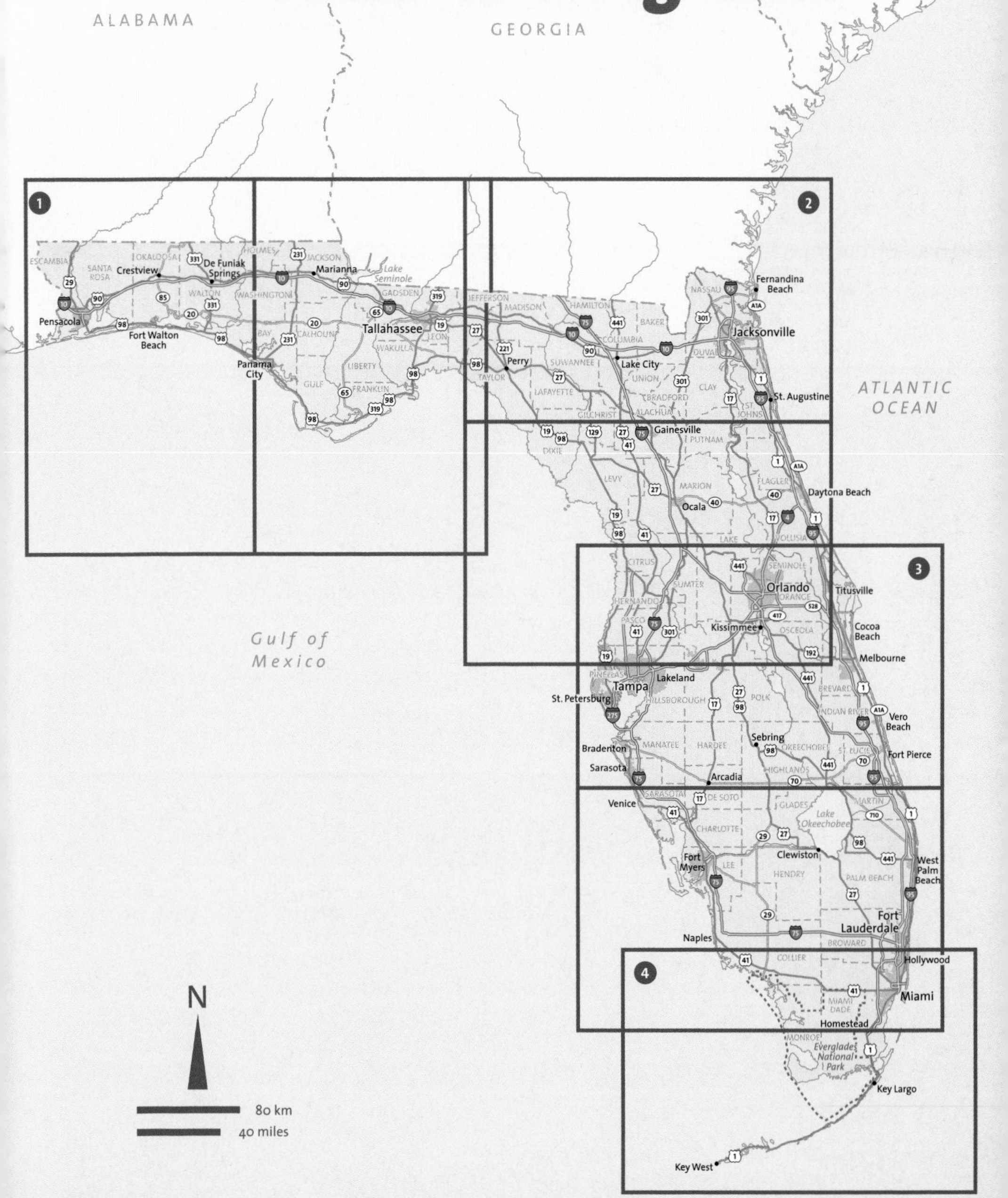

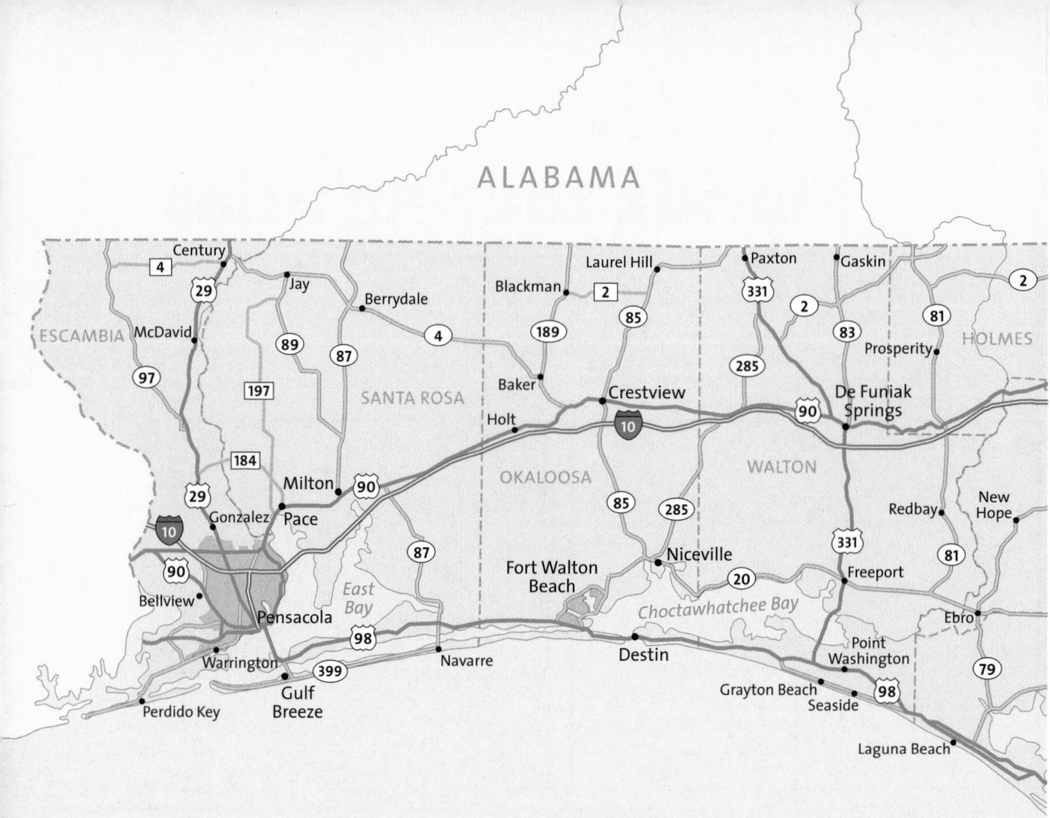

ALABAMA
Century
4
29
Jay
Berrydale
ESCAMBIA
McDavid
97
89
87
197
SANTA ROSA
184
Milton
90
Gonzalez
Pace
10
Bellview
Pensacola
East Bay
87
98
Warrington
399
Navarre
Gulf Breeze
Perdido Key
Laurel Hill
Blackman
2
189
85
Baker
Holt
Crestview
OKALOOSA
85
285
Fort Walton Beach
Niceville
20
Choctawhatchee Bay
Destin
Paxton
Gaskin
331
2
83
81
HOLMES
Prosperity
285
De Funiak Springs
WALTON
Redbay
New Hope
331
81
Freeport
Ebro
Point Washington
79
Grayton Beach
Seaside
Laguna Beach
Gulf of Mexico

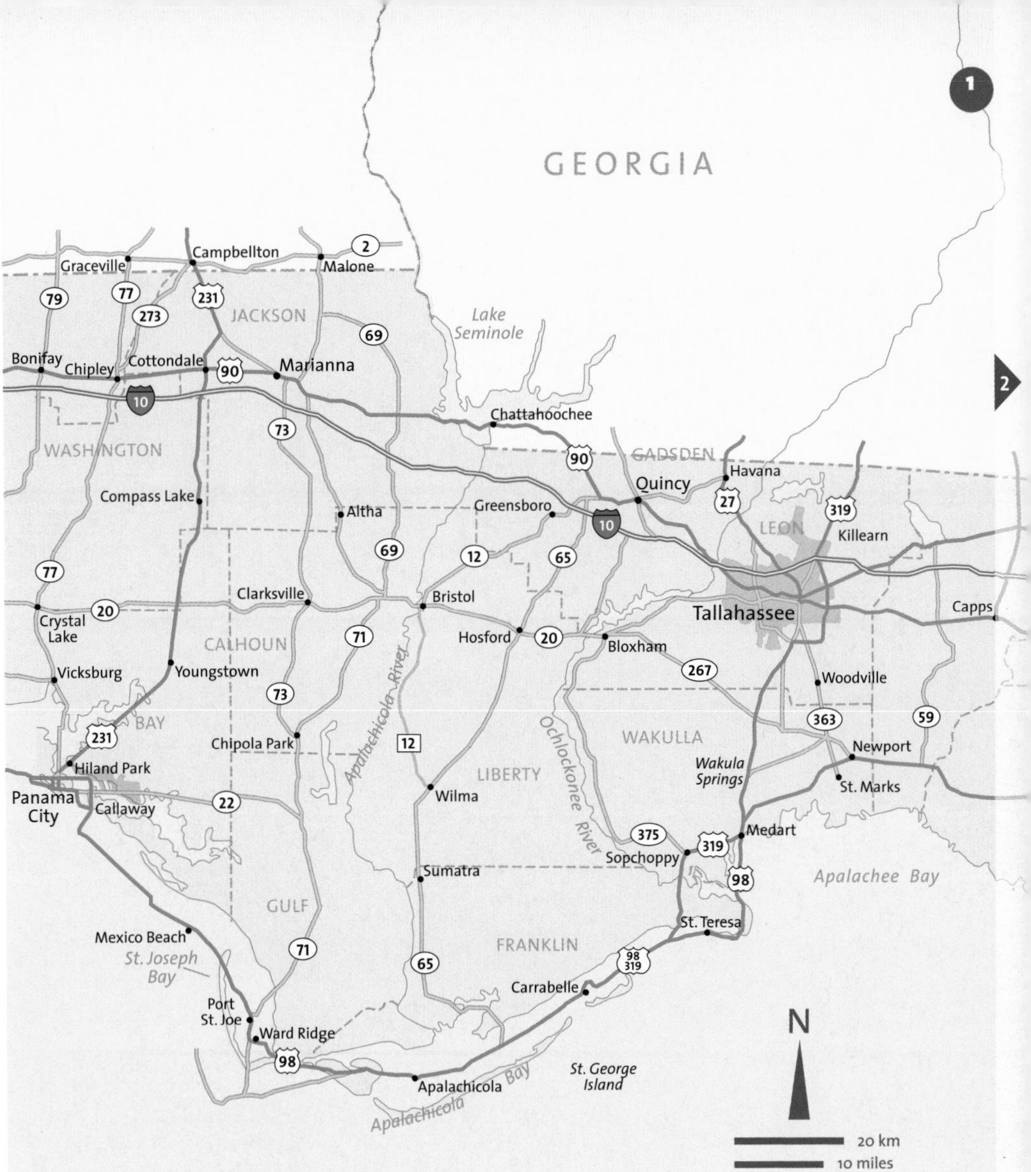
1
2
GEORGIA
Graceville
Campbellton
Malone
JACKSON
Lake Seminole
Bonifay
Chipley
Cottondale
Marianna
Chattahoochee
WASHINGTON
GADSDEN
Havana
Quincy
Compass Lake
Altha
Greensboro
LEON
Killearn
Clarksville
Bristol
Tallahassee
Capps
Crystal Lake
Hosford
Bloxham
CALHOUN
Vicksburg
Youngstown
Woodville
BAY
Chipola Park
WAKULLA
Newport
Wakula Springs
Hiland Park
LIBERTY
St. Marks
Panama City
Callaway
Wilma
Apalachicola River
Ochlockonee River
Medart
Sopchoppy
Sumatra
Apalachee Bay
GULF
St. Teresa
FRANKLIN
Mexico Beach
St. Joseph Bay
Carrabelle
Port St. Joe
Ward Ridge
N
St. George Island
Apalachicola
Apalachicola Bay
20 km
10 miles

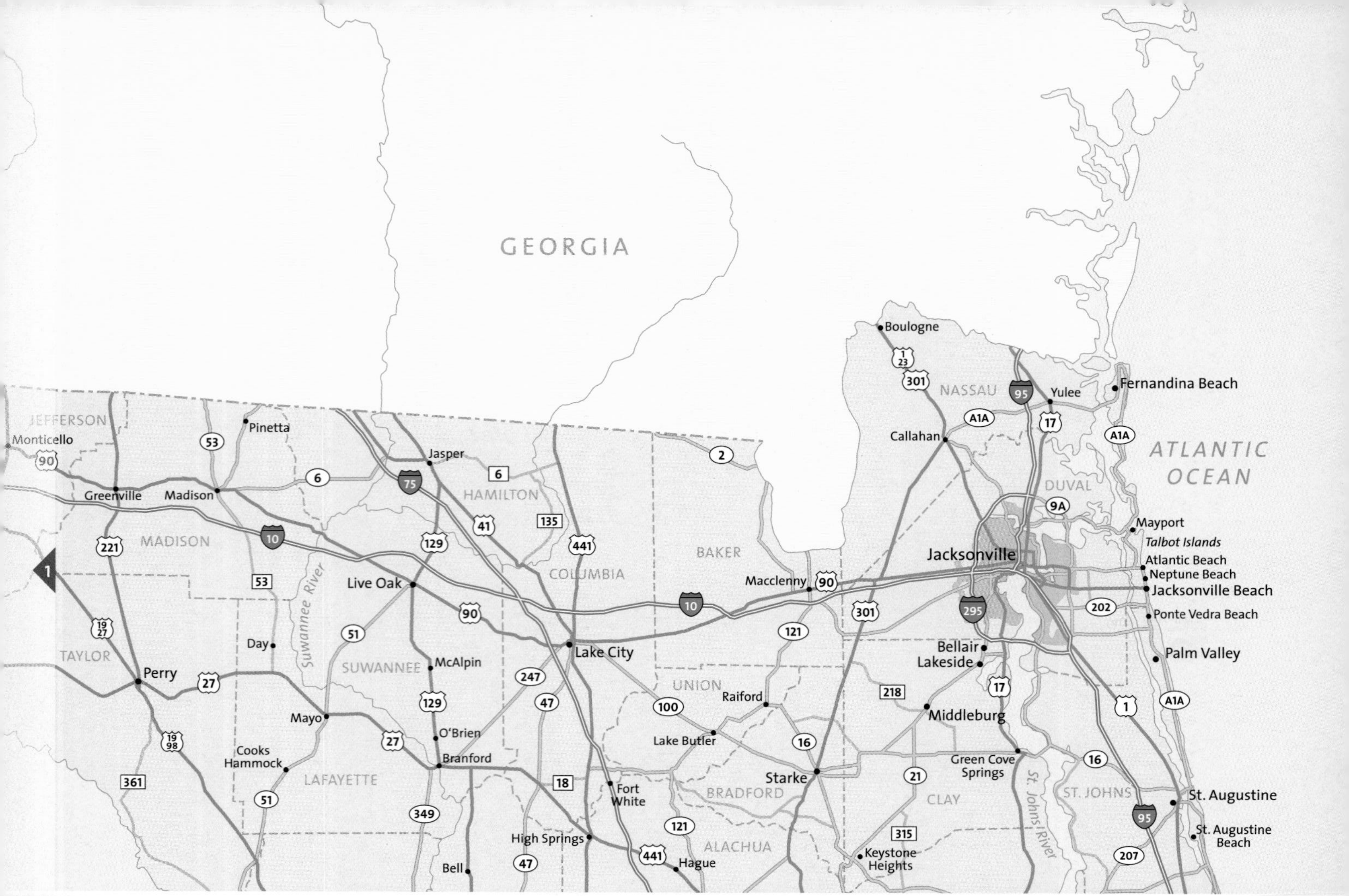
GEORGIA
ATLANTIC OCEAN
JEFFERSON
MADISON
TAYLOR
HAMILTON
SUWANNEE
LAFAYETTE
COLUMBIA
BAKER
UNION
BRADFORD
ALACHUA
NASSAU
DUVAL
CLAY
ST. JOHNS
Suwannee River
St. Johns River
Monticello
Greenville
Madison
Pinetta
Jasper
Live Oak
Day
Perry
Mayo
Cooks Hammock
McAlpin
O'Brien
Branford
Bell
High Springs
Fort White
Hague
Lake City
Macclenny
Raiford
Lake Butler
Starke
Keystone Heights
Boulogne
Callahan
Yulee
Fernandina Beach
Jacksonville
Mayport
Talbot Islands
Atlantic Beach
Neptune Beach
Jacksonville Beach
Ponte Vedra Beach
Palm Valley
Bellair
Lakeside
Middleburg
Green Cove Springs
St. Augustine
St. Augustine Beach
1

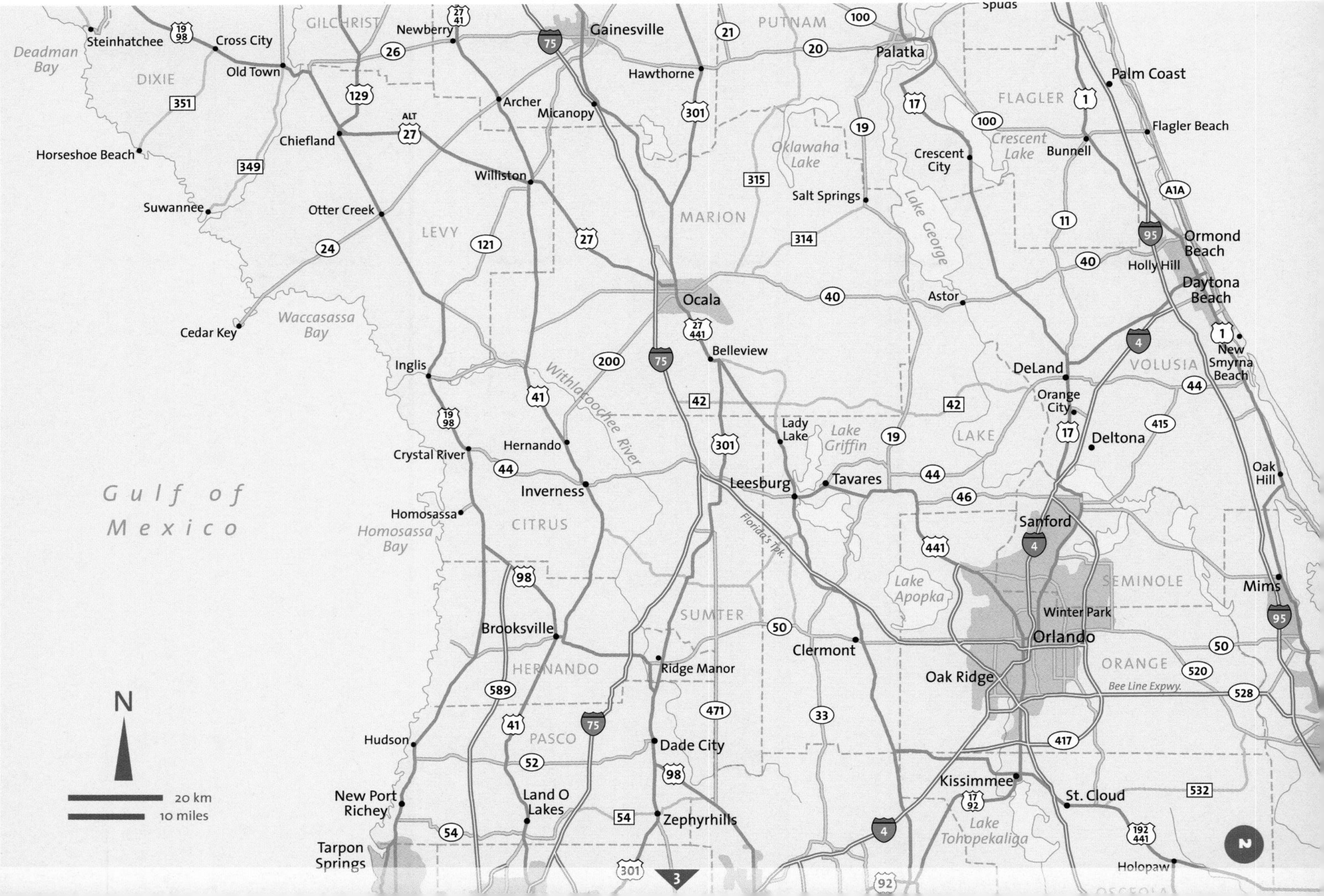

Gulf of Mexico
Deadman Bay
Steinhatchee
Cross City
Old Town
DIXIE
Horseshoe Beach
Suwannee
Cedar Key
Waccasassa Bay
GILCHRIST
Newberry
Gainesville
Archer
Micanopy
Chiefland
Williston
Otter Creek
LEVY
Inglis
Crystal River
Homosassa
Homosassa Bay
Hernando
Inverness
CITRUS
Withlacoochee River
Brooksville
HERNANDO
Hudson
New Port Richey
Tarpon Springs
PASCO
Land O Lakes
Zephyrhills
Dade City
Ridge Manor
SUMTER
Hawthorne
PUTNAM
Palatka
MARION
Ocala
Belleview
Oklawaha Lake
Salt Springs
Lake George
Astor
Lady Lake
Lake Griffin
Leesburg
Tavares
Florida's Tpk.
Clermont
LAKE
Lake Apopka
Oak Ridge
Orlando
Winter Park
Sanford
SEMINOLE
ORANGE
Bee Line Expwy.
Kissimmee
Lake Tohopekaliga
St. Cloud
Holopaw
DeLand
Orange City
Deltona
VOLUSIA
Crescent City
Crescent Lake
FLAGLER
Bunnell
Palm Coast
Flagler Beach
Ormond Beach
Holly Hill
Daytona Beach
New Smyrna Beach
Oak Hill
Mims
N
20 km
10 miles
2
3

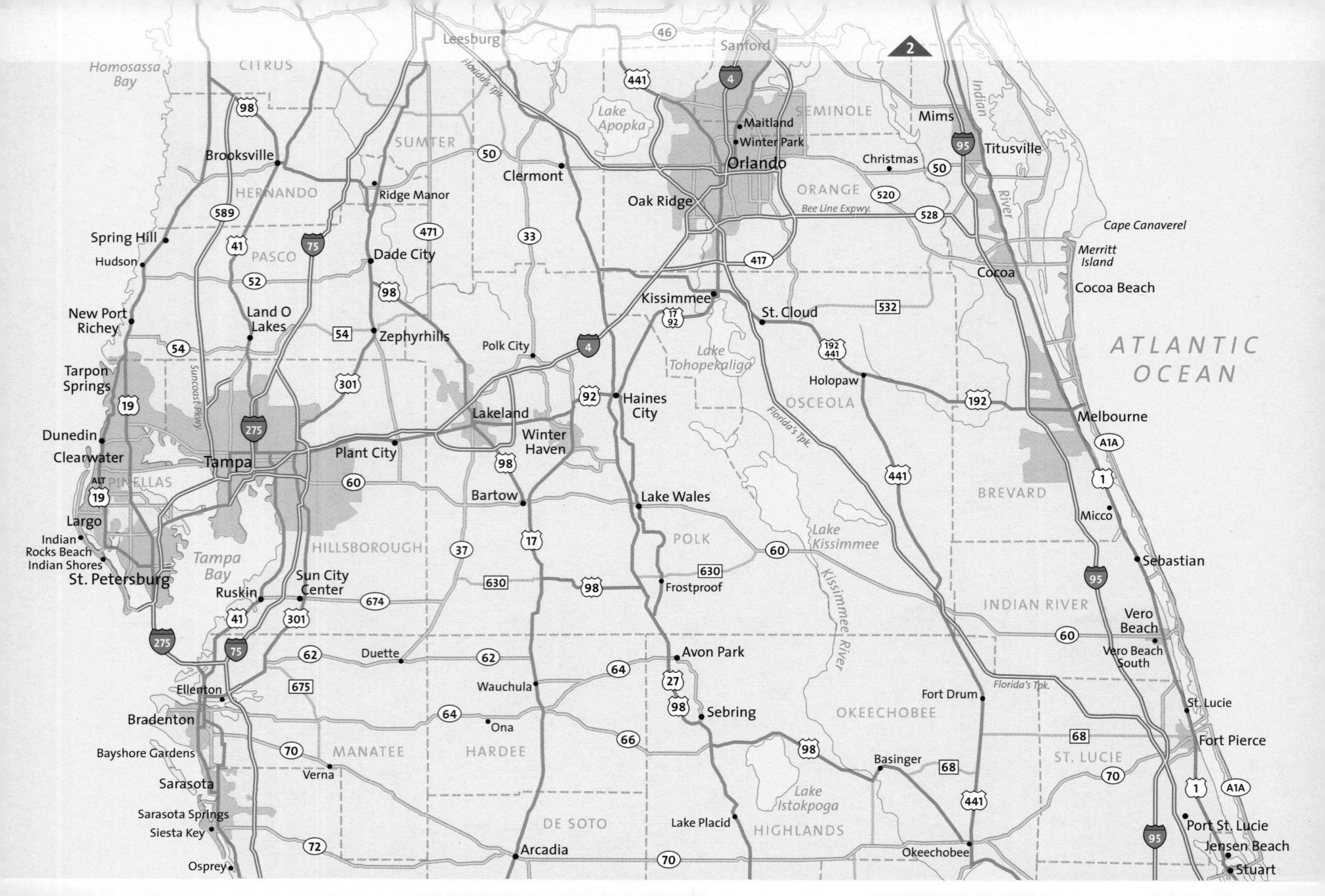

2
ATLANTIC OCEAN
Homosassa Bay
CITRUS
SUMTER
HERNANDO
PASCO
PINELLAS
HILLSBOROUGH
MANATEE
HARDEE
DE SOTO
POLK
OSCEOLA
ORANGE
SEMINOLE
BREVARD
INDIAN RIVER
OKEECHOBEE
ST. LUCIE
HIGHLANDS
Leesburg
Sanford
Maitland
Winter Park
Orlando
Oak Ridge
Mims
Titusville
Christmas
Indian River
Cape Canaveral
Merritt Island
Cocoa
Cocoa Beach
Bee Line Expwy.
Florida's Tpk.
Lake Apopka
Brooksville
Ridge Manor
Clermont
Spring Hill
Hudson
Dade City
New Port Richey
Land O Lakes
Zephyrhills
Kissimmee
St. Cloud
Lake Tohopekaliga
Polk City
Tarpon Springs
Suncoast Pkwy.
Holopaw
Haines City
Lakeland
Winter Haven
Dunedin
Clearwater
Tampa
Plant City
Melbourne
Largo
Indian Rocks Beach
Indian Shores
St. Petersburg
Tampa Bay
Bartow
Lake Wales
Lake Kissimmee
Kissimmee River
Micco
Sebastian
Ruskin
Sun City Center
Frostproof
Vero Beach
Vero Beach South
Duette
Avon Park
Wauchula
Ellenton
Bradenton
Ona
Sebring
Fort Drum
St. Lucie
Fort Pierce
Bayshore Gardens
Verna
Basinger
Sarasota
Lake Istokpoga
Sarasota Springs
Siesta Key
Lake Placid
Port St. Lucie
Jensen Beach
Arcadia
Okeechobee
Osprey
Stuart